THE GREENWOOD ENCYCLOPEDIA OF

African American Literature

THE GREENWOOD ENCYCLOPEDIA OF
African American Literature

VOLUME IV

O–T

Edited by
Hans Ostrom and J. David Macey, Jr.

GREENWOOD PRESS
Westport, Connecticut • London

Library of Congress Cataloging-in-Publication Data

The Greenwood encyclopedia of African American literature / edited by Hans Ostrom and J. David Macey, Jr.
    p. cm.
  Includes bibliographical references.
  ISBN 0–313–32972–9 (set : alk. paper)—ISBN 0–313–32973–7 (v. 1 : alk. paper)—
ISBN 0–313–32974–5 (v. 2 : alk. paper)—ISBN 0–313–32975–3 (v. 3 : alk. paper)—
ISBN 0–313–32976–1 (v. 4 : alk. paper)—ISBN 0–313–32977–X (v. 5 : alk. paper) 1. American
literature—African American authors—Encyclopedias. 2. African Americans—Intellectual life—
Encyclopedias. 3. African Americans in literature—Encyclopedias. I. Ostrom, Hans A.
II. Macey, J. David.
  PS153.N5G73   2005
  810.9'896073—dc22   2005013679

British Library Cataloguing in Publication Data is available.

This book is included in the *African American Experience* database from Greenwood Electronic Media.
For more information, visit www.africanamericanexperience.com.

Library of Congress Catalog Card Number: 2005013679
ISBN: 0–313–32972–9 (set)
    0–313–32973–7 (vol. I)
    0–313–32974–5 (vol. II)
    0–313–32975–3 (vol. III)
    0–313–32976–1 (vol. IV)
    0–313–32977–X (vol. V)

First published in 2005

Greenwood Press, 88 Post Road West, Westport, CT 06881
An imprint of Greenwood Publishing Group, Inc.
www.greenwood.com

Printed in the United States of America

The paper used in this book complies with the
Permanent Paper Standard issued by the National
Information Standards Organization (Z39.48–1984).

10 9 8 7 6 5 4 3 2 1

CONTENTS

LIST OF ENTRIES

TOPICAL LIST OF ENTRIES

The following list of entries, organized according to topical categories, includes a complete list of author entries and provides a comprehensive overview of the *Encyclopdedia*'s coverage of the literary, critical, historical, cultural, and regional contexts of African American literature. Please consult the Index for assistance in locating discussions of specific literary texts and other topics.

Athletes and Sports

Ali, Muhammad (born 1942)

Basketball

Campanella, Roy (1921–1993)

Carter, Rubin "Hurricane" (born 1937)

Johnson, Jack (1878–1946)

Jordan, Michael Jeffrey (born 1963)

Louis, Joe (1914–1981)

Mays, Willie Howard, Jr. (born 1931)

Robinson, Jackie [Jack Roosevelt] (1919–1972)

Authors

Abernathy, Ralph David (1926–1990)

Adams, Jenoyne (born 1972)

Adoff, Arnold (born 1935)

Ai (born 1947)

Albert, Octavia Victoria Rogers (1853–1889)

Aldridge, Ira (1807–1867)

Alers, Rochelle (born 1943)

Alexander, Elizabeth (born 1962)

Alexander, Lewis (1900–1945)

Allen, Jeffrey Renard (born 1962)

Allen, Richard (1760–1831)

Allen, Samuel Washington (born 1917)

Allison, Hughes (1908–c. 1974)

Als, Hilton (born 1961)

Amos, Robyn (born 1971)

Anderson, Garland (1886–1939)

Anderson, Mignon Holland (born 1945)

Historical and Cultural Figures

Literary Movements, Schools, and Organizations

Music and Musicians

O

OBAC (Organization of Black American Culture). Arts organization. OBAC was formed in 1967 in **Chicago, Illinois,** by the Committee for the Arts, and was dedicated to developing Black artists and artistic expression in a community setting. The perspective was Afrocentric, centered in the **Black Arts Movement,** and focused on an emerging Black aesthetic. OBAC founder **Hoyt W. Fuller** recalled: "The idea was revolutionary . . . it suggested that the seeds of liberation—political and economic and social, as well as aesthetic—would be planted in the Black psyche through this new approach to artistic expression. The interest then was primarily political; art for the sake of Black empowerment was the principle" (Fuller, 17).

At its start the organization was devoted to community empowerment, to a "public approach to art" (Jackson-Opoku, xiv), and to a "special vision of how expression in the arts could be related to the basic problems of the community" (Fuller, 17). OBAC was named by Art Workshop's Jeff Donaldson, based on the Yoruba word for leader, *oba,* and pronounced oh-*bah*-see). OBAC was largely composed of writers, and its Writers' Workshop was its largest and only lasting movement. However, in the first year a community workshop, a visual art workshop, and a drama workshop joined the Writers' Workshop. Fuller remembers: "The Committee was convinced that, by releasing that natural, pent-up store of creativity within the community, by urging Black people toward an identification with and an acceptance of themselves and their images, their history, their humanity, art itself would achieve a fresh interpretation rooted in the lives, the aspirations—in a word, the experience—of the community" (Fuller, 17). The Visual Art Workshop was responsible for Chicago's Wall of Respect, the first community-based outdoor mural, a model which inspired the national mural movement that continues to this day—though the Visual Art Workshop didn't continue after completion of the Wall. By OBAC's second year, only the Writers' Workshop continued.

OBAC writers brought poetry to taverns and schools, to wherever people of the community gathered. Freed from White aesthetic standards and literary history, from "universal" subjects, their avowed focus was on the natural, the concrete, the specific subjects of the Black experience. Carole A. Parks describes the agenda as follows: "OBAC writers strive to say something well; they simply believe it even more important that they have something to say. Something that affirms our worth as a people" (Parks, xvii). A speakers' bureau was organized "to provide OBAC writers for school and community programs" (Fuller 19), and members also volunteered to work with the next generations of writers, through workshops and a reading program at the public library. After four years, only two of the original Writers' Workshop members remained active, but they were replaced by new members (Fuller, 20).

OBAC's Writers' Workshop is the oldest such organization in the United States, continuing as a membership committee of the arts, nurturing and promoting Black writers with twice monthly workshops, along with readings and publishing, over the years, the periodical **NOMMO**, the OBAC *Newslettah*, *Cumbaya*, and NOMMO anthologies published by OBAhouse, as well as work by individual members, such as Angela Jackson's *Heartfruit* (1978). (*See* **Afrocentricity**.)

Resources: Jeff Donaldson, "The Rise, Fall and Legacy of the Wall of Respect Movement," *International Review of African American Art* 15, no. 1 (1998), 22–26; Hoyt W. Fuller, "Foreword to NOMMO," repr. in Parks, ed., NOMMO, pp. 17–20; Sandra Jackson-Opoku, "Preface," in Parks, ed., NOMMO, pp. xiii–xiv; Carole A. Parks, ed., *NOMMO: A Literary Legacy of Black Chicago (1967–1987)* (Chicago: OBAhouse, 1987).

Carol Klimick Cyganowski

O'Daniel, Therman B. (1908–1986). Editor, literary critic, and college professor. Therman Benjamin O'Daniel, founding editor of two African American literary journals, was born in Wilson, North Carolina, and attended public schools in Greensboro, North Carolina. He earned a B.A. from Lincoln University in Pennsylvania (1930), an M.A. from the University of Pennsylvania (1932), and Ph.D. from the University of Ottawa, Canada (1956). O'Daniel, the recipient of General Education Board and Ford Foundation fellowships, conducted postdoctoral research at Harvard University, the University of Pennsylvania, the University of Chicago, and the University of Ottawa. During a career of forty-five years, he taught at four universities: Allen University (1933–1939), Fort Valley State College (1940–1955), Dillard University (1955–1956), and Morgan State University (1956–1978). O'Daniel held a variety of administrative positions at three of those institutions including chair of the English Department, chair of the Division of Languages and Literature, dean of the Liberal Arts College, and acting president at Allen University; chair of the English Department, registrar, and director of summer school at Fort Valley; and director of summer school at Morgan.

Though O'Daniel spent most of his impressive career as an educator at Morgan and was named Professor Emeritus in 1985, he is best known for his contributions to African American literary criticism. As the *College Language Association Journal*'s founder and first editor (1957–1978), O'Daniel provided a forum for African American literary scholars and led the publication to national and international prominence (*see* **College Language Association**). He founded the **Langston Hughes Society** in 1981 and was the first editor (1982–1984) of the organization's *The Langston Hughes Review*, the first literary journal devoted to an African American author. O'Daniel's book-length studies are *A Twenty-five-Year Author-Title Cumulative Index to the CLA Journal* (1957–1982), published in 1985, and three edited works: *Langston Hughes: Black Genius: A Critical Evaluation* (1971), *James Baldwin: A Critical Evaluation* (1977), and *Jean Toomer: A Critical Evaluation* (1988), which was completed after O'Daniel's death by Ann Venture Young and Cason L. Hill. Among O'Daniel's additional publications is an introduction to a 1970 reprint edition of *The Blacker the Berry*, a novel by **Wallace Thurman**. Honors bestowed upon O'Daniel include recognition from the College Language Association for "meritorious service" (1974, 1978), the Black Academy of Arts and Letters' Alice E. Johnson Memorial Fund Award (1978), and two tributes from the Middle-Atlantic Writers Association: the Distinguished Literary Critic Award (1984) and the title Dean-Editor of Afro-American Literary Criticism.

Resources: George Houston Bass, "Tribute to Therman B. O'Daniel," *The Langston Hughes Review* 5 (1986), 12–13; Arthur P. Davis, J. Saunders Redding, and Joyce Ann Joyce, eds., *The New Cavalcade: African American Writing from 1760 to the Present*, vol. 1 (Washington, DC: Howard University Press, 1991), 689–690; Burney J. Hollis, "This Was a Man! A Tribute to Therman B. O'Daniel," *The Langston Hughes Review* 5 (1986), 1–4; Linda Metzger, ed., *Black Writers: A Selection of Sketches from Contemporary Authors* (Detroit: Gale, 1989), 440; R. Baxter Miller, "'One Prime Obligation': The Example of Therman B. O'Daniel (1908–1986)," *The Langston Hughes Review* 5 (1986), 5–10; Ann Allen Shockley and Sue P. Chandler, *Living Black American Authors* (New York: Bowker, 1973), 119–120.

Linda M. Carter

Oklahoma. Ralph Ellison is quoted as saying that the American frontier was a land of "infinite possibilities." Ellison's far-reaching optimism—with regard to the frontier, at least—was due in great part to his identity as one of Oklahoma City's most famous natives. His having been born there in 1914 placed Oklahoma on the literary map once he became an acclaimed novelist. In fact, many critics ascribe the breadth of Ellison's epic *Invisible Man* (1952) to his Oklahoma origins, to his direct relationship with the birthplace of the land run and its importance as a component of the American dream, and the complicated, problematic role that dream played in the lives of Black Americans. Oklahoma and its connection to the iconography of the American

West, the land of the Conestoga wagon and the "Sooners" and "Boomers," is well known and well documented. Less known, however, is the important role that Blacks played in the history and homesteading of Oklahoma.

Present in what is now known as Oklahoma since accompanying Coronado there on his trek in 1548, African Americans became slaves of the Five Civilized Tribes who were relocated to Oklahoma from the Southeast along the "Trail of Tears" in 1838. By the 1864 census, 8,000 African American slaves lived with the tribes, and this number would dramatically increase after the Five Civilized Tribes signed treaties with the U.S. government in 1866 that forced them to free their slaves. As part of the treaties, the U.S. government required the Indians to "cede the area known as the Oklahoma District or Unassigned Lands" (Stein and Hill). These lands became a hotbed of controversy as many disparate groups, such as abolitionists and "radical" Republicans, sought to secure them for African Americans, in hopes of creating a Black colony. These hopes were dashed by a demand for land and by an intense hatred of Blacks by Whites and Native Americans alike.

The Unassigned Lands were opened for Anglo-European settlement on April 22, 1889, the date of the most famous Oklahoma land run, in Guthrie, Oklahoma. Where formerly the Black presence in Oklahoma was outnumbered only by that of Native Americans, after the initial land runs, Oklahoma was overrun by Whites and became the site of some of the most numerous and restrictive "Jim Crow" laws in America.

However, in spite of the refusal to deed over the Unassigned Lands to African Americans, the increasing number and widespread nature of Jim Crow segregation laws, and the remaining land runs from 1889 to 1895, which brought an immediate new population of 50,000 primarily Anglo-American "Boomer" and "Sooner" settlers, the African American presence in Oklahoma would continue to grow. Those Blacks who had successfully participated in the land runs advertised Oklahoma as a land-rich, opportunity-laden territory, and many African Americans were drawn to the state.

Rather than take up residence beside Whites, who were resentful of their presence on the frontier (indeed, by 1895, the presence of the Ku Klux Klan was widely acknowledged and endorsed by White Oklahomans), African Americans were either pushed out of existing cities or willingly departed them and began to band together to form cities and towns which were composed solely of Black residents. Forming effective business cooperatives, many of these black cities thrived; in all, more than twenty-seven (indeed, some sources record as many as fifty) all-Black cities and towns were recorded. Many of them, such as Boley, Langston, Lima, Tullahassee, and Clearview, still exist.

African Americans persisted in following their dream of property ownership and community in Oklahoma and succeeded in creating some of the most influential Black business districts in the United States. Ironically, these districts would prove to be the sites of some of the worst **race riots** and prolonged racial tension in American history. Tulsa's Black financial district, the Greenwood area of Tulsa also known as "Black Wall Street," was razed to the ground in the **race riots** of 1921, along with part of its residential district. Oklahoma City's "Reno" district would similarly be the site of unrest and ultimate extinction, and the business area known as "Deep Deuce" or "Deep Second" would likewise feel the pressure of racial tension, even as it became the cultural heartbeat of Oklahoma City.

By the late 1920s, "Deep Deuce" (Second Street) had become the cultural hub of Black business and culture in the Oklahoma City area. While New York and **New Orleans, Louisiana**, are consistently associated with jazz and other forms of twentieth-century Black art and culture, Oklahoma City was just as noteworthy for its identity as the epicenter for **jazz** in the American heartland. Drawing talented musicians from the all-Black towns and cities of Oklahoma, as well as from cities in Missouri, Kansas, and northern **Texas**, "Deep Deuce" became a mecca of clubs and jazz joints displaying the talents of jazz greats such as **Count Basie** and Lester Young. Jazz bands from all over Oklahoma and as far away as Kansas City played to "mixed crowds" during the 1920s and 1930s in perhaps the only setting of informal integration in an otherwise deeply and persistently segregated state. However positive jazz music's influence on the culture of Oklahoma City, it was not widespread enough to prevent Blacks from suffering greatly during the **Great Depression**.

When the Great Depression of the 1930s turned Oklahoma into part of the Dust Bowl that had once been American farming's heartland, Black Oklahomans were hit the hardest. Although Franklin D. Roosevelt's WPA program assisted over 4,000 African American families, many others were intentionally prevented from obtaining government assistance. Because of the grim economic and social climate of the early 1930s, many Blacks gave up Oklahoma residence and took off for Canada, which promised landownership. The only notable gain in the 1930s for Black Oklahomans was the prevention of a Muskogee/Oklahoma City school bond which would have only benefited Whites-only schools. There was an active chapter of the **Federal Writers' Project** in Oklahoma City, and participants in this project interviewed former slaves, recording their stories (Slater).

Oklahoma City's history is tied to **Martin Luther King, Jr.**, because the first ever sit-ins were conducted in Oklahoma City in the 1950s. The most notable of these protests was the first, which began on August 18, 1958, when ten-year-old Marilyn Luper took a seat at Katz's drugstore lunch counter in downtown Oklahoma City. After some discussion, Luper's mother and friends joined her at the counter and placed an order for thirteen colas, putting their money in plain view on the counter. This process continued at the Katz counter and others for several days, during which time history teacher and activist Clara Luper and the children received both death threats from Whites and encouragement from Blacks. On August 23, 1958, the Katz chain declared that it would cease lunch counter segregation at all of its stores in Oklahoma, Missouri, Kansas, and Iowa.

While the sit-ins of the 1950s and 1960s resulted in little physical harm and a great deal of success, previous race altercations in Oklahoma had been far bloodier. Of all the race riots from 1915 to 1935, the Tulsa riots were perhaps the worst, resulting in over 6,000 African Americans being arrested and imprisoned in "detention camps." These detentions were often prolonged, fueled by the power of the Ku Klux Klan's strong presence in Tulsa and Oklahoma City.

Eventually, the **Civil Rights Movement** overpowered the persistent and deep-rooted racial segregation in Oklahoma, but it was a long and painstaking process. Although desegregation truly began in 1961, Oklahoma City and Tulsa would not be fully integrated for another decade. While legislators deliberately slowed the progress of integration in schools and government institutions, its realization was inevitable. How long it would last was another matter. Even after a decade of forced busing and integration, urban areas of Oklahoma were persistent in their efforts to return to a segregated way of life. Although Blacks resisted a spate of anti-busing legislation, eventually it was passed, and the late 1970s and 1980s found Oklahoma City, Tulsa, and Lawton once again segregated; this time, however, the segregation was not illegal and so could not be forcibly altered. The Oklahoma City of the early twenty-first century is not much different; the result is an urban Black population, roughly 30 percent of which lives below the poverty line and whose schools are underfunded and overenrolled.

Like Ralph Ellison, the historian **John Hope Franklin** is a native of Oklahoma, as is **Joyce Carol Thomas**. Poet **Melvin B. Tolson** lived in Guthrie, Oklahoma, for a time, and later served as mayor of Langston, Oklahoma, where the historically black college Langston University is located.

The Oklahoma Center for the Book and the Oklahoma Library Association now offer the Ralph Ellison Award to honor individuals who contribute to Oklahoma's literary heritage.

Resources: Gene Aldrich, *Black Heritage of Oklahoma* (Edmond, OK: Thompson, 1973); Eugene Berwanger, *The Frontier Against Slavery: Western Anti-Negro Prejudice and the Slavery Extension Controversy* (Urbana: University of Illinois Press, 1967); Monroe Lee Billington and Roger D. Hardaway, eds., *African Americans on the Western Frontier* (Boulder: University Press of Colorado, 1998); Randolph Campbell, *An Empire for Slavery: The Peculiar Institution in Texas, 1821–1865* (Baton Rouge: Louisiana State University Press, 1989); R. Halliburton, Jr., *Red over Black: Black Slavery Among the Cherokee Indians* (Westport, CT: Greenwood Press, 1977); Robert W. Johannsen, *Frontier Politics on the Eve of the Civil War* (Seattle: University of Washington Press, 1955); William Loren Katz, *The Black West*, 3rd ed. (Seattle, WA: Open Hand, 1987); Daniel F. Littlefield, Jr., *Africans and Seminoles: From Removal to Emancipation* (Westport, CT: Greenwood Press, 1977); Oklahoma Center for the Book, http://www.odl.state.ok.us/ocb/pastelli.htm; Theda Perdue, *Slavery and the Evolution of Cherokee Society, 1540–1866* (Knoxville: University of Tennessee Press, 1979); Kenneth W. Porter, *The Negro on the American Frontier* (New York: Arno, 1971); James A. Rawley, *Race and Politics: "Bleeding Kansas" and the Coming of the Civil War* (Philadelphia: Lippincott, 1969); W. Sherman Savage, *Blacks in the West* (Westport, CT: Greenwood Press, 1976); Mary Ann Slater, "Politics and Art: The Controversial Birth of the

Oklahoma Writers' Project," *The Chronicles of Oklahoma* 68 (Spring 1990), 72–90; Howard F. Stein and Robert Hill, *The Culture of Oklahoma* (Norman: University of Oklahoma Press, 1993); Quintard Taylor, *In Search of the Racial Frontier: African Americans in the American West, 1528–1990* (New York: Norton, 1998).

Deirdre Ray

Opportunity (1923–1949). Magazine. *Opportunity, Journal of Negro Life* is a magazine associated with the National Urban League, and especially with the period in the life of that organization when the socialist and "cultural entrepreneur" **Charles Spurgeon Johnson** was one of the key organizers. The National Urban League emerged largely as a response to the **Great Migration** of African Americans from the post-**Reconstruction** South to industrial metropolises in the North. The League would help the immigrants settle into livable and productive situations in the urban centers of the North. Johnson, who had worked for the Urban League in **Chicago, Illinois**, as research director, came to New York as the Urban League's National Director of Research and Investigations and editor of *Opportunity*, the organ of the organization. Contrasting the **NAACP** with the Urban League, Hutchinson observes, "Whereas the NAACP undertook direct action and immediatism, the Urban tended toward diplomacy and gradualism" (171).

Opportunity was launched on January 19, 1923, with a view, as stated in that first issue, to "put[ting] down interestingly but without sugar-coating or generalizations the findings of careful scientific surveys and facts gathered from research." The maiden issue of the journal ran an editorial which stated that in a "new effort," the journal would work to advance "the weary struggle of the Negro population for status through self improvement and recognition, aided by their friends." Some of the social questions that the journal covered included social work, migration, religion, housing, integration, labor, educational opportunities and problems, and public health.

Although *Opportunity* was not founded as a literary journal per se, Johnson had a literary projection for the journal's future. He had in mind a program much more elaborate than the issuing of records of the Urban League's rehabilitative operations. **The Crisis**, the organ of the NAACP, had offered a model for the new journal's literary activities. Headed by the versatile scholar-intellectual **W.E.B. Du Bois**, *The Crisis* had in 1919 hired **Jessie Redmon Fauset** as literary editor. Fauset's editorial responsibility was mainly to scout the United States for African American literary talent, and to accord it an outlet through the pages of *The Crisis* and its sister publication, **The Brownies' Book**. In this way, Fauset and Du Bois had begun to lay the foundations for the movement that would soon come to be known as the **Harlem Renaissance**. They had made encouraging contacts with such soon-to-be stalwart Harlemites as **Langston Hughes, Claude McKay**, and **Countee Cullen**. Fauset was also in correspondence with **Jean Toomer** whose 1923 novel, *Cane*, along with Claude McKay's 1922 collection of poetry, *Harlem Shadows*, was touted as the inaugurating publications of the Harlem Renaissance.

In tacit approbation of the lead provided by *The Crisis*, Johnson commenced a more aggressive literary program at *Opportunity*. In March 1924, he convened a highly symbolic event at the Civic Club, the only elite club in New York that did not have color or sex restrictions. Here Black intellectuals and their White counterparts frequently arranged to meet. The ostensible reasons for the March 21 gathering were a dinner and the celebration of a new novel. That novel, Jessie Fauset's first, had an eye-catching title: *There Is Confusion*. The novel served an important function, representing the Negro middle class, which had not been widely portrayed in fiction, but on the evening in question, it became an awfully fitting title for the real tenor adopted by the organizers. For far from foregrounding Fauset's signal achievement, the *Opportunity* editor gave the occasion over to Howard University professor **Alain Locke**, to formally inaugurate the **New Negro** Movement. The more than 100 attendees regarded Fauset less as the reason for the gathering, and more as one of the several potential sources of a projected flowering in Negro art and literature.

The Civic Club event was the Renaissance's all-important collaborative effort between Johnson's *Opportunity* and Paul Kellogg's **Survey Graphic**. The meeting inspired Johnson to increase exponentially the literary and artistic content of *Opportunity*, giving as much weight to artistic matters as to social or economic issues. Hitherto, apart from some book reviews and Countee Cullen's 1923 poem "Dance of Love," most of *Opportunity*'s articles had read like excerpts from Johnson's sociological treatise *The Negro in Chicago*, a work that greatly resembled Du Bois's *The Philadelphia Negro*. Kellog offered to devote the entire March 1925 issue of his magazine to a formal display of Negro literature and art in Harlem, and Johnson rose to the challenge of meeting Kellogg's offer. Alain Locke, master of ceremonies at the 1924 Civic Club dinner, edited the *Survey Graphic* issue. He collected an assortment of literary and artistic material for this Harlem number (1925), which he titled *Harlem, Mecca of the New Negro*.

In September 1924, Johnson announced that *Opportunity* would offer prizes for outstanding creative achievement. Johnson made this announcement at the peril of offending Du Bois and *The Crisis* management, who had informally reported the imminent inauguration of an annual *Crisis* literary contest.

The prizes were to be awarded in May 1925, during a gala occasion at the Fifth Avenue Restaurant. Many distinguished Whites agreed to serve as judges. When it came, the contest was consistent with its billing. Over 300 people attended the event and the quality of contest entrants was quite high, with some winners having already achieved literary renown through magazines other than *The Crisis* and *Opportunity*. Cullen's poem "Shroud of Color" had been featured in H. L. Mencken's *American Mercury*. After sharing the poetry third prize with Langston Hughes, Cullen won the second prize, and the first went to Hughes for his poem "The Weary Blues." The poem received authoritative recital that night from the venerable NAACP General Secretary, **James Weldon Johnson**. Subsequently, Cullen became the literary editor of *Opportunity*. This position gave him a platform, through his "Dark Tower" column, to influence readers' thinking on matters artistic, literary and political. Johnson's White connections were impressed by the quality of the material featured at the contest, and offered encouraging words. Over the years, Langston Hughes published at least fifty-one poems in *Opportunity* (Ostrom, 298). The journal frequently carried reviews of visual art, such as that produced by Winold Reis, Miguel Covarrubias, and Aaron Douglas.

Four months after the 1927 contest, however, the Urban League decided to suspend the contests. At its peak circulation, *Opportunity* sold a mere 11,000 copies a month. At that time, in 1928, *The Crisis* sold 60,000 copies a month, far below its own peak circulation point of over 100,000. Hitherto, *Opportunity* had been run on funds the Urban League received from the Carnegie Corporation in the form of a five-year annual grant of $8,000. In 1927, the Carnegie Corporation declined to renew the grant, arguing that the Urban League should be able, after five years of operation, to support its own publication. Charles Johnson petitioned Julius Rosenwald (a friend) for finances to continue running the journal, but the latter refused. The stock market crash was looming, and Johnson, apparently fearing that the journal might soon cease operations, quit his position as editor and joined the academic world at Fisk University. Here he would serve in two important capacities, initially as head of the Sociology Department and eventually as the institution's President.

But *Opportunity* proved to be resilient in the midst of the bad economic times, and lived on after the departure of its founding editor. By 1932, the journal had resumed its annual contests through personal donations. Then the journal boasted a list of judges that included Harlem Renaissance luminaries **Sterling A. Brown**, John Day of John Day Publishing Company, and Fannie Hurst of *Imitation of Life* fame. The journal continued operations until 1949, two years after a celebration of its twenty-fifth anniversary. In 1999, an anthology of literature that had appeared in *Opportunity* was published (Wilson).

Resources: Suzanne Churchill, *Housing Modernism: A Study of Little Magazines* (Davidson, NC: Davidson College Press, 2004); Harold Cruse, *The Crisis of the Negro Intellectual: A Historical Analysis of the Failure of Black Leadership* (New York: Quill, 1984); Countee Cullen, *My Soul's High Song: The Collected Writings of Countee Cullen*, ed. Gerald Early (New York: Anchor, 1991); George Hutchinson, *The Harlem Renaissance in Black and White* (Cambridge, MA: Belknap Press of Harvard University Press, 1995), esp. 168–175; David Levering Lewis, *When Harlem Was in Vogue* (New York: Oxford University Press, 1989); Hans Ostrom, *A Langston Hughes Encyclopedia* (Westport, CT: Greenwood Press, 2002); Arnold Rampersad: "Introduction," in *The New Negro: Voices of the Harlem Renaissance*, ed. Alain Locke (New York: Atheneum, 1992); *The Life of Langston Hughes*, vol. 1, *I, Too, Sing America* (New York: Oxford University Press, 1986); Hortense Spillers, "Sterling Brown's Literary Chronicles" [in *Opportunity*], *African American Review* 31, no. 3 (Fall 1997), 443–447; Sondra Kathryn Wilson, ed., *The Opportunity Reader: Stories, Poetry, and Essays from the Urban League's Opportunity Magazine* (New York: Modern Library, 1999).

Mzenga Aggrey Wanyama

OyamO (born 1943). Playwright, poet, author, and educator. Born Charles F. Gordon, OyamO took on his nickname (coined by neighborhood children) in the early 1970s to avoid being confused with another African American playwright with a similar name. OyamO's work blends surrealism, expressionism, and realism with African American music, dance, and poetry. His dramas generally focus upon an "everyman" who must face the pervasive nature of racism despite the promises of a "free" society.

In 1963, he enrolled at Miami University in Ohio, but soon left to join the U.S. Naval Reserves. Shortly thereafter, OyamO moved to New York to become active in the theater. To make a living while learning his craft, he took positions as a lighting technician and electrical technician for the New Lafayette Theatre and the Negro Ensemble Company, respectively. At these venues he was able to associate with other African American playwrights, including **Ed Bullins** and **Amiri Baraka**. OyamO was a frequent participant in Bullins's Black Theatre Workshop, which led to his collaboration in the creation of the Black Magicians' Theatre Company.

OyamO received his M.F.A. from Yale in 1981. In the same year, *The Resurrection of Lady Lester* premiered at the Yale Repertory Theatre. He has since had several plays produced around the nation: *Let Me Live* (1990), *I Am a Man* (1992), *Pink and Say* (adapted from the children's book by Patrick Polacco; 1996), *Famous Orpheus* (1998), *The White Black Man* (1998), *Liyanja* (1998), *Kickin' Summit* (2001), and *Harry and the Streetbeat* (2001). OyamO began teaching in 1979 at the College of New Rochelle, and through the 1980s held various positions at Emory University, Princeton University, the University Playwright's Workshop, the New Dramatists in New York City, and the Frank Silvera Writers' Workshop. He has received a Rockerfeller playwright-in-residence grant, a Guggenheim fellowship, a McKnight Foundation fellowship, and three National Endowment for the Arts fellowships. Since 1989, he has taught at the University of Michigan.

Resources: OyamO: *Hillbilly Liberation: (A Grossly Understated Prayer of Theatrical Spectacles, Social Positions and Poetry)* (New York: OyamO Ujamaa, 1976); *I Am a Man = Powa ta da Peepas* (New York: Applause Theatre and Cinema Books, 1995); *The Resurrection of Lady Lester: A Poetic Mood Song Based on the Legend of Lester Young* (New York: Green Integer, 2000); Jim Snyder, "Playwright with a 'Wild Side,'" *Chronicle of Higher Education*, Apr. 14, 1995, p. A6.

Michelle LaFrance

Oyewole, Abiodun (born c. 1946). Poet. Oyewole was one of the founders of the performance group **The Last Poets**. At fifteen, in a Yoruban ceremony, Charles Davis of Queens, New York, was renamed Abiodun Oyewole. He taught at Shaw University until he was arrested for armed robbery. While Oyewole was at Shaw, he established a Yoruba village in Sheldon, South Carolina, to preserve the culture and art of Nigeria.

Oyewole always responded to his world with poetry, but began in earnest with the death of **Martin Luther King, Jr.** Influenced by Shakespeare and

Langston Hughes, Oyewole is a rhythm poet, focusing on beat rather than rhyme. In explaining the Last Poets' "Nigger" poems to Daniel Kane, he says that "nigger" is the negative persona in Black people who needs to be destroyed in order to progress. Oyewole's own contribution is "Run Nigger."

Oyewole's motivation to write poetry comes from his desire to change the world around him and the perception of others. Influenced by such songwriters as Smokey Robinson, he began to see poetry as a medium for performance, to be spoken aloud. In 1968, with Gylan Kain and David Nelson, he was an original member of the Last Poets. Oyewole created the album *The Last Poets*, released in 1970, and *This Is Madness* (1974). Many recordings followed with the various artists who have comprised the Last Poets since the group's inception. In 1994 he released his solo recording *25 Years*.

Resources: "Daniel Kane Interviews Abiodun Oyewole," *Teachers and Writers*, Aug. 1999, www.writenet.org/poetschat/poetschat_aoyewole.html; Abiodun Oyewole, Umar Bin Hassan, and Kim Green, *On a Mission: Selected Poems and a History of the Last Poets* (New York: Henry Holt, 1996).

Patricia Kennedy Bostian

P

Packer, ZZ (born 1973). Short story writer. ZZ Packer, whose given first name is Zuwena (which in Swahili means "good"), is the author of the collection of short stories, *Drinking Coffee Elsewhere*. Born in **Chicago, Illinois**, to immigrant parents, Packer grew up in **Atlanta, Georgia**, and Louisville, Kentucky. She earned her B.A. degree at Yale University, then attended the Writing Seminar at Johns Hopkins University and the prestigious Iowa Writers' Workshop, where she studied under such respected authors as Frank Conroy and the Pulitzer Prize-winning African American writer **James Alan McPherson**. Packer has received the Whiting Writers Award, the Rona Jaffee Foundation Writers Award, and the Wallace Stegner/Truman Capote fellowship at Stanford University. She has also been a fellow at the illustrious MacDowell Colony.

Although Packer had her first short story published at age nineteen, in *Seventeen*, it took several more years before she honed her talent enough to be noticed by the mainstream literary establishment. After *The New Yorker* included one of her stories in its debut fiction issue in 2000, rival publishers engaged in a furious bidding war for the rights to bring out Packer's first collection, which earned the author a $250,000 advance. Since then, reviewers have consistently listed Packer among the rising stars on the American literary scene. According to a writer for the *Village Voice*, "The short stories in *Drinking Coffee Elsewhere* feel refreshingly subtle and unresolved. They don't call attention to themselves; in fact, they shun irony and linguistic bravado." Rather than making the characters seem unrecognizable, such unadorned writing only makes them "feel inseparable from the messy sociopolitical landscape, feet firmly planted in our world" (Press). This is a perspective shared by other reviewers of the collection. The *New York Times* writes, for instance, that Packer's collection "reminds us that no stylistic tour de force—or authorial gamesmanship, or flights of language—can ground a story like a well-realized character. This is the old-time religion of storytelling, although Packer's prose supplies plenty of the edge and energy we expect from contemporary fiction" (Thompson).

Such edginess and energy permeate the collection. With the exception of the poignantly tragic "The Ant of the Self," which is narrated by a precocious teen who makes an impromptu road trip from Kentucky with his formerly incarcerated father to sell exotic birds at the Million Man March in the nation's capital, the rest of the collection revolves around the experiences of Black women or—in some cases—young girls. Packer exhibits a near-flawless ear for capturing the trials and tribulations that Black women encounter in a society dominated by men and by Whites. These characters range from a group of teenage Girl Scouts on a camping trip who learn a hard lesson about prejudging others because of the color of their skin ("Brownies"), to a student teacher whose dream of saving inner-city youths from the environmental ills that plague them suddenly backfires ("Our Lady of Peace"), to the series of life disappointments that greet a sensitive and disgruntled first-year student at Yale ("Drinking Coffee Elsewhere"). In perhaps the collection's most disturbing story, and its longest, a fourteen-year-old runaway, a girl whose drug-addicted mother abandoned her years earlier, falls in with a charming but scheming pimp and loses far more than she bargained for ("Speaking in Tongues"). After reading these by turns harrowing and epiphany-laced narratives, it will come as no surprise to anyone that Packer's favorite author is the Nobel laureate **Toni Morrison**.

Resources: ZZ Packer, *Drinking Coffee Elsewhere* (New York: Riverhead Books, 2003); Joy Press, "Brownies and Yalies," *Village Voice*, Mar. 4, 2003, p. 58; Jean Thompson, "Notorious in New Haven," *New York Times*, Mar. 16, 2003, p. 7.

Guy Mark Foster

Paris, France. Paris served as a center of exile for numerous African American writers seeking a place to work and live free from racial tension and segregation during the first three quarters of the twentieth century. **Expatriate writers**, artists, and musicians formed an active enclave in the city during these years, drawn by the French capital's reputation as a place of freedom in the arts.

In the early nineteenth century, study in French universities was a rite of passage for sons of wealthy **creole** families in **New Orleans, Louisiana**, and the latter half of the nineteenth century saw African Americans including the playwright **Victor Séjour** and the scholar **W.E.B. Du Bois** making trips to Paris. (DuBois went on to pursue graduate studies in Europe at the University of Berlin.) But it was the 200,000 African American servicemen who came to France during **World War I** who brought the first permanent expatriate African American residents to Paris. This first community of mainly male expatriates was small, consisting of about thirty members who settled in the area of Montmartre, then a working-class suburb of the city. Many soldiers returned to the United States with stories of the lack of racism in Paris, a city where interracial marriage hardly raised eyebrows, and people of any color were accepted in restaurants, theaters, and public transportation. Not only did France provide social freedoms unknown in the United States at the time, but events at home were particularly grim for African Americans. To cite just one example, seventy-eight **lynching**s were recorded in the United States in 1919. In the same year Paris hosted the Pan African Congress, opposed by the U.S. Department of State. The high value of the U.S. dollar and the fact that touring musicians were often paid up to three times more in Paris than in the United States factored into the decision of some African Americans to make France their permanent home.

Parisians often saw these first settlers as seekers of political asylum, but a Parisian fascination with primitivism and American culture also made social acceptance easy during the 1920s. The literary salon of Martinique journalist Paulette Nordal attracted many visiting African American writers, and her *Revue du Monde Noir* published works by **Jessie Redmon Fauset, Langston Hughes, Claude McKay,** and **Walter White.** (In 1924, after working on a freighter, Hughes lived in Paris, working as a waiter, for several months; part two of his first **autobiography**, *The Big Sea*, is devoted to his experiences in Paris.) African American expatriates, usually isolated from their White counterparts, formed a close society, but by the 1930s economic pressures had forced many to return to the United States. Paris during the next decades was one center for discussion of **"Négritude"**—the idea that all descendants of Africans share a common culture. Claude McKay's semioautobiographical novel *Banjo* (1929), set in Marseilles, was attacked by **Harlem, New York,** writers for its insistence on a pan-Black culture (Chaney; Kaye).

By the 1950s, there were nearly 500 African American veterans studying at French universities on the GI Bill, and the center of African American Paris shifted from the night clubs of Montmartre to the cafés of the Left Bank, as Paris eclipsed Harlem as the center of African American literary life. **William Gardner Smith**'s *The Stone Face*, **Chester Himes**'s **autobiography** *My Life of Absurdity*, and **Richard Wright**'s unfinished novel *Island of Hallucinations* provide detailed descriptions of life as a Black expatriate in postwar Paris during these years. Yves Malartic's *Au Pays du Bon Dieu* describes a Harlem-born soldier's experience in France after the war. Several Black newspapers in the United States employed American correspondents after the war.

Toward the middle of the century, the African American literary movement in Paris centered on Richard Wright, who arrived in 1947, embittered by failed attempts to purchase property in the United States due to racial discrimination. Wright, already successful as a novelist, continued to write fiction set in the United States, but was heavily influenced by French existentialism. He became increasingly politically active after his arrival, forming the French-American Fellowship with the journalist William Rutherford to fight racism and promote the arts, and organizing the Congress of Negro Artists and Writers at the Sorbonne in 1956. Wright also served as unofficial ambassador to visiting and newly arrived African American writers in Paris, one of whom, **James Baldwin,** arrived in 1948. Baldwin's relationship to Wright was complex and sometimes stormy. Problems between the writers began with Baldwin's 1949 essay "Everybody's Protest Novel," which criticized Wright's *Native Son.* During their famous quarrel in a Left Bank brasserie, described by Baldwin in his essay "Alas, Poor Richard," Wright accused Baldwin of betrayal. (One of Baldwin's biographers discusses the extent to which accounts of the quarrel vary considerably; see Campbell.) Baldwin continued to attack Wright's caricatures of African Americans in other essays, meanwhile writing his own novels in Paris and publishing in New York. *Giovanni's Room* is the story of a homosexual love affair between an American and an Italian, set in Paris. His *Nobody Knows My Name* and *Another Country* also deal with expatriation and identification, as does his essay "The Discovery of What It Means to Be an American." His play *The Amen Corner*'s Parisian run was more successful than its New York run. Baldwin returned to the United States to meet **Martin Luther King, Jr.,** and work with civil rights activists, but eventually settled in France, purchasing a home in the South of France, where he died in 1987.

Chester Himes arrived in Paris in 1953, after French critics lauded the translation of his *Lonely Crusade,* which had been criticized harshly by both Black and White American reviewers as being too explicit in its portrayals of both political struggles and sex. Himes eventually began publishing mystery novels in France, happy to be freed from what he and others perceived to be the puritanical publishing world in the United States, the result of **McCarthyism.** His *A Case of Rape* (1957) breaks the myth of a France devoid of racism and describes Black expatriate life in Paris.

Other African American writers who moved to Paris during this period include William Gardner Smith, **Frank Yerby, Carlene Hatcher Polite, Barbara Chase-Riboud, Ted Joans,** and **Melvin Van Peebles.** With the death of Richard Wright in 1960 and notable advances arising from the **Civil Rights Movement** in the United States, the symbolic importance of African American exile began to fade. For many writers, expatriation had been a political statement, but expatriates now found themselves geographically distanced from the very struggles they supported. The film version of *Paris Blues* (1961) poignantly describes the dilemma facing African Americans in France during this period. Among contemporary African American writers living in Paris, the best known is the scholar and poet **James A. Emanuel,** author of *Black Man Abroad: The Toulouse Poems.*

Resources: James Campbell, *Talking at the Gates: A Life of James Baldwin* (1991; repr. Berkeley: University of California Press, 2002), 29–32, 62–70; Michael A. Chaney, "Traveling Harlem's Europe: Vagabondage from Slave Narratives to Gwendolyn Bennett's 'Wedding Day' and Claude McKay's *Banjo,*" *Journal of Narrative Theory* 32, no. 1 (Winter 2002), 52–76; Langston Hughes, "II: The Big Sea," in *The Big Sea* (New York: Knopf, 1940), 101–214; Jacqueline Kaye, "Claude McKay's *Banjo,*" *Présence Africaine* 73 (1970), 165–169; J. Gerald Kennedy, *Imagining Paris:*

Exile, Writing, and American Identity (New Haven, CT: Yale University Press, 1993); Jean Méral, *Paris in American Literature*, trans. Laurette Long (Chapel Hill: University of North Carolina Press, 1989); Tyler Stovall, *Paris Noir* (Boston: Houghton Mifflin, 1996).

Joshua Parker

Parker, Charlie. *See* **Gillespie, Dizzy, Charlie Parker, and Thelonious Monk**.

Parker, Pat (1944–1989). Poet, performance artist, and health care worker. One of the first African American poets to write openly about women's attraction to other women, Pat Parker helped give a literary voice to Black lesbians in the 1970s. According to **Barbara Smith**, Parker showed "that it was not only possible to survive as a Black lesbian, but that it was possible to be an out Black lesbian writer as well" (Parker 1999, 39).

Born to a working-class, Southern Baptist family on January 20, 1944, in Houston, **Texas**, Parker moved to California after graduating from high school. She initially wrote short stories, but after marrying playwright **Ed Bullins** in 1962, she turned to poetry. Coming out as a lesbian in the late 1960s, Parker achieved critical acclaim through readings at women's bookstores, coffeehouses, and festivals. She developed a national audience for her poetry through recording the album *Where Would I Be Without You?* with poet Judy Grahn in 1976 and taking part in the Varied Voices of Black Women concert tour in 1978.

Parker wrote five books of poetry: *Child of Myself* (1972), *Pit Stop* (1973), *Womanslaughter* (1978), *Movement in Black* (1978)—which includes many of the poems in her first three collections—and *Jonestown and Other Madness* (1985). In 1999, ten years after Parker's death, Firebrand Books released a new edition of *Movement in Black* with previously unpublished work, and with tributes and remembrances from ten other Black women writers.

"Racial identity and vigilance against racism were as central to Parker's writing as her love of women and her defiance against sexism and homophobia," states poet Michelle Parkerson (Parker 1999, 35). For example, "Movement in Black," considered by many to be her signature piece, chronicles the struggles and accomplishments of Black women. Other widely reprinted poems include "Where Will You Be?", a call to action against the oppression of lesbians, gay men, and bisexuals, and "For the Straight Folks Who Don't Mind Gays but Wish They Weren't So BLATANT," an insightful examination of heterosexual privilege.

Parker was also a pioneer in women's health care. She served as the medical coordinator of the Feminist Women's Health Center in Oakland, California, from 1978 until 1987, when she became too ill to continue working. She died on June 17, 1989, from breast cancer. (*See* **Lesbian Literature**.)

Resources: Pamela Annas, "A Poetry of Survival: Unnaming and Renaming in the Poetry of Audre Lorde, Pat Parker, Sylvia Plath, and Adrienne Rich," *Colby Library Quarterly* 18, no. 1 (1982), 9–25; Brett Beemyn, "Bibliography of Works by and about

Pat Parker (1944–1989)," *Sage* 6, no. 1 (1989), 81–82; Pat Parker: *Movement in Black*, enl. ed. (1978; Ithaca, NY: Firebrand Books, 1999); *Jonestown and Other Madness* (Ithaca, NY: Firebrand Books, 1985); Pat Parker and Judy Grahn, *Where Would I Be Without You? The Poetry of Pat Parker and Judy Grahn* (Los Angeles: Olivia Records, 1976); "Pat Parker," *FemmeNoir Online*, ed. A. D. Odom, http://www.femmenoir.net/weblogonlinediary/id149.html; Kate Rushin: "Pat Parker: Creating Room to Speak and Grow," *Sojourner*, Oct. 1985, 28–29; "With Fire in Her Eyes: A Farewell to Pat Parker," *Gay Community News*, Sept. 3–9, 1989, pp. 8–9, 12.

Brett Beemyn

Parks, Gordon (born 1912). Photographer, filmmaker, novelist, poet, and autobiographer. Gordon Parks is best known as a photographer, but in general he is respected for being a direct, conscientious, and passionate artist with a talent for recording life as it unfolds. Parks's intimate associations and relationships with his subjects have evoked not only the personal challenges which the poor and the marginalized experience, but his lens (and his writing) also capture those daily triumphs that keep them waking up each morning.

Gordon Parks (right) in December 1968 directing the filming of *The Learning Tree*. Parks was not only the producer and director, but also wrote the screenplay from his own novel and composed the musical score. AP/Wide World Photos.

Maintaining his steadfast commitment to scrutinizing and partaking in the essence of life, as well as the solitude and the finality of death, Parks has made many contributions to the field of literature. His best-known novel is *The Learning Tree* (1963), and his autobiographical works are *A Choice of Weapons* (1966), *Born Black* (1971), *To Smile in Autumn: A Memoir* (1979), *Voices in the Mirror: An Autobiography* (1990), and *Half Past Autumn: A Retrospective* (1997). Other works include the novel *Shannon* (1981); two books about photography, *Flash Photography* (1947) and *Camera Portraits: The Techniques and Principles of Documentary Portraiture* (1948); and several artistic compositions of his photography set to the cadence of his poetry. These include *A Poet and His Camera* (1968), *In Love* (1971), *Gordon Parks: Whispers of Intimate Things* (1971), *Moments Without Proper Names* (1975), and *A Star for Noon* (2000). Films he has directed include *The Learning Tree* (1969), the highly influential crime drama, *Shaft* (1971), and *Leadbelly* (1976). Of all Parks's works, those that have received the most acclaim have been his reflective photographic essays and compilations appearing in *Life* magazine from the late 1940s and into the 1970s. In these essays, Parks was concerned with exposing the nature of poverty and the effects of racism, themes he had firsthand knowledge of.

Parks was born in Fort Scott, Kansas, in 1912. Marked by poverty, racism, and the promises of dreams deferred, he left Kansas at the age of fifteen and traveled north to Minneapolis, Minnesota, to seek out opportunities and to make something of himself. His need to find gainful employment led him to pursue many different careers, ranging from piano player and busboy to janitor and even, for a short time, semiprofessional basketball player. It was in St. Paul, Minnesota, that Parks began his more than fifty-year love affair with photography.

After he broke into the fashion industry, as a prodigy, Parks's opportunities blossomed. By 1941, he became the first photographer to receive the prestigious Julius Rosenwald fellowship for his masterful works. The following year, as a part of his fellowship, he moved to **Washington, D.C.**, to work as a documentary photographer for the Farm Services Administration. At the FSA, Parks learned about prejudice firsthand while developing his recognizable style of social commentary. By using imagery as a narrative unto itself, Parks's works successfully captured the humanity of those suffering under the brutality of racism, the cruelty of poverty, and the reality of a life for a majority of African Americans in the twentieth century.

Resources: Harry L. Fagget, "A Choice of Weapons," in *Negro American Literature Forum* 4, no. 1 (Mar. 1970), 34–35; Gordon Parks: *Born Black* (Philadelphia: Lippincott, 1971); *Choice of Weapons* (New York: Harper & Row, 1966); *Half Past Autumn: A Retrospective* (Boston: Little, Brown, 1997); *The Learning Tree* (1963; repr. New York: Fawcett, 1978); *A Star for Noon: An Homage to Women in Images, Poetry, and Music* (Boston: Bullfinch, 2000), includes compact disc; J.R.S., "Gordon Parks Reads His Own Work. The Learning Tree. A Choice of Weapons," *The English Journal* 59, no. 9 (Dec. 1970), 1315–1316; Elizabeth Schultz, "Dreams Deferred: The Personal Narrative of Four Black Kansans," *American Studies* 34, no. 2 (Fall 1993), 25–52.

Pellom McDaniels III

Parks, Suzan-Lori (born 1963). Playwright and author. Suzan-Lori Parks, the daughter of a career military father, was born on May 10, 1963, in Fort Knox, Kentucky. Her family moved frequently throughout her childhood. By the time she enrolled in high school in Germany, where her father was stationed at the time, she had lived in six different states. Following high school, she attended Mount Holyoke College, where she studied with the celebrated novelist **James Baldwin**. After graduating from college in 1985, Parks studied playwrighting at the Yale School of Drama.

Parks's professional playwrighting career began in New York City. Her first play, *Imperceptible Mutabilities in the Third Kingdom*, premiered at BACA Downtown in **Brooklyn, New York**. Mel Gussow, the senior theater critic of the *New York Times*, attended the production and wrote the following of Parks: "Ms. Parks' heightened, dreamlike approach is occasionally reminiscent of **Adrienne Kennedy** and **Ntozake Shange**. . . . But there is sufficient evidence of the playwright's originality. . . . Ms. Parks' identity as an artist is clear. [S]he is earnest about making political points but has a playful sense of language and a self-effacing humor." The play received the 1990 Obie Award for Best New American Play. Parks again won the Obie in 1996 for *Venus*, her play about the exhibition of Saartjie Baartman, "the Hottentot Venus." Her next major play, *In the Blood*, was a Pulitzer Prize finalist in 2001. Despite not winning the Pulitzer, Parks received the prestigious MacArthur Foundation "genius" award. She won the Pulitzer the following year for *Topdog/Underdog*.

Parks's popularity as a playwright anchors itself in her unique style of writing. Inspired by the rhythms of **jazz** music, her plays have a poetic style which is reminiscent of the choreopoems of Ntozake Shange. This style informs the content of her plays, which, to date, can best be divided into history and realist plays. The former category includes *Imperceptible Mutabilities in the Third Kingdom* (1989), *The Death of the Last Black Man in the Whole Entire World* (1990), *Devotees in the Garden of Love* (1992), *The America Play* (1993), *Venus* (1996), *Fucking A* (2000), and *In the Blood* (2000). These plays center on the history and the stereotypes African Americans in the United States and abroad. *Topdog/Underdog* is Parks's first realistic play. A "living room drama," it chronicles the tense relationship between two brothers, Booth and Lincoln.

Parks's writing career extends beyond the stage. In 1995, film director **Spike Lee** enlisted the playwright to write the screenplay for his film *Girl 6*. More recently, she worked on the teleplay adaptation of **Zora Neal Hurston**'s *Their Eyes Were Watching God* (2005). In addition, Parks wrote her first novel, *Getting Mother's Body*, in 2003. Throughout her writing career, she has maintained a close connection with American universities. During the years that *The America Play* and *Venus* were produced, she served as the resident playwright at the Yale School of Drama, where both plays premiered. Currently, she teaches in the theater program at California School for the Arts.

Actress S. Epatha Merkerson (left) and Suzan-Lori Parks attend the opening night party for Pulitzer Prize–winning playwright Suzan-Lori Parks's *Fucking A* at Canteen on March 16, 2003 in New York City. Bruce Glikas/Getty Images.

Resources: Steven Drukman, "Suzan-Lori Parks and Liz Diamond: Doo-a-diddly-dit-dit," *TDR—The Drama Review* 39, no. 3 (1995), 56–75; Harry J. Elam, Jr., and Alice Rayner, "Unfinished Business: Reconfiguring History in Suzan-Lori Parks's 'The Death of the Last Black Man in the Whole Entire World,'" *Theatre Journal* 46, no. 4 (1994), 447–462; Mel Gussow,

"Identity Loss in *Imperceptible Mutabilities,*" *New York Times,* Sept. 20, 1998, p. C24; Suzan-Lori Parks: *The America Play, and Other Works* (New York: Theatre Communications Group, 1995); *Getting Mother's Body* (New York: Random House, 2003); *Imperceptible Mutabilities in the Third Kingdom* (Los Angeles: Sun and Moon, 1989); *In the Blood* (New York: Dramatists Play Service, 2000); *Red Letter Plays* (New York: Theatre Communications Group, 2000); *TopDog/Underdog* (New York: Theatre Communications Group, 2001); *Venus: A Play* (New York: Theatre Communications Group, 1997); Alisa Solomon, "Signifying on the Signifyin': The Plays of Suzan-Lori Parks," Theater 21, no. 3 (1990), 73–80.

Harvey Young

Parody. "Parody," derived from Greek *paroidia,* originally meant "a song sung along with another." Hipponax of Ephesus, known for his parody of *The Iliad,* is credited as the father of this genre. In the fourth century B.C.E., it meant comic imitations or quotations of epic verses. Aristotle's *Poetics* renders the term as *parodia,* defined as a narrative poem in epic meter and diction with mock heroic subject matter. Cervantes used "parody" to mean a criticism or renewal of other works in comic or ironic fashion, as did Henry Fielding over a century later. Ben Jonson used the term to signify imitation of popular verse to make it seem more absurd. By the eighteenth century, parody was defined as a poem which imitated the style of another for humorous effects. Today the term applies to the mimicry of any work of art or activity in communication that is designed to ridicule. Whereas the burlesque, its kin, perverts the original into a caricature or a travesty, parody exploits the integrity of its target or exaggerates its vulnerability.

Parody comes to be because something else has been. It shadows the target without which it cannot exist, and converses in the worlds of both. A skilled parodist weaves deftly in and out of both works, with subtle signals for audience laughter. Comic discrepancy and incongruity resulting from the interplay of the two texts brings enlivening tension to parody. Parody speaks through its own coded ways and words to the reader who recognizes its "double face" and "double voice" (Rose, 39).

Roman rhetorical coaching included imitation drills of great models for aspiring writers or speakers. Longinus recommends emulation of great writers of the past as a means of attaining sublimity in writing. In epic compositions Homer was the prototype; he was "imitated" by Archilochus, the supposed inventor of the iamb, who in turn was the elected model of Horace. Virgil was the Renaissance model of classical perfection, but he wrote his *Aeneid* according to the Homeric norms.

In his **autobiography**, Benjamin Franklin says that he shaped his style through his painstaking imitation of Addison and Steele in *The Spectator,* the short-lived, eighteenth-century English newspaper. Even Ezra Pound, in his *ABC of Reading,* recommends parody as a skill-building strategy, testing both the poem and the parodist alike. Modern parody for the most part has shifted from emulation to "re-creation," which can be benign or hostile. The benign entertains with a purposive mismatch of style and content. The hostile pokes fun and hurts. "Wise Saws and Modern Instances, or Poor Richard in Reverse," in *The Cynic's Word Book* (1906) by Ambrose Bierce, an example of the benign, twists the famous maxims of Franklin for pleasant effect. Likewise, Bierce's larger work, *The Devil's Dictionary* (1911), mimics conventional lexicography with his own sardonic but seductively phrased aphorisms. The works of Theodor Suess Geisel, better known as Dr. Suess, have inspired parodies: Brent Fogel's *If Dr. Suess Wrote for ER*, Phil Frankelphel's *Deconstructing Dr. Suess*, and Erika Milo's *Norse of Course* are rich in humor, each parodying Dr. Suess in a variety of imagined contexts.

Parody will make complete sense only if the reader knows both the texts—the source and the mock version. Allusive richness of a work, as Northrop Frye and others have noted, makes it fit for a literary audience. Unlike parodies of Suess, works in the **literary canon** offer higher challenge—for example, in Donald Ogden Stewart's *A Parody Outline of History* (1921, 2002), which pretends to fill in what H. G. Wells's *Outline of History* (1920) appears to have missed about America. Rather than shadow a source text, Stewart uses the "manner" of various authors whose style and weltanschauung he attempts to reproduce, in "curiously irreverent treatment of American historical events." Each chapter of his history is "imagined" as narrated by "America's most characteristic contemporary authors," such as James B. Cabell, Sinclair Lewis, Scott Fitzgerald, Edith Wharton, and many more. Likewise, T. S. Eliot's *The Wasteland*, parodied by Samuel Hoffenstein in *The Moist Land*, assumes the reader's familiarity with Eliot's work, without which the parody will be flat.

Hostile parody predictably produces responses in kind. John Wilkes, a known rake but a man of political standing as a member of Parliament, made obscene parodies of Alexander Pope's work. Wilkes mocked Pope's *Essay on Man* (1734) with his *Essay on Woman*, "bawdy in the extreme," a joint effort with Thomas Potter; both men were members of the notorious Hell-fire Club, a name to match Pope's Scriblerus Club. *The Dunciad* was greeted with the unwelcome *The Female Dunciad* and *The Popiad* from the Grub Street book trader Edmund Curll. Curll is identified as publisher, pamphleteer, biographer, pornographer, scandal-monger, book seller, journalist, and plagiarist. Obviously, these occupations overlapped, and distinctions, if any, mattered little.

Modern-day parodists face risks that precursors such as Curll did not have to fear. When Samuel Richardson's *Pamela: or, Virtue Rewarded* (1740) appeared, all of Europe cheered it, some praising the author even as Homer's equal. The success of the work lured pirates to bring out sequel volumes, the third and the fourth, with which Richardson had nothing to do. Numerous "anti-Pamela" versions, deliberately pornographic but with a moral pretext, attacked Richardson and his work. *The True Anti-Pamela: or, Memoirs of Mr. James Parry* (1742); *The Fair Adulteress* (1744); *The Life of Miss Fanny Brawn: or, Pamela the Second* by John Piper (1760) are a few of them, all generated by the source name and content. The novel also was burlesqued by Henry Fielding under the title *An Apology for the Life of Mrs Shamela Andrews* in

1741. Fielding parodied Richardson's Pamela further through his *Joseph Andrews* (1742), with a gender-reversed story line, making Joseph, Pamela's brother, Lady Booby's domestic help. The full title of the novel is *The History of the Adventures of Joseph Andrews and of His Friend Mr. Abraham Adams, Written in Imitation of the Manner of Cervantes, Author of Don Quixote.*

George S. Schuyler's **Harlem Renaissance** novel, *Black No More*, can be read as a parody of novels about **passing**. **Langston Hughes** wrote parodies of cliché verse in such poems as "Autumn Note," "Poem d'Automne," and "Signs of Spring," and he published them under pseudonyms that were also mildly parodic: J. Crutchfield Thompson and Earl Dane (Ostrom). **Ishmael Reed**'s novel *The Free-lance Pallbearers* (1967) parodies "rags-to-riches" narratives.

The recent parody of Margaret Mitchell's *Gone with the Wind* (1936) in Alicia Randall's *The Wind Done Gone* (2001) is also a work with an authorial agenda. Randall, rejecting the portrayal of African American life of the **Civil War** era as one-sided and racist, retells the story with alterations of character names and roles. The Mitchell estate accused Randall of "wholesale theft" of the source text, and blocked the release of her work. Randall, supported by authors such as Harper Lee, **Toni Morrison**, and Arthur Schlesinger, argued that her work was like Fielding's *Shamela*, despite the closeness of characters and scenes. The court agreed, and the book was one of the *New York Times* best-sellers for many weeks.

Sometimes a parodist may use self or his or her society as the subject, overplaying their criticized weaknesses or stereotypical attributes. Bob Cole's and Billy Johnson's musical classic, *A Trip to Coontown* (1898), an African American production, ridicules the vanity of a Black man "who momentarily lost sight of his own subordinate status," but for African Americans, it is a statement of resistance in the form of a work that parodies racism and racist assumptions. (Krasner, 35).

Henry Louis Gates, Jr., in his book *The Signifying Monkey* (1988), discusses the history of African American wordplay in a variety of literary forms and the ways in which such "**signifying**" can be a form of parody.

Resources: Simon Dentith, *Parody* (New York: Routledge, 2000); Robert P. Falk, *American Literature in Parody* (New York: Twayne, 1955); Henry Louis Gates, Jr., *The Signifying Monkey: A Theory of African American Literary Criticism* (New York: Oxford University Press, 1988); Linda Hutcheon, *A Theory of Parody: The Teachings of Twentieth-Century Art Forms* (Urbana: University of Illinois Press, 2001); David Krasner, *Resistance, Parody and Double Consciousness in African American Theatre, 1895–1910* (New York: St. Martin's, 1997); Hans Ostrom, *A Langston Hughes Encyclopedia* (Westport, CT: Greenwood Press, 2002); Ishmael Reed, *The Free-lance Pallbearers* (1967; repr. New York: Avon, 1972); Margaret Rose, *Parody: Ancient, Modern, and Post-Modern* (New York: Cambridge University Press, 1993); George Schuyler, *Black No More* (1951; repr. New York: Modern Library, 1999); Archibald B. Shepperson, *The Novel in Motley* (New York: Octagon Press, 1967); William Zaranka, ed., *The Brand-X Anthology of Poetry* (New York: Consortium, 1981), an anthology of parodies.

Varghese Mathai

Passing. In the United States, racial difference is often cultivated on the color line between "Black" and "White" (*see* **Race**). This line, however, is not indelible. Individuals motivated by a desire to escape the enclosures of a race-conscious society are often compelled to traverse this racial boundary, and the elusive nature of racial identity enables them to do so. A prevalent theme in African American literature, passing, through its interrogation of essentialism, challenges people's perceptions of race. Originating during **slavery** and persisting into the twenty-first century, passing subverts notions of racial identity by calling into question prevailing assumptions about the determinacy (or, more accurately, the indeterminacy) of race. One kind of passing common to African American literature invovles an African American with a light complexion living his or her life as a White person, or "passing" as a White person (*see* **Color of Skin**), usually in a situation in which living as a recognized African American—or "Black"—person would involve significant consequences different from those connected with being perceived as White.

Although passing typically refers to the conscious decision to cross the socially constructed barrier that segregates Blacks from Whites, passing was not restricted to the color line during slavery. In an effort to gain full human status, slaves who could not pass as White would often try to pass as free. Those denied the anonymity afforded a Black person with White features sought anonymity through crossing the legally sanctioned boundary that divided slave from free. Unfortunately, the lot of the free person of color was not substantially better than that of the slave. Whereas the individual who successfully passed as White gained both freedom and privilege, the individual who passed as free still bore the indelible mark of a slave.

Because the system of slavery was inextricably linked to racial identity, the color of a person's skin marked his or her status. Many all-but-White slaves facilitated their escapes from bondage through the assumption of White and, thus, free racial identities (*see* **Slave Narrative**). In the *Life of William Grimes, the Runaway Slave, Written by Himself* (1825), William Grimes identifies himself as a forty-year-old man "who passes for a negro, though three parts white." In the harrowing tale of his thirty years in bondage, Grimes recounts several incidents in which his White complexion aided in his flight to freedom. Recalling the circumstances of his birth in *A Narrative of the Adventures and Escape of Moses Roper, from American Slavery* (1838), Moses Roper reveals that his "very white" complexion so enraged the mistress of the house that she tried to murder him in his mother's arms. Ironically, the very thing that almost cost him his life as an infant—his nearly White countenance—is what saves him from a life of slavery. In *Narratives of the Sufferings of Lewis and Milton Clarke, Sons of a Soldier of the Revolution, During a Captivity of More Than Twenty Years Among the Slaveholders of Kentucky, One of the So Called Christian States of North America* (1846), Lewis Clarke details how he suffered at the hands of his mistress for being "too white." Disgusted at his having been mistaken for a member of the family, Clarke's mistress forces him to do long hours of manual labor in the hot sun so that no one will mistake him for

White again. In his portion of the narrative, Lewis's brother, Milton, recalls how his own White complexion was the source of much debate at a trial following his failed escape attempt. Like Roper and Grimes before them, Lewis and Milton Clarke eventually escape from slavery by passing as White. In *Narrative of the Life and Adventures of Henry Bibb, an American Slave, Written by Himself* (1849), **Henry Walton Bibb** boards a steamboat on the Ohio River and, "being so near the color of a slaveholder," he is able to facilitate his escape by blending in with the other passengers. One of the most gripping tales of racial deception and disguise is found in **William and Ellen Craft**'s *Running a Thousand Miles for Freedom; or, the Escape of William and Ellen Craft from Slavery* (1860). The Crafts' cleverly executed escape involved Ellen masquerading as a White male slave owner and William posing as her slave. Their escape caused such a stir that for years to follow, young masters journeying north with a single slave were often harassed by authorities.

In the aforementioned narratives, the slaves' impetus for passing is abundantly clear: each is motivated by the desire to trade a life of bondage for one of freedom. In fictionalized accounts of passing, however, the passer's motives are as varied as the individuals themselves. In **William Wells Brown**'s *Clotel; or The President's Daughter: A Narrative of Slave Life in the United States* (1853), Clotel mirrors Ellen Craft's escape by disguising herself as a White male in an effort to free herself and her daughter. Unfortunately, Brown's heroine does not fare as well as Ellen Craft. Trapped by her pursuers, Clotel takes her own life rather than return to a life of slavery. Tragedy also befalls the passers of **Frank J. Webb**'s *The Garies and Their Friends* (1857). Both Mrs. Garie and her son, Clarence, meet tragic ends when the secret of their "true" racial identities is revealed. Providing a stark contrast with Brown's and Webb's depictions of the tragic **mulatto** figure is the character of Iola Leroy in **Frances Ellen Watkins Harper**'s *Iola Leroy; or, Shadows Uplifted* (1892). Although she possesses all of the physical and cultural attributes of a White woman, Iola Leroy rejects the temptation to marry a wealthy White doctor and pass for White. Instead, Harper's heroine embraces her Black heritage and dedicates herself to the betterment of her race.

Charles Waddell Chesnutt's interest in the color line and racial ambiguity was the inspiration for his first novel, *The House Behind the Cedars*. Published in 1900, Chesnutt's narrative recounts the experiences of two mixed-race siblings, John and Rena Walden, who pass in an attempt to access the power and privilege not afforded members of their race. While John's efforts are rewarded, Rena's decision to reject her White identity contributes to her untimely death. Chesnutt's *Mandy Oxendine* (published posthumously in 1997) breaks with the tragic mulatto tradition in that its heroine is not destroyed by her "transgression." Perhaps the most prominent passing novel, **James Weldon Johnson**'s *The Autobiography of an Ex-Colored Man* (1912), delineates the psychological effects of its unnamed narrator's decision to permanently "pass into another world." Although he is not devastated by his decision to align himself with the White race, the narrator confesses to feeling small and selfish for abandoning his race. Unlike Chesnutt and Johnson, who seem at times ambivalent toward the subject of passing, **Walter White** is unequivocal in his rejection of passing in his novel *Flight* (1926). There is no mistaking the sense of liberation Mimi Daquin feels at her decision to return to her family and her community after abandoning them for the White world.

In her novels *Quicksand* (1928) and *Passing* (1929), **Nella Larsen** uses passing as a tactic of self-discovery for her characters. *Quicksand*'s Helga Crane passes in an effort to unify the various facets of her identity. Unfortunately, Helga fails in her search for an authentic self and becomes trapped in a single, stifling Black identity. *Passing*'s Clare Kendry also uses passing as a means of self-exploration. Refusing to be confined by a unitary identity, Clare adopts a series of guises and masks. However, her journey of self-discovery ends tragically when she decides to renounce her White identity and rejoin the African American community. More radical in its approach to passing, **Jessie Redmon Fauset**'s *There Is Confusion* (1924) has its main character pass in order to expose the racist treatment of Black soldiers in the South. The perils associated with this kind of passing are delineated in Walter White's autobiography, *A Man Called White* (1948), which details White's experiences with passing during his undercover work for the **NAACP**. As with the hero of Fauset's novel, White poses as a White man to investigate the atrocities being committed against members of his race. In Fauset's second novel, *Plum Bun* (1929), the heroine, Angela Murray, discovers that she has paid too high a price for passing into the White world. Like White's Mimi Daquin, Angela revels in her decision to cross back over the color line and reclaim her Black heritage. In Fauset's *Comedy, American Style* (1933), the Cary family is torn apart by a self-loathing mother who forces her daughter to pass for White. Olivia Blanchard Cary's obsession with blending into White society is so intense that it ultimately destroys her son, Oliver, and dooms her daughter, Teresa, to a life of misery.

Langston Hughes's poem "The Ballad of Walter White" remarks on White's ability to pass and his having passed in order to investigate **lynching in the South**. Hughes's short story collection *The Ways of White Folks* (1934) includes the story "Passing," written in letter form. In it a son who chooses to pass as White is writing to his mother, explaining his reasons. The story "Who's Passing for Who?" presents passing from a comic, even farcical, point of view; it appeared in the collection *Laughing to Keep from Crying* (1952) (Ostrom).

Although there was a surge of interest in the theme of passing during the **Harlem Renaissance**, relatively little was written about the topic in the years that followed. While passing may have been passé in literary circles, the subject was very much in the public eye. In February 1948, *Ebony* magazine startled readers with the revelation that millions of individuals with a determinable African American ancestry were currently passing for White in the United States. According to the cover essay by the eminent African American journalist Roi Ottley, as many as "Five Million White Negroes" had reputedly crossed the color line. As if to convince readers of the truth of his claims,

Ottley's article included a series of photographs asking readers to identify who on the page was Black and who was White. Of the fair-skinned individuals depicted in the photo array, all, except the woman with the darkest complexion, were African Americans. Ottley approximated that some 40,000 to 50,000 individuals crossed the color line each year. Estimates from other scholars ranged anywhere from 2,000 to 30,000 per annum during the peak years for passing (1880–1940). The secrecy associated with passing is perhaps the best explanation for the large discrepancy in the estimates.

Some fifty years after the appearance of Ottley's *Ebony* article, Shirlee Taylor Haizlip published an article in *American Heritage*, "Passing" (February/March 1995). According to Haizlip, the article was inspired by public reaction to her family memoir, *The Sweeter the Juice* (1994), which chronicles Haizlip's search for generations of family members who disappeared across the color line over the years. Following the release of *The Sweeter the Juice*, Haizlip received thousands of phone calls and letters from people wishing to fill in the gaps of their own families. The fact that several of the individuals who contacted Haizlip confessed that they had no idea that they themselves were Black attests to the slipperiness of racial categories. This kind of inadvertent passing is the subject of Gregory Howard Williams's **autobiography**, *Life on the Color Line: The True Story of a White Boy Who Discovered He Was Black* (1995). Following the separation of his parents, Williams experiences a kind of racial redefinition when he learns the "truth" about his identity. In a reversal of the typical passing scenario, the ostensibly White Gregory Howard Williams must adjust to life as an African American.

Much of the scholarship on passing focuses on the premise that passing for White somehow masks or obscures an essential Black identity. The passing figure's ability to transcend his or her race, however, challenges the very notion of an authentic or true racial identity. In this way, passing proves a powerful lens through which to explore the subjective nature of **race**.

Resources: Judith R. Berzon, *Neither White Nor Black: The Mulatto Character in American Fiction* (New York: New York University Press, 1978); M. Giulia Fabi, *Passing and the Rise of the African American Novel* (Urbana: University of Illinois Press, 2001); Elaine K. Ginsberg, ed., *Passing and the Fictions of Identity* (Durham, NC: Duke University Press, 1996); Shirlee Taylor Haizlip, *The Sweeter the Juice* (New York: Simon and Schuster, 1994); Hans Ostrom, *A Langston Hughes Encyclopedia* (Westport, CT: Greenwood Press, 2002), 40, 210, 296, 424; Werner Sollors, *Neither Black Nor White Yet Both: Thematic Explorations of Interracial Literature* (New York: Oxford University Press, 1997); Gregory Howard Williams, *Life on the Color Line: The True Story of a White Boy Who Discovered He Was Black* (New York: Dutton, 1995).

Carol Goodman

Pate, Alexs D. (born 1950). Novelist, playwright, poet, and performance artist. Alexs Pate was born and raised in **Philadelphia, Pennsylvania**, in a neighborhood marked by both strong families and gang violence, a tension that serves as background for his novels and for his explorations into the homes and inner lives of the African American family. Pate came of age during the **Black Arts Movement** in the mid-1960s and early 1970s—a time focused on questioning the role of Black writers and their connection to the wider Black community. He earned a B.A. from Temple University and worked in the corporate world before setting out to be a professional writer. Observing the African American community through families and, more specifically, the interrelations of fathers and children has become a hallmark of Pate's work. Critics have noted his attention to African American fatherhood as rare in contemporary literature, and one reviewer applauded his novel *Finding Makeba* (1996) for "addresses[ing] crucial matters of fatherhood, the Black literary experience, and the Black family experience" (Ingraham, 90). His first novel, *Losing Absalom* (1994), won both the First Novelist Award of the American Library Association Black Caucus and the Minnesota Book Award. Pate is perhaps most known for writing the novel version of the film *Amistad* (1997), commissioned by Steven Spielberg. He is also the author of *Innocent* (poetry, 1998), *The Multicultiboho Sideshow* (novel, 1999), and *West of Rehoboth* (novel, 2001). A play version of *The Multicultiboho Sideshow* was performed in Minneapolis, and Pate and David Mura developed a performance piece—"Secret Colors"—that explores the complex relationships between African Americans and Asian Americans through the story of their friendship. Pate currently teaches in the African American and African Studies Department at the University of Minnesota.

Resources: "Alexs D. Pate," *Contemporary Authors* (Feb. 14, 2000), Literature Resource Center, Gale Group Databases, Gelman Library, George Washington University, http://galenet.galegroup.com; Laura Ingraham, "Review of *Finding Makeba*, by Alexs Pate," *Library Journal*, Nov. 15, 1996, p. 90; Katherine Link, "'Illuminating the Darkened Corridors': An Interview with Alexs Pate," *African American Review* 36 (2002), 597–610; Alexs D. Pate: interview, excerpt from *Literature and Life: The Givens Collection*, PBS Online, http://www.pbs.org/ktca/litandlife/resources/pate.hmtl; "The Invisible Black Family Man," *Journal of Blacks in Higher Education*, Summer 1994, 76–77; "Profile: Alexs Pate's Book 'West of Rehoboth,'" *All Things Considered*, National Public Radio, Sept. 7, 2001, http://www.npr.org/features/feature.php?wfId=1128642; "Secret Colors: A Performance Piece by Alexs Pate & David Mura," *The Loft Literary Center*, http://www.loft.org/PateMura604.html; Marian Gray Secundy, "Literature Annotations: *Losing Absalom*," *Literature, Arts, and Medicine Database*, June 28, 1999, http://endeavor.med.nyu.edu/lit-med/lit-meddb/webdocs/webdescrips/pate482-des-html; Sybil Steinberg: "Fiction," review of *Losing Absalom*, by Alexs Pate, *Publishers Weekly*, Mar. 14, 1994, p. 65; "Forecasts: Fiction," review of *Finding Makeba*, by Alexs Pate, *Publishers Weekly*, Nov. 4, 1996, p. 62.

Christy J. Zink

Patterson, Raymond R. (1929–2001). Poet and educator. A New York poet, Patterson is praised for his devotion to language and his use of **blues** rhythms. Growing up in **Harlem, New York**, during the **Great Depression** provided Patterson with the theme of much of his poetry: triumph over adversity.

After leaving the Army, he worked for the Youth House for Boys in New York. Patterson received a master's degree from New York University and taught at Benedict College. After a stint in public schools, he returned to New York and taught at the City University of New York. He won numerous awards for his writing, including a grant from the National Endowment for the Arts. Patterson was also deeply involved in the creative life of Long Island, establishing writing workshops and serving on the boards of many organizations, such as the Walt Whitman Birthplace Association.

Patterson's early unpublished poem "Dearest Phillis" was a tribute to **Phillis Wheatley**. With Lawrence Sykes, he produced a photographic essay titled *Get Caught* (1964). Sykes also illustrated Patterson's later volume *Elemental Blues* (1983). *26 Ways of Looking at a Black Man* (1969), Patterson's first published volume of poetry, explores the life of African Americans and the political milieu of the 1960s.

Patterson is best remembered for *Elemental Blues: Poems 1981–1982* (1983), which has been translated into several languages, including French. In "A Note on the Blues," he explains that the musical form of blues influences his poetry. For Patterson, the blues encompass all of life's stages and occasions. Elemental subjects such as cancer, funerals, nuclear bombs, and children are all given equal footing in his blues poems. The book also shows the influence of Walt Whitman, David Ignatow, and **Langston Hughes**.

Resources: Raymond R. Patterson: *Elemental Blues* (Merrick, NY: Cross-Cultural Communications, 1983); *26 Ways of Looking at a Black Man* (New York: Award Books, 1969); "Raymond R. Patterson," in *Contemporary Authors Online* (Detroit: Gale, 2002), http://galenet.galegroup.com/contemporary/authors.

Patricia Kennedy Bostian

Pennington, James William Charles (1807–1870). Minister, historian, and activist. Known primarily as an abolitionist, Pennington wrote one of the first histories of African Americans, an important **slave narrative**, and several **sermons** and **essays** and supported figures ranging from **Frederick Douglass** to **Ann Plato**. Born to slaves in Queen Anne's County, Maryland, and named James Pembroke, Pennington became a skilled blacksmith before escaping in 1827. He eventually moved to **Brooklyn, New York**, in 1829. Called to the ministry, he attempted to enroll at Yale, but was rejected because of his race. He was allowed, though, to attend lectures, and grew proficient in German, Latin, and Greek.

In 1840, Pennington took charge of the Talcott Street Congregational Church in Hartford, Connecticut. Active in support of the *Amistad* Africans, Pennington called a national meeting in August 1841 to discuss African Americans' role in aiding Africans. This same year, in addition to prefacing his parishioner Ann Plato's *Essays*, he wrote his own *A Text Book of the Origin and History, &c, &c, of Colored People*. It was one of the first histories of African Americans, and it often centered on instilling racial pride. A key sermon, *Covenants Involving Moral Wrong Are Not Obligatory upon Man*, followed in

1842. When he was chosen as a delegate to the World Antislavery Convention in London, Pennington's rise to the national—indeed, international—stage was complete.

In 1847, he moved to Shiloh Presbyterian Church in New York City; two years later, he traveled to Britain and published his slave narrative, *The Fugitive Blacksmith* (1849). It quickly went through several editions, but its timing put Pennington at risk: it divulged his fugitive identity only a year before the Fugitive Slave Law. Fearful of recapture, Pennington stayed abroad—first in Jamaica, and then in Britain, as a lecturer. Eventually, British friends raised the funds needed to secure his freedom; Pennington then returned to the United States and community activism.

He had few family connections; little is known of either of his wives—Harriet, who died in 1846, and Almira Way, who he married in 1848 and who died in 1866. He had no children, but seems to have adopted a son, Thomas H. Sands Pennington. Plagued by financial problems and by the revelation of alcoholism, he left the pulpit in the mid-1850s. Historians disagree on the extent of Pennington's struggles with alcohol, but agree that he never regained his national stature, though he penned important essays for the *Anglo-African Magazine*. In later life, he established a freedmen's school in Natchez, Mississippi, and founded a church in Jacksonville, Florida. (*See* **Abolitionist Movement**.)

Resources: R.J.M. Blackett, *Beating Against the Barriers: Biographical Essays in Nineteenth-Century Afro-American History* (Baton Rouge: Louisiana State University Press, 1986); James W. C. Pennington, *The Fugitive Blacksmith* (London: Charles Gilpin, 1849); David E. Swift, *Black Prophets of Justice: Activist Clergy before the Civil War* (Baton Rouge: Louisiana State University Press, 1989); Herman E. Thomas, *James W. C. Pennington: African American Churchman and Abolitionist* (New York: Garland, 1995).

Eric Gardner

Penny, Rob[ert] Lee (1941–2003). Poet, playwright, theater founder, and professor. Penny is best known for helping to establish theater groups and a writers' workshop in **Pittsburgh, Pennsylvania**, as well as the Africana Studies Department at the University of Pittsburgh. He was also, however, a playwright and a poet in his own right and participated in the **Black Arts Movement**. Penny was born in Opelia, Alabama, and moved to what is known as the Hill District of Pittsburgh in 1949 (Mock). The Hill District became his home for the rest of his life. With **August Wilson**, Penny founded both the Black Horizons theater group in 1968 and the Kuntu Writers Workshop in 1976 (Wilson). At this writing, both organizations continue to thrive; Black Horizons is now known as New Horizons ("Editorial"). In the late 1960s and early 1970s, Penny was active in the Black Arts Movement and well acquainted with **Amiri Baraka** and **Sonia Sanchez**. He was a participant in the Congress of African Peoples in 1970, and he successfully advocated for an Africana Studies Department at the University of Pittsburgh; it was founded in 1969. Penny was Professor of Africana Studies for thirty-four years there, and he was well known for teaching a course called "Black Consciousness" (Mock; Wilson). As a playwright, Penny was author of *Good Black Don't Crack*, *Boppin' with the Ancestors*, *Killin' and Chillin'*, and *Sun Rising on the Hill District*. At this writing, his plays have not been published. Penny was also a prolific poet; a volume of selected poems, *Romance, Rhythm, & Revolution*, runs 200 pages. One obituary observed of Penny, "He taught them [young writers, poets, and playwrights] to appreciate their responsibility to blacks in general and to themselves as artists in particular" ("Editorial"). (*See* **Afrocentricity.**)

Resources: "Editorial: Death of Poet: Rob Penny Told the Story of the Black Experience," *Pittsburgh Post-Gazette* online (Mar. 19, 2003), http://www.post-gazette.com/forum/20030319edpenny0319p3.asp; Brentin Mock, "Robert Lee 'Rob' Penny," *ChickenBones: A Journal* (Mar. 2003), http://www.nathanielturner.com/robpenny2.htm; Rob Penny, *Romance, Rhythm & Revolution: Selected Poems* (Pittsburgh, PA: Magnolia Press, 1990); Frances Lee Wilson, "Robert Lee 'Rob' Penny," *ChickenBones: A Journal* (Mar. 2003), http://www.nathanielturner.com/robpenny.htm.

Hans Ostrom

Perdomo, Willie (born 1967). Poet. Often associated with the **Nuyorican Poets Café**, Willie Perdomo is perhaps best known for his live readings, poetry-slam appearances, and poetry performances. He was one of the early Grand Slam Poetry Champs at the Nuyorican Poets Café and has been vital to the burgeoning spoken-word movement in New York City and throughout the country. He is the author of several books of poetry, including *Smoking Lovely* (2003), *Postcards of El Barrio* (2002), and *Where a Nickel Costs a Dime* (1996). In addition to these books and the CDs that often accompany them, Perdomo has been included in several anthologies, such as *Listen Up! Spoken Word Poetry* (1999), *Poems of New York* (2002), *Bum Rush the Page: A Def Poetry Jam* (2001), and *Aloud: An Anthology of Writing from the Nuyorican Poets Café* (1995). He has been featured on several PBS documentaries, such as *Words in Your Face* and *The United States of Poetry*, and on *Def Poetry Jam*, a program on the HBO network. In 1997, Perdomo was runner-up for the Poetry Society of America's first book award, and he was the recipient of the New York Foundation for the Arts Fiction fellowship 1996 and the NYFA Poetry fellowship 2001. He also cowrote an episode for the HBO animated series *Spicy City* and recorded on *Flippin' the Script: Rap Meets Poetry*.

Perdomo grew up in East **Harlem, New York**, only blocks from the home of one of his most significant literary influences, **Langston Hughes**, with whom he is often compared. He is author of a children's story, *Visiting Langston*, a picture book illustrated by Bryan Collier (2002), which tells the story of a young girl who visits Langston Hughes's house. Perdomo's poetry reveals a variety of influences in addition to his affinity for Hughes's work. These influences range from **jazz**, **rap**, and salsa to the work of Walt Whitman, **Amiri Baraka**, and **Sonia Sanchez**. His poetry is rich with the sights, sounds and smells of the streets of Harlem, and his language reveals a mixture of Spanish, English, Black dialect, and "Spanglish." This linguistic mixture is evidenced in the following passage from the prose poem "Where I'm From": "Where I'm from, it's sweet like the late night scratch of rats' feet that explains what my mother means when she says slowly, 'Bueno, mijo, eso es la vida del pobre'" (*Smoking Lovely*, 18). This passage also demonstrates some of the more significant themes that this poet explores, especially issues of **race**, poverty, oppression, and class. Junot Díaz suggests the following of Perdomo: "He's the Puerto Rican diaspora's unofficial poet laureate and what he knows about being of color, being between languages, being poor, being a man, being in trouble, could save your life" (2). His work grapples with cultural identity, violence, and drug addiction as much as it explores ideas about love, family, and community.

Resources: Zoë Anglesey, ed., *Listen Up! Spoken Word Poetry* (New York: One World, 1999); Junot Díaz, Comments on *Smoking Lovely*, by Willie Perdomo (Nov. 12, 2003); Tony Medina and Louis Reyes Rivera, eds., *Bum Rush the Page: A Def Poetry Jam* (New York: Three Rivers Press, 2001); Willie Perdomo: *Smoking Lovely* (New York: Rattapallax Press, 2003); *Visiting Langston* (New York: Henry Holt, 2002); *Where a Nickel Costs a Dime* (New York: Norton, 1996); Rattapallax Press, http://www.rattapallax.com/perdomo_about2.htm.

Mark Tursi

Performance Poetry. Performance poetry is the oral, and sometimes visual, presentation of poetry in front of a live audience. It is often a multimedia, or "intermedia," art form that explores the intersection of poetry with drama, music, dance, and visual arts, and it is a genre that is largely concerned with the relationship between the poet and his or her immediate audience. Performance poets break down boundaries between writer and reader, and between art and life, as well as the barriers between different art forms. By emphasizing the communicative relationship between the writer and the reader or listener, performance poets present a challenge to some concepts of literature and art. Performance poetry is bound to a tradition that is more concerned with process, possibility, improvisation, spontaneity, and community rather than with the finished text as an artifact of literature.

African American writers have been seminal to the promotion, development, and proliferation of performance poetry throughout America since the early 1930s. For example, **Langston Hughes** wrote poetry that was inextricably linked to the rhythms, music, and dialects of the Black community in **Harlem, New York**, and that was particularly suited to be read aloud. The same can be said of the poetry of **Sterling A. Brown**, one of Hughes's contemporaries. For Hughes, Brown, and many other African American writers after them, poetry was often connected to **jazz** music, Black **spirituals**, and **blues**. Today, performance poetry, or spoken word, is experiencing a significant renaissance which is largely due to its promotion and practice by African American writers and performers.

However, the performance of poetry is not a recent phenomenon. The recitation of poetry has a long history that is inextricably linked to the very emergence of literature itself. The ancient Greeks began the "laureate tradition" of awarding outstanding performance poets with laurel crowns, and those poets often traveled from place to place, reciting poetry to the accompaniment of a musical instrument, such as a lyre. The oral tradition was particularly significant in early African societies, where ancestral stories traveled along ancient trade routes and migrated with different cultural groups throughout the continent and beyond. Some early African societies were known for "**signifying**" contests or word battles that involved something similar to a public poetry performance. In most of these societies, poetic narratives connected past to present to future and preceded written texts. The mnemonic devices of rhyme, repetition, and rhythm, often found in poetry, formed a way to keep these stories and cultural mythologies alive. In this way, literature was enlarged and cultural history preserved.

In the Middle Ages, troubadours and traveling minstrels were commonplace throughout Europe and Asia. The famous Japanese poet Bashō traveled throughout Japan judging **haiku** contests, and medieval troubadours performed poetry in courts or in small theaters, often with a harp. In the early modern period and after, public recitations experienced a resurgence on the stage and on the street. Miguel Cervantes' classic *Don Quixote* makes several references to "poetical tournaments" and "poetical jousts" that involved the public performance of poetry. It is these types of literary performances that can be considered the precursors to the performance poetry we see and hear across university campuses, theaters, concert halls, and cafés in America today.

In terms of modern poetics, the connection between drama and poetry increased with artists from the Dada movement, who drew from drama, collage, comedy, and dance in an attempt to challenge the dominant paradigms regarding art and literature. African American writers became more noticeably interested in the oral presentation of poetry towards the middle of the twentieth century with poets such as Hughes, Brown, **Claude McKay**, and **Countee Cullen**—all poets of the **Harlem Renaissance**—who drew on the idiosyncrasies, music, speech, and day-to-day life of urban Blacks. Aimé Césaire, Léopold Sédar Senghor, and Léon Damas, who pioneered an international movement called **Négritude**, wrote poetry that combined aspects from French surrealism with Black dialects to challenge dominant representations of African societies. Both groups insisted that oral poetry and written poetry that featured the **vernacular** were a more accurate model for Black writers worldwide, and thus helped promote the performance of poetry by writers of African descent.

Charles Olson's *Projective Verse* (1959) linked the poetic line to the breath and voice, and sparked a renewed interest in the way poetry was read aloud. Shortly after its publication, a renaissance in the performance of poetry began. In the 1950s and 1960s Beat poets such as Allen Ginsberg, Jack Kerouac, Anne Waldman, and **Amiri Baraka** performed their work from **San Francisco, California**, to New York City. Baraka, an African American poet then called LeRoi Jones, was decisive in calling attention to the rhythms and intonations inherent in Black dialect, and in connecting poetic language to jazz music. He is famous for performances from the 1960s to the present day, where he reads poetry alongside famous jazz musicians, such as bassist Reggie Workman and saxophonist David Murray. Baraka's essay "How You Sound??" (1960) expanded on Olson's arguments, and it suggested further that the sound and musicality of language are directly linked to content and subject matter. A contemporary of Baraka's, **Dudley Randall**, began the **Broadside Press** (1965), which published poems on broadsides and recorded Black poets reading their work.

Other important Black writers at this time, and in the 1970s, include a group of protest poets who are sometimes referred to as **the Last Poets**: Mutabaruka, Linton Kwesi Johnson, and **Gil Scott-Heron**. Scott-Heron's "sound poems," such as "The Revolution Will Not Be Televised" (1971) and *Whitey on the Moon* (1971), were accompanied with jazz and percussion riffs, and challenged dominant White cultural values. These poets and many of the African American poets at this time called attention to the poverty, inequality, and injustice resulting from racism and oppression in America. In the late 1970s, when **rap** and **hip-hop** were just beginning to find voice and rhythm in New York, **Ntozake Shange** experimented with a mixture of poetry, dance, and music in San Francisco bars and clubs. Shange's performances eventually moved to Broadway (1975), where she enjoyed a wide audience for several years. Like Heron and others, she was interested in issues of **race** and **color of skin**, but her monologues also explored **gender** and sexuality.

In the 1980s, **Nathaniel Mackey** drew on African rituals and jazz music, and in his essay "Sound and Sentiment, Sound and Symbol" (1985) he argued that the origins of poetic language are the same as the origins of music. Mackey's poetry often enacts jazz rhythms in what he calls a "post bebop" lyric, in which he attempts to challenge the stereotype of Black musicians as exclusively artists of spontaneity. (Bebop was a style of jazz that emerged in the United States after **World War II**.) In the same decade, rap bands such as Public Enemy, Run-DMC, and rappers including **Tupac Shakur** and Ice-T, brought a new focus and attention to the lyrics, message, and musicality of the day-to-day language spoken within the African American community. These rappers provided a very high-profile example of Black expression that included rage and frustration. They also pointed to existing racist conditions and conflicts within the Black community. With regard to performance of the spoken word, therefore, a thread runs from the Harlem Renaissance through the **Black Arts Movement**, rap, and hip-hop to contemporary performance poetry and "spoken word." Poetry's connection to hip-hop and the development and proliferation of the "poetry slam," or performance poetry contests, reveals a strong subversion of and reaction to academic formalism, and a rejection of the poststructuralist attention to the written text. This recent surge in spoken word poetry, with its clear African American origins, demonstrates a keen awareness of a long history of racial and cultural oppression, as well as the suppression of colloquial speech and dialect. Spoken word undermines and rejects restrictions on language by focusing on the recitation and performance of poetry in front of an audience; in this way, it is connected as much to drama as it is to poetry.

With influences from Langston Hughes to contemporary poets, including Baraka and Mackey, the writers and performers from the **Nuyorican Poets Café** in New York and elsewhere in the country have changed contemporary definitions and expectations of poetry. The use of everyday speech, Black English, and Spanglish, and the incorporation of diverse dialects in spoken word, subvert dominant expectations of poetry. In their performances, these poets often take on inequality, gender inequity, class hierarchy, and sexual liberation. Spoken word poetry is filled with the rhythms, rhymes, and other sonic devices that are part of contemporary hip-hop. For spoken word, like earlier performance poetry, the relationship between the author and an audience becomes fundamental to the experience of "reading" a poem. The contemporary Black American writers **Paul Beatty**, Saul Williams, Tracie Morris, **Jessica Care Moore**, Soul Evans, and many others demonstrate the vitality and energy of this burgeoning movement.

Resources: Zoë Anglesey, ed., *Listen Up! Spoken Word Poetry* (New York: One World, 1999); Gary Mex Glazner, ed., *Poetry Slam: The Competitive Art of Performance Poetry* (San Francisco: Manic D Press, 2000); Monica Molarsky, "Word Fever," *American Theatre* 16, no. 9 (Nov. 1999), 59–65; Kevin Powell, ed., *Step into a World: A Global Anthology of the New Black Literature* (New York: Wiley, 2000); Ellen Marcia Zweig, *Performance Poetry: Critical Approaches to Contemporary Intermedia* (Ann Arbor: University of Michigan Press, 1980).

Mark Tursi

Perkins, Useni Eugene (born 1932). Playwright and poet. Born in **Chicago, Illinois,** Perkins earned a B.S. and an M.S. at George Williams College and did further graduate work at DePaul University. Trained as a social worker, he was employed in that capacity with various organizations, most notably the Better Boys Foundation Family Center, from 1959 to 1982. At the same time, he wrote and began to teach writing courses at such institutions as Roosevelt University, Lewis University, Triton College, and Chicago State College, as well as in Chicago-area high schools, libraries, and community centers, and in prisons.

In both his poetry and his plays, Perkins has sought to understand how the African and the American aspects of African American identity might be synthesized more completely and meaningfully, both for African Americans themselves and for the broader American society. He is also concerned with the effects of urban life on the psyche of those—particularly the marginalized racially, economically, and politically—who live in the city and are very much defined by the possibilities that it seems to offer them or deny to them.

For a part-time playwright, Perkins has been extraordinarily prolific. His full-length plays include *Turn a Black Cheek* (first produced 1965), *Assassination of a Dream* (1967), *Thunder Is Not Yet Rain* (1968), *The Image Makers* (1972), *Professor J. B.* (1973), *Brothers* (1974), *Ghetto Fairy* (alternate title,

The Black Fairy; 1974), *Cinque* (1975), *Quinn Chapel* (1975), *Pride of Race* (1984), and *Papa's Child: The Story of Etta Moten Barnett* (2001). In addition, he has written the one-act plays *The Legacy of Leadbelly* (1966), *Nothing but a Nigger* (1969), *Black Is So Beautiful* (1970), *Cry of the Black Ghetto* (1970), *Fred Hampton* (1972), *It Can Never Be in Vain* (1973), *God Is Black, but He's Dead* (1975), and *Our Street* (1975).

Perkins's best-known and most widely anthologized poem is "Who'll Sound the Requiem?" His collections of poems include *An Apology to My African Brother, and Other Poems* (1965), *Black Is Beautiful* (1968), *West Wall* (1969), *Silhouette* (1970), *When You Grow Up: Poems for Children* (1982), and *Midnight Blues in the Afternoon and Other Poems* (1984). In addition, selections of his work have been included in *Port Chicago Poets: A New Voice in Anthology* (1966), *Black Arts: An Anthology of Black Creations* (1969), *The Black Seventies* (1970), *Calling All Sisters* (1970), and *To Gwen with Love* (1971). Perkins has edited the collections *Black Expressions: An Anthology of New Black Poets* (1967), *Dark Meditations: A Collection of Poems* (1971), and *Poetry of Prison: Poems by Black Prisoners* (1972).

Perkins's nonfiction books include *Home Is a Dirty Street: The Social Oppression of Black Children* (1975), *Harvesting New Generations: The Positive Development of Black Youth* (1986), *Explosion of Chicago's Black Street Gangs* (1987), and *The Afrocentric Self-Inventory and Discovery Workbook* (1990). *Home Is a Dirty Street* has been regarded as a major contribution to sociology, and the three later books, along with *Hey Black Child and Other Children's Poems* (2003), reflect his deepening interest in the importance of cultural awareness as an agent of social change.

Resources: **Primary Sources:** Useni Eugene Perkins: *The Afrocentric Self-Inventory and Discovery Workbook* (Chicago: Third World Press, 1990); *An Apology to My African Brother, and Other Poems* (Chicago: Adams Press, 1965); *Black Fairy and Other Plays* (Chicago: Third World Press, 1972); *Black Is Beautiful* (Chicago: Free Black Press, 1968); *Explosion of Chicago Black Street Gangs* (Chicago: Third World Press, 1987); *Ghetto Fairy* (Chicago: Third World Press, 1972); *Harvesting New Generations: The Positive Development of Black Youth* (Chicago: Third World Press, 1986); *Hey Black Child and Other Children's Poems* (Chicago: Association for the Positive Development of Black Youth, 2003); *Home Is a Dirty Street: The Social Oppression of Black Children* (Chicago: Third World Press, 1975); *Midnight Blues in the Afternoon and Other Poems* (Chicago: INESU, 1984); *Silhouette* (Chicago: Free Black Press, 1970); *West Wall* (Chicago: Free Black Press, 1969); *When You Grow Up: Poems for Children* (Chicago: Black Child Journal, 1982). **Secondary Sources:** Patricia Corrigan, "Rite of Passage . . . Author, Role Model, Takes Young Black Males Through Ceremony of Afrocentric Awakening," *St. Louis Post-Dispatch*, Mar. 28, 1991, p. 7; R. Lamont Jones, Jr., "All Society Must Help End Gangs, Expert Says," *Pittsburgh Post-Gazette*, June 19, 1993, p. B1.

Martin Kich

Perrin, Kayla (born 1969). Novelist and short story writer. Perrin adds her voice to the landscape of contemporary romantic fiction. However, her novels are not the typical wistful romance; they are rife with intrigue and mystery. Her fiction belongs to a category more aptly termed romantic suspense. In her novels, Perrin also tells stories about how the bonds of friendship, male/female relationships, and forgiveness are tested. Her novels also focus on the value of female friendships.

Born in Jamaica, Perrin moved to Toronto, Canada, when she was a child. She always knew she wanted to be a writer, and at thirteen years old she submitted her first book to Scholastic Publications. At eighteen she received first place in the Silver Quill Literary Association's short story contest for "The Million Dollar Smile." She received her B.A. in English and sociology from the University of Toronto and a B.Ed. from York University. In July 1997 her first novel, *Everlasting Love*, was published by Kensington's Arabesque Romance. Perrin's novels explore issues of self-esteem, trust, and forgiveness in a fictional world filled with vivid characterization and detailed settings. She is adept at creating a visual atmosphere which matches the emotional and suspenseful journey on which her characters find themselves.

A prolific writer, Perrin has published fifteen books in seven years, including a children's book, *The Disappearance of Allison Jones*. She has also contributed short stories to several collections, and she has written about how to write **romance novels**. She has received many accolades for her novels from a number of African American publications and romance book clubs. In February 2001, *If You Want Me* was nominated for the Gold Pen Award. On October 11, 2002, Perrin won the Golden Leaf Award for *In An Instant* from the New Jersey Romance Writers.

Resources: Kayla Perrin: *Again, My Love* (Columbus, MS: Genesis Press, 1997); *The Delta Sisters* (New York: St. Martin's, 2004); *The Disappearance of Allison Jones* (Columbus: Genesis Press, 2000); *Everlasting Love* (New York: Pinnacle/Arabesque, 1997); *Flirting with Danger* (New York: BET Books, 2001); *Fool for Love* (Washington, DC: Arabesque, 2003); *Gimme an O!* (New York: Avon, 2005); *Holiday of Love* (Washington, DC: BET Books, 2000); *If You Want Me* (New York: Harper Torch Romance, 2001); *In a Heartbeat* (New York: BET Books, 2003); *In an Instant* (Washington, DC: Arabesque, 2002); "Kidnapped," in *The Best Man* (New York: St. Martin's, 2003); "Making Magic with Characters," *Romantic Times*, http://www.romantictimes .com/data/tips/808.html; "Maternal Instincts," in *A Very Special Love* (New York: BET Books, 2000); *Midnight Dreams* (New York: BET Books, 1999); "A Perfect Fantasy," in *Wine and Roses* (New York: BET Books, 1999); "The Political Correctness of Writing the Ethnic Romance," in *How to Write a Romance for the New Market and Get Published*, ed. Kathryn Faulk (Columbus: Genesis Press, 2000); *Say You Need Me* (New York: HarperTorch, 2002); *The Sisters of Theta Phi Kappa* (New York: St. Martin's, 2001); *Sweet Honesty* (New York: BET Books, 1999); *Tell Me You Love Me* (New York: HarperTorch, 2003).

Cameron Christine Clark

Perry, Charles (1924–1969). Novelist. Perry is best known for having written *Portrait of a Young Man Drowning*, a graphic, tautly written novel about a young African American's harsh life on the streets of **Brooklyn, New York**, in the late 1950s. The novel's protagonist is Harold Odum, who at age sixteen is already involved in organized crime and who descends even further into a life of violence and, ultimately, of madness. Perry also wrote plays and worked as a radio actor. He was at work on a book about the mysterious death of his son (age eleven) when he died in 1969 of cancer ("Behind the Scenes"). Perry's novel is sometimes compared with the work of **Robert Deane Pharr** and **Clarence Cooper, Jr.**

Resources: "Behind the Scenes," Web page for Old School Books, http://www.wwnorton.com/osb/drown.htm; Charles Perry, *Portrait of a Young Man Drowning* (New York: Simon and Schuster, 1962; repr. New York: Norton, 1996).

Hans Ostrom

Perry, Phyllis Alesia (born 1961). Journalist and novelist. Born in **Atlanta, Georgia**, and raised in Tuskegee, Alabama, Perry worked as a journalist for many years. She was on the staff of the *Tuskegee News*, the *Northeast Mississippi Daily Journal*, the *Alabama Journal*, and the *Atlanta Journal-Constitution*. During her time as assistant city editor for the *Alabama Journal* in Montgomery, she was a member of the team that was awarded the Pulitzer Prize in 1988 for their 1987 series investigating Alabama's infant mortality crisis. That series also received the Distinguished Service Award of the Society of Professional Journalists, Sigma Delta Chi (1988). More recently, she worked for ten years for the *Atlanta Journal-Constitution* as an editor, copy editor, and reporter. With the publication of her first novel, Perry shifted her career to full-time novelist.

In 1998, Perry published the historical novel *Stigmata*. Her first novel, it tells the story of a woman whose life is radically altered after she inherits her grandmother's trunk and handmade quilt. These items, from a grandmother she did not know, prompt a journey to learn the truth about her family's past. The novel was first published in Germany, then in the United States, Great Britain, the Netherlands, and Spain. *Stigmata* received nominations for the Quality Paperback Book Club New Voices Award, and in 1999, Perry received the Georgia Author of the Year Award for a first novel. Her second book, *A Sunday in June* (2004), is a historical novel that takes place in turn-of-the-twentieth-century Alabama and explores the tension in a family about letting go of traditions of the past in order to gain social advancement.

Resources: Phyllis Alesia Perry: *Stigmata* (New York: Hyperion, 1998); *A Sunday in June* (New York: Hyperion, 2004).

Esther L. Jones

Petry, Ann Lane (1908–1997). Author of novels, short stories, and juvenile fiction. By debunking stereotypes of **race**, class, and **gender**, Petry contributed significantly to the nonsentimental depiction of the socio-economic plight of African Americans in the 1940s and 1950s and thereby paved the way for contemporary African American women's writing.

Born in 1908 in Old Saybrook, Connecticut, Ann Petry graduated from the Connecticut College of Pharmacy in New Haven in 1931 and then worked at her family's drugstores. After marrying George D. Petry in 1938, she moved to New York City, where she wrote for the **Amsterdam News**. She also took up painting, writing short fiction, and acting in the American Negro Theatre. Later, she honed her writing skills by editing the woman's page of *The People's Voice* and by participating in Mabel Louise Robinson's creative writing workshop at Columbia University. The $2,400 from a Houghton Mifflin Library Fellowship enabled her to finish her first novel, *The Street* (1946), the first book by a Black woman writer to sell over a million copies. Petry published two more novels, *Country Place* (1947) and *The Narrows* (1953), a collection of short stories titled *Miss Muriel and Other Stories* (1971), several adolescent books, nonfiction articles, and some poetry. Among the many honors she received are the Doctorate of Letters from Suffolk University (1983) and the University of Connecticut (1988), the Lifetime Achievement Award at the Fifth Annual Celebration of Black Writers Conference in **Philadelphia, Pennsylvania** (1989), and the Connecticut Arts Award from the Connecticut Commission of the Arts (1992) (Ervin, xii–xviii).

Though Petry herself seemed to reject such categorizing, her works are often compared with the naturalistic works of **Richard Wright** and **Chester Himes** and with the tradition of **protest literature** represented by the **Chicago Renaissance** (Ervin, xv). In his 1987 study *The Afro-American Novel and Its Tradition*, Bernard Bell describes *The Street* as "a conventional novel of economic determinism in which the environment is the dominant force against which the characters must struggle to survive" (178). However, in addition to the characteristic "slice of life," the novel depicts the entire range of possible responses to the realities of life in the streets of **Harlem, New York**, and presents a subtle psychological analysis of the consequences of squelched desires.

Lutie Johnson's hopes spring from her first contact with Ben Franklin's *The Way to Wealth* philosophy at the home of her White employers in Lyme, Connecticut. Petry describes how creature comforts and consumer goods create artificial desires in Lutie, who naively believes that she will be able to escape the restrictions of her social position and provide her son Bub with a better life. She asserts that "anybody could be rich if he wanted to and worked hard enough and figured it out carefully enough" (43). Consequently, she strives to improve herself by taking night classes and studying for the civil service exam. Petry models Lutie's behavior upon Franklin's only to reveal that Lutie is mistaken in her belief that the American dream is accessible even to a poor Black woman.

The title of Petry's novel underscores the formative influences of New York's 116th Street on its inhabitants. On the first page of the novel, the wind whips Lutie around the street, blinding her so that she can barely make out the street signs. It heaps up the garbage and nearly freezes the blood in her veins. Merciless in the pursuit of those it can hurt, it is an elemental force, uncaring and brutal. Petry employs the wind as the symbol of a force that continually threatens to take hold of Lutie, attacks her physically, and dampens her spirits. The walls in her apartment seem to trap her. The fear of Jones, the janitor, who lusts after Lutie and eventually tempts her son to steal mail from the residents in the apartment building, coupled with the uncertainty of her future, compel her to seek escape at the Junto Bar and Grill. Petry's choice of name for this bar is noteworthy, considering that Ben Franklin's first men's club in Philadelphia was called the Junto and was to serve philanthropic purposes.

At the end of the novel, while sitting on the train that is to take her away from the scene of the murder she committed in order to get the money for a lawyer to plead Bub's case, Lutie draws intersecting circles on the window-pane. They seem to represent the vicious cycle from which she could not free herself. Remembering her schoolteacher's derogatory remarks, she begins to wonder why, indeed, she was ever taught to write when she was not given the chance to put her talents to good use.

Despite this grim picture, Petry suggests potential alternatives: whenever her ambitions lure her into danger, memories of her grandmother's common sense warn Lutie not to proceed, but she chooses to ignore these warnings. As Keith Clark points out, "It is precisely because Lutie has become so enslaved to the American Dream and the 'white' means of attaining it that she lacks the ability to modify and act accordingly" (500). Ben Franklin cannot be the right kind of adviser for the poor and disenfranchised of Harlem. Actually, his philosophy rings false in this environment. Community rather than rational individualism, and traditional folk wisdom rather than capitalism, look far more promising. A statement in Petry's essay "The Novel as Social Criticism" sums up her position: "In one way or another, the novelist who criticizes some undesirable phase of the status quo *is* saying that man is his brother's keeper and that unless a social evil (war or racial prejudice or anti-Semitism or political corruption) is destroyed man cannot survive but will become what Cain feared he would become—a wanderer and a vagabond on the face of the earth" (33).

Dismissed as an assimilationist novel by some critics because it features a group of White characters and does not overtly discuss racial issues, *Country Place* (1947) sets out to examine the hypocrisies of a small New England town. The narrative moves from Doc Fraser's first-person story to several

Ann Petry, 1948. Yale Collection of American Literature, Beinecke Rare Book and Manuscript Library.

third-person limited omniscient accounts, a method that allows Petry to investigate different points of view and illumine the "composite reality" of the community's identity (Holloday, 34). The otherwise traditional narrative unfolds in one week and is driven by the rise of a powerful storm. Doc Fraser, a sixty-five-year-old White druggist in Lennox, Connecticut, plays a unifying role reminiscent of George Willard's in Sherwood Anderson's *Winesburg, Ohio*. Assisted by the town gossip (the taxi driver Tom Walker, called Weasel), Fraser proposes to report accurately what happened to the townspeople, "this record of events contains, of course, something of life and something of death, for both are to be found in a country place" (5). The novel focuses on Johnnie Roane's brief return to Lennox after **World War II** and on his estranged wife, Glory, whose affair with Ed Barrell encourages Johnnie to move to New York and fulfill his dream of becoming a painter. Two minor plots concern the wealthy Mrs. Gramby's conflict with her greedy daughter-in-law and the decision by the servants Neola and Portulacca to get married.

Set mainly in a black neighborhood in Monmouth, Connecticut, *The Narrows* (1953) involves a more obviously sociological investigation of racial matters, which led Bernard Bell to remark that the novel's theme is "that our lives are shaped as much by contingency as they are by time and place" (181). With its modernistic shifts in narrative perspective, some stream-of-consciousness passages, and interesting word coinages, this novel constitutes a new development in Petry's oeuvre. According to Hilary Holloway, the novel's epigraph, taken from Shakespeare's *Henry V*, suggests that one place can easily be compared to another (77), as Petry does with the Black and White neighborhoods and families.

Indeed, the novel creates complex relationships among carefully developed Black and White characters. The main character, the twenty-six-year-old African American Link (short for Lincoln) Williams, an orphan and Dartmouth history graduate, is the novel's linking character between Black and White and rich and poor. He works at the Last Chance bar owned by Bill Hood, who on and off, despite his mob connections, serves as his father figure and instills in him a pride in his ethnic heritage. Abbie Crunch, a staunch New England lady, is Link's adoptive mother. Because of his love for Camilla Treadway Sheffield, alias Camilo Williams, the rich White heiress to a munitions company fortune, Link is murdered at the end of the novel. Neither the two lovers nor the community knows how to deal with their interracial relationship (Holloway, 88). In his article " 'Same Train Be Back Tomorrer': Ann Petry's *The Narrows* and the Repetition of History," Michael Barry observes that the novel questions "Western progress narratives" while sustaining hopes for moral improvement (143).

In addition to some uncollected short stories, Petry also published *Miss Muriel and Other Stories* (1971), the first short story collection by an African American woman, including thirteen pieces. The title story calls attention to the pernicious consequences of stereotyping and prejudice experienced by both Black and White characters. Ruth's is the only Black family in the fictional Wheeling, New York. The child narrator befriends the elderly shoemaker

Blemish, who develops a keen interest in Ruth's aunt Sophronia. When two Black suitors enter the scene, Blemish is run out of town and Ruth debates whether she would have found this White suitor acceptable for her aunt. "The New Mirror" features the same black family and comments again on their feelings of alienation as the only " 'admittedly' black family" in Wheeling (59). "Has Anybody Seen Miss Dora Dean?" employs the same first-person, middle-class narrator as the preceding two stories. However, as an adult she is more acutely aware of latent discriminations. In the course of the story, she is finally able to answer a question that has preoccupied her since childhood: Mr. Forbes, a butler, killed himself because he could no longer stand his servile position, his suicide implicitly devaluing the lives of all African Americans who struggled for a place in the community (Holloday, 106). "Doby's Gone" introduces Sue, whose imaginary friend disappears when she faces racist violence in school. In "Solo on the Drums," Kid James, a drummer whose wife has left him, puts all of his emotions into his music. Petry creates an eerily expressionistic musical sequence in this piece reminiscent of similar elements in **Ralph Ellison**'s work.

Petry also wrote children's books, such as *The Drugstore Cat* (1949) and *Legends of the Saints* (1970). Driven by a desire to debunk stereotypes of African Americans, she created, in *Tituba of Salem Village* (1964), a partly historical and partly fictional portrait of a young Barbadian slave woman who came to Salem Village with the family of the Reverend Samuel Paris. Petry sympathetically describes the heartbreak of leaving home and the daily drudgeries of making a living in the colonies, in a staunchly Puritan community where any sort of "otherness" raises suspicions of witchcraft. *Harriet Tubman, Conductor on the Underground Railroad* (1955) emphasizes **Harriet Tubman**'s early years, her escape from slavery, and her return to Maryland to free hundreds of other slaves. Each of the fictionalized chapters ends with a short historical commentary. As Petry explained in interviews, these two novels include none of the uncertainties and questions of her adult novels because she meant to supply children with viable African American role models.

Contemporary literary criticism of Petry's work transcends naturalistic inquiries. While Heather Holloday describes Petry as a "neighborhood" novelist who emphasizes community and family and complex relationships (44) instead of rigid individualism, others have examined Petry as a New England writer or studied her anticipation of strong African American women characters. Recent articles have also illustrated the depth and versatility of Petry's work by drawing attention to new critical approaches springing from the theories of Michel Foucault and Sigmund Freud, from the critical perspective known as New Historicism, and strategies of interpretation connected to **feminism**.

Resources: Primary Sources: Ann Petry: *Country Place* (Chatham, NJ: Chatham Bookseller, 1947); *The Drugstore Cat* (New York: Crowell, 1949); *Harriet Tubman, Conductor on the Underground Railroad* (1955; repr. New York: Pocket Books, 1971); *Legends of the Saints* (New York: Crowell, 1970); *Miss Muriel and Other Stories* (1971; repr. Boston: Beacon, 1989); *The Narrows* (1953; repr. Boston: Beacon Press, 1988); "The Novel as Social Criticism," in *The Writer's Book*, ed. Helen Hull (New

York: Harper, 1950), 32–39; *The Street* (1946; repr. Boston: Beacon Press, 1974); *Tituba of Salem Village* (1964; repr. New York: Harper Trophy, 1991). **Secondary Sources:** "Ann Petry," *Voices from the Gap*, http://voices.cla.umn.edu/newsite/authors/PETRYann.htm; Michael Barry, "'Same Train Be Back Tomorrer': Ann Petry's *The Narrows* and the Repetition of History," *MELUS* 24, no. 1 (Spring 1999), 141–160; Bernard W. Bell, *The Afro-American Novel and Its Tradition* (Amherst: University of Massachusetts Press, 1987); Robert Bone, *The Negro Novel in America*, rev. ed. (New Haven, CT: Yale University Press, 1965); Keith Clark, "A Distaff Dream Deferred? Ann Petry and the Art of Subversion," *African American Review* 26, no. 3 (1992), 495–505; Hazel Arnett Ervin, *Ann Petry: A Bio-Bibliography* (New York: G. K. Hall, 1993); Heather Hicks: "Rethinking Realism in Ann Petry's *The Street*," *MELUS* 27, no. 4 (Winter 2002), 89–96; "This Strange Communion: Surveillance and Spectatorship in Ann Petry's *The Street*," *African American Review* 37, no. 1 (Spring 2003), 21–38; Hilary Holladay, *Ann Petry* (New York: Twayne, 1996); Julia Mickenberg, "Civil Rights, History, and the Left: Inventing the Juvenile Black Biography," *MELUS* 27, no. 2 (Summer 2002), 65–93; Marjorie Pryse, "'Pattern Against the Sky': 'Deism and Motherhood in Ann Petry's *The Street*," in *Conjuring: Black Women, Fiction and Literary Tradition*, ed. Marjorie Pryse and Hortense Spillers (Bloomington: Indiana University Press, 1985), 116–131; Mary Helen Washington, ed., *Invented Lives: Narratives of Black Women 1860–1960* (Garden City, NY: Anchor, 1987).

Susanna Hoeness-Krupsaw

Pharr, Robert Deane (1916–1989). Novelist. Pharr's novels present an unflinching, witty picture of crime and poverty in the urban African American experience. Born in Virginia to a schoolteacher mother and minister father, Pharr graduated in 1937 from Virginia Union College. He spent the next twenty-two years supporting himself as a waiter at resorts and hotels all along the eastern seaboard. After several failed attempts at playwriting, Pharr became inspired by the example of Sinclair Lewis and turned his hand to **novels**. While working at the Columbia University Faculty Club, he made the contacts necessary to publish *The Book of Numbers* (1969), a chronicle of the bloody struggle of two young men to dominate the numbers racket of a fictionalized Richmond, Virginia. Critics widely praised the novel for its sharp dialogue, dark humor, and frank depiction of the African American ghetto. Pharr's second book, *S.R.O.* (1971), depicts the residents of a run-down, single-room-occupancy hotel in **Harlem, New York**. While some reviewers again praised Pharr's realism, many were put off by the novel's blunt, lengthy portrayal of alcoholics, addicts, and prostitutes. Pharr's next two novels, *The Welfare Bitch* (1973) and *The Soul Murder Case* (1975), suffered critical and public rejection and went out of print almost immediately. Pharr scored a final success with *Giveadamn Brown* (1978), the surreal comic adventure of a young man who becomes the kingpin of a Harlem drug empire.

Resources: *Contemporary Authors*, new rev. series, vol. 75 (Detroit: Gale, 1984); Robert Deane Pharr: *The Book of Numbers* (Garden City, NY: Doubleday, 1969); *Giveadamn Brown* (Garden City, NY: Doubleday, 1978); *The Soul Murder Case* (New

York: Avon, 1975); *S.R.O.* (Garden City, NY: Doubleday, 1971); *The Welfare Bitch* (Garden City, NY: Doubleday, 1973); Richard Yarborough, in *Dictionary of Literary Biography*, vol. 33, *Afro-American Fiction Writers after 1955* (Detroit: Gale, 1984), 208–214.

David Yost

Philadelphia, Pennsylvania. Affectionately known as the City of Brotherly Love, Philadelphia is one of the most diverse cities in the northeastern United States. Its culturally rich history is represented by a mixture of nationalities contributing to its diverse appeal. Its reputation as the nation's birthplace of democracy promotes the value of freedom and an expression of it through the arts. Many groups have contributed to this diversity, and the African American community has made considerable artistic contributions to Philadelphia. From the perspective of art imitating life, the literary works represented by Philadelphia often speak to the regional developments that were influenced by larger national movements. Important historical eras shaping these developments include **slavery**, the **Civil War** and **Reconstruction**, the **Harlem Renaissance**, and the post–Harlem Renaissance period.

The Era of Slavery (1700s–1865)

African American heritage has had a strong presence in Philadelphia since the late seventeenth century. Some of the earliest commercial sales of African slaves took place in Philadelphia in the 1680s. Primarily inhabited and governed by the Quakers, Philadelphia was one of the first Northern cities to object to slavery. To promote the objection to slavery, the Quaker community granted manumission with the passage of the Gradual Abolition Act of 1780. This enactment was the beginning of a movement for freedom in the North. The passage of this act was the impetus for the **Abolitionist Movement** of the early nineteenth century, that supported the emancipation of Southern Blacks and their hope for a better life in the North. For Philadelphia, and many other northeastern cities, the conflict in **the South** and the Civil War would be the catalyst of inspiration for the literary movement of the late nineteenth century. Many freedmen and women flocked to this city to improve their lives. Many arrived with no formal education and made literacy one of the primary objectives in creating a better life. Hence, reading and writing were an important part of the social and cultural development during this period. Other major social developments in the city during this time include the founding of the first Black church and the use of newspapers within the community.

The newspaper was one of the most influential vehicles of written text in the late 1700s for Philadelphia's African American community. This is largely due to development of the Black church. The Black church in many ways was the birthplace of writing in Philadelphia. One of the oldest Black churches in the United States, the Mother Bethel African Methodist Episcopal Church, was founded in 1797. Attendance restrictions at traditional White churches encouraged African Americans to worship elsewhere. Dismayed by these restrictions, native-born Philadelphians—Reverend **Richard Allen**, Absalom Jones, and James Forten—encouraged community members to form their own congregations. To convey this message, and other religious themes, to the community at large, Allen, Jones, and Forten formed *The Christian Recorder* newspaper, one of the earliest African American religious publications.

Allen, Jones, and Forten continued to make significant contributions to the battle to abolish slavery. For example, they were staunch opponents of the Fugitive Slave Act of 1793, which gave slave owners the right to pursue and recover runaway slaves from Northern states to which they had escaped. To give voice to this opposition, their views were often reflected in articles written for *The Liberator*, one of the first antislavery newspapers in the country. Their work as advocates for freedom in the North continued for generations to come. For example, writing about her experiences as a nurse to freed slaves before and after the Civil War, James Forten's daughter, **Charlotte Forten Grimké**, wrote *A Free Black Girl Before the Civil War* (1854), a diary shedding light on the transition Southerners made to Philadelphia. In addition, James Forten's son-in-law Robert Purvis worked to support the efforts of the Anti-Slavery Society and the **Underground Railroad** by writing pamphlets to support their causes. In addition, Frances Jackson Coppin (known as **Fanny Marion Jackson Coppin**), educator and activist, later continued the efforts of the antislavery movement by writing articles for the paper frequently. *The Christian Recorder* also served as a forum to share news about to the Abolitionist Movement and stories about the Underground Railroad.

In addition, Philadelphia is recognized for the first publication of poetry by an African American woman in 1773, **Phillis Wheatley**'s *Poems on Various Subjects, Religious and Moral*. A native of Africa residing in **Boston, Massachusetts**, Wheatley saw her poetry break barriers for many other African American writers and poets in Philadelphia.

The literary dimensions of this period were characterized primarily by the quest for freedom and the experiences of slavery, and the social conditions of the South. Many of the works during this period were created from the oral traditions of storytelling that were an important aspect of African American culture.

The Post–Civil War Era and Reconstruction (1865–1920)

The period after the Civil War was filled with uncertainty for many African Americans. While the Reconstruction Act of 1867 provided federal protection for African Americans in the South, a poor economic situation made life very difficult. As a result, the migration to the North continued, and Philadelphia remained a major stop in the Northeast. As the numbers of new settlers in the city grew, so did their desire to be literate and more educated. Authors continued to write about this experience of the journey north. In 1872 *The Underground Rail Road* was written by **William Still**. Still's work is an account of life and the trials and tribulations on the Freedom Trail. Still is also known for his narrative about the discriminatory treatment of African Americans on the railway system in Philadelphia.

One of the best-known examinations of African American life and culture in Philadelphia is **W.E.B. Du Bois**'s *The Philadelphia Negro* (1899). Perhaps no other literary work examines the early social experiences of African American life in Philadelphia more extensively. It is regarded as the first account of social scientific research focusing on African American urban life in the United States. Du Bois provides an in-depth examination of "Negro Life" as it existed in that time. His findings include background and statistical information on the economic condition, the educational institutions, and the development of Philadelphia's first Negro hospital. According to Elijah Anderson, Du Bois's work was well ahead of its time.

Also among the literary works during this period which captured the social life of Philadelphia was **Gertrude Bustill Mossell**'s *Women's Era*, a nationally acclaimed newspaper during the late nineteenth century. Her work gave voice to the experiences of African American women in Philadelphia. Her first book, *The Work of the Afro-American Woman* (1894), celebrates the achievements of Black women. Much of her work spoke to the importance of racial identity and consciousness. Her efforts in this area also led her to help organize Philadelphia's branch of the National Afro-American Council, which later became National Association for the Advancement of Colored People (**NAACP**).

Toward the end of this period, Southerners continued to migrate North to make Philadelphia their home. The city still welcomed many freedmen and women and provided a venue of expression for many writers.

The Era of the Harlem Renaissance (1920s–1930s)

During the early 1900s, the desire of Southerners to move north grew considerably. The **Great Migration** consisted of an enormous number of African Americans who desired to create better lives for themselves. In addition to New York, **Chicago, Illinois**, and **Detroit, Michigan**, Philadelphia was a destination for many, a location promising improved economic conditions. The mass exodus of African Americans from the South, combined with the ending of **World War I**, created a new consciousness among African Americans, prompting a new collective consciousness which would be the beginning of what is known as the Harlem Renaissance.

One of the most influential figures of the Harlem Renaissance was the Philadelphia native, **Alain Locke**. Locke, an English and philosophy scholar, is credited with creating the term "Harlem Renaissance" (Worley and Perry). The "rebirth" of Harlem was characterized by the **New Negro** Movement, which embodied the celebration of a new collective consciousness among African Americans and its expression through the arts. Locke served as a mentor, assisting young African American writers by nurturing and publishing their work. Nathan Huggins, in his book *Harlem Renaissance*, asserts that Locke believed that transformation of the American Negro was largely dependent on freedom from the past and the rediscovery of himself. Much of Locke's influence was shared in ***The New Negro*** (1925), a publication dedicated to the New

Negro movement. It was a forum for artists to express themselves during this cultural revolution. Other works by Locke include *A Collection of Congo Art* (1927) and *Negro Speaks for Himself* (1924). He edited *Four Negro Poets* (1927), *The New Negro: An Interpretation* (1925), *Plays of Negro Life: A Source-Book of Native American Drama*, edited with Montgomery Gregory (1927), and *The Negro's Contribution to American Art and Literature* (1928).

Philadelphia's Literary Contributions Post–Harlem Renaissance (1930s to the Present)

Literary expression after the Harlem Renaissance period is characterized by a renewed sense of commitment to the African American community. This commitment relates to the raised levels of cultural awareness and pride that were explored artistically during the Harlem Renaissance. Still confronted by national issues of inequality, social and economic injustices, the voices of African American writers continued to capture the experiences of their communities. Historical developments such as the **Civil Rights Movement** and the **Black Power Movement** would serve to cultivate a new generation of writers who would significantly impact the literary world during the twentieth and twenty-first centuries.

African American trolley car conductors standing in front of car no. 52, Philadelphia, Pennsylvania, 1940. Courtesy of the Library of Congress.

For example, in his *Philadelphia Fire* (1990), **John Edgar Wideman** presents a fictional account of the Move fire tragedy that illustrates the issues of **race**, sex, and class as they existed during the early 1980s in the city of Philadelphia. This story received international acclaim and brought Wideman a Pen/Faulkner award for fiction. Born in **Pittsburgh, Pennsylvania**, in 1941, Wideman has relied on his experience in the African American community as a motivation for his fiction. Other books by Wideman include *Two Cities, Hurry Home, The Lynchers, Hiding Place, Sent for You Yesterday*, and *A Glance Away*.

Philadelphia's educational institutions have been recognized for their literary scholars and contributions. At the University of Pennsylvania, scholars such as **Lorene Cary** and Elijah Anderson have presented facets of Philadelphia life. Cary's *The Price of a Child* (1995) is a depiction of a freed slave's life in Philadelphia set in the mid-1800s. She is also author of *Black Ice* (1991), an autobiographical story of her Philadelphia adolescence and her experiences in other social circles, and *Pride* (1998), a story dedicated to African American women and the bonds of friendship.

The University of Pennsylvania is also home to the sociologist Elijah Anderson, who provides current interpretations of Du Bois's *The Philadelphia Negro*. Anderson's examination of African American urban life is also presented in *A Place on the Corner: A Study of Black Street Corner Men* (2004), *Streetwise: Race, Class, and change in an Urban Community* (1990), and *Code of the Street: Decency, Violence, and the Moral Life of the Inner City* (1999).

Leading the nation in the study of Afrocentricism is Molefi Asante, a leading theorist of **Afrocentricity**. Asante's *Afrocentricity* (2nd ed., 2003) is a comprehensive guide to understanding elements of this philosophy. Other works by Asante include *100 Greatest African Americans* (2002) and *Erasing Racism: The Survival of the American Nation* (2003).

Temple University is the academic home of **Sonia Sanchez**, a prolific poet and writer. Sanchez's work has received much acclaim due to her unique use of language and melodic voice. Her history as an activist has often been the motivation for her writing. Critical recognition of her work evolved during her participation in the **Black Power** movement of the late 1960s to the mid-1970s, during which time her poetry served as a model of artful expression for the era. Some of her most famous work includes *Homegirls & Handgrenades* (1984), a collection of autobiographical prose poems; *Three Hundred and Sixty Degrees of Blackness Comin at You* (1972); *Home Coming* (1969); and *We a BaddDDD People* (1970).

Philadelphia has served as a great historical reference for and about African American literary contributions. The regional developments that were influenced by national movements helped to make Philadelphia a model of creativity from which writers have derived and will derive great lessons of history and creativity. Today Philadelphia continues to generate literary greats such as **Bebe Moore Campbell**, whose *Brothers and Sisters* (1994), *Successful Women, Angry Men: Backlash in the Two-Career Marriage* (1986), *Your Blues Ain't Like Mine* (1992), and *What You Owe Me* (2001) have won several honors such as the Los Angeles Times Best Book Award of 2001 and the NAACP Image Award for literature.

Resources: **Primary Sources:** Anthony Davis, "Our Philadelphia Story: Today's Active African American Literary Scene in the City of Brotherly Love Has Deep Roots in a Proud Legacy," *Black Issues Book Review*, Jan.–Feb. 2002, http://www .findarticles.com/p/articles/mi_m0HST/is_1_4/ai_82511040; Nathan Huggins, *Harlem Renaissance* (New York: Oxford University Press, 1971); Demetrice A. Worley and Jesse Perry, Jr., *African American Literature: An Anthology*, 2nd ed. (Lincolnwood, IL: NTC, 1998). **Secondary Sources:** "Alain Locke," http://www.africawithin.com/bios/ alain_locke.htm; Elijah Anderson, *Streetwise: Race, Class, and Change in an Urban Community* (Chicago: University of Chicago Press, 1990); Molefi Asante, *Afrocentricity* (Trenton, NJ: Africa World Press, 1988); Lorene Cary, Web site, http://www .altrue.net/site/lorenecary/; W.E.B. Du Bois, *The Philadelphia Negro*, www2.pfeiffer.edu/ ~Iridener/DSS/DuBois/pntoc.html; Mari Evans, ed., *Black Women Writers 1950–1980: A Critical Evaluation* (Garden City, NY: Doubleday, 1984); "Mossell, Gertrude E. H. Bustill, 1855–1948," http://www.alexanderstreet2.com/nwldlive/bios/A7911BIO.html.

Pamela Felder Thompson

Phillips, Carl (born 1959). Poet and professor. In the relatively short time since the publication of his award-winning first book, *In the Blood* (1992), Carl Phillips has been widely recognized as a significant American poet. A prolific writer, he has subsequently published six additional books of poetry, as well as a book of essays. Phillips was born in 1959 to an African American father and an English mother; his family moved often due to his father's Air Force career. Phillips studied classics at Harvard and did not begin seriously writing poetry until adulthood. His success in the poetry world was immediate, and has led to many publications, awards, and honors. Phillips is currently a professor of English at Washington University in **St. Louis, Missouri**.

Phillips's work has been particularly important in demonstrating that Black poets need not write in modes or on topics that fit into established stylistic and thematic categories of Black literature, and need not act out or prove their Blackness in their work. Only two of his poems, both published in *In the Blood*, directly address racial questions. In the poem "Passing," he explicitly rejects the **blues** and Alabama as examples of the material the "Famous Black Poet" is expected to address and embody. **Passing** is a term used to refer to Black persons pretending to be White in order to avoid social stigma and prejudice. Phillips uses the term ironically, because the poem implies that if he were to write in the manner of the "Famous Black Poet," he would be passing as or pretending to be Black in a narrowly and artificially defined sense. Such a poem indicates a strong desire to carve out an independent individual and poetic identity not limited by social categories.

Though strongly rooted in history, Phillips's work tends to skip over the more immediate past (Black oppression and resistance in America, for example) in favor of reaching back to the founding stories of Western culture in ancient Greece and Rome. The biggest influence on his poetry has been classical Greek and Roman literature. He has spoken of the ancient Greek lyric poet Sappho and the ancient Roman lyric poet Catullus as very important to his work. Both were writers whose poetry combined powerful emotion with a strong sense of verbal music, and both were writers whose work centered on sexual desire and passionate love. Phillips has been praised for the way he brings new life to Classical materials, and for his integration of such material into a contemporary framework.

Phillips is gay as well as Black, and in his subject matter he is much more of a gay poet than a conventionally defined Black poet. Sexuality, rather than **race**, is the major topic of his poetry. Phillips has said that he did not begin reading African American literature until he began to teach it. The only other contemporary African African poet with whom his work shows affinities is **Reginald Shepherd**, whose work is also strongly influenced by classical literature and myth, and whose poetry frequently deals with homosexual desire. Phillips (like Shepherd) does not approach homosexuality in an explicitly political manner; his work is focused on the individual, not on society. Instead, Phillips uses sexuality to explore the relations and distances between people, especially between lovers, and as a springboard to explore the often difficult relations of the body and the mind, and of the material world and the spiritual world. In his poems, sex sometimes joins and sometimes separates body and soul, matter and spirit. Phillips's poems are full of lovers who find themselves at a spiritual or emotional remove from one another, a space they often try to fill with words. The poem both tries to close this gap and confirms that it can never be bridged. Indeed, Phillips's poems suggest that, regardless of a speaker's intentions, words sometimes widen the space between speaker and listener.

The conflict between body and soul is a major theme of Phillips's work. In many poems, Phillips mixes sexual and religious imagery in a manner reminiscent of and clearly influenced by the poetry of the biblical author of the Song of Songs, the sixteenth-century Spanish mystical poet St. John of the Cross, the 17th century English metaphysical poets John Donne and George Herbert, and the nineteenth-century American poet Emily Dickinson, among other forebears.

But Phillips's carefully crafted poems cannot be reduced to subject matter. They are at least as interested in how a thing is said as in what is said. His mastery of a highly flexible syntax (the arrangement of words into phrases and clauses), for which many critics have praised him, allows him to pace the reader's progress through a poem and to relate the materials of the poem in new and unexpected ways. This syntactical skill also allows him to gracefully shape the poems in the absence of more traditional structures such as rhyme and meter. Because Phillips's poems often take an indirect approach to their subject matter, they are sometimes considered difficult. The poems demand active participation from the reader. Some of the difficulty may arise from the calm and distanced manner in which Phillips approaches his often highly emotional material, much of which seems intensely personal. This calm, reserved approach can be called classical, which puts a great value on restraint, as opposed to a more openly expressive Romantic style. Such a classical style is one way for a writer to maintain artistic control over material that might otherwise be overwhelming.

Though Phillips continues to be regarded as a striking and unique writer, some observers have found the high seriousness of his work to be occasionally overbearing or ponderous, and his highly individual style to seem mannered, monotonous, or self-indulgent at times (Gilbert; Hoffert; Logan; Muratori). Phillips has expressed a lack of interest in formal or thematic innovation (highly valued by Modernist writers). Instead, he cites as his models such poets as Emily Dickinson, who found a style and a set of subjects early and spent their careers refining and going more deeply into them, rather than inventing new styles or looking for new subjects. Phillips seems willing to risk having his poetry seem repetitive in order to consistently pursue his vision. He remains a significant and distinctive figure in the contemporary American poetic landscape, and his poetry continues to receive acclaim.

Resources: Primary Sources: Carl Phillips: *Coin of the Realm: Essays on the Life and Art of Poetry* (St. Paul, MN: Graywolf Press, 2004); *Cortège* (St. Paul, MN: Graywolf Press, 1995); *From the Devotions* (St. Paul, MN: Graywolf Press, 1998); *In the Blood* (Boston: Northeastern University Press, 1992); *Pastoral* (St. Paul, MN: Graywolf Press, 2000); *The Rest of Love* (New York: Farrar, Straus and Giroux, 2004); *Rock Harbor* (New York: Farrar, Straus and Giroux, 2002); *The Tether* (New York: Farrar, Straus and Giroux, 2001). **Secondary Sources:** Juda Bennett, "Carl Phillips," in *Contemporary Gay American Poets and Playwrights: An A-to-Z Guide*, ed. Emmanuel S. Nelson (Westport, CT: Greenwood Press, 2003); Roger Gilbert, "Post-Love Poetry," *Michigan Quarterly Review* 41, no. 2 (Spring 2002), 309–328; Christopher Hennessy, "An Interview with Carl Phillips," *Writer's Chronicle* 34, no. 2 (Oct./Nov. 2001), 52–62; Barbara Hoffert, "The Tether," *Library Journal*, Apr. 15, 2001, p. 99; William Logan, "Folk Tales," *The New Criterion* 19, no. 10 (June 2001), 68–75; Fred Muratori, "Rock Harbor," *Library Journal*, July 2002, p. 85; Charles H. Rowell, "An Interview with Carl Phillips," *Callaloo* 21, no. 1 (Winter 1998), 204–217; Max Thomas, "Mighty Lines," *Iowa Review* 30, no. 2 (Fall 2000), 169–175.

Reginald Shepherd

Phillips, Gary (born 1955). Novelist. Born in **Los Angeles, California**, Gary Phillips attended San Francisco State University and completed a B.A. from California State University in Los Angeles. He has been employed as a labor organizer, a community activist, a political consultant, and an instructor within penal institutions for juvenile offenders.

Phillips is most widely known for his detective novels featuring Los Angeles private investigator Ivan Monk. An African American, Monk is involved with a Japanese American judge, and the series as a whole has a very multicultural slant. In an unusual turn to the formula for detective novels—especially those set in Los Angeles, from Chandler's Marlowe novels to Robert Campbell's Whistler novels—Monk owns and operates a doughnut shop rather than being a regular customer. All of the Monk novels are highly politicized. For instance, in *Violent Spring* (1994), the first of four novels in the series, Monk investigates the murder of a Korean store owner at the site of a new mall in South Central Los Angeles. In the aftermath of the riots that destroyed much of the district, the need for economic development cannot circumvent the long-standing tensions between African American residents and Korean entrepreneurs. Other novels in the series are *Perdition, U.S.A.* (1996), *Bad Night Is Falling* (1998), and *Only the Wicked* (2000).

Phillips has also developed a series around a former Las Vegas showgirl named Martha Chainey, who now works as a courier for organized crime. The novels are fast-paced variations on the "caper" genre, and the main character is both streetwise and free-spirited. The novels in this series are *High Hand* (2000) and *Shooter's Point* (2001).

Phillips' nonseries crime novels have included *The Jook* (1999), *The Perpetrators* (2002), and *Bangers* (2003). He has also written several **graphic novels**—*Desecrator* (1999), *Shot Callerz* (2003), and *Midnight Mover* (2004)—each of which has been illustrated by a different artist.

Resources: Brian Gilmore, "Going for Broke," *Washington Post Book World*, Jan. 2, 2000, p. 7; Chris Jackson, "Fiction Reviews," *Black Issues Book Review* 2 (Jan.–Feb. 2000), 50; Gary Phillips: *Bad Night Is Falling* (New York: Berkley, 1998); *Bangers* (New York: Dafina, 2003); *Desecrator* (Mission Viejo, CA: A.S.A.P, 1999); *High Hand* (New York: Kensington, 2000); *The Jook* (Los Angeles: Really Great Books, 1999), *Midnight Mover* (Portland, OR: Oni Press, 2004); *Only the Wicked* (Aurora, CA: Write Way, 2000); *Perdition, U.S.A.* (New York: Berkley, 1996); *The Perpetrators* (Los Angeles: UglyTown, 2002); *Shooter's Point* (New York: Kensington, 2001); *Shot Callerz* (Portland, OR: Oni Press, 2003); *Violent Spring* (Portland, OR: West Coast Crime, 1994).

Martin Kich

Photography. Invented in the mid-nineteenth century, photography bears a particularly strong relationship to literature, which embraced the new artistic mode quickly. The two are linked etymologically, photography loosely meaning "writing with light." Connections between literature and the art form were made early in its existence, from Henry Fox Talbot's *Pencil of Nature* (1824), which featured a photograph of a section of library books, to such early commentators as Edgar Allan Poe and Nathaniel Hawthorne. Photography's documentary quality, its appeal to truth, quickly attracted writers with aims of portraying reality accurately, whether for artistic or political reasons. Whether as proof of wealth, station, and breeding for the American middle class (equivalents of Renaissance paintings for that period's merchant class); as reminders of loved ones; or as evidence of the daily lives of the poor, the rural, and the aged, photography appealed to the growth of socially oriented artistic movements.

One of the earliest connections between photography and African American literature was *Poems of Cabin and Field* (1899), a collection of poems by **Paul Laurence Dunbar** accompanied by Hampton Camera Club photos of rural Black life in the late nineteenth century. This genre was to be emulated, in form if not in content, often during the twentieth century. **Langston Hughes**, for example, wrote a story to accompany photos by the **Harlem, New York**, photographer Roy DeCarava (the first Black recipient of a Guggenheim fellowship) in *The Sweet Flypaper of Life* (1955). The book, which, according to DeCarava, had a text due to economic necessity and his desire to have his work reach the widest audience, "was written only from what was seen and felt in the photographs.... Langston had over four hundred pictures to work with and selected those pictures that had a special meaning for him and translated these feelings into the words which grace the pages of our book" (White and DeCarava, 390). **Harlem Renaissance** portrait photographer **James Van Der Zee** published *The Harlem Book of the Dead* in 1978, which featured poems by **Owen Dodson**, interviews with Van Der Zee conducted by Camille Billops, and an introduction by **Toni Morrison**. One of the pictures from this book would later inspire Morrison's novel *Jazz* (1992).

Hughes was engaged in other combinations of word and image, writing an introductory essay to an exhibition of the photographs of Henri Cartier-Bresson (Hughes's roommate in Mexico City and a lifelong friend) and Manuel Alvarez Bravo ("Pictures More Than Pictures: The Work of Manuel Bravo and Cartier-Bresson," 1935) and working on two nonfiction books that merged the photographic image and the word in collaboration with Milton Meltzer, *A Pictorial History of the Negro in America* (1956) and *Black Magic: A Pictorial History of the Negro in American Entertainment* (1967). **Richard Wright** used photography similarly in some of his nonfiction works. After his use of **Great Depression** photos from the Farm Security Administration (FSA) in *Twelve Million Black Voices: A Folk History of the Negro in the United States* (1941), Wright became a photographer himself, taking photos in Ghana for *Black Power: A Record of Reactions in a Land of Pathos* (1954) and in Indonesia for *The Color Curtain: A Report on the Bandung Conference* (1956). Many of these photos accompany European editions of these books, though they are absent from American editions.

Gordon Parks's autobiographies form a third type of interaction between literature and photography. Parks, a *Life* magazine photojournalist, fashion photographer, writer, and filmmaker (including 1971's *Shaft*), was greatly influenced by the FSA photos. By 1937 his freelance work had earned him an internship with the agency. During this time Parks was urged by his mentor, Roy Stryker, to verbalize his experience of prejudice and other injustices as an aid to his photography (*Choice of Weapons*, 226–227), a practice that linked word and image in his work from then on. His autobiographical novel *The Learning Tree* (1963), the film version of which he wrote and directed (1969), was followed by a number of autobiographies, including *A Choice of Weapons* (1966), *To Smile in Autumn* (1979) and *Voices in the Mirror* (1990). In *A Poet and His Camera* (1968) he also united his callings as a poet and a photographer.

The works of **John Edgar Wideman** represent a fourth type of interaction between literature and photography. Wideman meditates on photography in many of his works, including the novel *Reuben* (1987), in which the innovative serial photographs of animal and human motion of nineteenth-century British photographer Edweard Muybridge influence the title character's view of life. One of the main characters in *Two Cities* (1998), Mr. Mallory, is an elderly photographer who puzzles over the divide between his memories of occasions in his life and the photos of those events, which he finds increasingly foreign. In *Hoop Roots: Playground Basketball, Love, and Race* (2001), photographs serve as an aide-mémoire for an essay about Wideman's grandmother Freed, "One More Time." Missing her, he marvels at the power of the photograph, which he compares to the game that serves as the main topic for his book. He writes, "The photo's art, like the art of the hoop, is deceptively simple. What you see is what you get and it seems to end there, if you don't penetrate past the surface. Like the best naturalistic paintings, the photo, the game are layered. What appears to be an ordinary, familiar slice of life . . . is just that, a scene the viewer is able to identify immediately with those snapshots of the world the eyes continuously consume every waking day. Just that but then more if we are paying attention, because we'll also hear the artist saying, Stop. Let's think about what's in front of our eyes. Maybe it's not so simple, so familiar. Or more familiar, more intimately familiar and revelatory than you'd ever guess at first glance" (232). For Wideman, writing, too, has this power to make us reconsider the world, built on the past and yet completely new at the same time (194–195).

Resources: Roy DeCarava and Langston Hughes, *The Sweet Flypaper of Life* (1955; repr. Washington, DC: Howard University Press, 1984); Paul Laurence Dunbar, *Poems of Cabin and Field* (New York: Dodd, Mead, 1899); Langston Hughes, "Pictures More Than Pictures: The Work of Manuel Bravo and Cartier-Bresson," in *Literature and Photography: Interactions 1840–1990*, ed. Jane M. Rabb (Albuquerque: University of New Mexico Press, 1995), 277–279; Langston Hughes and Milton Meltzer: *Black Magic: A Pictorial History of the Negro in American Entertainment* (Englewood Cliffs, NJ: Prentice-Hall, 1967); *A Pictorial History of the Negro in America* (1956; repr. New York: Crown, 1983); Toni Morrison, *Jazz* (New York: Knopf, 1992); Gordon Parks: *A Choice of Weapons* (New York: Harper & Row, 1966); *The Learning Tree* (New York: Harper & Row, 1963); *A Poet and His Camera* (New York: Viking, 1968); *To Smile in Autumn: A Memoir* (New York: Norton, 1979); *Voices in the Mirror: An Autobiography* (New York: Doubleday, 1990); James Van Der Zee, Owen Dodson, and Camille Billops, *The Harlem Book of the Dead* (Dobbs Ferry, NY: Morgan & Morgan, 1978); Minor White and Roy DeCarava, "Correspondence, November 1955," in *Literature and Photography: Interactions 1840–1990*, ed. Jane M. Rabb (Albuquerque: University of New Mexico Press, 1995), 388–392; John Edgar Wideman: *Hoop Roots: Playground Basketball, Love, and Race* (Boston: Houghton Mifflin, 2001); *Reuben* (New York: Henry Holt, 1987); *Two Cities* (Boston: Houghton Mifflin, 1998); Richard Wright: *Black Power: A Record of Reactions in a Land of Pathos* (New York: Harper, 1954); *The Color Curtain: A Report on the Bandung Conference* (Cleveland, OH: World Publishing, 1956); *Twelve Million Black Voices: A Folk History of the Negro in the United States* (New York: Viking, 1941).

Ian W. Wilson

***Phylon* (1940–1987; 1992–present).** Interdisciplinary journal. Since its founding by **W.E.B. Du Bois** in 1940, *Phylon*, a scholarly journal focusing on issues of **race** and culture, has been an important publication medium in African American Studies. Originally known as *Phylon: The Atlanta University Review of Race and Culture*, it has since also been called *The Phylon Quarterly* and, since 1992, *Phylon: The Clark Atlanta University Journal of Race and Culture*. Du Bois started the journal at Atlanta University, where he taught in the Department of Sociology. In the inaugural issue, he states that *Phylon* will "study and survey the field of race and culture, and of racial and cultural relations. It uses both designations more or less interchangeably; because it would emphasize that view of race which regards it as cultural and historical in essence, rather than primarily biological and psychological" ("Apology," 3). The first editorial board, with DuBois as Editor in Chief, consisted of Ira De A. Reid (sociology), **William Stanley Braithwaite** (literature), Mercer Cook (romance languages), Rushton Coulborn (history), William H. Dean, Jr. (economics), Oran W. Eagleson (psychology) and Rufus E. Clement (history). Du Bois was a frequent contributor and wrote a regular column, "A Chronicle of Race Relations," until his retirement from Atlanta University and *Phylon* in 1944, when he turned over editorial control to Ira Reid.

To serve the purpose of studying race and culture, *Phylon* has consistently included works from a variety of disciplines, predominantly the social sciences. It contains literary criticism to a large extent, but, unlike some earlier African American periodicals, it does not focus exclusively on artistic and or aesthetic concerns. The connection between literature and culture is a key emphasis. To that end, most of the early editions of *Phylon* contained a section subtitled "Books and Race." Beginning with the third quarter edition in 1944, however, that section was renamed "The Literature of Race and Culture," but it continues to feature books reviews, commentary, and creative writing relevant to those interested in race relations. In particular, the journal has been an effective place to raise the profile of African American writers. This purpose was assisted by **Alain Locke**, who from 1947 to 1953 conducted an annual review of Black literature, a tradition that *Phylon* kept up for ten years after his death in 1954. Given that there were few publications offering critical discussions of African American literature, this annual review was a significant forum. Over the years *Phylon* has published many significant African American scholars and writers, including **Langston Hughes, Charles Spurgeon Johnson, Alain Locke, Countee Cullen, Ann Petry, Margaret Abigail Walker,** Wendell Johnson, **James Weldon Johnson, Martin Luther King, Jr.,** and **Addison Gayle, Jr.**

Publication of *Phylon* ceased with the Winter Quarter issue of 1987, due to cutbacks by Atlanta University. Publication resumed in 1992, through Clark Atlanta University, the merged institution of Clark College and Atlanta University, but it is on an irregular schedule. Back issues from 1940 through 1992 are available online through the J-Stor database. The current editor is Clark Atlanta University sociology professor Dr. Jeffrey Porterfield.

Resources: Herbert Aptheker, ed., *Selections from* Phylon (Millwood, NY: Kraus-Thomson, 1980); W.E.B. Du Bois: "Apology," *Phylon: The Atlanta Review of Race and Culture* 1 (1940), 3–5; *The Autobiography of W.E.B. Du Bois: A Soliloquy on Viewing My Life from the Last Decade of Its First Century* (New York: International Publishers, 1968); Trudier Harris-Lopez, ed., *Afro-American Writers, 1940–1955* (Detroit: Gale, 1988); Alexa Benson Henderson and Janice Sumler-Edmond, eds., *Freedom's Odyssey: African American History Essays from* Phylon (Atlanta: Clark Atlanta University Press, 1999); David Lewis, *W.E.B. Du Bois* (New York: Holt, 2000); *Phylon*, online access 1940–1992, J-Stor, http://www.j-stor.org/journals/08856818.html.

Shelley Martin

Pinckney, Darryl (born 1953). Novelist and essayist. Pinckney's work has been recognized for the intense and productive self-scrutiny it directs at African American culture and identity. Born and raised in Indianapolis, Indiana, Pinckney studied at Columbia University and Princeton University. As a frequent contributor to the *New York Review of Books* since 1977, Pinckney has examined and synthesized a range of texts central to African American history and literature. **Hilton Als** comments, "With his fine critical intelligence, Pinckney furrowed the historical field. Writing of everyone from [Langston] Hughes to [Amiri] Baraka, he created a 'geographic'" (667). In the novel *High Cotton* (1992), Pinckney explores the challenges facing the "Also Chosen," the suburban progeny of the Black elite descended from **W.E.B. Du Bois**'s "**Talented Tenth.**" Characterized by **Gail Lumet Buckley** as a "serio-comic *Bildungsroman* of nationality, class, and religion, as well as **race**," *High Cotton* won the *Los Angeles Times* Art Seidenbaum Award for First Fiction (1). **Henry Louis Gates, Jr.,** commends the "pitiless and unsparing vision that . . . gives [*High Cotton*] a formidable kind of moral solidity" (1). Pinckney wrote the text for theatrical productions of *The Forest* (1988), *Orlando* (1989) and *Time Rocket* (1995); his 2001 *New Yorker* essay "Busted in New York," detailing an arrest for marijuana possession, was selected for *The Best American Essays of 2002*. Other publications featuring his work include *Granta*, the *New York Times*, the *New York Review of Books*, *The New Yorker*, *Vanity Fair*, *Vogue*, and the *American Poetry Review*. In 1994, Pinckney received an award for distinguished prose from the American Academy of Arts and Letters. Referring to the scope of Pinckney's authority within the field of African American literature, Gates has observed, "Resisting the urge toward ethnic cheerleading, Pinckney has served as one of our most important critical consciousnesses" (1).

Resources: Hilton Als, "Word!—*High Cotton* by Darryl Pinckney," *The Nation*, May 18, 1992, pp. 667–680; Gail Lumet Buckley, "Review of *High Cotton*," *Los Angeles Times*, Nov. 8, 1992, p. 1; Jan Garden Castro, "Darryl Pinckney: An Interview," *American Poetry Review* 23, no. 6 (Nov.–Dec. 1994), 9–14; "Darryl Pinckney," *Contemporary Authors* (Detroit: Gale, 2001), http://galenet.galegroup.com; Henry Louis Gates, Jr., "The Great Black Hope," "Review of *High Cotton*," *Washington Post*, Feb. 23, 1992, sec. X, p. 1; Darryl Pinckney: *High Cotton* (New York: Farrar, Straus and Giroux, 1992); *Out There: Mavericks of Black Literature* (New York: BasicCivitas,

2002); *Sold and Gone: African American Literature and U.S. Society* (New York: Farrar, Straus and Giroux, 2005); Alexandra Schultheis, "Traumatic Legacy and the Psychoanalysis of Race: African-American Masculinity in Darryl Pinckney's *High Cotton,*" in *Regenerative Fictions* (New York: Palgrave, 2003), 73–104.

Alex Feerst

Pinkney, Sandra (born 1971) and Myles Pinkney (born 1971). Children's author and photographer. Sandra and Myles Pinkney have collaborated on several children's books that emphasize diversity within and between races. *Shades of Black: A Celebration of Our Children* (2000), their debut collaborative work, celebrates diverse hair textures and skin and eye color in African American children. *A Rainbow All Around Me* (2002) pairs bright colors with children from around the world. Both books are acclaimed for their approach to diversity, rhythmic language, and engaging photography. *Shades of Black* won the 2001 **NAACP** Image Award for Outstanding Children's Literature.

Sandra Pinkney, daughter of Alfred and Frances McRae, received her degree in early childhood development from Duchess Community College. She is a member of several organizations concerned with childhood development, and the director of Lil' Praiser's Christian Day-Care. Myles Pinkney received his B.A. in communications from Marist College and is a member of the Professional Photographers Society of New York. In addition to illustrating books, he works as a freelance photographer.

Sandra and Myles are the third husband-and-wife publishing team in the Pinkney family. Myles's parents, Jerry and Gloria Pinkney, have collaborated for over twenty-five years. Brian, his brother, has illustrated a number of books, including those of his wife, Andrea. Despite the established tradition in the Pinkney family, it was not easy for Sandra and Myles to enter the publishing world. In a roundtable discussion for *Authors on the Web*, Sandra and Myles noted that it was difficult for them to find a publisher for *Shades of Black* because "many publishing houses did not understand the importance or significance of showing various skin colors of blacks in a book." They persisted until they found a publisher: "Having been teased as a child for our skin color, it was important [to us] for children to feel positive about how they look." (*See* **Color of Skin.**)

Resources: Rudine Sims Bishop, "The Pinkney Family: In the Tradition," *Horn Book*, Jan./Feb. 1996, 42–49; "Black History Month Author Roundtable," *Authors on the Web* (2002), http://www.authorsontheweb.com/features/0202-african-american .asp; Sandra and Myles Pinkney: *A Rainbow All Around Me* (New York: Scholastic, 2002); *Shades of Black: A Celebration of Our Children* (New York: Scholastic, 2000).

Sarah Antoinette Miller

Pittsburgh, Pennsylvania. City founded in 1758, located at the confluence of the Allegheny, Monongahela, and Ohio rivers in southwest Pennsylvania. Long associated with manufacturing and industry, the city was an important stop on the **Underground Railroad** and a center for the northern migration of

African Americans after the **Civil War** and especially after **Reconstruction**. Since its founding, the city has played an important role in the development of African American culture.

Pittsburgh was once considered the gateway to the West. While Blacks were among the earliest settlers of the city, in the years preceding the Civil War, Pittsburgh's Black community was small, numbering only 2,000, less than 5 percent of the city's population. Jobs were few, and discrimination kept many Blacks away. Despite the low Black population, Pittsburgh played a significant role in the fight for Black emancipation. In Pittsburgh, the **abolitionist movement** was centered in the city's famous Hill District, and some estimates say nearly 10,000 Blacks escaped slavery through stations in western Pennsylvania.

Two important African American authors and activists associated with the abolitionist movement in Pittsburgh are **Martin R. Delany** and **George Boyer Vashon**. Martin Delany, who has been called "the Father of Black Nationalism," was born in Charles Town, Virginia, in 1812. In 1822, the family moved to Chambersburg, Pennsylvania, and in 1831, Delany went to Pittsburgh. In 1843, he started one of the earliest **African American newspapers**, *The Mystery*, a paper devoted to the abolition of slavery. It ceased publishing in 1847, and that year Delany moved to Buffalo, New York, to work as coeditor of **Frederick Douglass**'s paper, *The North Star*. In 1849, Delany was one of the first Blacks to enter Harvard Medical School, but was not allowed to graduate. In 1852, he published *The Condition, Elevation, Emigration, and Destiny of the Colored People of the United States, Politically Considered*. In this work, Delany argued that due to the normalization of discrimination, African Americans should live outside the United States. Later in his life, Delany became a prominent politician and spoke out against such issues as the Fugitive Slave Law. While his residence in Pittsburgh ended in 1847, Delany returned numerous times to speak out against slavery and racial discrimination.

Another important abolitionist associated with Pittsburgh is George Boyer Vashon. Vashon was born in Pittsburgh in 1824, the son of John B. Vashon, a barber and an activist with the Underground Railroad. In 1844, Vashon became the first Black graduate of Oberlin College. He attempted to practice law in Pittsburgh, but was denied admission to the bar. He then moved to Syracuse, New York, in 1848, and was admitted to the bar in New York state, the first Black to do so. Throughout his career, Vashon was a frequent contributor to Frederick Douglass's paper, *The North Star*. Although Vashon is known as a reformer rather than an author, one of his poems, "Vincent Oge," is considered the first narrative, nonlyrical poem by a Black American writer in the United States. This epic poem of 139 lines is a tribute to the Haitian revolutionary Vicente Oge, and it inspired the French poet Aimé Césaire, who was associated with the **Négritude** movement.

After the Civil War, Pittsburgh underwent tremendous changes. Great numbers of European immigrants arrived, and the combination of natural resources and cheap labor enabled Andrew Carnegie, Henry Clay Frick, and

Thomas Mellon to build their industrial empires. Despite the economic growth of the city, Pittsburgh's Blacks remained on the outside, banned from working in the city's mills. Because of this ban, most Blacks were forced to work menial jobs. However, despite the lack of opportunities, during this period the city's Black population continued to grow, and by 1900 the African-American population reached 20,000 residents, the sixth largest in the nation.

During **World War I**, the demand for steel increased dramatically, and Pittsburgh's industries continued to grow. Due to the need for workers, Blacks had become eligible to work in the city's mills, and Southern Blacks converged upon the city. By 1919, Pittsburgh's Black population numbered 55,000. The influx of new citizens added a new vitality to the region, and Pittsburgh's music scene became world famous. The city boasted some of the most famous jazz musicians of that era, including Billy Strayhorn, Art Blakey, Earl "Fatha" Hines, Mary Lou Williams, and Lena Horne, and the Hill District became so famous in the Black community that **Claude McKay** called the intersection of Wylie and Fullerton in the Hill District the "crossroads of the world." In addition to the musical scene, after World War I, Pittsburgh's Black population helped create a number of Black sports teams. The most famous, the Pittsburgh Crawfords, included some of the most famous Black baseball players, among them Hall of Fame members Satchel Paige, Josh Gibson, and "Cool Papa" Bell. The Crawfords, along with the Homestead Grays, helped make Pittsburgh famous for Black baseball.

One of the most influential developments in Pittsburgh's Black cultural scene was the founding of the ***Pittsburgh Courier*** in 1907. Under the guidance of editor Robert Vann, the *Courier* the paper became one of the most important African American newspapers of the twentieth century. The paper focused on social and cultural issues relating to the Black community, and numerous African American writers and intellectuals contributed to the *Courier*, including "the black [H. L.] Mencken" **George Schuyler**, **W.E.B. Du Bois**, **Marcus Garvey**, and **Zora Neale Hurston**. The influence of the *Pittsburgh Courier* should not be underestimated. Many leading Black intellectuals and artists, including George Washington Carver, W.E.B. Du Bois, **Alain Locke**, **Countee Cullen**, and **Langston Hughes**, all participated in lecture programs in the Hill District sponsored by the paper.

Despite the growth of Black culture in Pittsburgh, racial discrimination was widespread, and many Blacks toiled in the mills with little chance for advancement. One novel that documents the struggles of Black mill workers is **William Attaway**'s *Blood on the Forge* (1941). The novel is the tragic story of three Black brothers who leave the rural South for the steel mills of Pittsburgh in 1919, and who are swallowed up in the violence of the labor movement. In this novel, Attaway explored the obstacles faced by Blacks in the South and North, and many of the struggles of the labor movements.

After **World War II**, the city continued to grow, but opportunities for Blacks remained limited. After the collapse of the steel mills in the 1980s, the city attempted to shift its economic focus from manufacturing to more service-related areas. Two of the more important modern writers to emerge from Pittsburgh during the post–World War II era are novelist **John Edgar Wideman** and playwright **August Wilson**. While neither currently resides in the city, the two remain connected to Pittsburgh, and both have centered many of their works around Pittsburgh's African American community.

John Edgar Wideman was born in **Washington, D.C.**, in 1941. Before he turned one, his family moved to Homewood, an African American neighborhood in Pittsburgh, where he lived until he was ten. Wideman became a star athlete, both in high school and at the University of Pennsylvania, where he studied English. He matriculated at Oxford University as a Rhodes Scholar, and later earned tenure as an English professor at the University of Pennsylvania. Although he has moved from Pittsburgh, Wideman returned to Homewood as the setting for many of his works. His first book of stories, *Damballah* (1981), along with *Hiding Place* (1981) and *Sent for You Yesterday*, (1983) formed his Homewood Trilogy. All three describe the community of Homewood, and explore the lives of African Americans in the neighborhood. In 1984, Wideman published his memoir, *Brothers and Keepers*, which tells the tragic story of his younger brother Robbie, who was sent to prison for life for participating in a robbery that left one man dead. Wideman is currently a professor of English at the University of Massachusetts at Amherst.

One of the most important authors to emerge from Pittsburgh is the award-winning dramatist August Wilson. Born on April 27, 1945, he grew up in the Hill District of Pittsburgh, and his experiences serve as the basis for many of his plays. His first major work, *Ma Rainey's Black Bottom*, opened in 1984, and was voted Best Play of the Year (1984–1985) by the New York Drama Critics Circle. The drama, Wilson's first in a ten play, ten decade cycle about the twentieth-century African American experience, is set in the **Chicago, Illinois**, recording studio of blues legend Ma Rainey, and explores race relations between Blacks and Whites in 1920s America. Wilson's next play, *Fences*, is set in Pittsburgh in the 1950s, and is the story of Troy Maxon, an angry former Negro League baseball player-turned-garbage collector. *Fences* brought Wilson his first Pulitzer Prize. In April 1988, Wilson's next play, *Joe Turner's Come and Gone*, opened on Broadway. Set in the 1910s in a boardinghouse in Pittsburgh, the play is the story of Harold Loomis, a Black man freed from prison after serving seven years. Now free, Loomis searches for his wife, Martha. *The Piano Lesson*, again set in Pittsburgh's Hill District, is the story of Boy Willie and his sister Berniece. Willie dreams of buying the Mississippi land that his ancestors once worked as slaves, but in order to raise the money for this purchase, Willie must convince his sister to sell the family's piano, an heirloom symbolic of the family's past. *The Piano Lesson* was named Best Play of the Year by the New York Drama Critics Circle. It also brought Wilson his second Pulitzer Prize for drama. Other important works include *Two Trains Running* and *Seven Guitars*, both set in Pittsburgh.

While Wideman and Wilson are the best-known Pittsburgh African American writers, other important figures include the late **Rob Penny**, the poet, activist, and teacher who founded the Kuntu Repertory Theater, and the poet **Toi Derricotte**, who was born in **Detroit, Michigan**, but currently teaches at the University of Pittsburgh. Derricotte's books of poetry include *Tender* (1997), *Captivity* (1989), *Natural Birth* (1983), and *The Empress of the Death House* (1978). In 1997, she published *The Black Notebooks*, a literary memoir.

Although Pittsburgh is not known for large numbers of African American authors, the city functioned as an important center for the African American cultural experience. Pittsburgh was at the forefront of the abolitionist movement, and the city was an important stop on the Underground Railroad. In addition, as the city's industries grew, and as Blacks became eligible to work in the mills, the city's African American culture expanded. Pittsburgh's long history of **jazz** greats, the influential *Pittsburgh Courier*, the city's two Negro League baseball teams, and the number of authors who visited Pittsburgh in the early twentieth century attests to this importance of Pittsburgh's African American population. Today, such authors as August Wilson, John Edgar Wideman, and others continue to focus on African American culture in Pittsburgh, and to explore the Black experience in America.

Resources: Andrew Bunie, *Robert L. Vann of the Pittsburgh Courier: Politics and Black Journalism* (Pittsburgh: University of Pittsburgh Press, 1974); Laurence Glasco, "Blacks in Pittsburgh," in *A Legacy in Brick and Mortar: African-American Landmarks in Allegheny County* (Pittsburgh: Pittsburgh History and Landmarks Foundation), 3–37; Peter Gottlieb, *Making Their Own Way* (Urbana: University of Illinois Press, 1987); Raymond E. Janifer, "Looking Homewood: The Evolution of John Edgar Wideman's Folk Imagination," in *Contemporary Black Men's Fiction and Drama*, ed. Keith Clark (Urbana: University of Illinois Press, 2001); Kim Pereira, *August Wilson and the African-American Odyssey* (Urbana: University of Illinois Press, 1995); Rob Ruck, *Sandlot Seasons: Sports in Black Pittsburgh* (Urbana: University of Illinois Press, 1987); Sandra G. Shannon, *The Dramatic Vision of August Wilson* (Washington, DC: Howard University Press, 1995); Joe William Trotter, Jr., and Eric Ledell Smith, eds., *African Americans in Pennsylvania* (University Park: Penn State University Press, 1997).

James A. Jaap

Pittsburgh Courier (1907–1965). Influential African American newspaper based in **Pittsburgh, Pennsylvania**. The *Pittsburgh Courier* was one of the most widely circulated Black newspapers during the early twentieth century, and focused on social and cultural issues relating to the Black community. Numerous African American writers and intellectuals contributed to the *Courier*, helping the paper become one of the most important African American newspapers of the twentieth century.

Edwin Nathaniel Harleston, a security guard at the Heinz food packing plant, founded the *Pittsburgh Courier* in 1907. In the first year, Harleston printed several editions, which consisted primarily of Harleston's poems, and only about ten copies of each edition were printed. In 1909, Harleston sought financial backers for the paper, and enlisted the help of Robert Vann, a young

African American attorney, to serve as legal counsel. On January 15, 1910, the *Courier*'s first substantial run of 500 copies was published. After the paper was incorporated on May 10, 1910, Harleston quit, upset over what he felt was a lack of compensation for his efforts. Shortly thereafter, Vann was named editor and publisher, a position he held until his death in 1940. Despite a constant struggle to obtain funding, under the leadership of Vann the *Pittsburgh Courier* flourished, and became one of the most popular Black newspapers of the time.

From its earliest beginnings, the *Pittsburgh Courier* focused on social and economic issues relating to African Americans. The paper consistently called for changes in the social and economic conditions of Black society. Some issues that the *Courier* advocated included proper housing and education for African Americans, proper medical facilities for African Americans, and enough Black physicians to treat Black patients. During these early years, the *Courier* also advocated educational opportunities for Black teachers and students, and the improvement of conditions for African American workers.

During the 1930s, the *Pittsburgh Courier* began one of its first major campaigns as a national opinion leader for the African American community. Upset over the racial stereotypes of *The Amos-n-Andy Show*, a nationally broadcast radio program, Vann and the *Courier* petitioned for the removal of the show from the airwaves. Though the effort eventually failed, the action established the *Courier* as a voice for the Black community.

The *Courier* was also highly influential in politics. In 1932, the paper criticized Republican president Herbert Hoover for not ending the **Great Depression**, and for enabling racial discrimination in government relief projects. The *Courier* therefore urged African American voters to switch their allegiance from the Republican Party to support the Democrat, Franklin D. Roosevelt.

After the death of Vann in 1940, Ira Lewis, who had worked closely with Vann on the paper since 1914, was named editor. Under Lewis's leadership, the *Courier* reached its highest circulation, estimated at over 350,000. With the cooperation of **A. Philip Randolph**, the founder of the Brotherhood of Sleeping Car Porters, the *Courier* was smuggled throughout the South by a network of Black Pullman car porters, who would hide the paper in the floors of railroad cars, and drop off approximately 100,000 copies each week outside of every major Southern city.

Lewis also directed several of the paper's most successful campaigns. The first was the "Double V" campaign, subtitled "Democracy: Victory at Home, Victory Abroad." Beginning in 1942, the "Double-V" campaign argued that Blacks serving the nation in **World War II** should receive full citizen rights at home. A logo was designed and many other Black newspapers, including the **Chicago Defender**, supported the campaign. The second important campaign was the fight against segregation in sports. In 1947, Wendell Smith, a sportswriter for the *Courier*, used his column to criticize segregation in professional sports. The efforts of Smith and the *Courier* to desegregate baseball led directly to **Jackie Robinson** signing with the Brooklyn Dodgers.

To present these controversial stances, the *Pittsburgh Courier* employed many of the leading African American writers and intellectuals as columnists. **George Schuyler**, author of the satirical novel *Black No More*, was the *Courier*'s leading editorialist and one of its most popular columnists. He joined the staff in 1925 and wrote a weekly column, "Views and Reviews." Late in 1925, Schuyler began on a nine-month tour of the South and wrote a series of columns he called "Aframerica Today." Other prominent Black figures who contributed materials to the *Courier* include Joel A. Rogers, **Marcus Garvey**, **W.E.B. Du Bois**, **Zora Neale Hurston**, and Elijah Muhammad. Rogers, a prominent Black journalist and African American historian, became the first Black war correspondent in U.S. history, and wrote a regular column that focused on African American history. Marcus Garvey contributed a serialized autobiographical column beginning on February 15, 1930. In 1936, Du Bois, after his resignation from the **NAACP** and *The Crisis* in 1934, wrote to Robert Vann stating his desire to publish a column of his observations. Du Bois's weekly column, "A Forum of Fact and Opinion," ran from February 8, 1936, to January 23, 1938, and covered a wide range of topics, from politics to Europe to African American history. Du Bois also traveled to Berlin to cover the 1936 Olympic Games for the *Courier*. In 1952, Zora Neale Hurston was hired by the *Courier* to cover the trial of Ruby McCollum, a wealthy African American wife who murdered her lover, Dr. C. Leroy Adams. Between 1956 and 1963, Elijah Muhammad, the leader of the **Nation of Islam**, contributed columns to the paper.

The combination of social issues and the use of prominent Black leaders helped the *Pittsburgh Courier* grow to become one of the best-selling Black newspapers in the country. In tackling social and cultural issues relating to the Black community, the paper became a force for social change. However, after Ira Lewis died in 1948, the paper's circulation declined. In 1965, the *Courier* was sold to John Sengstacke, the owner and publisher of the **Chicago Defender**. Today, the paper remains an important source for African American news, and is published under the name *New Pittsburgh Courier*.

Resources: James H. Brewer, "Robert Lee Vann, Democrat or Republican: An Exponent of Loose Leaf Politics," *Negro History Bulletin* 21, no. 5 (1958), 100–103; Andrew Bunie, *Robert L. Vann of the Pittsburgh Courier: Politics and Black Journalism* (Pittsburgh: University of Pittsburgh Press, 1974); Charles W. Eagles, "Two Double V's: Jonathan Daniels, FDR, and Race Relations During World War II," *North Carolina Historical Review* 59, no. 3 (1982), 252–270; Chris Lamb, "'What's Wrong with Baseball': The *Pittsburgh Courier* and the Beginning of Its Campaign to Integrate the National Pastime," *Western Journal of Black Studies* 4 (Winter 2002), 189–192; Armistead S. Pride and Clint C. Wilson II, *A History of the Black Press* (Washington, DC: Howard University Press, 1997); Patrick S. Washburn: "The Pittsburgh Courier's Double V Campaign in 1942," *American Journalism* 3, no. 2 (1986), 73–86; *A Question of Sedition: The Federal Government's Investigation of the Black Press During World War II* (New York: Oxford University Press, 1986).

James A. Jaap

Plato, Ann (c. 1820–?). Poet and essayist. Ann Plato was the second African American woman, after **Phillis Wheatley**, to publish a book in the United States. She was also the only African American woman to publish a book between 1840 and 1865. Little is known about Plato, other than that she was a devoted member of the Colored Congregational Church and that she was a schoolteacher in the Zion Methodist Church School of Hartford, Connecticut. She published only one book, *Essays: Including Biographies and Miscellaneous Pieces, in Prose and Poetry* (1841), with an introduction by her pastor, the Reverend W. C. Pennington.

Plato's book consists of several essays, biographical sketches, and poems. She writes about education, death, and religion, and gives godly counsel to her peers. Many of these works were written when she was in her teens. William H. Robinson, in *Early Black American Poets* (1969), describes Plato's work as "melodramatic to excess" and "pretentious" (113). He also criticizes her for referring "only obliquely to things racial," even though **slavery** still existed in **the South** and was a burning topic within her African American community, many of whose members supported abolitionist activities (113–114). Allusions to race are found only in two poems—"To the First of August," a tribute to the abolition of slavery in the West Indies (1838), and "The Natives of America"—and in one biographical sketch that makes a brief mention of racist laws (113–114). Robinson does credit Plato for having "[engendered] a few rewarding passages," as well as for her "most appealing" love poem, "Forget Me Not" (113–114).

In Plato's defense, **Ann Allen Shockley**, in *Afro-American Women Writers* (1988), states "that the author's subjects were objects of her concern and were part of her daily life," and that "her importance as a young black female seeking to express herself through literary endeavors during the colonial period of black bondage and female constraints is of great significance" (27). In *Notable Black American Women*, Nagueyalti Warren acknowledges the value of Plato's biographies as a "glimpse of what life must have been like for young, middle-class black women of New England" (854).

Resources: Janet Gray, ed., *She wields a Pen: American Women Poets of the Nineteenth Century* (Iowa City: University of Iowa Press, 1997); Ann Plato, *Essays: Including Biographies and Miscellaneous Pieces, in Prose and Poetry* (Hartford, CT: Printed for the author, 1841; repr. New York: Oxford University Press, 1988); William H. Robinson, Jr., *Early Black American Poets: Selections with Biographical and Critical Introductions* (Dubuque, IA: William C. Brown, 1969); Joan R. Sherman, ed., *African-American Poetry of the Nineteenth Century: An Anthology* (Urbana: University of Illinois Press, 1992); Ann Allen Shockley, ed., *Afro-American Women Writers 1746–1933: An Anthology and Critical Guide* (Boston: G. K. Hall, 1988); Nagueyalti Warren, "Ann Plato," in *Notable Black American Women*, ed. Jessie Carney Smith (Detroit: Gale, 1992).

Gladys L. Knight

Plumpp, Sterling D. (born 1940). Poet, playwright, and fiction writer. While exploring the **blues** and its literary dimensions, Plumpp's body of work underscores the wide range of possibilities which this expressive mode generates. Contributing to a long-standing dialogue on Black music and African American cultural production, Plumpp's writing illustrates the power and adaptability of the blues while demonstrating how the idiom functions as a repository of experience and memory constituting African American life in the United States. Best known for his poetic collections, including *Blues: The Story Always Untold* (1989), *Ornate with Smoke* (1997), and *Velvet Bebop Kente Cloth* (2003), Plumpp is distinguished by his informed engagement with music from the blues continuum and an unwavering interest in examining Black culture and politics, on the global and local levels.

Born in Clinton, Mississippi in 1940, Plumpp was reared, along with his half brother, Wardell Johnson, by his material grandparents, Victor and Mattie Emmanuel. His early life experience was typical of young Black male coming of age in the rural South during the mid-twentieth century. Enduring chronic poverty and laboring in fields that his grandfather worked as a sharecropper, Plumpp's access to primary education was hampered by the demands of the agricultural cycle and the distance between his grandparents' home and the nearest segregated schoolhouse. Plumpp estimates that he was eight years old before he began attending school with regularity. Despite these encumbrances, Plumpp earned a scholarship to the Holy Ghost Grammar School in Jackson, Mississippi, at the age of fifteen. After graduating from Holy Ghost High School, he received a scholarship to Saint Benedict's College in Atchison, Kansas, in 1960. While a student at St. Benedict's, Plumpp began his literary studies, which included reading works by the African American writers **James Baldwin** and **Richard Wright**.

Plumpp left St. Benedict's in 1962 to begin his career as a writer. Settling in **Chicago, Illinois**, he took a job in the post office and continued to read voraciously. After serving in the U.S. Army in 1964–1965, Plumpp returned to Chicago and resumed his education, earning bachelor's and master's degrees in psychology from Roosevelt University. His political activity with the Congress of Racial Equality eventually brought him an invitation to join **OBAC** (Organization of Black American Culture), a Chicago-based Black arts group formed by **Hoyt Fuller**. Early meetings of this group, held at the home of **Gwendolyn Brooks**, brought Plumpp into contact with other young Black writers who were also grappling with issues and ideas of the day and participating in what is known as the **Black Arts Movement**. Through OBAC, Plumpp developed working relationships with a number of Chicago writers, including **Carolyn M. Rodgers** and **Haki R. Madhubuti** (then known as Don L. Lee). His first two collections of poetry, *Portable Soul* (1969) and *Half Black, Half Blacker* (1970), were among the first volumes published by Madhubuti's fledgling **Third World Press**.

Although Plumpp's association with OBAC came to an end in the mid-1970s, an abiding concern for advancing the Black freedom struggle, both in the United States and internationally, continues to define his body of work. His commitment to this proposition is evident in the poetic collections he assembled in the early 1980s: *Somehow We Survive: An Anthology of South African Writing* (1982) and *The Mojo Hands Call, I Must Go* (1982). It is further sustained in his celebrated *Blues Narratives* (1999) and *Johannesburg and Other Poems* (1993). Acknowledging Plumpp's distinctive voice and his ability to translate a lived African American experience into a visionary literature of the African diaspora, the South African poet Keorapetse Kgositsile writes, "The city is a strange place. Sterling Plumpp knows that with a brutal clarity and he shows it to be that way with admirable skill, pushing the word to song past the hasty loudness of ranters."

Since his retirement from the faculty of the University of Illinois at Chicago in 2001, Plumpp has maintained a rigorous writing and reading schedule. He resides in Chicago, where he is an active member of the city's literary and musical communities.

Resources: Sterling Plumpp: *Blues: The Story Always Untold* (Chicago: Another Chicago Press, 1989); *Blues Narratives* (Los Angeles: Tia Chucha Press, 1999); *Half Black, Half Blacker* (Chicago: Third World Press, 1970); *Johannesburg & Other Poems* (Chicago: Another Chicago Press, 1993); *The Mojo Hands Call, I Must Go* (New York: Thunder's Mouth Press, 1982); *Ornate with Smoke* (Chicago: Third World Press, 1997); *Portable Soul* (Chicago: Third World Press, 1969); *Velvet BeBop Kente Cloth* (Chicago: Third World Press, 2003); Sterling Plumpp, ed., *Somehow We Survive: An Anthology of South African Writing* (San Francisco: Publishers Group West, 1982).

Michael A. Antonucci

Poetics. Poetics is the study of poetry as a genre, and it encompasses theories of poetry, criticism, poets' statements about poetry, and traditions of technique, as well as poetic texts. Within the Western literary tradition, from Aristotle's *Poetics* (c. 350 B.C.E.) to **Houston A. Baker, Jr.**'s *Afro-American Poetics* (1988) and **Kevin Powell**'s anthology, *Step into a World: A Global Anthology of the New Black Literature* (2000), poetics has played a central role in shaping, directing, and interpreting literary tastes and trends. African Americans, whose poetic traditions run deep, have made significant, distinctive contributions to poetics at least since the eighteenth century, and their contributions to the field have become even more important since the beginning of the twentieth century.

The roots of African American poetics are not to be found on the North American continent, but rather in Africa. Just as in ancient Greece songs constituted an important form of poetry, so early African poetry consisted of chants. Poets, often taking the histories of tribes, places, and wars as their subjects, worked orally either by improvising their poems to cater to local tastes or by memorizing and reciting the same poem or variants of it from generation to generation, sometimes as court griots or bards (Southern and Wright). Several myths about early African poetry can cause misunderstanding. First, African poetry is not composed of "rhythmic prose," as was commonly supposed until the end of the nineteenth century, but rather of discrete lines of short and long syllables with or without accents. At the same time, the important role that rhythm (and often music and dance) plays in these poems cannot be underestimated. Second, poetry from different regions in Africa does not necessarily form a homogeneous whole. In ancient as in modern times, African poetics has been inherently heterogeneous, drawing from many different languages (some estimates range upwards of 3,000) and many different styles on an enormous continent. Third, current knowledge of these early poems is limited, since only about 200 examples are extant, and little or no commentary has been handed down to us from the times in which these poems were written. As a result, it is impossible to advance definitive claims about early African poetry.

With the rise of **colonialism**, the history of African poetry in one sense comes to an end because colonialism affected African culture so broadly, disrupting literary practices and traditions. In another sense, the history of African poetry continued, but underwent enormous changes and fused with literary histories outside of Africa. During the colonial period, African writers began to emigrate to foreign, often hostile countries, sometimes willingly but more often as slaves. They began using languages other than their native ones, chiefly English and French. As a result of this **diaspora**, African Americans shaped English to fit African poetics, and African poetics to fit Anglo-American contexts.

"Bars Fight," by **Lucy Terry**, is commonly thought to be the first poem written by a Black person in America, although it was not published until 1855. The poem, written in twenty-eight (another edition has thirty) lines of rhymed tetrameter couplets, may be understood as the inauguration of one vein of African American poetics, which uses traditional English poetic styles, such as **ballads** and **sonnets**, to give voice to a **"Negro"** perspective. A more famous poet in this formal vein is **Phillis Wheatley**, born in Senegal, who is generally considered to be the first major African American poet. At the age of thirteen, Wheatley composed "On Being Brought from Africa to America" (1768), and four years later she published her celebrated *A Poem by Phillis, a Negro Girl in Boston, on the Death of the Reverend George Whitefield*. Wheatley's most important work, *Poems on Various Subjects, Religious and Moral* (1773), was published in England, where Wheatley had moved for health reasons. This more formal vein of poetics was more commonly practiced by African Americans in the North than those in **the South**, in part because African American literacy was not prohibited as strictly in the North as it was in the South, although it was often difficult for newly freed slaves to become literate. **Jupiter Hammon**, who published the first known work of African American literature in 1760, and **George Moses Horton**, who is credited with being the first professional African American poet, may be grouped with Terry and Wheatley. **Countee Cullen** and **Georgia Douglas Johnson**, **Harlem Renaissance** writers, can also be placed in this formal, Anglo-American vein; both, for instance, worked comfortably in the sonnet form.

The other major vein of African American poetics springs from the mostly oral, song-oriented tradition that developed because of the circumstances of **slavery**. This vein is sometimes referred to as the **vernacular** tradition. After the **Revolutionary War**, literacy was legally denied to Black slaves; Negro poetry, rather than being stifled by such laws, flourished in the South, though in different guises. It had its roots in orally transmitted field hollers, work songs, and **spirituals**. **Paul Laurence Dunbar** works with the vernacular extensively in *Lyrics of Lowly Life* (1893). The vernacular informs some of the innovations in rhythm and idiom provided by **blues** and **jazz** in the nineteenth and twentieth centuries, and it continues in the intricate rhyme schemes, sampling, street language, and layering of voices in contemporary **performance poetry**, including the work of **Gil Scott-Heron**, and in **hip-hop**. The vernacular vein of African American poetics is intimately linked to the history of African American music, though it is in no way limited to this context. During the pre–**Civil War** era, rhyming aphorisms were used to communicate common complaints as well as secret messages across work fields, such as "I aants a piece a hoecake I wants a piece o' bread./Well, Ise so tired an' hongry dat Ise almos' dead" (Talley, 280). One of the most prominent features of the field holler, which was to be taken up by the blues later on, is the call-response structure, in which one person says a line and another person or group of people answer according to certain lyrical prescriptions. During the post-Civil War era, Christian spirituals became a vehicle of increasing importance for African American poetic expression. Often as subversive as they were spiritual, these songs had been used during the antebellum period as codes in the **Underground Railroad**, as well as in devotional meetings that were actually planning sessions to help slaves escape to the North.

From the late nineteenth century to the interwar period, blues artists (including **Bessie Smith**), **ragtime** performers (including Scott Joplin), Dixieland musicians (such as King Oliver and Louis Armstrong), and bebop jazz artists (such as Charlie Parker) played an important part in shaping the poetic sensibilities of Black and White audiences across America. For example, **Langston Hughes**'s first book of poems, *The Weary Blues* (1926), draws heavily on blues language, structure, and sensibility (Tracy; Ostrom). The poetry of **Sterling A. Brown** and **Fenton Johnson** shows similar influences (Henderson). Hughes's essay "The Negro Artist and the Racial Mountain," although chiefly concerned with encouraging African American writers to write about what they know, makes an indirect statement about the need for a poetics that celebrates African American culture, including the blues and colloquial expression.

In the early twentieth century, Modernism had an enormous impact on all literature, including African American poetics. Critics often refer to "High" and "Low" Modernism. High Modernist poets include Ezra Pound and T. S. Eliot, whose work is structurally complex, full of allusions to other literary texts, often multilingual, sometimes surrealistic, and concerned broadly with cultural decay. The African American writers **Jean Toomer** (whose novel *Cane* includes poetry) and **Melvin B. Tolson** are associated with High Modernism. Low Modernists include Carl Sandburg, William Carlos Williams, Robert Frost, and **Langston Hughes**; their work is more accessible than that of Eliot and Pound, more colloquial, more at ease with themes related to everyday life, less densely allusive, and aimed at a broader audience.

In the postwar or **Cold War** era, the **Black Arts Movement** significantly influenced African American poetics, encouraging African American poets to explore African American experiences, politics, history, and language as fully as possible (Gayle). Poets connected with the Black Arts Movement include **Amiri Baraka, Haki R. Madhubuti, Gwendolyn Brooks, Carolyn M. Rodgers, Dudley Randall, Sonia Sanchez,** and **Etheridge Knight**. After the Black Arts Movement, African American poetics seems both to have exploded and to have imploded. It has exploded in the sense that it has become part of an everyday, global culture, but it has imploded in the sense that African American poetics has become more self-consciously distinct. On the popular front, musical metamorphoses into the free jazz of **Sun Ra**, the disco funk of Grand Funk Railroad, and the early **rap** of the Sugar Hill Gang and Grand Master Flash and Furious Five brought about a concomitant change in poetic tastes, and it is easy to discern the combined influence of Black Arts poetics, jazz, and rap in contemporary performance poetry.

Although tracing two strains of African American poetics—the formal and the vernacular—can be useful, many poets participate in both strains. For example, Countee Cullen preferred to work in traditional forms of English poetry, but his poetry addresses fundamental concerns of African American people, and his diction is chiefly contemporary. Langston Hughes's poetry is squarely in the vernacular tradition, but Hughes often deploys rhyme schemes and imagery common to an Anglo-American tradition, and the range of diction he deploys is deceptively broad. The poetry of **Rita Dove** and **Michael S. Harper**, to take just two examples, blends aspects of the vernacular and formal strains to such an extent that sharp distinctions become more difficult to make.

Poetry is always changing dynamically both in form and in content, and therefore poetics, or the set of ideas about poetry, is also extremely dynamic. The role that African American poetics has played in American literature and aesthetics cannot be underestimated. It has brought elements from a long oral tradition to American poetry, it has adapted and improvised on Anglo-American verse forms, and it has injected a sense of political urgency and of linguistic freedom into African American literature and American literature in general. (*See* **Blues Poetry; Prose Poem.**)

Resources: Klaus Benesch, "Oral Narrative and Literary Text: Afro-American Folklore in *Their Eyes Were Watching God,*" *Callaloo* 11 (1988): 627–635; Benjamin A. Botkin, ed., *Folk-Say,* vol. 1 (Norman: University of Oklahoma Press, 1930), a periodical; Charles T. Davis and Henry Louis Gates, Jr., eds., *The Slave's Narrative* (New York: Oxford University Press, 1985), esp. "Charles Chesnutt and the WPA Narratives: The Oral and Literate Roots of Afro-American Literature," 37–49; Sascha Feinstein, *Jazz Poetry: From the 1920s to the Present* (Westport, CT: Greenwood Press, 1997); Karen J. Ford, "These Old Writing Paper Blues: The Blues Stanza and Literary Poetry," *College Literature* 24, no. 3 (1997), 84–97; Addison Gayle, Jr., *The Black Aesthetic* (Garden City, NY: Doubleday, 1971); Stephen E. Henderson, "The Heavy

Blues of Sterling Brown: A Study of Craft and Tradition," *Black American Literature Forum* 14 (1980), 32–44; James Weldon Johnson, with J. Rosamond Johnson, eds., *The Book of American Negro Spirituals* (New York: Viking, 1925; repr. New York: Da Capo Press, 1989); Hans Ostrom, *A Langston Hughes Encyclopedia* (Westport, CT: Greenwood Press, 2002); Kevin Powell, ed., *Step into a World: A Global Anthology of the New Black Literature* (New York: Wiley, 2000); Alex Preminger and Terry V. F. Brogan, eds., *The New Princeton Encyclopedia of Poetry and Poetics* (Princeton, NJ: Princeton University Press, 1993); Eileen Southern and Josephine Wright, comps., *African-American Traditions in Song, Sermon, Tale, and Dance, 1600s–1920: An Annotated Bibliography of Literature, Collections, and Artworks* (Westport, CT: Greenwood Press, 1990); Pauline Turner Strong, *Captive Selves, Captivating Others: The Politics and Poetics of Colonial American Captivity Narratives* (Boulder, CO: Westview Press, 1999); Thomas W. Talley, *Negro Folk Rhymes: Wise and Otherwise* (New York: Macmillan, 1922); Steven Tracy, *Langston Hughes and the Blues* (Urbana: University of Illinois Press, 1988); M. Lynn Weiss, *Gertrude Stein and Richard Wright: The Poetics and Politics of Modernism* (Jackson: University Press of Mississippi, 1988).

Antony Adolf

Poetry. *See* **Ballad; Blank Verse; Blues Poetry; Dialect Poetry; Epic Poetry/The Long Poem; Formal Verse; Free Verse; Haiku; Lyric Poetry; Narrative Poetry; Performance Poetry; Poetics; Prose Poem; Sonnet; Surrealism; Villanelle.**

Polite, Carlene Hatcher (born 1932). Novelist, dancer, educator, and political activist. Carlene Hatcher Polite was born in **Detroit, Michigan**. After graduating from high school and leaving Michigan for Sarah Lawrence College in New York, Polite began a diverse career in the arts that included nearly ten years as a professional dancer (1955–1963) and the publication of two groundbreaking novels. The novels, *The Flagellants* (1967; English version) and *Sister X and the Victims of Foul Play* (1975), address the relationships between African American men and women; activism in the African American community; and the peculiarities of American racism during the height of the African American revolutionary movements of the 1960s and 1970s. Prior to the publication of *The Flagellants*, Polite was active in civil and human rights causes in Michigan. Frank E. Dobson, Jr., notes her participation by stating, "[s]he coordinated the Detroit Council for Human Rights and participated in the . . . November 1963 Freedom Now Rally to protest the Birmingham, Alabama, church bombings" (384). The church bombings in the American South killed four African American girls and incited many Northern volunteers and activists to protest the inhumanity of desegregation and racism.

In 1964, Polite moved to **Paris, France**, to begin her writing career. Her self-removal from the United States followed in the footsteps of such great African American artists as **Josephine Baker**, **Richard Wright**, **James Baldwin**, and Nina Simone, to name a few. Like these artists, Polite was in search of a foreign muse that would liberate her creativity. While abroad, Polite wrote and published a French edition of *The Flagellants* in 1966, and upon her return to the

United States in 1971, she began her teaching career at the State University of New York at Buffalo. Shortly thereafter, in 1975, she published her second novel, *Sister X and the Victims of Foul Play*, which is set in France. In the novel, the main characters reminisce on the life and times of "Sister X," or Arista, a friend and performer. The novel's themes parallel the progressive attitudes of the African American community during a period of vast social change. More recently, Polite's work has been anthologized in *Black Satin: Contemporary Erotic Fiction by Writers of American Origin* (July 2004) and there has been an increased interest among scholars in her novels and personal activism.

Resources: Frank E. Dobson, Jr., "Carlene Hatcher Polite," in *Contemporary African American Novelists: A Bio-Bibliographical Critical Sourcebook*, ed. Emmanuel S. Nelson (Westport, CT: Greenwood Press, 1999), 384–390; Carlene Hatcher Polite: *The Flagellants* (New York: Farrar, Straus and Giroux, 1967); *Sister X and the Victims of Foul Play* (New York: Farrar, Straus and Giroux, 1975); Margaret Reid, "The Diversity of Influences on Carlene Hatcher Polite's *The Flagellants* and *Sister X and the Victims of Foul Play*," *Connecticut Review* 18 (Spring 1996), http://www.ctstate.edu/univrel/ctreview/spring96/martdich.html.

Kalenda C. Eaton Donald

Popel [Shaw], Esther A. B. (1896–1958). Poet and educator. Born in Harrisburg, Pennsylvania, Popel graduated Phi Beta Kappa from Dickinson College in Carlisle, Pennsylvania. She taught for two years in **Baltimore, Maryland**, before settling in **Washington, D.C.**, where she began publishing poetry in **Opportunity**. Like **Lewis Alexander** and **Anne Spencer**, Popel is considered a relatively minor poet of the **Harlem Renaissance**. Nonetheless, Popel's poetry appeared in *Opportunity* from 1925 to 1934. Roses and Randolph describe her poetry as being categorized into three groups: lyrical, religious, and political.

The lyricism of such poems as "Night Comes Walking" (1929), "October Prayer" (1933), and "Little Grey Leaves" (1925) is based on the beauty of Popel's evocation of natural imagery. **Race** is almost always evident in her poetry. Popel's poem "Flag Salute" (1934) tells the story of a 1933 **lynching**, chillingly intertwined with a class recitation of the Pledge of Allegiance. Lynching is also the subject of "Blasphemy—American Style" (1934), in which the fears of a lynching victim cause him to forget how to pray.

Popel was also a popular speaker in the Washington, D.C., area and in New York City. *Personal Adventures in Race Relations*, published in 1946, was the result of the YMCA's Women's Press's interest in her speech delivered at the Woman's Club in Lawrenceville, NY.

Resources: Esther Popel: *A Forest Pool* (Washington, DC: Modernistic Press, 1934); "Our Thirteenth—in Ohio, 1936," *Journal of the National Association of College Women* 13 (1936), 61–63; *Personal Adventures in Race Relations*, 2nd ed. (New York: Woman's Press, 1946); "The Tenth Milestone," *Journal of the National Association of College Women* 11 (1933–1934), 29; Lorraine Elena Roses and Ruth Elizabeth Randolph, *Harlem Renaissance and Beyond* (Boston: G. K. Hall, 1990), 268–269.

Patricia Kennedy Bostian

Porter, Connie Rose (born 1959). Novelist, essayist, short story writer, children's writer, and poet. Porter uses **realism** to describe the various types of isolation that African Americans, especially women, confront every day. Born in Lackawanna, New York, in 1959, Porter has taught English and creative writing and has written two adult novels, a children's novel series, and essays, short stories, and poetry. Her first novel, *All-Bright Court* (1991), describes the

run-down neighborhood outside Buffalo where African American steel workers live in the 1960s. Porter traces several families in the neighborhood, focusing on the rift between generations' Southern traditions and Northern aspirations. The novel is both bleak and beautiful, and it incorporates elements of magical realism. In Porter's second novel, also set near Buffalo, *Imani All Mine* (1999), teenage Tasha Dawson delivers a girl she names Imani, or "faith," after she is raped. While Tasha doggedly pursues her studies under the burdens of motherhood, she copes with the divisions of **race** and the mysteries of her religious faith. When her baby is killed in a drug-related shooting, she begins anew. This novel may be read in conjunction with an earlier short story, "Primos" (1992), with which it shares some fig-urative and plot elements; similarly, *All-Bright Court* expands themes broached in "Hoodoo" (1988). Porter also writes the *Addy: An American Girl* children's series (beginning in 1993), in which Addy, an escaped slave girl, grows up in

Undated portrait of Connie Porter. Courtesy of the Library of Congress.

Philadelphia, Pennsylvania, in 1864. Moreover, concerned with the challenges of African American womanhood, Porter writes essays based on personal experiences. Her careful research and dedication to realism have won Porter many awards for her writing.

Resources: Ian Elliot, "Connie Porter: Telling It the Way It Was," *Teaching K–8* 25, no. 2 (Oct. 1994), 40–42; *Meet Connie Porter: An American Girls Author*, videorecording (Pleasant Company, 1993); Mickey Pearlman, *Listen to Their Voices: Twenty Interviews with Women Who Write* (New York: Norton, 1993); V. R. Peterson, "Connie Porter," *Essence* (Sept. 1991), 50; Connie Porter: "The Age of Miracles," *Callaloo* 13, no. 4 (Autumn 1990), 746; *All-Bright Court* (Boston: Houghton Mifflin, 1991); "Beauty and the Beast," in *Minding the Body: Women Writers on Body and Soul*, ed. Patricia Foster (New York: Doubleday, 1994), 175–185; "GirlGirlGirl," in *Between Friends*, ed. Mickey Pearlman (Boston: Houghton Mifflin, 1994); "Hoodoo," in *Centers of the Self: Stories by Black American Women from the Nineteenth Century to the Present*, ed. Judith A. Hamer and Martin J. Hamer (New York: Hill and Wang, 1994); *Imani All Mine* (Boston: Houghton Mifflin, 1999); "The Language of the Fat Woman," in *The Strange History of Suzanne LaFleshe and Other Stories of Women and*

Fatness, ed. Susan Koppelman (New York: Feminist Press, 2003); "Primos," *Bilingual Review* 17, no. 2 (May–Aug. 1992), 137–154.

Laura Smith

Postmodernism. Literary movement and cultural and political aesthetic. Postmodernism is considered by many scholars to be more a practice than a methodology. It reacts first and foremost to the self-assured air of Modernism. Euro-American cultural Modernism emerged from the Enlightenment (1700s), which emphasized empiricism, material progress, rational thought and reason, ideals of organic and universal truth, and increasing democratization that invested heavily in (or took its shape from) ideologies of the nation-state. Postmodernism also refers loosely to the cultural era after **World War II**. For the African American tradition, the most significant event of the modern era was the trade in African slaves. The trade not only helped to create the African **diaspora** and establish the permanent presence of Africans in the New World; it also powered Western economic systems and served as the impetus behind the solidification of doctrines of inequality founded on pseudoscientific theories of Black racial inferiority (*see* **Race**; **Slavery**). Thus, as Stephen Jay Gould (1981) has pointed out, the apex of the modern ideological moment might be described as the historical intersection (in 1776) of Thomas Jefferson's Declaration of Independence, Adam Smith's *The Wealth of Nations*, and Johann Blumenbach's *On the Natural Varieties of Mankind*. Jefferson's work limned the ideals of an emerging nation; Smith's book detailed the finer points of individualist economics; and Blumenbach, through his schema of racial classification and his coining of the term "Caucasian" as a racial descriptor for persons of European descent, unwittingly set into motion a slew of racist doctrines. The social and intellectual economy of the time was strongly informed by the intersection of the ideas put forward in these three documents, yet eighteenth-century black writers such as **Olaudah Equiano** and Quobnah Cugoano did not hesitate to contest these notions and to present their own accounts of Black life in the modern era.

The modern era stretched from the late eighteenth century to the mid-twentieth, and the subsequent terms "postmodern" and "postmodernism" seemed to convey, with appropriate vagueness, the new sense of crisis that many experienced after World War II. The feeling that modernist literature (composed by T. S. Eliot, Virginia Woolf, and others) was no longer relevant to a dramatically changed social and intellectual situation was growing steadily among the younger generations. Interestingly, postmodernism was embraced as the battle cry of a new optimism, populist and apocalyptic, sentimental and irresponsible, which is perhaps best articulated in the notion of a "counterculture." Ihab Hassan, one of the most authoritative commentators on the postmodern, writes that in the 1870s, the English painter John Watkins Chapman used the term in a manner similar to our use of "Post-Impressionism." The term *postmodernismo* was used as early as 1934 by the Spanish writer Federico de Onís. "Post-Modernism" later appeared in the final installations of Arnold Toynbee's multivolume work *A Study of History* (1934–1954). For Toynbee, "postmodernism" indicated anarchy and chaos, irrationality and indeterminacy—clearly negative connotations. Thus, Toynbee employed the term in a pejorative fashion.

It is important to differentiate between "postmodernism" and "postmodernity." While the former refers to an aesthetic or cultural practice, the latter indicates periodization. The "postmodern," as both period and practice, came to be theorized only in the 1970s. There are two veins of the postmodern that we may follow in the African American tradition: the aesthetic and the cultural.

Cornel West and **bell hooks** are among the best-known African American theorists of the postmodern. While he makes little effort to differentiate between postmodernism as practice and postmodernity as period, West, in his essay "Black Culture and Postmodernism" (1989), places the movement on a historical continuum that begins in 1945. Emphasizing the fall of Europe and the rise of the United States as a military and economic power, the slow resurgence and opposition of former European colonies in Africa and the Caribbean are significant for West. He harshly criticizes postmodern icons such as Jean-François Lyotard and Jacques Derrida. Lyotard's analysis of the "postmodern condition" is, to West's mind, "rather parochial and provincial—that is, narrowly Eurocentric" (391). Derrida fares no better under West: he neglects to include "Third World peoples, women, gays, lesbians—as well as their relative political impotence in creatively transforming the legacy of the age of Europe" (391). Indeed, Michel Foucault and Jürgen Habermas (who is no fan of postmodernists such as Derrida) likewise draw criticism from West, each proffering analyses that have "remained inscribed within narrow disciplinary boundaries, insulated artistic practices, and vague formulations of men and women of letters" (392). What is needed, West argues, is a push toward a radical reconsideration of historical methodologies and periodizations, which may lead us forthrightly to "issues of politics and ideology" (392). West encourages theorists to pluralize, historicize, and contextualize the postmodernism debate.

hooks, in her widely read essay "Postmodern Blackness" (1990), appears to apply a certain pragmatism in her view of postmodernism. That is, for her, postmodernism should serve as a foundation upon which and a space wherein Black intellectuals reaffirm their connections to the Black folk community, a locus wherein the various points and tenets of postmodernist thought—fragmentation, exile, and marginalization—converge and intersect. At this nodal point, hooks tells us, oppositional strategies of resistance, strategies informed by the historicity of the Black presence in America as well as the postmodern work of countercultural movements, can agitate in favor of the goal of Black liberation.

African American practitioners of the postmodern aesthetic have often gained attention through their use of literary devices that underscore a sense of fragmentation and that question the very possibility of representation.

Black literary postmodernism turns away from the essentialist identity politics of the 1960s (practiced by the Black Arts school) and turns instead toward conceptions of identity that emphasize pluralism and contingency, double-coding and self-reflexivity. **Ralph Ellison**'s *Invisible Man* (1952) is an early example of a novel that not only deals with the issues of selfhood and existence, but also interrogates and subverts traditional ideas of the novel as form. The bibliography, necessarily selective, includes contemporary African American writers considered to be significantly "postmodern," including **Toni Morrison, Ishmael Reed, Samuel R. Delany, Ishmael Reed**, and **John Edgar Wideman**. Cultural studies, Whiteness Studies, and critical race theory are among the discourses that come under the Black postmodernist umbrella. All examine the construction and maintenance of social power, and because Blackness is often posited as the oppositional social value of Whiteness, the examination of White supremacy through the lens of postmodernism is absolutely necessary.

Resources: Sandra Adell, "The Crisis in Black American Literary Criticism and the Postmodern Cures of Houston A. Baker and Henry Louis Gates, Jr.," in her *Double-Consciousness/Double Bind: Theoretical Issues in Twentieth-Century Black Literature* (Urbana: University of Illinois Press, 1994); Hans Bertens, *The Idea of the Postmodern: A History* (New York: Routledge, 1995); Samuel Delany, *Stars in My Pockets like Grains of Sand* (New York: Bantam Books, 1984); Madhu Dubey, *Signs and Cities: Black Literary Postmodernism* (Chicago: University of Chicago Press, 2003); Robert E. Fox, *Conscientious Sorcerers: The Black Postmodern Fiction of Leroi Jones Amiri Baraka, Ishmael Reed, and Samuel R. Delany* (Westport, CT: Greenwood Press, 1987; Stephen Jay Gould, *The Mismeasure of Man* (New York: Norton, 1981); Philip Brian Harper, *Framing the Margins: The Social Logic of Postmodern Culture* (New York: Oxford University Press, 1994); Ihab Hassan, *The Dismemberment of Orpheus: Toward a Postmodern Literature*, 2nd ed. (Madison: University of Wisconsin Press, 1982); W. Lawrence Hogue, *Race, Modernity, Postmodernity: A Look at the History and the Literatures of People of Color Since the 1960s* (Albany: State University of New York Press, 1996); bell hooks, "Postmodern Blackness" (1990), in *A Postmodern Reader*, ed. Joseph Natoli and Linda Hutcheon (Albany: State University of New York Press, 1993); Linda Hutcheon, *A Poetics of Postmodernism: History, Theory, Fiction* (New York: Routledge, 1988); Fredric Jameson, *Postmodernism, or the Cultural Logic of Late Capitalism* (Durham, NC: Duke University Press, 1991); Jean-François Lyotard, *The Postmodern Condition: A Report on Knowledge*, trans. Geoff Bennington and Brian Massumi (1979; Minneapolis: University of Minnesota Press, 1984); Brian McHale, *Postmodernist Fiction* (London: Metheun, 1987); Kobena Mercer, *Welcome to the Jungle: New Positions in Black Cultural Studies* (New York: Routledge, 1994); Toni Morrison: *Beloved* (New York: Knopf, 1987); *Paradise* (New York: Knopf, 1998); Ishmael Reed, *Mumbo Jumbo* (New York: Simon and Schuster, 1996); Cornel West: "Black Culture and Postmodernism," in *A Postmodern Reader*, ed. Joseph Natoli and Linda Hutcheon (Albany: State University of New York Press, 1993), 390–397; *Prophetic Thought in Postmodern Times* (Monroe, ME: Common Courage Press, 1993); John Edgar Wideman, *Reuben* (New York: Henry Holt, 1987); Howard Winant,

"Postmodern Racial Politics: Difference and Inequality," *Socialist Review* 20, no. 1 (Jan./Feb. 1990), 121–147.

Rebecka Rychelle Rutledge

Poststructuralism. A type of literary and cultural criticism, poststructuralism may be described as a philosophy that attempts to disrupt our reliance on language as something that guarantees meaning. It is largely associated with **deconstruction**, as well as with psychoanalysis (as used by the critics Frantz Fanon, Julia Kristeva, and others), French **feminism**, and cultural studies. Any understanding of poststructuralist thought must begin with the work of Jacques Derrida, whose 1966 lecture at Johns Hopkins University, "Structure, Sign and Play in the Discourse of the Human Sciences," and three books, *Of Grammatology*, *Speech and Phenomena*, and *Writing and Difference*, all published in 1967, precipitated the revolution against structuralism. Structuralist theory, predicated on the work of the Swiss linguist Ferdinand de Saussure, evolved from the formalism of the Prague School (led by the Russian linguist Roman Jakobson and the Viennese critic René Wellek) in the period between 1926 and 1948. Heavily influenced by the Moscow Linguistic Circle, the structuralists imagined the literary text to be a set of formal relations, a gestalt comprising multiple elements which, nonetheless, allowed for a unified whole. The term "structuralism," coined by Jakobson, refers not simply to a theory or a method, but to a way of seeing the world, a weltanschauung that insists upon an organic concept of reality and knowledge. Specific elements of this whole were considered to be both present and absent—present to the extent that they appear before us, yet absent insofar as they necessarily constitute factors of a larger system which we cannot fully grasp, but of which each existing ingredient, including we ourselves, forms a part. Structuralism was interested in neither individuality nor history; instead, it was concerned with relationships of meaning.

Derrida's early works initiated the turn away from language as a full and adequate representation of meaning, a principle central to the structuralist project. The quest for absolute meaning had long been the goal of Western metaphysics, and language, as a major constituent of the meaning-making process, had preoccupied Western thinkers from the time of Plato and Aristotle. The Platonic theory of Forms denigrated writing as a degenerate and inadequate representation of speech, and the French structuralists of the 1950s (Claude Lévi-Strauss and Jacques Lacan being quite prominent among them) were only the latest group to carry forward a program insisting upon the absolute ability of language to convey full meaning. Derrida, in working to collapse the binary opposition between speech and writing, also worked to "deconstruct" the notion of transcendental Truth, which had, for quite some time, powered metaphysics.

Poststructuralism came to the United States largely through the Yale School, a collective of scholars at Yale University who, led by Paul de Man, translated the French texts of Derrida and introduced them to American scholars and students. African American theorists and critics soon became invested in poststructuralist theory. In working to dismantle the notion of absolute Truth, a Eurocentric concept, they worked vigorously to disable the idea of a normative discourse of self and identity which posited people of color as "Other," as the inferior term in Hegel's famous dialectic of master and slave in his *Phenomenology of Spirit* (1806–1807). Without doubt, African Americanists had not waited for the work of Derrida to inaugurate a radical discourse of opposition and deconstruction. **Olaudah Equiano**, in his 1789 *Narrative of the Life of Olaudah Equiano*, strove to demonstrate the contradictions and gaps inherent in universalist theories of national identity. **W.E.B. Du Bois**'s idea of double consciousness, expounded at length in *The Souls of Black Folk* (1903), corrects Hegel's dialectic by insisting not only upon an account of the forces of history (including the legacies and realities of **slavery**, peonage, and Jim Crow), but also upon a theory of materialism that questioned the Enlightenment notion of Progress. Double consciousness read clearly is not a resignation to a sense of alienation in national life; rather, it is the recognition of a multiple self with multiple identities to be negotiated. Du Bois's double consciousness may be seen at work in the Martinican psychoanalyst Frantz Fanon's *Black Skin, White Masks* (1952), specifically in the widely read essay "The Fact of Blackness."

Du Bois's work is, arguably, foundational to contemporary Black poststructuralism in the United States. While the **Black Arts Movement** produced structuralist and formalist dicta on an authoritarian "Black English" and a "true Black Subject" during the 1960s, poststructuralist theorists such as **Houston A. Baker, Jr.**, made the shift away from Black structuralism. Baker, among his many projects, worked to link the cultural and social theory of Du Bois to language and experimental writing in the work of **Ralph Ellison** (who was both novelist and critic) in order to produce a poststructuralist theory of a **blues** idiom. Although **Barbara Christian**, the late doyenne of twentieth-century Black women's literary criticism, disparaged theory and called for a return to close readings in her essay "The Race for Theory" (1987), Mae Gwendolyn Henderson, in "Speaking in Tongues: Dialogics, Dialectics, and the Black Woman Writer's Literary Tradition" (1989), embraced poststructuralist theories of language by insisting upon the heteroglossic (or polyphonic) nature of Black women's writing.

Poststructuralism is viewed by many as a political method of reading texts and analyzing culture, and thus it serves as a vehicle through which to defer or even eclipse authoritarian Western discourse. The Frenchman Roland Barthes's announcement of the "Death of the Author" (1968) at the very historical moment of accession by Blacks to fuller social representation in the United States (including the passage of the 1964 Civil Rights Act and the establishment of **Black Studies** departments in colleges and universities in the late 1960s) alarmed many African Americanists. Likewise, poststructuralism's view of the fragmented and unstable subject at a time when Blacks were, in many arenas, laying powerful claim to full subjectivity has caused critics such as **Joyce Anne Joyce** to denounce poststructuralism and its cognate movement, **postmodernism**, as antihumanist and as anathema to Black literature and culture. Nevertheless, poststructuralism's potential to defer the Western logic of identity and legitimation continues to attract numerous adherents, and has contributed to the development of such intellectual enterprises as cultural studies, Whiteness studies, and critical **race** theory.

Resources: Michael Awkward, "Appropriative Gestures: Theory and Afro-American Literary Criticism," in *African American Literary Theory: A Reader*, ed. Winston Napier (New York: New York University Press, 2000), 331–338; Houston A. Baker, Jr., "Belief, Theory, and Blues: Notes for a Post-Structuralist Criticism of Afro-American Literature," *African American Literary Theory*, pp. 224–241; Barbara Christian, "The Race for Theory," in *African American Literary Theory*, pp. 280–289; Frantz Fanon, *Black Skin, White Masks*, trans. Charles Lam Markmann (1952; New York: Grove Press, 1967); Henry Louis Gates, Jr.: "'What's Love Got to Do with It?' Critical Theory, Integrity, and the Black Idiom," *African American Literary Theory*, pp. 298–312; "Writing 'Race' and the Difference It Makes," in *"Race," Writing, and Difference*, ed. Henry Louis Gates, Jr. (Chicago: University of Chicago Press, 1986); Mae G. Henderson, "Speaking in Tongues: Dialogics, Dialectics, and the Black Woman Writer's Literary Tradition," in *African American Literary Theory*, pp. 348–368; Joyce A. Joyce, "The Black Canon: Reconstructing Black American Literary Criticism," in *African American Literary Theory*, pp. 290–297; Deborah McDowell, "Black Feminist Thinking: The 'Practice' of Theory," in *African American Literary Theory*, pp. 557–579.

Rebecka Rychelle Rutledge

Powell, Kevin (born 1969). Author, poet, journalist, essayist, public speaker, political activist, and **hip-hop** historian. Powell grew up in Jersey City, New Jersey, and overcame countless obstacles to attend Rutgers University in the 1980s, where he studied political science and English. He went on to battle the problems of the inner city as a social worker in Newark, New Jersey, and later became an English instructor at New York University's Saturday high school program. By the late 1980s, Powell started to write freelance articles for *The Black American, San Francisco Weekly, Rolling Stone, Interview, YSB, Emerge*, and ***The Amsterdam News***. Later Powell's articles, essays, and reviews appeared in a range of publications including *Newsweek, Code, Essence*, and the *Washington Post*. In 1992 Powell published his first book, *In the Tradition: An Anthology of Young Black Writers*, which he edited with **Ras Baraka**, son of **Amiri Baraka**.

Powell is best known to the general public for his time in 1992 as a cast member of MTV's first season of *The Real World* (New York City) and as a senior writer for *Vibe* magazine from 1992 to 1996. He expressed his lyrical talent with a volume of poetry, *Recognize: Poems* (1995). Powell's other books include *Keepin' It Real: Post-MTV Reflections on Race, Sex, and Politics* (1997); *Step into a World: A Global Anthology of the New Black Literature* (2000); *Who's Gonna Take the Weight?* (2003), which contains three essays, "The Breakdown," "Confessions of a Recovering Misogynist," and "What Is a Man?"; and

Who Shot Ya? Three Decades of Hip-hop Photography (2002), on which he worked with the photographer Ernie Paniccioli. Powell met Paniccioli while he was serving as guest curator of the Brooklyn Museum of Art's "Hip-Hop Nation: Roots, Rhymes, and Rage." Powell is the founder/chairperson of "Hiphop Speaks," a college speaking tour that emphasizes the history and four elements of hip-hop (the DJ, the MC, the graffiti writer, and the dance element), as well as the political and social responsibilities of hip-hop. Powell is hailed as one of the most important voices of his generation for his analytical approach and accessible style as a social commentator, community leader, cultural critic, and college lecturer.

Resources: Kevin Powell: Ras Baraka and Kevin Powell, eds., *In the Tradition: An Anthology of Young Black Writers* (New York: Writers & Readers, 1992); *Keepin' It Real: Post-MTV Reflections on Race, Sex, and Politics* (New York: One World, 1997); *Recognize* (New York: Writers & Readers, 1995); *Step into a World: A Global Anthology of the New Black Literature* (New York: Wiley, 2000); *Who's Gonna Take the Weight?* (New York: Three Rivers, 2003); "Kevin Powell," *African American Literature Book Club*, author's profiles, http://aalbc.com/authors/kevin.htm; Ernie Paniccioli and Kevin Powell, eds., *Who Shot Ya? Three Decades of Hip-hop Photography* (New York: Amistad, 2002); Laurie Rodwell "Kevin Powell to Lecture on Multiculturalism in America," *Hendrix Today* (2003), http://www.hendrix.edu/Multicultural/Kevin%20Powell.htm.

eboni treco

Prison Literature. Prison literature conveys both the hardships and the accomplishments of prisoners through their **autobiographies, essays**, fiction, letters, poetry, and plays. While Anicius Boethius's *Consolation of Philosophy* (525/524 B.C.E.) has been recognized as one of the earliest examples of prison writing, other renowned contributions include works by European authors such as Miguel de Cervantes, the Marquis de Sade, Fyodor Dostoevsky, Alexander Solzhenitsyn, and Jean Genet. Influential models for contemporary prison writers are Genet's prison-inspired works *Our Lady of the Flowers* (1944), *Miracle of the Rose* (1946), *The Thief's Journal* (1949), and *Deathwatch* (1949). In the United States, prisoners have written captivity narratives and **slave narratives** (Franklin, 6), but they have also written about capital punishment, poverty, racism, mental health, addiction, disease, sexuality, and violence.

African American prison literature begins with the early plantation songs that collectively embody "the most poignant evidence of the continuity from pre–**Civil War** chattel slavery to the twentieth-century prison" (Franklin, 29). In the 1920s and 1930s, prison writers would reach larger audiences due in part to such liberal publications as *Esquire* and *American Mercury* magazine. Moreover, H. Bruce Franklin, one of the most important critics of prison literature, notes that as "the Depression made poverty and crime intrude more and more into everyday life, prison literature continued to gain a wider and more appreciative audience" (11). Works of prison-inspired literature by the ex-convict **Chester Himes**, *If He Hollers Let Him Go* (1945) and *Cast the First*

Stone (1952), helped to make him an important African American writer and also a pioneer of a new literary category, African American hard-boiled detective fiction (*see* **Crime and Mystery Fiction**).

In the context of the racial tension of the 1950s and 1960s and the assassinations of **Malcolm X** in 1966 and **Martin Luther King, Jr.,** in 1968, prison literature by African Americans informed a wide variety of American audiences. In the 1970s and 1980s, notorious autobiographies by **Angela Y. Davis**—*Angela Davis: An Autobiography* (1974)—and Assata Shakur—*Assata* (1987)—served to condemn what such writers saw as an unfair prison system that was part of a larger industrial enonomic and social system. Such a critique had already been advanced by Malcolm X in *The Autobiography of Malcolm X* (1965). Referred to as "Satan" before his conversion to Islam while in prison, Malcolm X inspired many confinement narratives. "After the assassination [of Malcolm X]," writes Franklin, "prison writers acknowledged him as both their political and spiritual leader; he is conventionally compared to Moses, Jesus, even Allah" (148). Like Davis and Shakur, American prison writers tend to echo Malcolm X's insistence upon the dire need for alternative modes of discourse inside what they regard as America's overtly patriarchal facilities.

Pivotal works by radical political prisoners include those by **Black Panthers George Lester Jackson** (*Soledad Brother*, 1970, and *Blood in My Eye*, 1972) and **Eldridge Cleaver** (*Soul on Ice*, 1967, and *Soul on Fire*, 1978). Other important works of African American prison literature are *Dopefiend* (1971), *Black Gangster* (1972), and *Daddy Cool* (1974) by **Donald Goines**; *Poems from Prison* (1968), *Born of a Woman* (1980), and *The Essential Etheridge Knight* (1986) by **Etheridge Knight**, and works by **Iceberg Slim**. Described by Holloway House as America's "most read" African American author, Iceberg Slim (born Robert Beck) remains an innovator in prison writing and crime fiction. His works are *Trick Baby* (1967), *Pimp: The Story of My Life* (1969, with introductions by both **Sapphire** and Ice-T), *Mama Black Widow* (1969), *The Naked Soul of Iceberg Slim* (1971), *Long White Con* (1977), *Death Wish* (1977) and *Airtight Willie & Me* (1979). Slim's raw **vernacular** and street-wise style make him an important precursor to **rap** and **hip-hop**, but they also serve as examples for younger prison writers.

Franklin was largely responsible for bringing American prison writing into academic institutions with the publication of *The Victim as Criminal and Artist* (1978). However, throughout the 1970s and the 1980s, prison regulations prohibited many prison writers from publishing their work. In his 1998 anthology, Franklin alludes to both the 1977 "Son of Sam" law and Title 28 of the Code of Federal Regulations, Section 540.20(b), which states: "The inmate may not receive compensation or anything of value for correspondence with the news media" (15). After a number of prohibitive laws were finally deemed unconstitutional, new prison literature emerged in the 1990s. Works by ex-gang members such as Sanyika Shakur—*The Autobiography of an L.A. Gang Member* (1993)—and Stanley "Tookie" Williams—*Life in Prison* (1998)—blend Malcolm X's theoretical discourse and Iceberg Slim's flare for storytelling. Writers such as Shakur and Williams also resurrect many of the arguments put forth by radical 1960s prisoners such as Davis, Jackson, and Cleaver, particularly theories promoting "prisoner-of-war" status for African-American prisoners.

Controversial prison writers have had to spend time in isolation cells and have experienced immediate transfers to remote facilities, with no access to writing supplies (Chevigny, 99). Mumia Abu-Jamal, a cofounder of the Philadelphia chapter of the Black Panthers and a death row inmate since 1982, had all writing privileges taken away after the release of his compilation *Live from Death Row* (1995) (Franklin, 351). Jamal's major works of nonfiction—*Death Blossoms* (1997), *All Things Censored* (2000), and *Faith of Our Fathers* (2003)—have dealt with prison topics pertaining to isolation, sexuality, violence, and the power hierarchy. In *Prison Masculinities* (2001), an anthology of writing by both prisoners and prison experts, Jamal comments on the issue of celibacy inside prison walls and reveals the consequences of homosexuality being detected by prison officials, many of whom he characterizes as homophobic. As American prison writers continue to reaffirm, both convicts and officials tend to target prisoners who chronicle the experiences of homosexually active and HIV-positive prisoners. *ManRoot* magazine founder and prison writer Paul Mariah was determined to describe the constant struggles of gay prisoners in the 1960s. The publication of Dannie Martin's essay "AIDS: The View from a Prison Cell" (1986) was deemed an intentional violation of Title 28 (Franklin, 14).

Incarcerated female writers such as Diane Hamill Metzger, author of "Uncle Adam" (1985), and Susan Rosenberg, author of "Lee's Time" (1993), critique what they regard as the "phallocentric" perspectives of prison authorities (Chevigny, xxv). Like other minority writers, including the Latino writer Miguel Pinero, women prison writers accuse officials of manipulating prisoners' bodies through acts that range from physical abuse to intentional overcrowding. These writers confirm that "bodies of color" are particularly susceptible to abuse.

While captives with firsthand experiences have written nearly all the works of prison literature, an exception to the rule remains Michel Foucault's *Discipline and Punish: The Birth of the Prison* (1975). In describing strategies imposed by those atop prison hierarchies in numerous nations, the French theorist indirectly validates works by African American prison writers. Ted Conover's *Newjack* (2000), winner of the National Book Critics Circle Award for Nonfiction, is a critique of both prisoners and prison officials—specifically, those who live and work in New York State's Sing Sing Prison. Posing and working as a prison guard, Conover observed the same institutionalized acts of violence, mistreatment, and blatant racism that prison writers have been documenting since the first prison narratives appeared. Notable contributions such as Nathan C. Heard's *House of Slammers* (1983), Kim Wozencraft's *Notes from the Country Club* (1993), and Jimmy A. Lerner's *You Got Nothing Coming* (2002) further serve to highlight one of Foucault's most significant contentions, that invisible bodies can be "transformed" into state-owned commodities (136).

As Patricia O'Connor states in *Speaking of Crime* (2000), such writers will utilize their memoirs and semifiction in order to establish connections outside of prison. O'Connor specifically observes "the ways prisoners...present themselves in autobiographical discourse, not only positioning themselves in their criminal pasts but narratively constructing past selves and potentially new selves in society" (153). While virtually all statutes enacted to censor prison literature have been deemed unlawful, a large number of prison writing programs have been dismantled due to insufficient funding (Chevigny, 98). However, both celebrated and lesser-known works continue to appear in contemporary anthologies and collections, including Bob Gaucher's *Writing as Resistance* (2002). Also, much prison literature remains accessible due to the existence of prison libraries and the work of such organizations as the PEN American Society and the Fortune Society.

Resources: Bell Gale Chevigny, *Doing Time: Twenty-five Years of Prison Writing* (New York: Arcade, 1999); Michel Foucault, *Discipline & Punish: The Birth of the Prison* (New York: Pantheon, 1977); H. Bruce Franklin, *Prison Writing in 20th-Century America* (New York: Penguin, 1998); Patricia E. O'Connor, *Speaking of Crime: Narratives of Prisoners* (Lincoln: University of Nebraska Press, 2000).

Stephen M. Steck

Prose Poem. The prose poem is found in ancient Hebrew writings, in biblical psalms, and in the literature of many other cultures. Prose poetry in Europe and the United States is well represented from the nineteenth century through the present, and a best-selling book of the twentieth century is a book of prose poems, Kahlil Gibran's *The Prophet* (1923). The prose poem is frequently associated with Charles Baudelaire, a French poet, critic, and translator. Baudelaire's *Little Poems in Prose* was published in 1869, but Aloysius (Louis) Bertrand had introduced the form into French literature almost three decades earlier, with *Gaspard of the Night* (*Gaspard de la nuit*, published posthumously in 1842). Bertrand experimented with short, volatile works that he called "fantasies." Predating French Symbolism and French **Surrealism**, Bertrand's poems were not read widely by his peers, even in literary circles, but the form continues to influence poets from many countries, notably Russia, North and South America, Italy, and Denmark.

"Prose" designates "consciously shaped writing and, in the broadest sense, consists of all forms of expression that do not have regular patterns of rhythm and rhyme" (Holman and Harmon, 379). The natural rhythms and absence of repeated themes in prose are distinguishing characteristics separating prose from the reiteration and metrical schemes of free verse, but "a clear line between prose and poetry is difficult to draw" (Holman and Harmon, 379). Medieval hymn sequences are occasionally called "proses," perhaps based on "quantitative" and "qualitative" verse distinctions regarding rhythm as duration of sound. ("Quantitative" refers to the number of syllables and/or stressed syllables, whereas "qualitative" refers to the length of syllables, as in a short vowel sound versus a long vowel sound.)

In its modern form, the prose poem is a condensed hybrid form that combines the qualities of prose and poetry. The form is rationally resisted by some who reluctantly concede that even prosaic writing becomes poetry when the author calls the work a poem. Holman and Harmon further observe that titling a work a "prose poem" prompts readers to apply the same attention to detail reserved for poetry (380). Incorporating elements of poetry, including rhythm, rhyme, sound patterning, and imagery, into the constraints of expository or narrative prose, the prose poem produces a heightened sensory or affective response to the occasionally startling imagery. What is and is not prose poetry is debatable. The classification is generally applied to a short work marked by recognizable poetic elements, a longer poetic work presented in prose format, or a prose work titled as verse. Prose poetry is characterized by prominent rhythms, rich language, and universal significance. James Joyce's *Finnegans Wake* is considered by some to be an example of this contradictory form in which words "inhabit more than one world," simultaneously capturing emotion and memory and representing concrete objects (Deutsch, Preface). Baudelaire and others demonstrate the suppleness of the prose poem, a form that allows the poet to apply lyrical language to ordinary themes. The distinctively dual, inward and outward, focus of the prose poem effectively accommodates a poet's creative experimentation and rational expression of a worldview.

In world literature, prose poetry is frequently used to focus on intensely emotional and complex cultural and historical events. Cultural and universal themes, including the disenfranchisement, spiritual malaise, and resistance addressed in the prose and poetry of many African American writers (such as **Phillis Wheatley**, **Frederick Douglass**, and **Zora Neale Hurston**), address autobiographical issues related to morality, education, and freedom. **Sterling A. Brown**, **Langston Hughes**, **James Baldwin**, **August Wilson**, and other Black writers further investigate these themes of literacy and identity in a variety of forms. Sterling Brown, familiar with the tensions of middle-class marginalization and the challenges of minority scholarship, notes in the work of Edwin Arlington Robinson, Robert Frost, Carl Sandburg, and Vachel Lindsay the power of **vernacular** language to express ordinary experience. Like Frost, Brown combines vernacular speech, folk forms, and traditional forms to explore cultural stereotypes and to depict authentic folk heroes. Experimenting with vernacular language as a literary and cultural tool, Brown, like Frost and other New American poets, demonstrates that language and cultural identity are inseparable. In *Negro Caravan* (1941), Brown extensively documents the linguistic experimentation and literary history of Black writers.

Langston Hughes, unofficial Black Poet Laureate, is recognized for his portraits of Black life in North America. Identifying with the black experience and with the music and language of distress marking the racial divide, Hughes gives that experience a voice. Drawing from folk and traditional sources, in prose and poetry he narrates racism, poverty, and the playfulness of the race's collective experience in two languages, Standard English and Black vernacular. Influenced by lyric and narrative forms, Brown's and Hughes' works offer dual models of liberation and endurance. **James Weldon Johnson** observes that the poet's characteristic use of the **Negro**'s common speech infuses Brown's poetry with the undiluted genuineness of the culture.

Robert Bly, a twentieth-century American poet who both works in and writes about the prose poem form, characterizes it as an "evolving" form, so although Wheatley, Douglass, Hurston, Brown, Johnson, and Baldwin did not publish prose poems per se, they arguably prepared the way for the use of the form by infusing lyric poetry with narrative elements and infusing prose with heightened rhythms and striking imagery Hughes's longer work *Ask Your Mama* (1961) represents his explicit experimentation with a kind of prose poetry. *Cane* (1923), by **Jean Toomer**, a work that mixes poetry and highly compressed, evocative narratives, is also arguably a work of prose poetry. Of European and African heritage, Toomer lived alternately as Black and White as a child and teenager. He was a symbolist and idealist, and his contribution to American and the African American literature was influenced by imagist aesthetics, by Baudelaire's prose poetry, and by Walt Whitman's mystical concept of the self.

The literary compression of the prose poem provides African American writers, including Toomer, an adaptive genre for addressing the intensity and range of cultural experience and knowledge. The form accommodates a range of prose and poetic techniques and creative processes, language choices, diction, rhythm, and rhyme. Prose poetry, positioned between prose and free verse, has fewer boundaries or definitive rules for meter and rhyme than traditional verse. Poetic devices, alliteration, assonance, and visual effects, achieved through line breaks and arrangement, produce the patterns of poetry. The rhythmic patterns of prose are generally less distinct. An example is **Bob Kaufman**'s prose poems, consisting of long lines composed of surrealistic imagery and vigorous rhythms. The orality and musical quality of Kaufman's poetry are characteristic of the **Beat Movement** and resemble the improvisations of **jazz** observed in the poetry of Langston Hughes and **Harryette Mullen**, consisting of similar linguistic improvisations and ironic, alternative readings of cultural issues through imagery.

Yusef Komunyakaa also uses startling imagery to investigate realistic and surrealistic themes. Almost two decades after completing his military service, Komunyakaa began recording his war experiences in verse, earning recognition as a soldier and a poet, and was awarded the Pulitzer Prize for poetry in 1994. Komunyakaa exemplifies the poet's skilled use of single images to convey experience. His work, like that of most African American poets and prose writers, is shaped by a proud heritage, rich jazz-**blues** tradition, shifts in culture, and the poetic challenge to compose these chaotic elements. This influence is evident in Komunyakaa's "Facing It," in the colliding, visceral images of "brushstrokes" and "black granite" and the poet's use of named and nameless individuals to focus the images.

The prose poem has become a widely used cultural and literary lens for many African American writers investigating aesthetic and practical issues defining the culture. The duality of the form appropriately expresses the culture's complexity, enabling preservationists to address the culture's static elements rooted in **folklore** and leaving other writers to consider dynamic elements that, like the culture's roots in jazz, are better developed and expressed by improvisation and multivocal patterns. Poetic or dramatic license enables writers to suspend conventional rules; to depart from form, fact, and other elements of realism; to represent cultural truths from creative or imagined perspectives. Various literary devices are used by prose poets to support this artistic freedom. The vividly imaginative imagery and vigorous rhythms characteristic of poetic prose make the medium attractive for expression of emotionally charged or sensory rich language, but some critics regard the form as flawed and unsatisfactory as either prose or poetry (McArthur, 790).

Resources: William L. Andrews et al., *The Oxford Companion to African American Literature* (New York: Oxford University Press, 1997); Charles Baudelaire, *Little Poems in Prose*, trans. Aleister Crowley, ed. Martin P. Starr, rev. ed. (Chicago: Teitan Press, 1995); Louis Aloysius Bertrand, *Gaspard de la Nuit*, trans. John T. Wright, 2nd ed. (Lanham, MD: University Press of America, 1994); Robert Bly, "The Prose Poem as an Evolving Form," in his *Selected Poems* (New York: Perennial Library, 1986); Babette Deutsch, *Poetry Handbook: A Dictionary of Terms*, 4th ed. (New York: Funk & Wagnalls, 1974); Kahlil Gibran, *The Prophet* (New York: Knopf, 1923); C. Hugh Holman and William Harmon, eds., *A Handbook to Literature*, 6th ed. (New York: Macmillan, 1992; Langston Hughes, *Collected Poems of Langston Hughes*, ed. Arnold Rampersad (New York: Knopf, 1994); James Joyce, *Finnegans Wake*, reiss. ed. (New York: Penguin, 1999); Tom McArthur, ed., *The Oxford Companion to the English Language* (New York: Oxford University Press, 1992); Emmanuel S. Nelson, ed., *African American Authors, 1745–1945: A Bio-Bibliographical Critical Sourcebook* (Westport, CT: Greenwood Press, 2000); Aldon Lynn Nielsen, ed., *Reading Race in American Poetry: An Area of Act* (Urbana: University of Illinois Press, 2000).

Stella Thompson

Protest Literature. Protest literature condemns what its authors perceive to be injustice and incites its audience to fight the same. From this perspective, much of African American literature, from its inception to the present, can arguably be called protest literature, in that it rejects the racist ideology that sustained **slavery**, segregation, racism, and oppression. Protest literature asserts the equality between Blacks and Whites, at times calling for militant action to effect the changes deemed necessary to ensure this equality.

The **slave narrative** was the first type of protest literature in African American letters. Having escaped from **the South** to the North, former slaves wrote about the physical and psychological cruelty of Southern slavery, the hunger for freedom, the difficult journey from bondage to freedom, and the moral urgency to abolish slavery. In his *Narrative of the Life of Frederick Douglass, an American Slave* (1845), **Frederick Douglass** eloquently describes the annihilation wrought by slavery upon the slave's body and spirit, but also, following a well-established tradition in autobiographical writing, he traces a trajectory from a sense of denied humanity and identity within slavery to the recovery of freedom. His writing is a rhetorical tour de force that convincingly describes and condemns slavery in Christian America.

Slave narratives, then, condemned an unjust system that treated human beings as chattel and mere commodities, but they also denounced the hypocrisy of the young American republic, a nation that claimed to be Christian and yet embraced the brutal institution of slavery. For example, to shame those who supported or tolerated slavery, **William Wells Brown**, in his 1853 novel *Clotel; or, the President's Daughter*, uses irony and sarcasm, two central tropes in protest literature. Several episodes in the novel echo the famed **satire** of Jonathan Swift in "A Modest Proposal" (1729).

Harriet Ann Jacobs's *Incidents in the Life of a Slave Girl* (1861) is another example of narratives from the antebellum years that show the evils of slavery. It focuses on the female slave, who, in addition to the usual brutality, also has to endure continuous sexual harassment and the agony of not being able to fulfill the moral expectations placed on the nineteenth-century woman. Jacobs's is a remarkable example of a Black woman's condemnation of, and resistance to, the brutality of slavery.

After the slave narrative, literature associated with early manifestations of **Black Nationalism** is probably the most ideologically articulated form of protest in African American letters. Already in the antebellum period, **Martin R. Delany** and **Alexander Crummell**, among others, had articulated the reality that Africans in America shared the brutal experience of slavery, the common tie to motherland Africa, exclusion and alienation from the American society, the necessity of a united front to overcome the ravages of slavery and racism, and the possibility of creating a great nation on the African continent. The realization that the end of the **Civil War** did not make African Americans any more acceptable in American society led to new nationalist discourses. Post-**Reconstruction** writers such as **Sutton E. Griggs, Pauline Elizabeth Hopkins, Frances Ellen Watkins Harper, Charles Waddell Chesnutt**, and **James Weldon Johnson** used their fiction to ponder and sometimes unequivocally advocate cultural nationalism and political separation in the face of continuing oppression. The most vocal message of protest against the state of Post-Reconstruction race relations probably came from **W.E.B. Du Bois**, whose work, notably his *The Souls of Black Folk* (1903), forcefully protested legalized segregation and large-scale violence against African Americans. He argued that the Jim Crow laws in the South and the accommodationist approach of some Black leaders (especially **Booker T. Washington**) created a steady course of disenfranchising African Americans and perpetuating the supposed inferiority of Blacks.

The cultural, literary, and artistic flowering of the **Harlem Renaissance** expressed aesthetic views rooted in race consciousness and pride, and it countered old stereotypes by presenting the complexity of Black people in America and in the world. Writers and artists such as **Alain Locke, Claude McKay, Langston Hughes, Countee Cullen,** Louis Armstrong, **Billie Holliday,** and **Zora Neale Hurston** offered America new and original forms of expression rooted in the African American experience, such as the **blues, jazz,** and African American **folklore.** This cultural display was an implicit protest against the inferior status that had been hitherto imposed on Black literary and artistic creativity by the dominant culture. In this period, **Marcus Garvey** reproved White oppression and racism, and proclaimed the oneness and greatness of people of African descent. He promoted self-help, race consciousness, and pride, as well as the liberation of the African continent from European colonial power. His ideology of Black nationalism called for the separation of the races as a way of protesting racism and oppression that had barred African Americans from total acceptance in the American society. Garvey led a **back-to-Africa movement.**

After the Harlem Renaissance, Langston Hughes produced politically alert work influenced greatly by socialist ideas. Many of the stories in his collection *The Ways of White Folks* (1934) implicitly protest how "some white folks," as Hughes puts it, treat African Americans, and he especially emphasizes themes of sexuality and class conflict. The poem "Dear Mr. President" (1943) protests the fact that while Black soldiers are fighting tyranny abroad, they must endure segregation within the American military (Ostrom). Much of Hughes's work in the 1930s and 1940s qualifies as protest literature (Berry).

The publication of **Richard Wright**'s novel *Native Son* in 1940 was hailed as a blunt portrayal of race matters in America. Fittingly, the novel opens with an alarm clock, symbolically calling America to pay attention to what centuries of enslavement and racism have wrought on the life of Bigger Thomas, a young man who lives in the Black belt of South Side **Chicago** in a small, rat-infested apartment he shares with his mother and his two siblings. In the novel, Wright deploys naturalism, which combines the literary technique of focusing on realistic detail with a worldview that focuses on human beings as victims of social forces that they cannot control. Wright portrays Bigger as a person conditioned to kill and as one ultimately executed by the same environment that created his criminal behavior in the first place.

A contemporary of Wright's, **Chester Himes,** who is better known for his work in **crime and mystery fiction,** also produced novels in the protest literature category.

In spite of significant African American contribution to the war effort, the period following **World War II** failed, as other periods had failed, to bring social justice to African Americans. Out of this period emerged the **Civil Rights Movement** of the 1950s and 1960s. Fighting to end racial segregation and inequality between the races, the movement was spearheaded by diverse figures and movements, including **Martin Luther King, Jr., Malcolm X,** the **Black Arts Movement,** and the **Black Power** movement.

Martin Luther King, Jr.'s fight is probably best conveyed through his speech "I Have a Dream," delivered on August 26, 1963, at the Lincoln Memorial in

Washington, D.C. One century after the Emancipation Proclamation, African Americans had not seen an end to racial injustice. King envisaged a society that would reject racism and segregation, and embrace true Christian love, brotherhood, and mutual acceptance. Another leader of the movement, Malcolm X, proclaimed that African Americans were not really Americans, but Africans who happened to be in America because America had never accepted them as full members of the society, instead repeatedly oppressing them. In a speech delivered in Cleveland, Ohio, on April 3, 1964, "The Ballot or the Bullet," Malcolm X proposed Black Nationalism as a remedy to White racism and oppression. He called for Black unity and argued the necessity for African Americans to elect politicians who would address their concerns and aspirations, appealed to African Americans to own and support businesses in their communities, and underscored the obligation to deal with social evils such as drugs, prostitution, and alcoholism that were destroying African American communities.

On the literary front, the Black Arts Movement (BAM) of the 1960s and early 1970s included much protest literature. **Amiri Baraka**, **Larry Neal**, **Sonia Sanchez**, and **Nikki Giovanni**, to name only a few writers of the period, promoted and practiced literary expression in the service of the Black community. The BAM aesthetic was probably best conveyed through an anthology edited by Baraka and Neal: *Black Fire: An Anthology of Afro-American Writing* (1968), and through Neal's essay "The Black Arts Movement" (1968). Contributors to the collection called for Black art and literature to reflect the needs of the Black community and promoted cultural nationalism. Baraka called the BAM writers "soldier poets," a term that reflected the nature of protest literature as a weapon against racism and oppression, and Neal described the BAM as "the aesthetic and spiritual sister of the Black Power concept" (62).

Even after the fading of the militant BAM ideology in the mid-1970s, there is still an underlying element of protest in African American literature. Arguably, because racism in some form or other continues to affect African Americans, many African American writers will, out of necessity, produce works that protest current social and political situations. At the same time, protest literature has always attracted the claim that it is propaganda or otherwise too explicitly political. Whether protest literature, or any artistic expression, is "political" or "too political" depends largely upon the definition of art and the belief about the function of art.

Resources: Amiri Baraka and Larry Neal, eds., *Black Fire: An Anthology of Afro-American Writing* (New York: Morrow, 1968); William Wells Brown, *Clotel; or, The President's Daughter: A Narrative of Slave Life in the United States* (1853; repr. New York: Carol Publishing Group, 1995); Frederick Douglass, *Narrative of the Life of Frederick Douglass, an American Slave, Written by Himself* (1845; repr. Boston: Bedford Books, 1993); Addison Gayle, *The Black Aesthetic* (Garden City, NY: Doubleday, 1971); Langston Hughes, *Good Morning, Revolution: Uncollected Social Protest Writings*, ed. Faith Berry (Secaucus, NJ: Carol, 1992); Harriet Jacobs, *Incidents in the Life of a Slave Girl, Written by Herself* (1861; repr. New York: Norton, 2001); Larry Neal, "The Black

Arts Movement," in *Visions of a Liberated Future: Black Arts Movement Writings*, ed. Michael Schwartz (New York: Thunder's Mouth Press, 1989), 62–78; Hans Ostrom, *A Langston Hughes Encyclopedia* (Westport, CT: Greenwood Press, 2002); Robert E. Washington, *The Ideologies of African American Literature: From the Harlem Renaissance to the Black Nationalist Revolt. A Sociology of Literature Perspective* (Lanham, MD: Rowman & Littlefield, 2001).

Aimable Twagilimana

Publishers and Publishing. Historical barriers to literacy, capital, and the institutions of cultural production have prevented African American publishing practices from being consolidated into a full-fledged industry within the United States. Despite these barriers, which are not necessarily issues belonging only to the past, Black organizations in the nineteenth and early twentieth centuries, as well as late twentieth-century entrepreneurs, have made it possible for African Americans to publish books without "**White**" or repressive editorial interference. By "White," **Zora Neale Hurston**, in her classic essay "What White Publishers Won't Print" (1950), implicates less a biologically racialized people and more the racist structure of social dominance in which consolidated U.S. publishers, "the accredited representatives of the American people," commission, manufacture, and distribute books that propagate stereotypes of Black cultural inferiority. Thus the promise held out by African American publishing practices is one of self-determination and self-authorization, whereby Blacks will be able to set their own terms for literary and cultural production.

The scholar and bibliographer Donald Franklin Joyce has documented African American publishing activity from its origins in the context of **slavery** to the present day. In condensing his findings, it is important to note at least three practices that were critical to Black book publishing prior to the post–**World War II** period. First, and most basically, African Americans were forced to self-publish much of their writing because their access to White-owned print technologies was severely restricted under slavery and for decades thereafter. **David Walker** managed to self-publish his fervent abolitionist *Appeal* (1829) in pamphlet form in **Boston, Massachusetts**, and, more impressively, to see it distributed to major Southern cities via post and secret carriers. **Harriet Ann Jacobs** struggled to find a publisher for her *Incidents in the Life of a Slave Girl* (1861) in both England and the U.S. North. The White editor and abolitionist Lydia Maria Child finally secured Jacobs a contract with a Boston firm, but after the firm went bankrupt, Jacobs elected to publish the **slave narrative** herself. In 1901 the Baptist minister and political novelist **Sutton E. Griggs** went so far as to establish Orion Publishing in **Nashville, Tennessee**, to release his own work, much of which sought to counter the racist stereotypes deployed by romantic plantation literature.

Second, the Black church stepped in to provide the infrastructure that any collective publishing enterprise requires. The religious presses emerged and were based in key centers of African American civic and cultural life: the

1331

African Methodist Episcopal (A.M.E.) Book Concern of **Philadelphia, Pennsylvania**, founded in 1817; the A.M.E. Zion Publishing House of Charlotte, North Carolina, founded in 1841; the National Baptist Publishing Board of Nashville, founded in 1896; and the Sunday School Publishing Board of the National Baptist Convention, also of Nashville, founded in 1916. These well-organized, community-funded presses published guides and manuals for denominational worship, but they also produced literary and informational periodicals, political essays, history textbooks, autobiographies, and a good amount of poetry. This practice was essential for those writers who were not closely identified with the mainstream abolitionist movement in the antebellum United States or with the **Harlem Renaissance**. For example, in the post–**Civil War** United States, the Southern activist and fiction writer William Pickens and the Midwestern poet and dramatist **Katherine Tillman** had their work published by the A.M.E. Book Concern and the National Baptist Convention, respectively.

Finally, post-**Reconstruction** political, civil rights, and professional organizations reserved portions of their business costs for publishing material that supported their causes. Joyce has identified the most active of these publishing organizations: the American Negro Academy (ANA), founded in 1897; the National Association for the Advancement of Colored People (**NAACP**), founded in 1910; the National Urban League (NUL), founded in 1911; and **Marcus Garvey**'s Universal Negro Improvement Association (UNIA), founded in 1918. Some of the NAACP's earliest publications were young-adult novels and children's literature that instilled a sense of pride and mobility in young readers' minds. However, the ANA, NAACP, and NUL were ultimately committed to printing critical studies of African Americans' plight under racist structures of social dominance, particularly amidst the violence visited upon Black bodies in the form of **race riots** and **lynching**s in the early years of Jim Crow segregation. One might say these monographs, along with **W.E.B. Du Bois**'s scholarly output, essentially constructed African American social-scientific discourse, which was and continues to be one of the primary sites of intervention in U.S. political culture. Not to be outdone, Amy Jacques Garvey edited her husband's philosophical and political treatises for publication by the UNIA between 1923 and 1925. The two-volume *Philosophy and Opinions of Marcus Garvey* was at that time the most comprehensive collection of insurgent nationalist and Pan-Africanist ideology the world had ever seen.

In emphasizing political tracts, history textbooks, religious manuals, and general works that supported **racial uplift**, it is clear that early Black book publishing was oriented around a comparatively elite African American middle-class readership, especially those politically active and culturally engaged readers who constituted what Du Bois would call the **Talented Tenth**. Though not exactly out of step with the national trend, this particular tendency was exacerbated by the fact that low literacy levels among Blacks in general and limited institutional and technological support forced publishers to target people who could read and afford their books. Publishing selections were thus quite delimited by the racist structure of social dominance in the United States.

It was not until the U.S. Supreme Court's 1954 *Brown v. Board of Education* decision, which outlawed school segregation and legislated equal access to education for all citizens, that a more diverse African American reading public could take shape. Black book publishers responded only as hard-fought civil rights measures began to produce tangible, lasting results. In the U.S. academy, **Howard University Press**, reinstituted in 1972, published studies of African American history and literature to lend scholarly support to student demands for the creation of **Black Studies** departments on college campuses across the nation. Though not a university press, Joseph Okpaku's Third Press in New York City published critical monographs alongside popular biographies, children's books, and translations of foreign literature. In the trade paperback market, **Dudley Randall**'s **Broadside Press**, based in **Detroit, Michigan**; **Naomi Long Madgett**'s **Lotus Press**, also based in Detroit; and **Haki R. Madhubuti**'s **Third World Press**, based in **Chicago, Illinois**, all founded between 1965 and 1972, were committed to publishing **Black Arts** poetry that had been routinely rejected or dismissed as insignificant by mainstream houses. These small, independent, and Black-run presses printed the most revolutionary verse of the period, composed by the likes of **Nikki Giovanni, Lance Jeffers, Etheridge Knight, Sonia Sanchez, Amiri Baraka, Jill Witherspoon Boyer**, and Randall and Madhubuti. There is no Black aesthetic without them.

Similarly, no account of the Black popular writing tradition is complete without consideration of Holloway House, based in **Los Angeles, California**. Founded in the late 1960s in the ferment of Black Nationalism and racial unrest in major U.S. cities, this press's mass-market paperbacks were aimed for reading and purchase not just by the African American middle class but by the black underclass as well. In particular, Holloway House authors **Donald Goines** and **Iceberg Slim** originated the hard-boiled "ghetto aesthetic" of street/urban literature that, in its cheaply bound book form, would prove attractive to and affordable for so many poor and working-class readers. The appeal of such titles as Slim's *Pimp* (1967) and *Trick Baby* (1967), or Goines's *Dopefiend* (1971) and *Whoreson* (1972), lay in the way readers could identify with their (anti)heroes, whether as Black masculine icons, victims of racist structures of social dominance, or intelligible combinations of the two. Here the Black aesthetic was not so much read as consumed by way of grounded, material practices of literary production and reception. Holloway House encourages such consumption to this day, supplementing reprints of Goines's and Slim's texts with historical novels, biographies, studies of **Afrocentricity**, collections of folk wisdom, **erotica**, and pornography.

It was not until the boom in African American romance publishing in the early 1990s that Holloway House faced stiff competition from other Black mass-market presses. **Terry McMillan**'s *Waiting to Exhale* (1992) sparked the mainstream U.S. publishing industry's interest in Black popular writing. Throughout the decade, African American romance novels and **crime and mystery fiction** were integrated into the massive catalogs of conglomerates such as Penguin and Random House. Arguably the most influential privately owned Black cultural medium in the United States, Black Entertainment Television (BET), acquired Kensington Publishing's famed African American romance line, Arabesque, in 1998, signaling that powerful company's immersion in the genre mainstream. On a different but parallel scale of development, the Columbus, Mississippi-based and romance-focused **Genesis Press**, which began operations in 1993, now boasts a fiction and nonfiction catalog as extensive, varied, and intriguing as Holloway House's. With such titles as Giselle Carmichael's *Magnolia Sunset* (2002), Barbara Keaton's *An Unfinished Love Affair* (2002), and Wanda Y. Thomas's *Passion's Journey* (2002), Genesis sells well among Black women who prefer steamier romances to those that are offered by Arabesque and the McMillan mainstream.

The story does not end there, however. In 1999 **rap** artist **Sister Souljah**'s best-selling *The Coldest Winter Ever* heralded not only a renaissance in street/urban literature but also that movement's correlative flourishing through nonmainstream independent and self-publishing practices. This may have been a case of Souljah's debut novel coming out at just the right time. Historically situated at the nexus of hardcore **hip-hop**, cheap softcover printing technologies, and growing African American incarceration rates, the book identified an audience ripe for narratives about street violence, urban poverty, and prison life (Rosen). Thus a significant gap in the publishing industry's literary output had to be filled. Black Print Publishing (BPP), based in **Brooklyn, New York**, stepped in with Wahida Clark, a federal women's prison inmate whose *Thugs and the Women Who Love Them* (2002) and *Every Thug Needs a Lady* (2003) are gritty, entertaining, and above all affordable. Newcomer BPP has also published Asante Kahari's controversial *Homo Thug* (2004). After self-publishing *Let That Be the Reason*, which she began writing while serving a prison term, in 2001, Vickie Stringer founded Triple Crown Publications (TCP) in Columbus, Ohio. TCP is now home to such urban literary artists as Tracy Brown, Shannon Holmes, Nikki Turner, and K'wan. Finally, most of the profits of Teri Woods's eponymous imprint come from sales of her first, self-published novel, *True to the Game* (1998), and Holmes's debut *B-More Careful* (2001).

For the time being, these small presses rely mainly on their own labor and means to distribute their books. Other independent publishers look to mainstream houses to handle promotion of their authors, several of whom have cultivated well-established national followings. **Erotica** writer **Zane** self-published her provocative *The Sex Chronicles* and founded Strebor Books International (SBI) in 1999. The enormous demand for SBI's titles led Zane to Simon and Schuster for distribution. Among SBI's authors are Shonell Bacon, Laurel Handfield, Allison Hobbs, Rique Johnson, Jonathan Luckett, and Franklin White. **Carl Weber**, on the other hand, has always directly entrusted his romance novels to Kensington's Dafina Books imprint. When he created an imprint of his own, Urban Books, Weber wanted to guarantee quality distribution for his authors, and therefore signed a worldwide distribution agreement with Kensington. La Jill Hunt's *Drama Queen* (2003) is Urban Books's first title.

Not all independent and self-publishing practices have been devoted to street/urban literature. Since 1997, such African American Christian book publishers as Walk Worthy Press, BET's New Spirit imprint, and Literally Speaking Publishing House (LSPH) have marketed their products as spiritually based alternatives to "worldly," even misguided, fare. Interestingly enough, novelists such as **Michele Andrea Bowen, Sharon Ewell Foster**, T. D. Jakes, Stephanie Perry Moore, Victoria Christopher Murray, and Jacquelin Thomas have become household names among both religious and nonreligious readers. Sales show that African American Christian fiction has tremendous secular crossover appeal, something that has eluded many of the books the White-dominated Christian Booksellers Association (CBA) chooses to promote (Patrick). Christian fiction writer S. James Guitard, whose *Mocha Love* was published by LSPH in 2002, observes of this trend: "CBA is a different market of books. They're often historical books, white, for an evangelical Christian audience. Our books are purposely targeted toward the 'sick.' People who might read Zane—we make it so they can read ours, too. We are trying to go after *that* reader" (Patrick, 37). Guitard's proselytizing motive may not sit well with all readers, but his valuation of inspirational and faith-based books brings to light a crucial, potentially progressive link between the modern Black church and popular literacy.

The surge of African American independent and self-publishing ventures at the dawn of the twenty-first century defies the odds of the way today's global publishing networks are coordinated and part of corporate conglomerations. For now it seems author-publishers such as Zane and Weber will oversee editorial decisions while relying on major companies to distribute their books. And one can only hope that BPP, TCP, and others will continue to turn a reasonable enough profit to compete with their mainstream counterparts in local, grassroots, and, perhaps most important, word-of-mouth circuits. Weber has stated, "I spend a lot of time in bookstores to find out what people are looking for and what self-published authors are doing. I haven't found anything exciting in the last [ten] years that hasn't been self-published" (Rosen, 34). Weber overstates the case here, but he does touch upon the importance of fostering nonmainstream publishing practices as a means not only of enriching U.S. literary culture but also of democratizing reading practices for all segments, classes, and strata of U.S. society. (*See* **Censorship; Children's Literature; CQ Comics Group; E-Zines, E-News, E-Journals, and E-Collections; Federal Writers' Project; Johnson Publishing Company; Just Us Books; Kitchen Table: Women of Color Press; Knopf, Alfred A.; Literary Canon; Magazines, Literary; Milestone Comics/Milestone Media; Newspapers, African American; OBAC; Redbone Press; Romance Fiction.**)

Resources: Bernard W. Bell, *The Afro-American Novel and Its Tradition* (Amherst: University of Massachusetts Press, 1987); Dickson D. Bruce, Jr., *The Origins of African*

American Literature, 1680–1865 (Charlottesville: University Press of Virginia, 2001); Zora Neale Hurston, "What White Publishers Won't Print," *Negro Digest* 8 (1950), 85–89; Donald Franklin Joyce: *Black Book Publishers in the United States: A Historical Dictionary of the Presses, 1817–1990* (Westport, CT: Greenwood Press, 1991); *Gatekeepers of Black Culture: Black-Owned Book Publishing in the United States, 1817–1981* (Westport, CT: Greenwood Press, 1983); "Publishing," in *The Oxford Companion to African American Literature*, ed. William L. Andrews, Frances Smith Foster, and Trudier Harris (New York: Oxford University Press, 1997), 604–610; Diane Patrick, "Let the Readers Say 'Amen,'" *Publishers Weekly*, Dec. 13, 2004, pp. 36–38; Judith Rosen, "Street Lit: Readers Gotta Have It," *Publishers Weekly*, Dec. 13, 2004, pp. 31–35; Robert E. Washington, *The Ideologies of African American Literature: From the Harlem Renaissance to the Black Nationalist Revolt* (Lanham, MD: Rowman & Littlefield, 2001).

Kinohi Nishikawa

Q

Queer Theory. Queer theory is a branch of critical theory that describes human sexuality as a socially constructed, historically based form of pleasure and analyzes art, culture, and knowledge based on that assumption. Queer theory has made two significant contributions to African American literary studies. It has brought to light the experience of African American people who are gay, lesbian, bisexual, and transgendered, and it has shown how **race** and racism are established and perpetuated through the regulation of sex and **gender**.

Because queer theory examines an exceptionally wide range of cultural phenomena and experiences, it makes sense to begin by discussing what queer theory does, instead of what it is. Queer theory uses the ostensibly marginal existence of homosexuality to interrogate and account for other, seemingly unimportant ways in which pleasure is expressed, such as the tone of voice in a sentence, a certain look between actors in a film, or an unspeakable sex crime referred to in a court transcript. Queer theory, however, doesn't just point these things out; it demonstrates how they are essential to the larger process of creating knowledge. We often think, for example, that heterosexuality is natural and must have existed before homosexuality deviated from it, but Michel Foucault, in a famous observation that grounds much of queer theory, points out that the specific concept of "heterosexuality" appears *after* the term "homosexual" emerged into scientific literature (101). This observation has two consequences: first, for heterosexuality to be represented, it needs to distinguish itself from something else, thus becoming dependent on that something else; second, in order for the power of heterosexuality to be established and maintained, it has to hide the appearance of its dependency on its proscribed other. It does so by elevating itself to the realm of the natural and the normal, while reducing the other term, homosexuality, to the realm of the deviant and unnatural. If this is how the heterosexuality/homosexuality binary functions, it is also how other binaries seen in representations of sex or pleasure function: love/promiscuity; normal/perverse; gender/drag; information/gossip; reality/art. Many people value terms such as "love," "normal," "gender," "information," and "reality" as natural while they devalue terms such as "promiscuity," "perverse," "drag," "gossip," and "art" as unnatural. What queer theory does is to revalue these historically devalued terms, which it recognizes as integral to the construction and interpretation of the terms ("love," "normal," "gender," etc.) to which they are set in binary opposition.

Queer theory is linked to **poststructural** critical theory, especially Michel Foucault's studies of sexuality and Jacques Derrida's deconstructive textual interpretations. In *The History of Sexuality*, Foucault studies homosexuality as a name or category rather than as an innate human identity or characteristic. He finds that sexuality is not simply hidden, waiting to be unrepressed or uncovered, but is produced through what he calls "discourse," by which he means the vocabularies, categories, and tools by which we describe the world around us. Foucault argues that sexuality is not a biological entity that remains the same throughout history. Instead, it has several biological components that acquire importance through the ways in which they are talked about and through the types of knowledge they facilitate, including medicine, anthropology, and population control. This emphasis on discourse also allows queer theory to draw from **deconstruction**. Deconstruction—a form of literary interpretation disseminated in the 1970s by Jacques Derrida—can be understood as a critique of binaries, combined with a celebration of the ambiguities of language. This emphasis on linguistic instability as opposed to fixed meanings distinguishes queer theory from gay/lesbian history. Queer theory claims that sexuality is changing, is dependent on historical circumstances, and can never mean one thing to two or more people, while gay/lesbian history sees sexuality as fixed throughout history, determined at birth, and resistant to the outside world. Finally, like Foucault and Derrida, queer theory has a complex relation to psychoanalysis. Queer theory critiques psychoanalysis for its homophobia and mainstream values, but it is heavily influenced by psychoanalysis. This is because psychoanalysis pays attention to precisely those things in a patient that a queer theorist studies in a text: slips of the tongue, sexual shame, unacknowledged desires, taboo subject matter. Psychoanalysis also provides one of the richest descriptions of human sexuality.

Eve Kosofsky Sedgwick and Judith Butler are two highly influential scholars who consolidated philosophies, including psychoanalysis and deconstruction, into queer theory and spread it within the academic community by the mid-1990s. Sedgwick uses deconstruction and psychoanalysis to argue that much of the energy in literature depends on erotic (but not necessarily sexual) connections between two male characters. Butler's *Gender Trouble* argues that gender is "performative," meaning that we learn gender by unconsciously imitating the way we see others perform it.

Queer theory also has roots outside the university, and any discussion of queer theory must acknowledge its ties to **Black feminism** and AIDS activism. While the male-dominated **Civil Rights Movement** generally emphasized changing laws to address overt acts of discrimination, post-civil rights Black feminists pointed out that racism was connected not only to laws but also to ideologies of sexuality and gender. In the early 1980s, "Third World feminists," such as **Angela Y. Davis**, **Barbara Smith**, **Audre Lorde**, and others explored links between race and sexuality, arguing not only against **White** racism but also against misogyny and homophobia within the Black community. In *This Bridge Called My Back*, Smith writes, "We are actively committed to struggling against racial, sexual, heterosexual, and class oppression and [to demonstrating how these] major systems of oppression are interlocking" (210). This "intersectional" analysis of race, sex, and gender has more recently empowered many scholars to use queer theory to illuminate how race came to be such an important component of American culture. Siobhan Somerville, in *Queering the Color Line*, argues that the nineteenth-century division between heterosexual and homosexual bodies was fundamentally related to the segregation of Black and White bodies during the same period. Another example is José Muñoz's book *Disidentifications*, which examines how Asian, Latino/a, and African American queers produce distinctive verbal and visual strategies for dealing with racial oppression.

Queer theory's interest in how bodies are visualized and how visual symbols influence people's perceptions also has a source in AIDS activism, exemplified by ACT-UP's efforts in the 1980s. One of the privileges that straight-identified people have over queer-identified people is the ability to talk about their sexuality publicly. Lacking this power, many people died from AIDS from the late 1970s into the 1980s because AIDS was associated with homosexuality and was viewed as a disease that should be kept "in the closet." The AIDS Coalition to Unleash Power (ACT-UP) was formed in New York City in 1987 to combat this situation. It raised awareness of AIDS through subtle but confrontational political slogans, symbols, and public protests. It deployed the famous pink triangle along with the words SILENCE=DEATH on pins, buttons, posters, and T-shirts as a way to use America's obsession with logos to spread its message visually. ACT-UP also staged "kiss-ins," at which men kissed men and women kissed women as a way to confront homophobes with their own fears of gay sexuality. Queer theory still draws from these sorts of protest in the way that it values humor, theatricality, and lack of shame as an antidote to political and intellectual quietism.

Queer theory's emphasis on textual ambiguity, its valuing of marginal types of knowledge, and its investment in nonserious art make it a unique form of critical thought. At the same time, those tendencies often make it difficult for queer theory to be taken seriously by more traditional disciplines. Like African American literary studies, queer theory constantly struggles to influence the core of more traditional disciplines even as it operates at their margins.

Resources: Henry Abelove, Michèle Aina Barale, and David H. Halperin, eds., *The Lesbian and Gay Studies Reader* (New York: Routledge, 1993); Judith Butler: *Bodies That Matter: On the Discursive Limits of "Sex"* (New York: Routledge, 1993); *Gender Trouble: Feminism and the Subversion of Identity* (New York: Routledge, 1990); Douglas Crimp, with Adam Rolston, *AIDS Demo Graphics* (Seattle, WA: Bay Press, 1990); Michel Foucault, *The History of Sexuality*, vol. 1, *An Introduction*, trans. Robert Hurley (New York: Pantheon, 1978); Judith Halberstam, *Female Masculinity* (Durham, NC: Duke University Press, 1998); Phillip Brian Harper, *Are We Not Men? Masculine Anxiety and the Problem of African-American Identity* (New York: Oxford University Press, 1996); Essex Hemphill, ed., *Brother to Brother: New Writings by Black Gay Men* (Boston: Alyson, 1991); Cherríe Moraga and Gloria Anzaldúa, eds., *This Bridge Called My Back: Writings by Radical Women of Color* (New York: Kitchen Table: Women of Color Press, 1983); José Esteban Muñoz, *Disidentifications: Queers of Color and the Performance of Politics* (Minneapolis: University of Minnesota Press, 1999); Eve Kosofsky Sedgwick: *Between Men: English Literature and Male Homosocial Desire* (New York: Columbia University Press, 1985); *Epistemology of the Closet* (Berkeley: University of California Press, 1990); Siobhan Sommerville, *Queering the Color Line: Race and the Invention of Homosexuality in American Culture* (Durham, NC: Duke University Press, 2000); Michael Warner, *The Trouble with Normal: Sex, Politics, and the Ethics of Queer Life* (Cambridge, MA: Harvard University Press, 1999).

David Woodard

R

Ra, Sun (1914–1993). Musician, composer, arranger, poet, and nonfiction writer. Sun Ra, whose original name was Herman Sonny Blount, was arguably one of the most controversial and certainly one of the most eccentric and prolific leading members of the Free Jazz movement, which began in the 1950s. Ra influenced writers in the **Black Arts Movement**, **science fiction** writers, and avante-garde writers after **World War II**, most notably **Amiri Baraka**. Although his self-nurtured legend has it that he was born on the planet Saturn, earthly records show that Ra was born in Birmingham, Alabama, to a family of restauranteurs (Szwed). He attended Industrial High School, where the influential music teacher John T. Whately singled him out as a Mozart-like prodigy. For most of the 1930s, Ra headed the Sonny Blount Band, which played mostly **swing** and **blues** music. While leading the band, he also attended Alabama A&M University in Huntsville as a music education major. Ra had to leave the university after one year (1935–1936), however, because his family, hit hard by the **Great Depression**, could not afford the tuition. By the 1940s, Ra was living and working in **Chicago, Illinois**, where he led a big band at the popular Club De Lisa. Sometime after this band broke up, his music and philosophical outlook on life and the cosmos changed drastically.

In 1950 he started his Space Trio, and he became interested in **Black Nationalism**. In 1952 he officially changed his name to Le Sony'r Ra. "Ra" represented the Egyptian Sun God. "Sony" is close in sound to "sunny" and was similar to his former middle name. He used the extra "r" so that there would be nine letters in his name, a number he considered lucky (Szwed). In the 1950s, Ra began writing poetry set to music, and his work began to influence other writers, including **Larry Neal**, **Askia M. Touré**, and certainly Baraka. Baraka

Sun Ra, 1991. © Christopher Felver/Corbis.

writes about Ra in *Blues People* (1963) and, obviously, in the essay "Sun Ra" (1995). Sun Ra changed his band's name to Arkestra in 1953. From about that point until his death, he was known as Sun Ra, rather than Le Sony'r Ra. Ra began to claim that he was not human, but of an angel race, and that he had been sent to Earth to serve as Cosmic Communicator for the Creator, bringing a message of peace and harmony though his music (Szwed). Many of his fans believed—and continue to believe—in his quasi divinity. For nearly forty years, Sun Ra toured the world with his band. His music attracted an especially large following in Europe. His performances often involved between thirty and a hundred performers, including musicians, dancers, poets, and actors. One performance occurred near the Pyramids in Egypt. A listing of Ra's numerous recordings appeared in the late 1990s, with a second edition in 2000 (Campbell and Trent). Ra's collected writings were published in 2004. (*See* **Performance Poetry**.)

Resources: Amiri Baraka: *Blues People: Negro Music in White America* (1963; repr. New York: Morrow, 1999); "Sun Ra," *African American Review* 29, no. 2 (1995), 253–261; Robert L. Campbell and Christopher Trent, *The Earthly Recordings of Sun Ra*, 2nd ed. (Redwood, NY: Cadence Jazz Books, 2000); Graham Lock, *Blutopia: Visions of the Future and Revisions of the Past in the Work of Sun Ra, Duke Ellington, and Anthony Braxton* (Durham, NC: Duke University Press, 1999); Stephen Quirke, *The Cult of Ra: Sun Worship in Egypt* (London: Thames & Hudson, 2001); Sun Ra: *Angels & Demons at Play/The Nubians of Plutonia* (1956; repr. Conshohocken, PA: Evidence Records, 1992), CD format; *Collected Works* (Sacramento, CA: Phaelos Books, 2004); *Supersonic Jazz* (Conshohocken, PA: Evidence Records, 1992), CD format; *We Travel the Spaceways/Bad, Beautiful* (1956; repr. Conshohocken, PA: Evidence Records, 1993), CD format; John F. Szwed, *Space Is the Place: The Life and Times of Sun Ra* (New York: Pantheon, 1997).

Antony Adolf

Race. Biologically defined, one species cannot breed with another species. Races, however, are distinct groups within a species; they can interbreed, but the existence of races indicates that this has rarely or only distantly occurred.

Racialism can be defined as the idea that the creation of human races occurs from the biological transmission not only of distinguishing physical characteristics but also intellectual, moral, and spiritual characteristics. Racism adds to "racialism" the false idea that one race of humans is verifiably superior to others, and this superiority justifies the superior race's domination of those inferiors. In Western thought, racism posits a race of **"White"**/Caucasian purity over impure, "non-White" races.

Human skin color is an ever-changing epidermal adaptation to sunlight. Skin must balance between being light enough to allow sufficient production of vitamin D (important to the maintenance of strong bones) and dark enough to prevent the destruction of folate (important to fertility and fetal development). Increased exposure to sunlight increases the skin's production of melanin, and this darkens the skin. The production of melanin thus can vary both in individuals over a lifetime and in populations over generations.

Current genetic research indicates that today's humans have descended from a common father who lived approximately 60,000 years ago (a mere 2,000 generations) and that the human migration out of Africa, which has resulted in most of today's skin colors, occurred only 40,000 years ago. Although these exact dates may change with future research, the essential point is that skin color is a superficial adaptation whose variations do not indicate human "races."

Not only are human skin colors a recent event in the evolutionary history of humans, but the idea of categorizing humans by **color of skin** is also a recent event in the cultural history of humankind. History tells us that humans have long categorized others, and groups tend to evaluate others as inferior. The supposed inferiority of other groups, however, has traditionally been based not on skin color but on such characteristics as language, religion, and customs. Although skin color has been an element of, for instance, the caste system of India, skin color as the primary basis for ranking groups (and ranking all groups throughout the world) is a European invention that began during Europe's "Age of Discovery."

European exploration of the world began in earnest in the 1400s. By the production of Shakespeare's *Othello* (c. 1603), we know that skin color had, for Europeans, become an important marker of difference. We also know, however, that early European travelers to Africa saw Africans more as trading partners than as inferiors or potential slaves. The European extermination of indigenous peoples of the Caribbean, however, necessitated the importation of a replacement workforce. Europeans used enslaved Africans to meet this need, and this dramatically different relationship with Africans required a new "story"—the story of dark-skinned (especially African) inferiority that we now call "racism."

European thinking at this time was a mix of Christianity and a revived Greco-Roman humanism that emphasized reason and visual perception. Reason and vision eventually manifested themselves in hierarchical classification systems in the natural sciences (e.g., Carl Linnaeus, 1735), and these systems usually included humankind. During the eighteenth and nineteenth centuries, a profusion of scientific studies and philosophical arguments strengthened European theories of race (and racism) by interconnecting race with such things as geography, nation, language, and material productivity. These interconnections meant that, to a large extent, to doubt the superiority of white skin was to doubt the superiority of Beethoven or question the preeminence of Versailles.

Europeans generally saw Africa as a "dark" continent of childish, uncivilized peoples whose limited potential for productivity could be achieved only through the firm hand of an enlightened "parental Europe." The "parental firmness" of **slavery**—so the story went—would bring order and Christianity to Africans, and this would result in a more productive and civil "African race." These ideas meant that dark skin became as much of an objective "proof" of the necessity of slavery as the object "horse" called for bridle and whip. The "parental firmness" of slavery was eventually replaced by such social interventions as colonization, Jim Crow separation (c. 1877–1964), and harsher prison sentences (vis-à-vis Whites with equal records). Although slowly diminishing, the belief that skin color isn't merely "skin deep" continues, and during times of perceived threat, race remains perhaps the most powerful trope for producing fear and anxiety among Americans.

How people of African ancestry have responded to Western ideas about "race" has varied, and any summary is necessarily reductive. As part of understanding these responses, it is important to keep in mind that many Euro-Americans used the supposed "truths" of such discourses as Christianity, science, evolution, and economics to argue the inevitability of hierarchical "race" relations. Because these discourses defined race, anyone arguing against racist thinking had to incorporate these discourses.

We see this, for instance, in the eighteenth-century writings of **Phillis Wheatley** and **Olaudah Equiano**, where both writers work within the dominant "White" logic of race. Both are humble, give thanks for their conversions to Christianity, and acknowledge the superiority of Western society. They largely maintain the dominant fiction of African inferiority, but with the admonition that Africans—contrary to much racist thinking at the time—could improve under *proper* tutelage (not slavery).

Both Equiano and Wheatley wrote to audiences within slaveholding societies. By the mid-nineteenth century, however, the audience for African American writers was largely abolitionist or at least slavery-ambivalent, and African American writers became less obsequious. They told how slavery went against both Christian and Enlightenment (e.g., Declaration of Independence) ideals, and this was detrimental to *all* of society. Up until the end of the **Civil War**, the idea of "race," however, was only obliquely addressed, in that the courage and self-educated eloquence revealed in such **slave narratives** as those by **Harriet Ann Jacobs** and **Frederick Douglass** implicitly argue against inherent "Black" inferiority.

Even most "White" abolitionists, however, accepted Black inferiority, and many fretted about what would be done with slaves if they were freed.

America's White abolitionists were sympathetic to the plight of African Americans, but this did not include a belief that African Americans were equal to people of European descent. Thus, although White abolitionists and postbellum reconstructionists were politically nearest to African Americans, even this end of the "White" political spectrum embodied what is probably the essential aspect of the discourse of "race," its foundation on binary logic. Under this logic, no matter what the characteristics, an African American remains excluded from the "normativity" that is the domain solely of "Whites" (an idea rooted in the *limpieza de sangre*—purity of blood—doctrine of fifteenth-century Spain).

This is the logic of the "one drop" theory of race—one drop of "Black blood" (i.e., one "non-White" ancestor) makes a person "Black." Science and vision come together in the system that declares half "Black" is **mulatto**, one-fourth is quadroon, one-eighth is octoroon, one-sixteenth is mustafina, and one-thirty-second is a whitewash. That "White" has no categories indicates its purity, and purity is by definition unattainable for any lineage once "contaminated." The violence of this logic is that it maintains eternal separation, endless division.

As the nineteenth century drew to a close, African Americans began to question the idea of race as a category. With such African Americans as **Alexander Crummell** "returning" to Africa, "race" began to strain as it expanded to address the complexities of a more global scope. The most significant thinking about race, however, came from **W.E.B. Du Bois**. When Du Bois states that "the problem of the Twentieth Century is the problem of the color-line" (1903), he acknowledges the problem of division. Du Bois's most important insight is that the division of racism is not only a division between "White" and "Black" but also a division *internal* to African Americans. Du Bois tells us that any African American sense of completeness, of being fully human, is continually disrupted by the discourse of racism whose binary logic posits the African American as lacking, as not human pure and simple but merely *Black* human. This he calls "double consciousness."

In addition, Du Bois's work on race includes a significant shift toward understanding race not as biologically determined but as more of a sociohistorical construction, and it replaces the idea of a racial hierarchy with "Whites" at the top with the idea that all races have unique and important contributions to make to the world. Du Bois leaves behind the late nineteenth-century argument of **Booker T. Washington** that the "**Negro** race" will employ hard work and patience to rise up and fill any job, essentially becoming "White." Du Bois does not doubt the ability of African Americans to join all levels of the workforce; his argument, however, is that the "Negro race" has a unique and important "message for humanity."

We see expressions of this shift during the **Harlem Renaissance**, where a dominant theme is that the African heritage expressed through African Americans offers the Western tradition, and especially White America, an emotional spirituality that it lacks. Outside America, the movement called **Négritude** was developing similar ideas. These somewhat philosophical and artistic "turns toward Africa" are complemented by the more politically "Africa focused" movement of **Marcus Garvey**'s United Negro Improvement Association (founded 1914). The nineteenth-century African American argument of the Negro race's "improvability" was thus replaced with a racial pride rooted in a continent of rich and important traditions.

Although **Langston Hughes**'s essay "The Negro Artist and the Racial Mountain" (published during the Harlem Renaissance) includes the word "racial," the essay actually urges African American writers to write about their experiences insofar as the experiences are an outgrowth of circumstance and history, not of essential "Negro" qualities. In a sense, Hughes argues that African American writers should "write what they know."

Since the Harlem Renaissance, African American ideas about race have become increasingly mixed. The 1930s saw the development of a Marxist (class-based) understanding of race not as biological but as a story used by those in power to divide and exploit workers. During the 1950s and early 1960s, such people as **James Baldwin** and **Martin Luther King, Jr.**, promoted the belief that the arts, religion, and political coalitions could eventually erase skin color from the equation of human relations.

However, with the violence of White responses to the late 1950s and early 1960s **Civil Rights Movement**, the violence of the **Vietnam War**, and the demise of colonial rule with the independence of numerous African and Caribbean nations, this "integrationist" vision of race's diminishing importance was overtaken by a return to race as both essential and a source of pride. During the 1960s, **Black Nationalism**, **Black Power**, **Afrocentricity**, and the **Black Arts Movement** expressed a "Black pride" that not only elevated the importance of race but—unlike the Harlem Renaissance—often promoted a politics of racial separation.

Like the early twentieth-century work of Du Bois, the 1960s mark a watershed for ideas about race with the development of Black pride, African Americans writing and performing for a mass Black (instead of narrow and largely White) audience, artistic use of African American **vernacular** traditions, a more international "Africana" sense of what it means to be African American, yet also the loss of a relatively monolithic understanding of race. Race became publicly complicated by **gender**, sexuality, and religion. After the 1960s, "Black" no longer equaled "heterosexual Black male."

Since the 1960s, people of Africa and African ancestry have increasingly become the prominent voices discussing race. Race still matters, as **Cornel West** declares in the title of his 1993 book, yet the general intellectual movement was toward the position of Paul Gilroy, who argued that skin color is, to state the obvious, only skin deep. But even if the idea of race based on skin color diminishes, this does not deny the existence of a "Black" (epistemological, social, musical, spiritual) heritage and experience, and from these come a wealth of ideas that remain both outstanding examples of the humanist tradition and vital resources for any person or group interested in a more peaceful and just world.

Resources: W.E.B. Du Bois, *The Souls of Black Folk* (Chicago: McClurg, 1903); Frantz Fanon: *Black Skin, White Masks* (1952; repr. New York: Grove, 1967); *The Wretched of the Earth* (1961; repr. New York: Grove, 1963); George M. Fredrickson, *Racism: A Short History* (Princeton, NJ: Princeton University Press, 2002); Henry Louis Gates, Jr., ed., *"Race," Writing and Difference* (Chicago: University of Chicago Press, 1986); Henry Louis Gates, Jr., and Cornel West, *The Future of the Race* (New York: Knopf, 1996); Paul Gilroy, *Against Race: Imagining Political Culture Beyond the Color Line* (London: Allen Lane, 2000).

Kevin M. Hickey

Race Riots. The term usually refers to rioting (in cities or large towns) precipitated by racial conflict, but it is also sometimes used to refer to other kinds of racial violence. By definition, race riots spring, in part, from a real or perceived inequality or oppression between members of different races.

Among the most notable race riots involving African Americans are the following: 1829: Cincinnati, Ohio; 1866: **Memphis, Tennessee**; 1868: **New Orleans, Louisiana**; 1898: Wilmington, North Carolina; 1903: Evansville, Indiana; 1906: **Atlanta, Georgia**; 1908: Springfield, Illinois; 1919: **Chicago, Illinois**, and Elaine, Arkansas; 1921: Tulsa, **Oklahoma**; 1923: Rosewood, Florida; 1935: **Harlem, New York**; 1942: **Detroit, Michigan**; 1943: Beaumont, **Texas**, Detroit, and Harlem; 1962: Oxford, Mississippi; 1964: Harlem; 1965: Watts (**Los Angeles, California**); 1966: Hunter's Point (**San Francisco, California**); 1967: Detroit; 1969: York, Pennsylvania; 1992: Los Angeles (Harley). Specific precipitating events vary in each case and are often matters of debate (Platt). They range from police brutality against African Americans (including murder), to Whites' reaction against attempted desegregation (Oxford, Mississippi, 1962; Williams), to African Americans' reaction to the results of a controversial trial (Los Angeles, 1992). Often clusters of events and reactions to them precipitate the rioting (Gooding-Williams; Platt). However, all these riots, and many others, can be traced more generally to the fact of the persistent oppression of and threats of violence against African Americans.

So much racial violence occurred in the summer of 1919 that it became known as the Red Summer (Tuttle). Much of the violence involved the **lynching** of African Americans. In the Rosewood, Florida, riot of 1923, the entire African American town was burned down by Whites (Singleton).

In 1873 the Colfax Massacre occurred in Grant Parish, Louisiana. A group of African Americans was attacked by a White mob in front of the courthouse there on April 13. At least sixty African Americans were killed and many more injured (Harned).

Accounts and images of racial violence have appeared in American and African American literature since the 1800s, including *Uncle Tom's Cabin* (1852) by **Harriet Beecher Stowe** and works by **Frederick Douglass**. The historical significance of racial tensions between African Americans and White Americans can be dated as early as the institution of **slavery** and the rebellions against it. Slavery was a culture held together by systematic violence

(Bryant, 9). The antebellum period of the master-slave relationship and its repetitiveness of public displays of violence led to outbreaks of violence across the nation while simultaneously influencing both the language of sentiment and the language of revolutionary liberation in this period (Bryant, 22). These images of racial tensions influenced writings of Frederick Douglass such as *Narrative of the Life of Frederick Douglass* (1845), *My Bondage and My Freedom* (1855), and *The Life and Times of Frederick Douglass* (1881).

The novel *Clotel* (1853), by **William Wells Brown**; the novel *Blake; or, The Huts of America* (1859–1862), by **Martin R. Delany**; and *The Garies and Their Friends* (1857), by **Frank J. Webb**, laid a foundation for understanding racial tensions and riots of the nineteenth century. In *Clotel*, Brown portrays the inhumane treatment of African American men, women, and children by Whites. He further describes this system of inhumane treatment as turning both races into brutes who indulge in waves of violence. Both Brown and Delany, unlike Douglass, illustrate a revolt against the entire slavery system, as opposed to the individual slave master. For example, in *Clotel*, we get an account of **Nat Turner**'s role in the Southampton County, Virginia, revolt as a "preacher amongst the Negroes" (33). Webb describes race riots of Whites against Blacks as a response to the economic success of African Americans in the North. In 1863, nearly ten years after Brown's, Delany's, and Webb's publications, one of the bloodiest outbreaks of violence occurred in New York City. Subsequently known as the Draft Riots, this violence created over $1.5 million of property damage, including the destruction of the Negro Orphan Asylum, and resulted in the slaying of many African Americans, many of whom were hanged from city lampposts. Approximately three years later, race riots occurred in Memphis, Tennessee.

Approximately three years after the U.S. Supreme Court's decision in *Dred Scott v. Sanford*, which effectively ruled against full citizenship—indeed, full humaniy—for Blacks, Webb published *The Garies and Their Friends*. The novel, published in London, focused on the caste system and the oppression that Blacks faced. Again, the writings of this era described the social climate of the century.

Appointed (1894), by Walter Stowers, is regarded as the first African American novel to portray the racism and racist ideologies of the Jim Crow era in the 1890s. This era signified that a so-called separate-but-equal ideology and the practices it led to were constitutional. These ideologies and practices would institutionalize oppression, which in turn would lead to violence in the next century.

The Marrow of Tradition (1901), written by **Charles Waddell Chesnutt**, illustrates how lynching played a vital and deadly role in a riot in Wilmington, North Carolina (1898), in which both Whites and Blacks perished. It explores this riot in three dimensions: the warrior, the avenger, and the forgiving Christian. According to Bryant (108), "[Chesnutt] shows the source of the riot in the feelings of whites and the state of affairs that conditions the blacks' response."

In 1942, race rioting erupted in Detroit at the Sojourner Truth Homes. A year later, outbreaks of rioting occurred in Beaumont, Texas; Harlem; and Detroit. The 1943 Detroit riot left more than thirty-four people dead and 1,000 injured resulting from disconnected incidents on Belle Isle (Platt, 201). Violence erupted in Columbia, Tennessee, and Athens, Alabama, in 1946.

Written during this period, **Langston Hughes**'s poem "Beaumont to Detroit: 1943" considers the irony of there being so much racial violence in the United States while African American soldiers are fighting in **World War II** (Ostrom, 31). Hughes also wrote "The Ballad of Margie Polite," which concerns the shooting of an African American soldier by a White policeman who had quarreled with one Margie Polite. The shooting precipitated a riot in Harlem on August 1–2, 1943. The soldier recovered from his wounds, but four citizens were killed in the riot, and 400 were injured (Ostrom, 21).

The eruption of civil unrest slowly dissipated after the 1970s and 1980s. However, a race riot occurred in Los Angeles after the March 3, 1992, acquittal of four police officers who were accused of beating an African American man, Rodney King. Unbeknownst to the officers, a citizen had videotaped the beating. The beating of a White truck driver, Reginald Denny, by African American rioters was captured on videotape.

Brenda Wall, Na'im Akbar, and **Michael Eric Dyson**, among others, have written about racial tensions leading up to and following the Los Angeles riots. Such authors analyze social and economic disparities between Whites and Blacks as well as sources of hope for the future. Their writings continue to explore issues of empowerment, liberation, and violence in the African American community and the impact these issues have on race relations in twenty-first-century America (Wall, 96).

Resources: Jerry H. Bryant, *Racial Violence in the African American Novel: Victims and Heroes* (Amherst: University of Massachusetts Press, 1997); Michael Eric Dyson: *The Michael Eric Dyson Reader* (New York: BasicCivitas, 2004); *Race Rules: Navigating the Color Line* (New York: Vintage, 1997); Robert Gooding-Williams, ed., *Reading Rodney King, Reading Urban Uprising* (New York: Routledge, 1993); Seymour L. Gross and John Hardy, eds., *Images of the Negro in American Literature* (Chicago: University of Chicago Press, 1966); Sharon Harley, *The Timetables of African-American History* (New York: Simon and Schuster, 1995); Buddy Harned, *Colfax Massacre*, http://spider .georgetowncollege.edu/htallant/courses/his312/bharned/opening_page.htm (2000); Tim Madigan, *The Burning: Massacre, Destruction, and the Tulsa Race Riot of 1921* (New York: St. Martin's, 2001); Hans Ostrom, *A Langston Hughes Encyclopedia* (Westport, CT: Greenwood Press, 2002); Anthony Platt, ed., *The Politics of Riot Commissions: 1917–1970* (New York: Collier, 1971); Amritjit Singh, *The Novels of the Harlem Renaissance: Twelve Black Writers, 1923–1933* (University Park: Pennsylvania University Press, 1976); John Singleton, dir., *Rosewood* (Los Angeles: Warner Brothers, 1997; DVD format, 2004); Walter Stowers, *Appointed* (1894; repr. New York: AMS Press, 1977); William M. Tuttle, Jr., *Race Riot: Chicago in the Red Summer of 1919* (New York: Wolff, 1997); Melissa Walker, *Down from the Mountaintop* (New

Haven, CT: Yale University Press, 1991); Brenda Wall, *Rodney King Rebellion: A Psychopolitical Analysis of Racial Despair and Hope* (Chicago: African American Images, 1992); Juan Williams, *Eyes on the Prize: America's Civil Rights Years, 1954–1965* (New York: Penguin, 1988); James O. Young, *Black Writers of the Thirties* (Baton Rouge: Louisiana State University Press, 1973).

Anita Bledsoe-Gardner

Race Uplift Movement. Race uplift refers to ways of thinking and modes of action that included not only the production of African American literature but also the work of Black churches, the educational policies of segregated all-Black schools, the activism of African American **women's clubs** and fraternal and benevolent societies, and the political organizing in African American communities to end **lynching** and racial violence and to transform America into a just society, peacefully, through legislation and the courts. Prominent figures associated with its pursuit were **Booker T. Washington, W.E.B. Du Bois, Ida B. Wells-Barnett**, and Lucy Craft Laney. Outlined in such classics as Washington's *Up from Slavery* (1901) and Du Bois's *The Souls of Black Folk* (1903), its themes encompassed hard and honest work, religion, ownership of home and land, thrift, hygiene, education, citizenship, the Black family, the betterment of the poor, and the advancement of the race. Uplift was not without its occasional tensions within African American groups, most notably a sense among the lower classes that they were being condescended to, and a discomfort among the more educated with the history of **slavery** and the perceived backwardness of the language, customs, and culture that characterized the lives of their Southern brothers and sisters.

It is difficult to pinpoint the exact inception of race uplift literature. Its beginning may be marked by the Emancipation Proclamation (January 1, 1863) and the works of **Frances Ellen Watkins Harper**, from her novel *Minnie's Sacrifice* (1868) to her *Poems* and *Idylls of the Bible* (1901). Signaling its close are *The Autobiography of an Ex-Colored Man* by **James Weldon Johnson** (1912) and Armistice Day (November 11, 1918), after which African Americans who had served in **World War I** returned to the United States expecting to be treated as heroes but encountered entrenched racism instead (Lewis, *When Harlem Was in Vogue*). Race uplift literature overlaps with and is inclusive of much of the literature of slavery, as well as that of the **Harlem Renaissance** in the twentieth century. The most important novelists, essayists, and poets who form this **literary canon** are Du Bois, Johnson, Washington, Wells-Barnett, **William Stanley Braithwaite, Charles Waddell Chesnutt, Anna Julia Haywood Cooper, James D. Corrothers, Paul Laurence Dunbar, Alice Moore Dunbar-Nelson, Sutton E. Griggs, Frances Ellen Watkins Harper, Pauline Elizabeth Hopkins**, and **Mary Church Terrell**. Their writings examine the conflicts between older ex-slaves and their children, sexual and racial violence, social and economic inequities, **passing** and racial identity, and the nature and substance of an African American artistic aesthetic.

While uplift writers were influenced by the experimentation of Walt Whitman and Emily Dickinson and the realism of **Mark Twain** and William Dean Howells, they also broke new ground. For example, in works such as *Iola Leroy; or, Shadows Uplifted* (1892) and *Poems of Cabin and Field* (1899), Harper and Dunbar, as well as Chesnutt, Corrothers, and Dunbar-Nelson used **dialect** to announce difference within African American communities, to demonstrate how mother wit and common sense could trump book learning, and to create honorable and dignified characterizations of the former slaves and Southern Blacks. By synthesizing the **blues, spirituals, conjuring, folktales**, and other **vernacular** expressions with traditional European forms and influences such as the sentimental, the neoclassical, and the genteel—Chesnutt's *The Conjure Woman, and Other Conjure Tales* (1899) and Du Bois's *Souls of Black Folk* exemplify this—race uplift literature also provocatively situated African American culture at the very center of American identity. And the leadership roles that African American women pioneered in the pre–**Civil War abolitionist movement**, as well as in temperance, suffrage, and other reform efforts, prepared them for their very strong representation among race uplift writers. They investigated themes of **gender** equity, motherhood, domestic and social violence, interracial friendships, and artistic and political autonomy.

Literary criticism since the 1990s has been characterized by an energetic rediscovery of forgotten or neglected race uplift literature. The 1890s novels of **Emma Dunham Kelley-Hawkins** and **Amelia E. Johnson** are representative of these recently recovered works that expand how we define African American literature through their use of racially ambiguous protagonists and their combination of evangelical and bohemian types. Post–Civil War race uplift **autobiography**, from **Elizabeth Keckley**'s *Behind the Scenes* (1868) to **Annie Louise Burton**'s *Memories of Childhood's Slavery Days* (1909), as the critic **William L. Andrews** has stated, emphasizes a reconciliation with **the South** that distinguishes it from earlier publications. Other scholars have investigated the influence of classicists such as William Henry Crogman, **Alexander Crummell**, and **William Sanders Scarborough** in defining an educational agenda, creating a literary canon, and delivering blows to racism through their systematic documentation of African Americans' achievements in collective biographies and biographical dictionaries. Black women's involvement in the churches and women's clubs was another source for this genre: **Gertrude Bustill Mossell**'s *The Work of the Afro-American Woman* (1908) is a noteworthy example. And misconceptions about the literature have been corrected. Not exclusively Northern or Southern, race uplift literature extends to the American West and includes works by such writers as the cowboy autobiographers Bass Reeves and **Nat Love**.

References: William L. Andrews, *African American Autobiography: A Collection of Critical Essays* (Englewood Cliffs, NJ: Prentice-Hall, 1991); Hazel V. Carby, *Reconstructing Womanhood: The Emergence of the Afro-American Woman Novelist* (New York: Oxford University Press, 1987); Frances Smith Foster, *Written by Herself: Literary*

Production by African American Women, 1746–1892 (Bloomington: Indiana University Press, 1993); Kevin K. Gaines, *Uplifting the Race: Black Leadership, Politics, and Culture in the Twentieth Century* (Chapel Hill: University of North Carolina Press, 1996); David Levering Lewis: *W.E.B. Du Bois: Biography of a Race, 1868–1919*, 2 vols. (New York: Henry Holt, 1993); *When Harlem Was in Vogue* (New York: Oxford University Press, 1989); Barbara McCaskill, "'To Labor . . . and Fight on the Side of God': Spirit, Class, and Nineteenth-Century African-American Women's Literature," in *Nineteenth-Century American Women Writers: A Critical Reader*, ed. Karen L. Kilcup (Malden, MA: Blackwell, 1998), 164–183; Barbara McCaskill and Caroline Gebhard, eds., *"Post-Bellum-Pre-Harlem": African American Literature and Culture, 1877–1919* (New York: New York University Press, 2005); Elizabeth McHenry, *Forgotten Readers: Recovering the Lost History of African American Literary Societies* (Durham, NC: Duke University Press, 2002); Elizabeth-Anne Murdy, *Teach the Nation: Pedagogies of Racial Uplift in U.S. Women's Writing of the 1890s* (New York: Routledge, 2003); Michele Valerie Ronnick, "Twelve Black Classicists," *Arion* 11 (2004), 85–102.

Barbara McCaskill

Racial Discovery Plot. A plot device first appearing in American literature, especially in novels, in the second half of the nineteenth century. Novels with a racial discovery plot feature protagonists who discover in adulthood that they are of mixed-race ancestry. These characters are often upper-class individuals, but whatever wealth or power they hold may become useless or inaccessible to them in light of their racial background. The racial discovery victim must reformulate his or her self-identity, as well as recover a position in society, after the revelation of mixed-race status.

The racial discovery plot can be found in works both by and about African Americans. African American female writers used it as part of a social protest agenda; for example, both **Frances Ellen Watkins Harper**'s *Iola Leroy* (1892) and **Pauline Elizabeth Hopkins**'s *Hagar's Daughter* (1901) use racial discovery to expand on the plight of the tragic **mulatto** character. Nearly identical plot twists appear in the work of White male authors. For example, William Dean Howells's *An Imperative Duty* (1891) and **Mark Twain**'s *Pudd'nhead Wilson* (1894) both depend on major characters who discover their own racial identity, although with less obvious political overtones. Racial discovery as a plot device also appears in **Charles Waddell Chesnutt**'s *The Quarry* (1999; completed in 1928) and William Faulkner's *Light in August* (1932).

While the racial discovery plot bears an obvious similarity to the well-known novel of **passing**, it may better be understood as a forerunner to that genre, which became common in the early twentieth century. The racial discovery plots can easily be distinguished in that they remove *volition* from the deception practiced by the protagonists. Some racial discovery characters eventually decide to pass, but initially they are completely ignorant of their ambiguous racial status. Both types of novels reflect changes in the structure of American society during the nineteenth century, when increased urbanization led to expanding cities full of strangers, and family reputations and social connections were increasingly unreliable. Questions of racial identity are just one part of social anxieties over identity and status, a topic explored fully by the literary scholar Karen Haltunnen.

The number of works featuring the racial discovery plot device around the turn of the twentieth century corresponds notably with the rise of legal segregation and an increasing number of Jim Crow laws in and beyond **the South**. The literary historian and critic Werner Sollors has called attention to legal segregation as a counter to an American culture which "strongly favored *achieved* rather than *ascribed* identity, and supported 'self-determination' and 'independence' from ancestral, parental, and external definitions" (*Beyond Ethnicity*, 37). Sollors sees racial identity at the heart of American debates over hereditary privilege versus meritocracy. The rising popularity of the racial discovery plot during the rise of Jim Crow laws suggests that both White and Black authors turned to literature to pose questions about how and by whom racial identity should be defined. By extension, these racial discoveries call into question how much heredity can and should determine the merit and success of any American.

Resources: M. Giulia Fabi, *Passing and the Rise of the African American Novel* (Urbana: University of Illinois Press, 2001); Karen Halttunen, *Confidence Men and Painted Women: A Study of Middle-Class Culture in America, 1830–1870* (New Haven, CT: Yale University Press, 1982); Werner Sollors: *Beyond Ethnicity: Consent and Descent in American Culture* (New York: Oxford University Press, 1986); *Neither Black Nor White Yet Both: Thematic Explorations of Interracial Literature* (New York: Oxford University Press, 1997).

Susan Hays Bussey

Ragtime. The word "ragtime," in its current historical, cultural, and musical sense, entered into the English language in the mid-1890s. It refers to the era in American history between about 1895 and the U.S. entry into **World War I** in 1917, and, more specifically, to the immensely popular African American instrumental music that this era produced. In the literature about ragtime the reader frequently encounters such descriptive words as "brash," "enthusiastic," "colloquial," "jaunty," "haunting," "swinging dance music," "elaborately syncopated," "vulgar," "faddish," "vibrant," and "abrasive." This music, largely compositional and usually played by a solo pianist, is characterized by rhythmically intricate, syncopated melodic lines running lyrically over a straightforward 2/4 or 4/4 accented "thump" or "stomp" in the bass line. Ragtime songs are typically structured by a progression of repeated (usually two) sixteen-bar phrases in AA BB CC DD form, with variations, that builds momentum toward an introspective concluding phrase. The precise etymology of the word is difficult to establish, but "ragtime" is likely a derivation of "ragged time." There is nothing ragged about the basic four-beats-to-the-measure time signature of the standard ragtime piece articulated by the player's left hand—a beat which often hits the listener as a kind of "oom-pah" precursor to the stride technique that **James P. Johnson** and others used to bring the ragtime piano idiom closer to the **blues** and **jazz** music of the early twentieth century. But in the complex polyrhythmic and polymetric melodic lines of these compositions the listener encounters a wealth of musical and emotional activity occurring just off the beat, in seemingly "ragged" syncopated patterns—a kind of musical expression more akin to African-based field hollers, coon songs, and jig band tunes than to the European classical orchestrations that gave American music the piano as a central melodic and harmonic instrument.

While musicologists and historians place the beginning of ragtime in the mid-1890s, the roots of the music reach back to before the **Civil War**. Slave-owning families that had no piano-playing members would sometimes allow musically inclined slaves access to a piano and some instruction so they could be summoned to the big house to play at social gatherings. The songs performed in this context were invariably popular **ballads**, hymns, and classical tunes, but these African American slave pianists would often subtly inflect the pieces with the peculiar (to those genres) African rhythmic structures and embellished, creative melodic interpretations that would come to characterize the jazz innovations of the following century. The emancipation of the slaves after the Civil War led to the establishment of a fairly active network of Black bars, saloons, juke joints, and honky-tonks throughout the Southern states, particularly in the towns along the Mississippi and Missouri rivers. A group of Black pianists found there a steady source of employment and a forum in which they could converse and play with each other, hone their skills, and develop their music.

These pianists were aware of a concurrent theatrical form, the minstrel show (**minstrelsy**), which traced its roots to the early nineteenth century circus performances and which was formalized in the late 1840s by such White actors as Thomas D. Rice and Daniel Decatur Emmett, who would perform in blackface. These variety shows featured stock characters named, for example, Jim Crow and Zip Coon, that reinforced White supremacist stereotypes of African Americans by depicting Blacks on the plantation in various demeaning situations. The first African Americans to break into the minstrel circuit were the Georgia Minstrels, organized by Charles Hicks in 1865, featuring Billy Kersands and Sam Lucas in the company. The Black American performers who took to the popular stage in the decades after the Civil War introduced White America to the "coon songs," music that accompanied the "coon shout," a boisterous, creative hollering match in which the contestants employed a form of musical braggadocio that is a precursor to certain modern day **hip-hop** and **rap** forms. Nancy Von Rosk has connected the "coon shows" to the work of **Paul Laurence Dunbar**.

Another plantation root of ragtime piano can be found in the cakewalk, a form of ensemble dance that became popular in the 1880s and first appeared on the professional stage in 1890 as the finale of Sam T. Jack's *Creole Show* at the Old Howard Theater in **Boston, Massachusetts**. This style of dancing featured lavishly dressed couples who would promenade, in step, to lively piano or orchestral music. The best of the "walkers" would "take the cake," and the best of the piano players on the saloon circuit were sought after in the parlors and dance halls where the cakewalk was becoming increasingly popular.

A final important influence upon the ragtime composers and pianists who emerged in the late nineteenth century were the European classical traditions being explored throughout the Continent by such piano virtuoso composers as Johannes Brahms in Germany and Austria, the young Sergei Rachmaninoff in Russia, and in the late work of Franz Liszt in Hungary. During the 1880s and 1890s these composers were blending conservative classical traditions with modern romantic impulses, and their innovations struck a chord with such composers as Scott Joplin, Tom Million Turpin, "Blind" John William Boone, and James "Eubie" Blake, who were forging a new use of the piano that was appropriate for the artistic worldview of late nineteenth-century African Americans. These young composers and their colleagues brought all of these influences together and produced ragtime, the first instrumental African American music that was not used merely as an accompaniment to something else, and that became an important precursor to the early jazz music of Jelly Roll Morton, King Oliver, Louis Armstrong, and **Edward Kennedy "Duke" Ellington**.

Ragtime piano was being performed by the late 1880s, if not sooner. But a ragtime composition was not available to the sheet music-buying public until Ben Harney, a White composer, published "You've Been a Good Old Wagon" in Louisville, Kentucky, in 1895, and this is the date that many historians mark as the beginning of the ragtime era. In January 1897 William Krell, also White, published the first instrumental rag, titled "Mississippi Rag." That the first publishers of this distinctly African American musical form were not themselves African Americans should come as no surprise. The profits made, for example, from Charles K. Harris's wildly popular composition "After the Ball" in 1892 indicated that there was a huge market for published sheet music in the United States and Europe. Due to the racist nature of the American marketplace, when ragtime entered this arena, it was difficult for Black composers to reap any of the profits. Most of the early African American ragtimers did not even try, and an important archive of American music has thus been lost. In December 1897, Tom Turpin became the first African American to publish a ragtime piece when he came out with "Harlem Rag." From this point forward, much in the manner that the history of **reggae** music is the history of the career of Bob Marley and the Wailers, or the history of **swing** can be traced through the odyssey of Duke Ellington, the arc of the ragtime era can be viewed by engaging the career of Scott Joplin. These are, of course, imperfect claims from the standpoint of historical research. But Joplin is the dominant composer of the era, and he holds a critically important place in the pantheon of American music.

Joplin was born in either 1867 or 1868 near what would later become Texarkana, **Texas**, and he died in New York City of tertiary syphilis on April 1, 1917. His life spanned the period from Congress's ratification of the Fourteenth Amendment to the U.S. entry into World War I. He attended the

Chicago World's Fair in 1893 along with many other leading ragtime composers, and spent many of his formative musical years in the 1890s in Sedalia, Missouri, where he published his first rag, titled "Original Rag," in March 1899. Six months later John Stark and Son published Joplin's "Maple Leaf Rag," which was probably composed in 1897 or 1898 and was likely the inspiration for the name of Sedalia's popular Maple Leaf Club. The "Maple Leaf Rag" sold hundreds of thousands of copies over ten years, bringing Joplin a modest but steady income throughout his life. To this day the song remains the most influential and most closely studied of any ragtime composition. Joplin spent the remaining years of his life mostly in **St. Louis, Missouri**, and New York City. Of his dozens of successful compositions in various genres, some of the most popular rags are "The Easy Winners" (1901), "The Entertainer" (1902), a tribute to President Theodore Roosevelt titled "The Strenuous Life" (1902), "The Cascades" (a hit at the 1904 St. Louis World's Fair), a collaboration with Joplin's immensely talented and tragically short-lived colleague Louis Chauvin titled "Heliotrope Bouquet" (1907), "Euphonic Sounds" (1909), and "Magnetic Rag" (1914).

While Joplin was, and remains to this day, the dominant musical presence of the ragtime era, other important composers during the period were Charles L. Johnson, James Scott, Joseph Lamb, and, of course, Ferdinand "Jelly Roll" Morton. Charles "Cow-Cow" Davenport, James P. Johnson, Earl "Fatha" Hines, Teddy Weatherford, and Duke Ellington—artists who pioneered such early jazz piano styles as boogie-woogie, stride, the "trumpet-piano" of the dixieland sound, and swing—all trace their roots to the work of the ragtime composers and performers. And such American classical composers as Igor Stravisnsky and Charles Ives, among others, acknowledged the influence of ragtime upon their work. Ragtime is alluded to in **James Weldon Johnson**'s novel *The Autobiography of an Ex-Colored Man* (1912).

After defining American popular music for more than two decades, when Joplin died in 1917 ragtime was being replaced by the thriving ensemble sound of dixieland jazz. While the "Maple Leaf Rag" would continue to sell and be performed throughout the 1920s and 1930s, it was not until after Jelly Roll Morton's death in 1941 that performers and academics would begin to revisit Joplin's work and the ragtime era, and acknowledge their importance to the history of jazz and American classical forms. Interest in ragtime continued to grow throughout the 1950s and 1960s. In late 1971 the New York Public Library issued a two-volume edition of Joplin's collected works, and Joplin's 1911 opera *Treemonisha*, never performed in its entirety during Joplin's lifetime, reached Broadway in October 1975. On New Year's Day 1973 Universal Studios released *The Sting*, a film that garnered seven Oscars, including one for Marvin Hamlisch's adaptation of several Joplin compositions that formed the basis for the soundtrack. In 1994 Oxford University Press published Edward A. Berlin's acclaimed biography *King of Ragtime: Scott Joplin and His Era*, and every June the Scott Joplin International Ragtime Foundation hosts the Scott Joplin Ragtime Festival in Sedalia, Missouri, that brings together scholars, performers, and ragtime enthusiasts. In 2002 a play by Oliver Mayer, *Ragged Time*, was produced in Los Angeles (Horstein). These are indications that ragtime now occupies a permanent place in American musical and cultural history, and that the haunting, euphonic sounds of Scott Joplin, Louis Chauvin, Joseph Lamb, and others will continue to challenge listeners to grapple with the problems and paradoxes of American history and racism, and the way these forces produced such a rich tradition of Black American music.

Resources: Edward A. Berlin: *King of Ragtime: Scott Joplin and His Era* (New York: Oxford University Press, 1994); *Ragtime: A Musical and Cultural History* (Berkeley: University of California Press, 1980); Rudi Blesh and Harriet Janis, *They All Played Ragtime* (New York: Knopf, 1950); Lawrence T. Carter, *Eubie Blake: Keys of Memory* (Detroit: Balamp, 1979); Susan Curtis: *Dancing to a Black Man's Tune: A Life of Scott Joplin* (Columbia: University of Missouri Press, 1994); "Scott Joplin and Sedalia: The King of Ragtime in the Queen City of Missouri," *Gateway Heritage* 14, no. 4 (Spring 1994), 4–19; John Edward Hasse, ed., *Ragtime: Its History, Composers, and Music* (New York: Schirmer, 1985); Scott Horstein, "Epic Ragtime Soul Music, the Legacy of Slavery: Oliver Mayer's *Ragged Time*," *Theatre Forum* 23 (Summer–Fall 2003), 12–17; David A. Jasen and Gene Jones, *That American Rag! The Story of Ragtime in the United States* (New York: Schirmer, 1999); David A. Jasen and Trebor Jay Tichenor, *Rags and Ragtime: A Musical History*, 2nd ed. (New York: Dover, 1989); James Weldon Johnson, *The Autobiography of an Ex-Colored Man* (Boston: Sherman, French, 1912); Vera Brodsky Lawrence, ed., *The Complete Works of Scott Joplin*, 2 vols., 2nd ed. (New York: New York Public Library, 1981); Alan Lomax, *Mister Jelly Roll: The Fortunes of Jelly Roll Morton*, 2nd ed. (1950; repr. Berkeley: University of California Press, 2001); Nancy Von Rosk, "Coon Shows, Ragtime, and the Blues: Race, Urban Culture, and the Naturalist Vision in Paul Laurence Dunbar's 'The Sport of the Gods,'" in *Twisted from the Ordinary: Essays on American Literary Naturalism*, ed. Mary E. Papke (Knoxville: University of Tennessee Press, 2003), 144–168; Terry Waldo, *This Is Ragtime* (New York: Hawthorne, 1976).

Mychel J. Namphy

Rahman, Aishah (born 1936). Playwright. Best known for her avant-garde stylistics, Rahman has written a number of experimental plays that have achieved great success Off Broadway and in regional theaters.

Born Virginia Hughes in 1936, Rahman spent her childhood and adolescence in New York City. In the mid-1960s, she enrolled at Howard University, from which she graduated with a B.S. in political science in 1968. She began her career as a professional playwright in the 1970s.

Rahman's most acclaimed play, *Unfinished Women Cry in No Man's Land While a Bird Dies in a Gilded Cage*, premiered at the New York Shakespeare Festival in June 1977. Set on June 12, 1955, the day that the jazz saxophonist Charlie Parker died, the play alternates its action between Parker's final hours in the posh apartment of his lover, Pasha, and five unwed mothers in the Hide-A-Wee Home who must decide whether or not to keep their babies. (*See* **Gillespie, Dizzy, Charlie Parker, and Thelonious Monk.**)

A number of Rahman's lesser known works center on the lives and careers of important figures in African American history, including *Lady Day: A Musical Tragedy* (1972), about **Billie Holliday**; *The Tale of Madame Zora* (1986), a **blues** musical about **Zora Neale Hurston**; and *The Opera of Marie Laveau* (with composer Akua Dixon Turre; later retitled *Anybody Seen Marie Laveau?*, 1989), a "pastiche of **folklore** and history . . . about the nineteenth-century French, Native American, and African New Orleans voodoo queen" (Margulis, 618). Other dramatic works by Rahman are *The Mojo and the Sayso* (1988) and *Only in America* (1993) (*see* **Mojo**).

In addition to her theatrical work, Rahman is an active educator and mentor to hopeful playwrights. Throughout the 1980s and early 1990s, she spent roughly a decade teaching drama and creative writing at Nassau Community College on Long Island. During this same time, she served as director of the Henry St. Settlements Playwrights Workshop. In 1992, she joined the creative writing faculty at Brown University, where she currently is a professor of playwriting and founder/editor in chief of *NuMuse*, a national journal of new plays by emergent authors.

Most recently, Rahman has turned her attention to nondramatic work, authoring a novel, *Illegitimate Life* (1996), and a memoir, *Chewed Water* (2001).

Resources: "Aishah Rahman," *Departments: English: Writing*, Brown University (Sept. 26, 2001), http://www.brown.edu/Departments/English/Writing/rahman.htm; Jennifer Margulis, "Aishah Rahman," in *The Oxford Companion to African American Literature*, ed. William L. Andrews et al. (New York: Oxford University Press, 1997), 618; Aishah Rahman: *Chewed Water: A Memoir* (Hanover, NH: University Press of New England, 2001); *The Mojo and the Sayso*, in *Moon Marked and Touched by Sun: Plays by African-American Women*, ed. Sydné Mahone (New York: Theatre Communications Group, 1994), 281–320; *Plays by Aishah Rahman* (New York: Broadway Play, 1997); *Unfinished Women Cry in No Man's Land While a Bird Dies in a Gilded Cage*, in *9 Plays by Black Women*, ed. Margaret B. Wilkerson (New York: Mentor, 1986), 199–237; "Rahman, Aishah," in *African-American Writers: A Dictionary*, ed. Shari Dorantes Hatch and Michael R. Strickland (Santa Barbara, CA: ABC-CLIO, 2000), 293.

Heath A. Diehl

Rampersad, Arnold (born 1941). Literary scholar, critic, biographer, and teacher. Arnold Rampersad is arguably best known for having written a two-volume definitive biography of **Langston Hughes** (1986–1988, 2nd ed., 2001). Born in 1941 in Trinidad, Rampersad came to the United States in 1965 to attend Bowling Green State University in Ohio, where he received B.A. and M.A. degrees in literature and history, respectively. His excellent showing at Bowling Green enabled him to gain admission to Harvard University, where he earned another M.A. and a Ph.D. Rampersad's academic career has taken him from Stanford to Rutgers, Columbia, Princeton (where for eight years he was the Woodrow Wilson Professor of Literature), and back to Stanford, where he holds the Sara Hart Kimball chair in the Humanities and serves as Cognizant Dean for the Humanities.

At the outset, Rampersad made clear that his scholarly province was going to be a comprehensive America by foregrounding the work of two representative figures, Herman Melville and **W.E.B. Du Bois**. But, deciding to focus his energies on studying "groups of people who had not been adequately represented or understood," Rampersad has become a **Black Studies** scholar with a distinct knack for writing prize-winning biographies. For instance, outside Du Bois's own autobiographical writings, Rampersad's *The Art and Imagination of W.E.B. Du Bois* presents the most lucid and comprehensive evaluation of the salient phases in the life of the great trailblazer of African American intellectual history and culture. The book illuminates the role of Du Bois and *The Crisis* magazine in the development of the radical philosophical foundations of African American scholarship and politics.

An important intellectual rationale underlies Rampersad's interest in biography. The more fashionable scholarly focus on ideas invariably provided lopsided impressions of the figures and personalities whose works were thematized in African American Studies projects. More of the practical lives of these figures needed to be brought to the fore to lend credence to the philosophical claims made about them. In the case of Du Bois, for instance, Rampersad demonstrates with amazing attention to detail how crucially Du Bois's formative experiences in New England shaped his public persona. In perhaps the most balanced fashion yet, Rampersad presents Du Bois's so-called racial ambivalence by implying that the latter's greater identification with his paternal ancestry than with the maternal lineage was determined by more than considerations of pigmentation. Alexander Du Bois's solid sense of self and personal pride that precluded any sort of subservience to the idea of White supremacy had won his grandson over, writes Rampersad. This observation was contrary to the simplistic idea then in tacit currency that Du Bois preferred the Du Boises to the Burghardts because the latter were darker than the former.

Perhaps the most starkly meritorious of Rampersad's prize-winning biographical works is the two-volume *The Life of Langston Hughes*, the best-known biographical production in Afro-African Studies. The work is informed by Rampersad's catholic apprehension of American literature and especially of African American literature as a particular branch of the larger national tradition. Profoundly intrigued by the persona of the **Harlem Renaissance** poet, Rampersad researched every rivulet leading into and out of Hughes's prolific creative fountain, and thus clarified some of the more mysterious aspects of the poet's creative persona. Apart from writing a book (in volume 1) that presents the history of the Harlem Renaissance in a manner as compelling as Hughes's own *The Big Sea* (the first of two autobiographies), Rampersad's work fills in gaps deliberately left by Hughes in his great **autobiography**. The biography sheds greater light on some of the most profound moments in Hughes's life, which the poet had been particularly reticent about. It shows, for instance, how truly devastating to Hughes was the rupture in his relationship with patron of the arts Charlotte Osgood Mason, and how reminiscent this event had been of another important rupture in Hughes's life: his falling out with his father. Subtly, and without committing himself to untenable psychoanalyses, Rampersad teases out a viable connection between Hughes's proneness to emotional collapse and his uncommon creative facility. Additionally, this analytical trajectory helped Rampersad broach a zone of Hughes's personality that had seemed impenetrable to his contemporaries—his sexuality. Citing innumerable and thrillingly gossipy hetero- and homosexual challenges the poet had to contend with at different times in his life, Rampersad concludes that Hughes had indeed been as asexual as it was possible to be and still appear to be "normal."

But Rampersad has not limited himself to literary figures in his biographical work. Some of his award-winning projects have thematized the lives of major sports figures, for example. In an uncannily timely collaboration, he coauthored *Days of Grace: A Memoir* with the legendary tennis player Arthur Ashe just months before the latter's succumbing to AIDS in 1993. A prominent feature of *Days of Grace* is Rampersad's fluidity of style, which makes the great tennis player come touchingly alive in the text's pages. *Jackie Robinson: A Biography* (1997) is another of Rampersad's projects devoted to the life of a sports figure. Of this book Rampersad once said, "At first I thought that someone else should write it, someone who had grown up playing baseball." But, pressured by Rachel Robinson to write a book "about her husband's life before baseball, [during baseball], and the fifteen years after baseball," Rampersad proceeded to take **Jackie Robinson** "as seriously as [he] would any other [literary] subject." At this writing, Rampersad is at work on a biography of **Ralph Ellison** and for some time has had almost exclusive access to the more revealing folders of the Ellison Papers in the Manuscript Department of the Library of Congress.

But over and above these biographical undertakings, Rampersad has an extensive résumé in the critical and editorial facets of Afro-American Studies. In two multivolume titles, *The Collected Poems of Langston Hughes* (1994) and *The Collected Works of Langston Hughes* (2001–2004), he has created a comprehensive and easily accessible depository of Hughes's creative and nonfictional oeuvre. He has also edited works by **Richard Wright** and **Zora Neale Hurston**. His two-volume Library of America edition of Richard Wright's works includes revised individual editions of *Native Son* and *Black Boy*. He has also coedited the Race and American Culture series published by Oxford University Press, and an anthology, *Slavery and the Literary Imagination* (1989), with **Deborah McDowell**.

Resources: Arthur Ashe and Arnold Rampersad, *Days of Grace: A Memoir* (New York: Knopf, 1993); E. Deborah McDowell and Arnold Rampersad, eds., *Slavery and the Literary Imagination* (Baltimore: Johns Hopkins University Press, 1989); Lucius Outlaw and Arnold Rampersad, "An Interview with Lucius Outlaw and Arnold Rampersad," *InterVU*, WRVU Radio (Nashville, TN, Oct. 29, 2000); Arnold Rampersad: *The Art and Imagination of W.E.B. Du Bois* (Cambridge, MA: Harvard University Press, 1976); *The Life of Langston Hughes*, 2 vols., 2nd ed. (New York: Oxford University Press, 2002).

Mzenga Aggrey Wanyama

Randall, Dudley Felker (1914–2000). Poet and publisher. Known as a poet who connected the **Harlem Renaissance** generation of the 1920s to the **Black Arts Movement** of the 1960s, Dudley Randall was born in **Washington, D.C.**, then moved with his family to **Detroit, Michigan**, when he was nine. At fourteen, he published a sonnet in the *Detroit Free Press*, and began reading the poetry of **Langston Hughes** and **Countee Cullen**. He worked for the Ford Motor Company before **World War II**, then served in the military, and attended Morgan State College after the war. In the 1950s he was a librarian at Lincoln University (Pennsylvania) and Morgan State College, then moved in 1956 to the Wayne County Federated Library System. His first well-known poem, "Ballad of Birmingham," was written in 1963 in response to a church bombing in Alabama in which four young girls were killed. It was set to music by the folk singer Jerry Moore. Randall founded **Broadside Press** as a way of publishing his and other African American poems in single-sheet broadsides, suitable for framing. The first collection published by the press, *Poem Counterpoem* (1966), consisted of thematically matched poems by him and **Margaret Esse Taylor Danner**, a poet he had worked with at Detroit's Boone House for the Arts. Besides "The Ballad of Birmingham," this collection includes "Booker T. and W.E.B.," a frequently anthologized poem which dramatizes the intellectual conflict between **W.E.B. Du Bois** and **Booker T. Washington** about how African Americans might best respond to their political and economic situations in the United States. In 1967, the press brought out *For Malcolm: Poems on the Life and the Death of Malcolm X*, which featured works by **Robert Hayden, Margaret Abigail Walker, Gwendolyn Brooks, Amiri Baraka** (LeRoi Jones), **Larry Neal, Sonia Sanchez**, and **Etheridge Knight**.

The late 1960s and early 1970s was a time of explosive growth for both Randall and the poets he championed through his press. *Love You* (1970) presented fourteen of his love poems, *More to Remember* (1971) collected fifty poems he had written throughout his life, and *After the Killing* (1973) brought together fifteen poems that touched on social issues. Meanwhile, he published early works by Don L. Lee (**Haki R. Madhubuti**), Sonia Sanchez, **Nikki Giovanni**, and **Audre Lorde**, among others. In 1971, he edited the landmark anthology *The Black Poets*, which remains in print. Randall sold the press in 1977, but continued to work for it as a consultant. In 1981, he published *A Litany of Friends: New and Selected Poems*, and was named the first Poet Laureate of Detroit. He died in 2000, at the age of eighty-six. He will be remembered not only as a pioneering African American publisher but also as a poet whose touchstones included **Malcolm X**, W.E.B. Du Bois, and **Frederick Douglass**, as well as T. S. Eliot, Shakespeare, and William Butler Yeats. Randall developed a literary aesthetic that is not narrowly racial, but open to all humanity.

Resources: Primary Sources: Dudley Randall: *After the Killing* (Chicago: Third World Press, 1973); *Broadside Memories: Poets I Have Known* (Detroit: Broadside Press, 1975); *Cities Burning* (Detroit: Broadside Press, 1968); *A Litany of Friends: New and*

Selected Poems (Detroit: Lotus Press, 1981); *Love You* (London: Paul Breman, 1970); *More to Remember: Poems of Four Decades* (Chicago: Third World Press, 1971); Dudley Randall, ed., *The Black Poets* (1971; repr. New York: Bantam, 1985); Dudley Randall and Margaret Danner, *Poem Counterpoem* (Detroit: Broadside Press, 1966); Dudley Randall and Margaret G. Burroughs, eds., *For Malcolm: Poems on the Life and the Death of Malcolm X* (Detroit: Broadside Press, 1967). **Secondary Sources:** Melba Joyce Boyd, *Wrestling with the Muse: Dudley Randall and the Broadside Press* (New York: Columbia University Press, 2003); D. H. Melhem, "Dudley Randall: The Poet as Humanist," in his *Heroism in the New Black Poetry: Introductions and Interviews* (Lexington: University Press of Kentucky, 1990), 41–60; R. Baxter Miller, "Dudley Felker Randall," in *Dictionary of Literary Biography*, vol. 41, *Afro-American Poets Since 1955*, ed. Trudier Harris and Thadious M. Davis (Detroit: Gale, 1985), 265–273; Julius E. Thompson, *Dudley Randall, Broadside Press, and the Black Arts Movement in Detroit, 1960–1995* (Jefferson, NC: McFarland, 1999).

Thomas J. Cassidy

Randolph, Asa Philip (1889–1979). Founder of a labor union and editor. Randolph founded the Brotherhood of Sleeping Car Porters. He was also a civil rights activist and editor of such publications as **The Messenger** and *The Black Worker.*

Asa Philip Randolph was born April 15, 1889, in Crescent City, Florida. His father was a minister and the family valued education, so Randolph attended and graduated from Cookman Institute in Jacksonville. Rejecting his father's suggestion that he pursue a career in the ministry, he found few employment opportunities in Florida beyond manual labor.

In 1911, Randolph moved to New York City, where he was attracted to the economic and political ideas of the Socialist Party. He and his friend Chandler Owen attempted to organize Black workers, and in 1917 they began to publish *The Messenger*, which argued that only through socialism and unionism could the economic status of the race be improved. The magazine also published the poetry and short stories of young African American authors. Randolph opposed U.S. participation in **World War I** and was briefly incarcerated for his pacifist views.

The Messenger staff was split over communism and the **Black Nationalism** of **Marcus Garvey**, both of which Randolph opposed. With the influence of socialism in decline, Randolph welcomed an opportunity to organize the Black-dominated Pullman porters, and *The Messenger* became the official organ of the Brotherhood of Sleeping Car Porters. Nevertheless, failure to carry through with a strike pledge in 1928 led to a decline in membership for the Brotherhood, and *The Messenger* ceased publication. Nonetheless, as Hutchinson suggests, *The Messenger* influenced the intellectual shape of the **Harlem Renaissance. George S. Schuyler** was involved with editing the magazine, and **Langston Hughes** published several poems in it (Ostrom).

However, the Brotherhood and Randolph gained a new lease on life with Franklin Roosevelt's New Deal encouragement of collective bargaining. Securing affiliation with the American Federation of Labor and launching a new publication, *The Black Worker*, Randolph and the Brotherhood negotiated a contract with the Pullman Company on August 25, 1937. Through *The Black Worker*, Randolph sought to unionize the Black working class.

With defense industries pulling the nation out of the **Great Depression**, Randolph demanded that President Roosevelt take action against racial discrimination so that African Americans could take advantage of new employment opportunities. In response to Randolph's threat of a march on Washington, the President issued Executive Order 8802, which established the Fair Employment Practices Commission.

In the postwar period Randolph's Committee Against Jim Crow in Military Service and Training pressured President Harry Truman to issue Executive Order 9981 and integrate the nation's armed forces. Randolph, along with his young associate Bayard Rustin, became increasingly active in the emerging **Civil Rights Movement**. He formed the Negro American Labor Council to challenge racial discrimination within the labor movement, and in 1963 proposed a March on Washington for Jobs and Freedom.

While the March on Washington was an important symbol for the Civil Rights Movement, Randolph antagonized many younger and more militant Blacks by embracing the liberal establishment. He supported President Lyndon Johnson's compromise to allow only two members of the Mississippi Freedom Democratic Party to be seated at the 1964 party convention.

In 1964 he formed the A. Philip Randolph Institute to foster his economic ideas. Believing that only full employment could address poverty, Randolph proposed the Freedom Budget for All Americans, an ambitious plan intended to eliminate poverty in the United States, but the expensive **Vietnam War** made implementation of Randolph's ideas impossible. Increasingly estranged from the growing militancy of the **Black Power** movement, Randolph never wavered from his belief that economic progress was essential for racial equality. Suffering from numerous health problems, he died on May 16, 1979. The motion picture *10,000 Black Men Named George* (2002) is based on Randolph's founding of the Brotherhood of Sleeping Car Porters. (*See* **Labor.**)

Resources: Jervis Anderson, *A. Philip Randolph: A Biographical Portrait* (Berkeley: University of California Press, 1986); William H. Harris, *Keeping the Faith: A. Philip Randolph, Milton P. Webster, and the Brotherhood of Sleeping Car Porters, 1925–37* (Urbana: University of Illinois Press, 1977); George Hutchinson, "Mediating Race and Nation: The Cultural Politics of *The Messenger*," in his *The Harlem Renaissance in Black and White* (Cambridge, MA: Belknap Press of Harvard University Press, 1995), 289–312; Theodore Kornweibel, Jr., *No Crystal Stair: Black Life and the Messenger, 1917–1928* (Westport, CT: Greenwood Press, 1975); Hans Ostrom, *A Langston Hughes Encyclopedia* (Westport, CT: Greenwood Press, 2002), 243–244; Paula F. Pfeffer, *A. Philip Randolph: Pioneer of the Civil Rights Movement* (Baton Rouge: Louisiana State University Press,

1990); Jack Santino, *Miles of Smiles, Years of Struggle: Stories of Black Pullman Porters* (Urbana: University of Illinois Press, 1989); Robert Townsend, dir., *10,000 Black Men Named George* (Los Angeles: Paramount Studios, 2002), DVD format.

Ron Briley

Rap. A musical genre initially introduced in the 1960s as an experimental form of poetry featuring spoken word and poetry over **jazz** music. Over time, rap evolved into various rhythmic and lyrical styles that use rhetorical content and nontraditional musical instruments not only to disseminate information concerning historical and contemporary Black or oppressive experiences, but also to evoke dance from an audience. Similar to the way **blues** and jazz were literary protests during the **Harlem Renaissance** and the **Black Arts Movement**, respectively, rap music's infancy was a literary vehicle to register the latter half of the **Black Power** movement. Since the 1970s, rap has remained one of the most indelible musical forms from which its crafters can foreground the Black experience in forums outside of music, including literature, theater, and art, and rap is **hip-hop** culture's foundation.

Although the Bronx, New York, is often named as the birthplace of rap music, literary evidence demonstrates that rap, like other musical genres created within African American culture, is planted in the soil of slave songs, work songs, field calls, protest songs, and slave **spirituals**. Rap music and its lyrics represent an outgrowth of the slave experience and form one of its residual branches. The rhythm of slave and work songs is a traditional call-and-response in which the leader makes a call, "We are going down to Georgia, boys," and the chorus offers a response, "Aye-Aye." Call-and-response in a rap format imitates that structure, as the lead calls, "Everybody say Hey! Ho!," and the audience replies, "Hey! Ho!" (Naughty by Nature). Additionally, rap lyrics share sociopolitical arguments and purpose with field calls, protest songs, and slave spirituals. Much of the historical discourse concerning race as seen in such songs, in some form or another, remains current. In other words, although racism today is practiced and spoken in a language differing from that of the nineteenth century, racial concerns of the past remain unreconciled, and rap music serves as a contemporary sounding board for those concerns.

Hailing the Sugar Hill Gang as rap's first artists is also an issue of contention in the historical account of the genre. However, publication of literature and lyrics produced and performed by **the Last Poets** and **Gil Scott-Heron** demonstrate that the latter are the first artists to combine poetic commentary and African rhythms and beats on an audio recording. In rap's infancy, lyrics articulated Blacks' response to specific social issues, such as police brutality, poverty, and institutional racism in a way that educated the mainstream public. Scott-Heron's "The Revolution Will Not Be Televised," first appeared in *New Black Poet: Small Talk at 125th and Lenox*, and was released on the Flying Dutchman label in 1970. Also released in a book of poetry of the same name that year, the poem/lyric argues that there will not be a technological or drug-induced escape from the ongoing Black revolution; rather, it will be "live," and by default, all Americans will participate in the discourse and actions concerning issues of **race**. The Last Poets' "Niggers Are Scared of Revolution," also released in 1970, is a scathing attack against Blacks who willingly participate in stereotypical activities rather than supporting the unavoidable movement at hand.

In 1979 the Sugar Hill Gang introduced what is known as Mickey Mouse rap, songs with lyrics addressing no particular social issue. The group's first album was also the first commercially released collection of rap songs, and their live shows introduced three groundbreaking ideas to rap performance. First, the Sugar Hill Gang popularized written poetry, in that they demonstrated how poems could be converted into rap songs with a beat. Second, the group's lyrical ability introduced labyrinthine lyrics to rap music, a competitive practice as seen in the work of Mystical and Twista today. Finally, the Sugar Hill Gang's performances evoked dance, rather than political thought, and made the music a commercial enterprise marketable to the mainstream public (Light). Their work not only spawned what would become the greatest revenue-generating market in music history, but they also initiated a lyrical form from which rap as an art could be measured: lyricism and danceability. Although maintaining the social objectives of rap music, groups such as Grand Master Flash and the Furious Five and Afrika Bambatta, as well as Big Daddy Kane and Rakim, incorporated acoustic African rhythms, DJ mixes of existing music, techno and synthetic beats, and poetry not only to enlighten Americans on racial oppressions plaguing the Black experience, but also to get their listeners to dance.

In the 1980s, rap music began branching off. As the audience grew internationally, rap music was being created in cultures outside of Black America. In America, since the 1980s, the Black aesthetic and experience have remained the corpus for rap music. Notwithstanding commercially viable performances of rap music by artists outside of African-American culture, such as the Beastie Boys, Vanilla Ice, Eminem, and Bubba Sparkxx, the Black experience and its agenda remain the foundational topics discussed in rap music. Rap's history, however, does not negate the multicultural participation that has always been present in rap music, particularly in marketing and production.

Rap music is inherently politically and racially charged. In 1988, Public Enemy, the most anthologized Rap group, began publishing lyrics that applied not only to Blacks' historical past but also to contemporary issues concerning the treatment of Blacks by White institutions and the American government. Their second album, *It Takes a Nation of Millions to Hold Us Back*, attacks a range of issues, from the introduction of crack cocaine into Black America to the military. "Black Steel in the Hour of Chaos" criticizes the disproportionate number of Black men in prison, and "Night of the Living Baseheads" relays Chuck D.'s positions on crack and its sale, distribution, and effect on the Black community. Similarly, Brand Nubian's lyrics for "Slow Down," from their 1990 album *One for All*, presents the effects of crack on Black women, and therefore on the **Black family**.

The years 1989–1992 were pivotal in rap music's critique of America's police departments. During this time, N.W.A., Ice-T, and Public Enemy released lyrical content directly addressing police brutality. N.W.A.'s "Fuck the Police" argued against racial profiling, Ice-T.'s "Cop Killer" stated that Blacks should defend themselves when attacked by police, and Public Enemy humorously presented the Black community's belief that contacting 911 in an emergency is "a joke." From local radio shows to members of Congress and the Reagan administration, mainstream America cited N.W.A., Ice-T, and Public Enemy as promoters of violence against police, and argued for a ban of rap music on radio and television. However, since the mid-1980s, Black activists and supporters of the First Amendment have cited documented accounts of police brutality against Blacks across America's urban centers. Their persistence and the lyrics of rap artists collectively relifted the veil shrouding the violence against and within the Black experience by revealing formidable racial realities to the mainstream. Rap's ability to bring local racial conflicts to an international forum, and pose questions regarding the state's relationship with the Black community, have been considered dangerous, having the potential to incite violence, which is also documented. However, in 1989, the Stop the Violence All-Stars, which consisted of KRS-One, Stetsasonic, Kool Moe Dee, MC Lyte, Just-Ice, Doug E. Fresh, Heavy D, Public Enemy, and Ms. Melodie, composed the lyric "Self Destruction," released on a twelve-inch recording. In the song, each rapper presents a resolution to violence, demonstrating that rap music's crafters have always been proactive in nonviolent discourse.

The notion of censoring and/or banning rap music has, for some, remained an important objective. Partisans of such action contend that rap affects America's youth in destructive ways that can influence the decision-making process. In the mid-1990s, C. Delores Tucker and Bob Dole launched an attack on rap's lyrical representation of women, targeting **Tupac Shakur** and Death Row Records. As rap music crossed over into middle-class White America, Eminem became a popular target for censorship.

Because rap music is produced and consumed predominantly by men, one of the central arguments for discarding the First Amendment in what are deemed extreme cases is that its representations of women are inherently subjective. Therefore, it is argued that when fielding and inscribing notions of womanhood, motherhood, rape, and sexuality, any lyrical content produced in such an illusory environment cannot be policed by its male crafters. Regardless of the ebb and flow of femininity in rap's discourse, the discussion has not gone unanswered by Black women, scholars and crafters alike. In both rap lyrics and African American literature, Black women have participated in the dialogue on issues of female representations. Robin Roberts's article "Ladies First: Queen Latifah's Afrocentric Feminist Music Video," examines Dana Owens's feminist approach to her lyrics and narrative. Salt-n-Pepa's 1990 album, *Black's Magic*, not only presents the rhetoric of **Black feminism**, but also represents Black womanhood and sexuality in ways standing in opposition to male-produced lyrics. In "None of Your Business," and "Let's Talk About

Sex," Salt-n-Pepa demand that their sexual preferences and activities remain personal, private, and unavailable for scrutiny by a male-dominated society. In the song "Independent," which appeared on their 1993 album, *Very Necessary*, the group addresses Black womanhood directly, presenting lyrics resisting any show of capitulating their authenticity, autonomy, or agency as Black women. MC Lyte presents a self-portrait of strength, confidence, and youth in her 1989 lyric "Cha Cha Cha," in which she claims to focus on surviving in the music industry despite it being dominated by men. In 1991, Queen Latifah, the most successful female rap artist, released "Ladies First," following up with "U.N.I.T.Y." in 1993. The latter repeatedly asks, "Who you callin' a bitch?" The former argues that women bear "the new generation of prophets, cuz it's ladies first."

Rap's survivability lies not only in the messages it relays, but also in its continued marketability and overwhelming profitability. Rather than banning the music outright, the option to record self-censored versions is popular among record companies housing Eminem, Ludacris, R. Kelley, and Lil' John and the East Side Boyz, who are easy prey for contemporary proponents of censorship. The music industry is unable to ignore rap music's ability to generate massive wealth, and calls to ban and dismantle rap have moved beyond the overt call for censorship into more covert responses, such as rescinding marketing deals and using delays of seven–eight seconds during live televised performances.

By the mid-1990s, as America settled into the realization that Rap music is not a fad, but a mainstay of American music, manifestations of rap were seen and heard throughout the arts. African American literature, the American mainstream, and mass media have been affected by rap music. In the late 1990s, after the murders of Tupac Shakur and the Notorious B.I.G. (Christopher Wallace), rap music, and the contemporary Black experience, generated not only new discourse but also new literary styles and language presented in Black writing. Rap music's language, an outgrowth of African-American **vernacular**, is demonstrated in scholarship, fiction, and poetry written and published by Blacks. Rappers and scholars alike access the language of rap music to argue the Black agenda and present the Black experience. Historically, poets, rap lyricists, and scholars bear these points out.

Poetry written by **Nikki Giovanni, Sonia Sanchez, Amiri Baraka, Carolyn M. Rodgers**, and **Ntozake Shange** are recited in rhythm, sometimes with Afrocentric beats and sounds, a further demonstration of the foundational links between Black poetry and rap music. Additionally, poets from the Black Arts Movement recognize and communicate the origins of rap music by contributing to literary discourse as essayists and cultural theorists, for instance, Giovanni's *Racism 101* and Baraka's "Somebody Blew Up America." Lyricists also publish **essays**, fiction, **autobiography**, and collections of poetry, and not only are a growing population of contributors to African American literature, but also have increased the readership of Black fiction. **Sister Souljah**, rapper-turned-lecturer, penned two novels in the 1990s, *No Disrespect* and *The Coldest Winter Ever*. In 1996 The Last Poets' published *On a Mission: Selected Poems and a History of the Last Poets*. After twenty years in the rap industry as producer, writer, and rapper, KRS-One published a book of essays, *Ruminations* (2003), a historical account of rap music and the relevance of the Black aesthetic to the art form's presentation, organization, and themes.

Increasingly scholars are incorporating rap music into their work, and for some, the music is the basis of their work. **Houston A. Baker, Jr.**'s *Black Studies, Rap, and the Academy* (1993) is one of the first scholarly works to argue that rap music represents an authentic Black experience and therefore should not be discounted in postsecondary **Black Studies** programs. Similarly, **Tricia Rose**'s *Black Noise: Rap Music and Black Culture in Contemporary America* (1994) postulates rap music as intellectual property and work, suggesting that rap is a viable discourse worthy of discussion and study. In *Open Mike: Reflections on Philosophy, Race, Sex, Culture, and Religion* (2002) and *Holler If You Hear Me: Searching for Tupac Shakur* (2001), **Michael Eric Dyson** either peppers the vernacular with the language of rap music or uses the music as the basis for his observations and arguments. Born from students' usage of Black **vernacular** and its relationship to the language of rap music, language diversity is often the subject of pedagogical theory. The discourse's response to students' language rights sometimes employs rap's language as a point of entry into the debate. Keith Gilyard's article "Holdin' It Down" states not only that the Black vernacular, and the experiences that accompany it, must be "demystified," but also that credible "vernacular educational theory" necessitates that the vernacular be understood as "intellectual activity."

Both the language and the themes of rap lyrics and video presentations have a place in the pages of contemporary Black fiction as well, further suggesting that rap music is a significant part of African American literature. Novelists such as **Omar Tyree**, **Terry McMillan**, Carol Taylor, **E. Lynn Harris**, and Jamis L. Dames access the intrasocial themes presented in rap. Topics including gang and police violence, paternity, monogamy, family, dating, homosexuality, and the underground economy are critiqued and framed in rap music. Rapping has bred a new wave of Black poets. Mos Def, Common, Cee-Lo, Jill Scott, and Floetry have successfully converted the art of spoken word, song, and lyricism into poetry and vice versa. The Roots, a Philadelphia rap acoustic band, incorporates the poetry of Ursula Rucker on their CDs, thereby packaging rap, spoken word, and poetry together. Similarly, Jill Scott packages poetry and spoken word with rhythm and blues and jazz. In essence, rap music is an integral part of Black art.

As such, rap music is the catalyst for a new generation of African American literature. From poems, songs, and lyrics to scholarship, literary criticism, and fiction, rap music informs, performs, and reports the Black aesthetic and experience to a global audience. Despite suggestions that rap is derogatory, denigrating, or demonizing, the music is responsible for maintaining an open forum discussion concerning events, social issues, and experiences pertaining to African Americans. Rap's contributions can be seen in African American literature, theater, film, television and marketing, art, politics, and of course music. Additionally, rap music provides a stage for social and racial debates that is heavily accessed by young and/or oppressed people who enter the discourse from diverse cultural environments. As a disseminator of cultural information, the music exports the Black experience throughout the world and imports the cultural experiences of others into the American psyche. Rap music has converted street rhymers into writers, poets, businessmen, and millionaires. Through rap music, myriad youth races, cultures, and languages have been integrated, helping proponents of the genre demonstrate not only the need for multicultural educational and social environments, but also their revenue-generating potential.

Resources: Houston A. Baker, *Black Studies, Rap, and the Academy* (Chicago: University of Chicago Press, 1993); Nelson George, *Hip Hop America* (New York: Penguin, 1999); Keith Gilyard, "Holdin' It Down," in *Rhetoric and Composition as Intellectual Work*, ed. Gary A. Olson (Carbondale: Southern Illinois University Press, 2002), 118–129; Cheryl L. Keyes, *Rap Music and Street Consciousness: Music in American Life* (Urbana: University of Illinois Press, 2002); Alan Light, *The Vibe History of Hip Hop* (New York: Three Rivers Press, 1999); Naughty by Nature, "Hip Hop Horray," by V. Brown, K. Gist, and A. Criss, on *19 Naughty III* (New York: Tommy Boy, 1993); "An Old Boat Song," in *Call and Response: The Riverside Anthology of the African American Literary Tradition*, ed. Patricia Liggins-Hill (Boston: Houghton Mifflin, 1998), 33; William E. Perkins, *Droppin' Science: Critical Essays on Rap Music and Hip Hop Culture* (Philadelphia: Temple University Press, 1996); Public Enemy, "911's a Joke," by W. Drayton, K. Shocklee, and E. Sadler, on *Fear of a Black Planet* (New York: Def Jam, 1989); Robin Roberts, "Ladies First: Queen Latifah's Afrocentric Feminist Music Video," *African American Review* 28, no. 2 (1994), 245–257; Tricia Rose, *Black Noise: Black Music and Culture in Contemporary America* (Middletown, CT: Wesleyan University Press, 1994).

Ellesia Ann Blaque

Rastafarian. A person who believes in the divinity of Haile Selassie I (1892–1975). In Amharic, an Ethiopian language, "Haile Selassie" translates as "Power of the Trinity." Selassie was also known as Tafari Makonnen, formerly Ras, which means, in Amharic, "Head/Duke/Prince" Tafari (Selassie's family name). Selassie was the last emperor of Ethiopia. He was crowned in 1930, deposed in 1974, and died in 1975; in 1992 Rastafarians from all over the world, including the United States, traveled to Ethiopia to celebrate the centenary of the late Emperor's birth. Rastafarianism, then, is a religion linked explicitly to the nation of Ethiopia, which was arguably the only African country to remain untouched by imperial powers at the height of European colonization. More recently it has suffered famines and civil wars. Rastafarianism can also be linked to the "prophetic" words of **Marcus Garvey**, founder of the United Negro Improvement Association. Before he left Jamaica for the United States in 1916, Garvey announced, "Look to Africa for the crowning of a Black King; he shall be the Redeemer" (Barrett, 81).

The crowning of Ras Tafari (Haile Selassie I) as Emperor was an event that attracted many dignitaries, including representatives of the British monarchy. Immediately after his coronation, the awareness of a potentially new era in Black history grew as far away as Jamaica. For example, Garveyites (followers of Garvey) in Kingston, Jamaica, such as Archibald Dunkley and Leonard Howell, became especially animated by the fact that Haile Selassie I referred to himself as "the Conquering Lion of the Tribe of Judah," an allusion to the apocalyptic writings of the New Testament (Revelation 5:5). They were also intrigued by his claim to be a direct descendent of King Solomon and the Queen of Sheba (1 Kings 10). By using an Amharic version of the Bible, first published between 1914 and 1918, these initial devotees went on to shape early Rastafarian belief and behavior. They noted, for example, that the Bible declares the Redeemer's Ethiopian origins: "I will make mention of Rahab and Babylon to them that know me; behold Philistia and Tyre, with Ethiopia; this man was born there" (Psalm 87:4). And again: "Princes shall come out of Egypt; Ethiopia shall soon stretch forth her hands unto God" (Psalm 68:31). On the basis of these and other biblical passages, such as Jeremiah 8:21 and Daniel 7:9, Rastafarians believed, and still believe, in Haile Selassie I's divinity. Basically, Rastafarians claim that Haile Selassie I is Jah (an abbreviated form of Jehovah) Rastafari, the Living God, even the reincarnation of Jesus. Another element of Rastafarian spirituality is the rejection of White dominance, especially in the form of European colonization and postcolonial influence, and the hope of an eventual return to Africa from the evils of the West (Babylon).

While countless early Rastafarians believed this exodus, or "movement of Jah people," was imminent and would be at the hands of the Emperor himself, many now favor rehabilitation. Some are all too aware of Africa's harsh living conditions, and others have heard of the modest success, at best, of Rastafarians who have repatriated. Thus the vast majority of Rastafarians currently reside in the Caribbean and the United States, where they work for the "Africanization" of the West. This Africanization involves, among many things, opposing racism and affirming **Black family** as well as community life. Since the 1960s and 1970s, Rastafarians in the United States have been growing in number (Hepner). One of the main contemporary scholars of Rastafarianism is the sociologist Randal L. Hepner. In an article that appears in perhaps the most comprehensive work on the Rastafarians, "Chanting Down Babylon in the Belly of the Beast" (1998), he draws from media announcements, law-enforcement reports, and his own detailed ethnographic work to show that Rastafarians are thriving in the eastern seaboard's urban centers, such as New York City and Miami, Florida, as well as in **Los Angeles, California**; the **San Francisco Bay Area, California**; **Chicago, Illinois**; and **Houston, Texas**. In these places, he says, Rastafarianism flourishes by crossing the usual lines of social marginalization (class, **race**, ethnicity, **gender**), largely, though by no means exclusively, through the success of **reggae** music, which numerous Rastafarians employ to communicate their convictions.

Rastafarianism attracts many young African Americans because a Black man's divinity provides a belief system that opposes traditional Christianity's perceived reliance upon, and basic support for, White dominance. The lifestyle, including reggae music, helps to identify Rastafarianism as a religion of protest against White capitalist and Christian values; indeed, it is not uncommon to hear Rastafarians speak of "chanting down Babylon," an allusion to undermining Western imperialism. Rastafarians have been depicted as characters in African American literary art. For example, they materialize as spiritual malcontents and dreamers in *The Children of Sisyphus* (1964), written by the Harvard scholar Orlando Patterson. Strongly influenced by the existential dread of Albert Camus's *The Myth of Sisyphus*, Patterson tells the tale of a Rastaman's desire to leave the West, Babylon, and travel to Ethiopia, the Black man's Vine and Fig Tree. More recent fictional treatments include Masani Montague's novel *Dread Culture: A Rastawoman's Story* (1995) and Geoffrey Philp's literary thriller *Benjamin, My Son* (2003). Montague focuses on the experience of a Jamaican family living in urban North America. Through the eyes of Johnnie and his sister Sheba, she addresses the struggle for identity, particularly religious identity, amid the senseless violence that marks inner-city housing projects. Philp updates, even retools, Dante's *Inferno* by centering on Jason Lumley, a Jamaican living in Miami, Florida, who meets a mentor Rastafarian and locksmith named Virgil. The end result is a horrifying vision of hell on earth. Kwame Dawes has edited an anthology of contemporary reggae poetry.

Resources: Leonard E. Barrett, *The Rastafarians: The Dreadlocks of Jamaica* (London: Heinemann, 1977); Barry Chevannes, ed., *Rastafari and Other African-Caribbean Worldviews* (New Brunswick, NJ: Rutgers University Press, 1998); Peter B. Clarke, *Black Paradise: The Rastafarian Movement* (Wellingborough, UK: Acquarian Press, 1986); Kwame Dawes, ed., *Wheel and Come Again: An Anthology of Reggae Poets* (Leeds, UK: Peepal Tree Press, 1998); Randal L. Hepner, "Chanting Down Babylon in the Belly of the Beast: The Rastafarian Movement in the Metropolitan United States," in *Chanting Down Babylon: The Rastafari Reader*, ed. Nathaniel Samuel Murrell et al. (Philadelphia: Temple University Press, 1998), 199–216; William F. Lewis, *Soul Rebels: The Rastafari*, ed. Joan Gregg (Prospect Heights, IL: Waveland Press, 1993); Masani Montague, *Dread Culture: A Rastawoman's Story* (Toronto: Sister Vision Press, 1994); Nathaniel Samuel Murrell, William David Spencer, and Adrian Anthony McFarlane, eds., *Chanting Down Babylon: The Rastafari Reader* (Philadelphia: Temple University Press, 1998); Joseph Owens, *Dread: The Rastafarians of Jamaica* (London: Heinemann, 1976); Orlando Patterson, *Children of Sisyphus* (1964; repr. New York: Addison-Wesley, 1987); Geoffrey Philp, *Benjamin, My Son* (Leeds, UK: Peepal Tree Press, 2003); Velma Pollard, *Dread Talk: The Language of Rastafari* (Kingston: Canoe Press/University of the West Indies, 1994).

Darren J. N. Middleton

Ray, Henrietta Cordelia (c. 1852–1916). Poet and biographer. A prolific African American poet of the nineteenth century, Ray first received national attention when William E. Matthews read her poem "Lincoln" at the dedication of the Freedmen's Monument in **Washington, D.C.**, in 1876. In 1926, **Hallie Quinn Brown** included a selection of Ray's work in *Homespun Heroines* and compared her literary talents and accomplishments with those of **Phillis Wheatley** and **Frances Ellen Watkins Harper**.

Ray was born in New York City into, as Brown describes it, "a family where birth, breeding and culture were regarded as important assets" (172). She was one of the seven children of Charlotte Augusta Burrough and Charles B. Ray, a Congregational minister, distinguished abolitionist, and editor of *The Colored American*. Following in the footsteps of her older sister Charlotte, who became the first African American women to earn a law degree from Howard University in 1872, Henrietta earned a graduate degree in pedagogy from the University of the City of New York in 1891, and is also believed to have attended the Sauvener School of Languages. She was a teacher in New York City public schools for nearly thirty years and continued to instruct small groups of students and teachers in mathematics and the arts well after her retirement.

Ray published many of her poems in periodicals during the last two decades of the nineteenth century and wrote a biography of her father, *Sketches of the Life of Rev. Charles B. Ray*, in 1887 with Florence Ray, the sister with whom she resided on Long Island throughout most of her adult life. She published her first collection of poetry, *Sonnets*, in 1893, and another titled *Poems*, which Brown deemed a testament to "her versatility, love of nature, classical knowledge, delicate fancy, an [*sic*] unaffected piety," in 1910 (175). While Ray's work is often compared with poetry written by Anglo-American women of the nineteenth century, Cheryl Walker points out that "her tributes to Lincoln and to **Paul Laurence Dunbar** prove that she was not insensitive to issues of race" (353). (*See* **Sonnet**.)

Resources: Primary Sources: Henrietta Cordelia Ray: *Lincoln: Written for the Occasion of the Unveiling of the Freedmen's Monument in Memory of Abraham Lincoln: April 14, 1876: By H. Cordelia Ray* (New York: J. J. Little, 1893); *Poems* (New York: Grafton Press, 1910); *Sonnets* (New York: J. J. Little, 1893); Henrietta Cordelia Ray and Florence T. Ray, *Sketches of the Life of Rev. Charles B. Ray* (New York: J. J. Little, 1887). **Secondary Sources:** Hallie Q. Brown, comp., *Homespun Heroines and Other Women of Distinction* (1926; repr. New York: Oxford University Press, 1988), 169–175; Joan Sherman, "Henrietta Cordelia Ray," in her *Invisible Poets: Afro-Americans of the Nineteenth Century*, 2nd ed. (Urbana: University of Illinois Press, 1989), 129–135; Cheryl Walker, "Henrietta Cordelia Ray," in *American Women Poets of the Nineteenth Century: An Anthology* (New Brunswick, NJ: Rutgers University Press, 1992), 352–353.

Kara L. Mollis

Raymond, Linda (born 1952). Novelist. Born and raised in Ohio, Raymond was initially educated as a respiratory therapist and for a long period worked in the neonatal unit of Children's Hospital in San Diego. Although she found the work very rewarding, she also found it emotionally draining. When her marriage involved relocating, she decided to switch careers. After attending American River College and California State University at Sacramento, Raymond earned an M.A. in creative writing from the University of California at Davis. Now a resident of Orangevale, California, where her husband has a veterinary practice, she has drawn on her own medical experiences, as well as on her grandmother's volunteer work in a hospital in Dayton, Ohio, to write her well-received first novel.

For *Rocking the Babies* (1994), Raymond has received an American Book Award, an Honor Award in Fiction from the Black Caucus of the American Library Association, and a Bay Area Award in Fiction. The film rights to the novel were acquired by the well-known producer Jerry Bruckheimer.

The novel focuses on two middle-aged women who do volunteer work in the neonatal unit of a hospital. The women could not be more different, and initially dislike one another. Nettie Lee Johnson is raising her grandson. With a rather hardscrabble background and a large extended family, she is outgoing and very down to earth. Martha Howard is a retired librarian with few close relations and a narrow circle of friends. Her work at the hospital is one of her major social outlets. Very reserved and very concerned with propriety, she initially regards Nettie Lee's amicable overtures as an affront. But one of the main duties of the volunteers is to rock the babies, and while engaged in this, the women cannot help but talk. Beyond the immediate story lines involving several of the infants in the unit, the women's reminiscences provide a colloquial but penetrating perspective on African American history and culture over much of the twentieth century. The novel provides a very direct demonstration of the power of a shared cultural heritage to bridge the gaps among African Americans of different social and economic classes.

At this writing, Raymond is working on a second novel, tentatively titled *Catalpa*, in which the central character is a woman of mixed race.

Resources: Debra Dennis, "Mothers Get a Second Chance Caring for Children's Children," *Cleveland Plain-Dealer*, Oct. 3, 1994, p. E6; Drew Limsky, "Fiction: *Rocking the Babies*," *Washington Post Book World*, Dec. 25, 1994, p. X6; Teresa Moore, "Trading Tales: Family Stories Bridge the Gap Between Two Different Women," *San Francisco Chronicle*, Jan. 15, 1995, p. 8; Linda Raymond, *Rocking the Babies* (New York: Viking, 1994).

Martin Kich

Realism. Mode of literature. Realism emerged in American literature as a reaction against romanticism (Abrams). Although critics do not agree on the exact time period in which realism flourished, they more or less agree that American realism arose between 1860 and 1914 and that **Mark Twain**, Williams Dean Howells, and Henry James are among its most important representative authors (McQuade). The distinction between realism and romanticism lies primarily in their portrayal of life and their treatment of fictional characters. Romanticism often emphasizes fantasy, yearning, dreams, nostalgia, sentiment, ecstatic states, alternate modes of reality, and escape, as evidenced in the poetry of such British poets as William Blake, William Wordsworth, John Keats, and Percy Bysshe Shelley, as well as of the American poet Henry Wadsworth Longfellow. By contrast, works in the realist mode create a different impression. (It is important to note that both romantic and realist works are composed of language which is at least once removed from "reality.") Works of realism create the effect of a factual, detailed, sometimes photographic, even gritty, representation, and they tend to focus on real-life situations and on characters with plausible personalities and motives who must confront believable ethical and moral choices. The diction of prose in the realist mode often includes colloquial speech or the **vernacular**, and the overt use of symbolism is rare.

One key work considered to be part of American Realism is Mark Twain's *The Adventures of Huckleberry Finn* (1885). Through the use of vivid imagery and the colloquial language of Huck, the narrator, Twain relates the adventures of Jim, the African American slave, and Huckleberry Finn as they float on a raft along the Mississippi River, each attempting to escape abuse, while learning about themselves, one another, and the world around them.

Charles Waddell Chesnutt is considered an important African American writer in the tradition of realism. His novel *The Conjure Woman* puts the White narrator and his wife in conflict with an African American **trickster/folklorist** named Uncle Julius. Chesnutt's short story "The Wife of His Youth" features a very light-skinned **mulatto** leader of the elitist Blue Vein Society. After years of separation from her, he acknowledges his dark-skinned plantation wife, thus triumphing over his prejudices. **James Weldon Johnson**'s novel *Autobiography of an Ex-Colored Man* (1912) is also written in the tradition of realism. Johnson uses the novel to explore the issue of **race** and identity of the African American.

Realism is vividly evident in the novel *Invisible Man* (1952) by **Ralph Ellison**, even though in other respects the novel is considered to be an excellent example of **Modernism**. In this novel, Ellison portrays the African American as "invisible" to White society. He also represents the anger and insignificance felt by African Americans, and therefore he represents psychological realism. Thus, works of literature written well after the era of realism (1860–1914) may still draw on elements of the realist literary mode.

The short stories and novels of **Zora Neale Hurston**, including *Their Eyes Were Watching God* (1937), come out of a realist tradition, use the vernacular, and focus on the predicaments of working-class African American women and men.

Langston Hughes's poetry often springs from a straightforward, accessible realist mode and concerns itself with the lives and situations of ordinary people. His novel *Not Without Laughter* (1930) is clearly in the realist mode, relating the **coming-of-age** of a young African American man in the Midwest. His poem "Mother to Son" (1922) concerns a life lesson a mother is relating to her son. She tells him that regardless of the troubles he encounters in life, he must continue to persevere in the face of social adversity. Hughes's poem "I, Too" (1925) uses a realistic analogy, placing the issue of racial equality in the context of a family in which the narrator is "the darker brother" who must "Eat in the kitchen." In the poem "Middle Passage," **Robert Hayden** recreates the history of Africans being brought to America aboard slave ships. Hayden's use of language includes names of slave ships, lyrics to "Trinity Hymnal #497," and vocabulary from the vernacular. His realistic portrayal elicits a deep, disturbing connection with the Africans on the ships, effectively juxtaposing the readers' consciousness with the experiences of the Africans during their journey through the historic **Middle Passage**. Similarly, **Arna Bontemps**, in the poem "Southern Mansion," implicitly suggests not only that **slavery** and its oppression of African Americans was cruel when it occurred but also that forms of African American enslavement and oppression persist. From Charles Chesnutt and James Weldon Johnson through Zora Neale Hurston, Langston Hughes, Arna Bontemps, Robert Hayden, and African American writers of today, realism remains a useful mode of literature.

Resources: M. H. Abrams, *A Glossary of Literary Terms*, 7th ed. (Fort Worth, TX: Harcourt Brace, 1999), 260–261; Russell Ames, "Social Realism in Charles W. Chesnutt," *Phylon* 14, no. 2 (Spring 1953), 199–206; Arna Bontemps, "Southern Mansion," in *American Negro Poetry: An Anthology*, ed. Bontemps (1963; repr. New York: Hill and Wang, 1995), 80; Charles W. Chesnutt, *The Conjure Woman* (Durham, NC: Duke University Press, 1993); Ralph Ellison, *Invisible Man* (1952; repr. New York: Random House, 1995); Henry Louis Gates, Jr., and Nellie Y. McKay, eds., *The Norton Anthology of African American Literature* (New York: Norton, 1996); Robert Hayden, *Collected Poems*, ed. Frederick Glaysher (New York: Liveright, 1996); Langston Hughes: "Mother to Son" and "I, Too," in *The Collected Poems of Langston Hughes*, ed. Arnold Rampersad (New York: Vintage Classics, 1994); *Not Without Laughter* (New York: Knopf, 1930); Zora Neal Hurston, *Their Eyes Were Watching God* (1937; repr. New York: HarperCollins, 1969); James Weldon Johnson, *The Autobiography of an Ex-Colored Man* (1912; repr. New York: Dover, 1995); Donald McQuade et al., eds., *The Harper Single Volume American Literature*, 3rd ed. (New York: Longman, 1999), 1354–2086; Mark Twain, *The Adventures of Huckleberry Finn* (1885; repr. New York: Pocket Books, 1973).

DaNean Pound

Reconstruction. The historical Reconstruction was a period of twelve years between the end of the American **Civil War** (in 1865) and 1877. A crucial cause of the Civil War had been the question of chattel **slavery** in **the South**. The industrial North, for economic and moral reasons, wished to see human bondage come to an end, while the agrarian South viewed the imminent end of slavery as a potentially devastating blow to its economic life. African American leaders such as **Frederick Douglass** and **Martin R. Delany**, seeing in the Civil War the most promising opportunity yet to release their people from bondage, urged President Abraham Lincoln to allow **Negro** men to enlist in the Union Army. These first Black Civil War soldiers acquitted themselves valiantly, thus encouraging the President to involve more of them after the Emancipation Proclamation in 1863. With the Confederate surrender at Appotomax Courthouse in 1865, Negro slavery in the United States effectively came to an end. The Thirteenth Amendment to the Constitution was ratified in that year, and the end of slavery was formalized. Subsequently, the Fourteenth Amendment of 1868 gave the Negroes equal rights before the law, and the Fifteen Amendment of 1870 extended voting rights to Negro men.

But to the extent that Reconstruction (formally authorized by an act of Congress in 1867) was a program of affirmation for Negro human rights in the United States, it started long before the cessation of hostilities. During the war, many volunteers from the North, both White and Black, headed south to undertake relief duties on the battleground and minister to the needs of the emancipated former slaves. When the Freedmen's Bureau (also enacted by Congress in 1867) established schools for the emancipated slaves and hospitals for soldiers, these volunteers from the North served as teachers and nurses.

But the twelve years of Reconstruction was a period that Southern Whites viewed as a continuation of the North's humiliation of them. After the war, Union troops stayed on in the South to enforce the victors' agenda, an important part of which was to ensure that the postwar constitutional amendments would be implemented. However, the Southern Whites accused the North of imposing Negro and carpetbagger rule on them, and did whatever they could to circumvent the provisions of the amendments regarding Negroes. In the presidential election of 1872, the Democrats showed more strength than the ruling Republicans had anticipated. Although President Ulysses Grant was reelected with a comfortable electoral majority, the strong performance of the Democrats forced the government to rethink its commitment to Reconstruction programs in the South. Thus, a gradual easing of legal protections for Blacks became evident. In assertive defiance of the Fourteenth Amendment, the Ku Klux Klan, constituted in 1866, turned the daily lives of Blacks into a living nightmare. (See **Lynching**.)

This situation was exacerbated in 1876 when President Grant chose not to run for reelection. His eight-year government had survived several charges of corruption, and he and his team were ready to let another group take over leadership. Thus, Rutherford B. Hayes became the Republican Party's presidential nominee to oppose the Democrat Samuel J. Tilden. The Hayes-Tilden contest was so close that Congress had to appoint a commission to determine the winner of the presidency. Hayes won the election by one electoral vote amid Democratic threats to filibuster the new government's legislative program. Compromise became inevitable. And since the Democrats' most important source of disenchantment was the presence of Union troops in the South, the President withdrew the troops in 1877 and thus effectively brought Reconstruction to its end. In an 1877 address in **Atlanta, Georgia**, to the freedmen, President Hayes justified the end of Reconstruction by saying that the Southern Whites would respect Negro interests and rights if the Southern states were "let alone" by the federal government. Henceforward, the expression "let alone" became a mantra of Southern Whites' sense of victory in their fight against Black interests.

But the end of Reconstruction was just one of the sources of hardship for the former slaves. For while Reconstruction had mitigated somewhat the harsher realities of Southern racism against the Negro, many of the pledges the Union government had made to the Negroes had not been fulfilled. For instance, the promise that former slave families would each receive forty acres of land and a mule had not been kept in spite of the fact that the government had adequate land for the purpose. Thus denied a modicum of economic independence and subject to the hostile whims of Southern Whites, the Blacks had little choice but to acquiesce in their systematic exploitation and impoverishment by White farmers. Ostensibly a system of contractually ceding a measure of economic independence to Blacks, sharecropping actually impoverished them further. The lien system was especially exploitative because it mortgaged the Black tenants' produce in advance of growth, and thus turned them into poorly compensated laborers masquerading as independent farmers. "It's owed before it's growed," lamented the sharecroppers. In other words, Reconstruction had started and ended with the Blacks still experiencing what Frederick Douglass graphically characterized thus (1882): the Negro, "though no longer a slave, [was] in a thralldom grievous and intolerable, compelled to work for whatever his employer was pleased to pay him, swindled out of his hard earnings by money orders redeemed in stores, compelled to pay the price of an acre of ground for its use during a single year, to pay four times more than a fair price for a pound of bacon and to be kept upon the narrowest margin between life and starvation" (*Life and Times of Frederick Douglass*, quoted in *Digital History*).

Formal reversals of Black civil rights legislation did not ensue soon after the end of Reconstruction since, to the White Southerner, the Blacks seemed defenseless enough as it was. Yet, in spite of the harassment and violence to which they were invariably subject, Blacks continued efforts to exercise their voting rights until the 1890s, when specific steps were taken by the Southern state governments to limit this suffrage. Led by Mississippi with its "understanding" clauses—whereby one voted only if one could read the constitution, or understand it when it was read—and Louisiana with its "grandfather clause"—only those could vote whose fathers had made the voting rolls in 1867—Southern states commenced to systematically legislate the Fifteenth Amendment off their statute books. The 1896 U.S. Supreme Court landmark decision of *Plessy v. Ferguson* made clear that in their campaign against Black civil rights, the Southern Whites were not acting alone but had the tacit support of the rest of the country. In that case, Homer Plessy of Louisiana contested the state's law that imposed racially segregated accommodations on public conveyances. The Supreme Court ruled against Plessy, asserting, in effect, that the colored was socially inferior to the White, and the nation's constitution was powerless to change that situation.

This combination of legislated and "understood" hostility toward the Negro in the South was responsible for migrations of Blacks to the northern and western cities of the United States in search of livable conditions. Frederick Douglass saw the migrations as a sign that the U.S. citizenship of the Black person was still in question. The government, he argued, should guarantee Black citizens legal protection in the South as well in the North and in the West. (*See* **Great Migration**.)

This was the sort of soil in which postbellum African American literature would be sowed. Although with the end of slavery the **Abolitionist Movement** had ceased to exist, the **slave narrative** continued to thrive in the postbellum years. But the challenge for postbellum African American literature was how to continue developing into genres other than the preponderantly biographical slave narrative. A number of writers produced representative works between the years of Reconstruction and the **Harlem Renaissance**. Some of these writers took advantage of what was generally known as the Black press to publish their works, but others were able, in spite of the difficulties engendered by racial discrimination, to find outlets for their work in the predominantly White-owned press. These writers included **Frances Ellen Watkins Harper, Charles Waddell Chesnutt, Paul Laurence Dunbar, W.E.B. Du Bois, Booker T. Washington**, and **James Weldon Johnson**. The struggles of Chesnutt and Dunbar to achieve published status best exemplify the publication ambiance in which Reconstruction and post-Reconstruction Black writers first found accommodation. Chesnutt crawled his way over what he called the "entering wedge" by initially writing in the somewhat apolitical plantation mode popularized by such White writers as Joel Chandler Harris. With the help of well-meaning and supportive White friends, Dunbar used borrowed funds in the printing of his first work of poetry (1893) before worming his way into the graces of some prominent White critics who would judge that he was able to "feel Negro Life Aesthetically" and "express it lyrically," and help him have his later works published by some of the best firms available.

Resources: James S. Allen, *Reconstruction: The Battle for Democracy 1865–1876* (New York: International Publishers, 1937); William L. Andrews, *The Literary Career of Charles Chesnutt* (Baton Rouge: Louisiana State University Press, 1980); Sean Dennis Cashman, *America in the Gilded Age: From the Death of Lincoln to the Rise of Theodore Roosevelt* (New York: New York University Press, 1984); Frederick Douglass, *Life and Times of Frederick Douglass* (Hartford, CT: Park, 1881), quoted in *Digital History*, http://www.digitalhistory.uh.edu/black_voices/voices_display.cfm?id=86; John E. Findling and Frank W. Thackeray, eds., *Events That Changed America in the Nineteenth Century* (Westport, CT: Greenwood Press, 1997); John Hope Franklin, *Reconstruction After the Civil War*, 2nd ed. (Chicago: University of Press, 1994); William Dean Howells, "Introduction to Lyrics of Lowly Life," in *William Dean Howells as Critic*, ed. Edwin H. Cady (Boston: Routledge & Kegan Paul, 1973); John White, ed., *Reconstruction After the Civil War: Seminar Studies in History* (London: Longman, 1977).

Mzenga Aggrey Wanyama

Redbone Press (1995–present). Publishing house. Lisa C. Moore is the chief editor at Redbone Press, which is the only Black lesbian publishing house in the United States. Although Moore did not originally intend to start a publishing house, that was the end result of her attempts to publish an anthology of Black lesbian "coming-out" stories, *Does Your Mama Know?*, in 1995. Moore, who holds bachelor's degrees in both accounting and journalism, had previously worked for *HealthQuest* magazine and the *Atlanta Journal-Constitution*, as an editorial assistant and copy editor, respectively. Assembling the anthology was an endeavor undertaken while working three part-time jobs to pay contributors. After assembling the anthology, composed of forty-nine accounts of Black lesbians coming to terms with their sexuality, Moore quickly realized that self-publishing the book would be the best way to preserve the integrity of the collection's message. After raising the money herself, she ordered a first run of 3,000 copies.

Moore pounded the pavement, networking with Black bookstores, gay bookstores, and Black lesbian organizations. She also set up readings throughout the country where anthology contributors lived, and sent hundreds of review copies to alternative media outlets. Her hard work paid off. The first print run sold out in six months. In the ensuing years, *Does Your Mama Know?* garnered two Lambda Literary Awards, for Small Press and for Lesbian Studies, and more than 8,000 copies are currently in print. The Lambda Awards not only increased the book's visibility but also led to Redbone Press acquiring a distributor.

Redbone Press's second title was released in 1998. *The bull-jean stories*, by **Sharon Bridgforth**, is a collection of short stories that chronicles the life and loves of a Black bulldagger in the 1920s ("bulldagger" is an African American **slang** term referring to a lesbian with what are thought to be masculine characteristics). Bridgforth's book met with success and has been released both as a paperback and as an audio book. *The bull-jean stories* received the 1998 Lambda Literary Award for Best Small Press Book and was nominated by the American Library Association for the Gay/Lesbian Book Award. With more than 4,000 copies in print, *The bull-jean stories* has been excerpted in *Girlfriends* magazine.

In September 2002, Redbone Press faced a serious setback when fire consumed Moore's apartment and destroyed most of the press's records. With the help of the Black gay and lesbian community, Moore has been able to rebuild much of what was lost. Though there have been setbacks, Redbone Press hopes to publish two to three fiction, nonfiction, and poetry titles a year. At this writing, an anthology titled *Spirited* is in the works; it will be a collection of essays by Black gay men and women on religion and spirituality, and how the two intersect with the lives of the Black gay community.

Resources: Sharon Bridgforth, *The bull-jean stories* (Austin, TX: Redbone Press, 1998); Lisa Moore, ed., *Does Your Mama Know?* (Decatur, GA: Redbone Press, 1997).

Roxane Gay

Redding, J. Saunders (1906–1988). Scholar, novelist, journalist, critic, historian, and essayist. Redding was born in Wilmington, Delaware, to a middle-class family that valued education highly. After a year at Lincoln

University, he transferred to Brown University. Years later, Redding would become the first African American professor at an Ivy League school, teaching at Brown in 1949. Shortly after graduation, by his own account not yet a fully formed writer, Redding taught at Morehouse College for three years, until he was fired for alleged radicalism. Throughout his life, Redding remained an integrationist, revering **W.E.B. Du Bois**'s stance on race in America and rejecting the school of thought, associated with **Booker T. Washington**, that called for separate African American institutions and universities. The idea of maintaining the status quo by creating a parallel society for the Blacks of America troubled Redding. His stance on being Black in the United States was multifaceted: he was well aware of the double standards and contradictions among Blacks and Whites, but he insisted that he considered himself an American writer above all else.

Redding's first book, *To Make a Poet Black* (1939), was an ambitious "history of **Negro** thought in America" (vii). This book would later help him secure a Rockefeller Foundation grant to "go out into Negro life in the South" and write on his experiences. This would later become his best-known work, *No Day of Triumph* (1942). His writing is neither obviously White nor Black but occupies a formal middle ground. In the following decades Redding stayed in academia, publishing his only novel, *Stranger and Alone*, in 1950. This novel, more critically acclaimed than commercially successful, tells the story of Shelton Howden, born to a Black mother and a White father, who refuses to deal with his own **race** and trades his heritage for career success.

Most of Redding's works were out of print until the rise of Black scholarship in the early 1960s. Redding was offered several chairs at respected universities, and eventually taught at Cornell. As Faith Berry notes in her introduction to *A Scholar's Conscience*, however, the "radical" integrationist of the 1930s was now considered conservative by his students (9). Redding rejected the **Black Arts Movement** and other forms of what he considered isolationism, provoking criticism from **Amiri Baraka**. Redding never changed his position, though some have argued that he never fully took a stand. In his life and in his prose, he always kept the distance of the scholar, the observer. He revered Du Bois but never claimed the center stage for himself. Redding remains, however, one of the clearest and sharpest nonfiction voices in contemporary African American literature.

Resources: Faith Berry, ed., *A Scholar's Conscience: Selected Writings of J. Saunders Redding, 1942–1977* (Lexington: University Press of Kentucky, 1992); Arthur P. Davis and J. Saunders Redding, eds., *Cavalcade: Negro American Writing from 1760 to the Present* (Boston: Houghton Mifflin, 1971); J. Saunders Redding: *The Lonesome Road: The Story of the Negro's Part in America* (Garden City, NY: Doubleday, 1958); *No Day of Triumph* (New York: Harper & Brothers, 1942); *On Being Negro in America* (New York: Bantam Books, 1964); *Stranger and Alone: A Novel* (Boston: Northeastern University Press, 1989); *They Came in Chains*, rev. ed. (Philadelphia: Lippincott, 1973); *To Make a Poet Black* (College Park, MD: McGrath, 1968).

Ryan Chapman

Redmond, Eugene B. (born 1937). Poet, journalist, and playwright. An extremely versatile writer, Redmond grew up in East St. Louis, Illinois. He got his start as a writer, in part, by working on his high school newspaper and penning songs for local doo-wop groups (Pettis, 275). Serving as a Marine from 1958 to 1961 enabled him to spend time in the Far East and learn spoken Japanese. Redmond next studied at Southern Illinois University, where he earned his B.A. in English literature in 1964. By 1966, he had completed his M.A. in English literature at Washington University. Redmond cofounded *The Monitor*, an East St. Louis weekly, in 1963, and held various editorial positions at the paper over a period of seven years (Pettis, 275). His dramatic talents came to the fore in 1967, when he began working alongside **Katherine Dunham** at Southern Illinois University's Performing Arts Training Center.

That same year Redmond met the African American writer-poet **Henry Dumas,** who at the time was poet-in-residence and director of language workshops for the university's Experiment in Higher Education Program. Dumas's mythic, Afrocentric fiction and his zeal for community outreach had a lifelong impact on Redmond. During the ten months that Dumas lived in East St. Louis, he and Redmond socialized often and frequented poetry readings in the city. After Dumas's death in 1968, Redmond became literary executor of his estate and a tireless promoter of Dumas's work.

At the same time, he devoted considerable energy to his own creative endeavors. Redmond published his first book of poems, *Sentry of the Four Golden Pillars*, in 1970, under the imprint of Black River Writers Press, a company he founded with Dumas and Sherman Fowler. In all, Redmond published five books of poetry during the 1970s, as well as *Drumvoices: The Mission of Afro-American Poetry. A Critical History* (1976), an ambitious chronicle of the African American poetic tradition from 1746 to 1976. The year *Drumvoices* was published, Redmond was named Poet Laureate of East St. Louis. Redmond's work reflects the political and cultural tumult of the 1960s in its focus on Black consciousness and in its many allusions to **jazz**, **spirituals**, and the **blues**, though many of his poems deal with more personal life themes. After two decades of teaching and performing poetry throughout the United States and abroad, Redmond returned to East St. Louis in 1990. He teaches English at Southern Illinois University and edits the multicultural magazine *Drumvoices Revue*.

Resources: Primary Sources: Eugene Redmond: "The Ancient and Recent Voices Within Henry Dumas," introduction to *Goodbye, Sweetwater: New and Selected Stories*, ed. Eugene Redmond (New York: Thunder's Mouth Press, 1988), xi–xx; *Drumvoices: The Mission of Afro-American Poetry. A Critical History* (Garden City, NY: Anchor, 1976); *The Eye in the Ceiling: Selected Poems* (New York: Harlem River Press, 1991); *In a Time of Rain and Desire: New Love Poems* (East St. Louis, IL: Black River Writers, 1973); *River of Bones and Flesh and Blood* (East St. Louis, IL: Black River Writers, 1971); *Sentry of the Four Golden Pillars* (East St. Louis, IL: Black River Writers, 1970). **Secondary Sources:** Joyce Pettis, "Eugene Redmond," in *Dictionary of Literary Biography*, vol. 41, *Afro-American Poets Since 1955*, ed. Trudier Harris and Thadious M. Davis (Detroit: Gale, 1985), 274–281; "Eugene Redmond," in *Contemporary Authors Online*, http://galenet.galegroup.com/servlet/BioRC.

Stacy Torian

Reed, Ishmael (born 1938). Novelist, short story writer, poet, essayist, dramatist, editor, and publisher. One of the most innovative, controversial, and prolific literary figures of his era, Reed describes himself in a 1968 interview as a literary "anarchist" (Sheppard, 6), one who aims to challenge Western literary conventions as well as the African American **literary canon**. Satiric in temperament and experimental in practice, Reed has little regard for many established literary conventions and seeks to create an alternative Black aesthetic (which he calls "neoamerican hoodooism") that relies on ancient African rituals such as **conjuring**, magic, and **voodoo** to counter dominant Western influences and to foster a multicultural consciousness in U.S. society. Although versatile and prolific, Reed is best known for his **postmodernist** novels, which satirize and parody the fundamental style of African American narrative, from the confessional mode of **slave narratives** to the modern autobiographical fiction of **Richard Wright**, **Zora Neale Hurston**, **James Baldwin**, and **Ralph Ellison**. As editor and publisher, Reed cofounded the Yardbird Publishing Company (1971), Reed, Cannon, and Johnson Communications (1973), and the Before Columbus Foundation (1976), all of which have promoted and helped to define U.S. multicultural literature. Since 1980, the Before Columbus Foundation has sponsored the American Book Awards, which have drawn considerable attention to outstanding texts of U.S. multiethnic literature.

Ishmael Scott Reed was born in Chattanooga, Tennessee, to Henry Lenoir and Thelma Coleman on February 22, 1938. His surname comes from his stepfather, Bennie Stephen Reed, an autoworker. In 1942, Reed moved with his mother to Buffalo, New York, where he grew up and attended public schools. From 1956 to 1960, he was enrolled in the University of Buffalo (now the State University of New York at Buffalo), but financial difficulties forced him to drop out without a degree (Boyer). In 1962, he moved to New York City to begin his career as writer and editor. In 1967, the same year his first novel, *The Free-lance Pallbearers*, was published, he moved to Berkeley, California, and took up a teaching position in the University of California. Although the University of California at Berkeley denied him tenure in 1977, Reed has continued to teach there. In 1979, he moved to a working-class neighborhood in Oakland. He also has taught at the University of Washington, the State University of New York at Buffalo, Columbia, Yale, Dartmouth, Harvard, and the University of California at Santa Barbara. Reed's prolific literary accomplishments (nine novels, five volumes of poetry, five collections of essays, four plays, and numerous edited volumes and articles on various subjects) have been widely recognized. Notable accolades include two nominations for the National Book Award (for *Mumbo Jumbo* and *Conjure*) and one for a Pulitzer Prize (for *Conjure*), a Guggenheim Memorial Foundation Award, a Rosenthal Foundation Award, and a Pushcart Award.

Critics have been generous in praising Reed's satiric talent and achievements. Robert Scholes, for example, has called him "a black Juvenal," comparing him to the great Roman satirist (2). Indeed, Reed is a rarity among satirists in that he satirizes not only the material conditions of society but also the discursive conventions that portray them. In *The Free-lance Pallbearers*, he burlesques the traditional confessional style of African American narrative through Bukka Doopeyduk's search for selfhood in a corrupt, cannibalistic society called Harry Sam. *Yellow Back Radio Broke-Down* (1969), his second novel, explores the themes of social strife. In *Mumbo Jumbo* (1972), his most successful novel, and *The Last Days of Louisiana Red* (1974), Reed creates a mythic hoodoo (voodoo) detective called Papa LaBas, who attempts to counter Judeo-Christian influences in African American life by "neoamerican hoodooism." The neoamerican hoodooism seeks to recast ancient Egyptian myths and West Indian magic and blend them. Set in **Harlem, New York**, and **New Orleans, Louisiana**, during the 1920s, *Mumbo Jumbo* depicts the conflict between two opposing forces of American society: Jes Grew, a spontaneous outburst of Black artistic energy in the form of dance, and Wallflower Order, embodiment of the Atonist faith that underlies White rationalism. *The Last Days of Louisiana Red* is set in Berkeley, California, and narrates the investigation of the murder of Ed Yellings, by Papa LaBas, who uses voodoo to cure

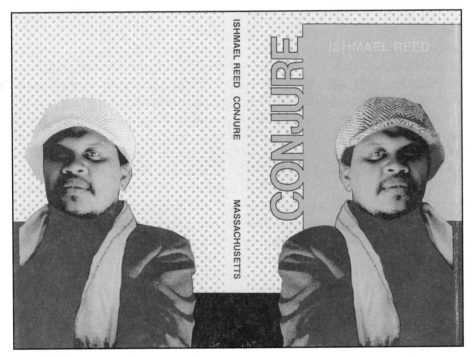

Front and back cover of Ishmael Reed's novel *Conjure*, 1972. Yale Collection of American Literature, Beinecke Rare Book and Manuscript Library.

Louisiana Red of a mental condition that causes conflicts within the African American community. However, it is the subplot about the Moochers (his name for radical Black feminists) that has drawn fiery outrage: **feminist** writers and critics vehemently deny Papa LaBas's charge that Black women conspire with the White establishment to hold Black men down.

In his later novels, Reed moves away from his "neoamerican hoodooism" and focuses on sociopolitical satire. Set in the **Civil War**, *Flight to Canada* (1976) satirizes both the traditional **slave narrative** and abolitionist-inspired novels (particularly **Harriet Beecher Stowe**'s *Uncle Tom's Cabin*) with a deliberate, playful anachronism: jumbo jets and television alongside Abraham Lincoln and Robert E. Lee frame runaway slave Raven Quickskill's escape to Canada. Reed's twin novels on social and racial politics, *The Terrible Twos* (1982) and *The Terrible Threes* (1989), take aim at the Reagan era cultural conservatism and rampant commercialism. Both rework Charles Dickens's *A Christmas Carol* to showcase the glaring disparity between the extravagance of the rich and the dire condition of the poor. In *The Terrible Twos*, President Clift (a former model turned president) is representative of a social elite supported by new money and unconcerned about the well-being of the working classes. In *The Terrible Threes*, Reed's indictment of capitalism's greed and callousness turns into a condemnation of the Neo-Nazi mentality of the government that conspires to purge the country of its "unwanted" citizens with nuclear weapons. Reed's two other novels, *Reckless Eyeballing* (1986) and *Japanese by Spring* (1993), deal with literary and academic politics. *Reckless Eyeballing* depicts a conspiracy between White male publishers and Black female writers to perpetuate racist stereotypes of Black men as rapists and muggers in literature. The novel is a variation, then, of the subplot of *The Last Days of Louisiana Red*. *Japanese by Spring* satirizes an opportunistic Black academic who, in an effort to gain tenure at his predominantly White institution, speaks out against affirmative action and multiculturalism.

Like his fiction, Reed's poetry demonstrates his preoccupation with developing an alternative aesthetic and fighting against the social, political, and economic injustices of U.S. society. Major collections include *catechism of d neoamerican hoodoo church: poems* (1970), *Conjure: Selected Poems, 1963–1970* (1972), *Chattanooga: Poems* (1973), *A Secretary to the Spirits* (1978), and *New and Collected Poems* (1988). In *catechism*, Reed shows a strong preference for the lowercase (as reflected in the title of the collection), omission of vowels and punctuation, and the use of typographical shorthand such as the slash and the ampersand in lieu of words, a practice that befits his agenda of challenging the dominant Judeo-Christian influence through neo-American hoodooism. *Conjure*, which includes most of the poems in *catechism*, is more varied in subject matter and typographical format. However, Reed continues to promote neo-American hoodooism (for example, in "For Cardinal Spellman Who Hated Voo Doo" and "New-HooDoo Manifesto") and to satirize the misdeeds of the capitalist "monster," the military-industrial complex. *Chattanooga*, Reed's most personal collection, explores the historical significance of the city of his birth as he imbues it with personal memory and reflection. In *A Secretary to the Spirits*, Reed adds a visual dimension to his multicultural aesthetic by incorporating Betye Saar's Egyptian collage illustrations, which complement Reed's verbal message. *New and Collected Poems* demonstrates Reed's broadened scope and vision. In "Points of View," the section containing his new poems, his subject matter includes the U.S. invasion of Grenada, a California earthquake, the British royal family, the Ayatollah Khomeini, and Jesus.

Reed's major collections of essays include *Shrovetide in Old New Orleans* (1978), *God Made Alaska for the Indians* (1982), *Writin' Is Fightin': Thirty-seven Years of Boxing on Paper* (1988), *Airing Dirty Laundry* (1993), and *Another Day at the Front: Dispatches from the Race War* (2003). Selections from these books appear in *The Reed Reader* (2000). His essays are often marked by a contentious style and complement his exploration of multicultural themes in his novels and poetry. (*See* **Black Arts Movement; San Francsico Bay Area, California.**)

Resources: Primary Sources: Ishmael Reed: *Another Day at the Front: Dispatches from the Race War* (New York: Basic Books, 2003); *Blues City: A Walk in Oakland* (New York: Crown, 2003); *Flight to Canada* (1976; repr. New York: Scribner's, 1998); *The Free-lance Pallbearers* (1967; repr. Normal, IL: Dalkey Archive, 1999); *Japanese by Spring* (1993; repr. New York: Penguin, 1996); *The Last Days of Lousiana Red* (1974; repr. New York: Harper, 1983); *Mumbo Jumbo* (1972; repr. New York: Scribner's, 1996); *Reckless Eyeballing* (1986; repr. Normal, IL: Dalkey Archive Press, 2000); *The Reed Reader* (New York: Perseus, 2000); *The Terrible Threes* (New York: Atheneum, 1989); *The Terrible Twos* (1982; repr. Normal, IL: Dalkey Archive Press, 1999). **Secondary Sources:** Jay Boyer, *Ishmael Reed* (Boise, ID: Boise State University Press, 1993); Bruce Dick and Amritjit Singh, eds., *Conversations with Ishmael Reed* (Jackson: University Press of Mississippi, 1995); Bruce Dick and Pavel Zemliansky, eds., *The Critical Response to Ishmael Reed* (Westport, CT: Greenwood Press, 1999); John Domini, "Ishmael Reed: A Conversation with John Domini," *American Poetry Review* 7, no. 1 (1978), 32–36, repr. in Dick and Singh, pp. 128–143; Henry Louis Gates, Jr., "The 'Blackness of Blackness': A Critique of the Sign and the Signifying Monkey," *Critical Inquiry* 9 (1983), 685–723; "Ishmael Reed," in *African American Writers*, ed. Lea Baecher and A. Walton Litz (New York: Scribner's, 1991), 361–377; Robert Scholes, "Review of *The Last Days of Louisiana Red*," *New York Times Book Review*, Nov. 10, 1974, p. 2; Elizabeth A. Settle and Thomas A. Settle, *Ishmael Reed: A Primary and Secondary Bibliography* (Boston: G. K. Hall, 1982); Walt Sheppard, "When State Magicians Fail: An Interview with Ishmael Reed," *Nickel Review* (28 Aug.–10 Sept. 1968), 72–75; Shamoon Zamir, "An Interview with Ishmael Reed," *Callaloo* 17 (1994), 1131–1157, repr. in Dick and Singh, pp. 271–302.

Wenxin Li

Reggae. Type of music. Reggae is a distinctive form of Caribbean music, developed in the 1960s by artists interested in blending Jamaican folk music and African American rhythm and blues (R&B). However, deeper sources of reggae lie in numerous Jamaican musical styles, such as mento, ska, and rock steady, which are united, for the most part, by the use of complex percussive arrangements, recurring guitar plucks, pounding bass effects, and song lyrics that are often political (Kaslow). Popular in the 1940s, mento performers fused African musical traditions with calypso music from the island of Trinidad, creating a hybrid sound that remained fashionable well into the 1950s, when it was replaced by ska, a more upbeat genre. Ska represented a musical merger of mento, American R&B, and the **jazz** of **New Orleans, Louisiana**. Jamaicans, including musicians, had become aware of R&B and jazz by means of shortwave radio broadcasts from Florida. Early ska was largely instrumental and emphasized the first and third beats in a four-beat musical measure. Pioneered by artists such as Prince Buster, Coxsone (also known as Downbeat), Don Drummond, Jackie Mittoo, and Rico Rodriquez, ska was very popular in Jamaica in the early 1960s, partly because vans equipped with record turntables, so-called sound systems, would travel to various parts of Jamaica, spinning the latest tunes. Ska's more melodious vocal form, rock steady, became popular in the mid-1960s. Rock steady also reflected a new era in Jamaican musical history, since rock steady groups, including Justin Hinds and the Dominoes, seemed more concerned than their musical forebears with confronting, by means of their music, what they perceived to be societal and political injustice. Emphasizing both drum and bass lines, rock steady eventually evolved into reggae, which first appeared in 1968 as a hybrid of rock steady and ska.

Reggae's evolution was accelerated by Jimmy Cliff, who became an international star in 1973 for his part in the reggae-inspired movie *The Harder They Come* (1972). Other influential reggae artists include Desmond Dekker and the group Toots and the Maytals, whose song "Do the Reggay" solidified the genre's name. Often associated with the **Rastafarian** religious movement, which became popular in Jamaica after the 1930 coronation of the last Emperor of Ethiopia, Haile Selassie I, reggae is now a worldwide phenomenon. It owes its global impact chiefly to one artist: the late Robert (Bob) Nesta Marley, the Jamaican singer-songwriter. In the late 1960s Marley teamed up with Peter Tosh, Bunny Wailer, and session musicians, the Wailers, to craft a lyrically potent sound that captured the heart of the Rastafarian credo, the belief that God is a living Black man (Haile Selassie I). By 1975, Marley and the Wailers were international recording stars, admired for albums such as *Catch a Fire* (1973), *Natty Dread* (1974), *Rastaman Vibration* (1976), and *Exodus* (1977), and Rastafarianism, Marley's professed religion, became enormously more visible on the world's cultural map.

Very generally, Rastafarian reggae music combines the deeply evocative appeal one associates with literary devices with a strident condemnation of the socioeconomic injustices perpetrated by those who are seen to control and sanction society's status quo. The social system, whether it be in Jamaica or the United States, is perceived as "Babylon": a social mechanism built upon secular principles deemed incongruous with "Jah Love" (Jah is the Rastafarian name for God), and hence in need of redemption. Equipped with an arsenal of powerful words and rhythms, the Rastafarian reggae singer and musician becomes a kind of contemporary prophet with at least two special tasks. First, she or he must highlight, expose, and condemn those inadequacies that society's poor and dispossessed are socialized into merely enduring. In this sense, Rastafarian reggae singers and musicians serve as critics of both personal and institutional transgression. They "chant down Babylon" or advance social revolution by speaking through their music. Second, each Rastafarian reggae singer and musician strives to raise the awareness of others, freeing them from mental slavery. Such dual aims come together in Marley's music, particularly in the songs "Redemption Song," "Buffalo Soldier," and "Exodus." More recent musicians, including Freddie McGregor, also embrace both objectives and take the torch, as it were, from Bob Marley and the Wailers.

The genre known as "dub reggae" came into its own in the mid-to-late 1970s, pioneered by eccentric record producers such as Lee "Scratch" Perry and King Tubby. Faced with the need to avoid the expense of recording a new song for the B side of a band or singer's 45 rpm single, Perry and Tubby stripped the A side song of its vocals and added reverb, echo, distortion, and other decorative effects, thereby creating a "dub version" of the original cut. Following such producers, various Jamaican sound system operators and disc jockeys, such as U-Roy and I-Roy, began adding their own lyrics, sometimes impulsively or spontaneously. This development led to what many now identify as the art of "toasting," which, after it was heard in **Los Angeles, California**, and New York City in the early 1980s, inspired both **hip-hop** and **rap** music.

Jamaican reggae took on a more electronic feel in the late 1980s and throughout much of the 1990s. Electronic subgenres of reggae include "dancehall" and "raga." Reggae music from these decades often features punched-up rhythms and sexually explicit lyrics, made famous by artists such as Shabba Ranks and Mad Cobra. However, reggae's politically potent themes of Black unification and emancipation were never entirely forsaken. Indeed, they surfaced in the form of "dub poetry," crafted and performed by Jamaican artists such as Linton Kwesi Johnson, Mutabaruka, and Benjamin Zephaniah. Today, reggae music is a permanent feature of world music and culture and has had considerable impact on American popular culture (Bilby). Reissues of Bob Marley's earlier work sell very well in the United States, established as well as upcoming reggae artists perform regularly in concerts in major American cities, and Grammy Awards are given to reggae artists annually. Reggae is also extremely popular over the airwaves and in the cinema, as evidenced by the soundtracks of Hollywood movies such as *Heartland Reggae* (1982), *Countryman* (1983), *Club Paradise* (1986), *Cool Runnings* (1993), and *New Jack City* (1991). Critics have also explored connections among reggae, rap, and African American **performance poetry** (Ross).

Resources: Steve Barrow and Peter Dalton, *The Rough Guide to Reggae*, 2nd ed. (1997; repr. New York: Rough Guides, 2001); Kenneth Bilby, "The Impact of Reggae in the United States," *Popular Music and Society* 5, no. 5 (1977), 17–23; Kevin

O'Brien Chang and Wayne Chen, *Reggae Routes: The Story of Jamaican Music* (Philadelphia: Temple University Press, 1998); Sebastian Clarke, *Jah Music: The Evolution of the Popular Jamaican Song* (London: Heinemann, 1980); Chuck Foster, *Roots, Rock, Reggae: An Oral History of Reggae Music from Ska to Dancehall* (New York: Billboard Books, 1999); Andrew Kaslow, "The Roots of Reggae," *Sing Out!: The Folk Song Magazine* 23, no. 6 (1975), 12–13; Stephen King and Richard J. Jensen, "Bob Marley's 'Redemption Song': The Rhetoric of Reggae and Rastafari," *Journal of Popular Culture* 29, no. 3 (Winter 1995), 17–36; Nathaniel Samuel Murrell, William David Spencer, and Adrian Anthony McFarlane, eds., *Chanting Down Babylon: The Rastafari Reader* (Philadelphia: Temple University Press, 1998); Andrew Ross, *Real Love: In Pursuit of Cultural Justice* (New York: New York University Press, 1998); Chris Salewicz and Adrian Boot, *Reggae Explosion: The Story of Jamaican Music* (New York: Harry N. Abrams, 2001); *The Story of Jamaican Music* (New York: Mango Records, 1993); Timothy White, *Catch a Fire: The Life of Bob Marley* (New York: Owl Books, 1998).

Darren J. N. Middleton

Reid-Pharr, Robert F. (born 1965). Social theorist, literary and cultural historian, journalist, and winner of the Randy Shilts Triangle Award for nonfiction in 2002. One of the most seminal new voices in the public intellectual community today, Reid-Pharr produces work reflecting a wide terrain of American life. His writing draws upon the methods and insights from a number of broadly conceived critical fields, most prominently African American Studies, cultural studies, and **queer theory**.

Reid-Pharr grew up in North Carolina and attended the University of North Carolina at Chapel Hill. He went on to complete two master's degrees at Yale University and then received his Ph.D. in American Studies at Yale in 1994. While a professor in the English Department at Johns Hopkins University between 1994 and 2001, Reid-Pharr became committed to literary retrieval, editing and reissuing a number of landmark cultural texts formerly out of print. Among these were *Miss Nume of Japan* by Onoto Watanna, the first novel published by an Asian American; *La Raza Cósmica* by José Vasconcelos, the first printed statement on the concept of Mexican *Mestizaje*; and *The Garies and Their Friends* by the complex, but often neglected, nineteenth-century African American novelist **Frank J. Webb**.

Academically, Reid-Pharr is known as one of the most influential contemporary scholars of antebellum nineteenth-century African American literature. His 1999 text *Conjugal Union: The Body, the House and the Black American*, is an intricate analysis of key antebellum Black writers, including **David Walker**, **William Wells Brown**, Webb, **Harriet E. Wilson**, **Martin R. Delany** and **Frederick Douglass**. The text begins by considering questions of Black representation, subjectivity, and Black American history. Reid-Pharr contends that for Black antebellum writers, the Black body was the necessary antecedent for any intelligible public presence. He states that it was during the antebellum period that the Black body came to operate for Blacks as a primary site in the negotiation of a specifically African American identity. He also argues that there is a clear nexus of body and household in the writings of Black antebellum intellectuals, who used homes and families as a way to negotiate the production of the Black body.

Much of Reid-Pharr's current work and journalism is invested in finding new access points into the study of sexuality and culture. In *Black Gay Man* (2001), a group of essays which includes a foreword by **Samuel R. Delany**, he treats topics as diverse as the Million Man March, interracial sex, anti-Semitism, and a range of African American literary figures from **W.E.B. Du Bois** to **James Baldwin**, **Audre Lorde**, and Frantz Fanon. His writing combines sharp political and cultural analyses with **autobiography, humor**, and, in his words, "an attempt to bring an erotic sensibility back into the study of American literature and culture." He wrote an introduction to a new edition of Frank J. Webb's novel *The Garies and Their Friends*. Currently Professor of English at the City University of New York Graduate Center, Reid-Pharr, in his most recent writing, continues to address questions about race, sexuality, cosmopolitanism, and performance. He states that a goal of much of his work has been to "help dismantle the American identity machine, to break its hold on the collective imagination" (Mulcahy). (*See* **Gay Literature**.)

Resources: Judith M. Mulcahy, unpublished interview with Robert Reid-Pharr, City University of New York, Dec. 8, 2004; Robert F. Reid-Pharr: *Black Gay Man* (New York: New York University Press, 2001); *Conjugal Union: The Body, the House and the Black American* (New York: Oxford University Press, 1999); "An Interview with Samuel R. Delany," *Callaloo* 14, no. 2 (Spring 1991), 524–534; "Introduction," in *The Garies and Their Friends*, by Frank J. Webb (Baltimore: Johns Hopkins University Press, 1997); "Tearing the Goat's Flesh: Homosexuality, Abjection, and the Production of a Late-Twentieth-Century Black Masculinity," in *Novel Gazing: Queer Readings in Fiction*, ed. Eve Kosofsky Sedgwick (Durham, NC: Duke University Press, 1997); "Violent Ambiguity: Martin Delany, Bourgeois Sadomasochism and the Development of a Black National Masculinity," in *Representing Black Men*, ed. Marcellus Blount and George Cunningham (New York: Routledge, 1996).

Judith Mulcahy

Remond, Charles Lenox (1810–1873). Antislavery lecturer. Remond helped to set the tone for the antislavery lecture circuit, urging both moral and political action against **slavery** and racial inequality.

Raised in Salem, Massachusetts, in an atmosphere of prejudice and segregation, and taught antislavery principles by his parents and their abolitionist visitors, Remond became a staunch participant in the **abolitionist movement**. He worked for several antislavery newspapers, including White abolitionist William Lloyd Garrison's *The Liberator*, and joined several antislavery societies, including the Massachusetts Anti-Slavery Society, which hired him as its first Black lecturer in 1838. In 1840, this society chose Remond as a representative to the World's Anti-Slavery Convention in London. When the convention refused to allow places for the women delegates, he joined the women in the observation gallery to protest their treatment. He eventually lectured throughout England, Ireland, and Scotland for nineteen months before returning home in December 1841.

Remond used his eloquence in letters and speeches, which were often published in abolitionist newspapers such as *The Liberator*, to advance the antislavery cause and to promote equality of **race**, class, and **gender**. In his speeches, Remond created a rhythm of increasing fervor, and his frank, sometimes ironic reasoning and anecdotes of personal experience revealed the folly and abomination of slavery and prejudice. Upon his return to the United States, he was seated in a "Jim Crow" railway car for the journey from **Boston, Massachusetts**, to Salem; he later protested this prejudicial treatment to the Massachusetts House of Representatives, which in 1843 eliminated such examples of segregation. He also fostered the lecture career of his younger sister **Sarah Parker Remond**, lecturing with her in New York in the 1850s, and he later acted as a recruiting agent for African American regiments (the 54th and 55th Massachusetts) for the Union Army in the **Civil War**. He eventually held positions as streetlight inspector and customs stamp clerk in Boston, and conducted his last lecture tour in 1867. He died in 1873. In her diary, **Charlotte Forten Grimké**, a family friend, noted his moodiness (Grimké 164, 252); his own letters attest to frequent ill health, possibly from consumption. Remond's eloquence as a lecturer and letter writer made him famous during his own time. After the arrival of **Frederick Douglass** on the lecture scene, however, Remond's popularity waned.

Resources: Jacqueline Bacon, *The Humblest May Stand Forth: Rhetoric, Empowerment, and Abolition* (Columbia: University of South Carolina Press, 2002); Charlotte Forten Grimké, *The Journals of Charlotte Forten Grimké*, ed. Brenda Stevenson (New York: Oxford University Press, 1988); Dorothy Burnett Porter, "The Remonds of Salem, Massachusetts: A Nineteenth-Century Family Revisited," *Proceedings of the American Antiquarian Society* 95 (1985), 259–295; Benjamin Quarles, *Black Abolitionists* (New York: Oxford University Press, 1969); C. Peter Ripley, ed., *The Black Abolitionist Papers*, vol. 1, *The British Isles, 1830–1865* (Chapel Hill: University of North Carolina Press, 1985); Louis Ruchames, *The Abolitionists: A Collection of Their Writings* (New York: Putnam, 1963).

Laura Smith

Remond, Sarah Parker (1824–1894). Antislavery lecturer. Remond delivered antislavery lectures that emphasized the sufferings of African American women and that urged moral action against the prejudices and policies underlying **slavery**.

Remond's status as a free Black woman in Salem, Massachusetts, could not protect her from the prejudice against her race. After passing the entrance exam to Salem's high school in 1835, she was refused entrance. In 1853, she was thrown out of two separate cultural events in **Boston, Massachusetts**, and **Philadelphia, Pennsylvania**; in the Boston incident, Remond pled her case in civil court and won damages. In the case of later injustices, Remond took her cause to the public, sharing letters and delivering speeches reported in antislavery newspapers. Remond finally devoted herself to this activism in 1856 when she joined her famous older brother and antislavery speaker, **Charles Lenox Remond**, on a lecture tour for the American Anti-Slavery Society.

The zenith of her lecture career occurred during a tour of England, Scotland, and Ireland in 1859. British and American newspapers reporting her speeches described her eloquence and ability to speak without notes, holding listeners' attention for more than an hour at a time. Her speeches employed figures of speech and anecdotes borrowed from antislavery rhetoric, such as a story about the auction of a female slave. Nevertheless, she established a unique sense of "sisterhood" with her female listeners by showing how slavery could affect women of all complexions. Her lecture style relied on an accumulation of sentiment, argument, and statistics, a style one critic has related to legal argument, direct and accumulative (Peterson, 139). In fact, Remond often used language of law and government, such as the Declaration of Independence (1776) or the Dred Scott decision (1857), to show the gap between professed democratic principles and actual practice.

With the end of the **Civil War**, Remond's lecture career ended. She continued her studies, earning a physician's diploma in 1871 from a hospital in Florence, Italy. She practiced medicine and later married Lazzaro Pintor. She died in 1894 and was buried in Rome. Remond's antislavery work may today be found in her 1860 autobiography (in *Our Exemplars*), her published and private letters, an 1864 tract (titled *The Negroes and Anglo-Africans as Freedmen and Soldiers*), and reported and transcribed speeches.

Resources: Ruth Bogin, "Sarah Parker Remond: Black Abolitionist from Salem," in *Black Women in American History: From Colonial Times Through the Nineteenth Century*, ed. Darlene Clark Hine, vol. 1 (Brooklyn, NY: Carlson, 1990); Charlotte Forten Grimké, *The Journals of Charlotte Forten Grimké*, ed. Brenda Stevenson (New York: Oxford University Press, 1988); Carla L. Peterson, *"Doers of the Word": African-American Women Speakers and Writers in the North (1830–1880)* (New York: Oxford University Press, 1995); Dorothy Burnett Porter, "The Remonds of Salem, Massachusetts: A Nineteenth-Century Family Revisited," *Proceedings of the American Antiquarian Society* 95 (1985), 259–295; Benjamin Quarles, *Black Abolitionists* (New York: Oxford University Press, 1969); Sarah Parker Remond: *The Negroes and Anglo-Africans as Freedmen and Soldiers* (London: Emily Faithfull, 1864); "Sarah P. Remond," in *Our Exemplars, Poor and Rich; or, Biographical Sketches of Men and Women Who Have, by an Extraordinary Use of their Opportunities, Benefited Their Fellow-Creatures*, ed. Matthew Davenport Hill (London: Cassell, Petter, and Galpin, 1861); C. Peter Ripley, *The Black Abolitionist Papers*, vol. 1, *The British Isles, 1830–1865* (Chapel Hill: University of North Carolina Press, 1985).

Laura Smith

Research Resources: Electronic Works. The refinement of digital technology has revolutionized access to information, making it possible for students and scholars to research an enormous and rapidly growing body of literature by and about African Americans. The *MLA* (Modern Language Association) *International Bibliography* is the premier database for literature in general, including African American literature. However, the overview of sources listed below focuses specifically on databases related to African American literature. The overview is not intended to be exhaustive, but instead to provide a reasonable range of databases that serve different research needs. Some of the databases are commercial products, while others are freely available on the World Wide Web.

The publisher Chadwyck-Healey offers a number of commercial products for researching African American literature. *African American Poetry, 1750–1900* is a collection of 3,000 poems by fifty-four African American poets writing in the late eighteenth and nineteenth centuries. It is based on William French's bibliography, *Afro-American Poetry and Drama, 1760–1975*. Poems by many well-known poets are included—**Paul Laurence Dunbar**, for example—as well as poems by lesser known authors, including **James Corrothers** and **Albery Allson Whitman**, author of *An Idyl of the South: An Epic Poem in Two Parts* (1901). The *Database of Twentieth Century African-American Poetry* provides access to the full text of thousands of poems written by the most important and influential African American poets from the early twentieth century to the present. The works of **Rita Dove**, **Robert Hayden**, **Audre Lorde**, and **Langston Hughes** are among those in the database. Biographical profiles accompany the text. *International Index to Black Periodicals Full Text* covers humanities-related disciplines drawn from more than 150 international journals, newspapers, and newsletters. The full text of over forty periodicals are included from 1998 forward. Titles include *The Langston Hughes Review*, *Obsidian*, *Research in African Literatures*, and the *African American Review*. *African American Biographical Database* brings together the biographical profiles of thousands of African Americans. The content is primarily drawn from *Black Biographical Dictionaries, 1790–1950* and includes extended narratives of African American literary figures. The commercial provider of database resources Biblioline offers the *Black Studies Database*, which includes material from over 150 journals, magazines, newspapers, newsletters, and reports between 1948 and 1986. (*See* **Black Studies**.)

The Schomburg Center for Research in Black Culture, a division of the Research Libraries of the New York Public Library, holds the country's largest collection of works by and about Africans and the people of African descent. In addition to books, the Center collects pamphlets, photographs, microforms, sound recordings, films, periodicals, art, and ephemera, from all countries and in all languages. The New York Public Library has made available *Black Studies on Disc*, an annually updated CD-ROM database that contains all the Schomburg catalogs. It is accompanied by the *Index to Black Periodicals*, an index to articles in black journals and magazines since 1989. *African American Women Writers of the 19th Century* is the Schomburg Center's digital collection of biography, autobiography, fiction, poetry, and essays written by Black women prior to 1920.

An independent not-for-profit organization, JSTOR, provides electronic access to back issues of important scholarly journals in the humanities, social sciences, and sciences. Within the *Language and Literature Collection*, there are extensive archives of core African American literary journals, including **Callaloo**, **Phylon**, *African American Review*, and the *Journal of Black Studies*.

The University of Virginia Library's Electronic Text Center has a long history of providing public access to electronic texts. *African American Writers: Online E-texts* is a browsable and searchable database of African American writers ranging from **Phillis Wheatley** to **Maya Angelou**.

Black Drama provides access to English-language plays written by Black authors from North America, the Caribbean, and Africa, from 1850 to the present. The database also includes selected playbills, production photographs, and other ephemera related to the plays. There is a concentration of materials from the **Harlem Renaissance**, contemporary African American authors, and twentieth-century African playwrights. (*See also* **Archives and Collections: 1828–Present**; **Archives and Collections: Notable Collections**.)

Resources: *African American Biographical Database* (Chadwyck-Healey, 2003), http:// aabd.chadwyck.com; *African American Poetry, 1750–1900* (Chadwyck-Healey, 1995), http://www.chadwyck.com; *African American Studies* (JSTOR, 2004), http://www.jstor .org; *African American Writers: Online E-texts* (University of Virginia Library Electronic Text Center, 2003), http://etext.lib.virginia.edu/subjects/African-American/html; *Black Drama* (Alexander Street Press and the University of Chicago, 2003), http://www .alexanderstreet2.com/bldrlive/; *Black Studies Database 1948–1986* (Biblioline, 2004), http://biblioline.nisc.com/scripts/login.dll?BiblioLine&dbname=QBLK; *Black Studies on Disc* (New York: G. K. Hall, 2003), CD-ROM; *Database of Twentieth-Century African-American Poetry* (Chadwyck-Healey, 1999), http://www.chadwyck.com/; *Digital Schomburg: African American Women Writers of the 19th Century* (Schomberg Center, New York Public Library, Center for Research in Black Culture, 1999), http://digital.nypl.org/ schomburg/writers_aa19/; *International Index to Black Periodicals Full Text* (Chadwyck-Healey, 2003), http://iibp.chadwyck.com; *MLA International Bibliography* (New York: Modern Language Association, 2004), http://www.mla.org/bibliography.

Lori Ricigliano

Research Sources: Reference Works. Reference works provide access to information about African American authors, their works, and criticism of their works.

Reference works are designed to provide access to specific items of information rather than to be read consecutively, the way a novel or a story is read, for example. Reference works may be in print or electronic form. For the purposes of this entry, print reference works will be discussed; for electronic sources, see **Research Sources: Electronic Works**.

For literature, reference works may be divided into two major categories: bibliographies/indexes and source works. A bibliography/index reference work is "a systematically produced descriptive list of records" (Katz, 7) that provides a citation or some indication of the existence of a work and where it may be found. Source-type works are synoptic; that is, they provide summaries or digests of information. They do so directly rather than simply pointing out where information may be found. Source works include almanacs, biographical sources, dictionaries, encyclopedias, handbooks, and yearbooks (summaries of events in a given single year, such as 1954 or 1989).

Reference works relevant to literature tend to focus upon biographical information about authors, to give an indication of the existence of works, to provide a plot summary and list of characters and themes of a particular work, or to give access to criticism and reviews of works. There are several reference sources specifically for African American literature. Many of the major literary reference sources include references to at least a few writers of African descent. Literary reference sources may be retrospective, covering authors, works and criticism of the past, or current, covering contemporary authors, works, and criticism.

A selected list of reference works for African American literature, with brief annotation, follows. The list is divided into bibliography/index sources and dictionary/encyclopedia/handbook sources. A brief description follow each item. Items are listed alphabetically by the title of the work.

Bibliographic and Index Sources

African-American Literature: Overview and Bibliography. Paul Q. Tilden, ed. New York: Nova Science Publishers, 2003. This work provides an overview of African American literature as well as a bibliography of literature and criticism of works by African American authors.

Afro-America Fiction, 1853–1976: A Guide to Information Sources. Edward Margolies and David Bakish. Detroit: Gale, 1979. This source provides a checklist of novels, anthologies, and short stories, and an annotated list of bibliographies on Black fiction. It has author, title, and subject indexes.

The Afro-American Novel, 1965–1975: A Descriptive Bibliography of Primary and Secondary Material. Helen Ruth Houston. Troy, NY: Whitston, 1977. This volume provides biographical notes about fifty-six African American writers as well as listings of their novels, criticism, and reviews of their works.

Afro-American Poetry and Drama, 1760–1975: A Guide to Information Sources. William P. French et al. Detroit: Gale, 1979. This work provides a listing of poetry and dramatic works and criticism.

The Afro-American Short Story: A Comprehensive, Annotated Index with Selected Commentaries. Preston M. Yancy, comp. Westport, CT: Greenwood Press, 1986. This source provides an index to 800 short stories, by over 300 authors, written between 1950 and 1982.

Best Literature by and About Blacks. Phillip M. Richards and Neil Schlager. Detroit: Gale, 2000. This source is a selective bibliography of literary works by and about African Americans.

A Bibliographical Guide to African-American Women Writers. Casper LeRoy Jordan, comp. Westport, CT: Greenwood Press, 1993. This is one of the most comprehensive bibliographies of writing by African American women, with entries on 900 writers. Listings of primary and secondary sources are provided.

Black American Women in Literature. Ronda Gliken, comp. Jefferson, NC: McFarland, 1989. This volume provides bibliographic coverage of 300 African American women writers.

Black American Writers, 1773–1949: A Bibliography and Union List. Geraldine O. Matthews, comp. Boston: G. K. Hall, 1975. A bibliography and union list of monographs by 1,600 African American authors.

Black Authors: A Selected Annotated Bibliography. James Edward Newby. New York: Garland, 1991. This source is a selected bibliography of 3,000 books, monographs, and essays published between 1783 and 1990. The annotations vary in length but tend to be brief, and are arranged in nine broad categories. There is a title index and an author index.

Black Image on the American Stage: A Bibliography of Plays and Musicals, 1770–1970. James Vernon Hatch. New York: DBS, 1970. This source provides a bibliography of plays, musicals, reviews, and operas either written by an African American or containing at least one African American character or theme from 1767 to 1970. There is an author index.

Black Literature, 1827–1940. Henry Louis Gates, Jr., ed. Alexandria, VA: Chadwyck-Healy, 1990. This source, is a printed guide to a microfiche collection of 3,000 sources. Author, title, and genre indexes are on separate microfiches. Over 50,000 separate items are listed.

Books by African-American Authors and Illustrators for Children and Young Adults. Helen E. Williams. Chicago: American Library Association, 1991. This source is arranged by age range and provides an annotated bibliography to children's and young-adult literature and sources by African American authors and illustrators written between 1900 and 1989.

The Harlem Renaissance: An Annotated Bibliography and Commentary. Margaret Perry. New York: Garland, 1982. This work provides an annotated bibliography of articles and books about the Harlem Renaissance. Major authors are highlighted. There is an author index and a title index.

Index to Black American Writers in Collective Biographies. Dorothy Campbell. Littleton, CO: Libraries Unlimited, 1983. This volume provides an index to nearly 270 biographical sources published from 1837 to 1982. There are over 1,900 authors listed in this work.

The Pen Is Ours: A Listing of Writings by and About African-American Women Before 1910 with Secondary Bibliography to the Present. Jean Fagan Yellin and Cynthia D. Bond, comps. New York: Oxford University Press, 1991. This source provides a bibliography of writing by and about African American women with an emphasis on coverage of items appearing from 1773 to 1910. The items are arranged in five broad categories; there is also a name index.

Southern Black Creative Writers, 1829–1953: Bio-Bibliographies. Mamie Marie Booth Foster, comp. Westport, CT: Greenwood Press, 1988. This volume provides brief biographical notes for 200 African American writers and a bibliography of monographs, periodicals, and anthologies. There are author, state, and period indexes.

Dictionary, Encyclopedia, Handbook Sources

African American Dramatists: An A-to-Z Guide. Emmanuel Nelson, ed. Westport, CT: Greenwood Press, 2004. This source is a biographical dictionary of African American dramatists. A bibliography of their works and criticism is included.

African American Poets: Lives, Works, and Sources. Joyce Owens Pettis. Westport, CT: Greenwood Press, 2002. This source is a biographical dictionary with bibliographies of selected poets from the eighteenth century to contemporary times.

African American Writers. Lea Baechler and A. Walton Litz, eds. New York: Scribner's, 1991. This source provides biographical and critical essays about thirty-four African American authors.

African-American Writers. Philip Bader. New York: Facts on File, 2004. This is a biographical guidebook to selected African American writers.

Black Authors and Illustrators of Children's Books: A Biographical Dictionary. Barbara Rollock. 2nd ed. New York: Garland, 1992. This is a biographical dictionary of 150 writers and illustrators of children's books published between 1930 and 1990.

Black Literature Criticism: Excerpts from Criticism of the Most Significant Works of Black Authors over the Past 200 Years. James P. Draper, ed. Detroit: Gale, 1992. This source provides biographical and critical information on 125 writers of African descent. Each entry provides a biographical sketch of an author, a listing of his/her works, and excepts from authoritative critical essays.

Black Plots & Black Characters: A Handbook for Afro-American Literature. Robert L. Southgate. Syracuse, NY: Gaylord, 1979. This source provides plot summaries of 100 works (speeches, novels, plays, and long poems) by African American authors appearing between 1619 and 1978. There is an author index and a chronological index.

Contemporary African-American Novelists: A Bio-Bibliographical Critical Sourcebook. Emmanuel S. Nelson, ed. Westport, CT: Greenwood Press, 1999. This source provides biographical essays and critical analyses of the works of seventy-nine contemporary authors.

The Handbook of African American Literature. Hazel Arnett Ervin. Gainesville: University Press of Florida, 2004. This source provides entries on themes (ambiguity, memory, representation, signification, etc.) relevant to African American literature.

Masterpieces of African-American Literature. Frank N. Magill, ed. New York: HarperCollins, 1992. This volume provides the plot summary, list of characters and excerpts of critical analyses of 149 titles by 96 African American writers. It includes an author index and a title index.

Modern Black Writers. Steven R. Serafin, ed. New York: Continuum, 1995. This volume contains excerpts of criticism of the works of 125 literary authors from 32 countries with an emphasis on works published in English and French during the twentieth century.

The Oxford Companion to African American Literature. William L. Andrews et al., eds. New York: Oxford University Press, 1997. This volume provides brief biographical sketches of 400 authors and plot descriptions for over 150 books and literary characters. There are also entries on issues pertinent to literature, genres, and themes. The coverage is from the colonial times to the present.

(*See also* **Archives and Collections: 1828–Present**; **Archives and Collections: Notable Collections**.)

Resources: Robert Balay, *Guide to Reference Books*, 11th ed. (Chicago: American Library Association, 1996); Ron Blazek and Elizabeth Aversa, *The Humanities: A Selective Guide to Information Sources*, 5th ed. (Englewood, CO: Libraries Unlimited, 2000); William A. Katz, *Introduction to Reference Work*, 8th ed., vol. 1 (New York: McGraw-Hill, 2002).

Kimberly Black-Parker

Rhodes, Jewell Parker (born 1954). Novelist, nonfiction writer, and professor. Rhodes has written highly regarded historical novels and two books about writing and publishing. She was born and raised, until the age of eight, in **Pittsburgh, Pennsylvania**. She subsequently lived in California, then returned at sixteen to Pittsburgh to embark on her college career as a drama student. From Carnegie-Mellon University she has earned a B.A. in drama criticism, an M.A. in English, and a Doctor of Arts in creative writing. She teaches at Arizona State University, where she has directed the M.F.A. program in creative writing. She has won numerous awards, including the Yaddo creative writing fellowship, the National Endowment for the Arts Award in Fiction, and the Fiction Award of the Black Caucus of the American Library Association, and she is a two-time Pushcart Prize nominee.

As a child, Rhodes sought refuge in creative writing, the world of the theater, and avid reading to free herself from the reality of a home life made tumultuous with an absent mother. She has said that her paternal grandmother has been her biggest single source of inspiration, likening her to a griot, a wondrous oral storyteller (*Free Within Ourselves*). While Rhodes's three novels to date have focused on historical figures and settings, Rhodes acknowledges that there is also a personal impulse at work in her novels. *Voodoo Dreams*, she came to realize, was about her beloved grandmother's power and a daughter's search for a mother. *Magic City*, ostensibly about the Tulsa **race riot** of 1921 rendered in compelling magic realist mode, was impelled by Rhodes's response to the 1992 Los Angeles riots and her exploration of her son's **coming of age** in contemporary America. *Douglass' Women* is centered on **Frederick Douglass**'s African American wife, Anna Murray, and his German Jewish mistress, Ottilie Assing. Rhodes has said that historical fiction, for her, is a way of understanding what has been in order to armor oneself against what will be (*Free Within Ourselves*). For Rhodes, therefore, writing is a kind of charm and talisman, creating life for future wisdom.

While Rhodes has not yet written an autobiographical novel, two of her short works of memoir can be found in her books dedicated to informing and inspiring beginning writers. "Block Party," a remembrance of her Pittsburgh neighborhood, is anthologized in *Free Within Ourselves*, and "Georgia on My

Mind" is reprinted in *The African-American Guide to Writing and Publishing Nonfiction*. In both works, Rhodes's intention appears to be to foster an understanding that writing can be a way of celebrating the self and the community. Additionally, her short fiction has appeared in such journals as **Callaloo**, *Feminist Studies*, *Calyx*, and *The Seattle Review*, and she has published essays, most notably in *Ms.* magazine.

Resources: Jewell Parker Rhodes: *The African American Guide to Writing and Publishing Nonfiction* (New York: Broadway Books, 2001); *Douglass' Women: A Novel* (New York: Atria Books, 2002); *Free Within Ourselves: Fiction Lessons for Black Authors* (New York: Main Street/Doubleday, 1999); *Magic City* (New York: HarperCollins, 1997); *Voodoo Dreams: A Novel of Marie Laveau* (New York: St. Martin's, 1993).

David A. Boxwell

Rice, Patty (born c. 1976). Novelist and poet. Rice's first publication, *Manmade Heartbreak* (1998), is a collection of romantic, erotic poetry that touches the heart with the silent and subtle power of love. Rice's first novel, *Somethin' Extra* (2000), is a romantic tale that explores the nuances of male-female relationships using humor, wit, and stylish evocations of sensuality. Rice espouses the healing power of putting the past into perspective in order to move confidently into the present as her protagonist, Genie, has affairs with "safe" married men in order to stay in control of her heart. When Genie meets David, they are both swept toward the charm and radiance of real love and acceptance while letting go of the past. Through Genie's musings, Rice comments on the media's idealistic construction of love and the unrealistic expectations those messages instill in women.

Rice's second novel, *Reinventing the Woman: A Novel* (2001), is infused with feminine self-help wisdom. Camille flees her abusive boyfriend and goes to live with her sister's family, where she slowly begins to learn about herself and her life choices. Rice again explores male-female relationships and especially women's recovery from unrealistic expectations about love. Camille's compelling journey to recover not only from her recent abuse by her boyfriend, but also from her past abuse at the hands of her mother, gives this story a special message of grace and redemption. Each chapter opens with a "reinventing rule" that becomes a theme of self-discovery and self-validation for Camille as she learns self-confidence and autonomy at the hands of Nora Jordan, her sister who is a motivational speaker. Rice's feisty style and wit, coupled with her underlying affirmations of feminine autonomy, give her works a special luminosity. Rice is the cofounder of My Sister Writers, a **Washington, D.C.**-based African American women writer's group.

Resources: Hazel V. Carby, *Reconstructing Womanhood: The Emergence of the Afro-American Woman Novelist* (New York: Oxford University Press, 1987); Anne duCille, *The Coupling Convention: Sex, Text, and Tradition in Black Women's Fiction* (New York: Oxford University Press, 1993); Patty Rice: *Manmade Heartbreak* (Washington,

DC: Ye Olde Front Shoppe, 1998); *Reinventing the Woman* (New York: Simon and Schuster, 2001); *Somethin' Extra* (New York: Simon and Schuster, 2000).

Debbie Clare Olson

Richardson, Willis (1889–1977). Playwright, nonfiction writer, editor, theatrical director, and teacher. Richardson is considered an important figure of African American **drama** during the **Harlem Renaissance**. Richardson was born in Wilmington, North Carolina, but he moved with his family shortly thereafter to **Washington, D.C.** One of his teachers in high school there was **Mary ("Mamie") Powell Burrill**, who encouraged him to write (Gray; Martin). Although Gray characterizes Richardson as a "forgotten" pioneer of African American theater, his achievements were nonetheless crucial. He was, for example, the first African American to have a dramatic play (as opposed to a musical play) produced on Broadway—*The Chip Woman's Fourtune* (1923). Earlier he had published plays in both **The Brownies' Book** and **The Crisis**, publications closely tied to **W.E.B. Du Bois** and the Harlem Renaissance. A play of his was included in **Alain Locke**'s influential anthology *The New Negro* (1925). In *The Chip Woman's Fortune, Broken Banjo: A Folk Tragedy* (1925), *The Bootblack Lover* (1926), and numerous other plays, Richardson portrays the lives of ordinary African Americans realistically, so his sensibility is close to that of his contemporary **Langston Hughes**. Richardson was among the many writers who frequented **Georgia Douglas Johnson**'s Washington, D.C., home, which was a hub of literary activity in the 1920s (Martin). He contributed essays about African American theatre to *Opportunity* and *The Messenger*, and he edited anthologies of black drama. As a playwright, director, and teacher, he worked with various theater companies, including the Howard Players at Howard University and the **Gilpin Players**.

Resources: Primary Sources: Willis Richardson: *The Broken Banjo,* in *The Crisis Reader,* ed. Sondra Kathryn Wilson (New York: Modern Library, 1999); *The Chip Woman's Fortune,* in *Anthology of the American Negro in the Theatre,* ed. Lindsay Patterson (Washington, DC: Association for the Study of Negro Life and History, 1967); *Compromise: A Folk Play,* in *The New Negro,* ed. Alain Locke (New York: Boni, 1925); *Mortgaged,* in *The New Negro Renaissance: An Anthology,* ed. Arthur P. Davis and Michael W. Peplow (New York: Holt, Rinehart and Winston, 1975); "The Negro Audience," *Opportunity* 3 (1925), 123; *A Pillar of the Church,* in *Lost Plays of the Harlem Renaissance, 1920–1940,* ed. James V. Hatch and Leo Hamalian (Detroit: Wayne State University Press, 1996); "Propaganda in the Theatre," *The Messenger* 6 (1924), 353–354; Willis Richardson, comp., *Plays and Pageants from the Life of the Negro* (Washington, DC: Associated Publishers, 1930), includes Richardson's plays *The Black Horseman, The King's Dilemma,* and *The House of Sham*; Willis Richardson and May Miller, *Negro History in Thirteen Plays* (Washington, DC: Associated Publishers, 1935). **Secondary Sources:** Christine Rauchfuss Gray, *Willis Richardson, Forgotten Pioneer of African American Drama* (Westport, CT: Greenwood Press, 1999); Helen R. Houston, "Richardson, Willis," in *The Oxford Companion to African*

American Literature, ed. William L. Andrews, Frances Smith Foster, and Trudier Harris (New York: Oxford University Press, 1997), 632; George-McKinley Martin, "Willis Richardson," in *The Black Renaissance in Washington* (Washington, DC: Public Library, June 20, 2003), http://www.dclibrary.org/blkren/bios/richardsonw.html; Patsy Perry, "Willis Richardson," in *Dictionary of Literary Biography*, vol. 51, *Afro American Writers from the Harlem Renaissance to 1940*, ed. Trudier Harris (Detroit: Gale, 1987); Bernard L. Peterson, Jr., "An Evaluation—Willis Richardson: Pioneer Playwright," *Black World* 26 (April 1975), 40–48.

Hans Ostrom

Ridley, John (born 1965). Novelist and screenwriter. John Ridley's versatile output includes creative work in radio, television, movies, and fiction. Born and raised in Milwaukee, Wisconsin, Ridley received a B.A. in East Asian languages and culture from New York University. His began writing professionally for situation-comedy series on television, including *The John Larroquette Show*, *The Fresh Prince of Bel-Air*, and *Martin*. Ridley's other television work includes the series *Third Watch* and the **hip-hop** drama *Platinum*. His television appearances include stand-up comedy performances on the *Tonight Show with Johnny Carson*, *The Late Show with David Letterman*, and the Comedy Central channel's *Comic Remix*, as well as cameo acting appearances on *The Fresh Prince of Bel-Air* and the Australian soap opera *Neighbors*. Ridley's hard-boiled detective novels include *Stray Dogs* (1997); *Love Is a Racket* (1998), which was included in the *Los Angeles Times*'s Ten Best Books of 1998; *Everybody Smokes in Hell* (1999); *A Conversation with the Mann* (2002), which is currently being adapted for film; *The Drift* (2002); and *Those Who Walk in Darkness* (2003). Ridley's work in film includes adapting the novel *Stray Dogs* into the film *U-turn* directed by Oliver Stone; directing *Cold Around the Heart* (1997), for which Ridley won Best Director at the New York Urbanworld film festival; writing the story for the **Gulf War** satire *Three Kings* (1999); and adapting *Those Who Walk in Darkness* as an animated film. His online animated series *Undercover Brother*, a **parody** of spy and **blaxploitation** genres, was adapted as a feature film, for which Ridley co-wrote the screenplay. Ridley is a frequent contributor to the program *Morning Edition* on National Public Radio, where his work has included cultural criticism, insider accounts of the entertainment industry, and political commentary. (*See* **Crime and Mystery Fiction.**)

Resources: Brian Egeston, "Review of *Those Who Walk in Darkness*," *Black Book Review* 10, no. 6 (Dec. 31, 2003), 4; "John Ridley," *Contemporary Authors Online* (2003), http://galenet/galegroup.com; Mark Lindquist, "Nights in the Gulag L.A." (Review of *Love Is a Racket*), *New York Times Book Review*, Oct. 11, 1998, p. 20; John Ridley: *A Conversation with the Mann* (New York: Warner, 2002); *The Drift* (New York: Knopf, 2002); *Everybody Smokes in Hell* (New York: Knopf, 1999); *Love Is a Racket* (New York: Knopf, 1998); *Stray Dogs* (New York: Ballantine, 1997); *Those Who Walk in Darkness* (New York: Aspect, 2003).

Alex Feerst

Riley, Len. Novelist. Born and raised in **Harlem, New York**, Riley established himself as a television writer for situation comedies such as *Good Times*, *The Jeffersons*, and *Benson*.

In his first novel, *Harlem* (1997), Riley provides a narrative that proceeds on two levels. The novel is a family saga following the progress of the Lamberts, a Harlem family, over the tumultuous decades of the 1920s and 1930s. Recent arrivals from the Deep South, the Lamberts have exchanged a familiar rural poverty for an urban poverty so startlingly beyond their previous experience that they might just as well have emigrated to a foreign country. Indeed, the Lamberts' experience is a microcosm through which Riley can explore largely forgotten aspects of the **Great Migration** of African Americans to the industrial centers of the Northeast and Midwest. The one thing that the Lamberts do find in Harlem that was unavailable to them in the segregated South is a much greater freedom of cultural expression.

The Lamberts arrive in Harlem during the period that would later come to be known as the **Harlem Renaissance**. The narrative link between the Lamberts and the musical and literary figures of the Harlem Renaissance is provided by their cousin Geneva. A liar on all sides, she has passed herself off as a member of a prominent African American family in order to marry a wealthy club owner in Harlem, and to glamorize her life in her letters to her family, she has greatly exaggerated the opportunities available in Harlem. After they come to Harlem, she hardly wants to acknowledge that they are her relatives, but she is so self-involved and unscrupulous that she eventually schemes to seduce her cousin's husband.

Through the link that Geneva provides, Riley is able to present cameo characterizations of historically important musicians and writers, as well as largely forgotten entrepreneurs and underworld figures. The vibrancy of the cultural life and of the high life in Harlem during this period is thereby contrasted with the mundane issues of daily life confronting ordinary families like the Lamberts. So, however melodramatic the complications involving Geneva are, they serve to link, tonally as well as dramatically, the two levels on which Harlem was experienced and understood.

Resource: Len Riley, *Harlem* (New York: Doubleday, 1997).

Martin Kich

Ringgold, Faith (born 1930). Painter, lecturer, and children's writer. Ringgold is perhaps best known for creating "story quilts," vivid quilts with narrative themes. She was born and raised in the Sugar Hill area of **Harlem, New York**. In 1948, Ringgold enrolled in the City College of New York to study art, but her education was interrupted midway by her first marriage in 1950, the birth of her two daughters in 1952, and, shortly after, a divorce that was finalized in 1956. She resumed her studies, completing a B.S. in fine arts and education in 1955 and an M.A. in arts in 1959. After completing her B.S., she began teaching art in New York public schools (1955–1973). By the 1960s her work developed, reflecting her growing political consciousness, her studies of

African arts and history, and the influence of the writers **James Baldwin** and **Amiri Baraka**. In 1962 Ringgold remarried. In 1963, she began a body of paintings called the *American People* series, which expressed the **Civil Rights Movement** from a female perspective.

In the 1970s Ringgold created African-style masks, painted political posters, lectured at feminist art conferences, and actively sought the racial integration of the New York art world. Among Ringgold's most renowned works, her "story quilts" were inspired by the Tibetan *tankas* (paintings framed in cloth). She painted these quilts with narrative images and original stories set in the context of African American history. These pieces include "Who's Afraid of Aunt Jemima?" (1984) and "Tar Beach" (1988), which Ringgold later adapted into a children's book. She has written and illustrated eleven children's books, including *Aunt Harriet's Underground Railroad in the Sky* (1992), *Dinner at Aunt Connie's House* (1993), *My Dream of Martin Luther King* (1995), *Bonjour Lonnie* (1996), *The Invisible Princess* (1999), *If a Bus Could Talk: The Story of Rosa Parks* (1999), and *Counting to Tar Beach* (1999). Ringgold has received more than seventy-five awards, fellowships, citations, and honors, including two National Endowment for the Arts awards and seventeen honorary doctorates, one of which is from her alma mater, the City College of New York.

Resources: "Faith Ringgold," *Britannica Concise Encyclopedia*, Encyclopaedia Britannica Premium Service (2004), http://www.encyclopediabritannica.com/ebc/article?eu=402253; Faith Ringgold: *Aunt Harriet's Underground Railroad in the Sky* (New York: Crown, 1992); *Bonjour, Lonnie* (New York: Hyperion, 1996); *Counting to Tar Beach* (New York: Crown, 1999); *Dinner at Aunt Connie's House* (New York: Hyperion, 1993); "Faith Ringgold: May I Introduce Myself" (Art in Context Center for Communications, 2003), http://www.faithringgold.com/ringgold/default.htm; *If a Bus Could Talk: The Story of Rosa Parks* (Simon and Schuster, 1999); *The Invisible Princess* (New York: Crown, 1999); *My Dream of Martin Luther King* (New York: Crown, 1995); *Tar Beach* (New York: Crown, 1991).

eboni treco

Rivers, Conrad Kent (1933–1968). Poet. The critic Edwin L. Coleman II suggests that the enduring influence of Conrad Rivers's work "lies in the fact that he spoke for a generation of young blacks forced to make the transition from the helpless, often hopeless 1950s to the chaotic, rage-filled 1960s" (Coleman, 282). The 1960s presented possibilities and choices that had previously been beyond the reach of African Americans. Rivers's poetry embraces such opportunities, but it expresses the idea that ultimately death is the only source of freedom available. Ultimately he worked to provide literary structures that would give solace to young writers asking the same questions as he has throughout his poetry.

Born in Atlantic City, New Jersey, to Cora McIver and William Dixon Rivers, Rivers and his brother grew up in **Philadelphia, Pennsylvania**. From 1953 to 1955, Rivers served in the Army. His uncle, Ray McIver, encouraged Rivers's interest in poetry and his desire for higher education. In 1960, he graduated from Wilberforce University, where he had met **Langston Hughes**, a major influence on his poetry. **Gwendolyn Brooks** influenced him as well, with her focus on **Chicago, Illinois**, as a metaphor for social change. Between 1961 and 1967, Rivers attended graduate school at Chicago Teachers College, Indiana University, and Temple University (Coleman, 284). He was an English teacher at Roosevelt High School in Gary, Indiana, at the time of his death in 1968.

Critics such as Blyden Jackson and Louis Rubin suggest that Rivers and his contemporaries wrote from a politically active stance. James C. Hall's extensive analysis examines the influence of the turbulent 1960s on African American writers. He points out a "turn toward a fundamental disbelief in the inherent goodness of the offerings of modernity, indeed, an antimodernism" (Hall, 4). He notes the influence of **Richard Wright** had on Rivers's poetry. During the late 1940s, a significant number of African American intellectuals left the United States for Europe, disaffected with the racial strife prevalent in American cities. Rivers was among many of the "postwar African American creative intelligentsia" to travel for the sake of his art (Hall, 11), spending the summer of 1963 mostly in **Paris, France**.

Rivers participated in the formation of a dynamic discussion group during the 1960s, with the journalists **Ronald L. Fair** and David Lorens, and the organizer Gerald McWhorter. Bigsby suggests that these men were out to change the world, but could not agree on where to begin (*The Black American Writer*, 102–103). Many writers, such as **Angela Jackson**, participated. Eventually, this movement became the seed group for the formation of the Organization of Black American Culture, or **OBAC**. The tragedy of his life cut short is eased by the legacy that he left to African American writers.

Resources: Primary Sources: Conrad Kent Rivers: *Dusk at Selma* (Cleveland, OH: Free Lance Press, 1965); *Perchance to Dream* (Wilberforce, OH: Wilberforce University Press, 1962); *The Still Voice of Harlem* (London: Paul Breman, 1968); *These Black Bodies and This Sunburnt Face* (Cleveland, OH: Free Lance Press, 1965); *The Wright Poems* (London: Paul Breman, 1972). **Secondary Sources:** C.W.E. Bigsby, *The Second Black Renaissance: Essays in Black Literature* (Westport, CT: Greenwood Press, 1980); C.W.E. Bigsby, ed., *The Black American Writer*, vol. 2, *Poetry and Drama* (Deland, FL: Everett/Edwards, 1969); Paul Breman, comp., *You Better Believe It* (New York: Penguin, 1973); Edwin L. Coleman II, "Conrad Kent Rivers," in *Dictionary of Literary Biography*, vol. 41 (Detroit: Gale, 1985), 282; Mercer Cook and Stephen E. Henderson, *The Militant Black Writer in Africa and the United States* (Madison: University of Wisconsin Press, 1969); James C. Hall, *Mercy, Mercy Me: African-American Culture and the American Sixties* (New York: Oxford University Press, 2001); Blyden Jackson and Louis D. Rubin, Jr., *Black Poetry in America: Two Essays in Historical Interpretation* (Baton Rouge: Louisiana State University, 1974); Abby Arthur Johnson and Ronald Mayberry Johnson, *Propaganda and Aesthetics: The Literary Politics of Afro-American Magazines of the Twentieth Century* (Amherst: University of Massachusetts Press, 1979); Don L. Lee, *Dynamite Voices I: Black Poets of the 1960's*

(Detroit: Broadside Press, 1971); Clarence Major, *The Dark and Feeling: Black American Writers and Their Work* (New York: Third Press, 1974).

Martha Modena Vertreace-Doody

Robeson, Paul (1898–1976). Actor, singer, autobiographer, and political activist. Paul von Blum calls Robeson "arguably the greatest Renaissance person in American history and one of the central cultural figures of the twentieth century" (213). Paul Robeson was born in Princeton, New Jersey. His father, William Drew Robeson, was an escaped slave from North Carolina who graduated from college and became a Presbyterian minister. Robeson's mother, Maria Louisa Bustill, was a schoolteacher who died when Paul was only six years old. An outstanding scholar and athlete, Robeson entered Rutgers College, as the only Black student, on scholarship in 1916. He graduated in 1919 and moved to **Harlem, New York**, to study law at Columbia University. He was admitted to the bar in 1923, and briefly practiced in a law firm, before turning to acting, where he enjoyed a brilliant career on stage and in film. Robeson's portrayal of the title character in Shakespeare's *Othello* was widely lauded.

Paul Robeson, 1942. Courtesy of the Library of Congress.

Robeson took an interest in socialism in the 1930s and caused national controversy in 1949 by stating that it was "unthinkable" that Black Americans would participate in a war against the Soviet Union, a country he felt had treated Blacks much better than his own (Sellman, 1626). This outraged many Americans and was the catalyst for a mob of White men attacking concertgoers later the same year at an outdoor Robeson concert near Peekskill, New York. Robeson's memoir, *Here I Stand* (1958), is a blend of **autobiography** and political activism. His wife, Eslanda Goode Robeson, published *Paul Robeson, Negro* (1930), which focuses on his career and their relationship. Lenwood Davis has compiled *A Paul Robeson Research Guide* (1982) and *A Paul Robeson Handbook* (1998). These include Robeson's speeches, interviews, and filmographies, his quotations and sayings, and a vast number of bibliographical references to materials about Robeson. *Paul Robeson: Essays on His Life and Legacy* (2002) is a collection of papers delivered at a 1998 academic conference. Biographies of Robeson include Martin B. Duberman's *Paul Robeson: A Biography* (1988) and Susan Robeson's pictorial biography *The Whole World in His Hands* (1981). Robeson has also been the inspiration for creative literature. **Phillip Hayes Dean**'s 1978 play *Paul Robeson* starred James

Earl Jones in the title role and was performed at the Booth Theatre in New York. Earl Schenck Miers's novel *Big Ben* (1942) is a fictional account of Robeson's years at Rutgers University. Outside the literary sphere, Paul Robeson produced many audio recordings, such as "Ol' Man River," and starred in feature films, such as *King Solomon's Mines* (1937).

Resources: Sheila Tully Boyle and Andrew Bunie, *Paul Robeson: The Years of Promise and Achievement* (Amherst: University of Massachusetts Press, 2001); Phillip Hayes Dean, *Paul Robeson* (Garden City, NY: Doubleday, 1978); Richard Dyer, *Heavenly Bodies: Film Stars and Society* (Basingstoke, UK: Macmillan, 1986); *King Solomon's Mines*, dir. Robert Stevenson (1937; MGM/UA Home Entertainment, 2003), DVD; Rebecca Larsen, *Paul Robeson: Hero Before His Time* (New York: Franklin Watts, 1989), for young adults; "Paul Robeson Home Page" (Rutgers University: Electronic New Jersey), http://www.scc.rutgers.edu/njh/PaulRobeson; Sterling Plumpp, *Paul Robeson* (Chicago: Third World Press, 1992); Lois Potter, *Othello* (New York: Manchester University Press, 2002); Paul Robeson, *Paul Robeson Sings "Ol' Man River" & Other Favorites* (EMI, 1987), CD; James Clyde Sellman, "Robeson, Paul," in *Africana: The Encyclopedia of the African and African American Experience*, ed. Kwame Anthony Appiah and Henry Louis Gates, Jr. (New York: BasicCivitas, 1999); *Speak of Me as I Am: The Story of Paul Robeson*, dir. Rachel Hermer (1998; NJN Public Television, 1999), videocassette; Jeffrey C. Stewart, ed., *Paul Robeson: Artist and Citizen* (New Brunswick, NJ: Rutgers University Press, 1998); Paul Von Blum, "Expanding the African-American Studies Curriculum: 'Paul Robeson: An American Life,'" in *Paul Robeson: Essays on His Life and Legacy*, ed. Joseph Dorinson and William Pencak (Jefferson, NC: McFarland, 2002), 213–218.

Mark Wadman

Robinson, C. Kelly (born 1970). Novelist. Born and raised in Dayton, Ohio, Robinson completed a B.S. in business administration at Howard University and an M.S. in business administration at Washington University in **St. Louis, Missouri**. He was subsequently employed by Price Waterhouse and Emerson Electric. Although he has continued to work as a financial analyst, he has increasingly concentrated on his writing, taking courses and workshops in fiction writing, reading a number of guides and handbooks on the topic, and participating in local and online writers' groups. Although he now has a prominent literary agency to market his work, he and his wife, Kyra, founded the publishing company Against the Grain Communications in part to publish his work. Aiming, more broadly, to promote more positive images of African Americans, their initial titles included his wife's nonfiction book *No Ways Tired: The Public Historically Black College Dilemma* and Robinson's first novel, *Not All Dogs* (1997).

Drawing on Robinson's experience at Howard University, *Not All Dogs*—republished as *Between Brothers* (1999)—concerns the efforts of four seniors at a historically Black college to save a community center. Robinson borrows elements from the suspense genre in making the antagonist a local drug lord. But his attention to characterization and his awareness of the nuances in social issues make this more than simply a genre novel. Indeed, the thematic points that the novel makes are more subtle and complex than they might otherwise be because involvement in this project affects each of the young men quite differently.

The title of *No More Mr. Nice Guy* (2002) refers to one of the main characters, a nice guy who becomes so frustrated by the ways in which women have abused his sensitivity that he transforms himself into a "player." His story is juxtaposed with that of a young woman who has become so tired of dealing with "players" that she yearns for a relationship with a nice guy. Out of this ironic pairing, Robinson creates a fairly fast-paced, perceptive, and witty story.

In *the Perfect Blend* (2004), Robinson focuses on a young man who seems to have achieved everything that he has wanted and finds his life rather crowded as he attempts to balance his commitments to his family, his friends, and his profession.

The Strong Silent Type (2005) centers on a former pro football player who finds his transition into life after football complicated by his stuttering. When he sees a speech therapist to correct the problem, a romance develops, but it is every bit as complicated as his redefinition of himself as something other than an athlete.

Resources: C. Kelly Robinson: *No More Mr. Nice Guy* (New York: Villard/Strivers Row, 2002); *Not All Dogs* (Dayton, OH: Against the Grain, 1997), repr. as *Between Brothers* (New York: Villard, 1999); *The Perfect Blend* (New York: New American Library, 2004); *The Strong Silent Type* (New York: New American Library, 2005); Glenn Townes, "Review of *The Perfect Blend*," *Black Issues Book Review* 6 (May/June 2004), 48.

Martin Kich

Robinson, Jackie [Jack Roosevelt] (1919–1972). Professional athlete, political activist, business executive, and autobiographer. Robinson helped to revolutionize professional athletics in the United States by breaking through "the color barrier." Born in rural Georgia, the youngest of five children, Jackie Robinson grew up in Pasadena, California, after his mother, Mallie, moved her family west in 1920. He was a star athlete in four different sports at the University of California at Los Angeles and briefly played professional football after college. Robinson entered the Army in 1942 and rose to the rank of lieutenant. He faced a court-martial following an altercation with a White bus driver at Camp Hood, **Texas**, who demanded that he move to the back of the bus even though Army regulations prohibited segregation. Cleared of the charges, Robinson was honorably discharged in 1944.

After playing for the Kansas City Monarchs of the Negro League in 1945, Robinson was signed to a contract by Branch Rickey of the Brooklyn Dodgers, in defiance of the major leagues' long-standing prohibition against African American players. He spent a season with Brooklyn's minor league team at Montreal, Canada, and then joined the Dodgers in 1947, thus integrating baseball. Robinson endured taunts, epithets, death threats, and other forms of intimidation from the general public, as well as hostility, threatened strikes, and dirty play from fellow players. He was immediately successful, earning the Rookie-of-the-Year award, and, in accordance with a strategy established by Rickey, did not retaliate against even the most vicious provocations. During his nine-year career Robinson won both a Most Valuable Player Award and a batting title, and he contributed to Brooklyn's only championship. After the silence of his first year, he increasingly spoke out against racism and more readily confronted those who challenged him. He retired in 1956 and was the first African American elected to baseball's Hall of Fame (1962).

Robinson worked on his public voice, and shaped his image, from the very beginning of his career, when he worked with the Black sportswriter Wendell Smith on *Jackie Robinson: My Own Story* (1948). The book sold well but contained errors that embarrassed Robinson and strained his relationship with Smith. Nevertheless, it was the basis of a modestly successful film, *The Jackie Robinson Story* (1950), starring Robinson as himself.

After retiring from baseball, Robinson worked as an executive for the Chock Full O' Nuts restaurant chain. His 1964 book, *Baseball Has Done It*, reflected his deep interest in civil rights, and included not only reflections on his own career but also statements from other players (Black and White) about the impact of integration on their lives. His entry into major league baseball was, he wrote, "a sociological experiment which has revealed certain truths about human relations, a research laboratory and proving ground for democracy in action" (10).

Robinson, once a prominent Republican, moved away from the party because of its record on civil rights. He was an active public figure who frequently commented on political and social events. In 1963, for example, he famously exchanged letters with the more radical **Malcolm X** in the pages of **The Amsterdam News**. Robinson remained a centrist figure throughout his life, emphasizing economic empowerment for the Black community and working with the **NAACP** and **Martin Luther King, Jr.**, at various times.

In later years, Robinson collaborated with Alfred Duckett on two autobiographies. *Breakthrough to the Big League* (1965), a book for young adults, is part of the large body of children's and adolescent literature that typically frames Robinson as

Back cover of the Jackie Robinson comic book, 1951. Courtesy of the Library of Congress.

a transcendent hero. *I Never Had It Made* (1972), a true memoir, offers self-examination that is provocative and painful more often than inspirational. Robinson explicitly describes the effect of racism on his life, explaining in the Foreword, "I know that I am a black man in a white world. In 1972, in 1947, at my birth in 1919, I know that I never had it made" (12). Less than half of the book is devoted to Robinson's baseball career; the rest focuses on politics, civil rights, equality, and personal development. The narrative offers a moving account of the death of his son, Jackie, who was successfully overcoming heroin addiction when he was killed in a car accident in 1971. Robinson's own untimely death occurred a year later. **Arnold Rampersad**'s important biography of Robinson was published in 1997.

From his dramatic entry into the major leagues to the present day, Robinson has been an iconic figure used to define the struggle for civil rights and equality. In his books and public statements, Robinson acknowledged the symbolic power of his accomplishments in baseball, but he also consistently connected what he had done to the cause of larger social change. In his foreword to a later edition of *I Never Had It Made*, **Cornel West** argues that Jackie Robinson "took on the awesome burden of symbolizing black humanity. . . . not because he wanted to *be* somebody but, rather, because he was already a great *somebody* in a land where all black folk were nobody to most white people." Robinson, as a player and later a writer, used his public image and voice to combat such a stifling invisibility.

Resources: *The Jackie Robinson Reader: Perspectives on an American Hero*, ed. Jules Tygiel (New York: Dutton, 1997); Arnold Rampersad, *Jackie Robinson* (New York: Knopf, 1997); Jackie Robinson, *Baseball Has Done It*, ed. Charles Dexter (Philadelphia: Lippincott, 1964); Jackie Robinson with Alfred Duckett: *Breakthrough to the Big League: The Story of Jackie Robinson* (New York: Harper & Row, 1965); *I Never Had It Made* (New York: Putnam, 1972); Jackie Robinson with Wendell Smith, *Jackie Robinson: My Own Story* (New York: Greenberg, 1948); Jules Tygiel, *Baseball's Great Experiment* (New York: Oxford University Press, 1997).

Robert D. Sturr

Robotham, Rosemarie Angela (born 1957). Editor, novelist, short story writer, and journalist. Robotham was born in St. Andrew, Jamaica, and raised in the capital city, Kingston. She did her university studies in the United States in New York City at Barnard College, where she earned a B.A. in English and geography. Later she earned an M.A. from Columbia University's School of Journalism. Robotham was a staff writer for *Life* magazine, and as a freelance journalist, she has contributed to numerous publications. She has also worked as an editor for the publisher Simon and Schuster. As an editor, Robotham has helped develop collections of writing that offer different views about and voices from the African **diaspora**. She is also interested in issues concerning the **Black family**, women and sexuality, and the **Middle Passage** (*Spirits of the Passage*). Robotham received good reviews for her novel *Zachary's Wings*, a contemporary love story concerning issues of social class and mixed-race relationships. In the introduction to *Mending the World*, a collection of stories about Black families, Robotham emphasizes the importance of "kinship relationships" that have been "critical to our survival, helping us to create entirely new definitions of who we are—and who we might yet become in a world that does not always admit our possibilities or welcome our vision." At this writing, Robotham is Senior Editor-at-Large for *Essence* magazine.

Resources: Rosemarie Robotham: "Dreaming in Harlem," in *Beloved Harlem*, ed. Bill Banks (New York: Doubleday, 2003); "Jesse," in *Black American Short Stories*, ed. John Henrik Clarke (New York: Hill & Wang, 1993); *Spirits of the Passage: The Transatlantic Slave Trade in the Seventeenth Century* (New York: Simon and Schuster, 1997); *Zachary's Wings* (New York: Scribner's, 1998); Rosemarie Robotham, ed.: *The Bluelight Corner: Black Women Writing on Passion, Sex and Romantic Love* (New York: Three Rivers Press, 1999); *Mending the World: Stories of Family by Contemporary Black Writers* (New York: BasicCivitas, 2003).

Wilma Jean Emanuel Randle

Roby, Kimberla Lawson (born 1965). Novelist. Roby self-published her first novel, *Behind Closed Doors*, through Lenox Press; the book was later reissued by Black Classic Press in 1997 and then by the mass-market publisher Avon in 2004. Since then she has published several extremely popular novels that explore problems faced by middle-class African Americans, particularly but not exclusively women. Her novels often have an underlying Christian theme, but also confront such issues as class conflict, adultery, workplace racism, and addiction to gambling. The narratives appeal to readers of **romance novel**s as well as to readers interested in contemporary, thematically Christian fiction. *Casting the First Stone* and *Too Much of a Good Thing* both feature the protagonist Curtis Black, an African American pastor who must negotiate emotional and spiritual conflicts. Roby began writing in 1995 (Price). Concerning the novel *A Taste of Reality*, she has said, "I wanted to examine and portray what it would be like, dealing with two extremely emotional issues simultaneously and then show what any woman might do to overcome them" (Price). Roby attended Illinois State University and graduated from Cardinal Stritch University in Milwaukee, Wisconsin.

Resources: Loretta Price, "Interview with Kimberla Lawson Roby," *Angelfire: The Literary Word* (Dec. 2, 2002), http://www.angelfire.com/co4/interviews/kim.html; Kimberla Lawson Roby: *Behind Closed Doors* (Baltimore: Black Classic Press, 1997; New York: Avon, 2004); *The Best-Kept Secret* (New York: Morrow, 2005); *Casting the First Stone* (New York: Dafina, 2002); *Here and Now* (New York: Dafina, 1999); *It's a Thin Line* (New York: Dafina, 2001); *A Taste of Reality* (New York: Avon, 2004); *Too Much of a Good Thing* (New York: Morrow, 2004).

Hans Ostrom

Rodgers, Carolyn M[arie] (born c. 1945). Poet, prose writer, critic, publisher, and lecturer. A noted figure in the **Black Arts Movement** of the 1960s, Rodgers, based in **Chicago, Illinois**, is known for her innovation in poetic voice and form, and for her sensitive exploration of a range of thematic concerns: racism, revolution, **gender** roles, relationships, identity, family conflict, spirituality, and survival. Her poetry documents the struggle to speak authentically as an African American woman during an era of dramatic social change, in a genre long dominated by Anglo-European tradition.

Rodgers began writing poems early in her school career, but an encounter with **Gwendolyn Brooks** on the Roosevelt University campus served as inspiration to take her avocation seriously. While employed as a social worker in the mid-1960s, Rodgers worked on her B.A., attended workshops conducted by Brooks, and joined **OBAC** Writers Workshop. With fellow OBAC participants **Haki R. Madhubuti** (Don L. Lee) and Johari Amini (Jewel Latimore), she founded **Third World Press**, a vehicle for new work in the spirit of cultural revolution.

Encouraged by Brooks and by **Hoyt Fuller** (OBAC founder and the editor of **Negro Digest**), Rodgers had her first collection, *Paper Soul*, distributed by Third World Press in 1968. Her work earned her the first **Conrad Kent Rivers** Memorial Fund Award, and subsequent publications, *Two Love Raps* (1969) and *Songs of a Black Bird* (1969), brought her the Poet Laureate Award of the Society of Midland Authors and a grant from the National Endowment for the Arts. Rodgers's bold articulation of the tensions and contradictions in contemporary African American life led to a continuing series of lectureships and residencies at colleges and universities. It also triggered criticism from some of her poet peers, those discomfited by her unconventional spellings, her mix of street language and Standard English, and/or her expression of certain themes and attitudes associated with the militant Black male. Rodgers directly addressed the pressure to represent "the new Black Womanhood" as "a softer self" in "The Last M. F." (*Black Bird*), a poem that simultaneously acquiesces to the demands of her artistic community and defends (and reiterates) her linguistic choices.

How I Got Ovah: New and Selected Poems (1975), published by Doubleday's Anchor Press, marks Rodgers's abandonment of her earlier political persona and further development of more introspective themes. Nominated for the National Book Award, this collection addresses such topics as love, loneliness, religion, and family (especially maternal) ties. *The Heart as Ever Green* (1978) likewise explores an evolving, meditative self in the context of community, notably through images of the natural world. In the title poem, the speaker's resilient heart is "ever green," "like buds or shoots,/determined to grow."

After publication with Doubleday, Rodgers established Chicago's Eden Press with support from the Illinois Arts Council, and her subsequent collections have appeared under that imprint. Sustaining her commitment to higher education, she earned an M.A. from the University of Chicago in the early 1980s. Carolyn Rodgers's work as a writer and educator has continued to receive commendation, and among her honors are the Carnegie Award and multiple PEN awards. Her remarkable oeuvre includes fiction, essays, reviews, and musical compositions.

Resources: Primary Sources: *Eden and Other Poems* (Chicago: Eden, 1983); *Finite Forms: Poems* (Chicago: Eden, 1985); *For Flip Wilson* (Detroit: Broadside, 1971); *For H. W. Fuller* (Detroit: Broadside, 1970); *The Girl with Blue Hair* (Chicago: Eden, 1996); *The Heart as Ever Green: Poems* (Garden City, NY: Anchor-Doubleday, 1978); *How I Got Ovah: New and Selected Poems* (Garden City, NY: Anchor-Doubleday, 1975); *A Little Lower Than the Angels* (Chicago: Eden, 1984); *Long Rap/Commonly Known as a Poetic Essay* (Detroit: Broadside, 1971); *Morning Glory: Poems* (Chicago: Eden, 1989); *Now Ain't That Love* (Detroit: Broadside, 1970); *Paper Soul* (Chicago: Third World, 1968); *Salt* (Chicago: Eden, 1998); *Songs of a Black Bird* (Chicago: Third World, 1969); *A Train Called Judah* (Chicago: Eden, 1996); *Translation: Poems* (Chicago: Eden, 1980); *Two Love Raps* (Chicago: Third World, 1969); *We're Only Human* (Chicago: Eden, 1994). **Secondary Sources:** Fahamisha Patricia Brown, "Rodgers, Carolyn M.," in *American Women Writers: A Critical Reference Guide*, ed. Taryn Benbow-Pfalzgraf, 2nd ed. (Detroit: St. James, 2000); Jean Davis, "Carolyn M. Rodgers," in *Dictionary of Literary Biography*, vol. 41, *Afro-American Poets Since 1955* (Detroit: Gale, 1985); Mari Evans, ed., *Black Women Writers (1950–1980): A Critical Evaluation* (Garden City, NY: Anchor-Doubleday, 1984); Karen Jackson Ford, *Gender and the Poetics of Excess: Moments of Brocade* (Jackson: University Press of Mississippi, 1997); Barbara J. Griffin, "Carolyn Rodgers," in *Notable Black American Women*, ed. Jessie Carney Smith, vol. 2 (Detroit: Gale, 1996); Joyce Pettis, "Carolyn Rodgers," in her *African American Poets: Lives, Works, and Sources* (Westport, CT: Greenwood Press, 2002); "Rodgers, Carolyn (Marie)," in *African-American Writers: A Dictionary*, ed. Shari Hatch and Michael Strickland (Santa Barbara, CA: ABC-CLIO, 2000); "Rodgers, Carolyn M(arie)," in *Black Writers: A Selection of Sketches from Contemporary Authors*, ed. Sharon Malinowski, 2nd ed. (Detroit: Gale, 1994); Marsha C. Vick, "Rodgers, Carolyn M.," *The Oxford Companion to African American Literature* (New York: Oxford University Press, 1997); Jon Woodson, "Rodgers, Carolyn M.," in *The Oxford Companion to Women's Writing in the United States*, ed. Cathy Davidson and Linda Wagner-Martin (New York: Oxford University Press, 1995).

Janis Butler Holm

Romance Novel. One of the most popular literary forms the world over, the romance novel engages with the affective and sexual dynamics of human intimacy by way of recognizable narrative conventions. Romantic themes preoccupied even the earliest of African American novelists, but it was not until the late twentieth century that Black writers had the opportunity to take up or even have access to romance as a precise mode of genre writing. Contemporary African American romance novelists have moved beyond the form's historically White and heterosexist contexts and preoccupations to depict the fullness of Black love in its multiply racialized, classed, and gendered dimensions.

Early Black novels were prone to articulate critiques of **slavery** and White domination in romantic plots. **William Wells Brown**'s historical (anti)romance *Clotel* (1853) is loosely based on Thomas Jefferson's rumored liaisons with his slave **Sally Hemings**. The novel was originally published in London, and did not appear in the United States until the 1860s. In telling the story of Clotel, daughter of Jefferson and his slave mistress, Currer, Brown makes explicit the sexual violence visited upon Black women as a means of reproducing the institution of slavery. A forerunner to such more famous twentieth-century historical novelists as **Frank Yerby** and **Margaret Abigail Walker**, Brown shows how White men's falling in "love" with their slaves was ultimately a cover for socioeconomic interest and racial domination. **Frances Ellen Watkins Harper**'s *Iola Leroy* (1892) and **Pauline Elizabeth Hopkins**'s *Contending Forces* (1900) are sentimental novels that explore similar themes in postbellum contexts; their female characters are able to pass in middle-class society but ultimately become credits to their race according to a logic of virtuous Black womanhood. **Charles Waddell Chesnutt**'s widely read *The House Behind the Cedars* (1900) is a novel of **passing** in which the **mulatto** Rena Walden passes as the White Rowena Warwick to win the affection of the aristocrat George Tryon. Here Rena's desire is a function of upward mobility and heterosexual longing, with the tragic result being the impossibility of consummating her love for Tryon.

In the 1920s and 1930s, the **Harlem Renaissance** witnessed the publication of a number of modernist-realist romances that upend traditional notions of **race** and **racial uplift**. The bourgeois women of **Jessie Redmon Fauset**'s "novel without a moral," *Plum Bun* (1929), and **Nella Larsen**'s self-reflexively urbane *Passing* (1929) determine passing to be an extraordinary gift and a tiresome burden at the same time. The color of Angela Murray's skin in *Plum Bun* enables her to experience the pleasures and delights of the proverbial "New Woman," but at the cost of recognizing her own kin in the city. The famed encounter at the end of *Passing*, between Irene Redfield and Clare Kendry, which leaves Clare dead from a fall, is the culmination of Irene's anxious policing of her racial and sexual identities throughout the story. In contrast to Fauset's and Larsen's novels, **Jean Toomer**'s *Cane* (1923), **Claude McKay**'s *Home to Harlem* (1928), and **Zora Neale Hurston**'s *Their Eyes Were Watching God* (1937) reveal the thwarted and at times thriving loves of the Northern urban working class and the Southern rural folk, none of whom has the ability or the desire to pass. Their lusty, quasi-romantic narratives reveal a division in class and **labor** relations in the way African American novelists, even those writing today, deal with questions of affect and sexuality.

James Baldwin's *Giovanni's Room* (1956) would prove to be the most powerful yet unusual "Black" romance of its time, for all the main characters are White, the story is set in **Paris, France**, and the most convincing sexual bond develops between two men, the American expatriate David and the Italian bartender Giovanni. More than anything else, it may have been Baldwin's lyrical prose that signaled a new direction in the way African Americans engaged with the genre. Black romance novelists could now write about love's triumphs and tragedies without being overly sentimental in style or overly reductive in plot. Furthermore, following in the footsteps of McKay as well as Baldwin, they would not need to confine their writing to heterosexual romance. Interestingly enough, these developments came to fruition only after Black women writers responded to the misogynistic, antiromance sentiment of 1960s **Black Nationalism** in novels of their own: **Gayl Jones**'s *Corregidora* (1975) and *Eva's Man* (1976); **Alice Walker**'s *Meridian* (1976) and *The Color Purple* (1982); and **Gloria Naylor**'s *The Women of Brewster Place* (1982) and *Mama Day* (1988). In *Sula* (1974), *Tar Baby* (1981), *Jazz* (1992), and *Love* (2003), **Toni Morrison** has fashioned one of the most remarkable single-authored oeuvres in world literature about the various shades and contours of Black love.

On a different level of the field of literary production, which requires a slightly different definition of the romance genre, the industry-leading romance publisher Harlequin did not bring out its first book featuring African Americans in the lead roles until 1984. **Sandra Kitt**'s *Adam and Eva*, set in the Virgin Islands with a vacationing woman and a single father, opened the door for African American romance authorship in the genre-oriented mainstream. There was no turning back. Kitt would go on to produce several other novels, mostly starring White characters, for the Harlequin American imprint, and although her career there gradually tailed off, she became the first author to be published by Kensington Publishing's Arabesque imprint in 1994. That series was founded when the chairman overheard two Black women in a New York City bookstore complaining about the lack of romantic fare for them. Coupled with the amazing success of **Terry McMillan**'s *Waiting to Exhale* in 1992, which ushered in a renaissance of Black popular writing in the United States more generally, the Arabesque line helped turn Black romance publishing into a full-blown enterprise. Women writers in particular became household names: **Rochelle Alers**, **Gwynne Forster**, **Donna Hill**, and Margie Walker. Kensington managed to do this in a little less than five years; in 1998 the company sold Arabesque to Black Entertainment Television (BET), where it continues to flourish.

Like McMillan, **Connie Briscoe**, **Bebe Moore Campbell**, and other contemporary quasi-romantic novelists, African American men have gone beyond the genre's plot and character conventions to represent their unique perspectives on Black and interracial intimacy. **Omar Tyree**'s *Flyy-Girl* (1993) and *A Do Right Man* (1997) paved the way for Black male romance writing, with *A Do Right Man* introducing readers to a strong yet sensitive, attractive yet self-conscious, African American man in search of true love. **Eric Jerome Dickey**'s *Sister, Sister* (1996) and *Friends and Lovers* (1997) are renowned for their emotionally complex Black female protagonists; his *Milk in My Coffee* (1998) explores the interracial sexual and family dynamics between Jordan Greene, a Black urban professional, and Kimberly Chavers, a White artist. **Carl Weber** employs sharp humor to tackle serious issues of masculine anxiety in *Married Men* (2001) and *Baby Momma Drama* (2003). One might say work by these men serves as a generational counterpoint to representations of Black masculinity not only in structural state racism, particularly when it comes to racial profiling and incarceration rates, but also in the Black female-authored novels of the 1970s and 1980s, where African American men tended to exercise dominant, patriarchal authority.

E. Lynn Harris is arguably the most popular and important gay romance novelist in the United States today. *Invisible Life* (1991), *Just as I Am* (1994), and *And This Too Shall Pass* (1996) are heartfelt, intelligent explorations of contemporary Black sexuality, which Harris refuses to categorize as being either essentially heterosexual or deviantly homosexual. His African American men struggle to bridge the gap between personal attraction and social or familial expectations. They usually find themselves torn between stereotypically "straight" identities in public—the ladies' man in college, the professional athlete, the well-respected businessman—and ostensibly "gay" sexual practices, which they keep private at the expense of being honest with their wives or girlfriends. The covert practices have come to be known as "living on the down low" or "the DL" in American social and cultural politics. Harris takes pains not to pathologize his characters, but to understand and sympathize with their complex motivations. He handles such topics as adultery, promiscuity, and AIDS with an unflinching yet deeply mature aesthetic.

Romance novelists from Kitt to Harris have established diverse and loyal audiences for their work. Their success has led to increased opportunities for African American romance authorship on at least three levels. First, popular imprints of major U.S. publishing houses have dedicated significant portions of their catalogs to Black romance fiction. Random House's Villard Books has released **Tajuana Butler**'s *Hand-Me-Down Heartache* (2001), **C. Kelly Robinson**'s *Between Brothers* (2001), and Tracy Price-Thompson's *Black Coffee* (2002). Simon and Schuster's Atria Books has come out with **Jervey Tervalon**'s *All the Trouble You Need* (2002), **Zane**'s *The Heat Seekers* (2002), and the 2004 reprint of **Sister Souljah**'s *The Coldest Winter Ever* (1999). Since the sale of Arabesque to BET in 1998, Kensington has developed its Dafina Books imprint, which publishes the prolific novelists Roslyn Carrington, **Margaret Johnson-Hodge**, Timmothy B. McCann, **Mary Monroe**, Mary B. Morrison, and **Kimberla Lawson Roby**.

Second, and on a smaller but no less significant scale of production, independent presses have supported first-time, regional, and underground romance novelists whose work draws the avid, less crossover-minded reader. These books tend to embrace poor or working-class settings and protagonists more readily than their big-name counterparts. Of note here is **Genesis Press** of Columbus, Mississippi, the largest Black privately owned book publishing company in the United States, whose Indigo and Indigo Love Spectrum imprints compete quite well with BET's Arabesque and Kensington's Dafina series. An author of note is Wahida Clark, who, with the help of Black Print Publishing based in **Brooklyn, New York**, has penned hardcore "romances" of the street, *Thugs and the Women Who Love Them* (2002) and *Every Thug Needs a Lady* (2003), while incarcerated in a women's federal prison in Lexington, Kentucky.

Finally, online publishing practices as well as work, neighborhood, and circle-of-friends book clubs have democratized the literary field by forging communities of readers and writers who are in it for the books, so to speak. Black romance Web sites such as Zane's www.eroticanoire.com are at the forefront of the revolution in and outside of print, turning literary nonprofessionals into published authors. Moreover, African American women's reading groups have sprung up across the nation in response not only to the inaugural season of Oprah's Book Club (1996) but also to the need felt by mothers, daughters, sisters, and friends to come together to talk about their favorite stories about Black love.

Based on these observations alone, one might conclude that the romance novel has been the most influential literary form in making this a critical era for Black literary production, measured in terms of best-selling books written by African Americans. But it is also worth pointing out that the McMillan-romance boom has stirred interest in African American **erotica** in short stories and anthologies. Though not technically romance novels, volumes such as *Brown Sugar* (2001), *After Hours* (2002), and *Black Silk* (2002), among a host of others, collect daring narratives of Black lust and desire that take their cue from the previously cited texts. Erotica has always occupied the margins of the literary field, denounced as pornography in public yet consumed as art in private. Black erotica sees this sort of readerly transgression as an occasion to deconstruct long-standing stereotypes about the hypersexual African American body. It accomplishes this not by policing the bounds of Black lust or desire but by expanding them through representations of both raw sensuality and passionate feeling. Zane's *The Sex Chronicles* (1999) is the most illustrative single-author book of this sort; hers is also one of the more provocative depictions of the sexual fantasies of modern Black women.

Resources: Michael Awkward, *Inspiriting Influences: Tradition, Revision, and Afro-American Women's Novels* (New York: Columbia University Press, 1989); Houston A. Baker, Jr., *Workings of the Spirit: The Poetics of Afro-American Women's Writing* (Chicago: University of Chicago Press, 1991); Devon W. Carbado, Dwight A. McBride, and Donald Weise, eds., *Black Like Us: A Century of Lesbian, Gay, and Bisexual African American Fiction* (San Francisco: Cleis, 2002); Hazel V. Carby, *Reconstructing Womanhood: The Emergence of the Afro-American Woman Novelist* (New York: Oxford University Press, 1987); Barbara Christian, *Black Women Novelists: The Development of a Tradition, 1892–1976* (Westport, CT: Greenwood Press, 1980); Patricia Hill Collins, *Black Sexual Politics: African Americans, Gender, and the New Racism* (New York: Routledge, 2004); Robert Fleming, ed., *After Hours: A Collection of Erotic Writing by Black Men* (New York: Plume, 2002); Calvin C. Hernton, *The Sexual Mountain and Black Women Writers: Adventures in Sex, Literature, and Real Life* (New York: Anchor, 1987); Deborah E. McDowell, *"The Changing Same": Black Women's Literature, Criticism, and Theory* (Bloomington: Indiana University Press, 1995); Retha Powers, ed., *Black Silk: A Collection of African American Erotica* (New York: Warner, 2002); Marjorie Pryse and Hortense J. Spillers, eds., *Conjuring: Black Women, Fiction, and Literary Tradition* (Bloomington: Indiana University Press, 1985); Carol Taylor, ed., *Brown Sugar: A Collection of Erotic Black Fiction* (New York: Plume, 2001).

Kinohi Nishikawa

Rose, Tricia (born 1962). Scholar, nonfiction writer, editor, and teacher. Rose is an innovative scholar who specializes in African American culture, **race** politics, **hip-hop** culture, and women's issues. She has published three books: *Longing to Tell: Black Women Talk About Sexuality and Intimacy*, *Black Noise: Rap Music and Black Culture in Contemporary America*, and *Microphone Fiends: Youth Music and Youth Culture*. She edited the latter with Andrew Moss.

Black Noise offers a theoretical and cultural analysis of hip-hop culture and **rap** music. It addresses the origins and transformation of hip-hop music and culture, the effects of rap on the perception of women, and the politics of rap in American culture. *Black Noise* won an American Book Award in 1995.

Microphone Fiends is an anthology of essays, interviews, commentary, and criticism that addresses rap culture, music, and its effects. Rose's latest book, at this writing, is *Longing to Tell: Black Women Talk About Sexuality and Intimacy*. This ethnographic book collects oral histories from African American women from diverse backgrounds; the oral histories focus on the women's experiences with sexuality.

Rose has contributed articles on such subjects as hip-hop, popular culture, and **Sally Hemings** to periodicals including *Essence*, *Vibe*, the *Village Voice*, and the *Boston Book Review*.

Rose earned a B.A. from Yale University and an M.A. and Ph.D. from Brown University. She teaches at the University of California, Santa Cruz.

Resources: Tricia Rose, *Black Noise: Rap Music and Black Culture in Contemporary America* (Middletown, CT: Wesleyan University Press, 1994); Tricia Rose, comp., *Longing to Tell: Black Women Talk About Sexuality and Intimacy* (New York: Farrar, Straus and Giroux, 2003); Tricia Rose and Andrew Moss, eds., *Microphone Fiends: Youth Music and Youth Culture* (New York: Routledge, 1994).

Shondrika L. Moss

Rowe, George Clinton (1853–1903). Poet and editor. As a poet and a preacher, Rowe's work focused on God and the African American **race**. Born in Connecticut, he moved to **the South** in 1876 and never returned to New England.

Rowe apprenticed to the *Litchfield Enquirer* in Connecticut and continued in the newspaper trade when he moved to Charleston, South Carolina. Along with his editing duties at various **newspapers**, he was an ordained Congregationalist minister. Rowe also worked with many organizations to improve the lives of African Americans.

Rowe's poetry has been praised for its sincerity, if not for its virtuosity. Most of the poems in *Thoughts in Verse* (1887) are **sermons** put in verse. Poems such as "The Life Boat" and "The Christian Faith" exhort the reader to believe in God even when his ways are unclear. Hard work and faith are the keys to happiness in most of the poems in this volume.

The poems in *Our Heroes* (1890) are directed "toward the elevation of the race." In the book's preface, Rowe explains that race pride is a prerequisite for

racial uplift. The poems in *Our Heroes* serve this end. Rowe includes tributes to various fighting men, including Crispus Attucks and Toussaint L'Ouverture, and to godly men of the cloth.

In addition to these two volumes, Rowe published *Memorial Souvenir* pamphlets, which were verse tributes to people such as the president of Livingstone College in North Carolina. Although Rowe was not regarded as a gifted poet, his poetry has been praised for its ability to look into the consciences of its subjects.

Resources: Blyden Jackson, *A History of Afro-American Literature*, vol. 1, *The Long Beginning, 1746–1895* (Baton Rouge: Louisiana State University Press, 1989), 263–264; *George Clinton Rowe: A Memorial Souvenir of Rev. J. Wofford White* (Charleston, SC: Walker, Evans & Cogswell, 1890); *Our Heroes* (Charleston, SC: Walker, Evans & Cogswell, 1890); *Thoughts in Verse* (Charleston, SC: Kahrs, Stolze & Welch, 1887); Joan R. Sherman, *Invisible Poets: Afro-Americans of the Nineteenth Century*, 2nd ed. (Urbana: University of Chicago Press, 1989), 136–141.

Patricia Kennedy Bostian

Roy, Lucinda (born 1955). Professor and writer. Both a scholar and an artist, Lucinda Roy has served as a teacher and administrator who actively promotes the causes of African American students as she explores themes of **race** and identity within her creative work. She has served as a professor at Virginia Technical University since 1985, where she presently holds an Alumni Distinguished Professorship in English. She also codirects the creative writing program and teaches classes in poetry and fiction. Roy has served as Dean for Outreach, Curriculum, and Diversity in the College of Arts and Sciences and as the Gloria D. Smith Professor of Black Studies and chair of the English department. In 1992, she was the Margaret Bundy Scott Professor of English at Williams College in Massachusetts.

Roy has been a strong advocate for the use of technology as a tool which helps minority students improve their writing and circumvent the hierarchical classroom structures which have hindered them. Her tenure at Virginia Tech has been marked by service to students through initiation of several programs which use technology to serve African American students, women, and other minorities. Roy has also demonstated strong devotion to service learning and programs that benefit the community. She has received the Alumni Award for Teaching Excellence and is a cofounder of the Service-Learning Program and codirector of ACCESS, an information technology project funded by the Alfred P. Sloan Foundation.

Roy is the author of two books of poetry and of fiction. *The Humming Birds* (1995) won the 1994 Eighth Mountain Poetry Prize. In 1989 Roy's "Needlework," a **slave narrative** of several hundred lines, won the Baxter Hathaway Poetry Award. Her poems have appeared in literary journals including **Callaloo**, *American Poetry Review*, *Oxford Magazine*, and *Denver Quarterly*. Roy's first novel, *Lady Moses*, was published in 1998, and her second novel, *The Hotel Alleluia*, was published in 2000. *The Hotel Alleluia* focuses on racial and political issues as it brings an American businesswoman to West Africa, where she searches for her roots and encounters her mixed-race half sister. When both return to the United States, the sisters explore differences in racial identity. Despite their close biological tie, they confront differences posed by culture and continents. Roy's own background includes a White mother and an African father, and reviewers have suggested that Roy's own personal history is ghosted in this novel.

Roy received her B.A. in English from King's College, London, and her M.F.A. in creative writing from the University of Arkansas. In May 2000, she was awarded an honorary doctorate of letters by the University of Richmond. Roy also works as a visual artist and speaks on the significance of instructional technology.

Resources: Lucinda Roy: "Home Page," http://athena.english.vt.edu/~roy/roy.html; *The Hotel Alleluia* (New York: HarperCollins, 2000); *The Humming Birds* (Portland, OR: Eighth Mountain Press, 1995); *Lady Moses* (New York: HarperFlamingo, 1998); *Wailing the Dead to Sleep* (London: Bogle L'Overture, 1988).

Elline Lipkin

Rushin, [Donna K.] Kate (born 1951). Poet, lecturer, and teacher. Rushin became widely recognized in 1981 with the publication of "The Bridge Poem" in the highly influential anthology *This Bridge Called My Back: Writings by Radical Women of Color*. Her poetry and essays have appeared in a number of anthologies, literary magazines, and journals, including *The Black Woman's Health Book, Double Stitch: Black Women Write about Mothers and Daughters, Home Girls: A Black Feminist Anthology, An Ear to the Ground: An Anthology of Contemporary American Poetry, New Worlds of Literature, Ms.* magazine, *English Teaching Forum,* and **Callaloo**. In 1993, she published a collection of poems titled *The Black Back-Ups*, which was selected by the New York Public Library as one of the Books for the Teen Ager in 1994, and was nominated for a Lambda Literary Award. Rushin has received numerous awards and prizes, including a fellowship from the Fine Arts Work Center in Provincetown, Massachusetts (1977), an Artists Foundation poetry fellowship (1978, for which she was also a finalist in 1985), a residency at the Cummington Community of the Arts in Cummington, Massachusetts (1978–1980), the 1988 Grolier Poetry Prize, the Amelia Earhart Award (1989), an honorable mention in the 1994 Galway Kinnell Poetry Contest, and a Drylongso Award (1995), and a residency at Cave Canem African American Poets Workshop (1997, 1998, 1999). Rushin was the Connecticut Poetry Circuit Poet in 1997.

Rushin was born in Syracuse, New York, and grew up in Camden and Lawnside, New Jersey. She developed a love of poetry from a very early age, encouraged by various family members who supported her love of reading and writing. Rushin states that her writing is very much informed by her memories of "home": "Home is how I talk about being a woman, an African American, an artist, a political person" (Farrow, 13). Through the focus of "home" Rushin gained her first experiences of and insights about loss, and her community's struggles with racism, sexism, homophobia, and economic disenfranchisement. Influenced by **The Last Poets, Amiri Baraka, Carolyn M. Rodgers, Nikki Giovanni,** and **Audre Lorde,** among others, her work is written in **free verse,** in a style that captures the rhyming, repetition, and musicality so often found in African American expressive culture. Rushin's work belongs to a tradition that critically explores and offers commentary on contemporary struggles— particularly those that intersect with **race,** class, and sexuality. Professor Fahamisha Brown asserts that Rushin's work—along with that of other poets such as **Lucille Clifton, June Jordan, Toi Derricotte, Pat Parker,** and **Elizabeth Alexander**—"challenges assumptions, shatters stereotypes, overturns expectations" (*Migrating Words*, 184).

Kate Rushin received a Bachelor of Arts degree in communications and theater from Oberlin College in 1969, and a Master of Fine Arts in creative writing from Brown University in 1994. She has participated in numerous poetry readings, festivals, and community events, and has worked as a community radio broadcaster. She has taught courses on writing and Black women writers at Wesleyan University, Brown University, the Massachusetts Institute of Technology, Boston University, Curry College, the University of Massachusetts–Boston, the Omega Institute, and the Cave Canem Workshop in New York.

Resources: Fahamisha Brown: "I AM A BLACK WOMAN: Pan-African Feminism/ Feminist Pan-Africanism in Black Women's Poetry," in *Migrating Words and Worlds: Pan-Africanism Updated*, ed. E. Anthony Hurley, Renée Larrier, and Joseph McLaren (Trenton, NJ: Africa World Press, 1999); *Performing the Word: African American Poetry as Vernacular Culture* (New Brunswick, NJ: Rutgers University Press, 1999); Anne Farrow, "Writing Home," *Northeast*, June 26, 1994, p. 13; Evelynn H. Hammonds, "Kate Rushin," in *Contemporary Lesbian Writers of the United States: A Bio-Bibliographical Critical Sourcebook*, ed. Sandra Pollack and Denise D. Knight (Westport, CT: Greenwood Press, 1993); Kate Rushin, *The Black Back-Ups* (Ithaca, NY: Firebrand Books, 1993).

Laura Pirott-Quintero

Rux, Carl Hancock (born c. 1968). Poet, playwright, novelist, and performance artist. Carl Hancock Rux is an award-winning, critically acclaimed literary and performance artist who has been hailed by critics as a virtuoso whose written and recorded works have helped shape and redefine African American literature in the twentieth and twenty-first centuries.

Rux was born in **Harlem, New York,** to a mother who suffered from schizophrenia and was subsequently institutionalized for her illness. He did not know his biological father. At the age of four, Rux became part of the foster care system and was raised in the South Bronx. He characterized himself as a loner, and at age four began telling himself stories and drawing pictures because he "really did not have anybody to talk to" (www.fosterclub.com/funstuff/ fam_fosterKids/carlHancock.cfm). At the age of fifteen, Rux was adopted by a family in Harlem who gave him love and support "but had its own dysfunction" (www.fosterclub.com/funstuff/fam_fosterKids/carlHancock.cfm). Despite their dysfunction, Rux's adoptive parents, both avid **jazz** fans who frequented the clubs in Harlem, gave him an extensive and comprehensive music education. After graduation from high school, Rux attended Columbia University.

Rux began seriously writing in 1990. Ironically, his early homespun fantasies did not make their way into his work, though it is difficult to imagine that the act of creating stories at such an early age did not have any effect at all. Because of his acute sense of a wide variety and eclectic mix of musical styles and genres, including **hip-hop**, **gospel**, rock, and R&B, among others, along with frequent visits to the **Nuyorican Poets Café**, Rux became interested in "the sounds of words and what they communicated" (www.fosterclub .com/funstuff/fam_fosterKids/carlHancock.cfm).

Many sounds, words, and other details of Rux's life appear in his works; he has published widely in many media and genres and has won numerous awards, including a Village Voice Literary Prize for "Writers on the Verge," in *Pagan Operetta* (1998) and an Obie for his play *Talk* (2003). His other plays include *Smoke, Lilies, and Jade* (1999/2004) and *Singing in the Womb of Angels* (1992). Rux's poems, fiction, and essays have been published in numerous anthologies and collections, including *Aloud: Voices from the Nuyorican Poets Café* (1994) and *Fire & Spirit: African American Poetry* (1997). His recorded work includes *Rux Revue* (1999) and *Apothecary Rx* (2004). *Asphalt* (2004) is Rux's first novel.

Resources: Miguel Algarin and Bob Holman, eds., *Aloud: Voices from the Nuyorican Poets Café* (New York: Henry Holt, 1994); Carl Hancock Rux: *Asphalt* (New York: Atria, 2004); *Pagan Operetta* (New York: Fly by Night, 1998); *Rux Revue* (Los Angeles: Sony, 1999), CD format; *Talk* (New York: Theatre Communications, 2003); Web page, www.carlhancockrux.com.

Patricia E. Clark

S

Sage: A Scholarly Journal on Black Women (1984–1995). *Sage* was an interdisciplinary journal with an African American feminist and "womanist" stance. The journal was established, in part, to provide a forum for research on African American women; a significant number of articles in *Sage* addressed African American women writers, their literature, and criticism of their works.

Sage was established in April 1983 and housed at the Women's Center of Spelman College in **Atlanta, Georgia**. It was the brainchild of its founding members and first editorial staff: Ruby Sales, Patricia Bell-Scott, Beverly Guy Sheftall, Janet Sims-Wood and Jacqueline Jones Royster. The group founded the Sage Women's Educational Press (SWEP) and began publishing *Sage*. The first issue appeared in May 1984.

Sage made its entrance into the American intellectual dialogue at time when **Black Studies** programs and Women's Studies programs were beginning to win acceptance and to mature inside the academy. Despite the gains in recognition of the conditions of African Americans and women that were made by both fields, there was a failure to discuss the specific concerns of African American women. Black Studies tended to be male-focused and exhibited male biases, and Women's Studies tended to have an Anglo focus and exhibited racial biases. The development of Black Women's Studies and Black feminist thought began to challenge the positionality of these fields. African American women's literature was a critical component in the establishment of Black Women's Studies and *Sage*. According to the editors, *Sage* was founded, in part, as a reaction to the "Black Women's literary renaissance fueled by the creative energies of **Paule Marshall**, **Toni Morrison**, **Toni Cade Bambara** and **Alice Walker**" (Bell-Scott, "In Celebration," p. 2).

The journal had an interdisciplinary focus with a global and cross-cultural perspective. *Sage* had three main objectives—to exist as a forum for discussion of issues important to African American women, to promote feminist scholarship, and to disseminate scholarship about African American women. Many different types of scholarship were represented in *Sage*. It included the scholarly articles and book reviews that are standard in academic journals, but it also included less traditional types of articles, such as excerpts from women's diaries, personal reflections, bibliographies, sketches, and photo essays. The intended audience for *Sage* was broad and included not only academics but also students, teachers, researchers, community activists, and policy makers. Each issue was devoted to a theme, such as mothers and daughters, dance, the **diaspora**, "male kin," health, education, women as workers, artists and artisans, rural Africa, and science and technology. The Spring 1985 issue was titled "Black Women as Writers."

Many articles appearing in *Sage* were written by prominent cultural and literary critics and scholars of African American writing, such as **Gloria Wade-Gayles**, Renita Weems, **bell hooks**, Mae G. Henderson, Carole Boyce Davies, **Pearl Michelle Cleage**, **Alexis DeVeaux**, Claudia Tate, and many others. There were countless scholarly articles and books reviews about many of the significant African American and African women writers, past and present, including Paule Marshall, Buchi Emecheta, Toni Morrison, Bessie Head, **Phillis Wheatley**, **Zora Neale Hurston**, Alice Walker, **Nella Larsen**, **Octavia E. Butler**, **Sherley Anne Williams**, **Gloria Naylor**, and **Frances Ellen Watkins Harper**.

In addition to the journal, the *Sage* editorial group and SWEP were responsible for the publication of one anthology, *Double Stitch* (1991), and the establishment of the Sage Writer/Scholar Internship Program.

Despite an impressive publication run, there were some significant production problems with the journal. *Sage* officially ceased publication with Summer 1995 issue.

Resources: Patricia Bell-Scott, "In Celebration of Black Women's Scholarship," *Sage* 1, no. 1 (Spring 1984), 2; Patricia Bell-Scott, Beverly Sheftall, Jacqueline Jones Royster, Janet Sims-Woods, Miriam DeCosta-Willis, and Lucie Fultz, *Double Stitch: Black Women Write About Mothers and Daughters* (Boston: Beacon, 1991); Beverly Guy-Sheftall, "A Black Feminist Perspective on Transforming the Academy: The Case of Spelman College," in *Theorizing Black Feminisms: The Visionary Pragmatism of Black Women*, ed. Stanlie M. James and Abena P. A. Busia (New York: Routledge, 1983), 77–89; Jacqueline Jones Royster, "Capping a Sagestone: The Final Issue," *Sage* 9, no. 2 (Summer 1995), 2–4.

Kimberly Black-Parker

Salaam, Kalamu ya (born 1947). Poet, playwright, essayist, journalist, and literary and cultural critic. Kalamu ya Salaam has been described as one of the most prolific writers of **the South**. He has earned this distinction because of the wealth of literary material he has created, including prose, poetry, essays, and anthologies. He is also founder of numerous literary organizations and publications.

Salaam's literary productions, whether as poet, playwright, prose writer, or literary or cultural critic, all address one fundamental theme: *that art must be a vehicle to assist in the liberation of African people*. His first plays, produced by the **Free Southern Theater** (FST), reflect the style and subject matter of the **Black Arts Movement** of the 1960s and 1970s. His plays *The Picket* (1968), *Mama* (1969), *Black Liberation Army* (1969), *Happy Birthday Jesus* (1969), *Homecoming* (1970), and *Black Love Song* (1971) were his attempts to capture the communal spirit of African American life (Toombs, 640).

Salaam has built bridges between African Americans and communities in such diverse places as Tanzania, the People's Republic of China, Cuba, Barbados, and Surinam (Millican, 232). He served from 1968 until 1971 as a writer, director, and performer in the FST, which later became known as BLKARTSOUTH. Salaam's first seven one-act plays were performed at FST, and BLKARTSOUTH published his first book of poetry, *The Blues Merchant*, in 1969 (Millican, 232).

Kalamu ya Salaam was born March 24, 1947. He is the son of Vallery and Inola Ferdinand, and the name given to him at birth was Vallery Ferdinand III. In 1970, he changed his name to Kalamu ya Salaam, which means "Pen of Peace." Salaam grew up in the Ninth Ward in **New Orleans, Louisiana**. Salaam and his family live in that neighborhood, a predominantly working-class African American community.

Salaam attended Carlton College in Northfield, Minnesota, in 1964 and 1965, but left before completing his degree. He then served three years in the U.S. Army and returned to New Orleans in June 1968. He enrolled in Southern University but was expelled in April 1969 for participating in student demonstrations. He eventually earned an associate degree in business at Delgado Junior College, graduating in the autumn of 1970 (Millican, 232).

In May 1973, Salaam helped to found Ahidiana, a New Orleans–based Pan-African Nationalist Organization that operated an independent educational program for preschool children. He also directed Essence of Life, Ahidiana's poetry and music ensemble, and he represented Ahidiana throughout the United States and internationally until 1984, when the organization ceased to exist (Millican, 233).

In recent years Salaam has served as senior partner in the New Orleans–based public relations firm Bright Moments (1984–1996), and was cofounder (with Kysha Brown) of Runagate Multimedia, Inc. He is founder and director of **NOMMO**, a New Orleans–based writers' workshop. Salaam is also founder and moderator of e-Drum, an informational listserv for Black writers and supporters of literature worldwide.

Salaam received a Senior Literature Fellowship from the Fine Arts Work Center in Provincetown, Massachusetts (1999), a Louisiana Endowment for the Humanities Award (1998), and the Mayor Marc Morial Arts Award (1997).

Resources: Arthenia J. Bates Millican, "Kalamu Ya Salaam," in *Dictionary of Literary Biography*, vol. 38, *Afro-American Writers after 1955: Dramatists and Prose Writers*, ed. Thadious M. Davis (Detroit: Gale, 1985), 231–239; Kalamu ya Salaam: "Art for Life: My Story, My Song," *ChickenBones: A Journal for Literary & Artistic African-American Themes* (2004), http://www.nathanielturner.com/artforlife.htm; *Black Liberation Army* (New Orleans: Free Southern Theater, 1969); *Black Love Song #1*, in *Black Theatre USA: Plays by African Americans*, vol. 2, *The Recent Period, 1935–Today*, ed. James Hatch and Ted Shine, rev. and enl. ed. (New York: Free Press, 1996); "Essays, Poems, & Interviews," *ChickenBones: A Journal for Literary & Artistic African-American Themes* (2004), http://www.nathanielturner.com/kystable.htm; *Happy Birthday Jesus* (New Orleans: Free Southern Theater, 1969); *Homecoming* (New Orleans: Free Southern Theater, 1970); *The Magic of Ju-Ju: An Appreciation of the Black Arts Movement* (Chicago: Third World Press, 2004); *Mama* (New Orleans: Free Southern Theater, 1969); *The Picket* (one-act), produced in New Orleans at Free Southern Theater, 1968; "Somewhere in the World," in *Black Southern Voices: An Anthology of Fiction, Poetry, Drama, Nonfiction, and Critical Essays*, ed. John Oliver Killens and Jerry W. Ward (New York: Meridian, 1991); *What Is Life? Reclaiming the Black Blues Self* (Chicago: Third World Press, 1994); Kalamu ya Salaam, ed., *From a Bend in the River: 100 New Orleans Poets* (New Orleans: Runagate Press, 1998); Charles P. Toombs, "Salaam, Kalamu Ya," in *The Oxford Companion to African American Literature*, ed. William L. Andrews, Frances Smith Foster, and Trudier Harris (New York: Oxford University Press, 1997), 640–641.

John Greer Hall

Sambo. One of the more volatile and pervasive of derogatory signifiers for African Americans. The word "Sambo" stretches, in influence, from the early years of enslavement in the New World to the present day, when documents containing its stigma are generally banned from the educational curriculum. While commonly traced from Helen Bannerman's *Story of Little Black Sambo* (1899), the name and vestige of Sambo appear in literature, on stage, on screen, in public records, and on restaurant franchises.

The earliest records of the term have been traced to indigenous African cultures. It is impossible, however, to be certain that similar-sounding African words had any direct impact on the word's usage in the Americas (Major). Even if one assumes a direct derivation when the word is used by Spanish authorities as a term for the enslaved, or by Southern colonials to denote the child of a mixed-blood and a pure Black enslaved, or even in occasional instances of enslaved persons named Sambo, the term takes on quite a different significance when used in art.

Throughout the nineteenth and twentieth centuries, instances of the Sambo stereotype appear in American literature and performance. John Murdock's *The Triumph of Love* (1795) first used the "Sambo" character's name and ethnic characteristics. Previous examples of "**Negro** roles" exist in such works as John Leacock's *The Fall of British Tyranny* (1776), but Murdock's play is the first to equate the name Sambo with the role's dialect-centered antics

(Effiong, 5). **Minstrelsy**, one of the most influential popular theater forms in American history, a tradition which counterfeited Black American culture in a song, dance, and comedy showcase performed mainly by White actors in burned cork (an inexpensive black cake makeup), featured a Sambo clown in a number of performances.

Over time, Sambo came to be equated with a grinning child. While there were exceptions in the nineteenth century, such as the cruel slave Sambo in **Harriet Beecher Stowe**'s *Uncle Tom's Cabin* (1852), a far more considerable number of examples in minstrelsy, joke books, popular songs, and children's games established Sambo as derogatory and stereotypical, as either child or childlike (Boskin, 36–39). By the time Helen Bannerman's book was released in the United States (1900), the ground was well paved for Little Black Sambo's trademark characteristics.

Bannerman's *Sambo* was an unprecedented success thanks to the revolutionary format of its simple illustrations and compact text, which made it ideal for young readers (Yuill, 7). It told of a young child named Sambo, who convinces a band of tigers not to eat him by giving each an article of his fine outer garments (shoes, an umbrella, a coat, etc.). Eventually, the tigers fight over the clothing, their bout culminating in each latching its teeth onto the tail of another and chasing each other around a tree. While they spin faster and faster, Sambo slips away with his clothes. The tigers spin so fast they melt into butter, which becomes part of an impressive meal of pancakes at Sambo's household. *Sambo* was republished dozens of times in the twentieth century, inspiring many related children's stories. Well into the mid-twentieth century, reviewers and educational specialists cited it as an exceptionally well crafted and highly recommended story. Some went so far as to claim that the book helped raise racial consciousness in the minds of White children (Lanes, 161–162). Sambo was pervasive in twentieth-century popular culture, appearing in everything from humor books to puppetry productions.

Those who objected to the story grew to outnumber its defenders. Among the targets were the illustrations, which seemed to show Sambo's mother as "Aunt Jemima" or "Mammy," a stereotyped Southern Black domestic, and Sambo, in his finery, as a minstrel clown. Attempts to quell the controversy without sacrificing the book included renaming the book *Little Sambo* or *Little Brave Sambo* (Sambo is a White boy living in the African jungle), but the name was too associated with counterfeit ethnicity. By the mid-1970s, the title was removed from most lists of recommended books.

In 1957 a restaurant named Sambo's was opened in Santa Barbara, California. The name was invented from a combination of syllables from the two founders' names: Sam Battistone and Newel Bohnett. However, when the founders developed a chain of restaurants, they began to use advertising images reminiscent of Little Sambo. The chain went out of business in the 1970s, but the original restaurant, Sambo's, remains. As late as 1998, attempts were made to revive the restaurant chain under the name Sambo's, in spite of criticism about how insulting the name had come to be regarded as being (LaMotte).

Like its many partner stereotypes, such as the buck (a threatening male sexual presence) or the tragic **mulatto** (a mixed-breed female who is usually the love interest of a White hero), gratuitous examples of the comic Sambo have become quaint historical curiosities in the arts of past decades. **James Baldwin** declared the death of such classic clichés in his *Notes of a Native Son* (27). Yet, as many African American artists, writers, and cultural critics continue to realize, the heritage of Sambo and its like continues to influence the possibilities of Black art and literature as counterfeit roles that can be revised, contradicted, or even ignored, but never completely escaped.

Resources: James Baldwin, *Notes of a Native Son* (Boston: Beacon Press, 1955); Helen Bannerman: *The Story of Little Babaji* (New York: HarperCollins, 1996); *The Story of Little Black Sambo* (New York: Frederick A. Stokes, 1900); Joseph Boskin, *Sambo: The Rise & Demise of an American Jester* (New York: Oxford University Press, 1986); Daniel Braithwaite, *The Banning of the Book Little Black Sambo from Toronto Public Schools, 1956* (Toronto: Overnight Typing & Copy, 1978); Philip Uko Effiong, *In Search of a Model for African American Drama: A Study of Selected Plays by Lorraine Hansberry, Amiri Baraka, and Ntozake Shange* (Lanham, MD: University Press of America, 2000); Elizabeth Hay, *Sambo Sahib: The Story of Little Black Sambo and Helen Bannerman* (Totowa, NJ: Barnes & Noble, 1981); Greg LaMotte, "Sambo's Revival Runs into Hot Water," *CNN Interactive* (Jan. 28, 1998), http://www.cnn.com/US/9801/28/sambo.revival; Selma G. Lanes, *Down the Rabbit Hole* (New York: Atheneum, 1971); Daniel J. Leab, *From Sambo to Superspade: The Black Experience in Motion Pictures* (Boston: Houghton Mifflin, 1975); Orrie M. MacDonnell, *Sambo: Before and After the Civil War* (Macon, GA: J. W. Burke, 1924); John Murdock, *The Triumph of Love; or, The Happy Reconciliation* (Philadelphia: John Murdock, 1795); P. B. Power, *Sambo's Legacy* (Philadelphia: American Sunday-School Union, c. 1870); Harriet Beecher Stowe, *Uncle Tom's Cabin; or, Life Among the Lowly* (Garden City, NY: Doubleday, 1960); Bill Yoffee, *Black Sambo's Saga: The Story of Little Black Sambo Revisited at Age 98* (Kensington, MD: Children's Book Adoption Agency, 1997); Phyllis J. Yuill, *Little Black Sambo: A Closer Look* (New York: Racism and Sexism Resource Center for Educators, 1976).

Ben Fisler

San Francisco Bay Area, California. For centuries, romantic notions of freedom, both spiritual and literal, have drawn people to the San Francisco Bay Area. That has been true for African Americans, too. The African American population in the Bay Area, however, remained small until the post–**World War II** migration of 400,000 African Americans to its shipyards in the 1950s and 1960s.

In the late nineteenth century, Black writers began publishing their work in San Francisco. The abolitionist and orator poet **James Monroe Whitfield** had been published in the San Francisco Bay Area (Hill, 375). **Washington, D.C.,** native **Thomas Detter** wrote "Nelli Brown or The Jealous Wife, with Other

Sketches" while he was living in Elko, Nevada, in 1871, but his book was printed in the Bay Area (Whiteman, ii). Other contributors to early African American literature in the Bay Area include Mifflin W. Gibbs, who wrote about the 1850s in his **autobiography** *Shadow and Light*, and the San Francisco playwright **Garland Anderson** (Daniels, 216–217).

In 1874, a fugitive slave whose original name was John Thomas Evans published *Life and Adventures of James Williams: A Fugitive Slave*, a first-person account that includes a full description of the **Underground Railroad** and details of his arrival by ship in San Francisco, following a four-day trip across Panama, and his subsequent journey to Sacramento.

Such influential writers as **James Weldon Johnson** and Horace Clayton spent time in the Bay Area in the early twentieth century, but some natives were making names for themselves, too. The poet **Edward Smyth Jones** published another edition of his 1911 collection, *The Sylvan Cabin: A Centenary Ode on the Birth of Lincoln*, in 1915, while he was working as a waiter in the Faculty Club (Jones, preface). His work was nationally known and even attracted the attention of the *New York Times* in 1913.

By the mid-twentieth century, more African Americans were beginning to settle in the Bay Area. In 1948, Louisiana native **Ernest James Gaines**'s family moved to Vallejo, California. After attending Vallejo Junior College, writing an unsuccessful novel, and serving in the army for two years, Gaines went to San Francisco State University. He later won a prestigious Wallace Stegner fellowship to study writing at Stanford University in Palo Alto before going on to write several books, including the popular *Autobiography of Miss Jane Pittman* (Hill, 1599). The author and poet **Sapphire**, who was born in Fort Ord, California, attended San Francisco City College before she moved to New York in 1977.

Some notable writers—including the journalist and historian Thomas J. Fleming, a pioneering African American editor and writer who moved to the Bay Area in the 1920s, and the memoirist, novelist, and poet **Al Young**—stayed in the Bay Area for decades after they arrived. Others, among them the venerated poet and memoirist **Maya Angelou**, stayed in San Francisco only briefly before they moved elsewhere. The Bay Area has also been a welcoming environment for poets, including San Francisco Poet Laureate devorah major and the writer Opal Palmer Adisa. The award-winning poet Forrest Hamer, who resides in Emeryville, also has a psychotherapy practice in the area.

During the 1960s and 1970s, writers including **Amiri Baraka** and **Sonia Sanchez** were a part of the **Black Studies** movement at San Francisco State University. They were also a part of the **Black Arts Movement**, along with the poet **Sarah Webster Fabio**; **Ed Bullins**, a dramatist who enrolled in school in the Bay Area after serving in the U.S. Navy (Koolish, 18); and the playwright Marvin X. During this volatile time, **Huey P. Newton** and Bobby Seale established the **Black Panther Party**, and their literature helped inform the nation about their commitment to **Black Power**. The revolutionary figure **Angela Y. Davis**, who now teaches at the University of California, Santa

Cruz, south of the Bay Area, contributed texts about liberation, **feminism**, and her own life. The author, essayist, and editor magazine **Ishmael Reed**, who recently wrote a book about Oakland, moved to the Bay Area in 1967.

The San Francisco Bay Area has been home to queer writers and activists from the African American community who have given voice to the marginalization of gay and lesbian people of color. **Jewelle Gomez**, who is from **Boston, Massachusetts**, and is best known for her novel *The Gilda Stories*, is now a San Francisco resident. Houston native **Pat Parker** moved to the Bay Area in the early 1970s and became a prominent activist, working as a medical coordinator at the Oakland Feminist Women's Health Center and other organizations.

In 1971, the pioneering scholar **Barbara Christian** became an assistant professor at the University of California, Berkeley. She was the first African American woman to achieve tenure there and was instrumental in introducing such writers as **Toni Morrison** and **Alice Walker** to a broader audience. The University of California, Berkeley also attracted the poet **June Jordan**, who founded the Poetry for the People program there.

In 1974, New Jersey native **Ntozake Shange** premiered her Obie-winning play, *for colored girls who have considered suicide/when the rainbow is enuf*, in the Bay Area (Hill, 1827) after teaching at Sonoma State University and Mills College. Three years later, the Pulitzer Prize-winning novelist, poet, and activist **Alice Walker** moved to San Francisco. Later, she lived in Berkeley and in Mendocino County, a more rural part of the Bay Area, where she wrote *The Color Purple*. In the 1980s, the area became home to the author and journalist Evelyn C. White, who most recently completed *Alice Walker: A Life* (2004) and is also the editor of the groundbreaking *Black Women's Health Book*.

The newest generation of writers residing in the Bay Area includes **Terry McMillan**, the author of *Waiting to Exhale*, who lives in Danville, and the novelist **Mary Monroe**. Other authors in the Bay area include the short story writer **Z Z Packer**, the journalist and author Farai Chideya, and the novelist **April Sinclair**. Oakland native Danyel Smith, a pioneering **hip-hop** journalist and novelist, returns to her home city often. **Guy Johnson**, the son of Maya Angelou, resides in the Bay Area, as does Alice Walker's daughter, Rebecca Walker.

Established beacons of African American literature include the Lorraine Hansberry Theater in San Francisco and activist/editor Robert Allen's *The Black Scholar*.

Resources: Albert S. Broussard, *Black San Francisco: The Struggle for Racial Equality in the West, 1900–1954* (Lawrence: University Press of Kansas, 1993); Douglas Henry Daniels, *Pioneer Urbanites: A Social and Cultural History of Black San Francisco* (Berkeley: University of California Press, 1990); Patricia Liggins Hill, ed., *Call and Response: The Riverside Anthology of the African American Literary Tradition* (Boston: Houghton Mifflin, 1998), 375–377, 1598–1600, 1632–1634, 1654, 1668, 1827–1828; Edward Smyth Jones, *The Sylvan Cabin: A Centenary Ode on the Birth of Lincoln* (San

Francisco: Sunset, 1915); Lynda Koolish, *African-American Writers: Portraits and Visions* (Jackson: University Press of Mississippi, 2001); James M. Rose and Alice Eichholz, *Black Genesis: A Resource Book for African-American Genealogy*, 2nd ed. (Baltimore: Genealogical Publishing, 2003), 73; Maxwell Whiteman, *A Century of Fiction by American Negroes, 1853–1952: A Descriptive Bibliography* (Philadelphia: Library of Congress, 1955), ii; James Williams, *Life and Adventures of James Williams: A Fugitive Slave* (San Francisco: Women's Union Book…Office, 1874), 29–33.

Joshunda Sanders

Sanchez, Sonia (born 1934). Poet, activist, playwright, editor, and teacher. Sonia Sanchez was born Wilsonia Benita Driver in Birmingham, Alabama. Her mother died when she was one, and after the death of her grandmother, she spent several years with a variety of relatives before finally settling in New York City with her father, Wilson Driver, a successful **jazz** musician. From the age of nine, Sanchez was acquainted with the music of famous jazz musicians, including John Coltrane and Nina Simone. Shortly after she received her bachelor's degree in political science from Hunter College in 1955, she married Albert Sanchez, a Puerto Rican immigrant, whose surname she continues to use when writing. During the racial turbulence of the early 1960s, Sanchez was a supporter of integration and CORE (Congress of Racial Equality). However, Sanchez turned her attention to a more separatist view after considering the ideas of **Malcolm X**. After hearing Malcolm X's speeches, Sanchez became more acutely aware of the political predicament of Blacks during this era. During this same time, Sanchez began to study creative writing formally with Louise Bogan, who encouraged her to pursue a literary career. Sanchez initially published poetry in small magazines and Black periodicals, such as *The Liberator*, the **Journal of Black Poetry**, **Black Dialogue**, and **Negro Digest**. Sanchez later formed a writers collective along called the Broadside Quartet. The group consisted of young poets and was promoted by **Dudley Randall**, founder of **Broadside Press**.

Randall and Sanchez were associated with the **Black Arts Movement**. Sanchez is one of the most influential women members of that movement. **Joyce A.** Joyce asserts that "Sonia Sanchez remains one of the proudest and the most vibrant of those [Black Arts Movement] figures whose works manifest this spiritual link between art and politics" (62). Like the work of **Amiri Baraka** and **Haki Madhubuti**, Sanchez's poetry is chiefly in **free verse** and often uses the **vernacular**. Joyce observes, "If we are to appreciate Sonia Sanchez' poetry, we must wash away all Euro-American, middle class notions of what can and cannot be said in poetry and even of how a poem should look on the printed page. Abrasively strong in content and challenging in form, Sonia Sanchez' poetry addresses itself to the Black community" (64).

Sanchez began a long teaching career in 1965 at the Down Town Community School in New York and later moved to the **San Francisco Bay Area**, where she was a pioneer in developing **Black Studies** courses at San Francisco State University. In 1968, Sanchez married the activist/poet **Etheridge**

Knight, with whom she had three children; however, the marriage was troubled, and may have made her more acutely aware of the increasing tensions between Black men and Black women. This awareness may have been the impetus for many of her poems. Her first three volumes of poetry—*Home Coming* (1969), *We a BaddDDD People* (1970), and *It's a New Day* (1971)—include poems on the construction of the **Black family**, drug abuse, domestic violence, and interracial relationships. Sanchez was also a member of the **Nation of Islam** between 1972 and 1975; however, she left the Nation of Islam due mostly to what she considered its repression of women. In her book *Love Poems* (1973), her Islamic ideology is apparent, and she experiments with the **haiku** form. Sanchez has also written *Blues Book for Blue Black Magical Women* (1974). She joined the teaching staff of Temple University in **Philadelphia, Pennsylvania**, in 1977, serving as professor in the departments of English and Women's Studies. While Sanchez is best known for her poetry, she is also a playwright. Her plays include *Sister Son/ji* (1969), and *Uh Huh: But How Do It Free Us?* (1975).

Sanchez's later poetry reflects a shift toward an interest in **feminism** and women's rights. In 1978 she published *I've Been a Woman*, and in 1984, *Homegirls & Handgrenades* (1984), one of her most celebrated works and the winner of the 1985 American Book Award from the Before Columbus Foundation. *Under a Soprano Sky* (1987) and *Wounded in the House of a Friend* (1995) are more recent books. The latter concerns the devastation of rape and AIDS, but also the need for triumph and hope. Sanchez's other poetry volumes include *Does Your House Have Lions?* (1997), which was nominated for a National Book Critics Circle Award, *Like the Singing Coming off the Drums: Love Poems* (1998), and *Shake Loose My Skin* (1999).

Recently, much like the poet **Nikki Giovanni**, Sanchez has celebrated the contemporary **hip-hop** movement. In an article in *Black Issues Book Review*, she explains, with rapper Mos Def, why modern day **rap** artists should be taken seriously as poets and why the Black Arts Movement and hip-hop really exist on a continuum (Cook). Besides the American Book Award, Sanchez has received the prestigious Robert Frost Medal in poetry. Although Sanchez is arguably one of the most prolific women poets in American literary history, criticism and scholarship about her work is, at this writing, relatively scarce. Joyce writes, "The dearth of essays on Sonia Sanchez' craft as well as the simplistic and superficial reviews of her poetry testify to the lack of serious attention given to her 'vitriolic verse'" (63).

Resources: D. A. Cook, "The Aesthetics of Rap," *Black Issues Book Review*, Mar./Apr. 2000, 22–27; Joyce Ann Joyce, *Ijala: Sonia Sanchez and the African Poetic Tradition* (Chicago: Third World Press, 1996); D. H. Melhem, *Heroism in the New Black Poetry* (Lexington: University Press of Kentucky, 1990); Sonia Sanchez: *Blues Book for Blue Black Magical Women* (Detroit: Broadside Press, 1974); *Does Your House Have Lions?* (Boston: Beacon Press, 1997); *Home Coming* (Detroit: Broadside Press, 1969); *Homegirls & Handgrenades* (New York: Thunder's Mouth Press, 1984); *It's a New Day*

(Detroit: Broadside Press, 1971); *I've Been a Woman* (Sausalito, CA: Black Scholar Press, 1978); *Like the Singing Coming off the Drums: Love Poems* (Boston: Beacon Press, 1998); *Love Poems* (New York: Third Press, 1973); *Shake Loose My Skin* (Boston: Beacon Press, 1999); *Under a Soprano Sky* (Trenton, NJ: Africa World Press, 1987); *We a BaddDDD People* (Detroit: Broadside Press, 1970); *Wounded in the House of a Friend* (Boston: Beacon Press, 1995).

Gail L. Upchurch

Sanders, Dori (born 1930). Novelist. Dori Sanders is the acclaimed author of *Clover* (1990), *Her Own Place* (1993), and a country-style cookbook. Childhood and life on the family farm that she and her brother currently manage in South Carolina are her inspiration. Sanders grew up in segregation on eighty acres that her father, a school principal, had purchased. Her earliest memories include telling stories around the "storytelling rock," and then, years later, jotting story ideas on napkins and the backs of menus while working in a banquet hall (Smith). Algonquin Books rejected her first novel, a story about sharecroppers, because they felt it was "too melodramatic," and suggested she write from her own experiences (Smith). *Clover*, Sanders's first published novel, was a result of adopting that strategy.

The idea for *Clover* came to Sanders while watching two funeral processions. At the end of one procession was a young Black girl, and at the end of the other was a White woman. From this experience, Sanders created a story about overcoming grief and cultural differences as narrated by Clover, a ten-year-old African American girl who is being raised by Sara Kate, her White stepmother. *Her Own Place* is about an African American woman named Mae Lee Barnes and her single-handed struggle to run a farm and raise five children. This story takes place from the civil rights era through the 1980s. Sanders asserts that "Mae Lee represents all women who struggled after World War II" ("Dori Sanders"). Both novels, published by Algonquin, "have earned her comparisons to Alice Walker (1944), Zora Neale Hurston (1891–1960), and Eudora Welty (1909–2001)" (Smith).

Since food played a significant role in both novels, Algonquin requested that Sanders write a cookbook, and in 1995, they published *Dori Sanders' Country Cooking: Recipes & Stories from the Family Farm Stand*.

Resources: *Biography Resource Center*, http://galenet.galegroup.com/servlet/BioRC; Dori Sanders: *Clover* (Chapel Hill, NC: Algonquin, 1990); *Dori Sanders' Country Cooking: Recipes & Stories from the Family Farm Stand* (Chapel Hill, NC: Algonquin Books, 1995); *Her Own Place* (Chapel Hill, NC: Algonquin Books, 1993); home page, http://www.dorisanders.com; "A Writer from Filbert: Her Own Place," presented at Fifty-seventh Annual Meeting of the South Caroliniana Society, Columbia, 1993; "Dori Sanders," *South Carolina African American History Online*, http://www.scafricanamericanhistory.com/currenthonoree.asp?month=1&year=1994; Jessie Carney Smith, ed., *Notable Black American Women* (Detroit: Gale, 1992).

Gladys L. Knight

Sapphire [Lofton, Ramona] (born 1950). Poet, novelist, short story writer, and performance artist. Sapphire's publications defy easy classification for two reasons: each work involves a mixture of writing styles and literary genres; and her texts move outward from personal experience to confront cultural and political issues concerning sexuality, identity, **race**, and class. Whereas the second of these characteristics has brought Sapphire much recognition as a confessional writer committed to engendering positive social change, her achievement as a formalist warrants equal consideration. Relationships between literary form and narrative function play a pivotal role for Sapphire: the hybrid nature of her writing dramatizes the author's transformation of private reflection and expression into public discourse, at the same time provoking the reader to confront the political implications of the subject matter in each of her texts. Sapphire's publications, thus, are lyrical and dramatic—charged with a resistance against the status quo that underscores the author's wariness of being affiliated with politically "correct" notions of African American identities, communities, and literary traditions.

Ramona Lofton was born in 1950 in Fort Ord, California. She attended San Francisco City College during the mid-1960s, majoring first in chemistry, then in dance, and discovering along the way the works of **Ntozake Shange**, Jessica Hagedorn, and **Sonia Sanchez**, which would prove to have a formative influence on her own writing. Lofton changed her name to Sapphire and moved to New York in 1977. In the early 1980s she began writing poetry and reading her work at various Village venues, including the **Nuyorican Poets Café**. She also taught in literacy programs in the Bronx and **Harlem, New York**, and returned to school, graduating from City College in 1983 with honors in modern dance. When she was forty-three, Sapphire entered the M.F.A. program in poetry at Brooklyn College, where she studied with Susan Fromberg Schaeffer and Allen Ginsberg.

Combinations of prose and verse in Sapphire's publications complement the author's translation of personal trauma into public action, and thereby challenge the audience to acknowledge and engage with urgent social matters, such as urban poverty, drug addiction, and police brutality; homosexuality and AIDS; incest, rape, and sexual violence. Much of Sapphire's writing also embraces life-affirming themes, especially those of liberated sexuality, love, and friendship. Her first book, *American Dreams* (1994), a collection of poems and prose works, explores the legacy of childhood sexual abuse. *Black Wings and Blind Angels* (1999), a book of poetry, merges classical and experimental literary forms with memories and dreams in efforts to redeem personal and cultural history. Her debut novel, *Push* (1996), which has received much acclaim and criticism from the political right as well as from the left, tells the story of Precious Jones, an HIV-positive sixteen-year-old girl in Harlem who has two children by her father, endures sexual violation by her mother, and learns to read and write through the guidance and friendship of Blue Rain, a literacy teacher. In all three books, Sapphire's writing teaches through dance—that is, through the performance of narrative transfigurations of selves, characters, and readers.

Resources: Brenda Daly, "Seeds of Shame or Seeds of Change? When Daughters Give Birth to Their Fathers' Children," in *This Giving Birth: Pregnancy and Childbirth in American Women's Writing,* ed. Julie Tharp and Susan MacCallum-Whitcomb (Bowling Green, OH: Bowling Green State University Popular Press, 2000), 103–123; Gordon Fran, "Breaking Karma: A Conversation with Sapphire," *Poets and Writers,* Jan./Feb. 2000, 24–31; Jewelle Gomez, "Cutting Words," *Lambda Book Report: A Review of Contemporary Gay and Lesbian Literature* 4, no. 10 (1995), 6–7; Janice Lee Liddell, "Agents of Pain and Redemption in Sapphire's *Push,*" in *Arms Akimbo: Africana Women in Contemporary Literature,* ed. Janice Lee Liddell and Yakini Belinda Kemp (Gainesville: University Press of Florida, 1999), 135–146; P. J. Mark, "Giving Birth to the Self," *Quarterly Black Review of Books,* Sept. 1996, 8; Mark Marvel, "Sapphire's Big Push," *Interview,* June 1996, 28–30; D. T. Max, "Pushing the Envelope," *Harper's Bazaar,* July 1996, 133–136; Rachel Petter, "Sparkling *Sapphire,*" *Deneuve* 4, no. 3 (1994), 34–35; William Powers, "Sapphire's Raw Gem," *Washington Post,* Aug. 6, 1996, pp. B1+; Sapphire: *American Dreams* (New York: High Risk Books, 1994); *Black Wings and Blind Angels: Poems* (New York: Knopf, 1999); *Push* (New York: Knopf, 1996); Dinitia Smith, "For the Child Who Rolls with the Punches," *New York Times,* July 2, 1996, pp. C11+.

W. Scott Howard

Satire. Satire may be defined as a mode of writing that has at its heart an attitude of criticism of personal and social values and that aims to produce laughter as it highlights vice and folly. Working in many forms and genres, the satirist writes from the core values of his/her culture, attacking deviations from that core that he/she sees as sinful, foolish, aberrant, or otherwise detrimental to social order. The satirist, like the **trickster**, always carries a two-edged sword, as it were; his verbal instruments, including irony and exaggeration, can cut friend and foe alike if the subject seems to the satirist to have strayed from the acceptable paths of traditional culture.

The roots of African American satire go deep into the African and European pasts. In ancient times, in West Africa, the Near East, and Celtic Europe, the satirist's function was filled by priests or poets whose job it was to compose curses and spells against military enemies or to remind overweening rulers of their dependent relationships to the ancestors and the gods. In their homelands both the European and African ancestors of Americans knew a kind of verbal performance that featured mockery, **parody,** and ridicule. West African griots' service to their chiefs included the role of satirist, at times cursing and mocking the enemy, at other times suggesting that the chief or his advisers had lost touch with communal values. Like court jesters and carnival performers in European cultures, the griots, whose major function was to recite the legitimizing lineage of the leader and to praise his achievements, were at times permitted to speak the otherwise unspeakable. In the literate traditions of Europe, satirists often burst the bounds of class and station to mount their critiques, as did Jonathan Swift, an Anglican priest, in ironically proposing cannibalism as a solution to Irish poverty in *A Modest Proposal* (1729).

African American folk traditions exhibited the satiric impulse, even when the expression of views critical of slaveholders and supporters of "the peculiar institution" might be severely punished; the slaves found a voice in **folktales** and orature for criticism of Mr. Charley and Miss Anne, the prototypical master and mistress of the plantation. A satiric impulse is so well disguised in many of the animal fables in which small, powerless creatures such as rabbits and spiders defeat the large and powerful elephant and lion that they were absorbed into American **folklore** with little understanding of their mordancy. The slaves also created stories featuring John the trickster slave who continually outwitted his master. These tales show John winning the kind of small victories that reminded the powerless slaves that the master was not a god, but a fallible human being just like themselves. When African Americans began to write fiction, stories of this type soon surfaced; **Paul Laurence Dunbar**'s "Mr. Cornelius Johnson, Office Seeker" and **Charles Waddell Chesnutt**'s "The Passing of Grandison"—indeed, many of Chesnutt's stories—contain satiric elements drawn directly from the folk tradition of the trickster slave. Nor did the satiric impulse die out with emancipation. A line of folk narratives concerning Shine, an imaginary African American survivor of the *Titanic* disaster, reminds listeners that the high and mighty White folks on the doomed ship were as mortal, and perhaps less resourceful, than Shine the stoker. The captain and various passengers appeal to Shine for help, offering money, status, and sexual favors, but Shine tells them they are on their own; if they hope to be saved, he says, they would be advised to "get your ass in the water and swim like me."

During the **Harlem Renaissance** period, writers found satire an appropriate mode for the expression of their double-edged attitudes toward their equally double-edged experience. Many writers in the period felt that the enthusiasm for the work of African American artists expressed by White readers, critics, and supporters was based on racial fascination and paternalism, not on aesthetic judgments. **Wallace Thurman**, in his *Infants of the Spring* (1932), mocked the pretensions of fellow Black artists, even as he exposed the false amity of White admirers. **Rudolf J. C. Fisher**'s *The Walls of Jericho* (1928) explores class and color conflict among African Americans in Harlem through a satiric lens. The most distinguished satirist of the period was **George Schuyler**, who pilloried African Americans' desire for acceptance by whites in *Black No More* (1931), in which most of the African American population undergoes scientific treatment to turn them white. **Zora Neale Hurston**, in *Moses, Man of the Mountain* (1939), retells the Moses story in the idiom of the Black South, satirizing both White obsessions with the religiosity of African Americans and the presumption that the figures of Scripture and legend are best understood as Whites. Many of the short stories in **Langston Hughes**'s collections *The Ways of White Folks* (1934) and *Laughing to Keep from Crying*

(1952) exhibit a highly ironic, even satiric edge. In his newspaper sketches featuring Jesse B. Simple (the first spelling was "Semple," but Hughes changed it to "Simple" in all the later tales), Hughes gently commented on the gap between the ideals of educated Blacks and the common sense of the Black masses; in another set of newspaper sketches, later collected as *Like One of the Family*, **Alice Childress** dramatized the relationships between African American domestics and their bourgeois White employers.

While there are satiric elements in the fiction of **Richard Wright, Ralph Ellison**, and **James Baldwin**, the next generation of African American writers was more thoroughly engaged in satirizing American failures to achieve national values such as universal civil rights and African American deviations from core values. The prescriptions of the **Black Power** theorists that art should expose the enemy and further the revolution were responded to in various ways. **William Melvin Kelley**'s *dem* (1967) exposed the enemy—White supremacy—in a wildly comic tale of a casually racist young WASP advertising executive whose wife bears one White and one Black twin. **John Oliver Killens**'s *The Cotillion* (1971) contrasts the racial ambivalence of the Femmes Fatales with the trickster militancy of the narrator, Ben Ali Lumumba, in the struggle to win over the heroine. Fran Ross's novel *Oreo* (1974) used the myth of Theseus in a satiric send-up of such high culture fictions as James Joyce's *Ulysses* in an extravagant tale about a Black teenage Philadelphian in search of her Jewish father in New York. **Kristin Hunter Lattany**'s novels *The Landlord* (1966) and *The Lakestown Rebellion* (1978) both turn on the trickster element in African American culture to show how the community can defeat White power and authority. **Hal Bennett**'s novels, exemplified by *Lord of Dark Places* (1970), take up the American fascination with the Black male body. Bennett's hero worships his own phallic self, and services both men and women to survive molestation in childhood, Civil Rights Era assaults, the **Vietnam War**, and urban violence. Bennett ultimately indicts both Whites and Blacks for fetishizing the Black male body. **Douglas Turner Ward**'s one-act play *Day of Absence: A Satirical Fantasy* (1966), described as "a reverse minstrel show done in white face," and **Amiri Baraka**'s *The Great Goodness of Life: A Coon Show* (1967) both focused on mocking the stereotypical images used by the white majority to contain and suppress African Americans. Later plays, such as Robert Alexander's *I Ain't Yo Uncle* (1996), continued to work this satiric vein.

The major figure among African American satirists in the **Black Arts Movement** is **Ishmael Reed**. In poems and novels written between the late 1960s and the turn of the twenty-first century, Reed skewered many aspects of Anglo-American and African American culture, including western movies, the Nixon administration, Japan mania, even **Black Power** militants. His masterpiece, *Mumbo Jumbo* (1972), rewrites the history of Western civilization as a struggle between Jes' Grew, the principle of dance and spontaneity, connected to the ancient Egyptian, West African, and Haitian mysteries, and the Wallflower Order, representative of everything Nordic, overregimented, stiff, and authoritarian. Reed's impressive revisions of history, manipulations of racial stereotypes, and interpellation of scholarship, advertisements, journalism, drawings and photographs no more detract from the book's hilarity than does its imitation of the detective novel form. **Al Young**'s parodic fictional creation, the poet O. O. Gabugah, turned the tables on the Black Arts Movement's prescriptive theorizing in a series of mock revolutionary utterances that went undetected as frauds.

Writers of the post–Black Arts Movement period (since 1980) often write in a satiric vein. This so-called **hip-hop** satire retains affinities with such popular culture forms as rap music and experimental fictional forms while exploring the complexities of African American identity that result from increases in the experiences of integration, higher education, and miscegenation. These writers redefine and reuse the stereotypes created by both Blacks and Whites to define racial and cultural authenticity, and frequently write about racially isolated individuals. Thus **Trey Ellis**'s novel *Platitudes* (1988) used a Chinese box structure of narrative within narrative to explore adolescent sexuality and new possibilities for fiction. **Darius James**'s novel *Negrophobia* (1992) is a carnival of the grotesque, obscene, and scatological, designed to "subvert the perversion" of American racist culture. **Paul Beatty**'s *The White Boy Shuffle* (1996) explores enduring questions of African American leadership and the gap between the masses and the privileged that have been raised by predecessors like Hughes, Ellison, Killens, Kelley, and Reed. Beatty's hero finds himself as leader ironically advocating that African Americans commit mass suicide. These works all confront the despair arising from "a dream deferred," the failure of the nation to meet the expectations raised by the **Civil Rights Movement**. Like **rap** music and other artistic products of African American culture at the end of the twentieth century, they are in-your-face, bold, and uncompromising. Hilarious as they often are, these hip-hop satires are dark presences, reminding readers how much remains to be done before the nation achieves its democratic ideals, if it ever can—and how hard the work of getting there will be. (*See* **Humor**; **Signifying**.)

Resources: Darryl Dickson-Carr, *African America Satire: The Sacredly Profane Novel* (Columbia: University of Missouri Press, 2001); Alan Dundes, ed., *Mother Wit from the Laughing Barrel: Readings in the Interpretation of African American Folklore* (Englewood Cliffs, NJ: Prentice-Hall, 1973); Robert C. Elliott, *The Power of Satire: Magic, Ritual, Art* (Princeton, NJ: Princeton University Press, 1960); Ronald Paulson, *The Fictions of Satire* (Baltimore: Johns Hopkins University Press, 1967).

Joseph T. Skerrett, Jr.

Scarborough, William Sanders (1852–1926). Classicist. Among African American scholars whose work has been neglected, William Sanders Scarborough is one of academe's more glaring oversights. His *First Lessons in Greek* (1881) was a celebrated text for Greek study and the first scholarly publication in classic languages by an African American.

Born into slavery in Macon, Georgia, in 1852, Scarborough obtained an early education through collaboration among his parents, slaveholder William De Graffenried, and a J. C. Thomas. Later, Scarborough attended Lewis High School and Atlanta University. In these years, Scarborough encountered the infamous quip from John C. Calhoun that linked African Americans' humanity to their acquisition of Greek. He responded by obtaining his A.B. from Oberlin College in 1875 after rigorous study in the classics. Scarborough returned to teach at Lewis High, which was burned by arsonists. After comparable experiences in South Carolina, he left to obtain an M.A. at Oberlin. Scarborough became Professor of Ancient Languages at Wilberforce College, a position he later relinquished to **W.E.B. Du Bois**. In 1881, Scarborough married Sarah Bierce, an accomplished scholar in ancient and modern languages. She became his partner in scholarship as well, editing *First Lessons in Greek*.

First Lessons was hailed by students and professors and was employed in Black and White classrooms, including at Yale University. In 1882, the American Philological Association admitted Scarborough as its third Black member. His APA presentations are cataloged in the *Transactions of the American Philological Association*. Scarborough regularly lectured at APA, starting in 1884 with "The Theory and Function of the Thematic Vowel in the Greek Verb." At the 1885 APA meeting, Prof. James Harrison's racist evening paper "Negro English" was followed by Scarborough's morning lecture, "Fatalism in Homer and Virgil." Scarborough's *The Birds of Aristophanes: A Theory of Interpretation* was separately published in 1886. Scarborough gave a lecture at the racially inhospitable University of Virginia (home of Confederate apologist and classicist Basil Gildersleeve) in 1892. In addition, his substantial introduction to Prof. James M. Gregory's *Frederick Douglass: The Orator* (1893) helped launch the first attempt to collect and comment upon **Frederick Douglass**'s speeches. Scarborough and Gregory examined Douglass in comparison with classical orators.

Scarborough became the first Black member of the Modern Language Association, a member of the **NAACP**'s Committee of Fifty, and editor of the A.M.E. (African Methodist Episcopal) *Sunday School Quarterly*. He joined the African American intellectual pantheon, the American Negro Academy, which was dedicated to combating claims against Black intelligence, encouraging Blacks' intellectual development, debating issues of note to Blacks, and publishing work by Black scholars. In 1897, Scarborough became Vice President of Wilberforce University. He assumed the presidency in 1908 and served until 1920. Scarborough died in 1926, after a remarkable rise from slavery to scholarly renown. He dispelled one of the persistent and damaging myths about African Americans' intellect, mastering the ancient languages and shaping pedagogy in classics.

After much neglect, Scarborough's contribution to American scholarship has drawn new attention. Robert Fikes, **Dolan Hubbard**, and the classicist Michelle Ronnick have attempted to unearth elements of Scarborough's life and work, and the Modern Language Association recently named a literary prize in his honor.

Resources: **Primary Sources:** William Sanders Scarborough: "The Chronological Order of Plato's Dialogues," *Transactions of the American Philological Association* 24 (1892), vi–viii; "Fatalism in Homer and Virgil," *Transactions of the American Philological Association* 16 (1885), xxxvi–xxxvii; *First Lessons in Greek* (New York: A. S. Barnes, 1881); "The Theory and Function of the Thematic Vowel in the Greek Verb," *Transactions of the American Philological Association* 15 (1884), vi. **Secondary Sources:** Robert Fikes, "African-American Scholars of Greco-Roman Literature," *Journal of Blacks in Higher Education* 35 (2002), 120; E. A. Hairston, "The Ebony Column: Classics and the African-American Literary Tradition 1772–1910." Ph.D. diss., University of Virginia, 2004; Michelle V. Ronnick, "William Sanders Scarborough: The First Professional Classicist of African-American Descent," *Negro Educational Review* 47 (1997), 162–168.

Eric Ashley Hairston

Schomburg, Arthur A. (1874–1938). Scholar, activist, and bibliophile. Schomburg's dedication to Black history and his passion for collecting books and art led to the world's most comprehensive archive of materials documenting the African **diaspora**. Born in Puerto Rico to a freeborn Black mother and a father of German descent, Arthur (Arturo) Alfonso Schomburg described himself as "Afroborinqueño." He traced the impetus of his lifelong search for documents of African experience to a fifth-grade teacher who remarked to him that Black people had "no history, no heroes, no great moments" (Sinnette 13). Early on, Schomburg began studying Black history, admiring in particular the Haitian revolutionary Toussaint L'Ouverture. In Puerto Rico, he studied commercial printing at the Instituto Popular in San Juan, and later attended St. Thomas College in the Virgin Islands, where he studied Black literature. It was during this stage of his education, while studying and teaching in the Virgin Islands, that Schomburg began collecting books.

In 1891, Schomburg emigrated to New York City. He lived on the Lower East Side, where he was active in local revolutionary groups working toward the decolonization of Cuba and Puerto Rico. His activities included serving as secretary for the Caribbean group Las Dos Antillas from 1892 to 1896 and working with liberationists such as José Martí, Máximo Gómez, Antonio Maceo, and Ramón Betances. While holding jobs as an elevator operator, bellhop, printer, and porter, Schomburg attended night classes at Manhattan Central High School. Planning a career as a lawyer, Schomburg worked as a clerk at the law firm of Pryor, Mellis, and Harris from 1901 to 1906. When he was not allowed to sit the New York State Regents Law Certificate exam, however, Schomburg took a position at the Latin American division of the Bankers Trust Company, where he worked until 1929. During this time, he developed a friendship with the journalist John Edward Bruce, a fellow bibliophile who encouraged Schomburg's scholarship and developing book collection. As Schomburg's studies continued, his range of interest expanded from a focus on Black experience in the Caribbean to one that included all people of color who had been dispersed across the globe. His growing body of documentation emphasized debunking prevalent theories of racist pseudoscience while filling in erasures of Black cultural production and contributions to society.

In 1904, Schomburg published his first article, "Is Hayti [sic] Decadent?," in *The Unique Advertiser*. In 1911, Schomburg and Bruce founded the Negro Society for Historical Research. In 1914, he was inducted into the American Negro Academy, whose membership included intellectuals such as **W.E.B. Du Bois, Alain Locke,** Kelly Miller, and **Carter G. Woodson.** He would later serve as president of the America Negro Academy from 1922 until its disbanding in 1929. A member of the Freemasons, Schomburg was grand secretary for the Grand Lodge of New York from 1918 to 1926, keeping an extensive archive of Black Masonic documents. His enthusiasm for and mastery of African American literature made him an important figure in circles associated with the **Harlem Renaissance,** the **New Negro** movement, and **Marcus Garvey'**s Universal Negro Improvement Association. Through these he developed connections with Black writers and intellectuals such as Walter Page and **James Weldon Johnson,** and found a close friend in the poet and novelist **Claude McKay.** Schomburg's many published writings include "Racial Integrity: A Plea for the Establishment of a Chair of Negro History in Our Schools, Colleges, etc." (1913), *A Bibliographical Checklist of American Negro Poetry* (1916), "Economic Contribution by the Negro to America." (1916), and articles in *The Crisis, Opportunity, The Messenger, Negro World, Negro Digest,* The A.M.E. Review, New Century, and *Survey Graphic*.

Schomburg's service to the study of black history persists in the collection he amassed during a lifetime of searching for rare and unusual materials, which led some to call him the "Sherlock Holmes of Negro History" (Sinnette, 2). Among Schomburg's voluminous holdings were **slave narratives,** rare books (early editions of *Clotel,* by **William Wells Brown,** and the poetry of **Phillis Wheatley**), journals, broadsides, artwork, abolitionist sermons written by ex-slaves, and the almanacs published by **Benjamin Banneker.** In 1926, the New York Public Library purchased Schomburg's personal collection, comprising about 5,000 items, with the help of a $10,000 Carnegie grant, and added it to the Division of Negro Literature, History and Prints of the 135th Street branch. After returning in 1929 from four years of travel and book-collecting in Spain, France, Germany, and England, financed by the proceeds of selling his collection, Schomburg worked as director of acquisitions, and later as curator, of the Fisk University library's Negro collection in **Nashville, Tennessee.** In 1932 he became curator for the New York Public Library Division of Negro Literature, History, and Prints, a position he held until his death in 1938.

The collection was named in his honor in 1940, and renamed again in 1972, this time as the Schomburg Center for Research in Black Culture. In his essay "The Negro Digs Up His Past" (1925), Schomburg asserts: "The American Negro must rebuild his past in order to make his future.... History must restore what slavery took away" (670). Schomburg's obituary in the *Journal of Negro History* celebrates the "invaluable assistance which he rendered others," singling out his contributions of "knowledge and usefulness... widely known to the scores of persons who called upon him for service which he always unselfishly rendered" (404). The Schomburg collection, located in **Harlem, New York**, currently contains over 5 million items and serves as a preeminent archive for research in African American history. Reflecting on Schomburg's wider significance as a curator, scholar, and mentor, John Henrik Clarke declared: "Arthur A. Schomburg was the antecedent of the Black Studies Revolution and one of the ideological fathers of this generation" (9). (*See* **Archives and Collections: 1828–Present.**)

Resources: John Henrik Clarke, "The Influence of Arthur A. Schomburg on My Concept of Africana Studies," *Phylon* 49, no. 1–2 (Spring–Summer 1992), 4–9; Robert Knight, "Arthur 'Afroborinqueño' Schomburg," *Civil Rights Journal* 1, no. 1 (1995), 3–4; Alfred A. Moss, Jr., *The American Negro Academy* (Baton Rouge: Louisiana State University Press, 1981); Obituary of Arthur A. Schomburg, *Journal of Negro History* 23, no. 3 (July 1938), 403–404; Victoria Ortiz, *The Legacy of Arthur A. Schomburg: A Celebration of the Past, a Vision for the Future with a Biographical Essay of Arthur A. Schomburg* (New York: Schomburg Center, New York Public Library, 1988); Arthur A. Schomburg, "The Negro Digs Up His Past," *Survey Graphic* 6, no. 6 (Mar. 1925), 670–672; Elinor Des Verney Sinnette, *Arthur Alfonso Schomburg, Black Bibliophile & Collector: A Biography* (New York: New York Public Library, 1989); Mary Katherine Wainwright, in *Contemporary Black Biography*, vol. 9, ed. L. Mpho Mabunda (Detroit: Gale, 1995), 208–211.

Alex Feerst

Schuyler, George Samuel (1895–1977). Journalist, novelist, and satirist. Condemned by many for his views but also respected by many for his undeniable talent, George Samuel Schuyler has been extolled as "the premier Black journalist." According to Nicholas Stix, Schuyler is "the greatest black journalist this country has ever produced." His writings, although controversial, significantly influenced Black journalism in particular, and journalism in general. During his career, Schuyler traveled extensively overseas. He was one of the first Black reporters to serve as a foreign correspondent for a major metropolitan newspaper, the *New York Evening Post*. Schuyler's writing career included positions as reporter, associate editor, and columnist for the New York office of the **Pittsburgh Courier** (1924–1966). He also wrote for magazines and journals, including **The Messenger** (1923), *The Nation* (1926), *The New Republic*, **Opportunity**, **The Crisis**, *American Mercury*, *The Call*, and *American Opinion*.

Langston Hughes's landmark essay "The Negro Artist and the Racial Mountain," written during the **Harlem Renaissance**, was a response to an essay Schuyler had written, "The Negro-Art Hokum," in which Schuyler ridiculed some assumptions behind the notion of **"Negro"** writing. Both essays are included in *The Portable Harlem Renaissance Reader* (1994), edited by David Levering Lewis.

In the longer forms of literature, Schuyler had similar impact. His novel *Slaves Today: A Story of Liberia* (1931), and the satirical science fiction novel *Black No More* (1931), sometimes called the first science fiction work by an African American, featured fierce implicit social commentary. Schuyler wrote under several pseudonyms, including William Stockton, D. Johnson, Rachel Call, Edgecombe Wright, Verne Caldwell, and John Kitchen. Additionally, he wrote the serialized novels *The Black Internationale* and *Black Empire* for the *Pittsburgh Courier* (1936–1938) under the name Samuel I. Brooks. These novels helped to double the *Courier*'s circulation to 250,000. In 1991, *The Black Internationale* and *Black Empire* were published together in book form as *Black Empire*. Schuyler's political shift from the left to the extreme right became the theme of his **autobiography**, *Black and Conservative* (1966). Schuyler vigorously demonstrated his iconoclasm and highly unpopular ultraconservatism in his books, articles, pamphlets, reviews, and essays, including "The Negro-Art Hokum" (1926), "Blessed Are the Sons of Ham" (1927), "Our White Folks" (1927), "Our Greatest Gift to America" (1929), "The Caucasian Problem" (1944), "The Reds and I" (1968), and "Malcolm X: Better to Memorialize Benedict Arnold" (1973).

Schuyler's best-known work, the satirical science fiction novel *Black No More*, was considered pulp fiction during the 1930s. It deals with the **race** issue in America, featuring a Black doctor, Junius Crookman, who discovers a phenomenon that will change Black people into White people. Beginning with this science fiction premise, Schuyler examines the racial attitudes of everyone from White racists to Black intellectuals. He also offers caricatures of real-life individuals, such as **W.E.B. Du Bois** as Dr. Shakespeare Agamemnon Beard, **James Weldon Johnson** as Dr. Jackson, and Madame C. J. Walker as Madame Siseretta Blandish. The novel's protagonist is Max Dasher (a.k.a. Matthew Fisher), one of the first to embrace and undergo Dr. Crookman's discovery. Many Blacks find this discovery to be a welcome alternative to the everyday denigration they experience. The novel poses the question, "What would America be like if there were no Blacks?" Would racism cease? Dr. Crookman's newfound marvel allows Blacks to experience the daily amenities once experienced only by White America, and eventually results in an epiphany for people of all races.

George Samuel Schuyler was born on February 25, 1895, in Providence, Rhode Island, and was raised in Syracuse, New York. His father died when he was three. His mother later married a cook and porter. When he was still very young, Schuyler's mother taught him to read and write. In 1912 he dropped out of school and joined the army, serving in **World War I** until 1919 and obtaining the rank of first lieutenant. During his stint in the army, Schuyler went AWOL when a "Greek immigrant shoeshine man in Philadelphia called him the 'n' word, and refused to shine his shoes." Schuyler remarked, "I'm a son-of-a-bitch if I'll serve this country any longer." He eventually turned himself in and was convicted by a military court. Schuyler was sentenced to five years in prison, but because of good behavior he was released after serving nine months of his sentence. In 1919 Schuyler was discharged from the army. He never wrote about or discussed his AWOL, his subsequent conviction, or his time in military prison. After his discharge from the army and before returning to Syracuse, Schuyler moved to New York City, where he did factory work, washed dishes, and performed other unskilled work.

In 1928, Schuyler married Josephine E. Cogdell, an artist, journalist, and heiress of a prominent White **Texas** family. He was her second husband. Their daughter Philippa Duke Schuyler was born in 1931. Josephine fed young Philippa a diet that incorporated wheat germ, cod liver oil, and uncooked foods, including raw liver, in an effort to perpetuate her concept of hybridization as a source of superior vigor and intellect. Philippa was a piano prodigy who later became a journalist for the *Union Leader*. Like her father decades earlier, she experienced racial prejudice in America. This led her to travel abroad and, for a brief period, legally change her name to Felipa Monterro y Schuyler, and pass for White. Years later she resumed the name Philippa Schuyler. On May 9, 1967, while reporting in Vietnam and performing an unauthorized humanitarian rescue mission, Philippa died in a helicopter crash. Two years later her mother, distraught over her death, committed suicide.

Schuyler's extensive career was politically radical. In his early years he was a member of the Socialist Party. His conservative critiques and satiric depictions of the **Harlem Renaissance**, the **Civil Rights Movement**, and of a broad range of civil rights leaders, from W.E.B. Du Bois to **Martin Luther King, Jr.**, gained him attention, as did his affiliation with the far-right John Birch Society. Still, Schuyler's rhetorical powers demand respect, and his journey to ultraconservatism should not erase his earlier accomplishments as journalist and novelist. Additionally, in recent years there has been renewed interest in his fiction and admiration for his accomplishments, including a new edition of *Black No More* with an introduction by **Henry Louis Gates, Jr.** On August 31, 1977, Schuyler died in New York City at the age of eighty-two.

Resources: Henry Louis Gates, Jr., "A Fragmented Man: George Schuyler and the Claims of Race," *New York Times Book Review*, Sept. 20, 1992, pp. 42–43; Jennifer Hislop, "Phillipa Duke Schuyler: Child Prodigy," http://www.intermix.org.uk/ p%20d%20schuyler00.htm; Jennifer Jordan, "The New Literary Blackface," *Black Issues Book Review*, Mar.–Apr. 2002, 9, www.findarticles.com/p/articles/mi_m0HST/ is_2_4/ai_83553036; Mark Gauvreau Judge, "Justice to George S. Schuyler," *Policy Review Online*, Aug.–Sept. 2000, 26, http://www.policyreview.org/aug00/Judge_ print.html; David Levering Lewis, ed., *The Portable Harlem Renaissance Reader* (New York: Viking, 1994); *The Kaiser Index to Black Studies, 1984–1986*, vol. 4 (Brooklyn, NY: Carlson), 289; Richard A. Long, "Renaissance Personality: An Interview with George Schuyler," *Black World* 25, no. 4 (1976), 68–78; Emmanuel S. Nelson, "George Samuel Schuyler (1895–1977)," in *African American Autobiographers: A*

Sourcebook, ed. Nelson (Westport, CT: Greenwood Press, 2002), 323–327; Michael W. Peplow, "George Samuel Schuyler (1895–1977)," in *The Heath Anthology of American Literature*, ed. Paul Lauter, 4th ed. (Boston: Houghton Mifflin, 2002); Ann Rayson, "George Schuyler: Paradox Among 'Assimilationist' Writers," *Black American Literature Forum* 12 (1978), 102–106; John M. Reilly, "The Black Anti-Utopia," *Black American Literature Forum* 12 (1976), 107–109; Paul P. Reuben, "Chapter 9: Harlem Renaissance—George Schuyler," *PAL: Perspectives in American Literature—A Research and Reference Guide* (May 2003), www.csustan.edu/english/reuben/pal/chap9/schuyler.html; George S. Schuyler: *Black and Conservative* (New Rochelle, NY: Arlington House, 1966); *Black No More* (Boston: Northeastern University Press, 1989); Carolyn See, "So Young, So Gifted, So Sad," *Washington Post Book Review*, Nov. 24, 1975, www.washingtonpost.com/wp-srv/style/longterm/books/reviews/composit.htm; Nicholas Stix, "George S. Schuyler and Black History Month," *Enter Stage Right*, Feb. 23, 2004, p. 26, http://www.enterstageright.com/archive/articles/0204/0204schuyler.htm; Kathryn Talalay, *Composition in Black and White: The Life of Philippa Schuyler* (New York: Oxford University Press, 1977), also www.washingtonpost.com/wp-srv/style/longterm/books/chap1/composit.htm.

Yvonne Walker

Science Fiction. Type of literature. While many who attempt to define science fiction will insist on science and technological inventions (real or imagined) as necessary components of such literature, many others will claim that science is not a necessary element for a literary work to be considered science fiction. Usually a work of science fiction hypothesizes about positive as well as negative changes of all kinds in society and their outcomes, develops models of different worlds, and enables us to imagine situations that we normally cannot or will not face in our everyday lives. Science fiction does not, however, necessarily predict the future; in fact, although many works of science fiction speculate on possible futures, some writers set their stories in the past and/or present. Lester Del Rey offers a useful, broad definition of science fiction: "Science fiction is an attempt to deal rationally with alternate possibilities in a manner which will be entertaining" (5). He adds that science fiction largely plays with potentialities by asking "What if?" (11).

Hugo Gernsback, a science and technology enthusiast, helped bring science fiction to a larger audience in April 1926 when he published the first magazine devoted entirely to what he called "scientifiction." The title of his magazine was *Amazing Stories*. The publication of the magazine, and Gernsback's coining of the term "science fiction" three years later, resulted in his being known as the "father of magazine science fiction" (Del Rey, 43). Yet the term "science fiction" did not become widely used until 1938, when John Wood Campbell, one of the most popular writers in the field at the time, became the editor of another science fiction magazine, *Astounding Stories*, and changed its title to *Astounding Science Fiction*.

Although science fiction did not become a well-defined literary genre until the twentieth century, many contributed to its development before that time.

In *The True History* (175 C.E.), by Lucian of Samosata, the adventurers are lifted by an enormous waterspout to the moon, where they meet intelligent beings. The astronomer Johannes Kepler wrote a moon voyage, *Somnium* (1634), which takes place in a dream and the transportation to the moon is made possible by a lunar spirit. The first story about a flight to the moon written in English is *The Man in the Moone* (1638), by Francis Goodwin. Other influential works include *Voyage to the Moon* (1650), by Cyrano de Bergerac; *Gulliver's Travels* (1726), by Jonathan Swift; *Frankenstein* (1818), by Mary Wollstonecraft Shelley; some tales by Edgar Allan Poe, including "The Unparalleled Adventure of One Hans Pfaal" (1835); and *A Connecticut Yankee in King Arthur's Court* (1889), by **Mark Twain**.

Arguably the two writers who exerted the most influence on the evolution of science fiction are Jules Verne and Herbert George Wells. Franz Rottensteiner calls Verne "a timid extrapolator" (22) because of Verne's insistence on the scientific plausibility of his stories. To ensure scientific verisimilitude, Verne often consulted scientific publications to emphasize the authenticity of his novels. His works wonderfully capture the atmosphere of the nineteenth century, especially the excitement people felt about science and their hope in scientific and technological progress. In 1864, Verne published *A Journey to the Center of the Earth*, in which three travelers descend deep into the hollow Earth. Verne's moon voyages, *From the Earth to the Moon* (1865) and the sequel, *Around the Moon* (1870), describe the preparations and the actual voyage of two Americans and a Frenchman to the moon. Verne's probably most renowned novel, *Twenty Thousand Leagues Under the Sea* (1870), tells a story of three men who are imprisoned by Verne's famous character, Captain Nemo, on his submarine *Nautilus*. Some of his other novels include *Around the World in Eighty Days* (1873), *The Mysterious Island* (1875), *The Purchase of the North Pole* (1889), *The Castle of the Carpathians* (1892), and *The Floating Island* (1895). Although Wells authored around 120 books, he is most known for his science fiction. The first of his science fiction novels is *The Time Machine* (1895). *The Island of Dr. Moreau* (1896), described by Wells as "an exercise in youthful blasphemy" (Aldiss, 26), tells about Dr. Moreau's attempts, conducted on a Pacific island, to turn animals into humans. Another of Wells's stories, *The War of the Worlds* (1898), concerns Martians trying to gain control over the earth. When Orson Welles's radio version of the novel was broadcast in 1938, many horrified listeners thought that the Martians had actually attacked New Jersey, and panic ensued. A new film version appeared in 2005.

The first half of the twentieth century witnessed fast development in science fiction, mainly because of the many specialized magazines that were being published at the time. The period between 1938 and 1949 is usually referred to as the golden age of science fiction, and two of the noted science fiction writers who contributed widely to the magazines then were Isaac Asimov and Robert A. Heinlein. The audience for science fiction literature, composed chiefly of White males, grew significantly in this so-called golden age. Science fiction clubs were created in the United States, and in 1941 the

National Fantasy Fan Federation was formed. The phenomenon of science fiction conventions was another important step in contributing to the development of science fiction because they created publicity for the genre and allowed readers to meet writers. At the convention known as Philcon II, held in **Philadelphia, Pennsylvania**, in 1953, awards for the best science fiction novel, artist, magazine, and so on, were conferred. The award was named after Hugo Gernsback—the Hugo Award—and has come to represent the highest achievement in the field. Since 1965 the Association of the Science Fiction and Fantasy Writers of America has been awarding the Nebula Award for the best novel, novella, novelette, and short story for each year.

After **World War II**, the subject of a world catastrophe, including one caused by nuclear war, gained considerable strength in science fiction. Some examples of such works are *Shadow on the Hearth* (1950), by Judith Merril; *The Day of the Triffids* (1951), by John Wyndham; *Limbo* (1952), by Bernard Wolfe; and *The Long Loud Silence* (1952), by Wilson Tucker. This was a prolific period in science fiction, and aficionados of science fiction sometimes refer to the 1950s as "the big boom." Many new writers entered the scene, such as Mark Clifton, Philip K. Dick, Zenna Henderson, Frank Herbert, and Robert Sheckley. The 1960s brought new issues that caused numerous debates among science fiction writers and fans as the "New Wave" stories began appearing. This movement (initiated in Great Britain) emphasized style and narrative techniques instead of plot, and writing itself became the focus. Brian Aldiss, J. G. Ballard, John Brunner, Thomas M. Disch, and, to a degree, Harlan Ellison were some of the followers of the movement's ideas. Many women began publishing science fiction in the 1960s, including Marion Zimmer Bradley, Ursula K. Le Guin, Anne McCaffrey, Vonda N. McIntyre, Joanna Russ, Pamela Sargent, and Kate Wilhelm. In the 1980s, a new literary movement, cyberpunk, emerged, integrating high technology with techno and punk countercultures. The term "cyberpunk" was coined at the beginning of 1980s by Bruce Bethke in his short story of the same title. Probably the best-known cyberpunk novel today is *Neuromancer* (1984), by William Gibson, which introduced the term "cyberspace," presented the idea of a global information network (Matrix), and won the Hugo, the Nebula, and the Philip K. Dick Memorial Awards. In 2004, the entrepreneur Paul Allen opened the Science Fiction Museum and Hall of Fame in Seattle.

At this writing, **Octavia E. Butler, Samuel R. Delany, Stephen E. Barnes**, and Charles R. Saunders are considered the most prominent African American science fiction writers. Butler has published novels, short stories, and essays and has won numerous awards, including the Nebula and Hugo Awards and the MacArthur Fellows grant. Her Xenogenesis trilogy—*Dawn* (1987), *Adulthood Rites* (1988), and *Imago* (1989)—pursues a theme of the urgent need for change in society. In her Earthseed books—*Parable of the Sower* (1993) and *Parable of the Talents* (1998)—Butler uses a similar theme. She presents a community attempting to rebuild their lives after a catastrophe. Samuel

R. Delany is the most prolific African American science fiction writer today. He has won numerous awards, including the Hugo, the Nebula, and the Pilgrim. His novel *The Einstein Intersection* (1967) follows a theme that also appears in Butler's novels—the possibility of relocation to another planet in order for humans to start a new life. Some of Delany's other novels are *The Jewels of Aptor* (1962), *Babel-17* (1966), *Triton* (1976), and *Dhalgren* (1974). Besides science and other fiction, Delany also writes nonfiction. In addition to his numerous novels, Stephen Barnes has written screenplays and scripts for television shows, such as *The Twilight Zone, The Outer Limits*, and *Gene Roddenberry's Andromeda*. In his most recent novels, *Lion's Blood: A Novel of Slavery and Freedom in an Alternate America* (2002) and *Zulu Heart* (2003), Barnes introduces an alternate world history in which Africa colonized the Americas. Charles R. Saunders was born in the United States but emigrated to Canada to protest the **Vietnam War** in 1969. He won the Small Press Award for Best Writer of Fantasy in 1980. His Imaro trilogy—*Imaro* (1981), *The Quest for Cush* (1984), and *The Trail of Bohu* (1985)—is set in Africa and focuses on a Black warrior named Imaro. While these four writers differ in their literary styles and foci, their works share some common themes: domination and control, oppression and violence, traditions of ancient African nations, and the need for change.

Resources: Brian W. Aldiss, "H. G. Wells," in *Science Fiction Writers: Critical Studies of the Major Authors from the Early Nineteenth Century to the Present Day*, ed. Everett Franklin Bleiler (New York: Scribner's, 1982), 25–30; Marleen S. Barr, ed., *Future Females, the Next Generation: New Voices and Velocities in Feminist Science Fiction Criticism* (Lanham, MD: Rowman & Littlefield, 2000); Harold Bloom, ed., *Classic Science Fiction Writers* (New York: Chelsea House, 1994); David Cowart and Thomas L. Wymer, eds., *Twentieth-Century American Science-Fiction Writers* (Detroit: Gale, 1981); Lester Del Ray, *The World of Science Fiction, 1926–1976* (New York: Garland, 1980); Sandra M. Grayson, *Visions of the Third Millennium: Black Science Fiction Novelists Write the Future* (Trenton, NJ: Africa World Press, 2003); Therese Littlejohn, "Fest Is Mothership for African Americans in Science Fiction," *Seattle Times*, June 6, 2004, Arts & Entertainment sec.; Tom Moylan, *Scraps of the Untainted Sky: Science Fiction, Utopia, Dystopia* (Boulder, CO: Westview Press, 2000); Franz Rottensteiner, *The Science Fiction Book: An Illustrated History* (New York: Seabury Press, 1975); Charles R. Saunders: *Imaro* (New York: DAW, 1981); *The Quest for Cush: Imaro II* (New York: DAW, 1984); *The Trail of Bohu: Imaro III* (New York: DAW, 1985); Sheree R. Thomas, ed., *Dark Matter: A Century of Speculative Fiction from the African Diaspora* (New York: Warner Books, 2000).

Iva Balic

Scott-Heron, Gil (born 1949). Poet, novelist, pianist, and recording artist. Scott-Heron's body of work not only contributed to African American literature during the **Black Arts Movement** in the 1960s, but also influenced the development of **rap** as a genre of music in the 1970s. Scott-Heron was born in **Chicago, Illinois**, on April 1, 1949. His father, a professional soccer player, and his mother, a librarian, divorced when he was young. After their separation, Scott-Heron moved to Lincoln, Tennessee, with his grandmother, who taught him to play the piano. Scott-Heron graduated from South Jackson Elementary School and enrolled at Tigrett Junior High. His presence there, along two other Black children, desegregated the junior high in 1962. However, the pressure of racism frustrated Scott-Heron, and he moved to the Bronx with his mother when he was an adolescent. In 1967, he was accepted by Lincoln University, a historically Black college, and moved to Oxford, Pennsylvania. In his sophomore year Scott-Heron became preoccupied with completing his first novel. He did not finish his courses that semester, nor did he complete his undergraduate degree, but he did complete his book, titled *The Vulture* (1968). The novel's crime-mystery plot hinges on four stories, each told by a different male character, concerning the death of John Lee. However, underneath the primary plot are references to America's morality and political ethics, and to African Americans' sense of survival. The book was published by Payback Press in 1968 along with his first book of poetry, *A New Black Poet: Small Talk at 125th and Lenox*. The latter would become the foundation for and partially share a title with his second record album, *Small Talk at 125th and Lenox*, released on the Flying Dutchman label in 1970. The **jazz** album presents thirteen tracks of African rhythms mixed with modern jazz sounds, and includes several politically charged spoken-word poems, such as "Whitey on the Moon," and "The Revolution Will Not Be Televised," setting the tone for Scott-Heron's critique of White America, the media, and the federal government. The former is a 107-second live performance supported solely by African congas and Scott-Heron's poetic performance, which interrogates the ethical position of the American government's interests in space exploration as opposed to addressing problems surrounding race and class. The latter is a studio recording of strong bass lines, a flute, and African drumbeats overlaid with Scott-Heron's rhetorical spurning of the elite's concerns with whitening their teeth and avoiding razor burns in the wake of America's political, social, and economic unrest. In doing so, Scott-Heron foregrounds his idea that all Americans will be drawn into ongoing cultural conflict because "the revolution will be live."

Scott-Heron then produced a great deal of poetry, fiction, jazz compositions, and lyrics, including a 1974 song titled "We Beg Your Pardon (Pardon Our Analysis)," a reflection on the pardoning of former President Richard Nixon by President Gerald Ford. In similar political poetics, Scott-Heron's "B-Movie" (1981) critiques the politics of Ronald Reagan and the "trickle-down theory" of economics advanced by Reagan's administration. Beginning in 1974, Scott-Heron issued three twelve-inch vinyl singles, a trend popular in the rap industry, commercially releasing his songs "The Bottle" (1978), a lyric addressing addiction and alcoholism and its effects on the **Black family**, and "Johannesburg," which criticized apartheid in South Africa directly and bluntly. Between 1970 and 2001 Scott-Heron composed fifteen albums, which produced seven compilations, a mixture of previously released work and new titles.

Additionally, he published several books of poetry, including his 2001 title *Now and Then: The Poems of Gil Scott-Heron*. He also published another novel, *The Nigger Factory*. It concerns discrimination and White resistance to diversity on a college campus in Virginia in the 1960s. Most, if not all, of Scott-Heron's literature and lyrics express his political and social views concerning the conditions African American experience. His work not only has affected the political tone of literature of the time, but also has helped to voice **Black Power** and to influence African American literature and **rap** lyrics after the 1980s. By mixing **jazz** fusion with spoken word, Scott-Heron's rhetorical style and poetics are extremely culturally conscious. Rap groups, such as Public Enemy, emulate Scott-Heron's volatile tone and immerse their lyrics in ideas from Islam, Garveyism, and **Black Nationalism**.

Scott-Heron's work has influenced such rap artists as KRS-One, Lord Jamal of Brand Nubian, Common Sense, and **Tupac Shakur**, all of whom have written about inner-city conditions. The issues Scott-Heron raises in novels, poems, spoken-word recordings and nonfiction prose are revisited in other contemporary African American literature, such as Nathan McCall's *Makes Me Wanna Holler: A Young Black Man in America* (1994), Del Jones's *Culture Bandits II* (1993), and **Sista Souljah**'s *No Disrespect* (1994). Scott-Heron's influence on African American literature can also be heard in the work of contemporary poets, such as Speech (formerly of the group Arrested Development) and Ursula Rucker, a featured artist on the recordings by the rap group The Roots. Remaining popular within the Black community and among scholars, Scott-Heron's poetry and lyrics are often required reading in high school and college courses on African American literature. Scott-Heron operates his own recording company, TVT Records, but has not recorded on that label since *Spirits* (1994). At this writing, he continues to perform and tour.

Resources: Writings: Gil Scott-Heron: *A New Black Poet: Small Talk at 125th and Lenox* (London: Payback Press, 1971); *Now and Then: The Poems of Gil Scott-Heron* (Edinburgh, Scotland: Canongate, 2001); *So Far So Good* (Chicago: Third World Press, 1990); *The Vulture and the Nigger Factory* (London: Payback Press, 1971). **Discography** (Recordings are listed in chronological order): *A New Black Poet: Small Talk at 125th & Lenox* (Flying Dutchman, 1970); *Pieces of a Man* (Flying Dutchman, 1971); *Free Will* (Flying Dutchman, 1972); *The Revolution Will Not Be Televised* (Flying Dutchman, 1974); *Winter in America* (Strata-East, 1974); *The First Minute of a New Day—The Midnight Band* (Arista, 1975); *From South Africa to South Carolina* (Arista, 1975); *It's Your World—Live* (Arista, 1976); *Bridges* (Arista, 1977); *Secrets* (Arista, 1978); *The Mind of Gil Scott-Heron* (Arista, 1978); *1980* (Arista, 1980); *Real Eyes* (Arista, 1980); *Reflections* (Arista, 1981); *Moving Target* (Arista, 1982); *The Best of Gil Scott-Heron* (Arista, 1984); *Tales of Gil Scott-Heron and His Amnesia Express* (Peak Top, 1990); *Glory—The Gil Scott-Heron Collection* (Arista, 1990); *Minister of Information* (Peak Top, 1994); *Spirits* (TVT Records, 1994); *Ghetto Style* (Camden/BMG International, 1998); *The Gil Scott-Heron Collection Sampler: 1974–1975* (TVT Records, 1998); *Evolution (and Flashback) The Very Best of Gil Scott-Heron* (RCA,

1999). **Videography:** Robert Mugge, dir., *Gil Scott-Heron: Black Wax* (Los Angeles: Winstar Video, 1982), DVD; Gil Scott-Heron, *Freedom Beat: The Video* (Los Angeles: Pacific Arts Video, 1988), VHS format; James Taylor, dir., *No Nukes* (Los Angeles: Warner Video, 1980), VHS format.

Ellesia Ann Blaque

Scottsboro Boys, The. The name refers to nine young African American men who were involved in one of the most important court cases connected to the **Civil Rights Movement**. In the 1930s, the Scottsboro Boys' trials had an impact not only on African American writers but also on a variety of people concerned with racial equality.

On March 25, 1931, several young men and teenagers, some Black, some White, were hitching a ride on a freight train out of Chattanooga, Tennessee, when a fight broke out. Subsequently nine young Black men were arrested near Paint Rock, Alabama, charged with assault, and then taken to Scottsboro, the seat of Jackson County. Rape charges were added against all nine after two women, Victoria Price and Ruby Bates, claimed to have been been raped. The next day the boys were nearly lynched by a crowd of over 100 that had gathered. They pleaded not guilty to the twenty indictments against them. On April 9, 1931, an all-White jury in Judge E. A. Hawkins's court convicted and sentenced to death eight of the boys: Clarence Norris, 21; Charles Weems, 21; Haywood Patterson, 17; Olen Montgomery, 17; Ozie Powell, 16; Willie Roberson, 17; Eugene Williams, 13; and Andy Wright, 17. The trial of the ninth boy, Roy Wright, 13, ended in a mistrial when some jurors held out for a death sentence even though the prosecution had asked for a sentence of life imprisonment.

In March 1932, the Alabama Supreme Court affirmed the convictions of seven of the boys. The conviction of Eugene Williams, 13, was reversed because in 1931 he had been a juvenile. The U.S. Supreme Court overturned the convictions of all the boys in November 1932 in the case of *Powell v. Alabama*. The court ruled that the defendants had not been well represented by lawyers, as required by the Fourteenth Amendment. However, Alabama officials refused to drop the case and insisted on trying the young men again.

By this time, the boys' plight had gained worldwide publicity because many people believed the Scottsboro boys to be victims of racial prejudice. Such organizations as the National Association for the Advancement of Colored People (**NAACP**) and the International Labor Defense of the American Communist Party (ILD) hoped to represent the Scottsboro Boys. Demonstrations were held in Dresden, Leipzig, and Berlin, Germany, in support of the young men. An international collection of intellectuals and scientists, including Albert Einstein, signed a petition demanding their release.

On March 27, 1933, in Decatur, Alabama, before Judge James Horton, Haywood Patterson was the first to be retried. Samuel S. Leibowitz, one of the country's most prominent defense attorneys, was hired by the ILD to represent the nine young men. During the trial, one of the two supposed rape victims, Ruby Bates, retracted her testimony. (Leibowitz implied that Price and Bates were prostitutes.) Still, the jury convicted Patterson, and he was sentenced to death. On April 18, 1933, Judge Horton postponed the trials of the other Scottsboro Boys because of dangerously high local tensions. In May, thousands marched in **Washington, D.C.**, protesting the Alabama trials. In June, Judge Horton disagreed with the Patterson verdict and ordered a new trial. In October, the Scottsboro cases were removed from Judge Horton's jurisdiction and transferred to that of Judge William Callahan. In December 1933, Patterson and another defendant, Clarence Norris, were convicted of rape in a third trial and sentenced to death.

In February 1935, the U.S. Supreme Court, in *Norris v. Alabama*, overturned the convictions of the two because Blacks had not been allowed to serve on juries in Alabama. Again, Alabama officials refused to drop the charges against any of the defendants. In December 1935, the NAACP, the ILD, the American Civil Liberties Union, the League for Industrial Democracy, and the Methodist Federation for Social Service banded together to form the Scottsboro Defense Committee, which was chaired by Allan Chalmers. Once again in Judge Callahan's court, Haywood Patterson was convicted of rape for a fourth time in January 1936 and sentenced to seventy-five years in prison. In July 1937, Clarence Norris was convicted of rape and sentenced to death. Andy Wright, Charles Weems, and Ozie Powell were convicted and sentenced to long prison terms. Roy Wright, Eugene Williams, Olen Montgomery, and Willie Roberson were released and all charges were dropped. Over the next three years, Chalmers attempted to persuade the governor of Alabama, Bibb Graves, to pardon the remaining Scottsboro Boys, but nothing could be agreed upon. Between 1943 and 1946, four of those convicted were paroled. The fifth, Patterson, escaped to Michigan in 1948; the Governor of Michigan refused to surrender him to Alabama officials.

Among those involved in attempting to help the Scottsboro Boys was **Langston Hughes**, who visited eight of the boys in prison in 1932 and participated in a fund-raising event in San Francisco in 1934. He also published several works based on what happened to the boys: the play *Scottsboro Limited* (1932) and the poems "Justice," "Christ in Alabama," "Scottsboro," and "The Town of Scottsboro."

Resources: Dan T. Carter, *Scottsboro: A Tragedy of the American South*, rev. ed. (Baton Rogue: Louisiana State University Press, 1979); William Haltom, "The Scottsboro Boys," in *A Langston Hughes Encyclopedia*, ed. Hans Ostrom (Westport, CT: Greenwood Press, 2002), 343–345; James Haskins, *The Scottsboro Boys* (New York: Henry Holt, 1994); Arthur Garfield Hays, *Trial by Prejudice* (New York: Covici, Friede, 1933); Gerald Horne, *Powell v. Alabama: The Scottsboro Boys and American Justice* (New York: Franklin Watts, 1997); Langston Hughes: *Collected Poems*, ed. Arnold Rampersad (New York: Knopf, 1994); *Scottsboro Limited*, in *The Political Plays of Langston Hughes*, ed. Susan Duffy (Carbondale: Southern Illinois University Press, 2000); Clarence Norris and Sybil D. Washington, *The Last of the Scottsboro Boys* (New

York: Putnam's, 1979); Haywood Patterson and Earl Conrad, *Scottsboro Boy* (Garden City, NY: Doubleday, 1950).

Craig Loomis

Scruggs, Afi-Odelia E. (born 1954). Journalist, memoirist, and children's writer. After a full-time journalism career spanning the years 1987–2001, Scruggs gained prominence as a memoirist and author of a work of children's fiction.

Scruggs is the daughter of Max Walter Scruggs, an accountant, and Irene Daniel. Scruggs, who tested for a high IQ as a child, entered third grade as a seven-year-old and entered the University of Chicago at sixteen. After earning a doctorate in Slavic linguistics from Brown University and spending a year as a faculty member at the University of Virginia, she left academia to pursue a career in freelance writing. She worked as a journalist in Mississippi and Ohio, including as a metro columnist for the *Cleveland Plain Dealer*, and taught journalism at Ohio Wesleyan University and elsewhere.

Scruggs's most critically acclaimed work is her 2002 memoir *Claiming Kin: Confronting the History of an African American Family*. The memoir began as a book on **gospel music**, but grew into an autobiographical narrative about Scruggs's own family struggles and recovered traditions. Scruggs draws on her background as a journalist to uncover details of her slave ancestors and the roots behind her upbringing in Franklin and **Nashville, Tennessee**. Her memoir draws on the same spirit of inquiry as **Alex Haley**'s *Roots* (1976) in its attention to illuminating a family history made dim by slavery. Scruggs's inquiry leads her to surprises about the true origins of her family name and the details of her line of ancestry.

Scruggs is also the author of the children's book *Jump Rope Magic* (1999), about an African American girl who charms an elderly neighbor through her jump rope rhymes, and *Beyond Stitch and Bitch: Reflections on Knitting and Life* (2004), a humorous collection of essays about the life lessons learned from knitting.

Resources: Afi-Odelia Scruggs: *Beyond Stitch and Bitch: A Knitter Reflects on Life* (Hillsboro, OR: Beyond Words, 2004); *Claiming Kin: Confronting the History of an African American Family* (New York: St. Martin's, 2002); *Jump Rope Magic* (New York: Blue Sky, 2000).

Melissa Shields

Seacole, Mary (1805–1881). Afro-Caribbean autobiographer, nurse, and entrepreneur. Born Mary Jane Grant to a Scottish army officer and a free Afro-Caribbean woman, Seacole became a successful businesswoman, healer, and traveler. A widow for much of her life—she was briefly married to Edward Seacole, a sickly older man who died shortly after their marriage—she lived a remarkably independent and adventurous life. Her **autobiography**, *The Wonderful Adventures of Mrs. Seacole in Many Lands* (1857), is a witty, engaging, and highly readable chronicle of her eventful life in places as varied as Panama, England, and the Crimea.

Though it is a self-representational narrative, Seacole offers in her text only a truncated version of her early life in Jamaica. To her father she attributes her spirit of adventure and wanderlust; from her mother, she states, she learned entrepreneurial and medical skills. After a cursory overview of the first four decades of her life in colonial Jamaica, she briefly describes her days as a hotel owner in Panama. The bulk of the narrative, however, focuses on her work as a merchant and nurse in the Crimea. Initially her desire was to join the British army as a nurse and serve in the Crimean War; rejected by the British officers because of her color, she nevertheless moved to the Crimea independently, established a boardinghouse near the British military headquarters, and began to cater to the material and medical needs of the British troops. When the war ended, Seacole, now bankrupt, settled in England; with characteristic business acumen, she decided to write her **autobiography** in an attempt to earn royalties and pay off her debts.

Seacole's narrative, republished in 1988, offers a fascinating glimpse into the complex positioning of a nineteenth-century colonial woman of color within the framework of the British Empire. She never challenges the foundations of British imperialism; in fact, she subscribes to its "civilizing mission." Yet her angry response to racism and her self-confident disregard for the constraints of color contain an implicit form of resistance and reveal an articulate, if largely unintended, critique of colonialism.

Resources: Sandra Pouchet Paquet, "The Enigma of Arrival: *The Wonderful Adventures of Mrs. Seacole in Many Lands*," *African American Review* 26, no. 4 (Winter 1992), 651–663; Mary Seacole, *The Wonderful Adventures of Mrs. Seacole in Many Lands* (1857; repr. New York: Oxford University Press, 1988).

Emmanuel S. Nelson

Séjour, Victor (1817–1874). Playwright, poet, and short story writer. Although Séjour wrote exclusively in French and died virtually unknown in the United States, he was one of the most important dramatists of the mid-nineteenth century. His expatriatism paved the way for later generations of African American writers, and his work provided significant milestones both in nineteenth-century French theater and the canon of African American literature.

Juan Victor Séjour Marcou Ferrand was born to Juan Francois Louis Séjour Marcou and Eloisa Phillipe Ferrand, both free people of color, on June 2, 1817 in **New Orleans, Louisiana**. The second son, Victor was welcomed into a prosperous family. His father owned a thriving cleaning and dyeing business, and his success enabled him to provide numerous socioeconomic advantages for his son, including an education both in the United States and abroad.

Under the tutelage of Michel Seligny, a respected scholar, Séjour cultivated his interest in writing and literature at Sainte Barbe Academy, and in 1836, his parents sent him to **Paris, France**, to complete his education and begin his career. Paris lacked the hostile racist attitudes that saturated the United States, and thereby offered Séjour greater opportunities.

Soon after his arrival, Séjour published "Le Mulatre" (1837), a short story about a slave who kills his master and then discovers that the master is his father. The story offers a scathing critique of the "peculiar institution," and was one of the first antislavery pieces written. It was, however, the only time that Séjour's work would address matters of **race**. The reason for his abandonment of the topic is unclear, though many scholars argue that he subversively addressed the issue through other vehicles. It is argued, for example, that his play *Diegarias* (1844) focuses on intolerance through the example of religious persecution. Whether the theme of religious persecution was meant to substitute for racism is unknown, however; Séjour never said.

In 1841, Séjour entered the literary circles of Paris with the publication of his poem *Le Retour de Napoléon*, a tribute to France's fallen leader, which gained critical acclaim both in Paris and in the United States. Three years later, his reputation grew, but this time as a dramatist; his first play, *Diegarias*, was a triumphant success. Over the next fifteen years, Séjour became one of the most popular playwrights in Paris, writing and staging over twenty plays, including a version of *Richard III* in 1850. In these successful years, he received the Legion of Honor (1860), accumulated tremendous wealth, and had three children with three different women, none of whom he married.

In the mid-1860s, Séjour's popularity began to fade. Theatergoers became less interested in his work, and fewer directors were willing to stage his plays. By 1874, Séjour was destitute and dying of tuberculosis. Months before his death, *La Gaieté* agreed to produce Séjour's plays *Cromwell* (1874) and *Le Vampire* (1874). They were, however, never performed. On September 21, 1874, Séjour died. He was buried in Père-Lachaise Cemetery at the expense of a close friend.

Resources: Philip Barnard, "Séjour, Victor," in *The Oxford Companion to African American Literature*, ed. William L. Andrews, Frances Smith Foster, and Trudier Harris (New York: Oxford University Press, 1997), 647; Thomas Bonner, "Victor Séjour (Juan Victor Séjour Marcou et Ferrand)," in *Dictionary of Literary Biography*, vol. 50: *Afro-American Writers before the Harlem Renaissance*, ed. Trudier Harris (Detroit: Gale, 1986), 237–241; T. A. Daley, "Victor Séjour," *Phylon* 4, no. 1 (1943), 5–16; Charles Edwards O'Neill, "Theatrical Censorship in France, 1844–1875: The Experience of Victor Séjour," *Harvard Library Bulletin* 26, no. 4 (1978), 417–441; A. E. Perkins, "Victor Séjour and His Times," *Negro History Bulletin* 5, no. 7 (Apr. 1942), 163–166; J. John Perret, "Victor Séjour, Black French Playwright from Louisiana," *French Review* 52, no. 2 (Dec. 1983), 187–193; Bernard L. Peterson, *Early Black American Playwrights and Dramatic Writers: A Biographical directory and Catalog of Plays, Films, and Broadcasting Scripts* (Westport, CT: Greenwood Press, 1990), 172–174; Charles Barthelemy Rousséve, "Negro Literature in Ante Bellum Louisiana: Victor Séjour," in his *The Negro in Louisiana: Aspects of His History and His Literature* (New Orleans: Xavier University Press, 1937), 82–90.

Jennifer R. Coates

Senna, Danzy (born 1970). Novelist, journalist, essayist, and educator. A native of **Boston, Massachusetts**, Danzy Senna is best known for her first novel, *Caucasia* (1998). In this story of two sisters from a mixed-race family, Senna takes on the permeability of the color line and the mutable nature of racism. Birdie, the novel's first-person narrator, has the light complexion of her White mother, while her sister, Cole, is dark-skinned, like her father. As the story progresses, Birdie's mother moves her to a White suburb—which Birdie dubs "Caucasia"—and encourages Birdie to pass as White (*see* **Passing**).

Senna was able to draw from her own experiences in a mixed-race family for *Caucasia*. Her father, Carl Senna (a journalist) is Black and her mother, Fanny Howe (a poet and novelist), is White. While Senna had originally sought a career in the sciences, she eventually turned to writing as her true calling. In 1992, she graduated with a B.A. from Stanford University (with honors) and in 1996 received her M.F.A. from the University of California at Irvine. From 1992 to 1994, Senna was employed at *Newsweek* as a researcher/reporter. From 1996 to 1997 she was a contributing editor for *American Benefactor*. Senna also served as an instructor of writing and literature at the College of the Holy Cross. She has been awarded the MacDowell Colony fellowship (1997), the Stephen Crane First Fiction Award, Book-of-the-Month Club (1998), and the American Whiting Writers' Award (2002). Senna's nonfiction essays have been included in *To Be Real: Telling the Truth and Changing the Face of Feminism*, edited by Rebecca Walker (1995), and *Half and Half*, edited by Claudine C. O'Hearn (1998). Her most recent novel is *Symptomatic* (2004).

Resources: Claudine C. O'Hearn, ed., *Half and Half: Writers on Growing up Biracial and Bicultural* (New York: Pantheon, 1998); Danzy Senna: *Caucasia* (New York: Riverhead, 1998); *Symptomatic* (New York: Riverhead, 2004); Rebecca Walker, ed., *To Be Real: Telling the Truth and Changing the Face of Feminism* (New York: Anchor, 1995).

Michelle LaFrance

Sermons. The sermon is one of the most important sources of and for African American literature. Drawing from the oral tradition of **folk tale** and song, as well as the most influential written source in the Western world, the Bible, the African American sermon's legacy extends today into every genre of American literature. The method of preaching that developed during **slavery** is commonly referred to as the folk sermon. African American spiritual leaders at the time operated under the most difficult conditions. Aside from negotiating the laws and animosity of local governments and White citizens in order to reach their congregations, preachers confronted audiences who were largely illiterate. Performance and storytelling, therefore, were key skills for relating the message of the Gospel. Well-known practitioners of the folk sermon include Absalom Jones (1746–1818) and Rev. **Richard Allen**. Richard Allen described his sectarian leanings in a way that illustrates the straightforward spirit of the folk sermon, as well as the determination of those deprived of education to gain knowledge:

The Methodists were the first people that brought glad tidings to the colored people. I feel thankful that I ever heard a Methodist preach. We are beholden to the Methodists, under God, for the light of the Gospel we enjoy; for all other denominations preached so high-flown that we were not able to comprehend their doctrine. Sure am I that reading sermons will never prove so beneficial to the colored people as spiritual or extempore preaching. (Miller 1971, 226)

In his *Autobiography of an Ex-Colored Man* (1912), **James Weldon Johnson** described people walking long miles to a "big meeting" in bare feet, their good shoes strung over their shoulders to stay clean. The novelist then gives us an excellent description of the sermons:

As far as subject-matter is concerned, all of the sermons were alike: each began with the fall of man, ran through various trials and tribulations of the Hebrew children, on to the redemption by Christ, and ended with a fervid picture of the judgement day and the fate of the damned. But [one preacher] John Brown possessed magnetism and an imagination so free and daring that he was able to carry through what the other preachers would not attempt. He knew all the arts and tricks of oratory, the modulation of the voice to almost a whisper, the pause for effect, the rise through light, rapid-fire sentences to the terrific, thundering outburst of an electrifying climax. (Miller 1971, 227)

The existing transcriptions of folk sermons show that the first half of their performance (written out as prose) often kept to a calm style and relatively "standard" grammar. Soon, however, the tone shifted to a "whooping" or intoned chanting style marked on the page as verse and characterized by rhythmic repetition and calls to the congregation. This emotional and evocative mode allowed the preacher to take his rhetoric to often rapturous conclusions.

Despite its performative nature, the folk sermon was structured along the same formal lines as more scholarly, written sermons: introduction of the Scripture at hand; statement of the thesis or main idea for the sermon; the discussion, which forms the bulk of the sermon; and conclusion. The scholar Gerald L. Davis, in the most comprehensive study to date on the African American sermon, *I Got the Word in Me and I Can Sing It, You Know*, also describes the importance of the period leading up to the sermon. The preacher must first "line-up" his congregation by fulfilling his "duty to charge the preaching environment with dynamic energies and in so doing to induce the congregation to focus oral and aural mechanisms on the content and structure of the sermon performance." In this way, the preacher and the congregation come to a sort of unspoken agreement about the traditional structures which will be adhered to and, also, the extent to which they will be improvised upon (Davis, 17).

However it is parsed, it is just as essential that the sermon follow this formal structure as that the preacher make it his own. This combination of a set form (closer to the written) and the need, before a live audience, for improvisation (of the oral and performative) gives the sermon a distinctly **jazz**like quality. This quality allows the preacher to give his congregation the scriptural foundation they require while simultaneously responding to their reactions and needs in the here and now. Despite its access and recourse to a rich written theological tradition, the African American sermon fully manifests itself only with the accompaniment of a living audience. Riffs and repetition, elliptical pursuit of inspiration, and a calling up of the congregation's collective consciousness and memory are essential strategies of the sermon. In addition to the spoken word, a significant part of the sermon dynamic takes place on a nonverbal level between the preacher and his audience, by way of vocal and visual cues:

> During a performance, when both "performer" and "audience" are actively locked into a dynamic exchange, the audience compels the performer to acknowledge the most appropriate characteristics of the genre system—the "ideal" in terms of that particular performance environment—before permitting the performer sufficient latitude for the individuation of his genius and style. (Davis, 26)

In this sense, the preacher and congregation act together to reexperience or reenact a thing whose contours they already recognize and love. There are organic echoes in this process, then, of both the redemption of the Lord's Supper and the retribution of a judging God. A skillful preacher must be very attentive not only to the overall mood and momentum of the audience but also, specifically, to the cues of senior congregation members. Stern looks or nodding assent from the "amen corner" can lead the orator to cut passages short or extend elliptical riffs (Davis, 11).

These various strategies, rooted as they are half in the living moment of the congregation, almost require (as Jesus did) that sermons address not just spiritual but also worldly issues such as social justice, education, racism, and poverty. G. L. Davis writes that "any image culled from the Bible for use in a sermon must hold opportunity for the uniting of the sacred with the profane. Or at least there must be ample latitude, in the image, for the sacred example to be made obvious through profane illustration" (Davis, 2). Often, in the spontaneous delivery of sermons, this spiritual hierarchy can be subtly reversed, so that what is wrong or unjust in our profane lives is made obvious through sacred illustration. It is in this mode that the "speeches" of **Martin Luther King, Jr.,** and **Malcom X** are understood to be among the greatest American sermons. It should be no surprise that the African American sermon style resonates today even in the most mainstream of political speeches.

The lyrical elements of the sermon are most evident today in **rap** and **hip-hop**. Ironically, while appropriating the forms of the sermon genre for their own uses, hip-hop artists are often critical of the tradition of Christ-like suffering from which sermons draw. This phenomenon, taken together with the fact that sermon style maintains its structure across denominational lines more than across race and class lines, reveals African American homiletics to be largely cultural. Considering the sermon form's ability to operate as both prose and poetry (and even song), along with its substantial influence on such disparate poles of contemporary American experience as hip-hop and mainstream political speech, the African American sermon is one of the most influential genres in American literature.

Resources: Richard Allen, *The Life Experience and Gospel Labors of the Rt. Reverend Richard Allen* (Nashville, TN: Abingdon Press, 1983); James Baldwin, *Amen Corner* (New York: Dial Press, 1968); Gerald L. Davis, *I Got the Word in Me and I Can Sing It, You Know: A Study of the Performed African-American Sermon* (Philadelphia: University of Pennsylvania Press, 1985); Gerald L. Davis, producer, *The Performed Word* (Red Taurus Films, 1981); E. Franklin Frazier, *The Negro Church in America* (New York: Schocken, 1964); Dolan Hubbard, *The Sermon and the African American Literary Imagination* (Columbia: University of Missouri Press, 1994); Langston Hughes and Arna Bontemps, eds., *The Book of Negro Folklore* (New York: Dodd, Mead, 1958); Zora Neale Hurston, *Jonah's Gourd Vine* (New York: Perennial Library, 1990); Ruth Miller, *Blackamerican Literature 1760–Present* (Beverly Hills, CA: Glencoe, 1971); Bruce A. Rosenberg, *Can These Bones Live? The Art of the American Folk Preacher* (Urbana: University of Illinois Press, 1988); Michael Warner, ed., *American Sermons: The Pilgrims to Martin Luther King Jr.* (New York: Library of America, 1999); James Melvin Washington, ed., *Conversations with God: Two Centuries of Prayers by African Americans* (New York: HarperCollins, 1994).

Robert Strong

Sexual Revolution (c. 1960–1980). This is the term applied to the 1960s and 1970s in the United States and Europe when attitudes toward sexuality changed considerably. The legalization of birth control, the development and sale of birth-control pills, aspects of **feminism**, changing attitudes toward fashion, influences springing from the **Beat Movement** and the hippies, and a variety of other factors combined to create a widespread sense of freer sexuality and even promiscuity. The actual nature, extent, and appropriateness of the sexual revolution remain matters of debate, however.

At least two factors made the sexual revolution potentially problematic for African Americans. First, African Americans had always been "sexualized" by White Americans, often depicted or regarded as more primitive and hence more inherently sexual. Second, the sexual revolution was often depicted as a revolution that the White middle class was experiencing (Allyn).

In African American literature, writers struggled to challenge the image of Black sexuality long before the sexual revolution. This struggle began with **Sojourner Truth**'s *The Narrative of Sojourner Truth* (1850) and **Phillis Wheatley**'s *Poems on Various Subjects, Religious and Moral* (1773). Until these books, Blacks were affected by the widespread controlling mythological image that Black women are sexually promiscuous. Much later, **Lorraine Hansberry**'s dramatic representations of the plight of Black women in *To Be Young, Gifted* *and Black* (1969) affirms this image of Black women, showing the marginal status of Blacks that enabled otherwise silenced Blacks to express their understanding and conveying their emotions.

Writers in the **Black Arts Movements** (BAM), which was contemporary with the sexual revolution, set up a new realm of literary opportunities for Blacks to be read, criticized, and respected. Works from the BAM often deal with themes of beauty, change, and the history of Blacks, though women do so in a way different from their counterparts. The realistic emphases of these writings show the authors' cultural and racial commitments at a particularly vulnerable time in history. At the same time, they portray the same inspiration as many Black writers of the time, but advocating for Black women to take control of their social relationships and their bodies, and show Black women as being defined as more than their mere image or status in society (*see* **Sanchez, Sonia**).

Rape is a form of power in the sense that one is dealing with a dehumanized being who is separated from and who does not control her body. Rape is an instrument of sexual violence and exploitation directed against Black women. Challenging the lived experience of Black women enduring sexual violence by White males has long formed a recurrent theme in Black women's writings. Autobiographies such as **Maya Angelou**'s *I Know Why the Caged Bird Sings* (1970) and **Harriet Ann Jacobs**'s "The Perils of a Slave Woman's Life" (1861/1987), from *Incidents in the Life of a Slave Girl*, record examples of both actual and threatened sexual violence. The effects of rape on Black women is a recurrenting theme in Black women's fiction. **Gayl Jones**'s *Corregidora* (1975) and **Rosa Guy**'s *A Measure of Time* (1983) explore interracial rape of Black women. **Toni Morrison**'s *The Bluest Eye* (1970) and *Beloved* (1987), **Alice Walker**'s *The Color Purple* (1982), and **Gloria Naylor**'s *The Women of Brewster Place* (1980) examine rape within Black families and communities. Ironically, then, during the sexual revolution, these and other writers were exploring the complexities of sexuality as opposed to celebrating sexuality uncritically. These writings illustrate an effort to conceptualize sexual violence against Black women as part of a system of interlocking **race**, **gender**, and class oppression. The work of such writers as **Angela Y. Davis** and **bell hooks** suggests that sexual violence has been central to the economic and political subordination of Blacks overall. Similarly, the works of **Amiri Baraka** and **Ralph Ellison**, among others, critique the image of the Black male as a sexual predator and offer a reinvention of the image of Blacks that remains influential today.

It was not until the writings of **James Baldwin** that representations of homosexuality in Black literature began to emerge fully. His novel *Giovanni's Room* characterized a new phase of Black writing, although the main characters in the novel are White. Baldwin's novel *Another Country* is, to some degree, an early examination of the emergent sexual revolution.

George Chauncey's *Gay New York: Gender, Urban Culture, and the Making of the Gay Male World* (1994) further explores issues of ethnicity and sexuality.

J. L. King's *On the Down Low* (2004) examines bisexuality among Black males who reject the label of homosexuality. These groundbreaking writings are known for their omissions as much as for what they say about Blacks.

Although sexual behavior and attitudes toward sexuality certainly did change significantly during the sexual revolution, then, African American writers have necessarily had to examine linkages among sexuality, gender, and ethnicity almost from the beginning. Therefore, the sexual revolution was arguably less of a revolution from an African American perspective.

Resources: David Allyn, *Make Love, Not War: The Sexual Revolution: An Unfettered History* (Boston: Little, Brown, 2000); James Baldwin: *Another Country* (New York: Dial, 1962); *Giovanni's Room* (New York: Dial, 1956); Harold Bloom, ed., *Alice Walker* (New York: Chelsea House, 1989); Gwendolyn Brooks, comp., *A Broadside Treasury* (Detroit: Broadside Press, 1971); George Chauncey, *Gay New York: Gender, Urban Culture, and the Making of the Gay Male World, 1890–1940* (New York: Basic Books, 1994); John Henrik Clarke, *Black American Short Stories: A Century of the Best* (New York: Hill & Wang, 1993); J. L. King, *On the Down Low: A Journey into the Lives of "Straight" Black Men Who Sleep with Men* (New York: Broadway Books, 2004); Sonia Sanchez, *Homegirls & Handgrenades* (New York: Thunder's Mouth Press, 1984); Claudia Tate, ed., *Black Women Writers at Work* (New York: Continuum, 1983).

Aaron Peron Ogletree

Shackelford, Theodore Henry (1888–1923). Poet. Shackelford is remembered primarily because of **James Weldon Johnson**'s inclusion of his "The Big Bell in Zion" in his landmark anthology, *The Book of American Negro Poetry*. (Johnson spells the name Shackleford in that anthology, but Shackelford's books were published under a different, and presumably the correct, spelling of his last name.) Inspired by a brother's escape from **slavery**, the narrator declares, "Ise gwine to be real nice an' meek....Den I'll run away myself nex' week." Given Shackelford's family history, the poem may reflect the stories of his grandparents, former slaves who migrated to Canada, where he was born at Windsor, Ontario, in 1888.

Little is known about Shackelford except for brief biographical sketches by Johnson and by Robert T. Kerlin in *Negro Poets and Their Poems*. Though his formal schooling was limited to three years, he moved to Pennsylvania at the age of twenty-one and enrolled at the Downingtown Industrial Training School. He graduated four years later and continued his studies at the Philadelphia Museum of Art.

Shackelford's career as a poet was brief but productive. He published *Mammy's Cracklin' Bread* in 1916 and then reprinted the poems from that slim chapbook along with new material in a longer and more handsomely produced collection, *My Country and Other Poems* (1918). It included 118 poems, two of which were set to music. Both volumes were published in Philadelphia and featured Shackelford's own illustrations.

With an emphasis on humorous **folktales**, musicality, and religious or didactic messages, Shackelford follows in the tradition of **Paul Laurence**

Dunbar. Approximately a quarter of his poems are in **dialect**, including "Mammy's Cracklin' Bread," a sentimental (yet comic) portrayal of Southern family life. In the rest of his verse, Shackelford used a range of styles and forms, including pastoral lyrics, traditional **sonnets** and honorific poems. Condemnations of segregation and racial violence (often from a religious perspective) can be found in poems such as "God Will Make it Right" and "Despondent." Shackelford also dramatized the contribution of African American soldiers during **World War I** in a number of significant poems.

The settings and topical references in those war poems suggest that Shackelford either lived in or frequently visited New York as early as 1917. According to both Johnson and Kerlin, he died in Jamaica Plain, Massachusetts, on February 5, 1923.

Resources: James Weldon Johnson, ed., *The Book of American Negro Poetry* (New York: Harcourt, Brace, 1922); Robert T. Kerlin, ed., *Negro Poets and Their Poems* (Washington, DC: Associated Publishers, 1923); Theodore Shackelford: *Mammy's Cracklin' Bread and Other Poems* (Philadelphia: Klopp, 1916); *My Country and Other Poems* (Philadelphia: Klopp, 1918).

Robert D. Sturr

Shaik, Fatima (born 1952). Novelist. A native of **New Orleans, Louisiana**, Fatima Shaik attended Xavier University and completed her B.S. at Boston University and her M.A. at New York University. Returning to New Orleans, she was a reporter for two years with the *Times-Picayune*. From 1976 to 1988, she lived again in New York, working in several capacities for McGraw-Hill. Then, for two years, she was back in New Orleans as an instructor in the Journalism Department at Southern University. Since 1991, she has lived in the greater New York area, serving as an instructor in the Communications Department at St. Peter's College in northeastern New Jersey.

Shaik is the author of three highly regarded books for young readers. In *The Jazz of Our Street* (1997), two children join their neighbors in an impromptu celebration when a **jazz** band marches down their street. Set in Louisiana in the late eighteenth century, *Melitte* (1997) centers on the experiences of an orphaned slave girl who is abused by her master but is befriended by her master's daughter. When an opportunity to escape presents itself, her sense of release from an intolerable situation is undercut by the sense that she is deserting her only real friend. *On Mardi Gras Day* (1999) is a vivid description of the citywide celebration, emphasizing the ways in which it strengthens the bonds within the African American community.

Shaik's only book for adult readers, *Mayor of New Orleans: Just Talking Jazz* (1987), is a collection of three novellas, all set in New Orleans but treating very different subjects. In "Mayor of New Orleans," an African American trumpet players recalls how for four improbable months he served as chief executive of the city. "Climbing Monkey Hill" focuses on the experiences of an adolescent African American girl who is trying to understand herself against the backdrop of the highly charged integration of the city's school system. In "Before Echo," the main character is a sixteen-year-old Cajun girl who comes to New Orleans to locate her mother, who abandoned her to seek a better life in the city and had become a prostitute.

Resources: Matt Berman, "Brave Heart," *Times-Picayune* [New Orleans], Oct. 12, 1997, p. D8; Fatima Shaik: *The Jazz of Our Street* (New York: Dial, 1997); *Mayor of New Orleans: Just Talking Jazz* (Berkeley, CA: Creative Arts, 1987); *Melitte* (New York: Dial, 1997); *On Mardi Gras Day* (New York: Dial, 1999).

Martin Kich

Shakur, Tupac (1971–1996). Rap artist, actor, and poet. Born in New York City to a member of the **Black Panther Party**, Shakur was arguably destined to become an activist. In September 1983 his mother, Afeni Shakur, enrolled her son in the 127th Street Ensemble, a theater group in **Harlem, New York**. His first performance was as Travis in **Lorraine Hansberry**'s play *A Raisin in the Sun*. The play was produced to raise funds for **Jesse Jackson**'s 1984 presidential campaign. Shakur's childhood was nomadic. His mother moved him and his siblings from Harlem to the Bronx and back again, and from city to city. Shakur left New York permanently in 1986 and settled in **Baltimore, Maryland**. It was at this time that he wrote his first **rap** and called himself "M.C. New York." Shakur attended the Baltimore School for the Arts, where he studied acting and ballet. He began to explore his creativity at the school, and said of this time, "I was starting to feel like I really wanted to be an artist" (*2PacLegacy*).

Shakur's debut CD, *2Pacalypse Now*, was released in 1991. His feature-film acting debut came as Bishop in *Juice* (1992). Shakur continued to act and record at a feverish pace, appearing in seven feature films, two of which were released posthumously. He released three full-length CDs (*2Pacalypse Now*, and *Strictly for my N.I.G.G.A.Z.* in 1993, and *Me Against the World* in 1995), and a double CD (*All Eyez on Me* in 1995). Shakur died September 13, 1996, after being shot four times on September 7. His murder, shrouded in controversy and mystery, has yet to be solved. Many more recordings followed his death, most prominently *The 7 Day Theory*, under the pseudonym Makaveli (a play on the Italian political philosopher Niccolo Machiavelli). **Michael Eric Dyson** says Tupac Shakur "may be the most influential rapper to have lived" (138). In 1999 *The Rose That Grew from Concrete*, a book of poetry written by Shakur between 1989 and 1991, was published to critical acclaim. The book further revealed his artistic skill. Shakur was named by *Forbes* as one of the top-earning celebrities of 2003, ranking him with such other deceased cultural luminaries as Elvis Presley, Marilyn Monroe, and J.R.R. Tolkien. A documentary film, *Tupac: Resurrection*, was released in 2003, along with a soundtrack.

Resources: Michael Eric Dyson, *Holler if You Hear Me: Searching for Tupac Shakur* (New York: BasicCivitas Books, 2001); Jacob Hoye and Karolyn Ali, *Tupac: Resurrection* (New York: Atria, 2003); Tupac Shakur, *The Rose That Grew from Concrete* (New York: MTV Books, 1999); *Vibe* magazine, *Tupac Amanu Shakur* (New York: Three Rivers Press, 1998); Armond White, *Rebel for the Hell of It: The Life of Tupac*

Shakur (New York: Thunder's Mouth Press, 1997); www.2PACLegacy.com; www
.tupacfans.com.

D. Shane Gilley

Shange, Ntozake (born 1948). Playwright, poet, and novelist. Ntozake
Shange combines a cultural feminism with Pan-Africanism in her distincitive
contribution to African American arts. Her enormously popular choreopoem,
for colored girls who have considered suicide/when the rainbow is enuf (1975),
combines poetry, drama, and movement, and made Shange one of the preeminent African American poets.

Paulette Williams (Shange's original name) enjoyed a childhood of relative
security. Surrounded by the arts, she was introduced to a wide variety of
literary and artistic figures, from **Dizzy Gillespie** (*see* **Gillespie, Dizzy, Charlie
Parker, and Thelonious Monk**) and **Paul Robeson** to **Countee Cullen** and
William Shakespeare. She received a bachelor's degree from Barnard College
(1970) and an M.A. from the University of Southern California (1973), both
in American Studies. A transforming period in her life, graduate school gave
Shange more positive writing experiences. Her primary and secondary encounters were characterized by racial harassment, and debasement of Black or
female subjects. She taught classes in writing and socialized with dancers,
authors, and musicians. She underwent a spiritual transformation when two
South African friends re-baptized her in the Pacific Ocean with the Xhosa
(South African, Zulu) name Ntozake Shange, a combination of "she who
comes with her own things" and "she who walks with (or like) the lions."
Like other important African American writers, including playwright **Amiri
Baraka** (formerly LeRoi Jones), she considered it an act of self-identification
to relinquish her Anglo-American name in favor of a signification that iden-
tifies her exclusively as a Black woman and a feminist.

In the following two years, Shange taught humanities and women's studies
in the **San Francisco Bay area**. She participated in poetry recitals and experimented with African, Caribbean, and African American dance traditions.
She worked with the dance company of Halifu Osumare and was inspired
by Osumare's feminist/African aesthetics. Her "Stead Slingin Hash/Waltzin
Proper & Wanderin Demure" appeared in the collection *Time to Greez! In-
cantations from the Third World* (1975). In 1974, she worked with Paula Moss,
a dancer formerly with Osumare's company, The Sound Clinic (a brass trio),
and Jean Desarmes & his Reggae Blues Band. Their series of poems, dances,
and music would become *for colored girls*. Over the next two years, the group
presented "the Show" in bars, cafés, universities, and poetry centers, receiving
positive responses wherever they played. In 1976, Joseph Papp produced it at
New York's Booth Theatre, where it ran for 747 performances, won the Obie
and Outer Critics Circle Awards for Best Play (1977), and enjoyed successful
national and international tours.

According to later interviews, Shange never anticipated presenting *for
colored girls* as a mainstream theatrical production, intending only to share her

personal experiences as a Black woman with the female artists of her community. Paradoxically, it is its personal narrative and particular community appeal that has given the play its universality. Reviewers for the *Chicago Tribune*, *New York* magazine, and the *New York Times* hailed its ability to transcend the anger and suffering of being a Black woman in America, celebrated its multifaceted and dramatically viable portrait of the experience of growing up, and praised it for not losing sight of its target audience. The play also had its detractors. Some critics refused to accept its unconventional dramatic structure; others claimed it demonized Black men. Subsequent critical and scholarly opinion generally rejects a sexist reading, finding that the play, while attacking the behavior of abusive men, also holds some women responsible for allowing themselves to be victimized.

Ntozake Shange, 1978. Courtesy of the Library of Congress.

Seven performers share the text of three sections of stories on similar themes: a young Black girl comes of age, an adult Black woman deals with a debasing identity imposed upon her by outsiders, and the adult Black woman re-forms her own self-definition. Each story (poem/dance/song) moves from youth to adulthood, from ignorance to self-awareness, from particular experience to collectivity. In her rejection of linearity, Shange intends to disrupt the oppressive structures of Western language. In her emphasis on music and dance, she takes a stereotype of Blacks as performers and exploits it in revised form, attempting to reveal the cultural patterns of Black dance and song as nonverbal tools, offering protective and spiritual powers (Effiong, 124).

While no latter work achieved the impact of her first Broadway production, Shange continued to be a prolific stage writer for some years. She produced a *three Pieces* series: *Spell #7*, a choreopoem that attacks stereotypes of the past for continuing to limit racial equity by limiting possibilities in thought; *A Photograph*, an unconventionally structured piece that reaffirms the defensive powers of dance and exposes the self-destructiveness of nihilistic victimization; and *Boogie Woogie Landscapes*, an expressionistic work that brings to the surface the subconscious of "the average black girl." For many critics, these productions proved that Shange was a master poet but a mediocre playwright who had yet to find her dramatic voice.

Still, Shange had some important successes, earning a Tony award for her adaptation of Bertolt Brecht's *Mother Courage*, the *Los Angeles Times* Book Review Award for *Three Pieces*, and the Columbia University Medal of Excellence (all in 1981). Her most recent play, *Three Views from Mount Fuji/A*

Poem with Music, opened at the Lorraine Hansberry Theatre in 1987. Since then, Shange has turned to fiction and poetry, producing several novels. *Sassafrass, Cypress and Indigo* depicts the lives of three sisters in the aftermath of the **Civil Rights Movement**. Her most recently published works, *Daddy Says* and *Float Like a Butterfly*, are **children's literature**, drawing naturally on the **"coming-of-age"** themes developed in her early dramas.

As the second Black female playwright (after **Lorraine Hansberry**) to receive Broadway productions, Shange introduces a much-needed, self-consciously feminist agenda to the mainstream Black theater. From 1983 to 1986, she served as associate professor of drama at the University of Houston, and for one year as Distinguished Professor of Literature at Rice University. Currently, she resides in **Philadelphia, Pennsylvania.**

Resources: Primary Sources: *Betsy Brown: A Novel* (New York: St. Martin's, 1985); *Daddy Says* (New York: Simon and Schuster, 2003); *A Daughter's Geography* (New York: St. Martin's, 1991); *Ellington Was Not a Street* (New York: Simon and Schuster, 2002); *Float Like a Butterfly* (New York: Turnaround, 2003); *for colored girls who have considered suicide/when the rainbow is enuf* (New York: Macmillan, 1977); *From Okra to Greens/A Different Kinda Love Story* (New York: Samuel French, 1983); *How I Come by This Cryin' Song* (New York: St. Martin's, 1999); *If I Can Cook, You Know God Can* (Boston: Beacon, 1998); *Liliane* (London: Minerva, 1996); *The Love Space Demands: A Continuing Saga* (New York: St. Martin's, 1992); *Nappy Edges* (New York: St. Martin's, 1978); *Ridin' the Moon in Texas: Word Paintings* (New York: St. Martin's, 1987); *Sassafrass, Cypress and Indigo: A Novel* (New York: St. Martin's, 1982); *See No Evil: Prefaces, Reviews & Essays* (San Francisco: Momo's, 1984); *three pieces: Spell #7, A Photograph: Lovers in Motion, Boogie Woogie Landscapes* (New York: St. Martin's, 1981). **Secondary Sources:** Elizabeth Brown-Guillory, *Their Place on the Stage: Black Women Playwrights in America* (Westport, CT: Greenwood Press, 1988); Sean Carney, *Artaud, Genet, Shange: The Absence of the Theatre of Cruelty* (Ottawa: National Library of Canada, 1994); Mary K. DeShazer, "Rejecting Necrophilia: Ntozake Shange and the Warrior Re-Visioned," in *Making a Spectacle: Feminist Essays on Contemporary Women's Theatre*, ed. Lynda Hart (Ann Arbor: University of Michigan Press, 1989), 86–100; Philip Uko Effiong, *In Search of a Model for African-American Drama: A Study of Selected Plays by Lorraine Hansberry, Amiri Baraka, and Ntozake Shange* (Lanham, MD: University Press of America, 2000); Deborah R. Geis, "Distraught Laughter: Monologue in Ntozake Shange's Theater Pieces," in *Feminine Focus: The New Women Playwrights*, ed. Enoch Brater (New York: Oxford University Press, 1989), 210–225; Neal Lester, *Ntozake Shange: A Critical Study of the Plays* (New York: Garland, 1995); Carolyn Mitchell, "'A Laying On of Hands': Transcending the City in Ntzoke Shange's *for colored girls who have considered suicide/when the rainbow is enuf*," in *Women Writers and the City: Essays in Feminist Literary Criticism*, ed. Susan Merrill Squier (Knoxville: University of Tennessee Press, 1984), 230–248; Tejumola Olaniyan, *Scars of Conquest/Masks of Resistance: The Invention of Cultural Identities in African, African-American, and Carribean Drama* (New York: Oxford University Press, 1995); Bernard L. Peterson, "Ntozake Shange," in his *Contemporary Black American Playwrights and*

Their Plays: A Biographical Directory and Dramatic Index (Westport, CT: Greenwood Press, 1988), 417–421; Sandra L. Richards, "Ntozake Shange," in *African American Writers*, ed. Valerie Smith, 4 vols. (New York: Scribner's, 1991); Y. S. Sharadha, *Black Women's Writing: Quest for Identity in the Plays of Lorraine Hansberry and Ntozake Shange* (New Delhi: Prestige Books, 1998); Khalilah Watson, *Mothering the Self: The Novels of Ntozake Shange* (Albion, MI: Albion College Press, 1997).

Ben Fisler

Shannon, Angela (born 1964). Poet and teacher. Shannon's poetry is known in part for reflecting a keen sense of history. Born in **Oklahoma**, Shannon teaches poetry at the Loft (an arts organization) and at Hamline University, both in Minneapolis, where she lives. Shannon's poetry, collected in *Singing the Bones Together* (2003), is inspired by the poets **Countee Cullen** and **Gwendolyn Brooks**, and artists such as **Romare Bearden**, family stories, and African American history, especially the **Middle Passage**. Her characters remember, and sometimes try to forget, the hardships of **slavery** and segregation. But the pain is tempered with joy in Shannon's collection. "Sunday" evokes the church services of her childhood, the harmonica player wakes lost memories in his listeners in "Sugar Blue," and the carefully tended blooms in "Hydrangea" offer glimmers of hope and happiness. Shannon's poems have been published in many journals and anthologies, and were included in her choreopoem *Root Woman*, which premiered at the Fleetwood-Jourdain Theater in Evanston, Illinois, in 2001. *Singing the Bones Together* was nominated for the Minnesota Book Award in 2004. Other awards include a poetry fellowship from the Illinois Arts Council and a Mentor Award from the Loft. She also holds an M.F.A from Warren Wilson College. Shannon credits **Lucille Clifton**, **Sterling Brown**, and **Marilyn Nelson** for influencing her poetry.

Resources: Gregory Pardlo, "Review of *Singing the Bones Together*," *Black Issues Book Review* 5, no. 3 (May/June 2003), 59; Angela Shannon, *Singing the Bones Together* (Chicago: Tia Chucha, 2003); personal correspondence with Patricia Kennedy Bostian, Sept. 30, 2004.

Patricia Kennedy Bostian

Shannon, Ray (pseudonym of **Gar Anthony Haywood**). Historically, Blacks have contributed little to **crime and mystery fiction**. During the **Harlem Renaissance**, **Rudolph J. C. Fisher** and **Chester Himes** broke new ground for Blacks in this genre, but not until the late 1980s did the number of Black mystery writers increase substantially (Hamilton). These new writers include Ray Shannon, **Walter Mosley**, **Barbara Neely**, **Eleanor Taylor Bland**, and Gary Hardwick (Fleming, 256).

Ray Shannon has achieved significant acclaim, especially for his works based on private investigator Aaron Gunner. In these novels, Shannon addresses the "reemergence of black militancy, gangs in the inner city and the [relationship between] the African American community and the LAPD"

(Hamilton). Shannon has also produced a comedic detective series based on the lives of Joe and Dottie Loudermilk: *Going Nowhere Fast* (1994) and *Bad News Travels Fast* (1995). Shannon's most recent novels are *Man Eater* (2003) and *Firecracker* (2004). He has entries in *The Encyclopedia of Murder and Mystery* (1999) and *The Mammoth Encyclopedia of Modern Crime Fiction* (2002).

Resources: Mike Ashley, comp., *The Mammoth Encyclopedia of Modern Crime Fiction* (New York: Constable & Robinson, 2002); "Authors' Biographical Sketches," 1996 Program, California Librarians Black Caucus, http://www.clbc.org/aboutprog96/html; Robert Fleming, *The African American Writer's Handbook: How to Get in Print and Stay in Print* (New York: One World, 2000); Denise Hamilton, "Noir Wave," *Los Angeles Times*, Jan. 20, 1999, p. E1; "Ray Shannon," *Black History Month Author Roundtable*, http://www.authorsontheweb.com/features/0302-bhm/bhm-authors2.asp; Ray Shannon, "A Pseudonymous Author Takes on Hollywood: Interview with Ray Shannon," *Publishers Weekly*, Dec. 2, 2002, p. 32.

Gladys L. Knight

Sheffey, Ruthe T. (born c. 1926). Literary critic, editor, and college professor. Ruthe T. Sheffey, scholar and founder and president of the **Zora Neale Hurston** Society, was born in Virginia. She received a B.A. from Morgan State College (now Morgan State University) in 1947, an M.A. from Howard University in 1949, and a Ph.D. from the University of Pennsylvania in 1959. After teaching English and French at Claflin College in Orangeburg, South Carolina, in 1948–1949, she returned to Morgan in 1949 as an English Department faculty member and chaired the department from 1970 to 1974. Sheffey, who continues to teach at Morgan after more than fifty years and remains active in a variety of literary organizations, founded the Zora Neale Hurston Society in 1983 to promote appreciation of Hurston's life and works and to preserve the African American literary heritage. Sheffey is the editor of the Society's journal, *The Zora Neale Hurston Forum*. She also edited *A Rainbow 'Round Her Shoulder: The Zora Neale Hurston Symposium Papers* (1982), the collected papers of the first national Zora Neale Hurston Symposium, which was held at Morgan in 1981.

Sheffey's additional book-length publications are *Impressions in Asphalt: Images of Urban America in Literature* (1969), a textbook edited with **Eugenia Collier**; and *Trajectory: Fueling the Future and Preserving the African-American Literary Past* (1989). She has contributed articles to such periodicals as *The Black Scholar, Black World, College Language Association Journal, Drama Critique, Langston Hughes Review,* and *Studies in Philology.* Among her many honors are the Iva G. Jones Medallion for Outstanding Teaching at Morgan (1993–1995); Morgan's Department of English and Language Arts Ruthe T. Sheffey Award, established in 1998 in recognition of her scholarship, teaching, and service; and three awards from the **College Language Association** for the most original and distinguished scholarship (1962–1964), best scholarly production of the year (1974), and distinguished service (1996).

Resources: R. Baxter Miller, "Foreword," in *Trajectory: Fueling the Future and Preserving the African-American Literary Past, Essays in Criticism (1962–1986)*, by Ruthe T. Sheffey (Baltimore: Morgan State University Press, 1989), v–xiv.

Linda M. Carter

Shepherd, Reginald (born 1963). Poet, essayist, and **short fiction** writer. Shepherd was a key figure in the emergence of the gay Black voice in literature and identity politics in the late 1980s and the 1990s. His intricate and allusive verse and his essays on everyday concerns have established him as an important figure among African American writers of the new millennium. Born in New York City and raised in the housing projects of the Bronx, Shepherd went on to receive his B.A. from Bennington College and M.F.A degrees from Brown University and the University of Iowa. He has since taught at Northern Illinois University and Cornell University, and currently lives and writes in Pensacola, Florida. His key essays include "On Not Being White" (*In the Life*) and "Coloring Outside the Lines: An Essay at Definition" (*Fighting Words*). His best-known short story, "Summertime, and the Living Is Easy ...," was first published in 1994 and later was included in the anthology *Go the Way Your Blood Beats* (1996). Shepherd has published poems in such distinguished literary journals as *Black Warrior Review*, *TriQuarterly*, and *Poetry*.

In the early 1990s, Shepherd began collecting, arranging, and adding to his poetry in a series of books, all published by the University of Pittsburgh Press. In his poetry, Shepherd draws on Greek mythology, Continental philosophy, and the work of such poets as Wallace Stevens, Michael Anania, and Paul Celan. He blends these influences with the experiences of daily life as a gay Black man. In his poetry Shepherd attempts to get "something done, a new existence in the world, and not simply something said, mere commentary on what already is" (Prufer, 237). His first book of poetry, *Some Are Drowning*, won the 1993 Associated Writing Programs' Award in Poetry. His other books of poetry include *Angel, Interrupted* (1996), *Wrong* (1999), and *Otherhood* (2003). Shepherd has received grants from the National Endowment for the Arts, the Illinois Arts Council, and the Constance Saltonstall Foundation, among other awards and honors. (*See* **Gay Literature**.)

Resources: Kevin Prufer, ed., *The New Young American Poets: An Anthology* (Carbondale: Southern Illinois University Press, 2000), 237–239; Reginald Shepherd: *Angel, Interrupted* (Pittsburgh: University of Pittsburgh Press, 1996); "Coloring Outside the Lines: An Essay at Definition," in *Fighting Words: Personal Essays by Black Gay Men*, ed. Charles Michael Smith (New York: Avon, 1999); "A Nigger for Narcissus," in *Obsessed: A Flesh and the Word Collection of Gay Erotic Memoirs*, ed. Michael F. Lowenthal (New York: Plume, 1999); "On Not Being White," in *In the Life: A Black Gay Anthology*, ed. Joseph Beam (Boston: Alyson, 1986); *Otherhood* (Pittsburgh: University of Pittsburgh Press, 2003); *Some Are Drowning* (Pittsburgh: University of Pittsburgh Press, 1993); "Summertime and the Living Is Easy ...," in *Go the Way Your Blood Beats: An Anthology of Lesbian and Gay Fiction by African American*

Writers, ed. Shawn Steward Ruff (New York: Holt, 1996); *Wrong* (Pittsburgh: University of Pittsburgh Press, 1999).

Antony Adolf

Sherman, Charlotte Watson (born 1958). Short story writer, novelist, poet, housing administrator, and counselor. Sherman draws on both African culture and modern psychology in her writing. She received her B.A. in social sciences from Seattle University, and she has remained active in social work. In 1989 she was an emergency housing coordinator for the East Cherry YWCA, and in 1991–1992 she was a mental health specialist for Group Health Cooperative. In 1992–1993 Sherman taught writing workshops for the Seattle Education Center and YMCA.

Sherman has incorporated her experiences in dealing with psychological wounds into her literary works. Her first publication, *Killing Color* (1992), is a lyrical collection of folk-style short stories that weave together elements of traditional African legends and modern social messages. Sherman's works frequently explore the interconnectedness of the physical body and the more recent African American past and to ancient African ancestors. Her first novel, *One Dark Body* (1993), utilizes ancient African customs, rituals, and social symbolism to help the novel's modern protagonist, Raisin, achieve wholeness and healing. In 1994, Sherman edited *Sisterfire*, a richly textured collection of what she terms Black "womanist" fiction and poetry. Her second novel, *Touch* (1995), is a didactic tale of a woman's struggle to cope with her HIV-positive status and still maintain a sense of erotic sexuality and spirituality. *Touch* is a gratifying affirmation of the healing forces of love, hope, and the human touch. Sherman's other works include *Eli and the Swamp Man* (1996), a children's tale, and *Blues Ain't Nothing but a Good Woman Feeling Bad: Healing the Hidden Depression of Black Women*, in which Sherman debunks the stereotype of the Black "superwoman" and compassionately examines the modern Black woman's experience and those everyday elements that may contribute to Black women's depression.

In 1990, Sherman won the King County Arts Commission Publication Award; in 1992, the Seattle African-American Women's Achievement Award; and also in 1992, the Great Lakes College Association Award for *Killing Color* (1992). She has published in *Obsidian*, *The Black Scholar*, *CALYX*, *Painted Bride Quarterly*, and *Ikon*. Sherman's works are included in anthologies such as *When I Am an Old Woman I Shall Wear Purple* (1987), *Memories and Visions* (1989), and *Gathering Ground* (1984).

Resources: Charlotte Watson Sherman: *Blues Ain't Nothing but a Good Woman Feeling Bad: Healing the Hidden Depression of Black Women* (New York: HarperCollins, 1997); *Eli and the Swamp Man* (New York: HarperCollins, 1996); *Killing Color* (Corvallis, OR: Calyx, 1992); *One Dark Body* (New York: HarperCollins, 1993); *Touch: A Novel* (New York: HarperCollins, 1995); Charlotte Watson Sherman, ed., *Sisterfire: Black Womanist Fiction and Poetry* (New York: HarperPerennial, 1994); Nicholas Sloboda, "Retelling Our Selves: Collective Memory and the Body in Charlotte Watson

Sherman's *One Dark Body*," *African American Review* 32, no. 2 (1998), 317+; Kimberly Wallace-Sanders, ed., *Skin Deep, Spirit Strong: The Black Female Body in American Culture* (Ann Arbor: University of Michigan Press, 2002).

Debbie Clare Olson

Shine, Ted [Theodis] (born 1931). Playwright, editor, and scholar. Considered one of the "deans" of Black theater, Shine was born in Baton Rouge, Louisiana, and attended public schools in Dallas, **Texas**. He received his bachelor's degree from Howard University, where he was influenced and encouraged by the playwright **Owen Dodson**. He received his M.A. degree from the University of Iowa in playwriting and his Ph.D. from the University of California at Santa Barbara. A prolific writer, Shine is the author of several unpublished and published plays, including *Contribution*, *Shoes*, *Come Back after the Fire*, and *Herbert III*. He also penned many screenplays and had an all-Black "soap-Opera" (television drama) produced by the Maryland Center for Public Broadcasting in **Baltimore, Maryland**.

Shine wrote over sixty half-hour scripts for the PBS television program *Our Street*. In *Contribution*, produced by the Negro Ensemble Company in the 1968–1969 season, he explores generational conflict through comedy. Eugene, a young student involved in sit-ins in **the South**, challenges his grandmother's interest and dedication to the **Civil Rights Movement**, only to find that her "contribution" has been a surprisingly substantial one. In *Shoes*, the action centers upon a group of teens who make both wise and foolish plans for their summer earnings. When their mentor, Mr. Wisely, attempts to counsel one particular teen on the advantages of saving money, Shine crafts a conflict that displays the tragedy of conspicuous consumption that plagues many youths. A television adaptation was aired on PBS television and was produced by Barbara Shultz.

One of Shine's most notable works is the 1974 compilation of forty-five plays by Black Americans, titled *Black Theater USA*, edited by James Hatch with Shine as a consultant. In the later editions of the book, Shine was a coeditor with Hatch. Many of the plays in this landmark anthology were unpublished at the time, and the book is a primary text in African American theater and history classes at several colleges and universities.

Shine has taught at Dillard University in Louisiana, Howard University in **Washington, D.C.**, and Prairie View A&M University in Prairie View, Texas, where he is currently the Chair Emeritus in the Drama and Music Department.

Resources: Alice Childress, comp., *Black Scenes* (New York: Zenith Books, 1971); Owen Dodson, "Who Has Seen the Wind? III." *Black American Literature Forum* 14, no. 2 (Summer 1986), 54–59; James Hatch, ed., *Black Theater USA* (New York: Free Press, 1974); James Hatch and Ted Shine, eds., *Black Theatre USA: Plays by African Americans from 1847 to Today*, rev. and enl. ed. (New York: Free Press, 1996); Pamela F. Jackson and Karimah, eds., *Black Comedy: Nine Plays* (New York: Applause Theatre and Cinema Books, 1997); Whitney J. LeBlanc, "An Interview with Ted Shine,"

Studies in American Drama, 1945–Present 8, no. 1 (1993), 29–43; Ted Shine, *Contributions* (New York: Dramatist's Play Service, 1970).

Joan F. McCarty

Shockley, Ann Allen (born 1927). Journalist, editor, and novelist. Although Shockley's fiction is noteworthy for its frank treatment of lesbianism and of homophobia within the African American community, her nonfiction works have had a greater and more lasting impact, especially within the library profession.

Ann Allen was born on June 21, 1927, in Louisville, Kentucky. Her parents, social workers Henry and Bessie Lucas Allen, encouraged her interest in reading and writing. Later, Harriet La Forrest, a grade school teacher, also helped shape her literary aspirations. While attending Fisk University in **Nashville, Tennessee**, she worked as fiction editor and columnist on the *Fisk University Herald*. After graduating from Fisk in 1948, she married William Shockley. They had two children and were later divorced. In the 1940s and 1950s, Shockley contributed freelance pieces to several newspapers and journals, and began to write and publish short stories.

In 1959 Shockley took a library science degree at Western Reserve (later Case Western Reserve) University. She held librarian positions at Delaware State College (1959–1960), Maryland State College (1960–1969), then returned to Fisk University, where she served as special collections librarian and university archivist (1969–1998). Shockley contributed numerous pieces to the professional literature in librarianship, pointing out the need for collections of African American literature and the importance of well-trained African American librarians to create and manage these collections. *Living Black American Authors: A Biographical Directory* (1973), which she compiled with Sue P. Chandler, was a major addition to the African American reference literature. *A Handbook of Black Librarianship* (1977), edited with E. J. Josey, made a vital contribution to African American librarianship, bringing together elements of history, chronology, directory, and theoretical handbook. Arguably Shockley's most significant work is *Afro-American Women Writers 1746–1933: An Anthology and Critical Guide* (1988). Although not as important as anthologies compiled by **Alain Locke**, **Langston Hughes**, or **Amiri Baraka**, this work is a digest of a wide variety of critical and biographical material, and provides a literary sampling from many lesser-known authors.

Shockley's fiction is groundbreaking for its treatment of lesbian sexuality and the discrimination and homophobia faced by gay people in American society. *Loving Her* (1974), Shockley's first novel, explores the main character's growing sense of lesbian sexual identity. Renay, a gifted musician, marries the man who raped and impregnated her in college. His behavior after marriage is no less insensitive and brutal. Renay leaves her husband when she meets Terry, a wealthy White writer, at a nightclub where Renay performs. The two women face racial discrimination and homophobia as they try to establish a life together.

Shockley explores similar themes in the short story collection *The Black and White of It*. Many of the characters are professional women working out the difficulties of maintaining lesbian relationships. Shockley's second novel, *Say Jesus and Come to Me*, examines the life of a female minister who abuses her position to sexually exploit a young woman in the church choir.

Although potentially flawed by a tone that some readers may find melodramatic and lecturing, Shockley's fictional works are important documents in the history of the feminist and gay liberation movements. **Alice Walker** (1975) notes the importance of hearing this particular voice within the African American community. Elgie, however, believes that Shockley subtly perpetuates, rather than deconstructs, patriarchal/heterosexual societal norms. (*See* **Lesbian Literature**.)

Resources: Primary Sources: Ann A. Shockley and Sue P. Chandler, comps.: *Afro-American Women Writers, 1746–1933: An Anthology and Critical Guide* (Boston: G. K. Hall, 1988); *The Black and White of It* (Weatherby Lake, MO: Naiad Press, 1980); *Living Black American Authors: A Biographical Directory* (New York: R. R. Bowker, 1973); *Loving Her* (Indianapolis, IN: Bobbs-Merrill, 1974); *Say Jesus and Come to Me* (New York: Avon, 1982); Ann A. Shockley and E. J. Josey, eds., *A Handbook of Black Librarianship* (Littleton, CO: Libraries Unlimited, 1977). **Secondary Sources:** Rita B. Dandridge, *Ann Allen Shockley: An Annotated Primary and Secondary Bibliography* (Westport, CT: Greenwood Press, 1987); Le-Ann Elgie, "*Loving Her*" (book review), *MELUS* 26 (2001), 252–254; Helen R. Houston, "Ann Allen Shockley," in *Dictionary of Literary Biography*, vol. 33, *Afro-American Fiction Writers After 1955*, ed. Thadious Davis and Trudier Harris (Detroit: Gale, 1984); Alice Walker, "A Daring Subject Boldly Shared," *Ms.*, Apr. 1975, 120, 124.

Steven R. Harris

Short Fiction. The literary category of short fiction can be expanded to include tales, anecdotes, fables, jokes, **ballads**, parables, **myths**, legends, sketches, and **folktales**; however, since the early nineteenth century, short fiction has been thought of largely as fictional narratives in the range of roughly three to thirty pages—much shorter than the novella and the **novel**. Short fiction is also associated with a tradition in which character-driven (as opposed to plot-driven) narratives focus on ordinary people, often on their psychological and emotional lives and less on adventurous action. However, over almost two centuries, stylistic and philosophical approaches to short fiction have varied widely, from **realism** and naturalism to absurdism and **surrealism**. African American short fiction's history is rooted in Africa insofar as it springs from the union of an oral tradition and a written tradition. Writers who draw heavily on the **vernacular**, for example, explicitly connect their work to both traditions.

In his preface to **Terry McMillan**'s *Breaking Ice: An Anthology of Contemporary African-American Fiction* (1990), **John Edgar Wideman** asks, "What's the fate of a Black story in a white world of white stories?" (viii). The history, if not the fate, of the African American short story, as a written genre, arguably began in 1820 with the publication of **Lemuel Haynes**'s "Mystery Developed; Or, Russel Colvin (Supposed to be Murdered) in Full Life, and Stephen and Jesse Boorn, His Convicted Murderers, Rescued from Ignominious Death by Wonderful Discoveries." It is a story based on actual events which occurred in 1819, when two brothers, Stephen and Jesse Boorn, were accused and convicted of murdering their brother-in-law, Russel Colvin. Haynes, a Black minister with a predominantly White congregation in Vermont, served as the Boorn brothers' spiritual adviser. While Haynes holds the distinction as the first African American male to write short fiction, **Frances Ellen Wilkins Harper**'s publication of "The Two Offers" (1859), which concerns the issue of whether a woman should marry or have a career, probably makes her the first African American woman writer to publish a short story.

African American short fiction continued to develop as, in the late nineteenth century, Black writers made the transition from producing individual stories to publishing collections. **Paul Laurence Dunbar**'s *Folks from Dixie* (1898) is the first collection of short stories published by an African American man. The first Black woman writer to publish a collection of short fiction is **Alice Dunbar-Nelson**; her book *Violets and Other Tales* (1895) includes short stories, essays, poetry, and sketches. In Dunbar's "Anner 'Lizer's Stumblin' Block," the genuine cadence of African American speech is captured when a preacher says to his congregation:

> Now come, won't you sinnahs? De Lawd is jes' on de other side; jes' one step away, waitin' to receibe you. Won't you come to him? Won't you tek de chance o' becomin' j'int 'ars o' dat beautiful city whar de streets is gol' an' de gates is pearl? Won't you come to him sinnah? Don't you see de pityin' look he's a-givin' you, a-sayin' come, come? (8)

In "The Short Stories of Eight Black-American Masters: A Critical Assessment," Velma P. Harrison suggests:

> One of the reasons for our keen enjoyment of...fiction, is its ironic interconnectedness with life. As such, a work of fiction often embodies the identifying traits of a group of people bound by common customs and traditions, and acts as an insightful cultural statement. More often, the relationship between art and culture is marked by individuals who relate the details in stories to their personal circumstances or discover the motive of fellow human beings through examining the actions of literary characters. (134)

Charles Waddell Chesnutt's "The Wife of His Youth" serves as an example of the phenomenon Harrison describes. This story concerns Mr. Ryder, a man who wants to better his social and economic situation within the Blue Vein Society. He proposes to the most educated, wealthiest, and lightest-skinned Black woman in the group. Mr. Ryder is faced with a dilemma when his first wife, who has spent the past twenty-five years searching for him, shows up. Although the woman at first does not recognize Mr. Ryder as her lost husband, he eventually admits that he is the missing man. This story is replete with African American history in that, after emancipation, many Blacks spent years looking for lost relatives.

Additionally, Chesnutt's very famous story "The Goophered Grapevine" reflects the reality of African American life under the conditions of perpetual servitude. It is a story within a story. John and his wife, Annie, have moved from the North to **the South** because of Annie's health. John is interested in purchasing a vineyard in North Carolina. While surveying the old McAdoo plantation, John and Annie meet Julius McAdoo, who tells them the history of the vineyard. According to Julius, the vineyard was "goophered" by Aunt Peggy; that is, it has had a spell placed on it. Dugald McAdoo, the former owner of the plantation, paid $10 to Aunt Peggy to keep Blacks from eating his profits. Unfortunately, a slave named Henry, who was new to the plantation, and unaware of the goopher, eats the grapes and is transformed. (*See* **Conjuring**.)

Henry's transformation personifies the vineyard in that he takes on its seasonal characteristics. Dugald McAdoo takes advantage of Henry's condition by selling him for $1,500 in the spring, when he is young and strong. McAdoo buys Henry back for $500 in the winter, when Henry is old and weak. Thus, every year, McAdoo makes $1,000. In addition to selling and buying Henry, McAdoo follows the advice of a Northern stranger who convinces him that he can make more money if he uses the stranger's method for cultivating grapes. The technique proves disastrous and the vineyard is ruined. Unfortunately, once the vineyard dies, so does Henry.

This classic African American short story addresses the trinity of money, greed, and selfishness prevalent throughout American history. McAdoo's eagerness to buy and sell human beings, as well as his willingness to destroy the vineyard in an effort to satisfy his insatiable appetite for profit, exemplifies the point. The story reveals the magnitude of the problem when McAdoo uses Henry's youthful appearance to garner more wealth. In addition, the fact that the stranger in the story is a Northerner is significant, in that it implicates European Americans in the North in the exploitation of African American labor. In effect, some Black American short fiction writers become personifications of **tricksters** by exposing America's deep-seated denial and self-deception regarding the historical, cultural, social, psychological, and economic realities of African American life within the United States.

Like Chesnutt, **Frank J. Webb**, in his story "Two Wolves and a Lamb" (1870), refrains from making judgments or comments about the thoughts or actions of the characters. This lack of intrusiveness on the part of the author allows the characters to tell their own stories in their own words. For example, Walton of "Two Wolves and a Lamb" reveals a vengeful nature while giving his perspective concerning the appropriate sentence for a woman convicted of murder:

[I]f they wish to punish her the infliction of death will not effect that object. A woman who loves with such intensity of passion that she will commit murder to attain the object of her affections, must also be capable of feeling in the keenest manner the pangs of remorse. A woman like that should be made to live and be so environed, that every moment of her existence the evidences of her crime should be kept unavoidably before her. Had the lover of the murdered girl been else than a fool, he would have endeavored to suppress the evidence he gave which led to her conviction, and held it ever suspended over her like the sword of Damocles. He should have let her live; yet so live as to be each moment face to face with death. (Webb, 1870)

After this diatribe, the narrator, Phil Braham, comments: "That man, thought I, as I regarded the vindictive expression that crept over his face as he spoke, is not one to be safely offended" (Webb 1870). Walton's statement, as well as Phil's reaction to it, provides added insight into Walton's personality. Also, by allowing the reader to know his thoughts, Phil reveals himself as a perceptive and compassionate human being.

After Chestnutt and Webb, the African American short story continued to flourish. **Harlem Renaissance** writers who produced short fiction include **Zora Neale Hurston, Langston Hughes, Dorothy West, Gwendolyn Bennett, Richard Bruce Nugent, Rudolph Fisher, Jean Toomer,** and **Wallace Thurman**. Since Hurston was rediscovered in the 1970s, her collections of short fiction have remained in print, and her story "Sweat" is often anthologized. Hughes's first collection of stories, *The Ways of White Folks* (1934), has remained in print and includes several stories that continue to be admired: "Cora Unashamed," "The Blues I'm Playing," "Father and Son," and "Berry." Hughes went on to publish two more collections during his lifetime as well as several collections of tales featuring Jesse B. Simple, a character he created in a column for the *Chicago Defender* in the 1940s (A. S. Harper). Later Hughes edited an important anthology of short fiction, *The Best Short Stories by Negro Writers: An Anthology from 1899 to the Present* (1967). It includes stories by Chestnutt and Hurston, as well as by Ted Poston, **Alice Childress**, Lindsay Patterson, and **John A. Williams**. He also included "To Hell with Dying," an early story by **Alice Walker**.

The range of short fiction produced by writers of the Harlem Renaissance period is considerable. It includes earthy, folk-oriented stories such as those by Hurston, who drew heavily on the vernacular. It stretches from ironic, satirical, politically alert stories by Hughes to stylized ones by Nugent and Toomer. Nugent's "Smoke, Lillies and Jade," which was published in the magazine *Fire!!*, uses a stream-of-consciousness technique, while Toomer's *Cane* is a novel-in-stories that is considered an excellent example of Modernist prose. West's "The Typewriter," Bennett's "Wedding Day," and Thurman's "Cordelia the Crude" are naturalistic, tragic stories that show an acute awareness of issues connected with **race** and social-class. In addition to *Fire!!*, magazines that published short fiction by African Americans during the Harlem Renaissance included *The Crisis*, *Opportunity*, and *The Messenger*.

Since the Harlem Renaissance, African American short fiction has proliferated further. Though known more for their novels, **Ralph Ellison** and **Richard Wright** produced short fiction. Ellison's story, "King of the Bingo Game," is often anthologized, as is Wright's "The Man Who Lived Underground." Similarly, **James Baldwin**, known chiefly as a novelist and essayist, produced the acclaimed story "Sonny's Blues." **Ann Lane Petry**, also a member of this generation, wrote short fiction as well as novels.

More recently, **Maya Angelou, Toni Cade Bambara, J. California Cooper, Edwidge Danticat, Samuel R. Delany, Carolivia Herron, Charles R. Johnson, Randall Garrett Kenan, William Melvin Kelley, Jamaica Kincaid, James Alan McPherson, Paule Marshall, Gloria Naylor, Ntozake Shange, Alice Walker, John Edgar Wideman**, and **Sherley Anne Williams** have produced short fiction that is considered cutting-edge. The stylistic range of short fiction these and other African American writers have produced is as wide as, if not wider than, that produced in the 1920s. Short fiction by African American women, in particular, constitutes some of the most accomplished American literature produced in the era.

African American short fiction has a long history, but criticism about African American writing in this genre has yet to catch up with the richness and variety of the literature. Hans Ostrom's *Langston Hughes: A Study of the Short Fiction*, Henry B. Wonham's *Charles W. Chesnutt: A Study of the Short Fiction*, and Keith E. Byerman's *John Edgar Wideman: A Study of the Short Fiction* provide thorough analyses of the writings of three prolific African American writers of short fiction. Elizabeth Ammons has written *Short Fiction by Black Women, 1900–1920* (1991), but more criticism about individual women writers of short fiction is needed.

In *Down Home: A History of Afro-American Short Fiction from Its Beginnings to the End of the Harlem Renaissance*, one of the few works to attempt a historical as well as a critical analysis of this subject, Robert Bone traces the origins of African American short fiction in the United States to Joel Chandler Harris, the collector of the Uncle Remus tales: "It was a white man of the deep south who forged the missing link between the Afro-American folktale and the Afro-American short story" (19). Bone credits Harris with influencing the development of African American short fiction but admits that Uncle Remus is an inauthentic European-American stereotypical invention, and therefore highly problematic.

Studying African American short fiction necessarily involves assessing it in terms of its own cultural and literary histories and not relying solely on the European and Anglo-American traditions of the short story, traditions based largely on the work of Edgar Allan Poe, Guy de Maupassant, Anton Chekhov, Henry James, O. Henry, and Ernest Hemingway, for example (Puschman-Nalenz; Lohafer and Clarey).

Relatively recent anthologies of African American short fiction help to provide a more distinct sense of the achievement in this genre. The anthologies include *Breaking Ice: An Anthology of Contemporary African-American Fiction* (1990), edited by **Terry McMillan**; *Calling the Wind: Twentieth Century African-American Short Stories* (1993), edited by **Clarence Major**; and *Children of the Night: The Best Short Stories by Black Writers, 1967 to the Present*, edited by Gloria Naylor (1995). Preston M. Yancy has compiled *The Afro-American Short Story: A Comprehensive, Annotated Index with Selected Commentaries* (1986), and Charmaine N. Ijeoma has compiled "The African American Short Story, 1820–1899: An Annotated Bibliography" (2002). Wolfgang Karrer and Puschman-Nalenz have edited *The African American Short Story, 1970–1990: A Collection of Critical Essays* (1993).

Resources: Elizabeth Ammons, comp., *Short Fiction by Black Women, 1900–1920* (New York: Oxford University Press, 1991); Robert Bone, *Down Home: A History of Afro-American Short Fiction from Its Beginnings to the End of the Harlem Renaissance* (New York: Putnam, 1975); Peter Bruck, ed., *The Black American Short Story in the 20th Century: A Collection of Critical Essays* (Amsterdam: Grüner, 1977); Keith E. Byerman, *John Edgar Wideman: A Study of the Short Fiction* (New York: Twayne, 1998); Charles W. Chestnutt: "The Goophered Grapevine," in *Selected Writings*, ed. SallyAnn H. Ferguson (Boston: Houghton Mifflin, 2001), 118–128; "The Wife of His Youth," in *Selected Writings*, ed. SallyAnn H. Ferguson (Boston: Houghton Mifflin, 2001), 199–209; Paul Laurence Dunbar, *Folks from Dixie* (New York: Dodd, Mead, 1898); Alice Dunbar-Nelson, *Violets and Other Tales*, vol. 1 of *The Works of Alice Dunbar-Nelson*, ed. Gloria T. Hull (New York: Oxford University Press, 1988); Donna Akiba Sullivan Harper, *Not So Simple: The "Simple" Stories by Langston Hughes* (Columbia: University of Missouri Press, 1995); Frances E. W. Harper, "The Two Offers," in *The Anglo-African Magazine*, ed. William Loren Katz, vol. 1 (New York: Arno, 1968), 288–291, 311–313; Velma P. Harrison, "The Short Stories of Eight Black-American Masters: A Critical Assessment," Ph.D. diss., Northern Illinois University, 1987; Lemuel Haynes, "Mystery Developed; Or, Russel Colvin, (Supposed to be Murdered) in Full Life; and Stephen and Jesse Boorn, (His Convicted Murders) Rescued from Ignominious Death by Wonderful Discoveries," in *Black Preacher to White America: The Collected Writings of Lemuel Haynes, 1774–1833*, ed. Richard Newman (Brooklyn, NY: Carlson, 1990), 203–212; Langston Hughes, ed., *The Best Short Stories by Negro Writers: An Anthology from 1899 to the Present* (Boston: Little, Brown, 1967); Charmaine N. Ijeoma, "The African American Short Story, 1820–1899: An Annotated Bibliography," *Bulletin of Bibliography* 59, no. 3 (Sept. 2002), 121–126; Randall Kenan, *Let the Dead Bury Their Dead* (San Diego: Harcourt Brace Jovanovich, 1992); Susan Lohafer and Jo Ellyn Clarey, eds., *Short Story Theory at a Crossroads* (Baton Rouge: Louisiana State University Press, 1989); Clarence Major, ed., *Calling the Wind: Twentieth Century African-American Short Stories* (New York: HarperPerennial, 1993); Charles E. May, "Short Fiction: 1840–1880," in *Critical Survey of Short Fiction*, ed. Frank N. Magill, vol. 1 (Englewood Cliffs, NJ: Salem, 1981), 173–217; Terry McMillan, ed., *Breaking Ice: An Anthology of Contemporary African-American Fiction* (New York: Viking, 1990); Gloria Naylor, ed., *Children of the*

Night: The Best Short Stories by Black Writers, 1967 to the Present (Boston: Little, Brown, 1995); Hans Ostrom, *Langston Hughes: A Study of the Short Fiction* (New York: Twayne, 1993); Barbara Puschman-Nalenz, "Presentation in Prefaces and the Process of Canonization," in *The African American Short Story, 1970–1990: A Collection of Critical Essays*, ed. Wolfgang Karrer and Barbara Puschman-Nalenz (Trier, Germany: Wissenschaftlicher Verlag, 1993), 12–24; Frank J. Webb, "Two Wolves and a Lamb," *New Era: A Colored American National Journal* 1, no. 1–4 (Jan.–Feb. 1870); John Edgar Wideman, "Preface," in *Breaking Ice: An Anthology of Contemporary African-American Fiction*, ed. Terry McMillan (New York: Viking, 1990), v–x; Henry B. Wonham, *Charles W. Chesnutt: A Study of the Short Fiction* (New York: Twayne, 1998); Preston M. Yancy, comp., *The Afro-American Short Story: A Comprehensive Annotated Index with Selected* Commentaries (Westport, CT: Greenwood Press, 1986), xi–xiv.

Charmaine N. Ijeoma

Signifying. With regard to African American literature and culture, signifying refers to a broad range of linguistic practices, oral and written, that involve improvisation, playfulness, and irony. Used in this way, signifying is different from the term "signifying," which has to do with words-as-signs in structuralist literary theory and in semiotics, which is the study of signs. **Clarence Major**'s definition of signifying may be the most concise: "performance talk" and "speaking ironically." **Henry Louis Gates, Jr.**, in his landmark book *The Signifying Monkey: A Theory of Afro-American Literary Criticism* (1988), argues that particular kinds of African American linguistic improvisation are rooted in African traditions and may be found throughout African American literature. Therefore, Gates implicitly argues, understanding the tradition of signifying is a potentially powerful way to understand African American literature, and signifying can be seen less as a genre or mode, like **satire** or **parody**, and more as a verbal practice that influences all kinds of literature. "The dozens" or "playing the dozens" is an example of signifying, in which two or more people trade verbal insults, not so much to wound one another as to engage in competitive, inventive wordplay. The dozens directly influenced **Langston Hughes**'s long poem *Ask Your Mama* (1961), which Gates cites as one example of how the oral tradition of signifying is transferred to the written word. Hughes's comic tales featuring the character Jesse B. Simple also include a great deal of verbal play between Simple and the character Boyd, who functions as something of a straight man for Simple's comedy (Ostrom, 356–358).

"The Signifying Monkey" is also the title of a **ballad** from African American **folklore**; it concerns the **trickster** figure of the Signifying Monkey and, according to Gates and McKay, one "somewhat sanitized version of it" is in *The Book of Negro Folklore* (1958), edited by Langston Hughes and Arna Bontemps. Gates and McKay include a less "sanitized" version in *The Norton Anthology of African American Literature* (36–38), and in a footnote (36), they define signifying as "a wide variety of African American verbal games involving ritual insult, competition, innuendo, parody, and other forms of loaded expression."

Verbal improvisation related to signifying is found in a wide variety of works in African American literature, including the novel *Mumbo Jumbo*, by **Ishmael Reed**; in **blues poetry** by Langston Hughes and others; in stories by **Zora Neale Hurston** (Roberts) and **Gloria Naylor** (Alexander); in colloquial poetry by **Sterling A. Brown, Gwendolyn Brooks, Amiri Baraka, Nikki Giovanni**, and **Sonia Sanchez**; in **performance poetry**; and in **rap** and **hip-hop** (Costello and Wallace). Mason and others suggest that literary parody and "intertextuality," in which one work of literature plays subtly off a previous one, are forms of signifying that may be found in such works as *Incidents in the Life of a Slave Girl*, by **Harriet Ann Jacobs**; *Invisible Man*, by **Ralph Ellison**; *The Autobiography of an Ex-Colored Man*, by **James Weldon Johnson**; and *Beloved*, by **Toni Morrison** (Mason, 665–666). As this list suggests, literary works do not necessarily have to be comic in nature to employ signifying and may incorporate verbal and literary echoes into serious, even tragic, works. (*See* **Folktales**; **Jazz**; **Jazz in Literature**; **Multicultural Theory**; **Vernacular**.)

Resources: Roger D. Abrahams, ed., *Afro-American Folktales: Stories from Black Traditions in the New World* (New York: Pantheon, 1985); Lynn Alexander, "Signifyin(g) Sex: Gloria Naylor's *Bailey's Cafe* and Western Religious Tradition," in *He Said, She Says: An RSVP to the Male Text*, ed. Mica Howe and Sarah A. Aguiar (Madison, NJ: Fairleigh Dickinson University Press, 2001), 91–105; Houston A. Baker, Jr., *Blues, Ideology, and Afro-American Literature: A Vernacular Theory* (Chicago: University of Chicago Press, 1984); Mark Costello and David Foster Wallace, *Signifying Rappers: Rap and Race in the Urban Present* (New York: Ecco Press, 1990); Harry J. Elam, Jr., "Signifyin(g) on African-American Theatre: *The Colored Museum* by George Wolfe," *Theatre Journal* 44, no. 3 (Oct. 1992), 291–303; Henry Louis Gates, Jr., *The Signifying Monkey: A Theory of Afro-American Literary Criticism* (New York: Oxford University Press, 1988); Henry Louis Gates, Jr., and Nellie Y. McKay, eds., *The Norton Anthology of African American Literature*, 2nd ed. (New York: Norton, 2004); Langston Hughes, *Ask Your Mama: 12 Moods for Jazz* (New York: Knopf, 1961); Langston Hughes and Arna Bontemps, eds., *The Book of Negro Folklore* (New York: Dodd, Mead, 1958); Carol D. Lee, *Signifying as a Scaffold for Literary Interpretation: The Pedagogical Implications of an African American Discourse Genre* (Urbana, IL: National Council of Teachers of English, 1993); Clarence Major, ed., *Juba to Jive: A Dictionary of African-American Slang* (New York: Penguin, 1994), esp. "Dirty Dozens, The," 138, and "Signifying," 416; Theodore O. Mason, Jr., "Signifying," in *The Oxford Companion to African American Literature*, ed. William L. Andrews, Frances Smith Foster, and Trudier Harris (New York: Oxford University Press, 1997), 665–666; Hans Ostrom, *A Langston Hughes Encyclopedia* (Westport, CT: Greenwood Press, 2002), 11–12, 356–358; Brian R. Roberts, "Predators in the 'Glades: A Signifying Animal Tale in Zora Neale Hurston's *Their Eyes Were Watching God*," *Southern Quarterly* 41, no. 1 (Fall 2002), 39–50; Ashraf H. A. Rushdy, "Daughters Signifyin(g) History: The Example of Toni Morrison's *Beloved*," in *Toni Morrison*, ed. Linden Peach (New York: St. Martin's, 1998); Larry Scanlon, "News from Heaven: Vernacular Time in Langston Hughes's *Ask Your Mama*," *Callaloo* 25, no. 1 (Winter

2002), 45–65; Geneva Smitherman, *Black Talk: Words and Phrases from the Hood to the Amen Corner* (Boston: Houghton Mifflin, 1994).

Hans Ostrom

Simmons, Herbert (born 1930). Novelist, playwright, and poet. One of the first African American artists to commit the **jazz** aesthetic to written form, Herbert Simmons has slowly achieved something of a cult following despite his relative obscurity within the African American literary tradition.

Simmons was born in **St. Louis, Missouri**, in 1930 and wrote his first novel, *Corner Boy* (1957), with the assistance of the prestigious Houghton Mifflin Literary Fellowship. *Corner Boy* is a bildungsroman, or **coming-of-age** novel, and it is also forerunner to the Holloway House hard-boiled fiction of **Donald Goines** and **Iceberg Slim**. It follows the trials of eighteen-year-old Jake Adams, a freewheeling drug pusher whose penchant for material goods is caught up in a cycle of drugs, racism, and violence. The climax of the novel shows how flashy cars and tailored suits cannot protect Jake and his friends from the harsh reality of White domination.

In 1958 Simmons received his B.A. from Washington University in St. Louis, and subsequently devoted himself to artistic creation full-time. But with the poor critical reception of his second and only other novel, *Man Walking on Eggshells* (1962), Houghton Mifflin dropped Simmons from its ranks and he sought refuge in the underground arts scene. This novel, another bildungsroman, tells the story of Raymond Douglas, an aspiring jazz musician who must overcome poverty, racism, and family strife during the Depression to play his horn for the masses. Inspired by the jazz improvisation of Miles Davis and John Coltrane, Simmons wrote his novel with an ear for literary experimentation; reviewers did not take kindly to his protonationalist radicalism and his impressionistic prose style, which he has called "assimbilationalism."

Simmons was an early member of the Watts Writers Workshop and later taught creative writing at California State University at Northridge. Though he claims to be writing the two other novels that will constitute the *Destined to Be Free* trilogy, of which *Eggshells* is the first part, Simmons remains a marginal figure from the 1950s and 1960s Black avant-garde.

Resources: Herbert Simmons: *Corner Boy* (Boston: Houghton Mifflin, 1957); *Man Walking on Eggshells* (Boston: Houghton Mifflin, 1962).

Kinohi Nishikawa

Simmons, Russell (born 1957). Entrepreneur, music producer, and television producer. A native of Queens, New York, Russell Simmons has been described as the Godfather of **Hip-Hop** for his groundbreaking record company Def Jam. The label he founded with Rick Rubin brought the legendary **rap** artists Run-DMC and LL Cool J to the mainstream music audience. The enormous success of Def Jam led to Simmons's expansion into other business ventures, including film producing and the creation of the urban clothing company Phat Farm in 1992. In 1994 Simmons launched *Def Comedy Jam*, an urban-focused comedy hour for cable television. His commitment to highlight African American talent met with unparalleled success. Russell Simmons made African Americans a key marketing demographic and a viable entrepreneurial base.

Based on the successful niche *Def Comedy Jam* carved out, Simmons created a series of poetry slam performances called *Def Poetry Jam*. The combination of **performance poetry** and DJ-driven music created a 1990s hip-hop version of the poetry café. In 2002, Simmons, along with Stand Lathan, took *Def Poetry Jam* to Broadway. Matthew Murray's review of the Broadway version reveals that "this cacophony of voices is what makes *Def Poetry Jam* most exciting, and when it breaks free of its traditional mold to embrace true theatrical communication, it doesn't happen a moment too soon." The excitement resulted in a 2003 Tony Award for Best Special Theatrical Event. *Def Poetry Jam* then began touring the country with rhymes, rhythms, and reflections on identity, cultural trials and tribulations, and love. Expanding the franchise further, *Def Poetry Jam* came to television. In 2002, *Russell Simmons Presents Def Poetry* television special won a Peabody Award for moving "poetry from the periphery to the center, and proved that television can be as literate as any other media." Having completed its fourth season in 2004, *Def Poetry Jam* is available on DVD for committed fans of the series. *Def Poetry Jam*'s success depends upon its contention that poetry is a life force.

On its, Web site, http://www.defpoetryjam.com, *Def Poetry Jam* makes a conscious move to be inclusive and succeeds in creating a community bound by the power of poetry. The venerable poets **Amiri Baraka** and **Sonia Sanchez** have appeared on the program. The Web site offers poetry and **haiku** contests for its community members. Online chats, message boards, and regular poetry columns in the "Write On!" section encourage community members to participate and wax poetic. *Def Poetry Jam* has expanded to DPJ Radio, where Internet users can listen to spoken word poetry at their computers.

The outreach of *Def Poetry Jam* is indicative of Russell Simmons the man and businessman. When *Inc.* magazine named him one of the most fascinating entrepreneurs for its twenty-fifth anniversary issue, it specifically cited his powerful example. He himself has said, "I'm open-minded about sharing and partnering." (*See* **Nuyorican Poets Café.**)

Resources: http://www.defpoetryjam.com; http://www.peabody.uga.edu/archives/search.asp; Rod Kurtz, "Russell Simmons," *Inc.*, Apr. 2004, 137; Ellen McGirt, "Russell Simmons," *Money*, July 2004, 45; Matthew Murray, "Russell Simmons *Def Comedy Jam* on Broadway," *Talkin' Broadway Reviews*, Nov. 14, 2002; Russell Simmons with George Nelson, *Life and Def: Sex, Drugs, Money, and God* (New York: Crown, 2001).

Amy L. Darnell

Sinclair, April (born 1955). Novelist. Like many successful Black writers, April Sinclair got her start through promoting her writing herself, at the grassroots level. Originally from the South Side of **Chicago, Illinois**, she grew up during the height of the **Civil Rights Movement** and the **Black Power**

movements, the eldest of four siblings. By the early 1990s Sinclair had long been a community activist working to wipe out hunger in America and to increase literacy for among inner-city youth. She earned a bachelor's degree at Western Illinois University and has taken graduate courses at San Francisco State University. Calling upon her activist network in Oakland, California, where she still lives, Sinclair began to leaflet the city, promoting a reading at her favorite bookstore, Old Wives Tales. More than 125 people showed up for that first reading of the first twenty pages of her novel. On the heels of that initial success, she began to read her novel excerpt across northern California, creating a word-of-mouth following for her work.

Literary agents began to follow Sinclair to her readings, and soon she had sold her first, albeit unfinished, novel to Hyperion Press. When it came time to sell her second novel, she received a six-figure advance and was able to write full-time. Her work has been reviewed widely in publications such as the *Voice Literary Supplement*, *Chicago Times*, *San Francisco Chronicle*, *Kirkus Review*, *New York Times Book Review*, *Publishers Weekly*, and *Los Angeles Times*.

Sinclair's three novels tackle difficult subjects. *Coffee Will Make You Black* (1994) chronicles the coming of age of Jean "Stevie" Stevenson in the 1960s on the South Side of Chicago, the area in which Sinclair grew up. Stevie deals with racism, **gender** oppression, and the awakening of her sexual attraction to other girls. The American Library Association named *Coffee Will Make You Black* Book of the Year, and the novel has been published in Spanish. It also received the Carl Sandburg Award from the Friends of the Chicago Public Library.

The sequel, *Ain't Gonna Be the Same Fool Twice* (1996), follows Stevie as she moves to San Francisco and continues to explore her sexuality while coming to terms with her more traditional upbringing and the less constrained life she is leading on the West Coast. In her third novel, *I Left My Back Door Open* (1999), Sinclair introduces readers to a new heroine, Daphne Dupree, an overweight, forty-one-year-old deejay looking for love and grappling with the memories of surviving incest as a child. Throughout the novel, Daphne is a character who has time to counsel everyone but herself, though in the end, she learns to love herself and deal with her past.

Though her audience has tried to label Sinclair as a lesbian writer, and at times her writing has seemed very autobiographical, she has shunned labels and remains largely close-mouthed about her private life. Sinclair hasn't published a novel since 1999, but she has toured the country, speaking about writing and holding fellowships at the Djerassi, Yaddo, MacDowell, and Ragdale artist colonies.

Resources: Carleens Brice, ed., *Age Ain't Nothin' But a Number* (Boston: Beacon Press, 2003); Devon Carbado et al., eds., *Black Like Us: A Century of Lesbian, Gay, and Bisexual African American Fiction* (San Francisco: Cleis Press, 2002); Jacqueline C. Jones, "April Sinclair (1954–)," in *Contemporary African American Novelists: A Bio-Bibliographical Critical Sourcebook*, ed. Emmanuel Nelson (Westport, CT: Greenwood Press, 1999), 438–442; April Sinclair: *Ain't Gonna Be the Same Fool Twice* (New York:

Hyperion, 1996); *Coffee Will Make You Black* (New York: Hyperion, 1994); *I Left My Back Door Open* (New York: Hyperion, 1999).

Roxane Gay

Sister Souljah (born 1964). Novelist, political activist, educator, lecturer, humanitarian, and **hip-hop** artist. Born Lisa Williamson and raised in the Bronx, New York, by her mother, Sister Souljah grew up in subsidized government housing while she and her mother were aided by the public welfare system on and off for nearly fifteen years. While in high school, she was an intern at the House of Representatives and was the winner of the American Legion's Constitutional Oratory Contest. While attending Rutgers University, she worked for Rev. Benjamin Chavis of the United Church of Christ Commission for Racial Justice, a church-sponsored civil rights organization, and was a well-known political commentator and writer for the university's newspaper. She graduated with degrees in American history and African Studies. Sister Souljah also completed an advanced placement summer program at Cornell University and studied at the University of Salamamca in Spain. She worked at a medical facility in Zimbabwe and visited Mozambican refugee camps. She has traveled and lectured extensively throughout southern Africa, the former Soviet Union, England, France, Portugal, Finland, and Holland.

After receiving national attention and harsh criticism for her 1992 **rap** album, *360 Degrees of Power*, which is a compilation of her personal thoughts and professional experiences, and her video *Slavery's Back in Effect*, Sister Souljah became one of the most sought-after collegiate speakers. This video was designed to speak directly to the African American community about how the effects of **slavery** still haunt their lives. She has spoken at Harvard Law School, Howard University, and UCLA. She has appeared on such television shows as *The* **Oprah Winfrey** *Show*, *Geraldo*, *Donahue*, *The Today Show*, and *Good Morning America*.

Sister Souljah serves as the Executive Director of Daddy's House Social Programs, Sean "Puffy" Combs's not-for-profit organization that serves 600 children ages six to sixteen from New York, New Jersey, and **Philadelphia, Pennsylvania**. She was a featured speaker for the Million Woman March in Philadelphia. She was responsible for creating, organizing, financing (through hip-hop music), and preparing curriculum for the African Youth Survival Camp that served the children of homeless families. It was a six-week camp that existed for three years in Enfield, North Carolina. She continues to work with other hip-hop artists by designing and producing major summer camp events and programs. She also educates teenagers about pregnancy, womanhood, manhood, current events, and history.

Sister Souljah is the author of two best-selling books. *No Disrespect* (1995) critiques the relationships between Black males and females; women's issues; sexual, economic, and cultural politics; and issues regarding the hip-hop culture. Her first published novel, *The Coldest Winter Ever* (1999), tells the story of a young Black woman trying to survive on the streets of Brooklyn while living in the shadows of her drug kingpin father. In her writing, Sister Souljah expresses her anger at the injustices against Blacks in America.

Resources: James Bowman, "Plain Brown Rappers," *National Review*, July 1992, 36; Gordon Chambers, "Souljah's Mission," *Essence*, Dec. 1991, 60; Susan J. Douglas, "Race, Rap, and White Blindness," *The Progressive*, Aug. 1992, 16; Terry Eastland, "Redeeming the Race Card," *National Review*, Sept. 1996, 44–46; Elizabeth Gleick, "And the Heat Goes On," *People Weekly*, June 29, 1992, pp. 104–105; J. Leland, "Rap and Race," *Newsweek*, June 29, 1992, pp. 46+; Kim Neely, "Souljah's Bad Rap: Candidate Clinton Thrusts the Rapper-Activist into the Spotlight," *Rolling Stone*, Aug. 6, 1992, pp. 15+; Vinette K. Pryce, "Sister Souljah Leads Youth from Wall Street to South Africa," *New York Amsterdam News*, July 30, 1998, p. 20; Melanie Rehak, "The Drama of the Ghetto Child," *New York Times Magazine*, May 30, 1999, p. 13; Sister Souljah: *The Coldest Winter Ever* (New York: Atria, 2004); *No Disrespect* (New York: Crown, 1994); *360 Degrees of Power* (Los Angeles: Sony Records, 1992), CD; Jack E. White, Jr., "Sister Souljah Capitalist Tool," *Time*, June 29, 1992, p. 88.

Sharon D. Raynor

Slang. Slang is typically defined as components of language (specifically words and/or phrases) that may be understood by the general public or by a smaller segment of the population, but that may not be typically accepted as "standard" or "formal" language. There is, however, no universal definition of slang, no way of determining absolutely what is and is not slang. Our ideas of slang vary based on many concerns—the people conversing, the context of the conversation, the intent of the speaker or writer, and others. Many think that the use of "incorrect" English means a person is using slang (Baugh; Mufwene et al.; Rickford and Rickford; Smitherman). That is not necessarily true. Linguistically, there is no such thing as incorrect language, because as long as someone is talking and is being understood by the person(s) listening, then communication occurs between speaker and listener—making language neither wrong or right but communicative.

Everybody has numerous ways of speaking depending on the context of the interaction. Linguists, those who study language, call these different ways of speaking "variations" in language use or "varieties" of a person's language. People use different varieties for particular purposes and in different environments. Any one person can have an unlimited number of ways of speaking. A variety used with family or friends might be different from one used in a job interview or during a formal presentation. All of these various ways of speaking are true language, and their appropriateness is dependent on the situation.

Slang, however, is not a variety of English on its own. Rather, slang words or phrases can be used within any variety of English, spoken or written. Therefore, one could use slang with a more formal variety of language or in a casual setting when the **vernacular** (the most casual and comfortable language a person uses) is being used. However, when slang is used, the variety is probably a less formal one.

We tend to think of standard or formal written language as what is taught in an English class or the language used in textbooks. Speaking Standard or formal English is usually associated with those who are educated or those who hold prestige or power in a society. Speakers of any variety of English—or any other language, for that matter—can use slang. And there are many speakers who never use slang at all.

Slang terms or phrases are often already in existence but have taken on a new meaning. Examples include "chill," "cool," or "to be down." Each of these terms or phrases existed long before its use as a slang term, but over time it has been given meanings by various groups of people, meanings that differ from their original usage. Some may even take on a new spelling, such as "phat" for "fat." Slang language has a relatively short life—even 100 years in terms of language is short—since language in some from or another has been used since human existence. Although slang terms or phrases may exist in the same general form over a period of time (meaning their spelling or their word form may stay the same), their meaning may change significantly. For example, usage of "groovy" as a slang term may have begun as early as the mid-1930s, and continues today (Wentworth and Flexner), but its meaning has changed over time. *The Dictionary of American Slang* (1975) defines "groovy" as it was used in 1935 as being "in the state of mind or mood conducive to playing music, especially swing music, well; in rapport with the piece [of music], especially of swing music, being played" (Wentworth and Flexner, 162). However, *The Dictionary of Contemporary Slang* (1990) defines "groovy" as "satisfactory, satisfying, fine. A term of approval, sometimes in the form of mild exclamation from the *hippy* era.... It now sounds risibly dated, unless used ironically" (Thorne, 221). Even within 55 years, then, the meaning of the slang term "groovy" has changed, although its form has not.

Many people often confuse varieties other than a "formal" language with slang, but variation in language from the "standard" does not necessarily indicate the use of slang. Slang is not a language variety, a secret code, nor is it the "idiom of everyday speech," even if it does contain components of all of these (Thorne, iii). Speakers of any language, including the many varieties of English, will use slang at some point in their lives. Slang is most comparable to colloquial language or vernacular, which is a less formal language used in everyday conversation that the majority of the population can understand. Slang can be defined as components of a less formal language used for a particular purpose.

Slang can also be defined by the community in which it occurs. Slang can vary by region, **race**, culture, or **gender**. Various communities have slang that is particular to that environment. For example, people who identify with the **hip-hop** community may share slang terms such as "bling-bling" (jewelry or the display of wealth), "flip-side" (the opposite side of a rap record or presenting something differently than has been done before), or the "po-po" (the police), and members of a drug culture may be familiar with words or phrases such as "kiss the porcelain god" (to vomit), "rollin'" (to be high on X), or "detox" (the process of withdrawing from drug use). Anyone may be able to identify and/or understand these words or phrases, and many may use them even if they are not members of the given community. They are used, however, more by members of the community than by those not affiliated with it.

Although slang terms and phrases can come from any topic area, historically slang terms and phrases cover sex, drugs, body parts (usually sexually related), and language of crime (Thorne). Slang is often confused with jargon, which consists of terms and phrases used by a specific group and that are not usually understood by the general population. Jargon and slang seem to have similar definitions, but jargon is usually reserved for industry-specific terms, such as those used in technology or computers, whereas slang is used for culturally specific groups, such as "urban youth" or "hippies."

The African American community is often given credit for inventing numerous slang terms. "And in connection with this you may ask yourself why do so many apparently well-meaning white folks say with bubbling enthusiasm that black people are geniuses for having devised a colorful private way of communicating?" (Major, 9). Many who have studied African American English say that the genesis of many slang terms in the African American community is "another aspect of a long, painful struggle toward human freedom" in which African Americans have had always "pushed the linguistic envelope."

Although slang and African American English are not one and the same, slang does play a large role in the use of African American English. However, some words that seem like slang may not be slang. For example, "ashy" (dry skin), "kitchen" (the nappy hair at the nape of the neck), and "siddity" (uppity-acting Black people) might be understood by the majority of African Americans and not by non-African Americans. Still, that does not make the words slang. All three words have had a history in English, and are used and understood by African Americans from all age groups and economic levels. Additionally, these terms have existed over time and have maintained the same meaning; therefore, they are not slang, but are part of the lexicon (the stable, widely used vocabulary) of African American English.

Motivation for using slang in regular speech varies widely and may be hard to determine. Some believe that people use slang to show their connection to a particular community or to show their disconnection from another. Some linguists argue that it is used in response to the treatment African Americans have endured since **slavery**. Linguists, however, may never know why people use slang when speaking. However, in writing, motivation for using slang is often obvious.

African American authors have made use of slang (in addition to the vernacular) in their writing to give depth and dimension to their characters— to give them a realness that readers can relate to. The use of slang in literature enables the reader to find out more information about the characters. Authors are able to create different characters with different lifestyles and illustrate that just by the language used by characters. In *Mules and Men* (1935), an ethnography by **Zora Neale Hurston**, her participants/characters use slang often. This book is the write-up of Hurston's time spent in her hometown of Eatonville, Florida, collecting local **folktales** and stories of the community. Her participants use slang for various purposes, but specifically for emphasis in their stories. For example, in a story about a mid-eighteenth-century man who mistakes a frog for a creature of the night, the participant says, "A big old *booger* done got after me." The term "booger" was then slang for the "boogie-man," but has since come to mean something entirely different. The use of slang in this case helps the author define the storyteller better than the use of simple description would allow.

More recent books also make use of slang. *Let That Be the Reason*, by Vickie Stringer, is a fact-based novel about a female drug dealer in which a considerable amount of modern slang is used. For example, she refers to a female's hair weave as being "unbeweavable." She also uses the phrase "sippin' on some bubbly" to refer to the drinking of champagne. The author uses slang often in this book to help make the characters more realistic and believable.

The use of slang is not a new phenomenon. It might seem that way because of popular media, but the first dictionary of English slang was Francis Grose's *Classical Dictionary of the Vulgar Tongue* (1785). Since then, many dictionaries of different types of slang have been published, including *NTC's Dictionary of American Slang and Colloquial Expressions*, *Dictionary of Afro-American Slang*, *Black Talk*, and *Prison Slang*. Many more dictionaries of slang cover slang of all types, from hip-hop to country.

Resources: John Baugh, *Out of the Mouths of Slaves* (Austin: University of Texas Press, 1999); Clarence Major, *Dictionary of Afro-American Slang* (New York: International Publishers, 1970); Salikoko S. Mufwene, John Rickford, Guy Bailey, and John Baugh, *African-American English: Structure, History, and Use* (New York: Routledge, 1998); John Russell Rickford and Russell John Rickford, *Spoken Soul: The Story of Black English* (New York: Wiley, 2000); Geneva Smitherman, *Black Talk: Words and Phrases from the Hood to the Amen Corner* (Boston: Houghton Mifflin, 1994); Vickie Stringer, *Let That Be the Reason* (Los Angeles: UpStream Publications, 2002); Tony Thorne, ed., *The Dictionary of Contemporary Slang* (New York: Pantheon, 1990); Harold Wentworth and Stuart Berg Flexner, eds., *Dictionary of American Slang*, 2nd ed. (New York: Crowell, 1975).

Iyabo F. Osiapem

Slave Narrative. Slave narrative is a broad category of literature that encompasses a variety of works. These include autobiographies by escaped, manumitted, or emancipated slaves; narratives of the life experiences of former slaves recorded by the **Federal Writers' Project** as part of the Works Progress Administration in the late 1930s; and fictionalized accounts of life in **slavery**, written both during the time of slavery and since then. Also often included within the category of slave narratives are works not written by former slaves but "told to" or "related to" an editor or amanuensis (one who copies or writes from the dictation of another). Slave narratives written by former slaves reached their apogee in the pre–**Civil War** era. They were frequently commissioned by abolitionists to garner sympathy and support for the **Abolitionist Movement**, with nearly a hundred such narratives produced before the end of the Civil War in 1865. The first narratives were composed and published as early as 1772. Newly discovered slave narratives have emerged as recently as 2002, when **Henry Louis Gates, Jr.**, purchased at auction and subsequently published *The Bondwoman's Narrative* by **Hannah Crafts**. The slave narrative continues to serve important functions in African American literature as a powerful source of inspiration for autobiographical works and as the source for fictionalized accounts of slavery dependent upon the genre's originators and literary conventions.

A full understanding of slave narrative as a unique and powerful genre in African American letters requires examination of the genre's place in history, a survey of some of the dominant tropes that structure slave narratives, and analysis of the genre's impact on American literature and culture.

Nonfiction slave narratives can be divided into three distinct historical time periods: those written prior to 1830, those produced between 1830 and the end of the Civil War, and those created after the end of the Civil War and through the efforts of the Works Progress Administration's Federal Writers Project from 1936 to 1938.

Fictionalized accounts of slave narratives exist throughout American literary history, with those written after **World War II** best classified as neo-slave narratives.

All slave narratives combine elements of **autobiography**, history, and cultural critique in their telling of life in slavery. One of the first known slave narratives in English was published in 1772, *A Narrative of the Most Remarkable Particulars in the Life of James Albert Ukawsaw Gronniosaw, an African Prince*, by James Albert Ukawsaw (Gates and Andrews). Of the earliest slave narratives, **Olaudah Equiano**'s *The Interesting Narrative of the Life of Olaudah Equiano, or Gustavus Vassa, the African. Written by Himself* (1789) is perhaps best known (Gates and Andrews). In it, Equiano relates his capture in his native land (modern-day eastern Nigeria) and his subsequent travels to the West Indies, Europe, and the American colonies. Equiano's narrative is notable largely because of its being authored by Equiano himself, rather than told to an amanuensis or created with the aid of an editor or ghostwriter. Equiano's independence in this regard perhaps contributes to the story's frank treatment of the horrors of slavery and its insistence upon immediate abolition.

Many narratives from this first period were modeled upon criminal confession narratives or religious conversion narratives, the latter of which would strive to impress its White readership with the author's piety and forgiveness. Equiano made much of his own conversion to Christianity; at the end of his *Narrative* he expresses his desire to become a Christian missionary to Africa and thereby to lobby against the African slave trade. That is, he connects his Christianity with the project of abolition, implicitly arguing that individual salvation and worldly perfection are in fact not just compatible but intrinsically linked aims. This combination of individual belief and cultural critique became the hallmark of successful slave narratives in the decades that followed. Equiano's assertion of selfhood in the claim that his narrative was "written by himself" importantly evaded possible influence by White editors and ghostwriters, a concern associated with nearly all antebellum slave narratives.

If the narratives were not in fact written by former slaves who were literate enough to produce and validate their own works, then how might the participation of White abolitionists, as editors and publishers, alter the works? Although Equiano's assertion of authorship effectively counters this concern, his embrace of Christianity raises troubling concerns about narrative authenticity because his narrative, while critical, also supports forgiveness of his former captors and the superiority of Christianity to any African faith. Similar concerns continued to receive attention in the second historical period of slave narratives, 1830 to 1865. Some other notable slave narratives from this period include Solomon Bayley's *A Narrative of Some Remarkable Incidents, in the Life of Solomon Bayley, Formerly a Slave, in the State of Delaware, North America: Written by Himself* (1825), **Venture Smith**'s *A Narrative of the Life and Adventures of Venture, a Native of Africa: But Resident Above Sixty Years in the United States of America. Related by Himself* (1798), and George White's *A Brief Account of the Life, Experience, Travels, and Gospel Labours of George White, an African: Written by Himself, and Revised by a Friend* (1810).

Slave narratives from the middle period, 1830 to 1865, are marked by their increased contempt for the institution of slavery. Of the many narratives produced during this era, none is better known or more highly regarded than **Frederick Douglass**'s *Narrative of the Life of Frederick Douglass, an American Slave, Written by Himself* (1845). Douglass's narrative stands as a powerful and moving critique of American society for its tolerance of slavery amid its avowed Christian beliefs; additionally, Douglass (and others of this period) powerfully connected the power of slaves—intellectual, moral, and physical—with manhood, thus affirming the African American slave's humanity and countering widespread notions that Africans were an inferior race suited only to forced labor. While Douglass's first narrative followed many of the conventions of the slave narrative, most notably beginning with letters affirming the authenticity of the text and the trustworthiness of the author, his later narratives, including *My Bondage and My Freedom* (1855), further distanced him from his White supporters, replacing White-authored letters of authenticity with a preface and introduction of Douglass's own creation. Douglass also stressed the importance of literacy as the foundation for freedom and the effectiveness of physical resistance to counter slavery's oppression.

Other notable narratives from this period include **William Wells Brown**'s *Narrative of William Wells Brown, a Fugitive Slave* (1847) and **Henry Bibb**'s

Narrative of the Life and Adventures of Henry Bibb, an American Slave. Written by himself (1849) (Gates and Andrews). Moses Roper's *Narrative of the Adventures and Escape of Moses Roper from American Slavery* appeared in 1838; it is remarkable in part for the number of times Roper attempted to escape before finally succeeding. **James W. C. Pennington**'s *The Fugitive Blacksmith; or, Events in the History of James W. C. Pennington, Pastor of a Presbyterian Church, New York, Formerly a Slave in the State of Maryland, United States* (1849) also belongs to this era. These works made use of the many conventions familiar to readers of slave narratives while also incorporating **trickster**-like figures from African American **folktales**.

This period also saw the publication of some of the best-known narratives by African American women, including Mary Prince's *The History of Mary Prince, a West Indian Slave. Related by Herself. With a Supplement by the Editor. To Which Is Added, the Narrative of Asa-Asa, a Captured African* (1831). **Soujourner Truth**'s *Narrative of Sojourner Truth, a Northern Slave, Emancipated from Bodily Servitude by the State of New York, in 1828* was first published in 1850 (Gates and Andrews), and **Harriet Ann Jacobs**'s *Incidents in the Life of a Slave Girl, Written by Herself* was first published in 1861 (Gates and Andrews). Female-authored narratives borrowed more strongly from the sentimental literary tradition, striving to make personal their accounts of oppression and elicit sympathy in the reader through shared identification. These narratives also importantly unmasked the sexual oppression of Black women at the hands of White slave owners, often in brutal detail. Since African American women could not connect their humanity to the manly attributes of strength and determination, they instead grounded their humanity in the sentiment of feeling, stressing sympathetic identification. The combination of autobiographical accounts of life in slavery, historical details, and the sentimental literary tradition's focus on eliciting sympathetic feelings was a powerful combination, and a form that many saw as freely adopted in **Harriet Beecher Stowe**'s *Uncle Tom's Cabin* (1852), the best-selling novel of the nineteenth century widely credited with bringing abolitionism to a wider audience.

The third period of slave narratives encompasses post-emancipation works such as **Booker T. Washington**'s *Up from Slavery* (1901); Frederick Douglass's third autobiography, *Life and Times of Frederick Douglass Written by Himself. His Early Life as a Slave, His Escape from Bondage, and His Complete History to the Present Time* (1892); and **Josiah Henson**'s *"Uncle Tom's Story of His Life." An Autobiography of the Rev. Josiah Henson (Mrs. Harriet Beecher Stowe's "Uncle Tom"). From 1789 to 1876. With a Preface by Mrs. Harriet Beecher Stowe and an Introductory Note by George Sturge, and S. Morley* (1877). Also included in this time period are the more than 2,300 narratives collected and transcribed by the Federal Writers' Project. While most of the narratives were transcribed interviews, and few were published individually, they are a rich source for poignant and personal accounts of life in slavery, and a significant contribution to the genre of slave narratives.

A group of African American ex-slaves from the U.S. Works Progress Administration, Federal Writers' Project slave narratives collections, 1937. Courtesy of the Library of Congress.

While the great many slave narratives published in the United States over a period of more than a century speaks to their variety and durability, there are a few common motifs, or literary tropes, shared by a great many of the works. First and foremost, because establishing the authenticity of narratives of life in slavery as actually authored by African Americans was important, many narratives begin with prefatory letters by leading figures such as editors, authors, politicians, and abolitionists that vouch for the authenticity of the text, especially for those narratives that claimed to be written "by himself" or "by herself." Most narratives also begin in slavery in **the South** and conclude with successful travel to the North, where freedom awaits, often signaled by the selection of a new name (to counter the loss of the patronym in slavery), the reunion of separated family members, and frequently marriage to a lost love. Often the decision to escape from slavery is precipitated by some kind of personal crisis, such as the death of a loved one, sale of a loved one to another slave owner or removal to another state, or simply overwhelming feelings of despair. Many also conclude with some sort of dedication to the abolitionist cause, emerging free in the North dedicated to speaking against slavery's injustices.

Despite this common narrative arc, many narratives—especially those written in the antebellum era—are careful to exclude particular details of the narrator's escape from slavery, for fear of closing off a possible avenue to freedom for others still held in slavery. Many chronicles of life in slavery highlight the dehumanizing effects of slavery on the individual through physical and psychological abuse: forced beatings, difficult labor, insufficient food, the separation of family members, lack of knowledge about one's own birth and parentage, and related horrors. Another common trope in slave narratives—particularly of the middle period—is the esteem of literacy and religion as the pathways to freedom, often in direct disobedience of strict rules against learning to read or congregating as slaves. Additionally, particularly in later slave narratives, there is a concerted effort to connect the desire for individual freedom from slavery to the desire to break free from tyranny that served as the basis for the nation's independence from Great Britain, thus marking slaves and their desire for freedom as eminently patriotic and American.

The collective impact of all these various forms taken by slave narratives on American literature and culture is incalculable. First and foremost, widespread dissemination of slave-authored accounts of life in slavery countered Southern claims of slavery as a benevolent institution and credited African Americans with qualities long denied them and essential to their humanity: feelings, intelligence, and desire for freedom. Detailed accounts of the brutality of slavery coupled with condemnations of a nation that, on the one hand, esteemed freedom from tyranny as one of its cornerstones and, on the other, turned a blind eye toward the practice of slavery gave much needed momentum and ammunition to the abolitionist cause. The slave narrative also marks the emergence of the African American literary tradition, with slave narratives comprising the majority of African American-authored texts published in the nineteenth and early twentieth centuries. Slave narratives, with their autobiographical approach and narratives of individuals overcoming great odds to achieve individual freedom and salvation, also presaged the emergence of autobiography as a dominant mode in African American letters. The influence of the slave narrative can be witnessed in such works as **James Weldon Johnson**'s *The Autobiography of an Ex-Colored Man* (1912) and **Ralph Ellison**'s *Invisible Man* (1952). While these novels recall the slave narrative in their autobiographical approach and narratives of individual subjugation in a racist society, the slave narrative also gave rise to an entirely new category of literature, the neo-slave narrative or fictionalized account of life in slavery. Works such as **Gayl Jones**'s *Corregidora* (1975), **Ishmael Reed**'s *Flight to Canada* (1976), **Octavia E. Butler**'s *Kindred* (1979), **Charles Johnson**'s *Middle Passage* (1990), and John Sayles's film *The Brother from Another Planet* (1984) all can be read as neo-slave narratives, connected as they are to the form, structure, and content of the slave narratives that preceded them. In all of these works, the individual's triumph over racist oppression is chronicled while critique is simultaneously leveled against the nation that allows such practices to persist. The slave narrative thus constitutes a rich, varied, and ever present literary genre central to understanding both the origins and the present of African American literature.

Resources: William L. Andrews, *To Tell a Free Story: The First Century of Afro-American Autobiography, 1760–1865* (Urbana: University of Illinois Press, 1986); William L. Andrews, ed., *Six Women's Slave Narratives* (New York: Oxford University Press, 1988); Sterling Lecater Bland, ed., *African American Slave Narratives: An Anthology* (Westport, CT: Greenwood Press, 2001); Arna Bontemps, ed., *Great Slave Narratives Selected and Introduced by Arna Bontemps* (Boston: Beacon Press, 1969); Hannah Crafts, *The Bondwoman's Narrative*, ed. Henry Louis Gates, Jr. (New York: Warner Books, 2002); Charles T. Davis and Henry Louis Gates, Jr., eds., *The Slave's Narrative* (Oxford: Oxford University Press, 1985); Frances Smith Foster, *Witnessing Slavery: The Development of Ante-Bellum Slave Narratives* (Westport, CT: Greenwood Press, 1979); Henry Louis Gates, Jr., and William L. Andrews, eds., *Slave Narratives* (New York: Library of America, 2000); Charles J. Heglar, *Rethinking the Slave Narrative: Slave Marriage and the Narratives of Henry Bibb and William and Ellen Craft* (Westport, CT: Greenwood Press, 2001); William Katz, ed., *Five Slave Narratives: A Compendium* (New York: Arno, 1968); Deborah E. McDowell and Arnold Rampersad, eds., *Slavery and the Literary Imagination* (Baltimore: Johns Hopkins University Press, 1989); Moses Roper, *Narrative of My Escape from Slavery* (Mineola, NY: Dover, 2003); Valerie Smith, *Self-Discovery and Authority in Afro-American Narrative* (Cambridge, MA: Harvard University Press, 1987).

Matthew R. Davis

Slavery. The horror and wide-ranging impact of slavery plays an enormous role in African American literature from its inception to the present, and slavery informs the history of the United States as a whole. While slavery reached its apex in population and extent at the beginning of the nineteenth century in America, the practice of slavery in the British colonies began soon after the first European contact. Spain had implemented slavery in its colonies in South and North America, and Britain followed Spain's example, enslaving indigenous peoples whom they conquered in battle. During the earliest contact between English Puritans and early fortune seekers and the native peoples who inhabited what would later be New England and Virginia, Christian values condoned atrocities difficult to conceive outside a framework designed to neutralize the actions of the British. Similar values later helped slave traders and policy makers as they made slavery *in perpetua* both possible and lucrative.

While contemporary students of slavery are struck by the seeming contradictions between slaveholding and Christianity, early colonists were not. Puritans, who first enslaved Indians, firmly believed that non-Christian captives taken in a "just war" were righteously taken as slaves. They managed to justify war, capture, and enslavement despite the fact that they were the invaders. This hypocrisy of justification required extensive effort to reenvision the Native Americans, who were simply defending their lands, as savage pagans in need of conversion. These conceptualizations of "just" war and "just" slavery made warring against Native Americans even more economically lucrative for early colonists (they not only won land, but enslaved labor as well).

By positioning their invasion of North America as divinely sanctioned, all resistance to the newcomers could be defined as aggressive action against the chosen of God. Puritans benefited in almost every instance: disease often killed off entire villages of Native Americans, leaving fields and paths seemingly miraculously ready for the Puritans; war that resulted in Indian casualties had the same effect as disease, and any surviving defiant Indians could be made into slaves and kept or sold for profit. The indigenous populations did not far well under slavery and were weakened by disease and abuse.

Like other Europeans, early British colonists in American turned to Africa to provide laborers who were strong, experienced agriculturally, and subjected to an already existing system of slavery and brokering in human beings. In 1619, the first Africans to serve in the colonies were brought by a Dutch man-o'-war to Jamestown, Virginia. These twenty men and women were legally situated as indentured servants, in much the same way as poor Whites from

Britain were. Robert McColley reminds us that the terms "servant" and "slave" were directly related: an African could easily be referred to by either term. Both terms are derived from the Latin *servus*, and the term "slave" was used primarily in the antebellum South as a "technical term in the marketplace, the legislature, and economic treatises. Antislavery writers and publicists, not southern planters, insisted on using the term *slave* exclusively." These early Africans were not yet slaves, and they existed in a legal capacity of indentured servitude comparable with White indentured servants. Indentured servitude was a contract-based system of labor regulated by law. Over the course of the seventeenth century, the system of indenture was redefined by Virginia's House of Burgesses to become a two-tier system that privileged Whites as indentured servants contracted to serve for a set time, generally seven years, and African Americans as slaves, serving not only for the term of their own lives but also passing on the lifelong service to their children.

The 1630s saw a marked rise in immigration, predominantly among religious Protestants. During this period, several major wars were fought between the Puritans and the Pequods, leading to the almost total annihilation of the tribe. Shortly after this, in 1640, the Massachusetts Bay Company was granted a charter by Charles I to settle the area with the principal purpose of conversion of the natives (Debo, 47). Commerce and conversion link here in more obvious ways. In this way, Christian discourse served as rhetorical justification for Puritans' appropriations of land and people. The population of Africans in Virginia and Maryland doubled in the 1650s and again in the 1660s, going from 300 in 1648 to 1200 in 1662. By the close of the seventeenth century, in many Southern counties close to 48 percent of labor was slave labor (McColley).

The legal changes between 1620, when the first Africans arrived, and 1700 fully entrenched chattel slavery in the British colonies of North America. Court case precedents and rulings from Virginia's House of Burgesses set the tone for the colonies' treatment of free Blacks and enslaved Blacks all along the eastern seaboard. These legal changes came as a result of steadily increasing importation of Africans to the British colonies from West Africa, a part of the triangular slave trade.

For over 400 years, Europeans constructed a highly profitable triangular trade between Europe, Africa, and the New World. It was originally established by Portuguese and Spanish in the fifteenth and sixteenth centuries; England and other powerful European nations established colonies and ports along the west coast of Africa in order to exploit an existing internal African slave trade. The British, for example, carried finished products to Africa and traded them for human beings, whom they carried forcibly to the Caribbean, where they "seasoned" the newcomers. Some Africans resisted enslavement through shipboard mutinies and suicide. The mortality rate of Africans over the **Middle Passage** of the Atlantic Ocean was very high; historians calculate that 5 to 20 percent of Africans died during the journey (conservatively estimated to be 1.8 million over 350 years), and the survivors arrived in the

Western Hemisphere sick, tired, and at risk for dying (Foner). Seasoning was a method slave traders used to condition Africans to the new climate and the increased workload that their lives as slaves would require. After two seasons, these Africans were sold to plantations in the British West Indies or brought north to be sold in America. Here ships' captains took on raw resources provided by the plantation economy of the British colonies and some finished goods to be transported to Britain, thus completing the triangle of the slave trade.

Prior to the Revolutionary War, the population of Africans and their descendants rose at a relatively slow rate. The eighteenth century saw a greater increase in the population of slaves in North America. By the eve of the Revolution, slave constituted nearly 40 percent of the population of the South, with the largest population in South Carolina. Of all slaves in the British colonies in North America, 90 percent lived in **the South**. In the North, slaveholding was less common and masters usually owned fewer than five slaves. On Southern plantations, slaves constituted a large minority, and at times a majority, of the overall population. In general, however, most slaves lived on moderately sized properties with masters who owned between five and fifty slaves. These slaves served as guides, craftsmen, house servants, and agricultural laborers. They helped raise and harvest rice, cotton, tobacco, sugar, and other crops. Africans adjusted to life in America, making connections, speaking a common language, practicing a common religion, and raising families. By the eve of the American Revolution, only about 20 percent of American slaves were African-born (although the concentration of Africans remained higher in South Carolina and Georgia). The natural growth of the slave population shaped a distinctive slavery in the American South and hastened the transition among slaves from African to African American.

The abolition of the transatlantic slave trade was the first success of international abolitionists: the first European country to end the international slave trade was Denmark, in 1792; Britain followed in 1808, after twenty years of increasingly tightened regulation; and the United States ended the trade in 1807. By this time period, however, ending the slave trade was only a half measure. Slavery was a functioning and self-replicating system in the British colonies and in the nation that would come to be the United States. Scholars estimate that prior to the ending of the slave trade, 9 to 10 million slaves were imported into the Americas.

In the midst of the struggle for colonists' freedom from British rule, many Africans and White abolitionists noted the clear hypocrisy concerning the enslavement of Africans; there were many early and powerful advocates for the abolition of slavery. The Quakers formally declared themselves antislavery at the turn of the eighteenth century and were monumental in encouraging such major White figures as Benjamin Franklin to publicly follow their cause. George Fox, the English founder of the Society of Friends, announced as early as 1676 that Christ had died for all, for "the Tawnies and the Black, as well as for you that are called Whites." He encouraged slaveholders in the colonies to free slaves, as they did indentured servants, after a period of "faithfull"

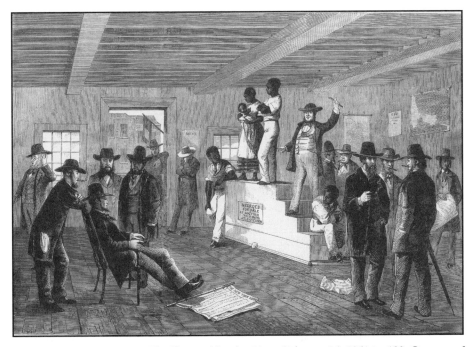

A slave auction in Virginia. *The Illustrated London News*, February 16, 1861, p. 139. Courtesy of North Wind Picture Archives.

servitude and to "let them not go away empty-handed" (Sorin, 26). Pennsylvanian Quakers passed the first official written group protest against slavery in North America in 1688.

A hundred years later, Anthony Benzenet sought to encourage members of the Church of England's missionary arm, the Society for the Propagation of the Gospel, to take an official stance against slavery, which they refused because they feared that White masters would then resist allowing Black slaves to convert. Benzenet began to agitate more publicly before the Revolution. Prior to 1770, no antislavery agitation was successful. A list of White patriots who were antislavery (at least in principle, even if some, ironically, owned slaves) includes Abigail Adams, John Adams, John Allen, Ben Franklin, Albert Gallatin, Alexander Hamilton, Patrick Henry, John Jay, Thomas Jefferson, James Madison, James Monroe, Harrison Gray Otis, Thomas Paine, and George Washington (Sorin, 30).

These White patriots were encouraged by free Blacks struggling for rights in the North who spoke against slavery. **Phillis Wheatley**'s poetry, as well as her correspondence with General Washington, was a public declaration of the humanity and Christianity of African Americans. Wheatley's *Poems on Various Subjects, Religious and Moral* is the first book published by an African American and the second book by a woman in America. In 1776, five free Black men took to court a case involving their refusal to pay taxes until they were given the right to vote (no taxation without representation), blurring their struggle with the White colonists. Rhode Island, Connecticut, and New York passed legislation between 1777 and 1779 that freed slaves who fought in the war on the patriots' side, or at least made it easier for White masters to free Black slaves to fight. In 1777, the Vermont Constitution abolished slavery. In 1783, the Massachusetts Supreme Court granted suffrage to Black tax payers, six years after New York. In 1787, the year that the Constitution was ratified and declared slaves to be the equivalent of three-fifths of a (White) human being, Absalom Jones and **Richard Allen** organized the Philadelphia Free African Society.

Noting the gulf between the Revolution's use of "oppression" and "slavery" and the reality of Black Americans' daily lives, the mathematician **Benjamin Banneker**, former slave-turned-entrepreneur, the autobiographer **Olaudah Equiano**, and others called direct attention to hypocrisy and violence. African Americans and White abolitionists who noted the reality of **race** in America portrayed the paradoxes of the "peculiar institution" that sought to create a world where White was equal to White (democracy) and White was always superior to Black (despotism). During the Revolution, Britain offered to free escaped slaves who fought against the colonists. In response, American forces offered freedom for Africans who supported their cause. Some were freed; those who supported the British and were vanquished, were transported to Canada to live in freedom far from family and known environs. The early nationalists, reformers who saw America as both site of crisis and utopia, sought to reconcile quintessentially American paradoxes through dramatic social change. The years following the Revolution would be impacted by the rhetoric and the ideals put forth by major nationalist figures.

While many White Protestants saw the contrast between an acceptance of slaveholding and their religious ideals, early proponents of abolitionism were often at odds with what the resolution following the abolition of slavery would entail. It was during this period that the American Colonization Society (ACS, formed in 1817) gained power. The ACS formalized years of considering colonization as a solution to race conflict and as an approach to the ultimate emancipation of Black slaves into the world of free Whites, an approach contingent on the swift removal of Blacks to Africa. Under this mantle of anxiety, the **abolitionist movement** slowed in force after the effective end of slavery in the North and did not rise again until the late 1820s,

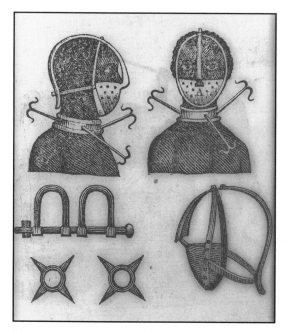

Illustration in an 1807 publication of an iron mask, collar, leg shackles, and spurs used to restrict slaves. Courtesy of the Library of Congress.

when it became obvious that the ideals of the Revolution would not extend to slaves. The argument moved from one of the "natural rights of man" to one of the immorality of slaveholding in a Christian nation.

Between the end of the Revolution and the 1820s, abolitionists promoted "gradualism" as the almost inevitable end to slavery, with so strong a sense of confidence that they nearly "smothered any sense of moral urgency" (Sorin, 39). Spurred by the moral drama of the Second Great Awakening, however, White abolitionists began to focus on individual morality and sought to rectify what they came to conceive of as a great national sin. This emphasis shifted the focus from the rights of people of African descent, as eighteenth-century natural rights rhetoric dictated, to the nature of virtue of White Americans, as the rhetoric of revivalism asserted. This newly constructed sense of moral urgency was termed "immediatism," which was not to be interpreted strictly as the immediate end to slavery, but rather as the immediate entry into the discourse concerning the appropriateness of freeing slaves. Abolitionists promoting immediatism supported the cause of immediate action against slavery in order that the nation would reap immediate benefit from activism. As a strategy, immediatism can be represented by this definition found in a letter signed by "Vigornius" in the *Boston Recorder and Telegraph* in 1825: "*The slave-holding system must be abolished*: and in order to the accomplishment of this end, *immediate* determined measures must be adopted for the *ultimate* emancipation of every slave" (Sorin, 39).

In contrast to this rather gradual approach to the immediate abolition of slavery, free Blacks and escaped slaves in the North were moving toward an ever-increasing militancy. Slaves in the South were fomenting rebellion as well. In 1822, a freeman named Denmark Vesey initiated what was ultimately a failed plot for overt rebellion on a plantation near Charleston, South Carolina. Revealed by a traitorous house servant, his plot ended with execution and threatening behavior by Whites. In the North, free Blacks were speaking up and being heard. In 1828, **David Walker**, son of a free mother and a slave father in North Carolina, delivered a radical speech to the Massachusetts General Colored Association. The following year he published an extended version of his oration. *Walker's Appeal, in Four Articles, Together with a Preamble, to the Colored Citizens of the World, but in Particular, and Very Expressly to Those of the United States of America* was published in Boston and disseminated to as many people in the Southern states as possible, using the mails and seamen traveling to southern ports. Southerners responded by passing legislation against seditious materials as well as further restricting literacy for slaves. The Georgia state legislature placed a price on Walker's head: $10,000 if he was delivered alive, $1,000 if dead (Walker, iii).

David Walker met with great resistance when his *Appeal* was published and distributed, not only from Southern slaveholding Whites, as he expected, but also from White abolitionists. William Lloyd Garrison and his followers argued that Walker had overstepped, supposedly because his work conflicted with the more pacifistic position of Garrison's ideals for antislavery, articulated in *The*

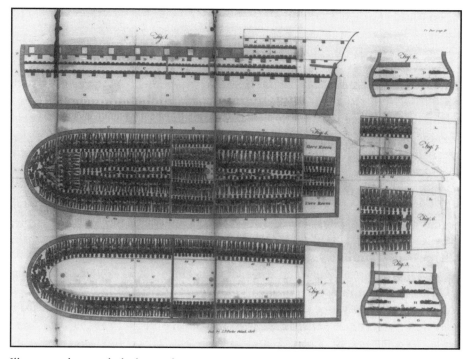

Illustration showing deck plans and cross sections of British slave ship *Brookes*, c. 1887. Courtesy of the Library of Congress.

Genius of Universal Emancipation, written in collaboration with Benjamin Lundy and published in the same year as Walker's *Appeal*. (Garrison would further formalize his ideas for abolition under his editorship of *The Liberator* and in his American Anti-Slavery Society, formed in 1833). The schism that resulted from the *Appeal* was indicative of the relationship between Whites' promotion of abolitionism as a securing of greater national virtue and Blacks' struggle for the liberty of selfhood and nationhood, a relationship born in the limits of White anti-Black racism.

Most of what we know of slavery comes from first-person accounts of slavery (**slave narratives**) written by former slaves and their free Black and White supporters. Charles T. Davis and **Henry Louis Gates, Jr.**, state in their Introduction to *The Slave's Narrative*: "From 1760 to the present, almost half of the Afro-American literary tradition was created when its authors and their readers were either slaves or former slaves" (xv). Between 1760 and 1865, hundreds of stories were written and transcribed. Many of the earlier narratives were dictated by illiterate slaves, and written down and edited by White amanuenses, for the purpose of proving the humanity of Blacks to a White, Northern audience not yet fully convinced of the horrors of slavery. Nearly 6,000 published narratives that described life in slavery, ranging from short accounts to book-length autobiographies, were produced by African American slaves. For decades historians have engaged in arguments concerning authenticity of the dictated narratives, some doubting the intentions of the

White editors or transcribers and some doubting the intentions of the slaves themselves. The popularity and reception of the slave narrative led to a reconfiguring of White abolitionists' strategies for representing slavery.

As an extreme example of public reception, **Frederick Douglass**'s *Narrative of the Life of Frederick Douglass, an American Slave* (1845) sold 5,000 copies in the first four months of publication and 11,000 in the following two years; by 1860, 30,000 copies of his work had been sold (Davis and Gates, xvi). With these narratives, abolitionists were able to portray the intimate experience of a life in slavery; with the self-authored narrative, the experience of a self in slavery could come into being. Free Blacks, influenced by both the slave narrative and the conversion narrative, came to incorporate first-person positioning in their rhetoric as well. Olaudah Equiano's early narrative and Douglass's first autobiography served to create a formula for the slave narrative that most male authors emulated afterward.

Harriet Ann Jacobs, the only African American woman to self-author a slave narrative prior to the **Civil War**, pseudonymously published her narrative, *Incidents in the Life of a Slave Girl* (1861). She frankly discusses how life was exceptionally hard for female slaves, who endured sexual assault, concubinage, and the condition of the mother, the legal precedent that declared the offspring of a female slave automatically were the property of her owner. While most of her narrative details her struggles to endure slavery and the unwanted advances of her unscrupulous master, Dr. Flint, Jacobs's narrative provides an interesting insight into the role that battles between the North and South played in the lives of slaves.

In discussing the Fugitive Slave Law of 1850, a part of the Compromise of 1850, Jacobs reveals how risky a process traveling outside of her New York employer's home is, even though she had escaped slavery years before. The potential for her to be recognized and "deported" underscores how mobility is a facet of citizenship and Whiteness. In this way, Jacobs reveals the constant threat of exposure fugitive slaves experienced: "It was the beginning of a reign of terror to the colored population. . . . the thrilling voices of poor hunted colored people went up, in an agony of supplication, to the Lord, from Zion's Church. . . . But what cared the legislators of the 'dominant race' for the blood they were crushing out of trampled hearts?" (286–287). New York comes to represent a state where selfhood is challenged, not only by slavery but also by the compromise of the law regarding slavery. Generations of escaped slaves lived in the cities of the North, and the Compromise of 1850 allowed slave hunters to travel north to recapture "stolen property" and return that property to the "rightful" owners. Even free Blacks were at risk of being taken by unscrupulous Whites who could later claim that such people were escaped slaves, and then sell them into slavery.

The cultural and social differences between the North and the South grew considerably in the antebellum era. Industry developed in the North, using skilled labor, and agriculture was less prominent. As the plantation economy grew in the South, Whites allowed themselves to become more dependent on the free labor that slaves provided. This economic difference worked to create cultural differences as plantation owners and other Whites connected to the plantation economy sought to justify the continued use of slave labor, despite Northern states' efforts to abolish the "peculiar institution." Using religion and racism to justify the enslavement of millions of people created an ideological schism among White American Christians. Slavery supporters argued that slavery was not only necessary for the nation but a benefit to African Americans, claiming it had saved them from heathenism and allowed them to be taken care of by a superior race. (This ideology is referred to as "paternalism," which positioned White men as fathers to White women and all people of color, and it assumed that White men were better suited for all positions of power.)

The decades before the Civil War were marked by increasingly hostile rhetoric between Whites over the issues of slavery and abolitionism. Southerners who were pro-slavery argued that their way of life was threatened. Northern abolitionists claimed that slavery was antithetical to Christianity and democracy, and feared that slavery was corrupting the moral fiber of the new nation.

African Americans writing during this period became increasingly assertive, frequently separating themselves from the prescribed role that White abolitionist movements had set aside for them. **Martin R. Delany** called for a return to Africa for emancipated and escaped slaves, believing that the only true freedom available for the Black nation existed on a continent slaves and free Blacks had never seen. **William Wells Brown**'s **autobiography** deviates from Frederick Douglass's arguably more romanticized notion of the slave as heroic, underscoring how slavery's hypocrisy impacted Blacks as well as Whites. Slavery permeated nearly every area of the nation's political, cultural, and social life.

Politicians struggled over new territories, working to claim more land for each side of the free state/slave state divide. A "Free-Soiler" and Republican, Abraham Lincoln, was elected President in 1860, a clear signal that slavery was no longer an issue on which the North and the South could compromise. Seven Southern states seceded from the Union, arguing that any limitation on slaveholding was a direct challenge to the Southern way of life. In April 1861, hostilities between the Union and the Confederacy began as four more states seceded. As troops battled over slavery, the Constitution, and states' rights, African Americans fled plantations, many of them joining Union forces. On January 1, 1863, Abraham Lincoln proclaimed slaves in the Confederacy free. The Emancipation Proclamation effectively ended slavery, though many slaves would not learn of their freedom for some time.

Following the North's victory over the Confederacy and the end of the Civil War, Congress passed three amendments to the Constitution that firmly entrenched freedom from slavery in the United States. The Thirteenth Amendment outlawed slavery, the Fourteenth Amendment granted equal protection under the law regardless of color, and the Fifteenth Amendment allowed Black men to vote. The period following the Civil War, **Reconstruction**, was a high point of national effort to right the wrongs of slavery. Unfortunately, that period and many of those efforts were short-lived, as a massive backlash against African American citizenship quickly arose in an effort to eradicate all rights of former slaves and free Blacks. (*See* **Bontemps, Arna**; **Brown, John**; **Haley, Alex**; **Morrison, Toni**; **Truth, Sojourner**; **Turner, Nat**.)

Resources: Patricia Bradley, *Slavery, Propaganda and the American Revolution* (Jackson: University Press of Mississippi, 1998); William Wells Brown, *Narrative of William W. Brown, a Fugitive Slave. Written by Himself* (Boston: Bela Marsh, 1849); Charles T. Davis and Henry Louis Gates, Jr., eds., *The Slave's Narrative* (New York: Oxford University Press, 1985); Angie Debo, *A History of the Indians of the United States* (Norman: University of Oklahoma Press, 1970); Frederick Douglass, *Narrative of the Life of Frederick Douglass, an American Slave. Written by Himself*, ed. Houston A. Baker, Jr. (New York: Penguin, 1986); Paul Finkelman, ed., *Slavery & the Law* (Madison, WI: Madison House, 1996); Eric Foner, *Slavery and Freedom in Nineteenth-Century America* (New York: Oxford University Press, 1994); Harriet Jacobs, *Incidents in the Life of a Slave Girl* (New York: Oxford University Press, 1988); Robert McColley, *Slavery and Jeffersonian Virginia* (Urbana: University of Illinois Press, 1973); Kenneth Morgan, *Slavery and Servitude in Colonial North America: A Short History* (New York: New York University Press, 2001); Gerald Sorin, *Abolitionism: A New Perspective* (New York: Praeger, 1972); David Walker, *Walker's Appeal in Four Articles with a Brief Preamble* (1829), intro. by William Loren Katz (Salem, NH: Ayer, 1969).

Pamela Ralston

Smiley, Tavis (born 1964). Author, radio and television host, and political analyst. While Smiley is perhaps best known for his work as a Black Entertainment Television host and his recent shows on National Public Radio and PBS, he is also an author of six books. Smiley grew up in Kokomo, Indiana, and attended Indiana University. He was actively involved with student and local government, and he graduated with a degree in law and public policy. He had an internship with, and later worked for, Tom Bradley, mayor of **Los Angeles, California**. Smiley sought a political career of his own but failed to be elected to the Los Angeles City Council, so he turned to writing and radio work by creating "The Smiley Report," a sixty-second radio commentary that quickly became syndicated. Smiley's first book, *Just a Thought: The Smiley Report* (1993), a collection of his radio commentaries, was followed by *Hard Left: Straight Talk about the Wrongs of the Right* (1996), which illustrates Smiley's liberal belief that Republicans can be blamed for America's evils. *Doing What's Right: How to Fight for What You Believe—and Make a Difference* (2000) is a collection of essays in which he examines society's problems and ways to solve them on the local and national levels. *How to Make Black America Better* (2001) opens with ten challenges related to money, education, and health that Smiley presents to the African American community. These themes are then addressed by well-known African Americans, with the discussion focusing on what needs to be done to improve Black America. Smiley's most recent work is

Keeping the Faith: Stories of Love, Courage, Healing and Hope from Black America (2002), a collection of essays written by Smiley and other well-known and everyday African Americans. They examine the role of faith, grief, healing, education, hope, and, especially, Black love in their lives. His most recent work, *On Air: The Best of Tavis Smiley on the Tom Joyner Morning Show, 2002–2003* (2004), is another compilation of his commentaries.

Resources: John L. Mitchell, "Los Angeles Profile. A Painful Failure in Politics Clears a Pathway to Success; Personality: Tavis Smiley Reinvented Himself as a Radio and TV Talk Show Host after Losing a City Council Race 10 Years Ago. Now He's Back in the Community, with a National Audience," *Los Angeles Times*, Aug. 21, 2001, home ed., p. B3; Diane Patrick, "The Smiley Factor," *Publishers Weekly*, Nov. 24, 2003, p. 17; Tavis Smiley: *Doing What's Right: How to Fight for What You Believe—and Make a Difference* (New York: Anchor/Doubleday, 2000); *Hard Left: Straight Talk about the Wrongs of the Right* (New York: Anchor/Doubleday, 1996); *How to Make Black America Better* (New York: Anchor/Doubleday, 2001); *Just a Thought: The Smiley Report* (Los Angeles: Pines One Publications, 1993); *Keeping the Faith: Stories of Love, Courage, Healing and Hope from Black America* (New York: Anchor/Doubleday, 2002); *On Air: The Best of Tom Smiley on the Tom Joyner Morning Show, 2002–2003* (Los Angeles: Pines One Publications, 2004).

Diane Todd Bucci

Smith, Amanda Berry (1837–1915). Evangelist, temperance leader, writer, and educator. In the context of literature, Smith is best known for her *Autobiography* (1893). Smith was born in **slavery** in Long Green, Maryland. Her parents purchased Amanda's freedom. She taught herself to read and write, and also had a few months of sporadic schooling. Widowed twice, Smith eked out a living as a washerwoman in Pennsylvania and New York until she joined the holiness movement and began to preach at camp meetings.

The better part of Smith's life starts with her 1868 experience of sanctification or the "second blessing," spiritual empowerment to resist sin and to demonstrate godly love. Attired in plain Quaker style, she began preaching in 1870 with a landmark African Methodist Episcopalian (A.M.E.) revival in Salem, New Jersey. Most of her future audiences would be prominent American White congregations and temperance societies at home and abroad.

Smith's participation in the 1878 Kesvick-Broadland Conferences in England transformed her into an international evangelist. For the next two years she traveled, preaching, throughout India, returning to England by 1881, her mind set on visiting West Africa. Smith spent the next eight years in West Africa, building churches, schools, and temperance sites in Liberia, Sierra Leone, and Nigeria. Successful, but in poor health, she returned to England in 1889 with Bob, her adopted son.

Upon her return to the United States in 1890, Smith stepped up her temperance work and was sponsored for a return tour to the United Kingdom in 1894. In the meantime she moved to Chicago and published her autobiography in 1893.

In 1899, Smith opened the Amanda Smith Orphan Home and Industrial School in Harvey, Illinois, the first colored orphanage in the state. Proceeds from the sale of her autobiography, which recounts her spiritual development, supported the orphanage. Though an acclaimed venture, the home proved too burdensome for her. In 1912, its governance was transferred to an interracial board and it was renamed the Amanda Smith Industrial School for Girls. However, the school went rapidly into bankruptcy and lost its certification. It was destroyed by fire in 1918.

Smith retired to Sebring, Florida, where the town's founder, George Sebring, had built a home for her. She died there on February 25, 1915. Sebring arranged for her burial in Homewood, Illinois. In 1991 the state of Illinois honored Smith by a special resolution.

Resources: William L. Andrews, ed., *Sisters of the Spirit: Three Black Women's Autobiographies of the Nineteenth Century* (Bloomington: Indiana University Press, 1986); Adrienne M. Israel, *Amanda Berry Smith: From Washerwoman to Evangelist* (Lanham, MD: Scarecrow, 1998); Amanda Smith, *An Autobiography* (New York: Oxford University Press, 1988).

Varghese Mathai

Smith, Anna Deavere (born 1950). Actor and playwright. Anna Deavere Smith was born on September 18, 1950, in **Baltimore, Maryland**. The daughter of an elementary school teacher and a coffee merchant, she graduated from Beaver College in 1971 and received an M.F.A. from the American Conservatory Theater in 1976.

Smith is best known for her "On the Road: A Search for an American Character" play series. These plays include *On the Road: A Search for an American Character* (1982), *Aye, Aye, Aye, I'm Integrated* (1984), *Fires in the Mirror: Crown Heights, Brooklyn, and Other Identities* (1992), and *Twilight, Los Angeles, 1992* (1993). They feature a range of personalities—all real, living people—played across Smith's singular body. For each of her plays, the playwright began her writing process by interviewing a large number of people and asking them to comment upon a single topic. She then condensed the tape-recorded interviews and her written notes of the interviews into a performance piece in which she, as an actress, played each of her interviewees. With the aid of an accessory, such as a hat or a tie, she performed an excerpt from each interview. The plays—the sum total of these edited, collected, and performed interviews—gave the viewer the opportunity to witness a number of differing perspectives upon often charged political issue. For example, both *Fires in the Mirror* and *Twilight: Los Angeles, 1992* center on racial prejudice and violence.

Smith has received numerous awards for her unique style of playwrighting. Both *Fires in the Mirror* and *Twilight, Los Angeles, 1992* won Obie awards. The former was nominated for the Pulitzer Prize. In 1996, Smith was awarded the prestigious MacArthur Foundation "genius" grant and was named the Ford Foundation's first artist-in-residence. The MacArthur Foundation, honoring the playwright, observed that she "has created a new form of theater—a blend of theatrical art, social commentary, journalism, and intimate reverie."

In 1997, Smith founded the Institute on the Arts and Civic Dialogue, a three-year pilot program sponsored by the Ford Foundation and hosted by Harvard University and the American Repertory Theater. The Institute brought together community activists, scholars, artists, and audiences with the goal of creating new artwork that engaged with social and political issues. It was a unique place where playwrights, actors, lawyers, professors, and community organizers worked together to create socially relevant theater.

Smith is also a successful actor. She has appeared in numerous films and televisions series: the films *The Human Stain* (2003), *The American President* (1995), *Philadelphia* (1993), and *Dave* (1993); the television series *The West Wing* (2000–2005); and the television version of *Fires in the Mirror* (1993). Throughout her career, Smith has maintained an affiliation with various colleges and universities. She has taught at Carnegie-Mellon, the University of Southern California, Yale, and Stanford. Currently, she teaches at New York University.

Resources: Richard Schechner, "Anna Deavere Smith: Acting as Incorporation," *TDR: The Drama Review* 37, no. 4 (1993), 63–64; Anna Deavere Smith: *Fires in the Mirror* (Garden City, NY: Anchor, 1993); *House Arrest and Piano: Two Plays* (Garden City, NY: Anchor, 2004); *Talk to Me: Listening Between the Lines* (New York: Random House, 2000); *Twilight: Los Angeles, 1992* (Garden City, NY: Anchor, 1994).

Harvey Young

Smith, Barbara (born 1946). Essayist, editor, activist, lecturer, and publisher. Barbara Smith's writing and speaking publicly about issues of social justice are her hallmark. Her work is influential, helping to inspire new considerations of African American subjectivity and identity, particularly as they intersect or conflict with established categories of and assumptions about identity.

Smith's essays began appearing in the 1960s and are now a fixture in most college-level Women's Studies curricula. Her politics are as multivalent as the identities she claims and the combinations of identities her work investigates. Smith is unsparing in her criticism of those individuals who are not willing to step outside of their own concerns in an effort to view the bigger picture— namely, how other people are affected by marginalization and oppression. Smith infuses Marxist and socialist perspectives throughout her writings as well as her lectures, shedding light on the condition of lower social classes in the United States and abroad.

As the cofounder and publisher of **Kitchen Table: Women of Color Press** (founded 1981), Smith is considered a pioneering publisher. Kitchen Table is the publisher of some of the most important feminist texts of the last two decades, including Cherríe Moraga and Gloria Anzaldúa's landmark anthology *This Bridge Called My Back: Writings by Radical Women of Color*, as well as *Home Girls: A Black Feminist Anthology*, which Smith edited. Although Smith no longer works directly with Kitchen Table, the press is going strong. Smith founded Kitchen Table with her cherished friend and colleague, **Audre Lorde**. When Smith gives lectures on college campuses and at professional conferences, she frequently includes anecdotes about working with Lorde at Kitchen Table. Doing so gives audiences a broader picture of the daunting work of maintaining a press devoted to publishing works by, for, and about women of color. Smith's anecdotes also keep Lorde's memory alive.

An additional way that Smith is viewed as a pioneer by many involves her lifelong work to broaden the concept of "feminist." In the early 1970s, she began critiquing the exclusive model of **feminism** that equated the concept with Whiteness. Foreshadowing her later determination to speak to identity intersections, she wrote numerous essays and gave public lectures about including women of other races, particularly Black women, under the label of feminism. In lieu of merely expanding the term to accommodate other cultures and ethnicities, Smith advocated a thorough discussion and/or investigation of the myriad differences between White feminism and feminism that might appeal to women of color. Drawing from this distinction, Smith is widely credited with being one of the first to conceive of Black Women's Studies in contradistinction to the more white-washed women's studies. Black Women's Studies addresses not only issues that are expressly related to racism and sexism, but also those issues that stem from the identity intersections that Smith speaks to. For instance, Black Women's Studies had a different (and arguably more compelling) critical view of the Anita Hill/Clarence Thomas Senate hearings in 1991 than did other feminist perspectives.

As a lesbian, Smith does not shy away from illuminating the abusive treatment—physical and ideological—that lesbian, gay, bisexual, and transgender (LGBT) individuals receive. She wrote and gave lectures about LGBT subjectivity long before it became fashionable to do so. Smith took quite a risk in speaking to these issues, for she often alienated some of her would-be supporters. This alienation only inspired Smith to continue her work. Some of her more compelling remarks about lesbian and gay subjectivity are featured in Marlon Riggs's award-winning documentary *Black Is, Black Ain't* (1985).

In 1998, Rutgers published a collection of Smith's essays, *The Truth That Never Hurts*. This text gathers many of her most famous treatises, placing them alongside newer works that examine police brutality, interlocking oppressions, and, of course, identity intersections. *Publisher's Weekly* lauded the work, reveling in its "stretches of sublime prose [that] translate [Smith's] crystalline intellect to the page, exciting both mind and senses."

Smith has worked as scholar-in-residence at the Schomburg Center for Research in Black Culture in New York and was also a Rockefeller Fellow at the City University of New York's Center for Lesbian and Gay Studies. She served as a general editor of *The Reader's Companion to U.S. Women's History*, working with other luminaries such as Wilma Mankiller, Gwendolyn Mink, Marysa Navarro, and Gloria Steinem. In 1999, *The Advocate*, which bills itself as the national gay and lesbian newsmagazine, named Smith as one its "Best and Brightest Activists for Lesbian and Gay Rights."

Resources: Gloria Hull, Patricia Bell Scott, and Barbara Smith, *All the Women Are White, All the Blacks Are Men, But Some of Us Are Brave: Black Women's Studies* (Old Westbury, NY: Feminist Press, 1982); Cherríe Moraga and Gloria Anzaldúa, eds., *This Bridge Called My Back: Writings by Radical Women of Color* (New York: Kitchen Table: Women of Color Press, 1983); Barbara Smith, *The Truth That Never Hurts: Writings on Race, Gender and Freedom* (New Brunswick, NJ: Rutgers University Press, 1998); Barbara Smith, ed., *Home Girls: A Black Feminist Anthology* (New York: Kitchen Table: Women of Color Press, 1983); Barbara Smith et al., eds., *The Reader's Companion to U.S. Women's History* (Boston: Houghton Mifflin, 1998).

Chris Bell

Smith, Bessie (1894–1937). Blues singer. Recognized as one of the greatest classic **blues** singers, Bessie Smith rose to stardom during the 1920s. Smith was equipped with a booming voice and commanding stage presence that endeared her to fans and earned her the title Empress of the Blues.

Smith was born in Chattanooga, Tennessee, on April 15, 1894. (She was known to claim different years of birth.) Her professional career began in 1912 as part of the chorus for a traveling show that featured Gertrude "Ma" Rainey. Rainey befriended Smith and became her mentor. By 1915, Smith was featured in her own shows and, amid her growing popularity, was tapped to make a "race record" in 1923. She continued to make successful records for about six years. By the 1930s, however, her career was suffering. Her hard drinking began to take a toll, as did the **Great Depression** and the public's shift in musical tastes.

Critics of the blues, both Black and White, claimed the music was too rough and uncultured. They were similarly critical of Smith's lifestyle. Throughout her career Smith was a notoriously heavy drinker, a feared fighter, and known for her affairs with men and women. She was a tall, dark-skinned woman who sang lyrics that were openly about love between Black people, as well as brashly sexual—none of which fit the stereotype of popular music.

During the height of her popularity and well after her death in 1937, Smith influenced various African American writers. Her powerful talent and defiant attitude were revered by the likes of **Langston Hughes**, **Amiri Baraka**, and **Alice Walker**, among others. In his controversial, landmark essay from the **Harlem Renaissance**, "The Negro Artist and the Racial Mountain" (1926), Hughes celebrates Smith as an example of a Black artist who

Undated portrait of Bessie Smith. Yale Collection of American Literature, Beinecke Rare Book and Manuscript Library.

expresses herself without shame and without accommodating the White mainstream. The poet **Robert Hayden** celebrated Smith in the poem "Homage to the Empress of the Blues" (1948). More recently, Walker recognized Smith for her place in a long line of Black women who defined themselves as valuable human beings and artists, despite what oppressive conventions dictated (*You Can't Keep a Good Woman Down*, 1982). Smith has become a symbol of agency and resistance for many feminists and queer writers, Black and White alike.

Resources: Chris Albertson, *Bessie* (New York: Stein and Day, 1972); Angela Y. Davis, *Blues Legacies and Black Feminism: Gertrude "Ma" Rainey, Bessie Smith and Billie Holiday* (New York: Knopf, 1999); Robert Hayden, "Homage to the Empress of the Blues," in *The Norton Anthhology of Modern and Contemporary Poetry*, vol. 2, *Contemporary Poetry*, 3rd ed., ed. Jahan Ramazani, Richard Ellmann, and Robert O'Clair (New York: Norton, 2003), 59; Langston Hughes, "The Negro Artist and the Racial Mountain," in *The Portable Harlem Renaissance Reader*, ed. David Levering Lewis (New York: Penguin, 1994), 91–95; Alice Walker, *You Can't Keep a Good Woman Down* (New York: Harcourt, Brace/Harvest, 1982).

Raquel Rodriguez

Smith, Effie Waller (1879–1960). Poet. Smith was one of the most important African American poets of the early twentieth century. The third of four children born to former slaves, Smith stated that her mother supplied the love that protected her from the harsh realities of the racial situation prior to 1900 (Andrews). She often alluded to these times in her poems, stating that her writing provided a safe haven from the realities of racial hatred and discrimination that she found in the outside world. She attended the Kentucky Normal School for Colored Persons in Frankfort, Kentucky, and worked as a teacher for several years. Smith published her first book of poetry, *Songs of the Months*, in 1904; its publication was financed by Mary Elliott Flannery, the first woman elected to a Southern state legislature. Her best-known poem, "Autumn 1896," shows that Smith was well read in classical literature and conscious of what other popular writers of her day were producing. Yet Smith was also aware of her situation in respect to racial origin and the difficulties that she would encounter because of her race. In 1909, she published two more volumes of poetry, *Rhymes of the Cumberland* and *Rosemary and Pansies*. These poems depict life in the Cumberland Mountains and include "Decoration Day" and "The Cornhusking."

Smith's poems often express the tension between her desire to be at one with nature and, at the same time, a student of school learning. One of her most powerful artistic statements about life, "The Faded Blossoms," appeared in *The Independent* magazine in 1911, just three months after her husband, Charles, a deputy sheriff from whom she was separated, was murdered while serving a warrant. Smith's later work focused on her love for the Appalachian Mountains. These poems show the origins of what is recognized today as "ecological feminism," a far-reaching philosophy that values the connections between humans and nonhumans and works for social and environmental justice. Her work last appeared in *Harper's* magazine in 1917. In the late 1920s, she adopted the daughter of a deceased friend and moved to Wisconsin, where she spent the rest of her life.

Resources: William L. Andrews, ed., *Two Biographies of African-American Women* (New York: Oxford University Press, 1995); Effie Waller Smith, *Collected Works of Effie Waller Smith* (New York: Oxford University Press, 1991); Karen J. Warren ed., *Ecological Feminism* (New York: Routledge, 1999).

Sarah Lynsey Williams

Smith, Mary Burnett (born 1931). Novelist. Since retiring in 1992 from teaching inner-city high school students in **Philadelphia, Pennsylvania**, Mary Burnett Smith has written two richly layered, psychologically complex **coming-of-age** novels set in small, segregated Black communities in the 1940s. In both novels adult women reflect upon the lessons learned at a pivotal time in their childhood. These are quiet, reflective novels about the joys of childhood, but they also incorporate adult themes, such as abortion, adultery, alcoholism, domestic violence, and interracial discrimination.

Set in 1948 rural Virginia, Smith's debut novel, *Miss Ophelia* (1997), focuses upon lonely, eleven-year-old Belly, whose pregnant best friend has been sent away. She reluctantly goes to help her Aunt Rachel, who is recuperating from surgery, and this turns out to be three paradisiacal weeks in which she is taught the piano as well as life lessons by kind Miss Ophelia, her mother's childhood friend. Belly learns about friendship when she must cope with pesky Jimmy, the boy next door, who is a victim of abuse, and the complexities of adult love, commitment, and sacrifice when she discovers that Ophelia is having an affair with her uncle.

In Smith's second novel, *Ring Around the Moon* (1998), nine-year-old Amy must deal with moving to a new neighborhood outside of Philadelphia in 1940 as her parents attempt to save their disintegrating marriage, which is beset by her father's alcoholism, gambling, and womanizing. However, the story also focuses on Amy's complicated relationship with her two brothers and her adjustment to a new school: making friends, acquiring a best friend, and dealing with racism due to her red hair.

Smith's two straightforwardly narrated, coming-of-age memoirs explore the complex adult issues children are frequently forced to deal with, but these are also novels of hope, survival, and the resilience of children.

Resources: Mary Burnett Smith: *Miss Ophelia: A Novel* (New York: Morrow, 1997); *Ring Around the Moon* (New York: Morrow, 1998).

Ymitri Jayasundera

Smith, Venture (1728/1729–1805). Autobiographer. In *Narrative of the Life and Adventures of Venture, a Native of Africa, But Resident above Sixty Years in the United States of America, Related by Himself* (1798), Smith details the African and the American sides of **slavery**, his entrepreneurial endeavors, and the disadvantages he suffered because he was illiterate. Born in Dukandarra, Guinea, the son of a prince, Smith (also known as Broteer Venture) was pressed into slavery at the age of eight. In a prelude that contrasts his experiences in Africa with his enslavement in America, Smith recounts his life with a farmer while his parents were estranged due to his father's third marriage. Although Smith was virtually a servant, the farmer treated him as a son. After reuniting with his family, Smith became the victim of a tribal war, saw his father tortured and killed, and was taken prisoner by still another tribe that had been armed by Europeans. While a servant to the leader of the conquering army, Smith fell victim to yet another tribal war. This conquering army sold him into slavery. Robert Mumford, a ship's steward, purchased the young boy for four gallons of rum and a piece of calico, and named him for "his own private venture."

Smith, one of the few surviving slaves not sold in Barbados, was transported to Rhode Island. There he became a house servant on Fisher's Island, performing such tasks as carding wool and pounding corn. His master and his mistress frequently beat him, and their son repeatedly harassed him. At twenty-two, Smith married Margaret (Meg), another slave in the household, and fathered four children. After an abortive escape attempt in which one of the escapees (Heddy) stole from the others, Smith redeemed himself by identifying Heddy as the ringleader. Smith was then sold to Thomas Stanton and moved to Stonington Point, Connecticut. Stanton, too, abused Smith and, when Smith was thirty-one, sold him to Colonel Smith.

Frugal and enterprising, Venture Smith earned money however he could—raising and selling vegetables, fishing, shining shoes—and purchased his freedom, adopting Smith's surname as his own. He continued to exhibit an entrepreneurial spirit, primarily as a woodcutter, watermelon farmer, and owner of a shipping business. Eventually he purchased freedom for his whole family, first buying his sons, and later his wife and daughter, as well as three unrelated Black men. Smith described the latter as ungrateful because they reneged on their agreement to repay his purchase money. Smith recounted additional instances of lending money to Blacks and Whites who failed to repay him, explaining that his illiteracy, particularly his inability to use figures, made him vulnerable; however, he also attributed his exploitation to racial inequality.

When he was sixty-nine, Smith dictated his *Narrative*—presumably to Elisha Niles, a schoolteacher—complaining that "though once straight and tall, measuring without shoes six feet, one inch and a half, and every way well proportioned, I am now bowed down with age and hardship." Smith's personal tales of his exploits revealed him to be a giant of a man, a "New England **John Henry**" (Kaplan and Kaplan, 255). His willingness to endure privation and hardship in order to accomplish his goal of freedom for himself, his family, and others underscored the power of personal effort while it also illustrated the obstacles free Blacks faced during the eighteenth century. The 1896 edition of Smith's *Narrative*—an expanded version published by a relative—included a supplement entitled *Traditions*. This addition featured accounts corroborating his larger-than-life image as a man who possessed superhuman strength and stature.

Resources: Jeannine DeLombard, "Smith, Venture," in *American National Biography*, ed. John Garraty and Mark Carnes (New York: Oxford University Press, 1999); Sidney Kaplan and Emma Nogrady Kaplan, *The Black Presence in the Era of the American Revolution*, rev. ed. (Amherst: University of Massachusetts Press, 1989); Venture Smith, *Narrative of the Life and Adventures of Venture, a Native of Africa, But Resident above Sixty Years in the United States of America, Related by Himself* (New London, CT: C. Holt, 1798).

Gloria A. Shearin

Smith, William Gardner (1927–1974). Novelist and journalist. Smith's novels examine the experiences of African Americans at home and abroad, and at least one of them represents a well-regarded, early example of **protest literature**. Smith was born and raised in **Philadelphia, Pennsylvania**, graduated second in his high school class (1944), and then worked as a reporter for the *Pittsburgh Courier*. After serving in postwar Berlin as a clerk for the U.S. Army, he returned to Philadelphia. While attending Temple University, Smith shaped his experiences abroad into a novel, *Last of the Conquerors* (1948), which recounts the stories of many Black soldiers who found greater freedom and opportunity in Germany than in the United States, for which they had fought. His second novel, *Anger at Innocence* (1950), narrates a doomed interracial romance in South Philadelphia. In 1951 Smith moved to **Paris, France**, and quickly developed ties there within the Black expatriate community, befriending such expatriate writers as **James Baldwin**, **Oliver Harrington**, and **Chester Himes**. In France, Smith worked as the English-language news editor for Agence France-Presse, contributed to *Ebony* and *Jet* magazines, and published his third novel, *South Street* (1954), which is considered by some critics to be among the earliest Black protest novels (Gayle). Though some reviewers had expressed misgivings about Smith's early fiction for emphasizing descriptive reportage over psychological depth and stylistic distinctiveness, *South Street* was praised for its skilled presentation of emotionally complex characters coming into militant self-consciousness. His other books include the novel *The Stone Face* (1963) and *Return to Black America* (1970), an examination of the **Black Power** movement in America. Smith was at work on a book on Ghana, having spent several years there working in television, when he died in 1974 in France. (*See* **World War II**.)

Resources: Jerry H. Bryant, "Individuality and Fraternity: The Novels of William Gardner Smith," *Studies in Black Literature* 3, no. 2 (Summer 1972), 1–8; Addison Gayle, Jr., *The Way of the New World: The Black Novel in America* (Garden City, NY: Doubleday, 1975), 239–247; LeRoy S. Hodges, *Portrait of an Expatriate: William Gardner Smith* (Westport, CT: Greenwood Press, 1985); Jacquelyn Jackson, "William Gardner Smith," in *Dictionary of Literary Biography*, vol. 76, *Afro-American Writers, 1940–1955*, ed. Trudier Harris (Detroit: Gale, 1988), 158–163; William Gardner

Smith: *Anger at Innocence* (New York: Farrar, Straus, 1950); *Last of the Conquerors* (New York: Farrar, Straus, 1948); *Return to Black America* (Englewood Cliffs, NJ: Prentice-Hall, 1970); *South Street* (New York: Farrar, Straus and Young, 1954); *The Stone Face* (New York: Farrar, Straus, 1963).

Alex Feerst

Smitherman, Geneva (born 1940). Linguist and educator, language-policy expert, and language consultant. Geneva Smitherman is a University Distinguished Professor of English and Director of the African American Literacy Program at Michigan State University. Educated in the **Detroit, Michigan**, public school system, she completed her B.A. and M.A. degrees in English and Latin at Wayne State University. She received her Ph.D. in English from the University of Michigan. An expert on Black English, language policy, education, and culture, Smitherman is the author or editor of fourteen books, forty-six chapters in books, sixty journal articles, seven book reviews, and numerous abstracts in academic journals.

One of her major publications is *Black English and the Education of Black Children and Youth*. It consists of the proceedings of a national symposium Smitherman convened in 1980 at Wayne State University. She was the principal expert witness and consultant on Black English for the parents and children in the court case *Martin Luther King Jr. Elementary School Children v. Ann Arbor School District Board*. The case became known as the "Black English" federal court case.

Some of Smitherman's other major works on Black English and education include *Talkin' and Testifyin': The Language of Black America* (1977), *Talkin' That Talk: Language, Culture and Education in African America* (2000); *Black Linguistics: Language, Society and Politics in Africa and the Americas* (2003); and *Language Diversity in the Classroom: From Intention to Practice* (2003).

Smitherman has held visiting professorships at Pennsylvania State's summer seminar in theory and culture (June 1994) and the Institute for African Studies, University of Ghana-Legon (1980), among others. She has conducted numerous workshops on Black English and language policy issues in Ghana, England, France, and West Germany. She has lectured on Black English at hundreds of colleges and universities throughout the world. As a linguist and Black language expert, Smitherman has received numerous awards for her works. Among them are the 2001 National Council of Teachers of English David H. Russell Research Award for *Talkin That Talk* and the 2000 Michigan State University Distinguished Faculty Award.

In addition to her distinguished professorship, Smitherman is currently the Director of My Brother's Keeper, a male mentoring program in the Detroit public schools. She is also a mentor of the Executive Committee of the Doctoral Program in African American Studies at Michigan State University. Since 1999, Smitherman has been engaged in faculty-mentoring in language education research, in partnership with the Department of English, North-West-Mmabatho, South Africa. She is also completing a monograph on language issues, titled *The Linguistic Democratization of South Africa*, and an autobiographical project, *Memoirs from a Daughter of the Hood*. (*See* **Slang**; **Vernacular**.)

Resources: Geneva Smitherman: *Black Language and Culture: Sounds of Soul* (New York: Harper & Row, 1975); "Ebonics, King, and Oakland: Some Folk Don't Believe Fat Meat Is Greasy," *Journal of English Linguistics*, spec. iss. on Ebonics (June 1998); *Talkin' and Testifyin': The Language of Black America* (Boston: Houghton Mifflin, 1977); *Talkin That Talk: Language, Culture and Education in African America* (New York: Routledge, 2000); "Toward a National Public Policy on Language," in *The Skin That We Speak*, ed. Lisa Delpit and Joanne Dowdy (New York: New Press, 2002); Geneva Smitherman, ed.: *Black English and the Education of Black Children and Youth: Proceedings of the National Invitational Symposium on the King Decision* (Detroit: Center for Black Studies, Wayne State University, 1981); Geneva Smitherman, David Kirkland, and Austin Jackson, "Leroy, Big D, and Big Daddy Speak in Ebonics on the Internet," *American Language Review*, Mar./Apr. 2001, 22–26; Geneva Smitherman, Sinfree Makoni, Arnetha Ball, and Arthur Spears, eds., *Black Linguistics: Language, Society and Politics in Africa and the Americas* (New York: Routledge, 2003); Geneva Smitherman and Victor Villanueva, eds., *Language Diversity in the Classroom: From Intention to Practice* (Carbondale: Southern Illinois University Press, 2003).

Ella Davis

Snoe, Eboni (born 1955). Writer of **romance novels**. Snoe was born Gwyn Ferris Williams in Gary, Indiana. She attended Fisk University in **Nashville, Tennessee,** for one year, then worked as a radio personality in **Memphis, Tennessee,** during the early 1980s, at which time she attempted to publish her first novel, *Sheik's Spell*. She was not immediately successful in placing the book, but by the early 1990s, she began to make her mark in the genre of romance writing. It was at this point that the pseudonym Eboni Snoe was created. The name is meant to symbolize her desire to create work that addresses people of color. In addition, she chose to use Snoe to represent the concept that love is universal rather than determined by racial or cultural criteria. The name Eboni Snoe, she has said, puts "the ends of the entire racial color spectrum side by side" (Web site). Snoe is considered a pioneer in the genre of ethnic romance. She has observed, "I want a reader to read my stories and enjoy them, be swept away within them, but I would also love for them to finish my books and think, *Is there any truth to this?* ... there is a consistent thread throughout every Eboni Snoe novel ... the grand possibilities of life, of existence. I'm not talking about evil things, or dark things, but glorious things that can fill us with joy and awe at being a human being, a part of creation, a part of the Creator" (Web site).

Resources: Eboni Snoe: *Beguiled* (Washington, DC: BET Books/Arabesque, 2000); *A Chance on Lovin' You* (Washington, DC: BET Books/Arabesque, 1999); *A Diamond's Allure* (Washington, DC: BET Books/Arabesque, 2003); *Emerald's Fire* (1997; repr. Washington, DC: BET/Arabesque, 2001); *Followin' a Dream* (Washington, DC: BET Books/Arabesque, 2001); *More Than You Know* (Washington, DC: BET Books/

Arabesque, 2004); *The Passion Ruby* (1995; repr. Washington, DC: BET/Arabesque, 2000); *Sheik's Spell* (Grass Valley, CA: Odyssey Books, 1992); *Tell Me I'm Dreamin'* (Washington, DC: BET Books/Arabesque, 1998); *The Ties That Bind* (Washington, DC: BET Books/Arabesque, 2002); Web site, www.ebonisnoe.com; *When Everything's Said and Done* (Washington, DC: BET Books/Arabesque, 2004); *Wishin' on a Star* (New York: Avon, 2000); Eboni Snoe, Sandra Kitt, and Francis Ray, *First Touch* (Washington, DC: BET Books/Arabesque, 2004).

Valerie Lynn Guyant

Sonnet. A highly structured poetic form originating in Italy and spreading throughout western Europe by the seventeenth century, the sonnet contains fourteen lines of regular length and meter and follows one of two rhyming patterns: (1) the Italian, or Petrarchan, sonnet, which consists of a set of eight lines (octet), rhymed *abbaabba*, followed by six lines (sestet) that are usually rhymed *cdecde* or *cdcdcd*; and (2) the English, or Shakespearean, sonnet, which presents three units of four lines each (quatrains) followed by a two-line closing (couplet), rhyming *ababcdcdefefgg*. The sonnet was a popular form among African American poets writing in the first half of the twentieth century. The earliest innovations to the sonnet by Black poets were largely focused on content; the sonnet form itself only gradually became the focus of experimentation and innovation. By the 1960s, however, the sonnet had been largely abandoned in favor of free verse and poetic forms more closely tied to African American **vernacular** traditions.

The sonnets written by African American poets in the opening decades of the twentieth century offer little evidence of formal experimentation or innovation. These sonnets closely follow the conventions set by their European models. **James Weldon Johnson** and **Paul Laurence Dunbar**, both at least as famous today for their **dialect poetry** as for their **formal verse**, adopt highly conventional diction and grammatical constructions in their sonnets. Dunbar's sonnet "Douglass" (1903) is addressed to the famous activist and **slave narrative** author **Frederick Douglass** and begins by stating that "we have fall'n on evil days/Such days as thou, not even thou didst know." Similarly, Johnson's "My City" (1923) recasts standard word order to fit the formal constraints of the sonnet when the speaker asks what he will miss most when dead: "Will it be that no more I shall see the trees?" Other examples of sonnets by African American poets in the early 1900s include **Alice Moore Dunbar Nelson**'s "Violets" (1917) and **William Stanley Braithwaite**'s sonnet series in *The House of Falling Leaves* (1908). **Joseph Seamon Cotter, Jr.**'s "Sonnet to Negro Soldiers" (1918) foresees the importance of the experiences of Black soldiers in **World War I** to the development of a new **race** consciousness in the 1920s: "from their trembling lips shall swell/A song of hope the world can understand."

The sonnet form was popular and widely employed among poets of the **Harlem Renaissance**, in part because the sonnet was well suited to reflect the refined language and sentiments these artists sought to convey to their

White readers. Examples of sonnets from the Harlem Renaissance include some of the best-known poems by **Countee Cullen** ("Yet Do I Marvel," "From the Dark Tower," and "To France"), **Helene Johnson** ("Sonnet to a Negro in Harlem," "Remember Not," and "Invocation"), Alice Moore Dunbar-Nelson ("Sonnet"), and **Claude McKay** ("Harlem Dancer," "The White House," and "If We Must Die"). James Smethurst has argued that with the exception of pieces by **Langston Hughes** in *Shakespeare in Harlem* (1942) and **Sterling A. Brown** in *Southern Road* (1932), the sonnets of the Harlem Renaissance poets are marked by formal conservatism, particularly when contrasted with those written by White modernists such as e.e. cummings and Wallace Stevens; nearly all of the sonnets written by Harlem Renaissance poets make use of exact and traditional end rhyme and are conservative in word choice, punctuation, and typography even as they concern contemporary issues confronting African Americans, as in the poems by McKay, Cullen, and Johnson noted above. Hughes's most conventional sonnet is arguably "Search," published in **Opportunity** in 1937 (Ostrom, 346).

By the 1940s, the sonnet form itself became the focus of experimentation and innovation. **Margaret Abigail Walker**'s *For My People* (1942) closes with what Smethurst has characterized as six sonnets whose very literariness problematizes their documentary purpose. Similarly, **Melvin B. Tolson**'s "A Legend of Versailles" (1944) presents highly politicized content alongside innovative rhymes. Finally, **Gwendolyn Brooks**'s *A Street in Bronzeville* (1945) closes with a sequence of twelve off-rhyme Italian and English sonnets on the realities of **World War II**, continuing the trend toward both new content and formal innovation.

Sonnets demonstrating both a commitment to tradition and a desire to innovate in both form and content have been produced by a few prominent writers in the latter half of the twentieth century. Examples include **Robert Hayden**'s learned sonnets "Those Winter Sundays" and "Frederick Douglass" (1962), Margaret Abigail Walker's elegiac "For Malcolm X" in *Prophets for a New Day* (1970), **Michael S. Harper**'s "Br'er Sterling and the Rocker" (1973), and **Rita Dove**'s mythologically inspired pieces such as "Persephone Abducted" and "Demeter Mourning," from *Mother Love: Poems* (1995).

Overall, however, the sonnet form has fallen out of favor among African American poets since the 1950s. In "Blueprint for Negro Writing" (1937), **Richard Wright** disparaged the writers of the Harlem Renaissance as compromised artists, and exhorted Black artists to create a new Black consciousness that was more emphatically urban, proletarian, and socially conscious. Wright thus implicitly rejected the elite and mannered form of the sonnet in favor of popular Black traditions, including the **sermon** and the folkloric **ballad** (such as those of **John Henry** and other Black folk heroes). These sentiments found widespread support in the **Black Arts Movement** of the 1960s and early 1970s, which pushed for poetry that was politically engaged and closely linked to African American vernacular traditions, including sermons and popular music.

Resources: William Stanley Braithwaite, *The House of Falling Leaves* (Boston: J. W. Luce, 1908); Gwendolyn Brooks, *A Street in Bronzeville* (New York: Harper & Brothers, 1945); Sterling Brown, *Southern Road* (New York: Harcourt, Brace, 1932); Joseph Seamon Cotter, Jr., *Complete Poems*, ed. James Robert Payne (Athens: University of Georgia Press, 1990); Countee Cullen, *On These I Stand* (New York: Harper & Brothers, 1947); Rita Dove, *Mother Love: Poems* (New York: Norton, 1995); Robert Hayden, *A Ballad of Remembrance* (London: Paul Breman, 1962); Langston Hughes, *Shakespeare in Harlem* (New York: Knopf, 1942); David Levering Lewis, ed., *The Portable Harlem Renaissance Reader* (New York: Viking, 1994) (contains poems by Brown, Cullen, Johnson, McKay); Hans Ostrom, *A Langston Hughes Encyclopedia* (Westport, CT: Greenwood Press, 2002); James Smethurst, *The New Red Negro: The Literary Left and African American Poetry, 1930–1946* (New York: Oxford University Press, 1999); Margaret Walker: *For My People* (New Haven, CT: Yale University Press, 1942); *Prophets for a New Day* (Detroit: Broadside Press, 1970); Richard Wright, "Blueprint for Negro Writing," in *The Portable Harlem Renaissance Reader*, ed. David Levering Lewis (New York: Viking, 1994), 194–205.

James B. Kelley

Soul. Since its inception, the concept of "soul" has referred to the spiritual, animating, and vital nature of humans. It was not part of the material world, but it was credited with the faculties of thought, action, and emotion, so that it could describe a person's emotional or moral nature or a strong, deeply felt emotion conveyed by a speaker, a performer, or an artist. Recently it has come to signify a sense of ethnic pride among Black people and especially African Americans, expressed in areas such as language, social customs, religion, and especially a style of music.

As a musical term, "soul music" is a blend of **blues**, **gospel music**, and rhythm and blues. It is composed of equal parts of the call-and-response of slave-era field hollers, the fervor of the Black Baptist church, and the blues of Southern African Americans. It is no surprise that the roots are religious to some extent. This gives soul some of its distictive features, such as the communal sense, its emotional tone, and the choral melody.

The movement from the religious idea of soul to a more secularized one was no doubt begun by music, but the turning point arguably came during the 1960s, when Motown, owned by Berry Gordy, recorded impressive hits by groups such as The Temptations, The Supremes, and The Four Tops. It was the first large African American record company, and it was established because, with a few exceptions, African Americans could not record their own music. Motown was part of the early impulse of Black pride.

If Blues was the music of the late nineteenth and early twentieth centuries, soul was the music for an urbanized African American population who lived mostly in cities such as **Detroit, Michigan**. It represented the move from rural to urban contexts. It was the medium to communicate young people's new experiences. It gave voice to the interests and hopes of a new generation that would come of age in the 1960s. Other artists of soul music include Wilson Pickett, Percy Sledge, and Aretha Franklin.

Yet the term "soul" never lost its religious sense. It has been present in African American literature from **sermons** and **spirituals** to **essays** and **novels**, and it has pointed to Black pride in a more or less overt fashion. *The Souls of Black Folk* (1903) by **W.E.B. Du Bois** is one of the most prominent examples. It is a collection of fourteen pieces in which Du Bois analyzes the psychological factors of African Americans both in their selves and in their relationship to White American society. For Du Bois the soul of the African Americans was their culture as expressed in their distinctive artistic practices, traditions, and communal values. These had to be recognized and conserved by American society.

Diana Ross with the president of Motown Records, Berry Gordy, in 1971. The man in the middle is unidentified. © Bettmann/Corbis.

As a consequence of the existing racism, Du Bois commented on "the color line": "The problem of the Twentieth Century is the problem of the color-line." He invented the term "double-consciousness" to refer to the dualities in African American self-perception. It must be noted that this perception is both individual and collective, and is the result of the hundreds of years of oppresssion that African Americans have suffered. Black Americans find it difficult to identify themselves, yet at the same time they realize that they are Africans and Americans and that their identities can be merged into a unity. The beginning and the end of the volume deal with the spiritual possibilities of Black America through its culture and folk music, anticipating the proliferation of blues music and the popularity of soul music.

Eldridge Cleaver's nonfiction book *Soul on Ice* (1967) is another important work on the issue. In 1957 he was imprisoned, and while in prison he affiliated with the Black Muslims and became a follower of **Malcolm X**. *Soul on Ice* deals with **race** and **gender** relations in American culture. It is also an articulation of African American nationalism of the 1960s, showing the force of the liberationist spirit of the time through autobiographical accounts, personal letters, and sociopolitical essays.

The pride in Black culture has been present ever since in African American culture, though most of the times it has been an underground feeling that could not move into the open for political and social reasons. It was in the 1960s that this pride rose to the surface with the **Black Arts Movement**. The **Civil Rights Movement** had already advocated for the dignity of African

Americans, but it was the Black Arts Movement that was closer to the concept of soul as an interaction between performers and audience, between the soloist and the choir (as in gospel choirs). Moreover, the traditions of Black popular culture were immensely influential in the movement. Poetry readings thrust it back to its oral origins and communal context. It was an experience in which readers and audiences could share deeply felt emotions, could feel parts of a single unity.

In 1964, **Amiri Baraka** organized In/Formation. The group included artists from the **Umbra Workshop**, painters such as Joe Overstreet, and the pianist Andrew Hill. They gave poetry readings and played jazz at St. Marks Playhouse. In 1965 they moved uptown to **Harlem, New York**, and established the **Black Arts Repertory Theatre/School**. The Black Arts Theatre was a conscious attempt to do art within an African American community, using the artistic and spiritual resources of this community. The Black Arts gave African Americans a new access to art, in which freedom and a new political awareness were fundamental concepts. The Black Arts supported Black nationalist ideas, looked back at African **folklore** practices, and called for an interactive relationship between the the performer and the audience. It was a "soulful" art that was communicated as directly and as easily as music was. It contained the expressions of the soul of African Americans, partly because it was produced from within the Black community. Through the Black Arts there arose a new sense of community and a new awareness of Black traditions and legacy at the same time that it took a political stance.

"Soul," then, may refer to a kind of music and the attributes of a musical performer, performance, or audience. It can also connote pride in African American culture, and it can refer to the spiritual essence of a person or of a people. In African American literature, it can be used to describe an essential or authentic quality in the literature, a quality that "rings true."

Resources: Houston A. Baker, *Afro-American Poetics: Revisions of Harlem and the Black Aesthetic* (Madison: University of Wisconsin Press, 1988); Gina Dent, *Black Popular Culture* (Seattle, WA: Bay Press, 1992); Nelson George, *Post-Soul Nation* (New York: Viking, 2004); Errol Hill, ed., *The Theater of Black Americans: A Collection of Critical Essays* (New York: Applause, 1987); David L. Lewis, *W.E.B. Du Bois: Biography of a Race*, vol. 1, *1868–1919* (New York: Holt, 1993); Bob Merlis and Davin Seay, *Heart & Soul: A Celebration of Black Music Style in America, 1930–1975* (New York: Billboard Books, 2002); Arnold Rampersad, *The Art and Imagination of W.E.B. Du Bois* (Cambridge, MA: Harvard University Press, 1976); Elliott M. Rudwick, *W.E.B. Du Bois, Voice of the Black Protest Movement* (Urbana: University of Illinois Press, 1982); Lorenzo Thomas, *Extraordinary Measures: Afrocentric Modernism and Twentieth-Century American Poetry* (Tuscaloosa: University of Alabama Press, 2000).

Santiago Rodríguez Guerrero-Strachan

South, The. Region of the United States. The idea of the South and Southern identity has a lot to do with how the region's inhabitants express their Southernness. African Americans participated in the making of the South's economy, society, and culture because historically the identity of the South hinged on the prevalence of chattel **slavery**. Southern literature and African American literature are inextricably linked with the region's social history. Initially, African Americans recorded their Southern experiences in **slave narratives**, early **novels**, and even poetry. **Frederick Douglass, Harriet Ann Jacobs, William Wells Brown**, and **George Moses Horton** all hailed from various parts of the South, and their experiences were just as different as the regional landscape. *A Voice from the South* (1892), early essayist and educator **Anna Julia Haywood Cooper**'s critique of the region, challenges perceptions of an all "white South" from the perspective of the Black woman, an unexpected spokesperson. In their fiction and nonfiction works, **Frances Ellen Wilkins Harper** and **Charles Waddell Chesnutt** successfully presented Blacks' struggle with problems in the South and set the stage for writers such as **Richard Wright, Zora Neale Hurston, Margaret Abigail Walker, Sterling A. Brown, Alice Walker**, and **Ernest James Gaines**. For many Black writers, a Southern sense of place influenced their works. **Langston Hughes**, a Midwesterner by birth and longtime resident of **Harlem, New York**, nonetheless set much of his work in the South, including the powerful short stories "Home" and "Father and Son." One of the most powerful novels to come out of the **Harlem Renaissance**—*Cane*, by **Jean Toomer**—is set partly in Georgia and evokes a distinctive, even exotic, African American culture of the South. Either in celebration of or to condemn their connections with the region, Black Southern writers' bittersweet relationship with the South is a hallmark of the literature.

On a map of the continental United States, the entire southeast region may be labeled "the South." It is outlined by rivers and large bodies of water: from the Gulf of Mexico north to the Potomac and Ohio rivers; the Atlantic Ocean is its eastern boundary. This section includes South Carolina, Mississippi, Louisiana, Florida, Georgia, Alabama, **Texas**, Arkansas, Virginia, Tennessee, and North Carolina—eleven of the Confederate states that seceded from the Union in 1860–1861 sparking the beginning of the **Civil War**. To this group Maryland, Delaware, Kentucky, Missouri, **Oklahoma**, and West Virginia are often added as the "border states" of the American South. The Mason-Dixon Line, a legendary symbol of regional distinction, determined the boundary between slave and free territories during the nineteenth century as well as other federal decrees to balance states' rights. De facto segregation in the South would also be determined in the twentieth century by this same imaginary line. However, despite emphasis on cultural distinctions—everything from language patterns and cuisine to religious dogma and politics—the geographical specificity of the American South remains unclear.

Today some individuals are reluctant, for instance, to claim all of Texas or southern Florida as parts of the South, but instead recognize only eastern Texas and northern Florida. These and other marginal areas are singled out due to their distance from the epicenter of the region, the "Deep South," which is the iconic representation of all things stereotypically Southern. (This section includes parts of Louisiana, Mississippi, Alabama, Georgia, and South Carolina.) Liberal estimations divide the region into "many Souths" or sub-regions characterized by specific geographical features (e.g., the Appalachian Mountains) or cultural elements (e.g., Louisiana's exotic Creoles and Cajun country). John Shelton Reed, a Southern sociologist, draws from a specific historical reference to characterize modern features of the region that persist. Statistical data show that agriculture, racial populations, poverty, illiteracy rates, and even **gender** roles distinguish the South as much as its geographical traits did during the days of the Confederacy. Thus, Reed takes a humorous approach to defining the region: "If we can use distinctive cultural attributes to find Southerners, then we can say the South is where they are found" (Reed, 6).

Resources: John B. Boles, *Black Southerners: 1619–1869* (Lexington: University Press of Kentucky, 1983); Trudier Harris-Lopez, *South of Tradition: Essays on African American Literature* (Athens: University of Georgia Press, 2002); John Oliver Killens and Jerry W. Ward, Jr., eds., *Black Southern Voices: An Anthology of Fiction, Poetry, Drama, Nonfiction, and Critical Essays* (New York: Meridian, 1992); John Shelton Reed, "The South: What Is It? Where Is It?" in his *My Tears Spoiled My Aim and Other Reflections on Southern Culture* (Columbia: University of Missouri Press, 1993), 5–28; Anissa Janine Ward, *Death and the Arc of African American Literature* (Gainesville: University Press of Florida, 2003).

Sherita L. Johnson

Southerland, Ellease (born 1943). Poet, novelist, essayist, and educator. Ellease Southerland (also known as Ebele N. Oseye) was born into a large family in **Brooklyn, New York**, and grew up in Queens, New York. Her earliest literary recognition came in the form of the Golden Award "for literary promise," which she received from Queens College during her junior year. Southerland earned a B.A. from Queens College (1965), and worked for the New York City Department of Social Services until 1971. She received an M.F.A. from Columbia University in 1974. Since the early 1970s, her poetry has been published in magazines including *Poet Lore, Soundings,* **Journal of Black Poetry** (selected by **Askia Touré** for inclusion in number 13 and by **Dudley Randall** for number 15) and *Black World*. Her first poetry collection, *The Magic Sun Spins* (1975), was published in the Heritage Series of Black Poetry. **Audre Lorde**, who also published a poetry collection in that series, expressed early admiration for Southerland's writing, and Lorde's writing was a source of inspiration to Southerland in her teaching. Southerland writes: "I would like for my poetry which is heavily rooted in ancient literature to inspire joy and deep appreciation for life." She also aims to capture her excitement at "the poetry I hear in daily speech." Southerland received the Gwendolyn Brooks Award for poetry in 1972.

The style of Southerland's fiction displays the gift of lyric compression which characterizes her poetry. Her first novel was *Let the Lion Eat Straw* (1979). The novel traces the life of Abeba Williams, abandoned in **the South** by her mother, who has gone to seek better opportunities in the North. Abeba develops an important relationship with Mamma Habblesham until her mother returns to take her to Brooklyn. A gifted pianist, Abeba falls in love with a singer named Daniel Torch and becomes consumed with the challenges of marriage and motherhood. The New York Public Libraries voted *Let the Lion Eat Straw* both a Notable Book and a title in the Black Heritage Series. In her second novel, *A Feast of Fools* (1998), the story of the Torch family continues and is expanded through the voice of Abeba's eldest daughter, Kora Ada. Kora Ada's relationship with Ibe Ikenna moves the story from Brooklyn to Nigeria and into the wider context of extended family.

Southerland officially took the name Ellease Ebele Noxolo Oseye in 1996, at which point her work became more richly imbued with African cultural and religious symbolism, philosophy, and nature. Her many visits to Nigeria, beginning in 1971, are vividly recounted in her memoir *This Year in Nigeria* (2001). During a trip to Nigeria in 1998, where she read from *A Feast of Fools*, she was made a fellow of the University of Nigeria at Nsukka. A diary of her first trip to Nigeria (1971) appeared as "Seventeen Days in Nigeria" in *Black World* (January 1972). Southerland is Professor of African Literature and Creative Writing at Pace University. Her awards include being voted Woman of the Year by the Delta Beta Zeta chapter of the Zeta Phi Beta sorority in honor of her essays on **Zora Neale Hurston** (2002). She has also received the Ankh Award (2002), the NAACP Image Award (2003), and a Citation of Honor for Literary Achievement from Claire Schulman, Borough President of Queens (1990).

Southerland/Oseye is a gifted writer in multiple genres who reflects her diasporic identity as an African American woman, joined with full consciousness of her African roots and their role as a source of emotional and artistic sustenance.

Resources: Ebele Oseye: *A Feast of Fools* (New York: Africana Legacy Press, 1998); *Let the Lion Eat Straw* (1979; repr. New York: Amistad, 2004); *Opening Line: The Creative Writer* (Jamaica, NY: Eneke, 2000); *This Year in Nigeria: A Memoir* (Jamaica, NY: Eneke, 2001); Ellease Southerland: "Egyptian Symbols and Contemporary Black Literature," *Black Scholar* 19, nos. 4–5 (1988), 13–17; *The Magic Sun Spins* (London: Paul Breman, 1975).

Lauri Ramey

Southern Studies. Academic discipline. Southern Studies take a multidisciplinary approach to understanding the culture and society of the American South as a geographical place and theoretical entity. It covers political movements and recognizes religious practices as well as speech and language patterns in **the South** that contribute to its regional identity. It includes the study of the people of the South, African Americans among them, as well as the products of people from the South, including literature, music, food, visual art, and **folklore**. One aspect of Southern Studies involves not only identifying the inhabitants but also examining their relationship to the land and their values, customs, and beliefs in order to give account of their experiences of being Southern. As an academic specialty, Southern Studies is a popular field that has generated an abundance of scholarship. One aim of the scholarship is to try to demystify the South while explaining America's preoccupation with the region. For scholars, students, and the general public, colleges and universities throughout the South have established centers for Southern Studies to preserve and promote the study of the region's history, life, and culture.

The South is perhaps the most distinctive region in the United States with its unique history of independence. Before the **Civil War**, its slave-based economy allowed the region to be prosperous and almost self-sufficient though the practice antagonized antislavery proponents in the North. The battle for the Confederacy, the rebel government formed by Southern states at the start of the Civil War, was one waged for states' rights separate from federal rule and, by and large, for the preservation of their economic base and, therefore, the continuation of **slavery**. Though the South lost the war, the quest for sovereignty remained a part of the Southern White ethos. For generations of many White Southerners, an undefeated spirit fueled the belief in a glorious, if mythic, agrarian past and created a sense of pride. Today, this is commonly known as "ancestral worship," and it overlooks the plight of African American slaves. During the late nineteenth century, the increase of national literary interests in regional culture commodified Southern writers. Ironically, while the South's literature was in vogue, its political affairs and hostile social atmosphere became infamous. After the brief **Reconstruction** (1865–1877), the South reinstated a new caste system (i.e., legal slavery was replaced by legal segregation, such as Jim Crow Laws, and unfair labor practices) that continued the oppression of African Americans until the middle of the twentieth century.

Throughout the South's complicated history, African Americans have made important contributions to the South and Southern Studies. From the Old South to the New South, during the Southern Literary Renaissance (1920s–1950s) and the contemporary period, African Americans actively participated in the making of the region at each epoch and challenged the mythic iconography of the South. As early as 1880, **William Wells Brown** surveyed the region in his My *Southern Home*, and in 1892 **Anna Julia Haywood Cooper**'s feminist manifesto A *Voice from the South* alerted the public to the **gender** and **race** discrimination regularly faced by Black women, especially in the South. The leadership of **Booker T. Washington** at Tuskegee Institute and nationwide provided one paradigm for successful African American citizenship and economic advancement. The fiction of **Charles Waddell Chestnutt** exposes the sociological conditions of the region during the late nineteenth century. When hundreds of thousands of African Americans migrated to the North, many retained their Southern cultural roots and planted them in urban areas, bringing the range of Southern Studies into a national focus. The works of **Richard Wright** reflect this transitioning. Considering the strong historical presence of African Americans in the South, Black cultural critic Thadious

Davis challenges the way the South (as a region and culture) still remained "White" in America's imagination. Based on the social order established during slavery, "whites in the South became simply 'Southerners' without a racial designation, but blacks in the South became simply 'blacks' without a regional distinction" ("Expanding the Limits," 4). Fortunately, the contemporary focus of Southern Studies acknowledges such discrepancies and denial of the past, and often attempts to identify the shared experience of being Southern regardless of race, gender, and/or sexual orientation, among numerous other factors.

One problem with examining the American South has always been a matter of inclusion, and defining *the* South is virtually impossible. The false, romantic picture of the antebellum South which prevailed in America's imagination since the mid-nineteenth century did not adequately represent or often even include a wide range of environments, diverse populations, and social relations that have always existed in the South. Popular images of plantations, a White aristocracy, and slavery are, of course, inadequate for defining the South. For instance, mostly small homesteads and a class of yeoman farmers populated the region while an elite few owned sprawling estates. Compared with White males (particularly those with property), women (of any race) and minorities were placed on the lowest levels of the patriarchal hierarchy established during slavery and upheld by law and regional customs for generations in the South. Scholars of Southern Studies point out, then, that until recently, regional history has been biased toward those of inherited economic, social, and ethnic privilege.

In recent years, one goal of Southern Studies has been to redefine the South by recovering archival materials and reinterpreting the historical development of the region. The monolithic "South" collapses when scrutinized by scholars working with such archival material and from a revisionist point of view. Their work closely examines common features of the region to understand the connection between the actual South and the *idea* of the South. Generally, the goal is to dismiss the myth altogether. Many critics launch investigations into legal definitions of race, class, and gender; who advanced these definitions; and who had a stake in maintaining them. Some scholars focus on how the law was used to regulate social relations that threatened notions of White supremacy. From the colonial period to the twentieth century, for instance, historians offer new evidence about the structure of Southern society that reveals how women and Blacks (enslaved and free) were actively involved in building communities and asserting their identities to define their status within these places. In Southern literary studies, women and minorities are valued for their contributions to regionalist writing more than ever before. Michael Kreyling, **William L. Andrews**, Patricia Yaeger, **Trudier Harris**, and Anne Goodwyn Jones are just a few literary critics who have invigorated Southern Studies with their scholarship.

Resources: William L. Andrews, Minrose C. Gwin, Trudier Harris, and Fred Hobson, eds., *The Literature of the American South* (New York: Norton, 1998); John

Blassingame, *Black New Orleans 1860–1880* (Chicago: University of Chicago Press, 1973); John B. Boles: *Black Southerners: 1619–1869* (Lexington: University Press of Kentucky, 1983); *The South Through Time: A History of an American Region* (Englewood Cliffs, NJ: Prentice-Hall, 1995); George Washington Cable, *The Negro Question: A Selection of Writings on Civil Rights in the South*, ed. Arlin Turner (New York: Norton, 1968); W. J. Cash, *The Mind of the South* (New York: Knopf, 1941); Dudley Clendinen, ed., *The Prevailing South: Life and Politics in a Changing Culture* (Atlanta: Longstreet Press, 1988); Anna Julia Cooper, *A Voice from the South by a Black Woman of the South* (1892; repr. New York: Oxford University Press, 1988); Allison Davis et al., *Deep South: A Social Anthropological Study of Caste and Class* (Chicago: University of Chicago Press, 1941); Thadious M. Davis, "Expanding the Limits: The Intersection of Race and Region," *Southern Literary Journal* 20 (1988), 3–11; Joe P. Dunn and Howard L. Preston, eds., *The Future South: A Historical Perspective for the Twenty-first Century* (Urbana: University of Illinois Press, 1991); Joseph M. Flora and Lucinda H. MacKethan, eds., *The Companion to Southern Literature: Themes, Genres, Places, People, Movements, and Motifs* (Baton Rouge: Louisiana State University Press, 2002); Eric Foner, *Reconstruction: America's Unfinished Revolution, 1863–1877* (New York: Harper & Row, 1988); Jimmie Lewis Franklin, "Black Southerners, Shared Experience, and Place: A Reflection," *Journal of Southern History*, Feb. 1994, 3–18; Glenda Elizabeth Gilmore, *Gender and Jim Crow: Women and the Politics of White Supremacy in North Carolina, 1896–1920* (Chapel Hill: University of North Carolina Press, 1996); Richard Gray, *Southern Aberrations: Writers of the American South and the Problem of Regionalism* (Baton Rouge: Louisiana State University Press, 2000); Larry J. Griffin and Don H. Doyle, eds., *The South as an American Problem* (Athens: University of Georgia Press, 1995); Gwendolyn M. Hall, *Africans in Colonial Louisiana: The Development of Afro-Creole Culture in the Eighteenth Century* (Baton Rouge: Louisiana State University Press, 1992); Jefferson Humphries, ed., *Southern Literature and Literary Theory* (Athens: University of Georgia Press, 1990); Tera W. Hunter, *To 'Joy My Freedom: Southern Black Women's Lives and Labors After the Civil War* (Cambridge, MA: Harvard University Press, 1997); *I'll Take My Stand: The South and the Agrarian Tradition*, by twelve Southerners (New York: Harper & Brothers, 1930); Anne Goodwyn Jones, *Tomorrow Is Another Day: The Woman Writer in the South, 1859–1936* (Baton Rouge: Louisiana State University Press, 1981); Anne Goodwyn Jones and Susan V. Donaldson, eds., *Haunted Bodies: Gender and Southern Texts* (Charlottesville: University Press of Virginia, 1997); John Oliver Killens and Jerry W. Ward, Jr., eds., *Black Southern Voices: An Anthology of Fiction, Poetry, Drama, Nonfiction, and Critical Essays* (New York: Meridian, 1992); Jack Temple Kirby, *Media-Made Dixie: The South in the American Imagination*, rev. ed. (Athens: University of Georgia Press, 1986); Michael Kreyling, *Inventing Southern Literature* (Jackson: University Press of Mississippi, 1998); Carol S. Manning, ed., *The Female Tradition in Southern Literature* (Urbana: University of Illinois Press, 1993); H. L. Mencken, "Sahara of the Bozart," in his *Prejudices, Second Series* (New York: Knopf, 1920); Ladell Payne, *Black Novelists and the Southern Literary Tradition* (Athens: University of Georgia Press, 1981); John Shelton Reed, *One South: An Ethnic Approach to Regional Culture* (Baton Rouge: Louisiana State University Press, 1982); Louis D. Rubin, Jr., ed., *The History of*

Southern Literature (Baton Rouge: Louisiana State University Press, 1985); Anne Firor Scott, *The Southern Lady: From Pedestal to Politics, 1830–1930* (Chicago: University of Chicago Press, 1970); Charles Grier Sellers, ed., *The Southerner as American* (Chapel Hill: University of North Carolina Press, 1960); Carol Stack, *Call to Home: African Americans Reclaim the Rural South* (New York: Basic Books, 1996); C. Vann Woodward: *The Burden of Southern History*, 3rd ed. (Baton Rouge: Louisiana State University Press, 1993); *Origins of the New South, 1877–1913* (Baton Rouge: Louisiana State University Press, 1951); Patricia Yaeger, *Dirt and Desire: Reconstructing Southern Women's Writing, 1930–1990* (Chicago: University of Chicago Press, 2000).

Sherita L. Johnson

Spellman, A. B. (born 1935). Poet, **jazz** critic, and arts advocate. Raised in Elizabeth City, North Carolina, Alfred B. Spellman attended Howard University, where he studied literature with **Sterling A. Brown** and playwrighting with **Owen Dodson**. By 1958, he had earned a B.A. in political science, entered Howard's law school, and begun graduate studies in English, while haunting the cafés and jazz clubs in uptown New York City.

By 1959, Spellman had moved to New York, found a job at Ted and Eli Wilentz's Eighth Street Bookshop, and begun to gain local fame as an FM radio host. Cofounder of **Umbra Workshop** and coeditor of *Umbra* magazine, Spellman performed scores of poetry readings in cafés and nightclubs with poets such as **Amiri Baraka**, the **Beat** poets, and **Sun Ra**. By 1964, **Langston Hughes** had included two of Spellman's poems in *New Negro Poets, U.S.A.*, and *Monthly Review* had printed Spellman's interview with **Malcolm X**.

In 1965, the Poets Press published *The Beautiful Days*, a volume of short, finely wrought poems; intensely personal, at times erotic, only their compression and vivid concreteness hinted at Spellman's early influences—"Eliot, Lorca, and Rilke." His later influences—"[Amiri] Baraka, Oppenheimer, Olson, Williams, and Neruda"—may have inspired such a vulnerable, intimate voice (Spellman interview). Despite the ardent activism of Umbra, Spellman notes, "my . . . topical, political poems seldom succeed. I do best [laying] out my confusions and contradictions." (Ridley interview).

Spellman was poet-in-residence at Morehouse College in 1967. The following year, with Baraka and **Larry Neal**, he founded *Cricket*, a music journal based in the East Village of New York, affirming Black "artistic and national unity" (Neal, 38). In 1969, he organized the Center for Black Art in Atlanta and cofounded *Rhythm*, a journal similar to *Cricket*.

Three more of Spellman's poems appeared in *Black Fire* (1968). In 1972, three new poems, including "Did Coltrane's Music Kill Him?," appeared in *Understanding the New Black Poetry*.

Spellman is best known as a jazz critic, and his *Four Lives in the Bebop Business* (1966), which consists of critical biographies of Ornette Coleman, Herbie Nichols, Jackie McLean, and Cecil Taylor, appears in all major jazz bibliographies. By 1972, Spellman had written liner notes for eighty jazz LPs, including John Coltrane's *Ascension*. He also occasionally hosts radio and television programs of jazz music and conducts interviews for NPR and PBS.

Spellman accepted the Assistant Directorship of the National Endowment for the Arts' (NEA) Expansion Arts Program in 1975 and is currently Deputy Chairman of the NEA. As a result, he has little time to write poems. What remains constant is his commitment to "strong art" as a "function of social consciousness" (Brooks, 17). In *Four Lives*, he argues, "Jazz is the great American art, yet it is treated as a cultural stepchild," and he quotes Cecil Taylor's challenge, forty years ago, that "No Negro jazz musician has ever gotten a grant" (16, 40). Spellman's advocacy of American art forms through the NEA has helped promote and support the national treasure of America's jazz artists.

Resources: Imamu Amiri Baraka (LeRoi Jones) and Larry Neal, eds., *Black Fire: An Anthology of Afro-American Writing* (New York: Morrow, 1968); Bonnie Brooks, "Reflecting and Encouraging American Culture" (interview with A. B. Spellman), *Dance/USA Journal* 9, no. 3 (1992); Stephen Henderson, *Understanding the New Black Poetry* (New York: Morrow, 1973); Langston Hughes, ed., *New Negro Poets, U.S.A.* (Bloomington, Indiana University Press, 1964); Larry Neal, "New Grass/Albert Ayler," *Cricket* 4 (1969), 37–39; Chauncey Ridley, personal interview with A.B. Spellman, July 2004; A. B. Spellman: *The Beautiful Days* (New York: Poets Press, 1965); *Four Lives in the Bebop Business* (New York: Pantheon, 1966); "Interview with Malcolm X," *Monthly Review* 16, no. 1 (1964); A. B. Spellman, Ronald Stone, and Ebon, eds., *The Journal Rhythm* (Atlanta: Center for Black Art, 1970).

Chauncey Ridley

Spence, Eulalie (1894–1981). Playwright. Spence was born on the Caribbean island of Nevis on June 11, 1894, and in 1902 came to the United States, where she became a pioneer in African American theater. She wrote about a dozen one-act plays and had several plays produced, winning five awards for her plays in **The Crisis** and **Opportunity** contests, more than any other dramatist. Her credo is laid out clearly in her essay "A Criticism of the Negro Drama" (*Opportunity*, June 1928): "We go to the theatre for entertainment, not to have old fires and hates rekindled." However, while most of her plays were comedies, they often had serious undertones. As Yvonne Shafer observes, "Her works are shot through with the social issues surrounding her" (282). Many of Spence's plays, such as *The Starter* (1927) and *Undertow* (1927), are set in **Harlem, New York**, depicting ordinary people from there; her female characters in particular are forceful personalities.

Spence's play *Fool's Errand* was produced by **W.E.B. DuBois**'s Krigwa Players in 1927, shortly before being entered in the National Little Theatre Tournament, where it was presented at the Frolic Theatre, thus making Spence the first Black woman to have her work seen on Broadway. Her only full-length play, *The Whipping* (1932), was sold to Paramount Pictures but never released as a film. Spence, who received an M.A. in speech from Columbia University in 1939, taught English and elocution at Eastern District

High School in **Brooklyn, New York,** from 1927 to 1958. One of her students there was Joseph Papp, now a producer associated with the Public Theater. She died in Gettysburg, Pennsylvania, on March 7, 1981.

Resources: Elizabeth Brown-Guillory, ed., *Wines in the Wilderness: Plays by African American Women from the Harlem Renaissance to the Present* (Westport, CT: Greenwood Press, 1990); Jennifer Burton, ed., *Zora Neale Hurston, Eulalie Spence, Marita Bonner, and Others: The Prize Plays and Other One-Acts Published in Periodicals* (New York: G. K. Hall, 1996); Freda Scott Giles, "Willis Richardson and Eulalie Spence: Dramatic Voices of the Harlem Renaissance," *American Drama* 5 (Spring 1996), 1–22; Kathy A. Perkins, ed., *Black Female Playwrights: An Anthology of Plays before 1950* (Bloomington: Indiana University Press, 1989); Bernard L. Peterson, Jr., *Early Black American Playwrights and Dramatic Writers: A Biographical Directory and Catalog of Plays, Films, and Broadcasting Scripts* (Westport, CT: Greenwood Press, 1990); Lorraine Elena Roses and Ruth Elizabeth Randolph, *Harlem Renaissance and Beyond: Literary Biographies of 100 Black Women Writers, 1900–1945* (Boston: G. K. Hall, 1990); Yvonne Shafer, *American Women Playwrights, 1900–1950* (New York: Peter Lang, 1995).

Louis J. Parascandola

Spencer, Anne (1882–1975). Poet. Born Anne Bethel Scales, and raised in and around the state of Virginia, Spencer was a precocious child who demonstrated a fascination with the written word at an early age. Her parents, who in Spencer's words "could read reading, but couldn't read writing," encouraged her to develop a love for books and literature (Lee, 18). When Spencer was fourteen, her mother enrolled the young poet at the Virginia Seminary at Lynchburg. Here she began her first efforts at writing poetry, excelled in liberal arts studies, and, upon graduation in 1899, gave the valedictory address. It was also at the seminary that she met Edward Spencer, whom she married in 1901. Spencer would spend the next sixteen years raising her children, developing the garden at her home, and working on her poetry.

In 1918 Spencer met **James Weldon Johnson,** who remained her close associate until his death in 1938. This contact was essential in introducing Spencer to the literary world beyond Lynchburg. Upon reading Spencer's poems, Johnson praised her efforts and forwarded her work to noted critic H. L. Mencken, with whom Spencer briefly corresponded. Later, Johnson arranged the publication of Spencer's poems in *The Crisis* and his own anthology, *The Book of American Negro Poetry* (1922), in which Spencer received considerable praise.

Spencer's poetry displays a predilection for natural images and an emphasis on transcendent imagination similar to that of Gerard Manley Hopkins and Samuel Taylor Coleridge. "Before the Feast of Shushan," for example, Spencer's first published poem, recalls the monologues of Robert Browning and the exotic language of the Romantics. Other poems focus on the natural scenes found in the Spencer's magnificent garden. Work on the garden and home, coupled with the effects of segregation, made the Spencer household a frequent stopping place for many significant Black figures of the era. During the years when Spencer was most socially active, she and her husband hosted James Weldon Johnson, **W.E.B. Du Bois**, **Paul Robeson**, **Sterling A. Brown**, and many other notables. Spencer last published in 1931, though she maintained an active social life until the late 1930s. In the 1940s and later, Spencer was less active in literary circles, although in her position as librarian at Lynchburg's Paul Lawrence Dunbar High School, she maintained some local influence. Spencer died in a nursing facility in Lynchburg in 1975.

Though she was a popular writer during her era, Spencer has remained understudied. Some attribute this to the absence of explicitly racial subject matter in her work despite the Jazz Age's fascination with stylized racial imagery. Spencer claims that this was so because while she easily wrote poetry about the things she loved, she had "no civilized articulation for the things I hate" (Greene, 138). This lack of articulation has left Spencer outside of some critical perspectives. Nevertheless, her work is some of the most vibrant and engaging to be published during the **New Negro** era. Spencer's papers, including poems, biographical sketches, and correspondence, are kept at the Anne Spencer House and Garden Historic Landmark, Lynchburg, Virginia.

Resources: J. Lee Greene, *Time's Unchanging Garden: Anne Spencer's Life and Poetry* (Baton Rouge: Louisiana State University Press, 1977); James Weldon Johnson, ed., *The Book of American Negro Poetry* (1922; repr. New York: Harcourt, Brace, and World, 1958).

Dennis Chester

Spillers, Hortense J. (born 1942). Literary critic, cultural theorist, and professor. Spillers is one of the most innovative and challenging African American literary critics working in the U.S. academy today. Her groundbreaking essays and articles have openly but cautiously incorporated **poststructuralism**, psychoanalysis, and postcolonial critique into analysis of literary and social texts in the African **diaspora**. Students of African American literature and culture have benefited from the sheer inventiveness of Spillers's cross-disciplinary critical vision. Yet in light of the astounding breadth of her scholarship, Spillers remains grounded in feminist theory and criticism and, correlatively, defends locally situated, site-specific critical protocols (*see* **Feminist, Black Feminist Literary Criticism**).

Spillers was born in **Memphis, Tennessee**, in 1942; she has spoken admiringly of the African American community of her youth that resisted White domination and Black self-defeat in the face of Jim Crow segregation through such institutions as the extended family and the church. This sense of community informs a good deal of Spillers's critical vision. She would have us approach community "intramurally," taking into account not only the external elements against which a community defines itself but also the interior dynamics that constitute a community's labor or ethos. Thinking community intramurally affords Spillers the space to engage feminist theory and criticism precisely within the historically masculinist field of African American literary criticism. It also allows her time to reflect on the broader U.S. academic community that enables, frames, and at times rejects her ideas and even her person.

Spillers earned her bachelor's and master's degrees from the University of Memphis in 1964 and 1966, respectively. She went on to do graduate work in the Department of English and American Literature at Brandeis University, at a time when the **Civil Rights Movement** had run its course, the **Vietnam War** had intensified, and public protest in the United States had been curtailed by extremist state repression. Spillers was politically active during this period but has not commented explicitly on her experiences. Of course, the insurgent spirit of that era infuses the compellingly wrought prose with which she has come to be identified. Politics is always a matter of artistic and writerly style for Spillers. But politics is also about pointing out egregious acts of injustice as they are visited upon the democratic body politic—"democratic" perhaps only in name, from her perspective. The 2002 article "Inauguration Day 2001," which appeared in the journal *boundary 2*, signals Spillers's continuing concern over matters of U.S. state policy. Here she sheds subtlety to condemn what she perceives to be the political corruption and imperial hegemony in the form of George W. Bush's "stolen" first-term presidency.

Spillers received her Ph.D. from Brandeis in 1974 with a dissertation titled "Fabrics of History: Essays on the Black Sermon." The African American oratorical tradition, especially as it has developed through the everyday practices of the church, is a site of fascination for Spillers, given its relation to community formation and radical politics. She revisits the tradition in "Moving on Down the Line" (1988), but we might conjecture more generally that her close readings of individual texts grasp the stylistic nuances of each author's craft to the extent that Spillers has long been attuned to the rhetorical dimensions of oral and written expression.

Spillers has taught at a number of institutions throughout her career, among them the University of Nebraska, Emory University, and Wellesley and Haverford colleges. She has also held a number of visiting appointments, including positions at Duke University and the John F. Kennedy-Institut für Nordamerikastudien, Freie Universität Berlin. The recipient of numerous grants, fellowships, and awards, Spillers is currently the Frederick J. Whiton Professor of English at Cornell University, where she has spent the bulk of her senior career.

Spillers's essays, articles, and reviews have been published and reprinted in a host of academic journals and anthologies. Her frequently collaborative editorial work has been equally influential in proposing major paradigm shifts in African American literary criticism. In 1985 she and Marjorie Pryse edited *Conjuring*, a landmark anthology that showcases the most original scholarship on Black women's literature of its time. *Conjuring* definitively announces Black women's rightful place in the annals and protocols of U.S. literary history, though what constitutes a Black women's literary tradition is open to debate. Pryse's rather essentialist introduction, a testament to the "ancient power" of Black womanhood, is keenly if not subversively qualified by Spillers's Afterword, "Cross-Currents, Discontinuities," which advocates poststructuralist flexibility in deriving any sense of tradition or coherence from such a diverse body of texts. Spillers has further practiced this approach to literary history as section editor and headnote composer for the much-lauded *Norton Anthology of African American Literature* (1996), edited as a whole by **Henry Louis Gates, Jr.**, and **Nellie Y. McKay**.

In "Who Cuts the Border?," the introduction to *Comparative American Identities* (1991), Spillers uses José Martí's and William Faulkner's figural representations of "America" to call for a postexceptionalist U.S. literary and cultural analysis. The process of negotiating national identity and cultural heritage in Martí and Faulkner represents for Spillers a "new area studies" inasmuch as "America" is understood to be a global signifier of paradoxical tensions: "home in exile," "borders and centers." Though the individual pieces in the book do not necessarily take up this theme, Spillers's speculative remarks stand as a relatively early gesture toward questions of diaspora and the postcolonial in African American literary criticism.

More than a decade later, "Peter's Pans," the panoptic introduction to the long-awaited collection of her own essays, *Black, White, and in Color* (2003), would render the field's turn to Pan-African texts in exquisite terms: the topic of Spillers's essay is eating—and eating sumptuously well—in and around the metropoles of the African diaspora. Though the political trajectory of this critical move may seem beyond the everyday gourmand's reach, we might again place emphasis on Spillers's lyrical prose in order to glance at the powerful implications of her argument. She notes that the "Cuisinart of the modern has blood on its hands, as the pillage and enslavement of millions are implicated in its development" (43).

Spillers is probably best known for her work on the psychoanalytic intersections of **race**, **gender**, and sexuality. Both "Mama's Baby, Papa's Maybe" (1987), initially published in *diacritics*, and "'All the Things You Could Be by Now, if Sigmund Freud's Wife Was Your Mother'" (1996), the expanded version of which appeared in *boundary 2*, revise Freudian impressions in a variety of guises—the anthropological approach of Claude Lévi-Strauss, the psychoanalytic approach of Jacques Lacan, and the ideological critique of Louis Althusser—to theorize the historical and cultural specificity of African American embodiment and subject formation. "Mama's Baby" in particular lays the foundation for Spillers's singular critical vision. The essay begins with a memorable litany of names that are forced upon Spillers as a Black woman intellectual in the United States. "My country needs me, and if I were not here, I would have to be invented" (65), she observes. The essay then sketches a genealogy of the Black body as it has been "invented" by the symbolic imaginary of U.S. social relations. Here Spillers deconstructs Jacques Lacan's theory of the subject's entrance into discourse by showing how the enslaved Black body confounds distinctions between the literal and the figurative, the Real and the Symbolic: "before the 'body' there is the 'flesh,' that zero degree of social conceptualization that does not escape concealment under the brush of discourse, or the reflexes of iconography.... If we think of the 'flesh' as a primary narrative, then we mean its seared, divided, ripped-apartness, riveted to the ship's hole, fallen, or 'escaped' overboard" (67). The haunting image of Being in the flesh brings to light a different symbolic order, an "American grammar," one that could account for the overdetermined strains of and on African American subjectivity. Spillers demonstrates the critical flexibility of her theory by at once deflating the pathological criticism aimed at Black mothers by the inflammatory "Moynihan Report," *The Negro Family, the Case for National Action* (1965), and teasing out the interdependent tropes of racial and gendered embodiment in **slave narratives** by **Frederick Douglass** and **Harriet Ann Jacobs**.

" 'All the Things'," something of a sequel to "Mama's Baby," urges recognition of the ethical imperative that lies behind a "psychoanalytic culture criticism" so conceived. What is at stake here is not simply the relation between reader and text but the relation between one reader and another and, indeed, the relations among and between a reader's noncorresponding desires, investments, and privations. Spillers calls this critical strategy "interior intersubjectivity," a relational mode of inquiry that bypasses standard subject/object relations to theorize a fundamentally generous critical reading practice. Her forthcoming *The Idea of Black Culture* promises to engage such methodological and pedagogical concerns in understanding a set of diasporic literary, social, and even culinary texts. In this project and others to come, Spillers is certain to continue to inspire readers in ways that occasion vibrant theoretical critique of African American literature and culture in their multiply lived, imagined, and felt dimensions.

Resources: Elizabeth Abel, Barbara Christian, and Helene Moglen, eds., *Female Subjects in Black and White: Race, Psychoanalysis, Feminism* (Berkeley: University of California Press, 1997); Christopher Lane, ed., *The Psychoanalysis of Race* (New York: Columbia University Press, 1998); Hortense Spillers, " 'All the Things You Could Be by Now, if Sigmund Freud's Wife Was Your Mother': Psychoanalysis and Race," *boundary 2* 23, no. 3 (1996), 75–143; *Black, White, and in Color: Essays on American Literature and Culture* (Chicago: University of Chicago Press, 2003); "Inauguration Day 2001," *boundary 2* 29, no. 1 (2002), 1–10; " 'The Little Man at Chehaw Station' Today," *boundary 2* 30, no. 2 (2003), 5–19; "Mama's Baby, Papa's Maybe: An American Grammar Book," *diacritics* 17, no. 2 (1987), 65–81; "Moving on Down the Line," *American Quarterly* 40, no. 1 (March 1988), 83–109; Hortense Spillers, ed., *Comparative American Identities: Race, Sex, and Nationality in the Modern Text* (New York: Routledge, 1991); Hortense Spillers and Marjorie Pryse, eds., *Conjuring: Black Women, Fiction, and Literary Tradition* (Bloomington: Indiana University Press, 1985).

Kinohi Nishikawa

Spirituals. A form of sacred music that was originally created by African Americans for African Americans during **slavery** times. In *The African American Almanac*, Christopher A. Brooks describes spirituals as "the most significant musical contribution of the enslaved African population in the nineteenth century" (958). Spirituals have served as the theme, focus, and inspiration for a large body of African American literature, both yesterday and today.

Spirituals are an amalgamation of West African traditions, Protestant Christianity, and the slave experience. When slaves adopted the religion of their captors, they created songs based on Christian principles, such as God, Heaven, Jesus, and biblical stories, but they expressed them in a manner indicative of their West African heritage, creating a distinct and even unique music not found anywhere else in the world. As a result, these songs included expressive and elaborate embellishments, improvisation, and call-and-response patterns. Call-and-response is a style of singing in which an individual sings a line and another individual or group echoes it. Slaves sometimes accompanied these songs with body swaying, hand-clapping, and foot-stomping. Songs were sung at work, in rare moments of leisure, and at camp meetings. Camp meetings generally took place in secret and were a place where slaves could worship freely among themselves. True to the oral tradition of their ancestors, slaves did not document these songs in hymnals or books. Nor did their creators claim individual ownership. Spirituals belonged to the community.

Spirituals served several functions within the slave community. They provided slaves a means to express their feelings and religious beliefs. Songs such as "Mary Had a Baby, Yes, Lord," established their faith in Scripture, while songs such as "O, Brother, Don't Get Weary" provided encouragement, joy, and hope. Some songs expressed their sorrow, such as "Nobody Knows the Trouble I See," and "Sometimes I Feel Like a Motherless Child," and other songs were used in praise and worship. Spirituals also provided a means of resistance and empowerment. Within these particular songs, slaves embedded coded messages that they kept secret from White slave owners. "Go Down Moses" is an example:

> Go down, Moses, Way down in Egypt land
> Tell old Pharaoh to let my people go
> When Israel was in Egypt land
> Let my people go
> Oppressed so hard they could not stand
> Let my people go
> Go down, Moses, Way down in Egypt land
> Tell old Pharaoh to let my people go
> "Thus saith the Lord," bold Moses said,
> "Let my people go; if not I'll smite your first-born dead
> Let my people go."
> Go down, Moses, Way down in Egypt land
> Tell old Pharaoh, "Let my people go!"

"Go Down Moses" illustrates how slaves used biblical references as coded words and how they perceived the world around them. The Hebrews represented the slaves. Egypt represented **the South,** and many attribute the Moses figure to **Harriet Tubman,** who led many slaves to freedom, and **Nat Turner,** who led a slave revolt. Harriet Tubman, called "The Moses of her People," was known to "[wander] along back southern roads" singing seemingly harmless spirituals (Altman, 251–252). In reality, she was singing secret messages to slaves. "Follow the Drinking Gourd" is an example of a spiritual she may have sung. This song was used to instruct slaves on how to travel north to freedom. The "drinking gourd" stood for the Big Dipper and, if followed, led north. Altogether, spirituals provided slaves a means to cope, survive, and "keep on keepin' on under the physical and psychological pressures of [slavery]" (Connor, 693).

Prior to the **Civil War,** many Northerners had never heard spirituals. Spirituals had been a phenomenon isolated in the slave quarters, within the confining walls of slavery. Still, Whites and African Americans made efforts to preserve these distinct songs and helped to expose them to wider audiences. Collection and documentation of spirituals began as early as 1801, when **Richard Allen,** founder of the African Methodist Episcopal Church, published *A Collection of Spiritual Songs and Hymns from Various Authors.* This collection was used in African American churches throughout the United States. Newly freed African Americans, such as **Frederick Douglass** and **Booker T. Washington,** wrote about spirituals in their **slave narratives.** Thomas Wentworth

Sheet music for the traditional spiritual, "Been A Listening." Published in 1938 by the Handy Brothers Music Co. Yale Collection of American Literature, Beinecke Rare Book and Manuscript Library.

Higginson, a Union colonel of a regiment of free slaves, first heard the spirituals during the Civil War and was moved to publish several songs in the *Atlantic Monthly*, as well as in his memoir, *Army Life in a Black Regiment* (1870).

By the 1870s, a new trend was sweeping through the United States and Europe, one which sparked a greater interest in spirituals than ever before. This trend occurred when singing groups from African American colleges, such as Fisk University, Hampton Institute, Calhoun College, and Tuskegee Institute, decided to go on tour to raise money. Spirituals were well received, particularly in the North, by former abolitionists and sympathizers with African American causes, and throughout Europe. Spirituals were so successful in Europe that Antonín Dvořák, a Czech composer, encouraged his students to compose and arrange spirituals (Brooks, 959). While composing his famous *New World Symphony* (1893), he wrote that "the so-called plantation songs are among the most striking and appealing melodies that have been found this side of the water" (Newman).

Interest continued through the end of the nineteenth century and into the twentieth. Many African Americans were arranging old spirituals and composing new ones. Some of the best-known composers include Hall Johnson, John W. Work, Florence Price, **Robert Nathaniel Dett**, Clarence Cameron White, and Harry T. Burleigh. In the literary world, writers were publishing works on and about spirituals. These works include *Hampton and Its Students* (1874), *The Story of the Jubilee Singers* (1877), *Plantation Melodies* (1888), and *The Book of American Negro Spirituals* (1925). The popularity of spirituals also gave rise to African American artists who could perform these songs without fear or shame. Some of the eminent artists are Marian Anderson, **Paul Robeson**, Robert McFerrin, Leontyne Price, and Jesse Norman.

As the status and fame of spirituals grew, so did the criticism. The bulk of this criticism can be categorized into two major camps: those who stressed a White influence and those who emphasized the West African contribution. Scholars such as Newman Ivey White, Guy B. Johnson, and George Pullen Jackson compared White and African American songs. They concluded that spirituals, though influenced by West African folk music, replicated White music, and that White songs are their "legitimate tune-and-words forbears" (Low and Clift, 593). This argument is presented in *American Negro Folk-Songs* (1928), *Folk Culture on St. Helena Island, South Carolina* (1930), and *White Spirituals in the Southern Uplands* (1933). There was, of course, a deluge of works providing an alternative perspective on the origin of the spiritual. These works include *The Souls of Black Folk* (1903) by **W.E.B. Du Bois**, *Afro-American Folksongs* (1914) by Henry E. Krehbiel, and *Sinful Tunes and Spirituals* (1977) by Dena Epstein. In these works, these writers and scholars credit and acknowledge West African culture and folk tradition as a significant influence in the making of spirituals. They point to how distinct West Africanisms influenced the tunes and expression of the music and how, when combined with Protestant Christian religion and its practices, a unique and distinct music not found anywhere else in the world was created.

More recently, commentators have focused on the role of the spiritual within the slave community rather than its origins in such works as James Cone's *The Spirituals and the Blues* (1972), John Lovell's *Black Song: The Forge and the Flame* (1972), and Lawrence Levine's *Black Culture & Black Consciousness* (1977) (Connor, 695).

Spirituals have played a significant role in the African American literary tradition, beginning as early as the slave narratives of the 1800s and extending to contemporary works more than a century removed from slavery. Several **Harlem Renaissance** writers, most notably **Langston Hughes** and **Zora Neale Hurston**, were influenced by spirituals. In *Moses, Man of the Mountain* (1939), Huston embellishes upon the biblical story and spiritual of "Go Down, Moses." Many other writers used spirituals as a way to "structure their plots [and their characters] and advance their themes" (Connor, 695). Examples include *Blake* (1859) by **Martin R. Delany**, *Jubilee* (1966) by **Margaret Abigail Walker**, *Invisible Man* (1952) by **Ralph Ellison**, *Song of Solomon* (1977) by **Toni Morrison**, and *The Amen Corner* (1968) and *Go Tell It on the Mountain* (1953) by **James Baldwin** (Connor, 695). Poets such as **Paul Laurence Dunbar** and **James Weldon Johnson** also modeled their works on spirituals.

Spirituals have come a long way. From the obscurity of slavery and from the mouths of nameless authors, spirituals thrive in the works of composers, performers, writers, and poets. As a result, spirituals are recognized the world over and forever entwined with African American culture and literature.

Resources: Primary Sources: Richard Allen, *A Collection of Spiritual Songs and Hymns from Various Authors* (Nashville, TN: A.M.E.C. Sunday School Union, 1987); M. F. Armstrong and Helen W. Ludlow, *Hampton and Its Students* (New York: Putnam, 1874); W.E.B. Du Bois, *The Souls of Black Folk*, ed. George Stade (1903; repr. New York: Barnes & Noble Classics, 2005); Dena Epstein, *Sinful Tunes and Spirituals: Black Folk Music to the Civil War* (Urbana: University of Illinois Press, 1977); Stephen Collins Foster, *Plantation Melodies* (Boston: J. Knight, 1888); Thomas Wentworth Higginson, *Army Life in a Black Regiment* (Boston: Fields, Osgood, 1870); Zora Neale Hurston, *Moses, Man of the Mountain* (Philadelphia: Lippincott, 1939); George Pullen Jackson, *White Spirituals in the Southern Uplands: The Story of the Fasola Folk, Their Songs, Singings, and "Buckwheat Notes"* (Chapel Hill: University of North Carolina Press, 1933); Guy B. Johnson, *Folk Culture on St. Helena Island, South Carolina* (Chapel Hill: University of North Carolina Press, 1930); James Weldon Johnson, ed., *The Book of American Negro Spirituals* (New York: Viking Press, 1925); Henry Edward Krehbiel, *Afro-American Folksongs: A Study in Racial and National Music*, 4th ed. (Portland, ME: Longwood Press, 1976); J.B.T. Marsh, *The Story of the Jubilee Singers, with Their Songs*, 7th ed. (London: Hodder and Stoughton, 1877); Newman Ivey White, *American Negro Folk-Songs* (Cambridge, MA: Harvard University Press, 1928). **Secondary Sources:** Susan Altman, "Harriet Tubman," in her *The Encyclopedia of African-American Heritage* (New York: Facts on File, 1997); James Baldwin: *The Amen Corner* (New York: Dial Press, 1968); *Go Tell It on the Mountain* (New York: Knopf, 1953); Christopher A. Brooks, "Sacred Music Traditions," in *The African American*

Almanac, 8th ed., ed. Jessie Carney Smith and Joseph M. Palmisano (Detroit: Gale, 2000), 957–964; James Cone, *The Spirituals and the Blues* (New York: Seabury Press, 1972); Kimberly Rae Connor, "Spirituals," in *The Oxford Companion to African American Literature*, ed. William L. Andrews, Frances Smith Foster, and Trudier Harris (New York: Oxford University Press, 1997); Martin R. Delany, *Blake* (Boston: Beacon Press, 1970); Ralph Ellison, *Invisible Man* (New York: Random House, 1952); Charles W. Joyner and Eileen Jackson Southern, "Music: Spirituals," in *Encyclopedia of Black America*, ed. W. Augustus Low and Virgil A. Clift (New York: McGraw-Hill, 1981), 591–598; Lawrence Levine, *Black Culture and Black Consciousness* (New York: Oxford University Press, 1977); John Lovell, *Black Song: The Forge and the Flame* (New York: Macmillan, 1972); Toni Morrison, *Song of Solomon* (New York: Knopf, 1977); Richard Newman, "African American Spirituals," *Africana* 19 (Oct. 2004), http://www.africana.com/research/encarta/tt_266.asp; Erskine Peters, ed., *Lyrics of the Afro-American Spiritual* (Westport, CT: Greenwood Press, 1993); Margaret Walker, *Jubilee* (Boston: Houghton Mifflin, 1966).

Gladys L. Knight

St. John, Primus (born 1939). Poet. Born in New York City and raised by his West Indian grandparents, Balbena and Primus St. Louis, St. John attended the University of Maryland and Lewis and Clark College. Prior to beginning his career as a teacher and professional writer, he worked as a civil servant, waiter, gambler, bartender, and construction worker. He began his teaching career at public schools in Tacoma, Washington, and at Mary Holmes Junior College in West Point, Michigan. In 1973, he accepted a professorship at Portland State University in Oregon, where he currently teaches Caribbean, African, and African American literature and creative writing. One of the five artists responsible for initiating the National Endowment for the Arts Poets in the Schools program, St. John has published numerous poems in anthologies and magazines. He is also the author of several collections of poetry: *Communion: Poems 1976–1998* (1999), which won a Western States Book Award; *Dreamer* (1990), which was a cowinner of the 1990 Hazel Hall Award for Poetry; *Love Is Not a Consolation: It Is a Light* (1982); and *Skins on the Earth* (1976). He was also nominated for a National Book Award.

St. John credits his grandparents with instilling in him a deep sense of social history and with adding the perspective of an elderly voice to his poetry. *Communion*, which incorporates poems from his previous volumes of poetry, is considered to be St. John's most polished collection "Dreamer," a poem of epic length in *Communion*, is one of his most highly acclaimed works. The piece is an exploration of **slavery** that uses two different voices—one that of an enslaved African artist in the **Middle Passage**, the other, and more dominant, that of ship captain John Newton, best known for writing the hymn "Amazing Grace"—and has obvious parallels to **Robert Hayden**'s "Middle Passage." While other poems by St. John also address slavery as well as his West Indian heritage, a greater part of his works addresses themes of religion, love, and time, and center around trying to understand what it is like to be an

African American male in a mostly **White** society. The poet William Claire cites a line from a letter he received from St. John that helps to explain the underlying sense of strength that most of his poems possess: "When the world gets you down, fool it with a poem" (Nin and Harms, 48).

Resources: American Academy of Poets, "Primus St. John" (Apr. 10, 2003), http://www.poets.org/poets/poets.cfm?45442B7C000C03050D; Edward Lueders and Primus St. John, comps., *Zero Makes Me Hungry: A Collection of Poems for Today* (New York: Lothrop, Lee & Shepard, 1976); Anaïs Nin and Valerie Harms, eds., *Celebration!* (Riverside, CT: Magic Circle Press, 1973); Primus St. John: *Communion: Poems 1976–1998* (Port Townsend, WA: Copper Canyon, 1999); *Dreamer* (Pittsburgh, PA: Carnegie Mellon University Press, 1990); *Love Is Not a Consolation; It Is a Light* (Pittsburgh, PA: Carnegie Mellon University Press, 1982); Ingrid Wendt and Primus St. John, eds., *From Here We Speak: An Anthology of Oregon Poetry* (Corvallis: Oregon State University Press, 1993); Al Young, ed., *African American Literature: A Brief Introduction and Anthology* (New York: HarperCollins, 1996).

Melissa Couchon

St. Louis, Missouri. St. Louis has long been a major crossroads in American history, not only in the transcontinental migration but also in the movement of African Americans from **the South** to the industrial centers of the Midwest. In many geographical, economic, political, and cultural senses, St. Louis has been the midpoint between **Chicago, Illinois**, and **New Orleans, Louisiana**. At first the northward movement of African Americans involved escape from **slavery** to freedom. It is symbolic of the city's place in this difficult but determined passage that Dred Scott's "home" was in St. Louis when Missouri was a slaveholding "border" state. In the early decades of the twentieth century, the **Great Migration** northward involved economic escape from the endemic poverty of sharecropping and tenant farming, as well as escape from the social, political, and cultural oppression of institutionalized racial segregation. Although most Midwest cities, including Chicago, were strictly segregated, the economic opportunities that the cities provided to African Americans eventually gave them a base from which to assert their civil rights and their right to cultural self-expression. Although the Gateway Arch faces east and west, St. Louis has been every bit as much a momentous crossroads for the south-to-north migration of African Americans and for the counter-movement of political and cultural ideas that eventually spelled the end of segregation in the South.

In 1900, St. Louis was the fourth largest city in the United States. Between 1950 and 2000, however, the city lost almost 60 percent of its population, the steepest decline in any city in the Western world since complete census records have been kept. Although some of the earliest and most prosperous settlers in the city's history were Haitian immigrants, for the most part African Americans in St. Louis were treated, at best, as second-class citizens. For many decades, they were denied access to any publicly supported education, and the adequacy of public education remains a volatile issue in St. Louis to this day.

Still, African Americans made a place for themselves in the city. In the first half of the twentieth century, the section of the city that included the Rosebud Café, the Plantation Club, the Black and Tan, the Booker T. Washington, and about 700 other clubs, cafés, saloons, and joints was a mecca for African American musicians playing everything from **ragtime** to **blues** and **jazz**.

It is hardly surprising that many African American writers have been born in the greater St. Louis area or have lived some or most of their lives there. Perhaps the most prominent of the writers with a connection to the city has been **Langston Hughes**. Born in nearby Joplin, Missouri, Hughes is supposed to have written his best-known poem, "The Negro Speaks of Rivers," while riding a train over the confluence of the Mississippi and Missouri Rivers at St. Louis. Since 1998, the city has annually hosted the Langston Hughes St. Louis World Black Poetry Festival, which has featured poets from throughout the United States and from countries across the **diaspora**. In 2001, Washington University in St. Louis hosted the conference "Black Heartland: The Growth and Development of African-American Culture in the Midwest."

The East St. Louis poet **Eugene B. Redmond** has written eloquently about African American history and contemporary life in the region. A faculty member at Southern Illinois University at Edwardsville and editor of the literary journal *Drumvoices Revue*, he has also been a prominent community activist and a cultural force in his promotion of the arts and literature throughout the greater St. Louis area.

St. Louis native **Quincy Thomas Troupe** has returned frequently to his hometown for poetry readings and other literary events, and his poetry has remained grounded in his formative experiences in the city. Troupe has received American Book Awards for *Snake-back Solos* (1978) and for his biography of Miles Davis, *Miles* (1989). Troupe has also served as editorial director of *Code*, the magazine commonly described as the "Black GQ." The position has come with some notoriety because *Code*'s publisher is Larry Flynt. Troupe himself became a controversial figure when, after he was named Poet Laureate of California, a background check revealed that he did not have the academic credentials that he had long claimed. Not only was the honor withdrawn, but he was forced to resign from his position at the University of California at San Diego.

A faculty member at Washington University in St. Louis since 1993, **Carl Phillips** is a widely published and much honored poet who explores African American and gay subjects and themes. For his collection *In the Blood* (1992), he received the Samuel Morse French Poetry Prize. For *Cortège* (1995), he was a finalist for a National Book Critics Circle Award and a Lambda Literary Award. For *From the Devotions* (1998), he was again a finalist for a National Book Critics Circle Award. For *Pastoral* (2000), he received a Lambda Literary Award, and for *The Tether* (2001), the Academy Award in Literature from the American Academy of Arts and Letters and the Kingsley Tufts Poetry Award.

The St. Louis poets Dahveed Nelson and **Abiodun Oyewole** were founding members of **The Last Poets**, who became well-known around the city in the 1960s and 1970s for their dynamic readings. St. Louis natives Chris Branch and Marsha Cann are young performance poets with growing national reputations.

Maya Angelou is a native of St. Louis but lived in the city only until she was three. Other highly regarded poets with connections to the St. Louis area include **Amiri Baraka**, Staceyann Chin, Reggie Gibson, Shirley LeFlore, and **Sonia Sanchez**. Longtime St. Louis resident Allan David Mahr is notable for having written more than 3,000 published poems and songs.

The theater scene has long been a prominent part of St. Louis's cultural life and, in particular, of the city's African American community. The St. Louis Black Repertory Company has a long and distinguished history as one of the preeminent venues for works by African American playwrights. **Ntozake Shange**'s play *Betsey Brown* (1985) is drawn from her experiences growing up in St. Louis during the 1950s and directly treats the racial divisions that created great tensions within the city in that period and beyond. Adapted for the stage from Shange's novel with the same title, the play has been successfully staged at several St. Louis high schools.

Born and raised in St. Louis, Keith Boykin is the author of *One More River to Cross* (1996), a well-received memoir of growing up as a gay African American. Another St. Louis native, **John R. Keene**, has treated the same subject in his experimental, autobiographical novel *Annotations* (1995), which won the Critics Choice Award from the *San Francisco Review of Books*. The novelist **David Haynes** also grew up in St. Louis, and although his novel *Somebody Else's Mama* (1995) is set in a small Missouri town, the characters have family and professional connections to St. Louis. The Christian romance novelist **Michele Andrea Bowen** has set her novels among the congregations of African American churches modeled after those she came to know while growing up in St. Louis.

Now a poet, a playwright, an essayist, and an author of books for young adults, **Jabari Asim** first came to attention as an arts writer for the *Get Out!* entertainment supplement of the *St. Louis Post-Dispatch*, and he became the book editor for the newspaper before moving on to the *Washington Post*. St. Louis native **Julius Lester** has written in a variety of genres. A faculty member at the University of Massachusetts at Amherst, he is most widely known for his historical fiction for children and young adults. For *To Be a Slave* (1968), he received a Newbery Honor Book citation and the Lewis Carroll Shelf Award. For *The Long Journey Home: Stories from Black History* (1972), he received the Lewis Carroll Shelf Award and was nominated for a National Book Award.

St. Louis native Albert J. Raboteau has written and edited five books on African American religions, including *Slave Religion: The "Invisible Institution" in the Antebellum South* (1978), *A Fire in the Bones: Reflections on African-American Religious History* (1995), and *Canaan Land: A Religious History of*

African Americans (2001). Howard Paige, a St. Louis native and science-fiction novelist who now lives in **Detroit, Michigan**, has successfully self-published three books on African American food: *African-American Cookery* (1987), *African-American Family Cooking* (1995), and *Aspects of African-American Foodways* (1999). In the same vein, Maya Angelou has edited *The Historical Cookbook of the American Negro* (2000).

St. Louis school principal Savannah Young entered the debate over Ebonics with the publication of her book *English: An African-American Handbook* (1997). She argues that African American students need to be taught in Standard English because the textbooks they use for every subject are written in Standard English. If students are not required to learn Standard English at a young age, they will be at a great disadvantage at every educational level and in their professional careers.

As St. Louis's population has declined, the proportion of African American residents has risen dramatically. Today, as in many cities, African Americans have a much greater voice in the city's governance and a more prominent place in its cultural life. But, at the same time, the general decline of the city has seemed to many to be symbolic of lost opportunities or, worse, an illustration of the dictum that a promise deferred is ultimately a promise denied.

Resources: Lorin Cuoco and William H. Gass, eds., *Literary St. Louis* (St. Louis: International Writers Center, Washington University/Missouri Historical Society Press, 2000); Lee Ann Sandweiss, ed., *Seeking St. Louis: Voices from a River City, 1670–2000* (St. Louis: International Writers Center, Washington University/Missouri Historical Society Press, 2000); Doris Wesley, *Lift Every Voice and Sing: St. Louis African-Americans in the Twentieth Century* (Columbia: University of Missouri Press, 1999); John Wright, *Discovering African-American St. Louis: A Guide to Historic Sites*, ed. Jean E. Meeh Gosebrink (St. Louis: International Writers Center, Washington University/Missouri Historical Society Press, 1994).

Martin Kich

Stepto, Robert Burns (born 1944). Scholar and memoirist. Stepto was born in **Chicago, Illinois**, the son of Robert Charles and Anna (Burns) Stepto. He attended Trinity College (B.A., 1966), and Stanford University (M.A., 1968; Ph.D., 1974). He has taught at Williams College, Dartmouth College, Princeton University, and the Bread Loaf School of English. He is currently Professor of English, African American Studies, and American Studies at Yale University.

Stepto's first book, *From Behind the Veil: A Study of Afro-American Narrative* (1979), announced the emergence of a new theoretical direction in the analysis of Black-authored literary works. Rejecting the sociologically inflected methodology of critics influenced by the **Black Arts Movement** of the late 1960s and early 1970s, Stepto turned to early poststructuralist modes of inquiry to unpack what he saw as the overlooked semiotic dimensions within African American written texts (semiotics is the study of "signs" or symbolic images, including words). Following Northrop Frye and Roland Barthes, he coined the term "pregeneric myths" to talk about the set of shared beliefs and stories that circulate within all cultures, including Black cultures, prior to written expression. For Stepto, the most prevalent pregeneric myth in Black America has been the longing for freedom and literacy.

Stepto identified two basic types of narrative expressions within major Black literary texts that he saw linked to this dominant **myth** and applied them to a broad range of canonical texts, from **slave narratives** to **Ralph Ellison**'s *Invisible Man* (1952). In "the narrative of ascent," the text's enslaved or naïve protagonist goes on a quest in the hopes of achieving literacy and therefore psychic well-being. Its companion, "the narrative of immersion," requires the questing figure to revisit **the South**, or one of its psychological surrogates, so as to become in the end an "articulate kinsman," someone who assumes the role of guide or mentor to the racially dispossessed. Stepto's reliance on White and European theoretical models would earn him criticism from other African Americanists. **Houston A. Baker, Jr.**, for example, castigated Stepto and similar scholars for their seeming elitism. Nonetheless, Stepto's careful and rigorous theoretical innovations eventually influenced an entire generation of highly regarded scholars in the burgeoning field of African American literary study.

Among Stepto's other works are *The Selected Poems of Jay Wright* (1987) and four coedited volumes on American and African American literature. The latter include (with Dexter Fisher) *Afro-American Literature: The Reconstruction of Instruction* (1979), (with **Michael S. Harper**) *Chant of Saints: A Gathering of Afro-American Literature, Art, and Scholarship* (1979), and (with D. McQuade et al.) *The Harper American Literature* (1993). In 1998, Stepto published his memoir, *Blue as the Lake*. Like his more explicitly critical writing, Stepto's memoir is deeply concerned with the lived impact of historical change and changing geography on the subjectivity of Americans of African descent. Relying on his own complex family history as the primary vehicle for engaging in a series of moving meditations on identity, parent-child relations, the **blues**, and place, Stepto manages to produce a jazzy word portrait of the many permutations of Blackness.

Resources: Robert B. Stepto: *Blue as the Lake: A Personal Geography* (Boston: Beacon Press, 1998); Robert B. Stepto and Michael S. Harper, eds., *Chant of Saints: A Gathering of Afro-American Literature, Art, and Scholarship* (Urbana: University of Illinois Press, 1979); *From Behind the Veil: A Study of Afro-American Narrative* (Urbana: University of Illinois Press, 1979); Robert B. Stepto, ed., *The Selected Poems of Jay Wright* (Princeton, NJ: Princeton University Press, 1987); Robert B. Stepto and Dexter Fisher, eds., *Afro-American Literature: The Reconstruction of Instruction* (New York: Modern Language Association, 1979).

Guy Mark Foster

Steptoe, John (1950–1989). Author and illustrator of children's books. Steptoe burst onto the national scene at age eighteen when *Life* magazine published his first children's book, *Stevie*, in its entirety (August 29, 1969).

Steptoe went on to write and/or illustrate numerous children's books before his death, in New York City, after a long illness, at the age of thirty-eight. The Library of Congress lists at least twenty books under his name. Among these are *The Story of Jumping Mouse*, which won a Caldecott Award from the American Library Association in 1985, and *Mufaro's Beautiful Daughters*, which won the same award in 1987. *Mother Crocodile*, written with **Rosa Guy**, won a Coretta Scott King Award in 1982. Steptoe was born in **Brooklyn, New York**, and grew up in its Bedford-Stuyvesant neighborhood. He attended the High School of Art and Design in Manhattan.

Resources: Rudine Sims Bishop, "Following in Their Fathers' Paths," *Horn Book* 74, no. 2 (Mar.–Apr. 1998), 249–255; Roni Natov and Geraldine DeLuca, "An Interview with John Steptoe," *The Lion and the Unicorn: A Critical Journal of Children's Literature* 11, no. 1 (Apr. 1987), 122–129; John Steptoe: *Mufaro's Beautiful Daughters* (New York: Lothrop, Lee & Shepard, 1987); *Stevie* (New York: Harper & Row, 1969); *The Story of Jumping Mouse* (New York: Lothrop, Lee & Shepard, 1984); *Train Ride* (New York: Harper & Row, 1971); *Uptown* (New York: Harper & Row, 1970).

Hans Ostrom

Stetson, Jeff (born 1949). Playwright and novelist. Stetson's first published play is the highly acclaimed and often produced *The Meeting*, which is based on an imagined meeting of **Martin Luther King, Jr.**, and **Malcolm X**. In the play, Stetson explores the philosophical differences between the leaders while emphasizing their humanity and respect for one another and for the struggle for equality and freedom. *The Meeting* has enjoyed more than 200 productions nationally and has been performed in South Africa, Kenya, London, and the Netherlands. Stetson has won the Louis B. Mayer Award and eight NAACP Theater Image Awards, including the Best Play and Best Writer Awards in 1987, for this work. The play was adapted for television in an *American Playhouse* production that aired in 1989.

Stetson, a native of **Harlem, New York**, also received the Theodore Ward Playwriting Award for his work *Fathers and Other Strangers*, in a competition sponsored by Columbia College of Chicago. He was a participant in the National Playwrights Conference at the Eugene O'Neill Center, administered by the noted director Lloyd Richards. His play *And the Men Shall Also Gather*, was produced at the Center in 1988, and Stetson adapted it as a pilot for FOX television. His play *Fraternity* won the Multi-Cultural Playwrights Festival sponsored by the Group Theater of Seattle in 1988. It has enjoyed successful productions in **Chicago, Illinois**, Oakland, California, **Atlanta, Georgia**, and several other cities in the United States.

Stetson, along with Jomandi Productions, received the National Theater Arts Residency Program grant to produce a work for the theater in Atlanta. *Keep the Faith* explores the colorful and intriguing life of Adam Clayton Powell, Jr. It premiered in 1998, directed by Marsha Jackson-Randolph, then co-artistic director of Jomandi Productions. Stetson is the author of several screenplays, including *Out of the Ashes* for Steven Spielberg's Amblin Productions and *The*

Buffalo Soldiers. His debut novel, *Blood on the Leaves* (2004), is a mystery that explores the ugly legacy of racism, **lynching**, and revenge.

Resources: Woodie King, Jr., ed., *The National Black Drama Anthology* (New York: Applause Books, 1995); Robert Kolker, "Residencies for Theater Artists Announced," *Backstage*, Nov. 1994; Jeff Stetson: *Blood on the Leaves* (New York: Warner Books, 2004); *The Meeting* (New York: Dramatist's Play Service, 1990).

Joan F. McCarty

Steward, Theophilus Gould (1843–1924). Theologian and historian. Theophilus Gould Steward wrote several autobiographical accounts, theological works, and church histories that provide an invaluable record of the early African Methodist Episcopal (A.M.E.) denomination. Steward was born on April 17, 1843, in Gouldtown, New Jersey. In 1863, he earned his preaching license. His first appointment was to the Macedonia A.M.E. Church in South Camden, New Jersey. Between 1865 and 1871, Steward led and established churches in South Carolina, Georgia, and Delaware. In 1873, he performed missionary work in Port-au-Prince, Haiti, and returned to the United States the following year to lead the African Wesleyan Methodist Episcopal Church in **Brooklyn, New York**. From 1874 to 1877, Steward contributed letters, sermons, and articles to the A.M.E. *Christian Recorder*, including sketches of biblical characters, articles on marriage, and a series of essays titled "Colored Society," which examined the economic status of African Americans in his congregation. His articles predated **Edward Franklin Frazier**'s *The Black Bourgeoisie* (1957). However, it was his *My First Four Years in the Itinerary of the African Methodist Episcopal Church* (1876) that brought him the most recognition in the A.M.E. Church.

After accepting the pastorate of Zion's Mission A.M.E. Church in **Philadelphia, Pennsylvania**, Steward reflected upon his mother's life in his work *The Memoirs of Mrs. Rebecca Steward* (1877). Between 1883 and 1885, Steward wrote several controversial theological works, including *Death, Hades and the Resurrection* (1883) and *The Divine Attributes* (1884). Steward caused more controversy by supporting the theory of evolution in his book *Genesis Re-read* (1885). He wrote another provocative work, *The End of the World; or, Clearing the Way for the Fullness of Gentiles* (1888) that challenged the ideology of White superiority. In 1891, Steward became the chaplain of the Twenty-fifth U.S. Colored Infantry. In 1894 and 1895, he wrote several essays that portrayed army life, such as "The Colored American Soldier," which advocated racial equality and was critical of racism in the military.

Steward wrote a Victorian novel titled *A Charleston Love Story; or, Hortense Vanross* (1899) which demonstrated the challenges of interreligious marriage. Steward published *The Colored Regulars in the United States Army* (1904), which demonstrated the patriotism and courage of African American soldiers. In 1906, he joined the faculty of Wilberforce University and served as Vice President of the college from 1908 to 1918. In 1912 and 1913, Steward worked with his brother William to write a history of their family, *Gouldtown, A Very*

Remarkable Settlement of Ancient Date (1913). He published his observations of Haiti in *The Haitian Revolution* (1914). In 1921, Steward penned his autobiography, *Fifty Years in the Gospel Ministry: From 1864 to 1914.* Throughout his final years, Steward remained an active writer, a dedicated teacher, and a skilled minister and historian.

Resources: **Primary Sources:** Theophilus Gould Steward: *A Charleston Love Story; or, Hortense Vanross* (New York: F. Tennyson Neely, 1899); *The Colored Regulars in the United States Army* (Philadelphia: A.M.E. Book Concern, 1904); *The Divine Attributes* (Philadelphia: Christian Recorder, 1884); *Death, Hades and the Resurrection* (Philadelphia: 1883); *The End of the World; or, Clearing the Way for the Fullness of Gentiles* (Philadelphia: A.M.E. Church Book Rooms, 1888); *Fifty Years in the Gospel Ministry: From 1864 to 1914* (Philadelphia: A.M.E. Book Concern, 1921); *Genesis Re-read* (Philadelphia: A.M.E. Book Rooms, 1885); *Gouldtown, A Very Remarkable Settlement of Ancient Date* (Philadelphia: Lippincott, 1913); *The Haitian Revolution, 1791 to 1804* (New York: T. Y. Crowell, 1914); *The Memoirs of Mrs. Rebecca Steward, Containing a Full Sketch of Her Life, with Various Selections from Her Writings and Letters* (Philadelphia: Publication Department of the A.M.E. Church, 1877); *My First Four Years in the Itinerary of the African Methodist Episcopal Church* (Brooklyn: 1876); **Secondary Sources:** Albert G. Miller, *Elevating the Race: Theophilus G. Steward, Black Theology, and the Making of an African American Civil Society, 1865–1924* (Knoxville: University of Tennessee Press, 2003); William Seraile, *Voice of Dissent: Theophilus Gould Steward (1843–1924) and Black America* (Brooklyn, NY: Carlson, 1991).

Julius H. Bailey

Stewart, Maria W. (1803–1879). Essayist, lecturer, abolitionist, and women's rights activist. Although Maria Stewart was the "first American woman to lecture in public on political themes and leave extant copies of her texts . . . a woman of profound religious faith, a pioneer black abolitionist and a defiant champion of women's rights . . . . she remains a significant historical figure hidden in plain sight . . . " (Richardson, xiii, xv). Born Maria Miller in 1803 in Hartford, Connecticut, Stewart was orphaned by age five and "bound out" as a servant to a minister's family until she was fifteen. Her life of drudgery and endless toil led to her conclusion later on that Blacks in the North were only "nominally free" (Richardson, xv). Afterward, she supported herself as a domestic servant and struggled to educate herself, mostly in Sunday School classes. In 1826, at the age of twenty-three, she married James W. Stewart, a veteran of the War of 1812 and a successful shipping agent in **Boston, Massachusetts**. The couple settled in a small but vibrant middle-class neighborhood near Beacon Hill and spent the next three years as activists focused on Black **racial uplift**. By the time she was twenty-six, however, Stewart was a childless widow. Exploited by unscrupulous White businessmen, she was cheated out of her husband's legacy and left virtually destitute.

Starting all over again, Stewart embarked on a three-year public career that produced her most important work as a writer, lecturer, and activist. She published a pamphlet in 1831, *Religion and Pure Principles of Morality*, and in

1832, a collection of religious writings titled *Meditations from the Pen of Mrs. Maria W. Stewart*; delivered four public lectures between 1832 and 1833; saw the appearance of a speech and a poem in *The Liberator*; and published an edition of her collected works in 1835, *Productions of Mrs. Maria W. Stewart*, a year after her move to New York.

Frances Smith Foster argues that Stewart was an early contributor to the African American women's literary tradition because "she was one of the first to proclaim herself a representative of and a model for others," a tradition that **Frances Ellen Watkins Harper, Elizabeth Keckley**, and **Charlotte Forten Grimké** would later join (5). Profoundly influenced by **David Walker** and his *Appeal...to the Coloured Citizens of the World* (1829) and the Briton John Adams's volume of women's history, Stewart quickly established herself as a "bold and militant orator..." speaking before "promiscuous" audiences of both men and women and addressing herself "squarely to black audiences" (Richardson, xiii, 12). Indeed, her first public lecture, "Why Sit Ye Here and Die?" is a call to action advocating Black defense even after **Nat Turner**'s rebellion the previous year. The most radical of her ideas, however, linked together **race** and **gender**, urging Black women to develop their intellectual abilities and play a public role in the advancement of Blacks in the United States (Ryan, 376). Stewart believed that women, particularly Black women, had a special responsibility "to take their place in the first ranks of black moral and political leadership" (Richardson, 19). Although her emphasis on education and women's influence on their children fell within the ideological bounds of True Womanhood, the very act of public speaking subverted women's confinement within the domestic sphere. Stewart's evangelism also figured prominently in her lectures and writings, both thematically and rhetorically, a result of her "born again" conversion sometime in the 1830s "that fueled her sense of mission" to Black women. In "Religion and Pure Principles of Morality," she addressed Black women directly, arguing, "O, ye daughters of Africa, awake! Awake! Arise! No longer sleep nor slumber, but distinguish yourselves. Show forth to the world that you are endowed with noble and exalted faculties. O, ye daughters of Africa! What have you done to immortalize your names beyond the grave?" (Foster, 4).

By 1834, Stewart had given up her career on the podium, but not her activism. She moved to New York, joined the Female Literary Society for Black women, became a teacher, and attended the Anti-Slavery Convention of 1837. In 1847, she was appointed assistant principal of a public school in the Williamsburg section of **Brooklyn, New York**. After the **Civil War**, she moved to **Washington, D.C.**, from **Baltimore, Maryland**, and became matron of the Freedman's Hospital. She also established a friendship with Elizabeth Keckley. In 1878, Stewart applied for a war widow's pension and used it to publish a new edition of her collected works in 1879. She died on December 17, 1879, and is buried in Graceland Cemetery in Washington, D.C.

Resources: Frances Smith Foster, *Written by Herself: Literary Production by African American Women, 1746–1892* (Bloomington: Indiana University Press, 1993); Carla

Peterson, *"Doers of the Word" African-American Women Speakers and Writers in the North (1830–1880)* (New Brunswick, NJ: Rutgers University Press, 1998); Marilyn Richardson, ed., *Maria Stewart: America's First Black Woman Political Writer: Essays and Speeches* (Bloomington: Indiana University Press, 1987); Barbara Ryan, "Maria W. Stewart," in *African American Authors, 1745–1945: A Bio-Bibliographical Critical Sourcebook*, ed. Emmanuel S. Nelson (Westport, CT: Greenwood Press, 2000), 375–378.

Rebecca R. Saulsbury

Still, William (1821–1902). Historian and political activist. Best known for his work with the **Underground Railroad**, Still also produced notable political tracts and one of the most important histories of the Underground Railroad.

The son of former slaves Levin and Charity Still, William Still was born in Burlington County, New Jersey. He never received a formal education and spent his youth working on the farms of his family and neighbors. In 1844, he moved to **Philadelphia, Pennsylvania**, where he met Letitia George.

The couple married in 1847, and that same year Still joined the Pennsylvania Society for the Abolition of Slavery, working as a clerk, and began his long association with the Underground Railroad. Active in Philadelphia's Vigilance Committee throughout the 1850s, Still aided hundreds of fugitive slaves escaping North. Perhaps one of the most famous cases, that of Jane Johnson, gained Still nationwide notoriety as part of the Passmore Williamson case. More recently, Johnson has returned to the spotlight because of her connection to **Hannah Crafts**'s *The Bondwoman's Narrative*, edited by **Henry Louis Gates, Jr.**, and published in 2002.

Although Still is best known for his work with the Underground Railroad, he was a champion of several reform causes, most notably equal rights for Northern free Blacks. He mounted a campaign against discrimination on public transportation in 1859 and organized the Pennsylvania Civil, Social, and Statistical Association—which gathered information about former slaves and fought for suffrage—in 1861. He sheltered **John Brown**'s family while Brown was imprisoned after his famous raid, and he aided a number of other prominent abolitionists. He also regularly reported his activities in the abolitionist press.

While fairly young, Still began purchasing real estate; when he left his clerk's position in 1861, he opened a successful coal business. These ventures afforded him a level of economic

William Still, 1879. Courtesy of the Library of Congress.

stability and helped fund his antislavery activities. They also allowed him to self-publish his history, *The Underground Rail Road*, in 1872. The book, based in large part on his own detailed records, was so successful that it quickly went through three editions. Critics since have recognized it not only as the sole work on the Underground Railroad by a Black participant, but also as a rich collection of information focused not just on abolitionists but on the fugitive slaves themselves. Records such as Still's are rare because many Underground Railroad activists destroyed records after the passage of the Fugitive Slave Law, or simply never kept records. Still's account has, therefore, provided a base from which most subsequent accounts of the Underground Railroad have drawn.

In addition to his journalism and *The Underground Rail Road*, Still published two pamphlets of note: *A Brief Narrative of the Struggle for the Rights of the Colored People of Philadelphia in the City Railway Cars* (1867) and *An Address on Voting and Laboring* (1874). He continued to advocate for a variety of reform causes until 1896, when weakening health forced him to retire from public life. (*See* **Abolitionist Movement**.)

Resources: John H. Bracey et al., eds., *Blacks in the Abolitionist Movement* (Belmont, CA: Wadsworth, 1971); Larry Gara: *The Liberty Line* (Lexington: University Press of Kentucky, 1996); "Still, William," in *American National Biography Online*, http://www.anb.org/articles/15/15-00657.html; William Still, *Underground Rail Road Records* (1892; repr. New York: Arno, 1968).

Eric Gardner

Still, William Grant (1895–1978). Composer, arranger, and conductor. Still was hailed as the "Dean of African-American Composers." His compositions include many settings of African American poetry and literature.

William Grant Still was born in Woodville, Mississippi, on May 11, 1895. When he was three months old, his father, for whom he was named, died. His mother, Carrie Lena Fambro Still, took him to Little Rock, Arkansas, to live with her mother. He stayed with his grandmother while his mother taught English in a local school. Carrie Still was both a dedicated teacher and a devoted, albeit strict, mother. In addition to her teaching, she participated in a number of cultural and community activities.

In 1904 Carrie Still married Charles B. Shepperson. Like Carrie, he was a patron of the arts. In 1912, Still's stepfather brought him some opera recordings along with a phonograph. Still was completely taken with this genre of musical **drama**. His love for the opera would last throughout his life.

Still graduated as valedictorian from M. W. Gibbs High School in 1911. According to his mother's wishes, he attended Wilberforce University (Ohio) in preparation for a career in medicine, though he would have preferred to study music. He became involved in several of the university's musical organizations, as both a performer and an arranger. In early 1915, Still left Wilberforce University before graduation in order to pursue a full-time career in music. He married Grace Bundy on October 4, 1915.

During the summer of 1916, Still found employment with W. C. Handy as a musical arranger. In 1917, he studied composition, theory, and violin at Oberlin Conservatory. Shortly thereafter, Still enlisted in the U.S. Navy. After he was discharged from the service, Still went to New York City to work for the Pace and Handy Music Publishing Company. In 1921, he performed in the pit orchestra for the Afro-American revue *Shuffle Along*. The show was highly successful, running in New York for 504 performances and having a successful road tour. While the show was playing in **Boston, Massachusetts**, Still studied composition with George Whitefield Chadwick at the New England Conservatory. In 1923, Still received an invitation from Edgard Varèse to study composition. Varèse introduced Still to many twentieth-century rhythmic and harmonic innovations.

The first performance of Still's *From the Land of Dreams* was on February 8, 1925. Varèse arranged this performance through the International Composers Guild. His next work, *Darker America*, was published in 1928, the year that Still won the Harmon Award for Distinguished Achievement among Negroes in Music. In 1929, Paul Whiteman hired Still as an arranger for the *Old Gold Hour*, a weekly radio show. Still met Verna Arvey, a concert pianist and writer, who eventually became his second wife. During 1940 Still completed his ballet, *Sahdji*, and composed the *Afro-American Symphony*. *Sahdji* was first performed by the Eastman Ballet and the Rochester Civic Orchestra under the baton of Howard Hanson on May 22, 1931. In the same year, Still's *Afro-American Symphony* received its first performance with the same orchestra. Still received a fellowship from the John Simon Guggenheim Memorial Foundation to compose an opera in 1934. That opera, *Blue Steel*, was completed in 1935.

Still moved permanently to **Los Angeles, California**, in May 1934. For six months he worked as a composer and an orchestrator for several notable films. The *Afro-American Symphony* received its New York Philharmonic premiere on November 20, 1935, with Hans Lange conducting. In 1938 Still began working on the opera *Troubled Island* with a libretto by **Langston Hughes** (who had written a play, *Troubled Island*, in 1936). Both works dramatize the life of Haitian revolutionary leader Jean-Jacques Dessalines. The opera was completed in 1941 and produced by the New York City Opera in 1949 (Ostrom). (*See* **Haiti**.)

Two important collaborations took place in 1940. The first was a choral ballad, *And They Lynched Him on a Tree*, with words by Katherine Garrison Chapin. Second, Still worked with **Zora Neale Hurston** on *Caribbean Melodies*. Throughout his composing career Still worked in partnership with many other writers and poets, including **Paul Laurence Dunbar**, Harold Bruce Forsythe, Virginia Brasier, Paul Webster, Ruth Page, Richard Bruce, **Alain Locke**, Albert Stillman, **Countee Cullen**, Philippe Thoby-Marcelin and **Arna Bontemps**. However, the poetry and libretti for many of Still's major works were written by his second wife, Verna Arvey. These works include the operas *A Bayou Legend* (1941), *Costaso* (1949–1950), *Highway 1, U.S.A.* (1962), *Minette Fontaine* (1959), *Mota* (1951), and *The Pillar* (1954–1955). Other works are *Christmas in the Western World (Las Pascuas)* (1967), *Lenox Avenue* (1938), *The Little Song that Wanted to Be a Symphony* (1954), *A Psalm for the Living* (1965), *Rhapsody* (1955), *Song for the Lonely* (1953), *Song for the Valiant* (1952), and *Those Who Wait* (1943).

Resources: Verna Arvey, *In One Lifetime* (Fayetteville: University of Arkansas Press, 1984); Hans Ostrom, *A Langston Hughes Encyclopedia* (Westport, CT: Greenwood Press, 2002); Hildred Roach, *Black American Music: Past and Present* (Malabar, FL: Krieger, 1992); Catherine Parsons Smith et al., *William Grant Still: A Study in Contradictions* (Berkeley: University of California Press, 2000); Eileen Southern, *The Music of Black Americans: A History*, 3rd ed. (New York: Norton, 1997); Judith Anne Still, ed., *William Grant Still and the Fusion of Cultures in American Music*, 2nd ed. (Flagstaff, AZ: Master-Player Library, 1995); Judith Anne Still, Michael J. Dabrishus, and Carolyn L. Quin, *William Grant Still: A Bio-Bibliography* (Westport, CT: Greenwood Press, 1996).

Marianne Wilson

Stowe, Harriet Beecher (1811–1896). Novelist and abolitionist. Stowe is best remembered for her 1852 antislavery novel *Uncle Tom's Cabin* (*UTC*), which Abraham Lincoln famously (and probably erroneously) is said to have credited with starting the **Civil War**. Her novel became an instant best-seller, galvanizing abolitionist feelings in the North. The work drew on published **slave narratives**, most notably **Josiah Henson**'s *Life* (1849), and it inspired any number of stage productions and imitations, and motivated a generation of African American writers to tell their experiences in and out of **slavery**. Stowe became a well-known public figure and an international representative of American abolitionism, despite coming late to the cause; in her younger years Stowe, like many Northerners, objected to the violent rhetoric of the **Abolitionist Movement**, a rhetoric which she found indicative of an unappealing radicalism. Her novel was nevertheless a complete triumph for the abolitionist cause, and Stowe became widely respected in the African American community.

One of nine children, Stowe was born into a politically active and intellectual family. Her father was the well-known essayist and minister Lyman Beecher, and several of her siblings also became published writers or well-known speakers. Stowe published stories, sketches, and a successful geography as a very young woman. She married the minister Calvin Stowe in 1836 and went on to have eight children of her own. Although *UTC* was Stowe's first and most successful novel, she continued writing for many years and published eight other novels. Eventually she became the primary breadwinner for her family. She interested herself in other causes after the Civil War, including women's rights.

Begun as a serial in 1851, *UTC* relates the adventures of the title character, a deeply religious and loyal slave who is sold, betrayed, or predeceased by a succession of masters, both kind and cruel. Tom's religious faith and passive acceptance in the face of adversity give him peace in all circumstances, and allow him to convert any number of acquaintances to Christianity. Within the framework of the sentimental genre, his experiences effectively argue against any possibility for religious or moral slaveholding. While *UTC* was mostly well received in the North, some African Americans objected to Stowe's advocacy of colonization in the book's final chapter, when the escaped slaves George and Eliza can find satisfaction only outside their native country, settling in Liberia. Nevertheless, the book sold 300,000 copies in the United States in its first year, and three times that number in England. Stowe's husband had negotiated a 10 percent royalty with a reluctant publisher; to everyone's surprise, those proceeds allowed their large family to live in style for a number of years.

While the novel presents Tom as a model of Christian beliefs and behavior, it also uses Tom and the other African American characters to establish some of the most enduring racial stereotypes in literary history. Stowe's novel includes the original wisecracking **tricksters**, Sam and Andy, as well as tragic intellectual **mulattoes**, George and Eliza. The title **"Uncle Tom"** itself has evolved in common parlance to mean an obsequious African American who accommodates White privilege to better himself at the expense of his race. This denigration of the term comes partly from increasing cultural standards of racial pride, but also results from the incredibly popular stage productions of the story, which gradually evolved into farcical comedies mocking Tom's subservience.

This same ambivalence toward Tom's character has been reflected in twentieth-century critical approaches to *UTC*. During the **Harlem Renaissance**, Stowe's work was criticized for racial stereotypes, but also fell short of the aesthetic standards established by **New Criticism** and African American critics such as **Alain Locke**, who sought to move away from a tradition of African American literature as a source of political propaganda. **Richard Wright** offered an unfavorable commentary on Stowe's legacy in the character name Bigger Thomas and in the title of his collection *Uncle Tom's Children*. In 1955, **James Baldwin** wrote "Everybody's Protest Novel," a legendary review of Wright's *Native Son* that compares Wright to Stowe, and finds them both lacking. He calls *UTC* "a very bad novel," and continues, "Bigger Thomas is Uncle Tom's descendant, flesh of his flesh, so exactly opposite a portrait that, when the books are placed together, it seems that the contemporary **Negro** novelist and the dead New England woman are locked together in a deadly, timeless battle." Baldwin's attitude toward the novel remained the accepted critical position until the **feminist/black feminist literary criticism** of the 1970s, when several noted scholars took up Stowe as an example of feminine cultural dominance during the nineteenth century. Both Ann Douglas and Jane Tompkins have used *UTC* to make formidable arguments about nineteenth-century American culture, although they hold very different estimations of the novel's merit as a work of literature. Their comments and the conversations that have grown up around them have come to be known as "The Stowe Debate": an ideological debate representative of ongoing disagreement in critical circles over the relative values of aesthetic merit and cultural impact.

Resources: James Baldwin, *Notes of a Native Son* (Boston: Beacon Press, 1955); Ann Douglas, *The Feminization of American Culture* (New York: Knopf, 1978); Joan D. Hedrick, *Harriet Beecher Stowe: A life* (New York: Oxford University Press, 1994); Joan D. Hedrick, ed., *The Oxford Harriet Beecher Stowe Reader* (New York: Oxford University Press, 1999); Eric J. Sundquist, ed., *New Essays on Uncle Tom's Cabin* (New York: Cambridge University Press, 1986); Jane Tompkins, *Sensational Designs: The Cultural Work of American Fiction, 1790–1860* (Oxford: Oxford University Press, 1985); Barbara Anne White, *The Beecher Sisters* (New Haven, CT: Yale University Press, 2003).

Susan Hays Bussey

Strange, Sharan (born 1959). Poet and educator. Strange's childhood, spent in Orangeburg, South Carolina, has influenced much of her poetry. The poems reflect her experience in the rural South, as well as her perspective on issues such as family, the self, and the past. Strange was educated at Harvard College, and received an M.F.A. in poetry from Sarah Lawrence College. She is a contributing and advisory editor of **Callaloo**, and in 1988 was cofounder of the Dark Room Collective and Reading Series, a forum for established and emerging African American writers. Strange has been a writer-in-residence at Yaddo, the Gell Writers' Center, and the MacDowell Colony, as well as at Fisk University, the University of California at Davis, and the California Institute of the Arts. She has lived in **Washington, D.C.**, where she taught writing, literature, and social studies at Parkmount, an alternative school that focuses on experiential learning. Currently, Strange is a lecturer at Spellman College in **Atlanta, Georgia**.

Strange is the author of *Ash*, winner of the 2000 Barnard New Women Poets Prize, selected by **Sonia Sanchez**. In her introduction to *Ash*, Sanchez describes what "tempers" Strange's poetry as "a subtle lyrical passion, that shimmers even when the self barely survives." The poetry of *Ash* is autobiographical but also outward looking. In an interview with **Toi Derricotte** featured in *Callaloo*, Strange explains that as a poet, reflecting on her childhood, her stance is that of a "documentary filmmaker," and the poems are meant to "bear witness to" the experiences of her childhood (292)—for instance, the poems "Jimmy's First Cigarette" and "The Stranger." In this way, she reserves any explicit emotional response while recording detail and action, as in a film. Her poems are also marked by her awareness that she is an individual among a community that includes humanity in general and her Black ancestors. As she explains to Derricotte, "ancestry" includes both one's family and the historic past.

Strange's influences include those from her family as well as such contemporary writers as **Toni Morrison** and **Yusef Komunyakaa** and "Black literary ancestors" such as **Frederick Douglass** and **Sojourner Truth**. It is perhaps because of her awareness of community that she is involved with

Callaloo, a literary magazine for Black writers around the world, and the Dark Room collective, whose community Strange considers "a way of overcoming isolation" (Derricotte, 297). Though the poems of *Ash* are lyrical and metered, Strange is interested in **prose poems**. Her poetry has appeared in a number of periodicals, including *Agenda*, *Agni*, *Black Bread*, *Best American Poetry 1994*, *Callaloo*, and *Radcliffe Quarterly*, and as well as anthologies: *The Garden Thrives: Twentieth-Century African-American Poetry* (1996), *Identity Lessons* (1999), *What I Never Said: Letter from Daughters and Sons to Their Fathers* (2001), and *Making Callaloo: 25 Years of Black Literature* (2001).

Resources: Toi Derricotte, "An Interview with Sharan Strange," *Callaloo* 19, no. 2 (1996), 291–298; Charles H. Rowell, ed., *Making Callaloo: 25 Years of Black Literature* (New York: St. Martin's, 2002); Sharan Strange, *Ash* (Boston: Beacon Press, 2001).

J'Lyn Simonson

Surrealism. Born in Europe in the years immediately following **World War I**, surrealism and other branches of **Modernism** directly influenced artistic production. The painter Marcel Duchamps (*Nude Descending a Staircase*), the writer Gertrude Stein ("A rose is a rose is a rose is a rose/she is my rose"), the photographer Man Ray (creator of the rayograph, camera-less photographic imaging), and the writer André Breton (French philosopher and self-described "founder of Surealism") focused their creative energy on moving beyond and away from traditional modes of writing, painting, sculpting, architecture, and photography. As Breton described it, "Surrealism is not interested in paying much attention . . . to anything whose end is not the annihilation of being and its transformation into an internal and blind brilliance which is no more the soul of ice than it is of fire" (Breton, 15).

At its height in the 1920s, European surrealism created a sense of artistic anarchism and chaos so intense that artists and writers across the globe took notice. Where formerly paintings were of clearly recognizable images (human figures, landscapes, objects) in natural colors, surrealist paintings were composed of shapes, angles, textures, and grossly distorted figures or objects rendered in wild primary colors. Often these paintings placed completely unrelated objects together or stretched known objects into twisted, asymmetrical shapes to reflect the strange and unrecognizable postwar social landscape (Salvador Dalí is infamous for his surrealist works incorporating melting or twisted timepieces, for example). Surrealist writers likewise worked to render language in ways that initially appeared arbitrary and meaningless in their attempt to illustrate the social, economic, and political upheaval around them. Often, surrealist works took on dreamlike or nightmarish qualities as artists and writers forced their audiences to recognize the nightmarish quality of twentieth-century life. Defamiliarization or disorientation, as the futurist Viktor Shklovsky called it in his *Art as Device*, was the aim of the surrealists and other Modernists in works that portrayed the persistent feeling that "there was no dividing line between sleep and the state of being awake" (Man Ray, *Self Portrait*). For the surrealists, there was never an escape from the nightmare, no waking relief from the horror of imagination. Instead, through their works the surrealists argued that the nightmare was now a constant state of being from which thinking humanity could not escape, and from whose revelation the critical artist could not relent.

To describe and define things as *surreal*, we really mean that they have taken on a sense of the *unreal* or the unbelievable reality we normally ascribe to dreams or nightmares. It is in this attempt at giving voice to the unbelievably tragic, wretched, or horrifying that surrealism is most persistently linked to the texts and experiences of Black American writers—indeed, to American writers in general.

Experiencing the **Great Migration** of Southern Blacks to the North, the **Great Depression**, and then the **race riots** in **Chicago, Illinois,** and other metropolitan areas, the young **Richard Wright** and other aspiring Black writers grew up identifying with the pain and confusion of these events. In *Uncle Tom's Children*, Wright's first published work of short fiction, the naturalism of Europe is blended conspicuously with the superrealism or surrealism of his own American experience. In this and all of Wright's literature that would follow, particularly in *Native Son* and *Black Boy*, characters sleepwalk through a nightmarish world of unchecked violence, depravity, racism, fear, and anxiety. Even as Bigger Thomas, Wright's most famous character, struggles to take ownership of his life, Wright's tragic text demonstrates the fallacy of control as the protagonist moves ceaselessly toward his doom; awaiting execution, Bigger epitomizes the helplessness of the individual in a world governed by personal, social, and economic machinery he doesn't understand.

Moreover, with Bigger and other characters like him, Wright demonstrates the particularly impossible situation for Blacks who are forced to straddle two worlds, **White** and Black, in an existence governed by anxiety so intense and constant that self-identity is virtually eliminated; instead, characters are defined by color and class, lost in a social structure in which they are doomed to failure. The social scenery of these works borders on the carnivalesque, as characters view themselves like twisted images in funhouse mirrors. This constant personal uncertainty and distrust of their self-image echoes the sentiments of **W.E.B. Du Bois** in his identification of "twoness," the impossibly strained coexistence of personal Blackness in a White society.

Ralph Ellison's novel *Invisible Man*, published in 1952 (its first chapter was published in *Horizon* in 1947), incorporates elements of **myth**, epic, ideology, fate, sociology, and **protest literature**. Perhaps because, as an author, Ellison attempts to transcend the boundaries set by his predecessors, *Invisible Man* is a long and convoluted tale peopled with characters representing a multitude of ideas and communities, and is set in places from the Deep South to the Northeast.

Known only to readers by the initial sentence of the novel in which the narrator states, "I am an invisible man," the main character's namelessness is our first indication that the novel will inhabit the dreamlike realms of surrealism. As in dreams or nightmares in which we cannot see ourselves and others do not call out to us by name, the novel's protagonist seems formless as his narration proceeds with a list of who and what he is not, followed by the line "Like the bodiless heads you see sometimes in circus sideshows, it is as though I have been surrounded by mirrors of hard, distorting glass. When they approach me they see only my surroundings, themselves, or figments of their imagination—indeed, everything and anything except me." Invisible Man is introduced to readers as the valedictorian of his Southern high school class who is sadistically thrown into a blindfolded boxing match with a group of other young Blacks for the amusement of local White businessmen. After surviving the match, Invisible's epic journey begins as he makes his way to college.

The complex and seemingly unreal events which connect the disparate threads of *Invisible Man*'s lengthy narrative are heightened by characters whose motivations are capricious or unexplained and whose names often play a vital role in identifying themes in the novel (Trueblood is the unwitting perpetrator of somnambulant incest, for example, and Mary, the mother figure, saves Invisible from homelessness and possible starvation). One of the largest sections of the novel places Invisible at the forefront of a Communist political sect as Ellison illustrates that party's manipulation of Blacks as political puppets. This is but one surreal sequence of events in a novel intentionally surreal from its beginning. With the coupling the naked White woman with the blindfolded young Black men for the entertainment of suited White businessmen in the opening chapter, readers are immediately anxious and disoriented (mimicking the dislocation identified by the surrealists so many years earlier), an experience shared by the main character. With this and subsequent scenes, Ellison paints a world in which all humans, not simply Blacks, are unreal, unseen, and unheard.

Among the contemporary Black writers who incorporate literary surrealism into their work, **Toni Morrison** is perhaps the most innovative and experimental, as she pushes the surreal beyond setting and character and extends it into form and narration. Most acutely surrealist in form and content is Morrison's Pulitzer Prize-winning novel *Beloved*, a **slave narrative** and ghost story combined. The surrealistic concepts of the unseen, the unknown, and the unrealized self are intensified by their relationship to a title character who has been literally and figuratively dismembered. Based on the actual tale of Margaret Garner, a former slave who murders her infant daughter and attempts the murder of her sons rather than see them returned to the cruelty and horror of **slavery**, Morrison's novel leaps pell-mell into the tale with little prefatory introduction or forewarning for the reader. Heightening the sense of nightmarish surrealism in a story already surreal in the extreme is a house possessed, to which readers are immediately introduced with the novel's first line: "124 was spiteful." The tale of Sethe, the Garner character, and Beloved, the infant daughter whose name is derived from the headstone on which it is inscribed, unravels quickly.

At differing points in the novel, numerous other characters inhabit the house at 124 Bluestone Road, as does the infant ghost of Beloved. The house is used as a narrative touchstone at the beginning of each of the three books into which the tale is broken, and readers get bits and pieces of Sethe's and Beloved's horrifying tale as the narrative progresses, in a manner mimicking the dismemberment of baby Beloved herself. With the same feeling of dislocation and disorientation of a dream, readers are uncertain in what order the events chronicled occur, and this sense of disorientation heightens as the narrative disintegrates toward its climax, which does not consist of an event, but is realized instead through the nearly unpunctuated monologues of Sethe, Denver, and Beloved. These monologues are followed by a series of poetic paragraphs that testify to the endlessness and timelessness of the traumatic specter of slavery. As disconnected as the tale is, through these poetic sequences Morrison ironically pulls together the spectral with the self, the past with the present, the known with the unknown, until even the reader must feel the pull of inclusion and tragedy. Upon reading these passages, we feel culpable as well as victimized.

Although the tale of slavery and its repercussions on subsequent generations is by far Morrison's most surrealist novel, others she has written can also be described as ventures into the surreal, such as *Song of Solomon*, whose focus is Milkman, a character seemingly at sea in a society which quickly disintegrates from a sense of community to one of chaos. As in *Beloved*, Morrison interweaves **folktale** with historicity as she chronicles the lives of Macon Dead and his offspring who live in a Northern **Negro** town and whose primary activities take place on Not Doctor Street. Once again, Morrison tries to articulate not what is seen and experienced, but instead what is thought to be, or felt, or told; with *Song of Solomon*, readers are again uncertain as to what, if anything, actually occurred to characters who know neither themselves nor each other. The novel progresses beyond its initial realism to a connection between the *here and now* and *the fable of us before* as Guitar, Milkman's best friend, tries to kill him. Instead, Milkman gives up his life as he leaps off a cliff into the darkness, to fly away like the character in the African American folktale or, even more possibly, to fulfill Shalimar's prophecy that "If you surrendered to the air, you could *ride* it."

African American literature's relationship to the surreal is inextricable. Black writers such as Richard Wright, Ralph Ellison, Toni Morrison, and countless others have grappled with the daunting task of giving voice to Blacks' positions in, outside, above, and beyond the fabric of Anglo-American society. Moreover, as active participants in the development not merely of African American literature and culture but also that of the mainstream as well, this experience has required an unrestrained narration and symbology, an unrestricted storytelling language that freely incorporates the seen and known with the equally important unseen and unknown. While its beginnings may have been in Europe in the early part of the twentieth century, surrealism was modified and reinterpreted by numerous Black writers to assist in the articulation of an experience beyond the scope of preceding literary movements.

African poets who have drawn on surrealistic techniques include **Langston Hughes**, especially in his long poems *Montage of a Dream Deferred* and *Ask Your Mama*. **Sonja Sanchez, Haki R. Madhubuti, Amiri Baraka,** and other writers of the **Black Arts Movement** used surrealistic techniques as well.

Resources: Saul Bellow, "Man Underground," *Commentary*, June 1952, 608–610; André Breton, *Manifestoes of Surrealism*, trans. Richard Seaver and Helen R. Lane (Ann Arbor: University of Michigan Press, 1969); Ralph Ellison, *Invisible Man* (New York: Vintage Books, 1990); Lucille Fultz, *Toni Morrison: Playing with Difference* (Chicago: University of Illinois Press, 2003); Henry Louis Gates, Jr., *Loose Canons: Notes on the Culture Wars* (New York: Oxford University Press, 1992); Renée Hubert, *Surrealism and the Book* (Berkeley: University of California Press, 1988); Toni Morrison: *Beloved* (New York: Plume, 1988); *Playing in the Dark* (New York: Vintage Books, 1992); *Song of Solomon* (New York: Plume, 1987); Man Ray, *Self Portrait* (New York: Bullfinch, 1998); J. M. Reilly, *Twentieth-Century Interpretations of Invisible Man* (Englewood Cliffs, NJ: Prentice-Hall, 1970); Hazel Rowley, *Richard Wright* (New York: Henry Holt, 2001); Jean-Paul Sartre, *What Is Literature? And Other Essays* (Cambridge, MA: Harvard University Press, 1988); Jonathan Veitch, *American Superrealism* (Madison: University of Wisconsin Press, 1997); Edmund Wilson, *The Boys in the Back Room: Notes on California Novelists* (San Francisco: Colt Press, 1941); Richard Wright: *Black Boy* (New York: Perennial Classics, 1998); *Native Son* (New York: Perennial Classics, 1998).

Deirdre Ray

Survey Graphic (1921–1948). Journal. One major aim of *Survey Graphic* was to explore social issues in the United States with the purpose of bringing about social reform. With regard to African American literature, it is best known for a special issue edited by **Alain Locke** in 1925.

Advances in manufacturing technology and mass production caused a shift in the distribution of capital in early twentieth-century America, increasing the gap between the wealthy and the working class. In addition, immigration and migration meant a larger labor pool fighting for the same resources. Magazines and journals began to appear that provided social workers with data and theories about such phenomena as well as recommendations about solving social problems and encouraging reform (Finnegan, secs. 1 and 2).

Paul Kellogg was a journalist, social reform activist, and editor of *Charities and the Commons*. After changing the journal's name to *The Survey* to reflect the more scientific approach being used in social reform, Kellogg and his brother Arthur formed Survey Associates in 1912. This advisory group of social-reform experts served as the publisher for the journal.

The Survey covered industrial issues such as safety, wages, and treatment of laborers, as well as social topics such as housing, insurance, women's suffrage, and discrimination. Unfortunately, the data presented in the journal were not in a format that was easily accessible or interesting to the average reader.

In 1921, Kellogg created *Survey Graphic* as a companion to *The Survey*. As its name suggests, *Survey Graphic* used charts, graphs, drawings, and photographs to provide the public with information similar to that in its companion journal, but in a format designed to have a more immediate impact on the reader.

Survey Graphic often devoted entire issues to important topics of the time. In the fall of 1924, Kellogg asked Alain Locke to assemble a collection of literary works to fill a special issue. Locke was a professor of English and philosophy who was a supporter of and mentor to a variety of African American artists of the time. The March 1925 issue of *Survey Graphic* was titled *Harlem: Mecca of the New Negro*, and it included stories, essays, and poetry by African Americans including **W.E.B. Du Bois**, **Countee Cullen**, **Claude McKay**, and **Langston Hughes**. The issue was read by an estimated 42,000 people—more than twice the journal's normal monthly circulation—and was significant because it brought the works of African Americans to a mostly **White** audience that was not fully aware of the literature, art, and music being produced in New York City during the **Harlem Renaissance** (Lewis, 115).

Throughout *Survey Graphic*'s history, the journal reported on topics directly related to African Americans, including the results of migration as African Americans moved north to fill labor needs during **World War II**, and escalating police violence as African Americans struggled to assert their civil rights. Two additional issues of Survey Graphic were devoted solely to the concerns of African Americans: *Color: The Unfinished Business of Democracy* (1942) and *Segregation: Color Patterns from the Past—Our Struggle to Wipe It Out* (1947) (Finnegan, sec. 25).

Financial difficulties forced *Survey Graphic* and *The Survey* (by now called *Survey Midmonthly*) to merge in 1948. However, the combined journal continued to struggle, and Survey Associates and the publication were dissolved in 1952.

Resources: Clarke A. Chambers, *Paul U. Kellogg and* The Survey: *Voices for Social Welfare and Social Justice* (Minneapolis: University of Minnesota Press, 1971); Cara Finnegan, *Social Welfare and Visual Politics: The Story of* Survey Graphic (New Deal Network, 2000), http://newdeal.feri.org; John Hope Franklin and Alfred A. Moss, Jr., *From Slavery to Freedom: A History of African Americans*, 7th ed. (New York: McGraw-Hill, 1994); David Levering Lewis, *When Harlem Was in Vogue* (New York: Oxford University Press, 1989); Jeffrey C. Stewart, *1001 Things Everyone Should Know About African-American History* (New York: Doubleday, 1996); *Survey Graphic* 6, no. 6, *Harlem: Mecca of the New Negro* (repr. Baltimore: Black Classic Press, 1980); University of Virginia, American Studies Department, *Portrait of America:* Survey Graphic *in the Thirties*, http://xroads.virginia.edu/~MA01/Davis/survey, an ongoing faculty and staff project begun in 1998 to study America in the 1930s through various media of cultural expression.

Michelle Mellon

Swindle, Renée. Novelist. Swindle completed an M.F.A. at San Diego State University, where she taught courses in composition and creative writing. She subsequently moved to Oakland, California, where she has taught fiction writing with the University of California at Berkeley's Extension Program.

Swindle's first novel, *Please Please Please* (1999), developed from a story that she submitted as a class assignment and then expanded into her M.F.A. thesis. *Please Please Please* is a romantic-triangle story with a maddeningly engaging narrator and several major ironic turns. The main character and narrator is called Babysister, and she is unabashedly self-involved, self-indulgent, and self-deluding. Her narrative is lively and unself-consciously self-caricaturing. Swindle's main accomplishment with this character is that she allows her some small room for growth without attributing more growth to her than might seem credible.

Babysister's best friend is a good-hearted, level-headed young woman named Deborah. Babysister is just barely able to keep the secret that she has, unconscionably, been having an affair with Deborah's fiancé, Darren. Yet, when Darren finally breaks off his relationship with Babysister and marries Deborah, Babysister is genuinely devastated. Ironically, out of her sense of betrayal and her emotional hurt, she finds the impetus to do some self-appraisal. So when Darren returns to her, overflowing with regrets and expressing a desire to resume their clandestine relationship, she is not entirely the same young woman he dumped.

The novel suggests, ironically, that the seemingly large gap between Deborah's and Babysister's perspectives and characters is narrower than it might initially appear to be. For Deborah, after all, has married Darren, whose character flaws run even deeper than Babysister's, and her best friend is Babysister. Regardless of how much Deborah is or is not willing to forgive, these two choices in close relationships make her a good deal less than perfect. And in the world in which Babysister and Darren operate, trying always to do the "right" thing accomplishes little beyond making one more vulnerable.

Swindle's work has been included in the collection *Best Black Women's Erotica* (2001).

Resources: Martha Southgate, "Speaking Volumes," *Essence*, July 1999, 95–100; Sabrina Sutherland, "Review of *Please Please Please*, "*Black Issues Book Review* 1 (July/ Aug. 1999), 30; Renée Swindle, *Please Please Please* (New York: Dial, 1999).

Martin Kich

Swing. A notable form of **jazz**, swing pointedly shaped the literary arts in what became known as the "Jazz Age." While there is no precise technical definition for "swing"—indeed, the incisiveness of "swing" and of jazz in general is that they resist static definitions—the term generally refers to a quality attributed to jazz performance, often related to the syncopated forward propulsion of rhythm and melody. Swing bands were often composed of ten to fifteen musicians, and they provided the music for what became known as swing-dancing, a fast-paced athletic dance first popular in **New Orleans, Louisiana**, and New York City in the 1920s and 1930s, before spreading to other major cities across the country, as well as one of America's most deeply entrenched expatriate communities: **Paris, France**. Some of the many prominent practitioners of early swing jazz included the bandleader Fletcher

Henderson and his star trumpeter, Louis Armstrong, **Edward Kennedy "Duke" Ellington**, Benny Goodman, Count Basie, and Jimmy Dorsey. A resurgence in interest in the art form took hold in the United States in the later 1980s and throughout the 1990s, as the film and music industries capitalized on a retrenched musical traditionalism being espoused by the prominent trumpeter and public persona Wynton Marsalis.

While jazz music and jazz aesthetics generally have profoundly influenced post-1945 literary movements (the **Beat Movement** and **Black Arts Movement** in particular), prewar influence is often overlooked. It is in the modern aesthetics of swing and swing's precursors that the likes of **James Weldon Johnson**, F. Scott Fitzgerald, **Langston Hughes**, and others found the images to capture the radical changes taking place in an America transformed by urbanization, quickened lifestyles, and, in general, the passage into a new and unstable era. Black aesthetic tradition at the heart of swing music blurred "high" and "low" culture, classical and popular, the universal and the provincial, to inform literary representation of change. Johnson's *Autobiography of an Ex-Colored Man* (1912) provides a precursor to the discourse about Black aesthetics and its co-optation by the White urban bourgeois, as the protagonist, an accomplished ragtime musician, sells his talents to a wealthy patron who pays him to travel the world and perform in his parlor. Fitzgerald, who gave the era its "Jazz Age" moniker, peppers such works as *The Great Gatsby* (1925) and *Tender Is the Night* (1934) with the representation of swing music, something dangerously modern, that is co-opted by the urban White bourgeois as a sign of their luxury. And Hughes, one of the best-known writers of the **Harlem Renaissance**, puts the swing cadences at the center of much of his poetry, including his early poem "The Weary Blues" and a later work, *Montage of a Dream Deferred* (1951), which looks back with dismay and concern at the era's unfulfilled visions for racial equality.

Resources: Robert O'Meally, ed., *The Jazz Cadence of American Culture* (New York: Columbia University Press, 1998); Robert O'Meally et al., eds., *Uptown Conversation: The New Jazz Studies* (New York: Columbia University Press, 2004).

Keith Feldman

Tademy, Lalita (born 1948). Novelist. Lalita Liane Tademy, author of the best-selling and critically acclaimed family narrative *Cane River* (2001), was born in Berkeley, California, and grew up in Castro Valley, California. She studied at Howard University on a full scholarship for two years before she transferred to the University of California, **Los Angeles**, where she earned a B.A. in psychology and statistics (1970) and an M.B.A. (1972). She held managerial positions at Bay Area Rapid Transit, Memorex, Tab Products, ITT/Qume, and Alps Electric USA before she accepted a job offer from Sun Microsystems, a Fortune 500 computer firm located in Silicon Valley, in 1992. Tademy, who was eventually promoted to vice president and general manager at Sun, was featured in *Black Enterprise*, **Ebony**, and *Fortune*, and was named an African American Innovator in the New Millennium at the Silicon Valley Tech Museum of Innovation.

In 1995 Tademy abandoned the career to which she had devoted two decades and, inspired by family lore, her memories of many childhood summers spent near Cane River in Colfax, Louisiana, and a two-page family history written by Tademy's great-cousin Gurtie Fredieu in 1975, began researching her family's genealogy. She traveled back and forth from California to Louisiana in order to talk to family members and local historians as well as to search archival and courthouse records. The result of Tademy's research is her debut novel, which is set in Cane River, a farming community named for the nineteen-mile river in central Louisiana that was populated in the 1800s by **Creole** French planters, free Blacks, and slaves. Spanning a period that stretches from **slavery** to freedom, from antebellum days to the 1930s, *Cane*

River is Tademy's tribute to four of her maternal ancestors: Elizabeth (b. 1799), Suzette (b. 1825), Philomene (b. 1841), and Emily (b. 1861).

Resources: Jabari Asim, "Families Torn Asunder: *Cane River* by Lalita Tademy," *Washington Post*, June 12, 2001, http://www.washingtonpost.com/ac2/wp-dyn? pagename=article&no; Jennifer Desai, "Menlo Park Author Leaves Tech World Behind and Discovers Her Roots," *The Almanac*, Mar. 28, 2001, http://www .almanacnews.com/morgue/2001/2001_03_28.cover28.html; Heather Knight, "Tracing Her Roots: Lalita Tademy Quit the Corporate Life to Write a Novel About Her Family History," http://sfgate.com/cgi-bin/article.cgi?f=/c/a/2001/06/01/PN213021 .DTL&hw=tracing+her+roots&sn=003&sc=462; "Lalita Tademy," *Contemporary Authors Online* (2003), http://www.galenet.com/servlet/LitRC?c=1&ai=1411597& ste=6&d; Lalita Tademy, *Cane River* (New York: Warner, 2001).

Linda M. Carter

Talented Tenth (c. 1900–1930). Social concept. The concept of the Talented Tenth is closely connected to **W.E.B. Du Bois**'s social and cultural theory. (Du Bois published the essay "The Talented Tenth," in 1903; see *The Negro Problem*). The concept represented his views about what kind of group might best represent African Americans when, at the beginning of the twentieth century, they occupied such a marginal position in American society. The concept was especially influential and relevant in the cultural movement known as the **Harlem Renaissance** of the 1920s. Du Bois and other architects of the movement believed it was the duty of intellectuals and writers to advance a satisfactory image of the African Amerian community, an image that would foster the integration of cultures on a national scale. Many of the writers especially—including **Wallace Thurman**, **Langston Hughes**, and **Zora Neale Hurston**—resisted this duty and believed that it impinged on artistic freedom (Lewis).

The origin of the term can be dated back to **Alexander Crummell** and his leading role in the American Negro Academy at the turn of the nineteenth century. Influenced by the ideas of the British intellectual Thomas Carlyle, Crummell was influential in the configuration of an African American "intellectual class" and in promoting the idea of **racial uplift**. This uplift, Crummell believed, would be achieved by means of education and cultural refinement. The intellectual class would serve as examples of this refinement, and they would also transmit it, according to Crummell's view. For Crummell, the only way to reach that aim—civilizing Blacks—was through the agency of the cultured men of the race—that is, the instructed minority that could guide the rest of the community with their knowledge and culture.

Du Bois, in turn, firmly believed that the Talented Tenth (his name for this group of cultural leaders) offered the only possibility for the African American community actually to assimilate fully into American society. According to him, "The Negro race, like all races, is going to be saved by its exceptional men" (Pascal, 31). Du Bois urged the forging of an aristocracy based on intelligence and morality, able to stand for the African American community with dignity and honesty. He encouraged African Americans to strive for a liberal style of education which would be clearly oriented to the uplift of the race: "Education and work are the levers to uplift a people" (Pascal, 50). For him, then, liberal education became the only way out of the desperate situation of the Black race in general and of African Americans in particular. For him it was the only effective means to ensure the desired integration. In Du Bois's view at the time, only an educated minority could lead the other African Americans in their pursuit of the ideal of civilization proposed by Crummell. Thus, education was assigned great importance in Du Bois's social and cultural agenda. This agenda was condemned as intellectual elitism by his political opponents, including **Booker T. Washington**.

Despite such criticism, Du Bois believed the Talented Tenth would benefit the entire African American community. As Arnold Rampersad observes, Du Bois believed that "the educated and moneyed classes had a strict responsibility to guide the masses...through their personal example of a respect for learning, whether in the arts, the sciences, or vocational skills" (58). For Du Bois, the key to the progress of the **race** lay in the Talented Tenth's acceptance of their leading role, especially in the forging of the aesthetic experience. They should also engage in establishing direct links with the White intellectual class, because "only by a union of intelligence and sympathy across the color-line in this critical period of the Republic shall justice and right triumph" (Du Bois, *Souls*, 132). Further, in Du Bois's view, the combination of talent and education should become the only valid yardstick by which to measure the worth and humanity of individuals, no matter what race they were classified in. Thus Du Bois subverted the racist ideology that depended on presumed racial differences (and even superiority) by proposing an alternative hierarchy which conferred primacy on intellectual and artistic abilities. **Harlem, New York**, intellectuals would then choose "neither religion (which symbolized the force of the Negro's past as the slave who endured) nor politics (which symbolized the Negro's present as quasi-participatory American citizen), but art (which symbolized the Negro's future as the new Westerner, the innovative imaginative force in the Western world)" (Early, 144). To excel intellectually was, in Du Bois's view, to pave the way for progress and for eliminating the effects of racial stereotypes. Art, especially literature, was deemed essential to articulate the so-called **New Negro** that would be born out of the ashes of the old and withered stereotypes.

In "The Talented Tenth: Memorial Address" (1948), Du Bois reevaluated his concept of the Talented Tenth and transformed it into "the doctrine of the Guiding Hundreth." Trying to respond to criticism the idea of the Talented Tenth had attacted, he emphasized the necessary virtues that should be possessed by the college-trained intelligentsia he had imagined: a willingness to sacrifice for the welfare of the race, honesty of character and far-seeing leadership, and especially a planned program (to be put into practice by a national organization) that could assure a better future for African Americans in the United States. The moral qualities of the intelligentsia were stressed in

Du Bois's 1948 version of the Talented Tenth. In this version, Du Bois was to some extent returning to Crummell's view of an elite group that would reform the race. In Crummell's and Du Bois's view, this group, as both scholars and philanthropists, would devote their lives to the task of reconstructing the race and disseminating their culture in a disinterested way. For African American writers, beginning with the Harlem Renaissance, the concept of the Talented Tenth raised many questions, including the following: To what extent should writers be seen, and see themselves, as part of an elite cultural group that would lead African Americans?

Resources: Alexander Crummell, *The American Negro Academy. Occasional Papers, 1–22* (New York: Arno, 1969); W.E.B. Du Bois, *The Souls of Black Folk* (1903; repr. New York: Bantam, 1989); W.E.B. Du Bois, Paul Lawrence Dunbar, Charles W. Chestnutt, et al., *The Negro Problem: A Series of Articles by Representative American Negroes of Today* (New York: J. Pott, 1903); Gerald Early, "Three Notes Toward a Cultural Definition of the Harlem Renaissance," *Callalloo* 14, no. 1 (1990), 136–149; David Levering Lewis, *When Harlem Was in Vogue* (New York: Knopf, 1981); Andrew Pascal, ed., *W.E.B. Du Bois. A Reader* (New York: Macmillan, 1971); Arnold Rampersad, *The Art and Imagination of W.E.B. Du Bois* (1976; repr. New York: Schocken, 1990); Eric Sundquist, ed., *The Oxford W.E.B. Du Bois Reader* (New York: Oxford University Press, 1996).

Mar Gallego

Tanner, Benjamin Tucker (1835–1923). Editor, theologian, and historian. As editor of the African Methodist Episcopal (A.M.E.) newspaper *The Christian Recorder* from 1868 to 1884, Benjamin Tanner shaped the direction of the A.M.E. Church following the **Civil War** and greatly influenced its denominational literature. Born in **Pittsburgh, Pennsylvania**, in 1835, Tanner was licensed to preach in the A.M.E. Church in 1858. Tanner's work, *An Apology for African Methodism* (1867), concerned the history of the A.M.E. Church and the role of early church leaders, such as **Richard Allen** and Absalom Jones, in gaining denominational independence. Tanner addressed the curse of Ham in *The Negro's Origin and Is the Negro Cursed?* (1869). In *The Christian Recorder*, Tanner used editorials, literary reviews, stories, and poetry, as well as letters and articles from leaders and members of the church, to convey and interpret local and national news for his readership. In 1884, Tanner was the first editor of the literary magazine *A.M.E. Church Review*, which showcased the intellectual ability of African Americans and A.M.E. members. In the same year, Tanner wrote *An Outline of Our History and Government for African Methodist Churchmen, Ministerial and Lay* (1884) to explain the church discipline to new members. In 1888, Tanner was elected bishop of the A.M.E. Church. From 1891 to 1895, Tanner wrote several theological works, including *The Divine Kingdom* (1891), *Theological Lectures* (1894), and *The Color of Solomon—What?* (1895), which challenged the notion that Solomon was White and instead asserted that he was of Asian descent. Tanner wrote *The Descent of the Negro* (1898), which made the case that, like all humans, African Americans were descended from Ham. In 1899, Tanner wrote another history of the church, *The Dispensations in the History of the Church and the Interregnum*. He wrote *The Negro in Holy Writ* (1900), which emphasized the role of Africans in the Bible. In the same year, Tanner wrote a pamphlet, *Hints to Ministers* (1900), in which he drew upon his own experiences to give advice to ministers. A committed teacher, Tanner wrote *Joel, the Son of Pethuel* (1905) for the students at Edward Waters College. An avid reader and prolific author, Tanner wrote, published, reviewed, and interpreted a wide range of literature for his religious denomination and the larger African American community.

Resources: Primary Sources: Benjamin T. Tanner: *An Apology for African Methodism* (Baltimore: [privately printed?], 1867); *The Color of Solomon—What?* (Philadelphia: A.M.E. Book Concern, 1895); *The Descent of the Negro* (Philadelphia: A.M.E. Book Concern, 1898); *The Dispensations in the History of the Church and the Interregnum* (Kansas City, MO: Benjamin T. Tanner, 1899); *Hints to Ministers* (Wilberforce, OH: Wilberforce University Press, 1900); *Joel, the Son of Pethuel* (Philadelphia: [privately printed?], 1905); *The Negro in Holy Writ* (Philadelphia: A.M.E. Book Concern, 1900); *The Negro's Origin and Is the Negro Cursed?* (Philadelphia: A.M.E. Book Depository, 1869); *An Outline of Our History and Government for African Methodist Churchmen, Ministerial and Lay* (Philadelphia: Grant, Faires & Rodgers, 1884); *Theological Lectures* (Nashville, TN: A.M.E. Church Sunday School Union, 1894). **Secondary Sources:** James T. Campbell, *Songs of Zion: The African Methodist Episcopal Church in the United States and South Africa* (Chapel Hill: University of North Carolina Press, 1998); William Seraile, *Fire in His Heart: Benjamin Tucker Tanner and the A.M.E. Church* (Knoxville: University of Tennessee Press, 1998); Clarence E. Walker, *A Rock in a Weary Land: The African Methodist Episcopal Church During the Civil War and Reconstruction* (Baton Rouge: Louisiana State University Press, 1982).

Julius H. Bailey

Tarpley, Natasha (born 1971). Children's author. Tarpley has received critical notice, a book award, and national recognition for a series of picture books for children, including *I Love My Hair!*, *Girl in the Mirror*, *Bibbity Bop Barbershop*, and *Joe-Joe's First Flight*. (E. B. Lewis is frequently the illustrator of Tarpley's books.) *I Love My Hair!* won the 1999 BlackBoard Children's Book of the Year Award ("Natasha Tarpley"). Tarpley was born and grew up in **Chicago, Illinois**, and later attended Harvard University, where she began to study German as her major subject but then shifted to African American Studies. In 1994 she received a grant from the National Endowment for the Arts. She has written since she was a child ("Natasha Tarpley"). Tarpley's books reflect a subtle understanding of children's psychology and ways of seeing the world (Gayle). Tarpley edited *Testimony: Young African-Americans on Self-Discovery and Black Identity*, and with Christen Satchelle edited *What I Know Is Me: Black Girls Write About Their World*. She was among ten writers who wrote the erotic narrative, *When Butterflies Kiss*, "edited" by the apparently apocryphal "Sekou." After living in New York City for many years,

Tarpley moved back to Chicago, where, at this writing, she is pursuing an M.F.A. in creative writing at the School of the Art Institute of Chicago.

Resources: Bridgett C. Gayle, "Interview with Natasha Tarpley," *Writer Online* (2000), http://www.writeronline.us/interviews/gayle10-17.htm; "Sekou," ed., *When Butterflies Kiss*, by Kiini Ibura Salaam, Elizabeth Clara Brown, T'kalla, Natasha Tarpley, Korby Marks, Shange, Kim Green, Mariahadessa Ekere Tallie, and Leticia Benson (Atlanta: Silver Lion Press, 2001); Natasha Tarpley: *Bibbity Bop Barbershop* (Boston: Little, Brown, 2002); *Girl in the Mirror* (Boston: Beacon, 1998); *I Love My Hair!* (New York: Little, Brown, 1998); *Joe-Joes's First Flight* (New York: Knopf, 2003); Natasha Tarpley, ed., *Testimony: Young African-Americans on Self-Discovery and Black Identity* (Boston: Beacon, 1995); "Natasha Tarpley," Dwyer & O'Grady (literary agency) Web site http://www.dwyerogrady.com/tarpley.html; Natasha Tarpley and Christen Satchelle, eds., *What I Know Is Me: Black Girls Write About Their World* (New York: Harlem Moon Press, 2005).

Hans Ostrom

Tarry, Ellen (born 1906). Children's author, journalist, and religious organizer. Best known as an advocate for both civil rights and the Catholic faith, Tarry was one of the first African Americans to publish positive representations of her race in books for children and young adults.

Born and raised in Birmingham, Alabama, Tarry described her childhood as happy and fulfilling (Smith). As a young girl she attended a Catholic boarding school for African Americans in Virginia and converted to Catholicism, a choice that is reflected in her writing and career.

Tarry attended Alabama State College, then began teaching at a segregated elementary school. In an effort to show her students they could achieve greatness, she wrote stories about successful local African Americans. These stories earned her a position writing a column, "Negroes of Note," for *The Birmingham Truth* newspaper. This theme also appeared later in her books for young adults, which include biographies of Katherine Drexel (1958, revised 2000), Martín de Porres (1963), and **James Weldon Johnson** (1967).

In 1929, Tarry moved to New York to pursue a career in writing and quickly became friends with major figures of the **Harlem Renaissance**, including **Claude McKay**, **Countee Cullen**, and **Langston Hughes**. With their support, she published several children's books that promoted ideals of interracial harmony and featured African American children as central characters. *Janie Belle* (1940), *Hezekiah Horton* (1942), and *My Dog Rinty* (1946) were praised for their beautiful pictures, interracial friendships, and realistic portrayal of **Harlem, New York**.

Tarry advanced her ideals on civil rights and interracial fellowship in a seminal work titled *The Third Door: The Autobiography of an American Negro Woman* (1955). She also cofounded Friendship Houses in both Harlem and **Chicago, Illinois**, served in vital roles in a number of Catholic organizations, and worked within the Department of Housing and Urban Development.

Resources: Helen Houston, "Ellen Tarry," in *Notable Black American Women*, ed. Jessie Carney Smith (Detroit: Gale, 1992), 1102–1103; Sister Mary Anthony Scally, *Negro Catholic Writers, 1900–1943: A Bio-Bibliography* (Detroit: Walter Romig, 1945), 108–111; Katharine Capshaw Smith, "From Bank Street to Harlem: A Conversation with Ellen Tarry," *The Lion and the Unicorn* 23, no. 2 (1999), 271–285; Bernard Sternsher and Judith Sealander, eds., *Women of Valor* (Chicago: Ivan R. Dee, 1990), 188–201; Ellen Tarry: *Hezekiah Horton* (New York: Viking, 1942); *Janie Belle* (New York: Garden City, 1940); *Katherine Drexel: Friend of the Neglected* (New York: Farrar, Straus and Cudahy, 1958); *Martín de Porres: Saint of the New World* (New York: Farrar, Straus and Cudahy, 1963); *The Other Toussaint: A Modern Biography of Pierre Toussaint, a Post-Revolutionary Black* (Boston: St. Paul Editions, 1981); *The Runaway Elephant* (New York: Viking, 1950); *The Third Door: The Autobiography of an American Negro Woman* (New York: David McKay, 1955); *Young Jim: The Early Years of James Weldon Johnson* (New York: Dodd, Mead, 1967).

Elizabeth A. Osborne

Tate, Eleanora Elaine (born 1948). Editor and author of fiction and poetry. Tate is recognized for writing books for middle grade readers that feature insightful and courageous African American girls attempting to make sense of the world and their place in it. Two of Tate's earlier works for middle grade readers—*Just an Overnight Guest* (1980) and the sequel, *Front Porch Stories at the One-Room School* (1992)—are set in the fictional small town of Nutbrush, Missouri, which is based on Tate's place of birth, Canton, Missouri. With a B.A. in journalism from Drake University in 1973, Tate began a career as a news reporter and news editor.

Tate has published poetry and fiction in several periodicals and contributed poetry, short stories, and essays to a number of collections, including **Rosa Guy**'s *Children of Longing* (1970) and Wade and Cheryl Hudson's *In Praise of Our Fathers and Our Mothers: A Black Family Treasury by Outstanding Authors and Artists* (1997). After publishing *Just an Overnight Guest*, Tate received a fellowship in children's literature from the Bread Loaf Writers Conference in Middlebury, Vermont. Tate's fiction addresses contemporary issues and concerns of African American girls: adolescence, identity issues, and family relationships, particularly between fathers and daughters. The importance of education, Black history and culture, self-esteem, and self-affirmation are also central themes in her novels.

Just an Overnight Guest, a story about Margie Carson and her resentment toward four-year-old Ethel, whom Margie later learns is her cousin, was made into a film in 1983 and listed as one of the "Selected Films for Young Adults" in 1985. Tate, who had attended first grade in a one-room school, used many of her personal experiences in *Front Porch Stories at the One-Room School*. In the book, Margie and Ethel listen as Margie's father tells stories of his childhood.

Myrtle Beach, South Carolina, is the setting of Tate's popular trilogy. In *The Secret of Gumbo Grove* (1987), Raisin Stackhouse searches for details about the history of the Black community in her South Carolina town; in *Thank You, Dr. Martin Luther King, Jr!* (1990), Mary Elouise struggles with issues concerning her racial identity; and in *A Blessing in Disguise* (1995), Zambia longs to develop a strong relationship with her father even as she attempts to come to terms with his irresponsible and dangerous lifestyle. Tate has received several awards for her novels, including a Parents' Choice Award in 1987 for *The Secret of Gumbo Grove* and "Pick of the Lists" awards in 1992 and 1996 for *Front Porch Stories at the One-Room School* and *A Blessing in Disguise*, respectively. While Tate worked on *African American Musicians* (2000), a book of biographical profiles of African American musicians, she discovered some of the background information she used to write her next book, *Minstrel's Melody* (2001), a **historical novel** set in 1904 in Calico Creek, Missouri. In addition to writing quality novels for young people, Tate has edited *Eclipsed* (1975, with her husband, Zack E. Hamlett III) and *Wanjiru: A Collection of Blackwomanworth* (1976).

Resources: "Eleanora E(laine) Tate," *Children's Literature Review* 37 (1996), 186–193; "Tate, Eleanora E(laine)," in *Major Authors and Illustrators for Children and Young Adults*, ed. Alan Hedblad (Detroit: Gale, 1998), 212–215.

KaaVonia Hinton-Johnson

Tate, Greg (born 1957). Essayist and critic. Greg Tate's writing enunciates a tone and elaborates a vocabulary for cultural criticism that is responsive to the rich and divergent forms of Black cultural production it considers. Tate attended Howard University in the late 1970s and began contributing to *The Village Voice* in 1986. Since then he has written numerous columns calling for "popular post-structuralism—accessible writing bent on deconstructing the whole of black culture" (*Flyboy*, 198). Tate's book *Midnight Lightning: Jimi Hendrix and the Black Experience* (2003) contextualizes **White** America's elevation of Hendrix by considering how Hendrix's life, music, and image relate in particular and unexpected ways to Black culture. Throughout his work, Tate has emphasized the necessity of critical writing that can keep up with the prolific varieties of Black expressive culture, arguing that "If Afro Americans have never settled for the racist reductions imposed upon them—from chattel slaves to cinematic stereotype to sociological myth—it's because the black collective conscious not only knew better but also knew more than enough ethnic diversity to subsume those fictions" (*Flyboy*, 153).

Introducing a collection of Tate's essays, *Flyboy in the Buttermilk* (1992), **Henry Louis Gates, Jr.**, remarks on Tate's ability to confound reductive positions with complex analyses that manage to "both celebrate the energizing pull of cultural nationalism *and* register its limitations, moral and intellectual" (13). Tate's work has appeared in the *New York Times*, *Rolling Stone*, the *Washington Post*, *Premiere*, *Downbeat*, *VIBE*, and *Artforum*; he is also a musician, producer, and cofounder of the Black Rock Coalition. His current projects include a book on African American rock titled *There's a Spectre Haunting Elvis: Further Invocations for the Dark Gods of Rock and Roll* and a collection of short **science fiction**, *Altered Spades, Fables of Harlem*.

Resources: Henry Louis Gates, Jr., "Foreword," in *Flyboy in the Buttermilk*, by Greg Tate (New York: Simon and Schuster, 1992), 13–14; Greg Tate: *Everything but the Burden: What White People Are Taking from Black Culture* (New York: Broadway Books, 2003); *Flyboy in the Buttermilk* (New York: Simon and Schuster, 1992); *Midnight Lightning: Jimi Hendrix and the Black Experience* (Chicago: Lawrence Hill, 2003); Greg Tate and Martin Dixon, *Brooklyn Kings: New York City's Black Bikers* (New York: PowerHouse Books, 2000).

Alex Feerst

Taulbert, Clifton LeMoure (born 1945). Author and entrepreneur. Taulbert was born February 19, 1945, in Glen Allen, Mississippi, and raised in an extended family that included his two brothers and four sisters, grandparents, and aunt. The experience of growing up in the racially charged and rapidly changing **South** formed the basis for Taulbert's widely acclaimed *Once upon a Time When We Were Colored* (1989). The experience of Civil Rights era Mississippi is visually rendered in the film adaptation of *Once upon a Time When We Were Colored* (1996) and the documentary *The Era of Segregation: A Personal Perspective* (1993), both of which Taulbert coproduced.

In 1963 Taulbert left the **Mississippi Delta** when he joined the Air Force. His Pulitzer Prize-nominated second memoir, *The Last Train North* (1992), continues his story from his decision to leave Mississippi after graduating from O'Bannon High School to his career with the Air Force, where he reached the rank of sergeant. He later moved to Tulsa, **Oklahoma**, to attend Oral Roberts University, then continued at Southern Methodist University, completing graduate work in banking.

His studies enabled Taulbert to recognize a trend in health consciousness, and he worked with the inventor of the Stairmaster, an exercise machine, to meet public demand. Taulbert's entrepreneurial successes include serving as President of Freemont Corporation. For his corporate achievements *Time* honored Taulbert by naming him an outstanding entrepreneur.

As in his memoirs, Taulbert's emphasis as an entrepreneur continues to be community building. In 1997 he published *Eight Habits of the Heart: The Timeless Values That Build Strong Communities*, which enumerates and emphasizes the universality of the lessons learned in Mississippi. Taulbert brings his message of community-building and leadership to public audiences by lecturing through the Building Community Institute, which he founded, and actively pursues his aims of community-building as a member of University of Tulsa board of trustees and the board of directors of the Tulsa Metropolitan Chamber of Commerce. Regardless of his role as public speaker, businessman, or entrepreneur, the affirming role of the community he narrated in *Once upon a Time When We Were Colored* remains.

Once upon a Time When We Were Colored and Taulbert's other nonfiction books, *Watching Our Crops Come In* (1997) and *The Journey Home: A Father's Gift to His Son* (2002), as well as his three children's books, have garnered both the **NAACP** Image Award for outstanding contribution to literature (1996) and his induction into the Oklahoma Writers Hall of Fame (2000).

Taulbert lives in Tulsa, Oklahoma, with his wife and son. He maintains a Web site that describes his ongoing work, www.cliftontaulbert.com.

Resources: "Ellen Gilchrist's and Clifton Taulbert's Portrayls of Glen Allen," *Notes on Mississippi Writers* 24, no. 2 (July 1992), 59–65; Onita Estes-Hicks, "The Way We Were: Precious Memories of the Black Segregated South," *African American Review* 27, no. 1 (Spring 1993), 9–18; Clifton Taulbert: *Eight Habits of the Heart* (New York: Penguin, 1999); *The Era of Segregation: A Personal Perspective* (New York: Knowledge Unlimited, 1993); *The Journey Home* (Tulsa, OK: Council Oak Books, 2002); *The Last Train North* (Tulsa, OK: Council Oak Books, 1992); *Little Cliff and the Porch People* (New York: Dial, 1999); *Once upon a Time When We Were Colored* (1989; repr. New York: Penguin, 1995); *Watching Our Crops Come In* (New York: Penguin, 1998).

Sean Harrington Wells

Taylor, Mel (born 1939). Novelist. Trained as a hair stylist, Mel Taylor saw his prospects unravel because of his addiction to cocaine. Along the way, he served several prison sentences. During his last incarceration, at the MacNeil Island Prison near Seattle, Washington, Taylor kicked his habit, earned his G.E.D., tutored other inmates, enrolled in a writing workshop, and helped to develop a theater workshop. After his release, he worked at a drug rehabilitation clinic in Seattle, and his efforts on behalf of other addicts were honored when he was asked to serve on the clinic's board of directors.

While enrolled in the prison writing workshop, Taylor began to conceive the story that would eventually become his only novel, *The Mitt Man* (1999). Originally, however, he wrote it as a screenplay, and when scriptwriter Tony Bill was a guest instructor at the workshop, Taylor showed him his early drafts. The two developed a friendship. Bill encouraged Taylor to continue working on the story and was instrumental in securing Taylor's early release from prison. While working at a film production office, Taylor gradually transformed his script into a novel. His progress was made more difficult by kidney failure, which still requires regular dialysis.

The Mitt Man is the story of two con men, James "King Fish" Cook and Jimmie Lamar. When the two meet in a Louisiana prison, Cook, who is old enough to be Lamar's father, has already served several decades of a life sentence for killing a White man who had assaulted his wife. Cook becomes Lamar's mentor, gradually instructing him in the subtleties of various confidence games and transforming the journeyman grifter into a master con artist. Eventually, Cook passes on his knowledge of how to work the ultimate con. The "mitt man" is a con man posing as a man of God to fleece true believers. The con requires that the mitt man never reveal, and yet never forget, that he is a swindler; it allows him to rationalize that however much he abuses the good faith of the believers, he is ultimately providing his victims with the conviction of salvation that they are seeking. When Lamar is released from prison and attempts to work the con, however, he is seduced by the faith of his intended victims and by the instinct that he might legitimately have a religious vocation. Such a role becomes too psychologically complicated for Lamar to sustain, and it all ends badly—ironically, because he has not been true to the con and to the code that governs it. Compared by several reviewers to *Elmer Gantry* and *Cool Hand Luke*, Taylor's novel shortens the distance between the licit and illicit in American life. (*See* **Prison Literature**.)

Resources: Richard Bernstein, "Preaching, and Picking Pockets, on a Racial Frontier," *New York Times*, Apr. 5, 1999, p. E6; Mel Taylor: *The Mitt Man* (New York: Morrow, 1999); *Murder by Deadline* (New York: Avon, 2005).

Martin Kich

Taylor, Mildred D. (born 1943). Children's writer and young-adult novelist. A leading writer of fiction for younger African American readers, Taylor has won many awards for her novels, notably the 1976 Newbery Medal, multiple Coretta Scott King Awards, *Boston Globe/Horn Book* Citations, and American Library Association ALAN Awards for significant contribution to young adult literature. Taylor was born in Jackson, Mississippi, on September 13, 1943, to Wilbert and Deletha (Davis) Taylor. Shortly after her birth, the family moved to Toledo, Ohio, where many friends and relatives had already made their homes. Taylor remained there until she graduated with a Bachelor of Education from the University of Toledo in 1965. She then joined the Peace Corps and taught English on a Navajo reservation in Arizona and history in Ethiopia. Upon returning to the United States in 1967, she worked as a Peace Corps recruiter and instructor in Maine. In 1969, she earned a Master of Arts at the University of Colorado's Graduate School of Journalism. As a member of the Black Student Alliance, she worked with students and university officials in structuring a Black Education program and then served as a study skills director in the program. After a brief return to Ethiopia, Taylor moved to **Los Angeles, California**, in 1971 and married Errol Zea-Daly in 1972; they had one child, and divorced in 1975 (Crowe, 5–6).

In California, Taylor worked temporary jobs while she focused on the writing she had been developing since she was a student. Inspired by family histories told by her father, family vacations in **the South**, and her time in Africa, Taylor's writing brings African American experience into literature for children and young adults. In 1973, Taylor entered a writing contest sponsored by the Council on Interracial Books for Children with a story about an African American father who defends his land against illegal logging by a White man. Told by eight-year-old Cassie Logan, *Song of the Trees* won the contest and was published by Dial Press (1975).

Taylor consistently juxtaposes themes of racism and hope, family and oppression, against the backdrop of African American culture, both historical and contemporary. While her novels most frequently tell the stories of the Logan family, *The Friendship* (1987) and *The Gold Cadillac* (1987) address racism from other perspectives. Taylor continued the Logan story with her second novel, *Roll of Thunder, Hear My Cry* (1976), which won the American Library Association's Newbery Medal; *Let the Circle Be Unbroken* (1981), *The Road to Memphis* (1990), and *Logan* (2004). *Mississippi Bridge* (1990), *The Well: David's Story* (1995), and *The Land* (2001) narrate the early Logan history, through **Reconstruction** and into the **Great Depression**.

Resources: Primary Sources: Mildred D. Taylor: *The Friendship* (1987; repr. New York: Puffin Books, 1998); *The Gold Cadillac* (1987; repr. New York: Puffin Books, 1998); *The Land* (New York: Phyllis Fogelman Books, 2001); *Let the Circle Be Unbroken* (New York: Dial, 1981); *Mississippi Bridge* (1990; repr. New York: Skylark, 1992); *The Road to Memphis* (1990; repr. New York: Puffin Books, 1992); *Roll of Thunder, Hear My Cry* (1976; repr. New York: Puffin Books, 1991); *Song of the Trees* (New York: Dial, 1975); *The Well* (1995; repr. New York: Putnam/Puffin, 1998). **Secondary Sources:** Chris Crowe, *Presenting Mildred D. Taylor* (New York: Twayne, 1999); Phyllis J. Fogelman, "Mildred D. Taylor," *Horn Book* 53, no. 4 (Aug. 1977), 410–414; Mary Turner Harper, "Merger and Metamorphosis in the Fiction of Mildred D. Taylor," *Children's Literature Association Quarterly* 13, no. 1 (1988), 75–80; Anita Moss, "Mildred D. Taylor," in *Writers of Multicultural Fiction for Young Adults: A Bio-Critical Sourcebook*, ed. M. Daphne Kutzer (Westport, CT: Greenwood Press, 1996), 401–413.

Roxanne Harde

Taylor, Regina (born 1959). Actress, playwright, and director. Taylor is an extremely versatile artist, enjoying success as an actor on stage, on television, and in film, as well as writing acclaimed plays. She was born in Dallas, **Texas**, and while she was still an undergraduate at Southern Methodist University, she appeared in a television movie about the **Civil Right Movement** and desegregation (*Crisis at Central High*, 1981). In 1992 she earned a Golden Globe Award for her performance in the dramatic television series *I'll Fly Away*. In 2000 she starred in the film adaptation of **Langston Hughes**'s short story "Cora Unashamed," from his collection *The Ways of White Folks* (1934). The film was directed by Debora Pratt. Taylor has also appeared in the films *The Negotiator* (1998), *Courage Under Fire* (1996), *Clockers* (1995), and *Jersey Girl* (1992), among many others. She also appeared on the highly popular television series *Law and Order*. On Broadway, she has played Juliet in *Romeo and Juliet*, and in **Los Angeles, California**, she appeared in the acclaimed dramatic work *The Vagina Monologues*. In 1999 she appeared in **Cheryl L. West**'s play *Jar the Door*, in **Chicago, Illinois**.

Taylor's own plays include *Watermelon Rinds* (1992), which mixes comedy and **drama** and concerns the internal politics of an African American family, and *Between the Lines* (1994), an experimental play. Her other plays include *The Ties That Bind: A Pair of One-Act Plays*, *Inside the Belly of the Beast*, *Escape from Paradise*, *Crowns*, *Night in Tunisia*, and *Oo-Bla-Dee*, which concerns a female African American **jazz** singer in the 1940s. In 2004 Taylor's adaptation of Anton Chekhov's *The Seagull* premiered on Broadway; it is entitled *Drowning Crow*. She has directed plays at the Goodman Theatre in La Jolla, California.

Resources: Kimberly Dawn Dixon, "Taking Place as We Speak: The Construction, Expression and Interpretation of Black Female Identity in the Careers of Regina Taylor, Anna Deavere Smith, and Suzan-Lori Parks," Ph.D. diss., Northwestern University, 2000; Deborah Pratt, dir., *Cora Unashamed* (Los Angeles: Warner Home Video, 2001), VHS format; Regina Taylor: *Crowns* (New York: Dramatists' Play Service, 2004); *Night in Tunisia* (New York: Dramatists' Play Service, 2004); *The Ties That Bind: A Pair of One-Act Plays* (New York: Dramatists' Play Service, 1995).

Hans Ostrom

Taylor, Susie King (1848–1912). Civil War veteran, teacher, and memoirist. Susie King Taylor is known to us for the single work she produced in 1902: *Reminiscences of My Life in Camp with the 33d United States Colored Troops Late 1st S.C. Volunteers.* In this book, she recounts her life as a regimental laundress and cook while also revealing fascinating details about regimental life and what the soldiers dealt with daily during the **Civil War.**

Taylor was born Susie Baker, a slave on a plantation in Georgia. While she does not seem to have been given her freedom officially, she was sent to live with her manumitted grandmother in Savannah, where she learned to read, write, and sew. When she was fourteen years old, the Civil War broke out and Susie found herself living with the "33rd United States Colored Troops," commanded by Col. Thomas Higginson, on St. Simon's Island. There she met and married a black soldier, Edward King, and she was asked to teach the forty or so children who were living behind the Union line. When the regiment joined the fighting, Susie went with them and proved herself invaluable as a laundress, nurse, cook, and aide-de-camp. That she was invaluable is proven by the introduction Col. Higginson wrote to her memoir. Edward King died after the war, and she remarried in 1879. Taylor spent the rest of her life engaged in social and political causes, most notably with initiatives concerning African American women.

When Taylor published her book, she joined a coterie of African American women activists in their attempts to show the strengths and contributions of African Americans in the United States. In detailing her experiences, Taylor was highlighting the intelligence, bravery, and significance of both the "colored troops" she had known during the war and of the African American women who worked alongside them; she was also indirectly showing that African Americans were an important part of American life. Her narrative recounts harrowing battles, but it also shows Black and White soldiers working together toward a common end. Taylor describes a softer side of the soldiers when she speaks of the sadness they all share at the death of a child. She stresses the commonalities of the Black and White soldiers. Published some thirty-five years after the end of the war, her memoir served to correct numerous racial stereotypes.

After the war, Taylor continued to work hard in many capacities, but "my interest in the boys in blue had not abated. I was still loyal and true, whether they were black or white" (133). Her belief in the struggle for freedom during the war became a fight against the injustices of racism after the war; Taylor felt acutely the division between White and Black Americans. In her writing, she implicitly asks why Blacks and Whites can't enjoy some of the same privileges while acknowledging that change will be slow to come. Taylor's memoir is a unique chronicle of the life of an American woman whose dismay at the treatment of people who fought for the nation's freedom becomes, ultimately, a call for justice for those same people "to be citizens of these United States" (151).

Resources: Joycelyn K. Moody, "Susie King Taylor," in *Dictionary of Literary Biography*, vol. 221, *American Women Prose Writers 1870–1920*, ed. Sharon Harris, Heidi Jacobs, and Jennifer Putzi (Detroit: Gale, 2000); Susie King Taylor, *Reminiscences of My Life in Camp with the 33d United States Colored Troops Late 1st S.C. Volunteers*, ed. Patricia W. Romero (1902; repr. New York: Marcus Wiener, 1999).

Marcy L. Tanter

Terrell, Mary Eliza Church (1863–1954). Writer, lecturer, and educator. In her role as an activist and as an advocate for the rights of Blacks and women, Terrell was a prolific writer. She wrote letters, editorials, essays, speeches, and her **autobiography**. Many of her numerous speeches were delivered in several regions of the United States and abroad. Her autobiography, *A Colored Woman in a White World*, was published in 1940. It was her seminal work.

Mary Church Terrell's life spanned almost a century. Her adulthood was spent as a tireless champion for the rights of African American women and other disenfranchised persons. By some standards, she was an unlikely activist. She was born in 1863 in **Memphis, Tennessee**, during the **Civil War** and died in 1954, shortly after the U.S. Supreme Court's two landmark decisions in the case commonly known as *Brown v. Board of Education*.

The parents of Mary Church Terrell, Robert Church, Sr., and Louisa Ayers Church, were former slaves. In spite of their humble beginnings, they became successful and wealthy. He was a businessman; she owned a hair salon. Her family's wealth made it possible for Mary Church to experience uncommon privileges. Yet those privileges did not protect her from the racial injustices and Jim Crow laws that were prevalent during that era.

In 1884 Terrell became one of the first Black women in the country to earn a college degree when she graduated from Oberlin College in Oberlin, Ohio. By 1888 she had earned a master's degree in languages from the same college. Her alma mater bestowed the honorary Doctorate of Humane Letters on her (1948). Later, she received honorary doctorates from Wilberforce University and Howard University. She returned to Memphis briefly before accepting a teaching assignment at Wilberforce College (now University) in Xenia, Ohio. Then she moved to **Washington, D.C.**, where she taught at the M Street High School. It was there that she met her future husband, Robert Heberton Terrell.

By 1890 Terrell had completed studying languages and traveling in France, Germany, Switzerland, Italy, and England. She became fluent in French and German. Her marriage to Robert Heberton Terrell followed on October 18,

1891, in Memphis. He was a graduate of the prestigious Groton Academy in Groton, Massachusetts, and a magna cum laude graduate from Harvard University (1884). He earned a degree from the Howard University Law School in 1889, and was class valedictorian. He practiced law in Washington, D.C., until accepting an appointment as the first Black judge in the Municipal Court of the District of Columbia.

Terrell lived in Washington and maintained a summer home at Highland Beach, Maryland. It was located next to the home of the noted abolitionist **Frederick Douglass**. She had met him through her father, and they had worked together on several civil rights projects.

By the turn of the century, Terrell was a well-known speaker and writer. She wrote many articles denouncing segregation, **lynching**, and unjust practices against women and Blacks. She is credited with writing the Delta Creed for Delta Sigma Theta sorority, which she

Mary Church Terrell, c. 1885. Courtesy of the Library of Congress.

assisted in forming on the campus of Howard University (1914).

Almost all of Terrell's activism is chronicled through her many writings. She rose to national prominence as President of the National Association of Colored Women (1897). She was a teacher and school principal, and eventually became the first African American woman to serve on the Washington, D.C., school board (1895–1919), and was one of the few Black women founders of the **NAACP** (1909). Terrell worked in the suffrage movement which led to the Nineteenth Amendment. She also led a successful effort to integrate the local chapter of the American Association of University Women. Terrell is perhaps best known for her success in desegregating restaurants in the nation's capital by filing a lawsuit after she and several others were refused service at Thompson Cafeteria (1950). The lawsuit challenged the ignoring of the lost antidiscrimination laws of 1872–1873, which had disappeared from the D.C. Legal Code. The case is known as *District of Columbia v. Thompson Restaurant Company*. On June 8, 1953, the U.S. Supreme Court ruled that segregated eating places were unconstitutional (McCluskey, 47). In the three years that the lawsuit was moving through the court system, Terrell led others in boycotts, sit-ins, and picketing of restaurants and stores in Washington, D.C. As a senior citizen, she was a pioneer of the **Civil Rights Movement** that fully developed a decade later.

On July 24, 1954, Terrell died in Annapolis, Maryland. An elementary school in Washington, D.C., bears her name. Combining a writing life with active efforts to improve societal conditions is the essence of Mary Church Terrell's legacy.

Resources: Dennis Brindell Fradin and Judith Bloom Fradin, *Fight On: Mary Church Terrell's Battle for Integration* (New York: Clarion Books, 2003); Audrey McCluskey, "Setting the Standard: Mary Church Terrell's Last Campaign for Social Justice," *Black Scholar* 29, no. 2–3 (1999), 47–53; Dorothy Sterling: *Black Foremothers: Three Lives*, 2nd ed. (New York: Feminist Press, 1988); "Mary Church Terrell," in *Notable American Women*, vol. 4, *The Modern Period* (Cambridge, MA: Harvard University Press, 1980); Mary Church Terrell: *A Colored Woman in a White World*, ed. Nellie Y. McKay (New York: G. K. Hall, 1996); "Lynching from a Negro's Point of View," *North American Review* 178 (1904), 853–868; *The Progress of Colored Women*, Address to the National American Women's Suffrage Association at the Columbia Theatre (Washington, DC: Smith Brothers, 1898).

Betty W. Nyangoni

Terry [Prince], Lucy (c. 1730–1821). Poet and orator. Most academic studies of African American literature date its origin at 1746, when the sixteen-year-old Terry wrote the first existing poem by an American of African descent. "Bars Fight" (1746) mourns the deaths of White colonists in an August 1746 Indian raid on Deerfield, Massachusetts. The twenty-eight-line occasional poem in irregular iambic tetrameter uses colloquial expressions and spellings, such as "bar" for "meadow" and "fout" for "fought." Its strong rhyme scheme and standard meter lend themselves to musical adaptation; however, the accompanying tune has not survived. The poem circulated in Massachusetts oral history until its publication in Josiah Gilbert Holland's *History of Western Massachusetts* (1855). Though the poem is the first extant work by an African American writer, it was not the first published one. Some of the colonial African American poets whose work was published in their lifetimes include **Jupiter Hammon, Phillis Wheatley**, and **Lemuel Haynes**. Ironically, "Bars Fight" chronicles some of the earliest racial tensions in the United States and commemorates the loss of White settlers, yet it was written by a young woman trapped in racial **slavery** by the same White colonists.

Lucy Terry, a resident of Deerfield, was kidnapped at approximately age five from Africa and purchased for sixty pounds off a Rhode Island slave ship by Ebenezer Wells of Deerfield in 1735. Terry met Abijah (or Obijah) Prince, a freed slave, in 1746. It took him ten years to earn the money to purchase her freedom, and they married in 1756. By 1769 the couple had six children: Cesar, Festus, Drucilla, Tatnai, Durexa, and Abijah, Jr. The Princes inherited land from Abijah's former master in Northfield, and later purchased property in Guilford and Sunderland. On two occasions their White neighbors attempted to appropriate their land, and both times Lucy Terry's oratorical skills successfully defended the family's rights. In 1785, she protested the Noyes family's encroachments before the Governor's Council, and in the 1790s she argued her case against Col. Eli Bronson in front of Supreme Court Justice Samuel Chase. Terry did not prevail in front of the board of trustees of Williams College, however, when she argued against the school's segregation policy in an attempt to enroll her oldest son in the early 1770s. Abijah Prince, several years Terry's senior, died in 1794. Local historians remember that Terry was known for her storytelling, and her home remained a gathering place for both African Americans and White Americans until her death in 1821. No other poems or works by Lucy Terry [Prince] have been discovered.

Resources: Dickson D. Bruce, Jr., *The Origins of African American Literature, 1680–1865* (Charlottesville: University Press of Virginia, 2001); Frances Smith Foster, *Written by Herself: Literary Production by African American Women, 1746–1892* (Bloomington: Indiana University Press, 1993); Blyden Jackson, *A History of Afro-American Literature*, vol. 1, *The Long Beginning, 1746–1895* (Baton Rouge: Louisiana State University Press, 1989).

Ann Beebe

Tervalon, Jervey (born 1958). Poet, novelist, screenwriter, playwright, and professor. Tervalon is a popular, versatile contemporary author. Whether as a poet, a novelist, a screenwriter, a playwright, or a professor, his use of the written word to animate the sense of a tragic or lost soul has led to his having received numerous awards. Born on October 23, 1958, Tervalon displayed literary talent in junior high school when he sold his first poem to *Scope/Scholastic Magazine*. He continued writing throughout high school in South-Central **Los Angeles, California**, and later studied as an undergraduate with the controversial Marvin Mudrick. Following his course with Mudrick, Tervalon committed to living a life dedicated to reading and writing books. Upon graduating with a B.A. in literature from the University of California at Santa Barbara, Tervalon spent five years teaching at one of the more brutal schools in Los Angeles. His experiences there led to his master's thesis at the University of California at Irvine and to the publication of *Understand This*. This first novel was nominated for the Barnes and Nobel Discover New Writers Award and won the 1994 New Voices Award for fiction.

Tervalon followed this dynamic exploration of racism in 1940s **New Orleans, Louisiana**, with *Dead Above Ground*, which won the 2001 Josephine Miles Award; *All the Trouble You Need* (2002); *Geography of Rage* (2002); and *Lita* (2003). In addition to his novel-length fiction, Tervalon has published numerous short fiction pieces and nonfiction articles in academic magazines as well as the *Los Angeles Weekly*. Adding still another dimension to his creative scope, his work as a playwright includes *Make the Break* (1994) and *Understand This* (1995), both commissioned by the South Coast Repertory Theater.

Tervalon's work vividly portrays the struggle of Black life without attempting to offer solutions. Instead, he takes the greater role as a writer and re-creates this uniquely oppressive way of American life for those who will never experience life in South-Central Los Angeles. His work reflects the difficult, the tragic, and the beautiful events of a people who do the best they can with the circumstances that have been given to them, in a prose style that is both nonjudgmental and unrelenting. He masters the art of reaching the reader's heart while reminding her that life continually renews itself even in the depths of disappointment, despair, and tragedy. Tervalon currently is the Remsen Bird Writer-in-Residence at Occidental College in Los Angeles.

Resources: Jervey Tervalon: *All the Trouble You Need* (New York: Simon and Schuster, 2002); *Dead Above Ground* (New York: Simon and Schuster, 2000); *Lita* (Simon and Schuster, 2003); *Understand This* (Berkeley: University of California Press, 2000).

Christine Marie Hilger

Texas. Texas possesses a rich tradition of African American literature. It has been the home of such notable literati as **Sutton E. Griggs**, novelist and essayist; Elizabeth Brown-Guillory, dramatist, critic, and professor; Thomas Meloncon, dramatist and poet; and **Lorenzo Thomas**, poet and professor. The stage of the Ensemble and Alley Theatre has hosted dramas by **Ntozake Shange** and **August Wilson**, and other smaller local theaters have also been active in support of African American dramatists. Of course, the dramatic stage, education, and publishing opportunities have not always been readily available to African American writers in Texas. Literary opportunities came as the result of hard work and innovative plans such as Houston's Ensemble Theater, the oldest Black theater company in **the South**. Texas has also been home to writers of history, criticism, romance novels, short fiction, and historical fiction. Among these are **J. California Cooper**, an acclaimed short story writer; Thomas Meloncon and Margie Walker, writers and professors at Texas Southern University; Anita Bunkley, a novelist; the critics Elizabeth Brown-Guillory and Lorenzo Thomas of the University of Houston; and Gladys Washington, Betty Taylor-Thompson, and Merline Pitre of Texas Southern University. Houston is also the home of the Romance Writers of America Association.

Texas academic communities continue to sponsor and inspire Texas writers. *Callaloo: Journal of African American and African Arts and Humanities* recently moved to its new home at Texas A&M University. Poets and writers of fiction find a forum for their works at lectures and workshops throughout the state. State branches of the National Endowment for the Humanities have sponsored workshops in African American Studies conducted by Professor Merline Pitre, and the National Endowment for the Humanities has granted resources to workshops for public school teachers on African American biography and the **Harlem Renaissance** conducted by Professors Betty Taylor-Thompson and Cary D. Wintz. Poetry readings and creative writing seminars and workshops are always available, as are the dramatic productions at Texas Southern University, Rice University, the University of Texas and its branches, Prairie View University, and the University of Houston and its branches. The Cultural Arts Council of Houston and Harris County supports six literary programs offered by literary nonprofits, including Inprint, Voices, Breaking

Boundaries, and Writers in School. These programs include African American writers and their works. The universities also have hosted writers-in-residence; for example, Ntozake Shange has been a visiting professor at both the University of Houston and Prairie View University. Celebrated speakers at Texas universities include **Nikki Giovanni**, **Alice Walker**, **Maya Angelou**, and **Cornel West**. Texas Southern University plays a significant role in providing an outlet for the production of African Americans in Texas. However, the arts in Texas go beyond the academic community. The Shrine of the Black Madonna Cultural Center and Bookstore in Houston, for example, is a frequent host for national African American writers, presenting literary lecturers and book signings. It also has branches in **Detroit, Michigan**, and **Atlanta, Georgia**.

In Dallas the Black Academy of Arts and Letters, a nonprofit founded by Curtis King in 1977, is modeled on the American Negro Academy. Its mission is to create an awareness and understanding of artistic, cultural, and aesthetic differences, using the framework of African American arts and letters. In 1977, the organization was renamed the Junior Academy of Arts and Letters, and Curtis King conversed with leading African American literary scholars, including **C. Eric Lincoln** and **John Oliver Killens** about forming an institution that would directly involve the aspiring young artists and scholars in Dallas. One of the objectives of the Academy is to sponsor a Literary Voices series and an annual book club publisher's luncheon. The Academy sponsors numerous literary events throughout the year.

However, the contemporary African American community is hardly a mirror of the sparse literary community available at the turn of the century, when racism and prejudice reigned throughout the state. It was in this earlier time that Sutton E. Griggs sought to find an audience for his militant novels and tracts written in the **protest literature** tradition of African American literature.

Sutton E. Griggs, although not well known or widely ready during his lifetime, has now come to the attention of the African American **literary canon** even though his novels have been largely been ignored by major critics. The noted critic and distinguished professor of literature **Arthur P. Davis** of Howard University included Griggs in his groundbreaking anthology *Cavalcade*, thereby enlightening a new generation of students as to his importance. Griggs was born in Chatfield, Texas, on June 19, 1872, and he became an orator, writer, minister, and a publisher. He was educated in Dallas and attended Bishop College, a historically Black college. He moved to **Nashville, Tennessee**, to serve as a pastor and denominational officer of the National Baptist Convention and later returned to Texas as pastor of a church in Denison, Texas.

In his novels, pamphlets, and political tracts the reader can easily discern the thematic concepts which dominated Griggs's literary efforts, including Black beauty, pride, militancy, and separatism. In his works, Griggs revealed his wide interest in world history and literature, politics, and government. The overwhelming theme of his novels is the protest against racial discrimination and racial violence in America. In his works the images of violence against the Black body and psyche dominate. Unfortunately, the bulk of Griggs's writings is out of print, and the text of only one novel, *Imperium in Imperio*, is available online. The *Norton Anthology of African American Literature* contains an excerpt from the novel *Overshadowed*, "The Blaze," in which the gory, violent, and sadistic details of **lynching** are presented. This particular excerpt, presented in both *Cavalcade* and *The Norton Anthology of African American Literature*, demonstrates the effects of racism on both the lyncher and the victim.

Griggs published numerous political and philosophical tracts and racially militant novels; the most significant novels are *Imperium in Imperio* (1899), *Overshadowed* (1901), *Unfettered* (1902), *The Hindered Hand; or, The Reign of the Repressionist* (1905), and *Pointing the Way* (1908). Of course, the opportunities for African American writers have expanded greatly since Griggs first wrote his novels; since the 1970s, literature by African Americans has found new and supportive audiences in Texas. Moreover, the Texas colleges and universities provide a haven for the creative talents of their professors.

Elizabeth Brown-Guillory, Lorenzo Thomas, and Thomas Meloncon, Margie Walker, and **Anita Bunkley** represent a younger generation of African American writers in Texas. Brown-Guillory is a playwright, performing artist, critic, and professor of English at the University of Houston. Besides teaching graduate and undergraduate course in African American literature and Women's Studies, she has published books on Black women playwrights and frequently publishes book chapters, reviews, and criticism in major journals. Moreover, she frequently lectures on **race**, class, and **gender** issues in Black women's literature. Brown-Guillory has had twelve plays produced in **Washington, D.C.**, New York City, Denver, **New Orleans, Louisiana**, Houston, Cleveland, and **Chicago, Illinois**. Her books include *Their Place on the Stage: Black Women Playwrights in America*, *Wines in the Wilderness: Plays by African-American Women from the Harlem Renaissance to the Present*, and *Women of Color: Mother-Daughter Relationships in Twentieth-Century Literature*. Brown-Guillory is the founder and faculty adviser/mentor to the Houston Showcase Theater, a faculty, staff, and student troupe committed to diversity in the arts at the University of Houston.

Poet and professor of English Lorenzo Thomas has likewise established himself as a significant contributor to state and national poetic arts achievement. His works have appeared in many journals, including *African American Review*, *Arrowsmith*, *Blues Unlimited (England)*, *Living Blues*, and many others. His poetic collections are *Chances Are Few*, *The Bathers*, and *Es Gibt Zeugen*. His critical books include *Sing the Sun Up: Creative Writing Ideas from African American Literature* and his most recent critical expository, *Extraordinary Measures: Afrocentric Modernism and 20th Century American Poetry* (2000). In a review of *Extraordinary Measures*, the reviewer praises the excellence of Thomas's research and review of the creative and scholarly origins of African American poetics. Thomas begins with **Phillis Wheatley**, giving a scholarly view of the "whole voice" of African American poets. Furthermore, he chronicles the academic, social, and artistic marginality of African American poets despite their enforced marginality in the American **literary canon** and American society. Thomas's book fills a critical void in the evaluation of African American poetics.

Texas Southern University, a historically Black college established in 1947, has also contributed to Texas letters. The chair of the Department of Fine Arts, Dianne Jemison Pollard, and her staff put on performances of new and standard works by African American writers. In addition, the university theater invites directors from other areas of the university who are interested in drama, as well as directors from the community. Gladys Washington, a retired faculty member, writes and produces plays for the public and the religious and the university community. Each year she serves as a guest director for the university theater group. Over the years, Washington has written and directed *The Cauldron*, *Harriet Tubman*, *The Christmas*, and *Star of Bethlehem*. She has also directed productions at Texas Southern University and the University of Houston.

Betty Taylor-Thompson, a member of the English Department at Texas Southern, writes reviews and scholarly and critical works for national journals on the subject of African American women writers. Merline Pitre has written two works covering African American history in Texas. Margie Walker has been writing successful romance novels since 1990. The first was *Love Signals*, followed by *Remember Me*, *Something to Celebrate*, *Sweet Refrain*, and *Conspiracy*.

In the area of popular fiction, Anita Bunkley's first novel, *Emily, the Yellow Rose*, is a study of the historical significance and the truth of the folk legend of the Yellow Rose of Texas, which inspired the popular song by the same name. Bunkley determined that the song was indeed about an African American woman. Bunkley has also written *Wild Embers*, a **World War II** story about a young nurse with lofty ambitions and a knack for re-creating her upbringing who finds herself in the midst of a scandal. The scandal coincides with the military's removal of the ban on racial barriers. The heroine opts to make a fresh start by enlisting as a military nurse and is stationed in Tuskegee, Alabama. During the war, relationships are forever changed, and the protagonist manages to assist the **NAACP** in integrating the local manufacturer. Bunkley is also the author of *Starlight Passage*.

The Ensemble Theatre/Audrey Lawson Theatre in Houston is the oldest and largest currently operating African American theater company in the Southwest. Founded in 1976 by the late George Hawkins, the company has grown rapidly and has a vast and dedicated following. In 1985, the Ensemble Theatre moved to its current location on Main Street; by 1993 the company had purchased the building, giving it the distinction of being one of the few African American theaters to own its facility. The building underwent renovations including an expanded main stage, additional seating, an arena, a dance floor, and a special events area. This renovation and expansion were largely due to the work of Audrey Lawson and a committee of Ensemble supporters; Mrs. Lawson's name has been added to the theatre in recognition of her unending work and support of this important artistic mecca for Houston. The Ensemble Theatre has hosted more than 200 shows and eight world premieres. Since 1976, The Ensemble Theatre presents works that entertain and offer insight into the African American experience and its intersecting points with other cultures. For example, it has produced *The Old Settler* by John Henry Redwood; *Black Nativity*, a gospel song-play by Langston Hughes, adapted by Marsha Jackson-Randolph; and *Camp Logan*, by Celeste Bedford Walker. *Camp Logan* has been touring for more than fifteen years, and won the **NAACP** Award for Best Drama in 1994. Walker collaborated with Audrey Lawson on the play *Harlem Nights*.

Thomas Meloncon, a playwright known nationally known for *Diary of Black Men* and *Whatever Happened to Black Love*, is a dramatist and poet, and a professor in the Department of Fine Arts at Texas Southern University. He is very actively involved with bringing innovative artistic programs in **jazz**, poetry, and drama to young people in the public schools. He has written plays especially for young actors, singers, and musicians at the High School for the Performing and Visual Arts in Houston, and has taken these students all over Texas for performances. The plays include *The Gospel According to Hip-Hop*, *Our Feet Can Tell a Story,* and *Where Were You in 1965*.

African American writers are a permanent fixture in the literary community in Texas. Not only have these writers, poets, lecturers, and teachers continued to engage in their personal writing careers, but they are dedicated to making the African American literary canon available to the public through critical writing, drama, poetry, and public forums.

Resources: "Black Academy of Arts and Letters, Dallas, Texas 2003–2004," http://www.tbaal.org; Arthur P. Davis and J. Saunders Redding, eds., *Calvalcade: African American Writing from 1760 to the Present*, vol. 1 (Washington, DC: Howard University Press, 1971); Arlene Elder, "Sutton Griggs," in the *Oxford Companion to African American Literature*, ed. William Andrews, Trudier Harris, and Francis Foster (New York: Oxford University Press, 1997); Peter Szatmary, "Ensemble Theater: Fulfilling Potential" (Sept. 1, 2004), http://houston.citysearch.com/profile/9832653/houston_tx/ensemble_theatre.html; Betty Taylor-Thompson: "Review of *Extraordinary Measures: Afrocentric Modernism and Twentieth-century Poetry*," by Lorenzo Thomas, *Choice*, July 2001; "Sutton Griggs," in *Dictionary of Literary Biography*, vol. 50, *Afro-American Writers Before the Harlem Renaissance*, ed. Trudier Harris and Thaodius Davis (Detroit: Gale, 1985); University of Houston, College of Arts and Sciences, "Elizabeth Brown-Guillory, Professor of English," http://www.class.uh.edu/English/Englishdpt/Elizabeth-Brown-Guilory.html; Cynthia Williams, "The Roots of Houston's Literary Life," *Cachh* (Cultural Arts Council of Houston/Harris County magazine), Spring 2004, 1–12.

Betty Taylor-Thompson

Theater. *See* **Drama**.

Thelwell, Michael (born 1939). Political activist, fiction writer, essayist, and educator. Thelwell is also known as Ekwueme Mike Thelwell. His significance to African American literature rests upon four decades of sociopolitical commentary advocating civil and human rights; critically acclaimed fiction dramatizing Black struggles; literary criticism delineating Black writers' responsibilities; and advancement of African American studies. After coming to Howard University in 1959, Jamaican-born Thelwell was awakened to the Black writer's responsibilities by the work of **James Baldwin**. Essays and short stories, including "The Organizer" (1968), collected in Thelwell's *Duties, Pleasures, and Conflicts: Essays in Struggle* (1987), recapture his 1963–1965 experiences working in the Deep South and **Washington, D.C.**, for the Student Nonviolent Coordinating Committee and the Mississippi Freedom Democratic Party. "The August 28th March on Washington" (1964) and "Fish Are Jumping an' the Cotton Is High: Notes from the Mississippi Delta" (1966) appear in *Reporting Civil Rights*, vol. 2, *American Journalism, 1963–1973* (2003).

Since 1965, Thelwell has forged a distinguished career as activist-educator at the University of Massachusetts-Amherst, where he founded the W.E.B. Du Bois Department of Afro-American Studies in 1970. Thelwell's Jamaican novel *The Harder They Come* (1980) is "one of the most important works of Caribbean literature" (Booker and Juraga, 76). "Modernist Fallacies and the Responsibility of the Black Writer" (included in *Duties, Pleasures and Conflicts*) advocates a socially responsible realist aesthetic. National and international periodicals and major African American projects, such as the television series *Eyes on the Prize, Part II* (1990) and **Toni Morrison**'s *Race-ing Justice, En-Gendering Power* (1992), feature Thelwell's contributions. Most recently, Thelwell edited *Ready for Revolution: The Life and Struggles of Stokely Carmichael* (2003).

Resources: M. Keith Booker and Dubravka Juraga, "Michael Thelwell: *The Harder They Come*," in *The Caribbean Novel in English* (Portsmouth, NH: Heinemann, 2001), 76–91; Clayborne Carson et al., eds., *Reporting Civil Rights*, vol. 2, *American Journalism, 1963–1973* (New York: Library of America, 2003); Toni Morrison, ed., *Race-ing Justice, En-Gendering Power: Essays on Anita Hill, Clarence Thomas, and the Construction of Social Reality* (New York: Random House-Pantheon, 1992); Michael Thelwell: *Duties, Pleasures, and Conflicts* (Amherst: University of Massachusetts Press, 1987); *The Harder They Come* (New York: Grove Press, 1980); "*The Harder They Come*: From Film to Novel," *Grand Street* 37 (1991), 135–165.

Cora Agatucci

Theology, Black and Womanist. With the publication of James H. Cone's *Black Theology and Black Power* in 1969, the term "Black theology" entered the vocabulary of Christian theology. Black theology is akin to the liberation theologies of Latin America in its message proclaiming the necessity of liberation for a historically and systematically suppressed people. In its first decade, Black theology specifically addressed the concerns of African Americans in the context of the United States. Black theology emerged as a meeting place between **Martin Luther King Jr.**'s commitment to the transformative power of suffering love and nonviolence and the social critiques of **Malcolm X**, who called for societal change "by any means necessary."

In its formation, the Black theology movement was a response by dissatisfied Black Christians who were sympathetic to the Student Nonviolent Coordinating Committee's (SNCC) demand for "Black power," echoing **Stokely Carmichael**. This led to the National Conference of Black Churchmen, wedding **Black Power** to Christian commitment in a statement published by the *New York Times*, providing the impetus for Cone to articulate a distinctively "Black theology." Some of the more important proponents of Black theology in its inception were J. Deotis Roberts, **C. Eric Lincoln**, Major Jones, Gayraud Wilmore, and Vincent Harding. Within academic circles, some Black scholars criticized Cone and Roberts for their reliance upon European and White American theologies, and upon their attempts to universalize their message to non-Blacks who also suffered racism and economic disenfranchisement. Such scholars insisted that the result was a watered-down Black theology which lost the force and effectiveness of its critique because it sought to be more "acceptable" to the ivory towers of academia. On the other hand, some critiques suggested that Black theology had accepted the tenets of Black Power uncritically, sacrificing the Christian message in favor of the dictates of a secular ideology.

These critiques brought a renewed effort by the progenitors of Black theology, along with the movement's second-generation scholars, to build stronger ties between what had become an overtly academic discussion and the mission and identity of Black churches. This brought a new commitment to the examination of the local, national, and international social issues that affected Black communities, and to reradicalize a theological movement that had become self-referential, in favor of a movement that sought to empower the very Black communities that it had sought to serve at its inception. A major figure in this reconfiguration of Black theology's priorities was **Cornel West**, who at the time was a faculty colleague of Cone's at Union Theological Seminary in New York City. West brought his philosophical training to the discussion, articulating Black theology as a Marxist critique of capitalism in America.

Other members of this second-generation movement in Black theology sought not only to address racism directed against Black people in the United States, but also to expand consciousness of oppression and identity out of the focus upon the present and into both the past and the future. Several important conversations grew out of this second generation's concerns with the enslaved ancestors and the children of Black America. One of these was the reclamation of Africa as a historical and cultural source for religious imagery and identity. Indigenous religions of Africa were mined for their pertinence to current Black religious practice and ritual. Another experience that grew to prominence for the second generation was the **"middle passage,"** both as a symbol for present cultural analysis and as a determining factor in the historical consequences of the brutality and loss of memory that occurred in the slave galleys. Still another vital source for theological construction was the Old Testament, in which the enslavement, liberation, and continued hardships of Israel made sense of the experiences of Black people in America. In the 1980s, Black theology's commitments expanded outside of the United States, becoming determinative in ecumenical conversations with Third World theologians, especially in Africa and Asia. As time passed, some proponents of Black theology argued that "Black" referred less to the specific experiences of African Americans in the United States, but addressed the plight of the underprivileged and disenfranchised throughout the world.

Another shift in Black theology occurred in the 1980s, as Black women scholars began to differentiate their theological voice from that of Black theology, deemed overtly male-oriented, and feminist theology, seen as overtly White-oriented. Delores S. Williams, Jacquelyn Grant, and Katie G. Cannon, all doctoral students of Cone's at Union Theological Seminary, became the forerunners of womanist theology, which drew intentionally on the social, cultural, and religious experiences of Black women as the fulcrum for their theological analysis of culture. The term "womanist" is derived from **Alice Walker**'s expression "womanish," referring to the daring, boldness, and courage of Black women who face the particular difficulties of their contexts in America. Although Walker did not use this term in a particularly religious capacity, these theologians embraced "womanist" as an important way to connect Christian theology to their cultural and personal experiences. Williams's *Sisters in the Wilderness* became the definitive work of womanist Christian systematic theology, and Grant's *White Women's Christ, and Black Women's Jesus* opened the Christological dimensions of Black culture and religion toward a messianic understanding of Christ synonymous with Black women's experiences and identity for present-day Black women Christians. Cannon became the womanist movement's first ethicist, drawing the narratives of literature and the performing arts into the methodology of Black theology and ethics, which inspired Emilie M. Townes's explication of womanist spirituality as social witness. (*See* **Feminism/Black Feminism**.)

Black and womanist theologies remain in a continuing process of redefinition and change, but their ideologies are an important part of the African American narratives concerning identity and community, incorporating interdisciplinary conversations into the meeting of the secular and religious lives of Black people in America. Increasingly, Black and womanist theologies are expanding from exclusive discussions on **race**, sex, and class, toward the inclusion of discourses concerning homophobia, anti-Semitism, and critiques of capitalism. These developments show the new dimensions of Black and womanist theology as embracing not merely social activism but also political engagement in dealing with the immediate and future concerns of Black people and communities in America. (*See* **Marxism**.)

Resources: Katie Cannon: *Black Womanist Ethics* (Atlanta: Scholars Press, 1988); *Katie's Canon: Womanism and the Soul of the Black Community* (New York: Continuum, 1995); James H. Cone: *Black Theology and Black Power* (1969; repr. Maryknoll, NY: Orbis, 1990); *A Black Theology of Liberation* (1970; repr. Maryknoll, NY: Orbis, 1990); *God of the Oppressed* (New York: Seabury Press, 1975); *The Spirituals and the Blues* (1972; repr. Maryknoll, NY: Orbis, 1991); James H. Cone and Gayraud S. Wilmore, eds., *Black Theology: A Documentary History*, 2nd ed., rev. vol. 1, *1966–1979*, vol. 2, *1980–1992* (Maryknoll, NY: Orbis, 1993); Jacquelyn Grant, *White Women's Christ and Black Women's Jesus* (Atlanta: Scholars Press, 1989); J. Deotis Roberts, *Liberation and Reconciliation: A Black Theology* (Philadelphia: Westminster, 1971); Emilie M. Townes: *In a Blaze of Glory: Womanist Spirituality as Social Witness* (Nashville, TN: Abingdon, 1995); *Womanist Justice, Womanist Hope* (Atlanta: Scholars Press, 1993); Cornel West, *Prophesy Deliverance! An Afro-American Revolutionary Christianity* (Philadelphia: Westminster, 1982); Delores S. Williams, *Sisters in the Wilderness: The Challenge of Womanist God-talk* (Maryknoll, NY: Orbis, 1993).

Stephen Butler Murray

Third World Press (1967–present). Since 1967, Third World Press has functioned as a literary beacon for Black culture and independent publishing. In that year **Haki R. Madhubuti** (formerly known as Don L. Lee), with the help of Johari Amini (also known as Jewel C. Latimore) and **Carolyn M. Rodgers**, laid the foundation for Third World Press. In conjunction with **NOMMO**, the publishing entity of the **Chicago, Illinois**, Organization of Black American Culture **(OBAC)** Writers' Workshop, Madhubuti and friends sought to celebrate the beauty of Blackness and bring new Black art into the community.

Third World Press has introduced the standard for progressive Black literature, books that focus primarily on issues, themes, and critiques related to the African American experience. Among the many authors published by Third World Press are the Pulitzer Prize recipient **Gwendolyn Brooks**; the poet and publisher **Dudley Randall**; the poets **Amiri Baraka, Mari Evans, Kalamu Ya Salaam**, and **Sonia Sanchez**; and the writers **Pearl Michelle Cleage, Sterling D. Plumpp, Woodie King, Jr.**, and Ruby Dee.

Over the years, Third World Press has served as adviser for the publishing branch of the Institute of Positive Education, a community resource and research center specializing in education and communications. Haki Madhubuti invested a $400 honorarium received from a poetry reading and used a mimeograph machine to create the first publications of Third World Press in a basement on the South Side of Chicago. Today Third World Press is the number one Black independent publishing company in America and has moved into a multimillion-dollar facility (Third World Press, Web site).

Publishing under the name Johari Amini, cofounder Latimore published three chapbooks of poetry: *Black Essence* (1968), *Images in Black* (1969), and *Let's Go Somewhere* (1970). Cofounder Rodgers published the books of poems *Paper Soul* (1968) and *Songs of a Black Bird* (1969) with the press, and cofounder Madhubuti has published numerous books at Third World Press. Like **Broadside Press** and **Lotus Press**, Third World Press has helped to shape the African American **literary canon** and to support younger writers, and has gone from modest beginnings to establish a national and even international reputation.

Resources: Johari Amini: *Black Essence* (Chicago: Third World Press, 1968); *Images in Black* (Chicago: Third World Press, 1969); *Let's Go Somewhere* (Chicago: Third World Press, 1970); Hoyt W. Fuller, "Foreword to *Nommo*," in *NOMMO*, ed. Carole Parks, pp. 17–20; Don L. Lee (Haki R. Madhubuti), "Black Poetics/for the Many to Come," in *NOMMO*, ed. Carole Parks, pp. 13–14; *NOMMO 2: Remembering Ourselves Whole* (Chicago: OBAhouse, 1990); Carole A. Parks, ed., NOMMO: *A Literary Legacy of Black Chicago (1967–1987)* (Chicago: OBAhouse, 1987); Carolyn M. Rodgers: *Paper Soul* (Chicago: Third World Press, 1968); *Songs of a Black Bird* (Chicago: Third World Press, 1969); Kalamu ya Salaam, *The Magic of Juju: An Appreciation of the Black Arts Movement* (Chicago: Third World Press, 2004); Third World Press, *History [of Third World Press]*, Web site, http://www.thirdworldpressinc.com/history.htm.

Earnest M. Wallace

Thomas, Joyce Carol (born 1938). Poet, playwright, novelist, and editor. Thomas was born in Ponca City, **Oklahoma**; her family moved to Tracy, California, when she was ten years old. She returns to the rural setting of her youth in several of her novels, including *Marked by Fire* (1982), *Bright Shadow* (1983), and *The Golden Pasture* (1986). Personal experiences such as picking cotton, participating in church activities, and forming relationships with community members also make their way into her work. **Folklore**, mysticism, magic, and tall tales are recurring elements in her stories, and African American history, heritage, culture, and community are important themes explored. Though Thomas has a number of books for babies, primary school children, and young adults to her credit, as well as her first novel for adults, *House of Light* (2001), which continues the Abyssina Jackson story, she began her professional writing career as a poet and playwright. By 1975, she had published three volumes of poetry: *Bittersweet* (1973), *Crystal Breezes* (1974), and *Blessing* (1975). *Inside the Rainbow* (1982), published in 1986, includes new and old poetry by Thomas. Of Thomas's talent as a poet, Toombs writes, "As a poet she is often praised for her seriousness of theme, thoroughness of treatment, faithful rendering of the black and human experience, and authentic persona" (245). In 1976, she wrote two plays, *Look! What a Wonder!* and *A Song in the Sky*. The former was produced in Berkeley, California, at the Berkeley Community Center; the latter was produced in **San Francisco, California**, at the Montgomery Theater.

Thomas earned a B.A. in Spanish and French at San Jose State University in 1966 and a master's in education at Stanford University in 1967. She taught creative writing at St. Mary's College, the University of California, Santa Cruz, Purdue University, and the University of Tennessee, Knoxville.

She has also served as an assistant professor of **Black Studies** at California State University and visiting associate professor of English at Purdue University.

Shortly after its publication, *Marked by Fire* (1982), which is arguably Thomas's most notable novel, was adapted into a musical by Ted Kociolek and Jim Racheef and titled *Abyssinia*. Other novels by Thomas include *The Golden Pasture* (1986), *The Water Girl* (1986), *Journey* (1988), and *When the Nightingale Sings* (1992). In 1998, Thomas published *I Have Heard of a Land*, a historical poetry picture book patterned after the migration experiences of her great-grandparents, and others like them, who settled in Oklahoma during the 1800s.

Thomas's work is highly acclaimed. She received the American Book Award (now known as the National Book Award) and the Before Columbus American Book Award, both for *Marked by Fire*; the Coretta Scott King Award for *Bright Shadow*; and the Coretta Scott King Honor Book Award for *Brown Honey in Broomwheat Tea*. She also received a Danforth Graduate Fellowship at the University of California at Berkeley, and the Djerassi Fellowship for Creative Writing at Stanford University. Thomas also has edited such notable anthologies as *A Gathering of Flowers: Stories About Being Young in America* (1990) and *Linda Brown, You Are Not Alone: Brown v. Board of Education* (2003). In early 2000, *The Gospel Cinderella*, a variation on the traditional Cinderella story set in a swamp and with a gospel convention rather than a ball, was published, and a collection of poems about African American identity titled *Blacker the Berry: Poems* appeared in 2002. As Toombs states, Thomas is certainly in the "forefront of serious black women writers" such as **Maya Angelou, Alice Walker, Toni Morrison**, and **Gloria Naylor**, among others (245).

Resources: Amy E. Earhart, "Joyce Carol Thomas," in *Contemporary African American Novelists: A Bio-Bibliographical Critical Sourcebook*, ed. Emmanuel S. Nelson (Westport, CT: Greenwood Press, 1999), 449–453; Charles P. Toombs, "Joyce Carol Thomas," in *Dictionary of Literary Biography*, vol. 33, *Afro-American Fiction Writers after 1955*, ed. Thadious M. Davis and Trudier Harris (Detroit: Gale, 1984), 245–250.

KaaVonia Hinton-Johnson

Thomas, Lorenzo (born 1944). Poet, critic, and professor. Thomas's writing, both creative and critical, uniquely reflects his Central American and African American identity. Born in Panama, Thomas moved to the United States as a young child, grew up in New York City, and attended Queens College (City University of New York). Difficulties with language early in his life caused Thomas to vow to improve his verbal skills, and this interest developed a poet's awareness of words. During the 1960s, Thomas was a founding member of the renowned **Umbra Workshop** on New York's City's Lower East Side, which paired involvement in the arts with political engagement. This is a source from which Thomas still draws inspiration. These years, which coincided with the **Civil Rights Movement**, are reflected within his poetry and its focus on African and folk history, as well as social criticism, through use of visual imagery, song, and allusion; his poems often center on civil rights and American culture. Thomas has also referred to the poet Aimé Césaire (from the island of Martinique), the first Afro-Caribbean poet of **surrealism** and an important figure in the **Négritude** movement, as an influence. He also attributes an aspect of his sometimes surrealistic style to the influence of André Breton. Thomas's sense of irony and the absurd and his social awareness are reflected in his poetry when he writes as a critic of the Western world, with sympathies toward folk culture and the oppressed.

In 1973 Thomas was invited to be the writer-in-residence at Texas Southern University in Houston, **Texas**, and decided to remain in the area. In the later 1970s he taught writing workshops, published widely, and became active with the Texas Commission of Arts and Humanities. Thomas has stated that his years in **the South** have enhanced his appreciation for Southern **blues** singers and folk music, and this influence can be seen within the inherent musicality of his work.

Thomas has stated in interviews that poetry should be "heightened speech" and not **vernacular** expression. He describes poetry as the "mental work that that occupies us when we are in a condition somewhere between sleep and waking." His most recent book of criticism, *Extraordinary Measures: Afrocentric Modernism and 20th Century American Poetry*, was named a Choice Outstanding Academic Book in 2001. In this book Thomas considers many historical and contemporary writers on a continuum of the African-American poetic tradition. He is also author of *Sing the Sun Up: Creative Writing Ideas from African American Literature*.

Poems and reviews by Thomas have been published in **Callaloo**, *African American Review*, *Ploughshares*, *The Paris Review*, and elsewhere. He has won several awards for his work, including two Poets Foundation awards (1966, 1974); a Committee on Poetry grant (1973); the Lucille Medwick Award (1974); and a National Endowment for the Arts creative writing fellowship (1983). Thomas served in the **Vietnam War** and also translated Vietnamese poetry, which is included in several anthologies.

Resources: Primary Sources: *Poetry:* Lorenzo Thomas: *The Bathers: Selected Poems* (Berkeley, CA: Reed, Cannon & Johnson, 1978); *Chances Are Few* (Berkeley, CA: Blue Wind Press, 1979); *Dancing on Main Street* (Minneapolis, MN: Coffee House Press, 2004); *Dracula* (New York: Angel Hair Books, 1973); *Fit Music* (New York: Angel Hair Books, 1972); *Framing the Sunrise* (n.p.: Sun Be/Am Associates, 1975); *Sound Science* (n.p.: Sun Be/Am Associates, 1978); *A Visible Island* (New York: Adlib Press, 1967); Lorenzo Thomas, ed., *ANKH: Getting It Together* (Hoston, TX: Hope Development, 1974). *Nonfiction:* Lorenzo Thomas: *Extraordinary Measures: Afrocentric Modernism and Twentieth-Century American Poetry* (Tuscaloosa: University of Alabama Press, 2000); *Sing the Sun Up: Creative Writing Ideas from African-American Literature* (New York: Teachers & Writers Collaborative, 1998); Lorenzo Thomas, Louis Guida, and Cheryl Cohen, *Blues Music in Arkansas* (Philadelphia: Portfolio Associates, 1982). *Articles:* Lorenzo Thomas, "The African-American Folktale and J. Mason Brewer," in

Juneteenth Texas: Essays in African-American Folklore, ed. Francis E. Abernethy (Denton: University of North Texas Press, 1996), 223–235; "Alea's Children: The Avant-Garde on the Lower East Side, 1960–1970," *African American Review* 27, no. 4 (Winter 1993), 573–578; "Authenticity and Elevation: Sterling Brown's Theory of the Blues," *African American Review* 31, no. 3 (Fall 1997), 409–416; "The Bop Aesthetic and Black Intellectual Tradition," *Library Chronicle of the University of Texas* 24, no. 1–2 (1994), 104–117; "'Communicating by Horns': Jazz and Redemption in the Poetry of the Beats and the Black Arts Movement," *African American Review* 26, no. 2 (1992), 291–298; "Poetry: The 1940s to the Present," *American Literary Scholarship: An Annual*, 1998, pp. 379–403; "The Shadow World: New York's Umbra Workshop & Origins of the Black Arts Movement," *Callaloo* 1, no. 4 (1978), 53–72. **Secondary Sources:** Peniel E. Joseph, "Black Liberation Without Apology: Reconceptualizing the Black Power Movement," *The Black Scholar* 31, no. 3–4 (Fall–Winter 2001), 2–19; Daniel Kane, "Interview: Lorenzo Thomas on Black Poetry and Modernism," *QBR—The Black Book Review* 9, no. 3 (May–June 2002), 31–33; Hermine Pinson, "An Interview with Lorenzo Thomas," *Callaloo* 22, no. 2 (Spring 1999), 287–304; Charles H. Rowell, "'Between the Comedy of Matters and the Ritual Workings of Man': An Interview with Lorenzo Thomas," *Callaloo* 4, no. 1–3 (Feb.–Oct. 1981), 19–35.

Elline Lipkin

Thomas, Piri (born 1928). Poet, novelist, autobiographer, and community worker. Born in the Spanish section of **Harlem, New York**, to Puerto Rican and Cuban parents, Thomas was accustomed to being called "negrito" and sometimes considered himself African American. Early on, Thomas became involved in criminal activity, was arrested and convicted, and spent time in prison. Released from prison in 1961 after serving six years, Thomas joined the Harlem Writers Guild and embarked on a literary career as one of New York's most inspirational autobiographical novelists. His acclaimed *Down These Mean Streets* (1967) includes aspects of race consciousness similar to those in **Eldridge Cleaver**'s *Soul on Ice* and *The Autobiography of Malcolm X*, by **Malcolm X** and **Alex Haley**. After the publication of this book, Thomas devoted his time to preventing troubled teenagers from following in his footsteps.

Because of his work with inner-city gang members, Thomas was featured in an award-winning documentary film called *Piri & Johnny* (1964). In addition, Thomas, like **Langston Hughes**, wrote personal accounts of life in Harlem. These appear in such works as *Savior, Savior Hold My Hand* (1972) and *Stories from El Barrio* (1978). *Seven Long Times* (1974) is a novel based on his time in prison, and it can be read as a powerful contemporary captivity narrative. In the book, Thomas describes the inhumane and racist practices he endured while incarcerated at Bellevue, Sing Sing, and Comstock. H. Bruce Franklin argues that *Seven Long Times* possesses a genuinely "developed political consciousness" (180). In the play *The Golden Streets* (1970), Harlem and its struggling masses are crucial concerns as Thomas pays homage to such archetypal figures as Hughes and **Claude McKay** by documenting not only the negative transformations but also the native splendors of the city. The sounds of Harlem left their own indelible marks on Thomas's artistic career; he recorded two collections of **performance poetry**: *Sounds of the Street* (1994) and *No Mo' Barrio Blues* (1996). The poetry is set to backgrounds of blended Latin rhythms, **blues**, and **jazz**. Thomas's work helped to inspire the literary movement associated with the **Nuyorican Café** that began in the 1970s. Thomas has been recognized by cultural critics as "the first of this generation to write of being made to feel ashamed of speaking Spanish and of looking neither quite white nor quite black" (Fox, 126). For his part, Thomas encourages younger generations with words of celebration: "Viva the children of all the colors! *Punto!*" (Thomas, "Afterword," 337). Thomas continues to speak at schools about how the self-worth of young people is damaged by racist institutions. At this writing, Thomas is working on a sequel to *Down These Mean Streets*.

Resources: Geoffrey Fox, *Hispanic Nation: Culture, Politics and the Constructing of Identity* (New York: Birch Lane Press, 1996); H. Bruce Franklin, ed., *Prison Writing in 20th-Century America* (New York: Penguin Books, 1998); Piri Thomas: *Down These Mean Streets* (1967; repr. New York: Vintage Books, 1997), an edition that includes Thomas's "Afterword to the Thirtieth-Anniversary Edition of *Down These Mean Streets*"; *Savior, Savior, Hold My Hand* (Garden City, NY: Doubleday, 1972); *Seven Long Times* (1974; repr. New York: New American Library, 1975); *Stories from El Barrio* (1978; repr. New York: Random House, 1992).

Stephen M. Steck

Thomas-Graham, Pamela (born 1963). Mystery writer. Thomas-Graham is one of the first writers to create an African American female sleuth who investigates murder and mayhem within the hallowed halls of academia. Veronica "Nikki" Chase, a thirty-year-old Harvard economics professor and amateur crime solver, is the heroine of Thomas-Graham's Ivy League Mystery series. The series is considered distinctive because the author weaves issues concerning **race**, class, and **gender** into each of her mysteries. The characters in her novels are multicultural and reflect a segment of the African American community that is rarely represented in literature—educated, middle- and upper-class, ambitious, and successful. (*See* **Crime and Mystery Fiction.**)

Thomas-Graham has been recognized for bringing the type of attention to higher education that John Grisham and Scott Turow have brought to the law, with more than a passing nod to Amanda Cross's academic sleuth Kate Fansler. Harvard, Yale, and Princeton universities have provided the settings for Thomas-Graham's mysteries and the detective work of amateur sleuth Nikki Chase. Each novel delves into issues and questions not found in most books of this genre. For example, can a smart and outspoken Black woman succeed at a predominantly White university (*A Darker Shade of Crimson*, 1998)? What happens when the issues of race, politics, and wealth intersect in academia (*Blue Blood*, 1999)? Is it possible to retain a sense of authenticity and identity while negotiating fierce competition within academe (*Orange Crushed*, 2004)?

Thomas-Graham is a Phi Beta Kappa graduate of Radcliffe College (1985), and a graduate of Harvard Business School and Harvard Law School (1989). She was the first Black woman to become a partner (1995) at McKinsey and Company, a global management consulting firm. In 1999, she joined NBC to become chief executive officer of CNBC.com, and in 2001, was named President and Chief Executive Officer of CNBC, which provides worldwide business news programming and financial market coverage.

Resources: Robyn D. Clarke, "Excellence by the Graham—CNBC President Pamela Thomas Graham," *Black Enterprise*, Sept. 2001, 78–87; Marina Dundjerski, "Businesswoman, Novelist, Donor: A Wealth of Role Models for Girls," *Chronicle of Philanthropy*, Nov. 4, 1999, pp. 58+; Adam Shell, "CNBC Leader Gives New Meaning to Multi-tasking," *USA Today*, Mar. 22, 2004, p. 38; Pamela Thomas-Graham: *Blue Blood* (New York: Simon and Schuster, 1999); *A Darker Shade of Crimson* (New York: Simon and Schuster, 1998); *Orange Crushed* (New York: Simon and Schuster, 2004).

Robin M. Dasher-Alston

Thompson, Era Bell (1905–1986). Autobiographer, journalist, editor, and travel writer. An overlooked figure, Thompson constitutes an important voice in American letters. Born in Des Moines, Iowa, she moved west with her family in 1914 to North Dakota. *American Daughter* (1946), the account of her childhood, adolescence, and young adulthood, relates a rare American experience: growing up African American on a homestead on the northern Great Plains. After her mother's death in 1918, Thompson and her father moved to a nearby farm and then to Bismarck in 1920. Although she never again lived on a farm, the plains had a profound effect upon her, and she devoted much of *American Daughter* to her and her family's rural life in North Dakota.

At Bismarck High School, Thompson excelled in athletics and academics, and published articles and poetry in the school newspaper. Too poor to attend college after graduation, Thompson entered a postsecondary business school in Mandan, North Dakota, where her father had opened a used-goods store. In 1925, she enrolled at the University of North Dakota (UND) in Grand Forks. Again, she excelled in athletics—breaking five UND track records—and academics, and she wrote for the college newspaper, the *Dakotah Daily Student*. A severe illness and financial difficulties forced her to leave before graduating.

In 1928 Thompson moved to **Chicago, Illinois**, took a position as a writer with a small Black magazine, and encountered the ideas, energy, and figures of the **Harlem Renaissance**. She returned to Mandan that summer to care for her ailing father, who died in July.

Thompson moved back to Grand Forks in 1930 and began working as a housekeeper for Rev. Robert O'Brian, a Methodist minister devoted to helping African Americans attain a college education. The O'Brians and Thompson moved to Sioux City, Iowa, where O'Brian had become president of Morningside College. Thompson graduated from Morningside in 1933 with a degree in social science. After graduation, she moved back to Chicago to pursue writing. In 1945 Thompson applied for a Newberry Fellowship to write a book about North Dakota. Recognizing the uniqueness of her experience, the committee encouraged her to write an **autobiography** instead. Thompson received the grant and began work on *American Daughter*, which was published in 1946 by the University of Chicago Press.

American Daughter was well received, including a complimentary review by **Ralph Ellison**. In *American Daughter*, Thompson portrays herself as an idealist and an optimist. One does not encounter the rage and bitterness found in other African American autobiographies of the period, such as *Black Boy*, by **Richard Wright**. Thompson attributed her optimism and idealism to having grown up in North Dakota, where prejudice was much less pernicious.

American Daughter opened doors for Thompson. Shortly after its publication, she accepted a position with **Johnson Publishing Company**, publisher of, among other things, the new magazine **Ebony**. She became co-managing editor in 1951 and international editor in 1964, a post she held until her death. In her years with Johnson, Thompson interviewed leading figures, Black and White, and traveled widely. In 1954, Thompson's second book was published: *Africa, Land of My Fathers*, a memoir about traveling throughout Africa. In 1963, with fellow *Ebony* editor Herbert Nipson, she published *White on Black: The Views of Twenty-Two White Americans on the Negro*, a collection of **essays** by people ranging from William Faulkner to Jack Dempsey.

Among other awards, Thompson received the Roughrider Award, the highest award given by the state of North Dakota, in 1976. And in 1979 UND changed the name of its Black Cultural Center to the Era Bell Thompson Cultural Center. Thompson died in Chicago in 1986.

Resources: Kathie R. Anderson, "Era Bell Thompson: A North Dakota Daughter," in *The Centennial Anthology of North Dakota History: Journal of the Northern Plains*, ed. Janet Daley Lysengen and Ann M. Rathke (Bismarck: State Historical Society of North Dakota, 1996), 307–319; Joanne Braxton, *Black Women Writing Autobiography: A Tradition Within a Tradition* (Philadelphia: Temple University Press, 1989); Kevin Cole and Leah Gruber, "Religion, Idealism, and African American Autobiography in the Northern Plains: Era Bell Thompson's *American Daughter*," *Great Plains Quarterly* 23, no. 4 (Fall 2003), 219–229; Ralph Ellison, "Stepchild Fantasy" (review of *American Daughter*, by Era Bell Thompson), *Saturday Review of Literature* 29 (June 1946), 25; Era Bell Thompson: *Africa, Land of My Fathers* (Garden City, NY: Doubleday, 1954); *American Daughter* (Chicago: University of Chicago Press, 1946); Era Bell Thompson and Herbert Nipson, eds., *White on Black: The Views of Twenty-Two White Americans on the Negro* (New York: Johnson, 1963).

Kevin L. Cole

Thompson, Robert Farris (born 1932). Educator, art historian, and theorist. Robert Farris Thompson is an acclaimed scholar and one of the foremost authorities on African, African American, Afro-Caribbean, and Afro-Atlantic art and culture. He is the Col. John Trumbull Professor of the History of Art and Master of Timothy Dwight College at Yale University, where he received his B.A. and his Ph.D.; he has been a professor of art history at Yale since 1961. Thompson focuses on the material culture and visual arts of various African ethnic groups, as well as the influence these groups have on the wider Atlantic world in terms of music, religion, art, dance, and philosophy. He is known for his captivating lecture style, in which he frequently breaks into dance and song. Along with his teaching and lecturing, Thompson is highly regarded for publications and art exhibitions. He has published such classics as *African Art in Motion, Face of the Gods: Art and Altars of Africa and the African Americas*, and his most widely popular book, *Flash of the Spirit: African and Afro-American Art and Philosophy*.

Thompson's theories about the essential connection between art and the culture of the artist have had a particularly strong impact in the world of art history. He took African art off the walls and sought to put it into its historical context. Thompson is credited with transforming the study of Africa and the African **diaspora** because he traces the background and the journey of the artwork, and he continues to link the material object to the cultural and philosophical origin and transformation.

Though critics have claimed that Thompson is too essentialist in his readings of African culture and/or that he occasionally makes leaps to prove some of his cultural connections, he has been consistently praised for his groundbreaking and enthusiastic research. Thompson believes that art and philosophy in the **Black Atlantic** world should be "intellectually perceived and sensuously appreciated," and his work strives to bring complex issues to the mainstream while debunking earlier **myths** and stereotypes about African art and culture. He goes beyond the generalized "African retention" claims of previous scholars who looked for African cultural influences in the Americas and engages in a more specific analysis that demonstrates traditions and inventions from Yoruba, Kongo, Dahomean, Mande, and Ejagham civilizations in Africa, and he explores their exact transformation and manifestation in the Americas. Thompson's research replaced a theory of passive retention with one of active retentions and, in the process, has pushed and expanded the ideas of African influence in the Americas.

Resources: Robert Farris Thompson: *African Art in Motion: Icon and Act in the Collection of Katharine Coryton White* (Los Angeles: University of California Press, 1974); *Face of the Gods: Art and Altars of Africa and the African Americas* (New York: Museum for African Art, 1993); *Flash of the Spirit: African and Afro-American Art and Philosophy* (New York: Vintage, 1984).

Emily McTighe Musil

Thurman, Howard (1900–1981). Preacher, theologian, essayist, and nonfiction writer. Howard Thurman was a minister and educator who wrote twenty-one books, mainly concerned with the theology of the Gospel. He helped found the Church for the Fellowship of All Peoples in **San Francisco, California,** and his *Jesus and the Disinherited* (1949) is said to have influenced

Martin Luther King, Jr., to such an extent that the famous preacher kept a copy in his briefcase (Thurman *With Head and Heart*, 255). Born in Daytona Beach, Florida, the son of Alice and Saul Thurman, Howard was cared for in part by his grandmother, who had been born a slave. The old woman was insistent that Thurman place education above all other priorities, and he became the first African American child in Daytona to complete the eighth grade. In an experience which he claimed greatly influenced him, an anonymous stranger paid the fee for Thurman's trunk when Thurman, short on funds, attempted to board the train for the Negro High School in Jacksonville, Florida (*With Head and Heart*, 24).

Thurman went on to receive an A.B. from Morehouse (1923) and a Bachelor of Divinity from Colgate-Rochester Theological Seminary (1926). After seeking out the mentorship of Rufus Jones, he studied under the great Quaker as a fellow at Haverford College. In the course of his lifetime, Thurman held posts at Oberlin, Morehouse, Howard; and from 1953 to 1965, he was Dean of Marsh Chapel at Boston University, the first African American to hold the post at this traditionally White institution. In 1935, while traveling in India, Thurman was invited to meet with Mohandas Gandhi. This meeting, at which Ghandi told Thurman that the greatest enemy of Jesus Christ in America was Christianity, planted the seed for Thurman's later involvement with the Fellowship Church—one of America's earliest interfaith and interracial churches.

Known for preaching sermons with a calm, learned intelligence, Thurman was always careful to place religion ahead of social protest. For a man who influenced the **Civil Rights Movement**, he preached few, if any, sermons directly concerning the race problem. His books, however, are notable for their attention, through the Gospel, to the disenfranchised. As he wrote in the essay "Good News for the Underprivileged," "Christianity, in its social genesis, seems to me to have been a technique of survival for a disinherited minority" (Brown et al., 687). *Jesus and the Disinherited*, considered by most to be the centerpiece of his life's work, offers a reading of the Gospel and the life of Jesus that helped lay the foundation of nonviolence for the American Civil Rights Movement. Thurman's foregrounding of faith and spirituality as key precursors to just action is illustrated in this passage from *Footprints of a Dream* (1959, 7): "The movement of the Spirit of God in the hearts of men often calls them to act against the spirit of their times or causes them to anticipate a spirit which is yet in the making. In a moment of dedication, they are given wisdom and courage to dare a deed that challenges and to rekindle a hope that inpires." (*See* **Theology, Black and Womanist.**)

Resources: Primary Sources: Howard Thurman: *The Creative Encounter: An Interpretation of Religion and the Social Witness* (New York: Harper, 1954); *Deep Is the Hunger: Meditations for Apostles of Sensitiveness* (New York: Harper, 1951); *Deep River: Reflections on the Religious Insight of Certain of the Negro Spirituals* (New York: Harper, 1955); *Disciplines of the Spirit* (New York: Harper & Row, 1963); *Footprints of a Dream: The Story of the Church for the Fellowship of All Peoples* (New York: Harper, 1959); *The*

Growing Edge (New York: Harper, 1956); *Jesus and the Disinherited* (New York: Abingdon-Cokesbury, 1949); *Meditations of the Heart* (New York: Harper, 1953); *With Head and Heart: The Autobiography of Howard Thurman* (New York: Harcourt Brace Jovanovich, 1979). **Secondary Sources:** Sterling A. Brown, Arthur P. Davis, and Ulysses Lee, eds., *Negro Caravan* (New York: Arno, 1969); Callie Crossley, prod., *This Far by Faith: African-American Spiritual Journeys* (Blackside and The Faith Project, 2003); Luther E. Smith, *Howard Thurman: The Mystic as Prophet* (Washington, DC: University Press of America, 1981); Elizabeth Yates, *Howard Thurman: Portrait of a Practical Dreamer* (New York: John Day, 1964).

Robert Strong

Thurman, Wallace (1902–1934). Novelist, editor, playwright, and screenwriter. Born in Salt Lake City, Utah, Thurman attended the University of Utah and the University of Southern California. While still living in Southern California, he founded the journal *Outlet*. Like several later well-conceived efforts to bring attention to African American writers and artists, it failed because of Thurman's recurring inability to manage the publication in a fiscally responsible manner.

In the mid-1920s, Thurman moved to **Harlem, New York**, where he did much to shape the dynamic confluence of literary, artistic, and cultural influences and energies that came to be known as the **Harlem Renaissance.** Thurman worked, in succession, for *The Looking Glass*, **The Messenger**, and *World Tomorrow*. He also founded the seminal journals **Fire!!** and *Harlem: A Forum of Negro Life*. Through such outlets, Thurman became one of the leading critics of what he saw as efforts to intellectualize, to politicize, and to commodify African American literary expression. He also became one of the most vocal champions of the work of many younger writers, in particular **Langston Hughes**. Although he sometimes expressed views that were more expedient than consistent, Thurman generally asserted the need for African American literature that reflected the broad spectrum of African American experience without any, even implicit, endorsement of racial stereotypes.

While working in editorial capacities for McFadden Publications and Macauley Publishing, Thurman wrote in several genres. With William Jourdan Rapp, he wrote the Broadway hit *Harlem* (1929). In the last years of his life, he began writing screenplays.

Thurman's most enduring literary works have been his novels. *The Blacker the Berry* (1929) explores the manifestations and nuances of racism within African American communities. Specifically, through its chronicling of the disheartening experiences of one dark-skinned young woman, the novel offers a scathing critique of the preference for lighter skin and other "White" features among many African Americans. *Infants of the Spring* (1932) is a roman à clef about the Harlem Renaissance that offers unflattering characterizations of some of its leading figures. Finally, *The Interne* (1932), with A. L. Furman, is a fictional exposé of corruption and incompetence at an urban hospital.

Thurman died of tuberculosis while seemingly still in the early stages of a multifaceted and very dynamically creative career. The variety of his interests, contacts, and contributions is reflected in the range of critical approaches to his work. More recently, the increased attention to gay and lesbian studies has led to a renewed interest in and some very fresh readings of his work.

Resources: Primary Sources: Wallace Thurman: *The Blacker the Berry: A Novel of Negro Life* (New York: Macauley, 1929); *Infants of Spring* (New York: Macauley, 1932); Wallace Thurman and A. L. Furman, *The Interne* (New York: Macauley, 1932). **Secondary Sources:** David Blackmore, "'Something…Too Preposterous and Complex to Be Recognized or Considered': Same-Sex Desire and Race in *Infants of the Spring*," *Soundings* 80 (Winter 1997), 519–529; Darryl Dickson-Carr, "Signs of Adolescence: Problems of Group Identity in Wallace Thurman's *Infants of the Spring*," *Studies in Contemporary Satire* 20 (1996), 145–159; SallyAnn H. Ferguson, "Dorothy West and Helene Johnson in *Infants of the Spring*," *Langston Hughes Review* 2 (Fall 1983), 22–24; Renoir W. Gaither, "The Moment of Revision: A Reappraisal of Wallace Thurman's Aesthetics in *The Blacker the Berry* and *Infants of the Spring*," *College Language Association Journal* 37 (Sept. 1993), 81–93; Granville Ganter, "Decadence, Sexuality, and the Bohemian Vision of Wallace Thurman," *MELUS* 28 (Summer 2003), 83–104; Freda Scott Giles, "Glitter, Glitz, and Race: The Production of *Harlem*," *Journal of American Drama and Theatre* 7 (Fall 1995), 1–12; Elisa F. Glick, "Harlem's Queer Dandy: African-American Modernism and the Artifice of Blackness," *Modern Fiction Studies* 49 (Fall 2003), 414–442; Gerald Haslam, "Wallace Thurman: A Western Renaissance Man," *Western American Literature* 6 (1971), 53–59; Mae Gwendolyn Henderson, "Portrait of Wallace Thurman," in *Remembering the Harlem Renaissance*, ed. Cary D. Wintz (New York: Garland, 1996), 289–312; David R. Jarraway, "Tales of the City: Marginality, Community, and the Problem of (Gay) Identity in Wallace Thurman's 'Harlem' Fiction," *College English* 65 (Sept. 2002), 36–52; Phyllis Klotman, "The Black Writer in Hollywood, Circa 1930: The Case of Wallace Thurman," in *Black American Cinema*, ed. Manthia Diawara (New York: Routledge, 1993), 80–92; Stephen Knadler, "Sweetback Style: Wallace Thurman and a Queer Harlem Renaissance," *Modern Fiction Studies* 48 (Winter 2002), 898–936; Eleonore van Notten-Krepel, *Wallace Thurman's Harlem Renaissance* (Amsterdam: Rodopi, 1994); Huel D. Perkins, "Renaissance 'Renegade'? Wallace Thurman," *Black World* 25, no. 4 (1976), 29–35; Daniel Walden, "'The Canker Galls…'; Or, the Short Promising Life of Wallace Thurman," in *The Harlem Renaissance Re-examined*, ed. Victor A. Kramer (New York: AMS, 1987), 201–211.

Martin Kich

Till, Emmett (1941–1955). The figure of Emmett Till and his violent murder at the age of fourteen appear in numerous and diverse African American writings that examine racially motivated violence, racial injustice, interracial sexuality, relations between **gender** and **race**, African American male bodies, and official or default segregation. While visiting Mississippi from **Chicago, Illinois,** Till was lynched by two White men, for allegedly whistling at a White woman, on August 28, 1955. The murderers, J. W. Milam and Roy Bryant, were acquitted by an all-White jury despite considerable incriminating evidence; they later confessed to a reporter under protection from double jeopardy. Before Till's story became a recurrent figure in African American literature, a photograph of Till's beaten and mutilated body circulated in many local and national magazines and **newspapers**, such as *Jet*, because Till's mother, Mamie Till, demanded a public funeral with an open casket. The photographs, which were often accompanied by political editorials, incited outrage and protests in various American communities.

Emmett Till and his mother, Mamie Bradley, c. 1950. Courtesy of the Library of Congress.

African American writers use the figure of Till as a barometer of the limits of American democratic institutions, as a trope of the sexuality of Black men and White women, and as a reminder of the origins of the **Civil Rights Movement** in the Jim Crow South. Against the backdrop of the failure of the court system to obtain justice for Till, Metress traces African American authors' divergent depictions of Till in the "court of literature" (2003, 101) as a sacrificial Christ figure, as a catalyst for organized resistance to racial injustice, or as a disturber of the peace. In the essay accompanying his poem "Mississippi—1955" (1955), **Langston Hughes** documents Till's **lynching** and questions a history of racial violence against young African Americans. Whereas the event had provoked many public protests in Black communities and urban centers, Hughes indicts senators for the lack of a congressional response. In her poem "A Bronzeville Mother Loiters in Mississippi. Meanwhile, a Mississippi Mother Burns Bacon" (1960), **Gwendolyn Brooks** assumes the voice of the accusing White woman while she casts Till's lynching against a background of dominant cultural myths of princesses, princes, and dark villains. In the course of the poem, the Mississippi Mother can no longer fit the image of the fourteen-year-old boy into the mold of stories of dark villains, and the violent husband no longer fits his role of rescuing prince. **James Baldwin** based his Broadway play *Blues for Mister Charlie* (1964) on Till's murder; a lynching victim lies in a ditch dividing Whitetown from Blacktown. Though the play opens with the scene of the lynching and ends with the acquittal in the courtroom, Baldwin uses flashbacks and a nonsequential story to explore the characters of Blacktown and Whitetown who interact across various lines of segregation, such as race, gender, class, and geography. In his collection of autobiographical prison writings, *Soul on Ice* (1968), **Eldridge Cleaver** cites Till's lynching, along with **Richard Wright**'s *Native Son* (1940), as a watershed moment in his analysis of his own sexuality and his conflicted attraction to figures of White femininity at the expense of African American women.

Literary works in which the figure of Emmett Till appears are typically polemical, and often evoke strong responses from critics and readers. Baldwin's play, for instance, lasted four months off-Broadway, and reactions to the play tended to be either extremely laudatory or extremely condemnatory, often along racial lines. Many criticized Baldwin for dwelling on race hatred, for resegregating or polarizing seemingly integrated audiences, for taking liberties with the historical record, or for portraying the murder as a purely sexual act. Baldwin, too, held adamant views regarding the intended audience of his play, demanding that ticket prices be affordable, thereby allowing more integrated audiences than at similar off-Broadway venues. Perhaps to explain the widely divergent reactions to the play, Baldwin contended, "I wanted to *upset* people—and I did" (quoted in Eckman, 238). Popular and critical reactions to Cleaver's text have been similarly intense and divisive.

The figure of Emmett Till informs subsequent literary examinations of racial violence, even if the story is not based directly on Till and his lynching. **Audre Lorde**'s poem "Afterimages" (1982) portrays Till as a haunting presence whose racial and sexual lessons we all "inherit," and whose story we continue to enact. In the poem, Till's story helps make sense of the story of a poor rural White woman flooded out of her Mississippi home whose image appears at newsstands and on television news programs. Many African American writers continue to evoke the figure of Till with stories of interracial sexuality coupled with scenes of violence and legal testimony. **Ishmael Reed**'s satirical and controversial novel *Reckless Eyeballing* (1986) tells the story of Ian Ball, who, after being roundly condemned for the sexism of an earlier play, writes a play about the excavation of the corpse of a lynched African American boy for a posthumous rape trial. **Bebe Moore Campbell**'s *Your Blues Ain't Like Mine* (1992) is a story about race, sexuality, violence, and the law set in the rural south of the 1950s that begins with a scene of a lynching strongly reminiscent of Till's.

The lessons of Till's story about interracial violence and sexuality have been partially revised or expanded, especially in the wake of highly publicized occurences of intraracial violence such as the Atlanta child murders (1979–1981), when Wayne Williams, an African American, was convicted of killing twenty-eight African American children. That event serves as the basis for the poem "The Good Shepherd: Atlanta, 1981" (1986), by **Ai**; Baldwin's final book-length essay, *The Evidence of Things Not Seen* (1985); and the posthumous novel *Those Bones Are Not My Child* (1999), by **Toni Cade Bambara**. (*See* **Lynching**; **Lynching in Literature**.)

Resources: Ai, "The Good Shepherd: Atlanta, 1981," in her *Sin* (Boston: Houghton Mifflin, 1986); James Allen, *Without Sanctuary: Lynching Photography in America* (Santa Fe, NM: Twin Palms, 2000); James Baldwin: *Blues for Mister Charlie* (New York: Dial Press, 1964); *The Evidence of Things Not Seen* (New York: Holt, Rinehart and Winston,

1985); Toni Cade Bambara, *Those Bones Are Not My Child* (New York: Pantheon, 1999); Gwendolyn Brooks, "A Bronzeville Mother Loiters in Mississippi. Meanwhile a Mississippi Mother Burns Bacon," in her *Selected Poems* (New York: Harper & Row, 1963); Bebe Moore Campbell, *Your Blues Ain't Like Mine* (New York: Putnam, 1992); Michael Eric Dyson, "Remembering Emmett Till," in his *Reflecting Black: African American Cultural Criticism* (Minneapolis: University of Minnesota Press, 1993), 194–198; Fern Marja Eckman, *The Furious Passage of James Baldwin* (New York: M. Evans, 1966); Clenora Hudson-Weems, *Emmett Till: The Sacrificial Lamb of the Civil Rights Movement* (Troy, MI: Bedford, 1994); Langston Hughes, "Emmett Till, Mississippi, and Congressional Investigations," in *Fight for Freedom and Other Writings on Civil Rights*, vol. 10 of *The Collected Works of Langston Hughes*, ed. Christopher C. De Santis (Columbia: University of Missouri Press, 2001), 248–251; Audre Lorde, "Afterimages," in her *Undersong* (New York: Norton, 1992); Christopher Metress, "'No Justice, No Peace': The Figure of Emmett Till in African American Literature," *MELUS* 28, no. 1 (2003), 87–103; Christopher Metress, ed., *The Lynching of Emmett Till: A Documentary Narrative* (Charlottesville: University Press of Virginia, 2002); Stanley Nelson, dir., *The Murder of Emmett Till*, *American Experience* series (PBS, 2004), DVD; Ishmael Reed, *Reckless Eyeballing* (New York: St. Martin's, 1986); Anne Sarah Rubin, "Reflections on the Death of Emmett Till," *Southern Cultures* 2, no. 1 (1996), 45–66.

Brian J. Norman

Tillman, Katherine Davis Chapman (1870–c. 1946). Essayist, fiction writer, poet, and playwright. Tillman was an extremely versatile writer active during the late nineteenth and early twentieth centuries. She was born February 19, 1870, in Mound City, Illinois, to Charles and Laura Chapman. The family moved to Yankton, South Dakota, where Tillman began her formal education at the age of twelve (Johns). After graduating from high school, she attended Kentucky State University in Louisville, South Dakota State University at Yankton, and Wilberforce University in Ohio. Records of what she studied or whether she graduated from any of the universities attended have not been found. Around 1893 she married Dr. George M. Tillman, an African Methodist Episcopal minister, and became active in both church and civic associations. The date of Tillman's death is uncertain. However, by the time the second edition of the *Centennial Encyclopaedia of the African Methodist Episcopal Church* was published in 1947, she and her husband both had died.

Tillman wrote for both religious and secular publications. Her works include *How to Live Well on a Small Salary* and *The Afro-American Queen*. She also wrote the play *Fifty Years of Freedom* and the poem, "Bring Me Flowers Now."

The Works of Katherine Davis Chapman Tillman (1991) includes essays, poetry, recitations, fiction, **drama**, and an anthology. The anthology section of the volume contains *Quotations from Negro Authors*. Tillman and her contemporaries were sometimes regarded as the first generation of "race women" because they sought to raise consciousness about African American heritage, inspire pride, and achieve civil liberties for African Americans. Like their male counterparts, including **W.E.B. Du Bois** and **Booker T. Washington**, Tillman and others anticipated the **Civil Rights Movement** of the 1950s and 1960s.

Resources: Robert L. Johns: "Katherine Davis Chapman," in *Notable Black American Women*, vol. 1, ed. Jessie Carney Smith (Detroit: Gale, 1992), 649–651; "Katherine Davis Chapman Tillman," *Biography Resource Center* (Gale Group, 2004), http://galenet.galegroup.com/servlet/BioRC; Katherine Davis Chapman Tillman, *The Works of Katherine Davis Chapman Tillman*, ed. Claudia Tate (New York: Oxford University Press, 1991); Richard R. Wright, Jr., ed., *Centennial Encyclopaedia of the African Methodist Episcopal Church* (Philadelphia: Book Concern of the A.M.E. Church, 1916; 2nd ed., 1947), see esp. "Tillman, Mrs. Katherine D.," p. 228 of 1st ed.

Deloice Holliday

Tokenism. The practice of using an individual to stand for a whole group and thereby to imply that the group is fully represented. The *Oxford English Dictionary* further defines it as "the practice or policy of making merely a token effort or granting only minimal concessions, esp. to minority or suppressed groups," and suggests that the word, used in this way, arose in the early 1960s, in the United States. But of course the practice of treating persons as tokens is virtually timeless. Tokenism can create a stigma placed on people of color that suggests they are not qualified for their positions, and that their presence is due to preferential treatment and substandard evaluation criteria (Fried, 142).

In the poem "We Wear the Mask," **Paul Laurence Dunbar** suggests how African Americans wear a figurative mask in order to function in a society that views them as tokens. He writes, "With his sneers and grins, we play the game as best we can." Dunbar seems to suggest that, when reduced to tokens, African Americans have had to behave as tokens to "play the game."

The issue of tokenism is connected to **affirmative action**. Many Blacks have decidedly mixed views about the effectiveness of affirmative action (Robinson, 69). For those who benefit from affirmative action programs, some would say that the "price" paid was low, especially if the one who benefits, let's say, received a Ph.D. from a prestigious school. Yet those who do not benefit will never know how it felt or feels to sit next to non–affirmative action students and wonder if they see you as their intellectual equal (Robinson, 66). Even more important, if you are Black, you wonder if you *are* their intellectual equal. The fear of "not being smart enough," which haunts all students, potentially becomes even more pronounced for an affirmative action student if the student wonders if she or he is a token. Also, attempts at ethnic representation in employment, the arts, and other venues can be interpreted as tokenism. For instance, if one African American character is included in a novel, a television series, or a feature film, readers or viewers could interpret the inclusion as appropriately representative or as tokenism, or even in yet another way. Tokenism, in any event, is a complicated phenomenon; it is potentially both a social and an artistic issue; and it depends significantly on context, perception, and interpretation.

Resources: Paul Laurence Dunbar, *The Complete Poems of Paul Laurence Dunbar* (New York: Dodd, Mead, 1913); Jane Fried & Associates, *Shifting Paradigms in Student Affairs: Culture, Context, Teaching, and Learning* (Lanham, MD: University Press of America, 1995); D. R. Kinder and L. M. Sanders, *Divided by Color: Racial Politics and Democratic Ideals* (Chicago: University of Chicago Press, 1996); P. Moreno, "The History of Affirmative Action Law and Its Relation to College Admissions," *Journal of the National Association for College Admissions Counseling*, Spring 2003, 14–21; *Oxford English Dictionary*, http://dictionary.oed.com/cgi/entry/00253948?single=1&query_type=word&queryword=tokenism&edition=2e&first=1&max_to_show=10 ("Tokenism"); J. L. Robinson, *Racism or Attitude? The Ongoing Struggle for Black Liberation and Self-Esteem* (New York: Insight, 1995); P. Rubio, *A History of Affirmative Action, 1619–2000* (Jackson: University Press of Mississippi, 2001); R. Tucker, *Affirmative Action, the Supreme Court, and Political Power in the Old Confederacy* (Lanham, MD: University Press of America, 2000).

Kimberley Buster Williams

Tolson, Melvin B. (1898–1966). Poet, journalist, and educator. Melvin Tolson is a problematic character within the story of African American literature. A lifelong writer, he was, nonetheless, over forty years old before he had his first literary work professionally published. Karl Shapiro said of him that he "writes and thinks in **Negro**" (*Harlem Gallery*, 1); however he is more typically associated with the "White" style of high **Modernism**. His densely allusive works have never gained the popular readership of such poets as **Langston Hughes** or **Amiri Baraka**. His work seemed to require a kind of critical rehabilitation from the White poets who wrote introductions to his collections. Tolson has more recently been granted a place among first-rate poets of the twentieth century, but is still largely ignored by both the popular and the scholarly communities.

Melvin Beaunorus Tolson was born on February 6, 1898, in Moberly, Missouri. His father, Alonzo Tolson, was an itinerant Methodist preacher, holding ministerial positions throughout the Midwest during Melvin's childhood. The elder Tolson was an autodidact, having taught himself a smattering of Hebrew, Latin, and Greek. Melvin's mother, Lera Hurt Tolson, seems to have been the motivation behind his educational and literary aspirations. From her, he got a strong sense of storytelling and an intriguing genealogy. In a personal notebook (quoted by Flasch, 21), Tolson described his mother's family as a clan of "gun-toting preachers and hallelujahing badmen."

In school, Tolson was studious and active in extracurricular organizations. He wrote poems for school publications and directed and performed in plays with the **drama** club. He graduated from Lincoln High School in Kansas City, Missouri, in 1918. He enrolled at Fisk University in the fall of 1918, but financial problems led him to transfer to Lincoln University in Oxford, Pennsylvania, for the fall term of 1919. At Lincoln, Tolson was again serious and studious, but he felt somewhat inhibited by the conservative curriculum and faculty. His growing interest in such modern poets as Carl Sandburg and

Edgar Lee Masters was discouraged. One positive result of his time at Lincoln, however, was his relationship with Ruth Southall, whom he met at a dance in 1921. They were married in 1922, and raised four children together.

After graduating from Lincoln University in 1923, Tolson accepted a position as professor of English at Wiley College in Marshall, **Texas**. Tolson became known among Wiley students as a rather stern motivator, encouraging them to read and study beyond the requirements of their courses. He also took over direction of the school debate team, which under his guidance became a powerhouse on the debate circuit, defeating the national champion University of Southern California in 1935.

During the 1931–1932 school year, Tolson took a leave of absence from Wiley to enroll in a master's degree program at Columbia University. Writers of the **Harlem Renaissance** had long fascinated him, but by the time Tolson arrived in New York City, the Renaissance, though still vigorous, was on its downward slope. Tolson met **Langston Hughes** and other writers, yet never became part of the movement. His thesis, "The Harlem Group of Negro Writers" (completed by the end of the year, but not submitted until 1940, due to Tolson's busy schedule back at Wiley College), is largely a reiteration of ideas found in **Alain Locke**'s *The New Negro*.

After returning to Texas, Tolson set to work on *A Gallery of Harlem Portraits*, a collection of over 150 poetic character sketches not unlike Masters's *Spoon River Anthology*. It describes an assortment of people, from heroes to rogues, saints to whores. The tone is ironic and humorous, with a great affinity for the **blues**. The poems often reveal inner thoughts and attitudes that the characters are unable to express. "Hester Pringle," for example, describes a secretary for the Deaconess Purity League who, after walking in on a man as he stands naked in the shower, cannot keep licentious thoughts from her mind:

> Hester saw herself naked,
> Pursued in the moonlight of a tropical garden
> By a bronze, hard-muscled body
> Glistening with beads of water. (47)

Tolson tried in vain to find a publisher for the collection, but it went unpublished until 1979, thirteen years after his death.

His failure to publish *A Gallery* dampened Tolson's poetic aspirations, but in 1937 he was invited to become a columnist for the *Washington Tribune*, a Black newspaper with a national readership. His columns, published between 1937 and 1944 (collected as *Caviar and Cabbage* in 1982), show a wide range of interests, an erudite manner, and an irascible humor. His strongest censure was often saved for ineffective Black politicians. In one column, he said that a particular Black Congressman did not have enough knowledge to "fill the belly of a prenatal bedbug" (130).

Tolson's poem "Dark Symphony" won first prize in a contest sponsored by the American Negro Exposition at Chicago in 1939, and was published in

Atlantic Monthly in 1941. "Dark Symphony" then formed the center of *Rendezvous with America*, a collection published in 1944. The book sold well, and Tolson experienced what would be his highest level of popular readership. The book owes a great deal to the style of Walt Whitman, down to the inclusion of a poem titled "A Song for Myself." Tolson's "for" contrasts with Whitman's "of" and signals a need for Tolson, and perhaps the African American male, to speak *for* himself. Other poems are reimaginings of Locke's **"New Negro,"** described by Tolson as "Hard-muscled, Fascist-hating, Democracy-ensouled" (40).

Tolson had two important life experiences in 1947: he was invited to become the Poet Laureate of Liberia and he left Wiley College for Langston University in Langston, **Oklahoma**. In Langston, Tolson became a prominent community figure, writing and directing plays for the university theater and being elected to several terms as mayor of the town. The position as Poet Laureate of Liberia, though largely symbolic, led to the publication of *Libretto for the Republic of Liberia* in 1953, and a major shift in Tolson's poetic style. *Libretto* uses an allusive, high-modernist style reminiscent of T. S. Eliot, and bristles with so many learned references to antiquity, sociology, philosophy, and foreign language that Tolson felt it necessary to include 737 explanatory notes. Despite its dense allusion, the book displays a strong sense of imagery, such as when Tolson describes Liberia as a "quicksilver sparrow that slips/The eagle's claw!" To write the introduction for the collection, a modernist of no less stature than Allen Tate was recruited. Tate noted that Tolson was "in the direct succession from [Harte] Crane," but the relationship between Tate, an unregenerate Confederate, as it were, and this African American poet seemed to confuse most critics and the public as well. (*See* **Modernism**.)

It would be twelve years before Tolson published another collection of poetry, but he did not relent from the modernist style established in *Libretto*. Tolson conceived *Harlem Gallery: Book I, The Curator* as the first in a multivolume epic that would "convey the reality of the black man's experience in America" and "act as one way of fixing a changing ethnic experience that might disappear altogether" (Russell, 9). The book utilizes all of Tolson's skills—dense allusion, sharp **humor**, clever characterization, and a strong ear for folk language—and fuses them in a sophisticated way not seen before. The poem observes the lives and attitudes of five main characters, the unnamed Curator, his friend Dr. Nkomo, the artist John Laugart, the musician Mister Starks, and the poet Hideho Heights. Through their achievements and weaknesses, the poem examines the significance of African American art and the artist's place in Black history:

> The Harlem Gallery, an Afric pepper bird,
> awakes me at a people's dusk of dawn.
> The age alters its image, a dog's hind leg,
> and hazards the moment of truth in pawn. (19)

In his introduction, Karl Shapiro makes the (now) embarrassing comment about Tolson writing "Negro," but also places him in a lineage with Eliot and Crane, and argues for the critical attention that has yet to be directed at his work (13). With *The Harlem Gallery*, Tolson attained great prominence among African American artists and established himself as a major poet. His erudite and modernist style, however, has insulated him from a greater audience. At a time when a developing sense of the Black aesthetic called for a more politicized approach to poetry, Tolson's style seemed old-fashioned and alienated him from a greater critical reception. He died of cancer in 1966, the epic sequence begun with *The Harlem Gallery* left unfinished.

Resources: Primary Sources: Melvin Tolson: *Caviar and Cabbage: Selected Columns by Melvin B. Tolson from the Washington Tribune, 1937–1944*, ed. Robert M. Farnsworth (Columbia: University of Missouri Press, 1982); *A Gallery of Harlem Portraits*, ed. Robert M. Farnsworth (Columbia: University of Missouri Press, 1979); *Harlem Gallery*, book I, *The Curator*, intro. Karl Shapiro (New York: Twayne, 1965); *Libretto for the Republic of Liberia* (New York: Twayne, 1953); *Rendezvous with America* (New York: Dodd, Mead, 1944). **Secondary Sources:** Michael Bérubé, *Marginal Forces/Cultural Centers: Tolson, Pynchon, and the Politics of the Canon* (Ithaca, NY: Cornell University Press, 1992); Robert M. Farnsworth, *Melvin B. Tolson, 1898–1966: Plain Talk and Poetic Prophecy* (Columbia: University of Missouri Press, 1984); Joy Flasch, *Melvin B. Tolson* (New York: Twayne, 1972); Mariann Russell, *Melvin B. Tolson's Harlem Gallery: A Literary Analysis* (Columbia: University of Missouri Press, 1980).

Steven R. Harris

Toomer, Jean (1894–1967). Poet, playwright, and short story writer. Toomer is best known for *Cane*, a book which mixes fiction and poetry and remains a significant Modernist text. Nathan Eugene Toomer was born in **Washington, D.C.**; his parents were Nina Pinchback, whose father, Pinkney Benton Stewart Pinchback, had been an important Louisiana politician after the **Civil War**, and Nathan Toomer, an older gentleman farmer from Georgia with a poor business reputation and a rumored heritage of mixed race. Pinkney Pinchback claimed to be of mixed race himself, though he could pass for White, and his wife was White. When Nathan Toomer abandoned his wife and child, Jean and his mother moved in with her parents. To his grandparents, who would play vital roles in his early life, Jean was known as Eugene Pinchback. He lived in Washington with his grandparents from 1896 to 1906. From 1906 until 1910 he lived in **Brooklyn, New York**, and New Rochelle, New York, with his mother, who had remarried. After the death of Toomer's mother in 1909, Jean moved back with his grandparents. He remained in Washington until 1914. The Pinchback family had fallen on hard times and abandoned their upper-middle-class home for one in a racially mixed area of Washington.

Toomer had been enrolled in Black schools at his grandfather's insistence the entire time he lived in Washington, but he was exposed to the daily lives of African Americans for the first time in his late teens. From 1914 to 1918 he briefly attended a number of colleges, including the University of Wisconsin at Madison, the Massachusetts College of Agriculture (now the University of Massachusetts at Amherst), the University of Chicago, the American College of Physical Training in **Chicago, Illinois**, New York University, and City College in New York City. He studied agriculture, physical education, history, sociology, and law, but never earned a degree. He moved around the country in 1918, then returned to New York City for two years. This period exposed him to radical politics and the New York literary scene. He briefly tried to spread the word of socialism to New Jersey longshoremen. In 1919 Toomer met Waldo Frank, who would be a prominent supporter of his work; at this point in his life, Toomer had decided to devote himself to writing. Around 1920 he adopted the name Jean, under which he would publish all his best-known works; in his later life he would go by Nathan Jean Toomer or N. Jean Toomer.

In 1920 financial problems forced Toomer to move back with his grandparents. He cared for them in exchange for a small allowance and continued to work hard on his writing. In the fall of 1921, he heard about an opportunity to serve as substitute teacher at a Black school in Sparta, Georgia, and he took the job. His experiences during this period and on another trip to **the South** in 1922 formed a crucial part of his artistic vision. The other main component of his vision was that of a mixed "American race," with Native American, African, and European roots; this understanding of **race** reflected Toomer's attitudes about himself and his work, and his search for a means to realize it would guide him through artistic pursuits, politics, and spiritual philosophies throughout his life.

Toomer's first trip to the South, which lasted until November 1921, was followed by the composition of his best-known plays, *Balo* (written in the winter of 1921–1922) and *Natalie Mann* (written in early 1922). *Balo* tells the story of the mixed-race Lee family, whose eldest son has a religious awakening and gives the play its name. During the play, which is filled with elements of Black folk culture, a White neighbor farmer, who is very similar to the patriarch Will Lee in concerns and outlook, visits; the play stresses both the similarities between those with different skin tones and the remaining historical separation that divides them. The Lee family—the father explicitly of African, European, and Native

Undated portrait of Jean Toomer. Yale Collection of American Literature, Beinecke Rare Book and Manuscript Library.

American origin, the mother described as having a yellow complexion—serve as exemplars of Toomer's vision of a hybrid American identity. *Balo* was performed at Howard University in 1923.

Natalie Mann tells the story of the title character, a middle-class Black woman who escapes the social restrictions placed on her by her cohort to live a nonconformist life in New York City; these strictures, the play indicates, derive from a desire to gain acceptance by mimicking White middle-class culture. Through the help and example of Nathan Merilh, a worldly, intellectual Black man who embraces Leo Tolstoy as well as the heritage of African American folk life (and who serves as another representation of Toomer's ideal American hybrid), Natalie rejects the strictures placed upon her. The play was never performed because producers found it unsuitable for the American stage (McKay, 81).

Cane, Toomer's best-known work and only published literary book, was begun in November 1921 and finished by the early fall of 1922. It combines poetry, short stories, and a **drama**, "Kabnis," which together form a portrait of African American life in the early twentieth century. A good deal of it was inspired by Toomer's time in Georgia, though portions take place in the North. The book has three parts which display unity of theme and create a whole. The first, highly lyrical part takes place in the rural South. It includes the well-known stories of women, "Karintha," "Becky," "Carma," "Fern," and "Esther"; and the poems "Song of the Son" (first published in the **NAACP**'s journal *The Crisis*) and "Georgia Dusk" (which was written early and sent to *The Liberator*). The second portion of the book focuses on the North, especially Washington, D.C., and Chicago. It portrays a much colder, urban life, though it also draws attention to relationships between men and women. This section is characterized by encounters in streets, theaters, and parks. The short play "Kabnis" is the third part. In it an educated Northerner living in the South struggles with his role in life.

Images of **nature** echo from one text to another in *Cane*, and many of its poems bear strong connections. All portions of the book touch on elements of African folk culture. *Cane* was published by Boni and Liveright in 1923 and made Toomer's reputation as an artistic innovator. Toomer's prose and poetry in the book are highly imagistic, subtle, and evocative. Though it did not sell well, *Cane* is acclaimed as a highlight of the **Harlem Renaissance**, and Toomer gained admirers such as **Langston Hughes**, **W.E.B. Du Bois**, **Countee Cullen**, Sherwood Anderson, and Kenneth Burke. Generations of writers following *Cane* were nudged toward experimentation in style and form thanks to his work. A second edition of the book appeared in 1927. The third and fourth editions appeared only in the 1960s, one with University Place Press (1967) and one with Harper & Row (1969). These editions were largely responsible for reintroducing *Cane* and the figure of Toomer at a crucial moment in the growth of the academic study of African American literature.

After the publication of *Cane*, Toomer mostly withdrew from the literary world, largely pursuing spiritual goals, influenced partly by the ideas of George

Gurdjieff. He published short stories and poems in journals such as *Little Review* and *The Dial*; *Balo* appeared in *Plays of Negro Life* (1927) and his novella *York Beach* in *The New American Caravan* in 1929; and he had a handful of aesthetic and political essays published in the 1920s and 1930s. Though he continued to write throughout his life, composing stories, novels, a play, and numerous partial autobiographies (including *Reflections of an Earth Being*, 1928–1930), the last literary pieces published during his lifetime were the poems "Brown River, Smile," which appeared in *Pagany* in 1932, and "The Blue Meridian," published in *The New Caravan* in 1936.

By late 1923 Toomer had become deeply involved with the teachings of George Ivanovitch Gurdjieff, an Armenian mystic philosopher who worked primarily in France. Toomer spent a summer at Gurdjieff's center and spread word of his philosophy in the United States. After meeting the White Modernist writer Margery Latimer, Toomer tried his hand at leading a Gurdjieff-inspired communal experiment near Portage, Wisconsin, Latimer's hometown. Latimer and Toomer married in 1931, living in Chicago and in an artists' colony in Carmel, California; she died days after giving birth to their daughter. In 1934 Toomer married Marjorie Content, a photographer and New York socialite, who moved in Toomer's circles. They moved to Doylestown, Pennsylvania, where Toomer lived until his death. He tried to develop another communal society in Doylestown, the Mill House Experiment, but it, too, failed. Though he distanced himself from Gurdjieff in the late 1930s, Toomer never completely abandoned his belief in the philosophy. He had become interested in the Society of Friends after moving to Pennsylvania, and after a trip to India and explorations of Scientology, Toomer joined the Quakers in 1940. He wrote for the Quaker journal *Friend's Intelligencer* and published two books on them, *An Interpretation of Friends Worship* (1947) and *The Flavor of Man* (1949).

Toomer's papers, formerly at Fisk University, are part of the James Weldon Johnson Memorial Collection at the Beinecke Rare Book and Manuscript Library at Yale University. (*See* **Modernism**.)

Resources: Geneviève Fabre and Michel Feith, eds., *Jean Toomer and the Harlem Renaissance* (New Brunswick, NJ: Rutgers University Press, 2001); Nellie Y. McKay, *Jean Toomer, Artist: A Study of His Literary Life and Work, 1894–1936* (Chapel Hill: University of North Carolina Press, 1984); Therman B. O'Daniel, ed., *Jean Toomer: A Critical Evaluation* (Washington, DC: Howard University Press, 1988); Hans Ostrom, "Jean Toomer" (poem), *Xavier Review* 23, no. 2 (Fall 2003), 46; Jean Toomer: *Cane* (1923; repr. New York: Liveright, 1975); *The Wayward and the Seeking: A Collection of Writings by Jean Toomer*, ed. Darwin T. Turner (Washington, DC: Howard University Press, 1980).

Ian W. Wilson

Touré, Askia Muhammad Abu Bakr el (born 1938). Poet. The poet and cultural activist Askia Touré was born Roland Snellings in Raleigh, North Carolina, but lived for most of his childhood and adolescence in Dayton,

Ohio. After serving in the U.S. Air Force from 1956 to 1959, he attended the Art Students League of New York from 1960 to 1962.

One of the driving forces behind the **Blacks Arts Movement** that profoundly shaped African American literature in the 1960s and 1970s, Touré was actively involved in the founding of such seminal organizations as the **Black Arts Repertory Theatre/School**, the Revolutionary Action Movement, and the Student Nonviolent Coordinating Committee. He also exerted a major influence on such periodicals as *Black Dialogue*, *Journal of Black Poetry*, *Liberator*, *Soulbook*, and *Umbra* (though this last was in existence before the Black Arts Movement took hold). (*See* **Umbra Workshop**.)

Touré has lectured on topics related to African history, African American Studies, and creative writing at colleges and universities throughout the United States, most notably Columbia University, Cornell University, Pennsylvania State University, San Francisco State University, the University of California at Berkeley, and Yale University.

In *JuJu: Magic Songs for the Black Nation* (1970), Touré and **Ben Caldwell** regenerate African **myths** within lyrical poems that draw heavily on the diverse rhythms of African American popular musical styles, from rhythm and blues to **gospel music** to **jazz**. Touré pays homage, in particular, to the influence of the innovative jazz musician John Coltrane. In *Songhai!* (1972), Touré reflects on what it means to be a Black Muslim and makes extensive use of materials drawn from African cultural and political history.

For the collection *From the Pyramids to the Projects: Poems of Genocide and Resistance!* (1990), Touré received an American Book Award. Pointedly exploring issues and events related to racism and "Black genocide," the collection came directly out of Touré's activism in **Philadelphia, Pennsylvania**, in the aftermath of the police department's controversial and devastating attacks on the radical sect MOVE.

In the twenty-one poems included in *Dawnsong! The Epic Voice of Askia Touré* (2000), Touré not only provides an Afrocentric interpretation of cultural history and a chronicle of salient events in early African history, but also suggests, with considerable lyrical force, how that history remains relevant for peoples of African ancestry throughout the world. Specifically, he conveys the great sense of spiritual integrity that comes with deep cultural awareness and attests to the ways in which the sacral elements of traditional African cultures have a continuing resonance and relevance. (*See* **Afrocentricity**.)

Resources: James Smethurst, "Review of *Dawnsong!*" *African-American Review* 36 (Summer 2002), 343–345; Askia Touré: *Dawnsong! The Epic Memory of Askia Touré* (Chicago: Third World Press, 1999); *Earth: For Mrs. Mary Bethune and the African and Afro-American Women* (Detroit: Broadside Press, 1968); *From the Pyramids to the Projects: Poems of Genocide and Resistance!* (Trenton, NJ: Africa World Press, 1990); *Songhai!* (New York: Songhai Press, 1972); Askia Touré and Ben Caldwell, *JuJu: Magic Songs for the Black Nation* (Chicago: Third World Press, 1970).

Martin Kich

Travel Writing. African Americans have long been among the myriad voyagers—the adventurers, missionaries, abolitionists, journalists, soldiers, novelists, poets, artists, historians, humanitarian aid workers, academics, students, politicians, political activists, and diplomats—who have written about their experiences while traveling in their own country and abroad.

Some of the writing is indistinguishable from writing done by those who are not African American, but in other instances what makes their writing distinct is the telling of the story from the specific point of view shaped in the context of the historic experience of race relations in America: where **race** is a factor, where race matters, and where there exists a direct or indirect referral back to America as the comparison point for the reception and experience encountered in this new environment.

The first Black people in America to document their travel experiences were those who were there involuntarily—as slaves. One of the first such works, *The Interesting Narrative of the Life of Olaudah Equiano; Or, Gustavus Vassa, the African. Written by Himself,* is credited with launching a new literary genre, the **slave narrative**. In it, **Olaudah Equiano** describes life in a village in Nigeria prior to his being kidnapped and sold into bondage. His writing offers a rare glimpse of life in Africa through the eyes of an African.

The mid-nineteenth century was a period of mobility in America and globally that was fueled by myriad ideologies, currents, and events. It was also a period that saw a flourishing of the writing of letters, journals, diaries, and newspapers as people on the move gave accounts of their voyages. Despite the restrictions imposed by the practice of **slavery** in America and the other social and economic constraints that African Americans faced, many of them were also a part of this movement of people within the country and outside its borders. From these travelers came reports and stories of their sojourns. The journey was to any place but **the South**, and usually was to the North—for some, as far north as they could go on the **Underground Railroad** and into Canada, or further to the south into Mexico, or, for a some, Europe. They included free Blacks, freed slaves, runaways, intellectuals, and abolitionists. Most were men, but there were women among them, too.

There were those who headed "out West" and those who, in the spirit of the **"back-to-Africa"** movement returned to Africa, to the country that would become Liberia. Others, free and runaway, reached Canada. Prominent abolitionists, artists, and intellectuals traveled to Europe. Many of these travelers wrote about their experiences. Most wrote simply, describing the places left behind. Others were more ambitious in the telling of the stories of their lives and adventures.

William Wells Brown, a former slave who became a prominent abolitionist and a man of letters, not only penned his **autobiography** but also wrote about his foreign travels in a book titled *Three Years in Europe*. Western pioneers and adventurers such as **James Beckwourth**, **Mary Seacole**, Mary Fields, **Nat Love**, and Bass Reeves left chronicles of their lives.

From the years following the **Civil War** and into the twentieth century, this domestic and global mobility continued and African Americans were increasingly in the mix. Artists, educators, entertainers, intellectuals, and political activists increasingly traveled abroad. African Americans were among the missionaries who went to Africa to bring the Christian gospel. Domestically, from the South to the North, the **Great Migration** began.

This mobility continued through the years after **World War I** and **World War II**, well into the twentieth century. It involved a growing range of African American travelers: students, teachers, journalists, diplomats, soldiers, development and humanitarian aid workers, adventurers, political activists, and seekers. Many of them wrote about their travel experiences and the lessons they learned about themselves and the world.

Among early and mid-twentieth century African American authors, those best known for writing about their travels are some of the key voices from the **Harlem Renaissance**, such as **Zora Neale Hurston, Arthur A. Schomburg, Richard Wright, Claude McKay, Jessie Redmon Fauset, Countee Cullen,** and **Langston Hughes**. Hughes's two autobiographies, *The Big Sea* (1940) and *I Wonder as I Wander* (1956), are filled with what is essentially travel writing, set in the many places Hughes visited, including western Europe, Russia, Asia, Mexico, and **Haiti**.

During the 1950s, Richard Wright wrote four nonfiction travelogues that looked at the world through the lens of a Black American male and in the context of his racial experiences and political and ideological perspectives. In the first of the four books, *Black Power: A Record of Reactions in a Land of Pathos*, in which he documents his first visit to Africa—to the Gold Coast, the country that would eventually become independent Ghana, in 1953—Wright managed to anger people on both sides of the Atlantic through his negative views about his experience. Though devoutly committed to the ideals of Pan-Africanism, Wright found no emotional bond with the Africa he encountered. "I'm of African descent and I'm in the midst of Africans, yet I can not tell what they're thinking. . . . So far my random observations compel me to the conclusions that colonialism develops the worst qualities of character in both the imperialist and his hapless victim." Wright also wrote about his travel to Indonesia for a gathering of African and Asian intellectuals and political activists in *The Color Curtain: A Report on the Bandung Conference*, and his views of Catholic Spain under Francisco Franco in *Pagan Spain* and a collection of essays in *White Man, Listen*.

In the generation following the Harlem Renaissance, **James Baldwin** wrote often of his life as an African American expatriate in Europe. In his classic essay "A Stranger in the Village," he writes about how it felt to be the only Black person living in a tiny Swiss hamlet and his realization that in terms of human relations, the world, including America, "is white no longer, and it will never be white again." (*See* **Essay**.)

In America and also in Canada, African American newspapers printed the stories of escaped slaves and émigrés from the American slave South. Mary

Ann Shadd, an African American whose parents fled to Canada and who is considered the first Black newspaperwoman in North America, published such tales in Canada's first antislavery newspaper.

The writings of two African American travel writers, the journalist **George Washington Williams** and Rev. William Sheppard, highlight another important distinction of African American travel writing: that in the early years most of this writing was not done specifically as a travelogue, yet often yields a wealth of valuable travel information. Thus, in examining African American travel experiences, one must explore myriad sources such as letters, biographies, and autobiographies.

George Washington Williams, a journalist and a man of many talents and professions—he was a former soldier, a lawyer, a politician, a minister, and a historian—traveled to the Congo (now Zaire) in 1890, at the time a colony of Belgium, to write stories he hoped would muster support for his idea (in the back-to-Africa spirit) to lead a group of African Americans to settle there. Instead, he ended up documenting the brutality that was inflicted on the people there. He penned an "Open Letter to the King of Belgium" and made his views known in work that that has been called "a milestone in human rights literature and investigative journalism." Unfortunately, his crusade against this cruelty was cut short by a fatal illness.

Almost a decade later, Rev. William Sheppard, the Southern Presbyterians' first Black missionary to the Congo, was horrified by the forced slavery and abuse of Congolese villagers that included chopping off the hands of those who would not work, so that other males would be persuaded to work in the rain forest, tapping trees for the rubber that was a precious export commodity for Belgium. Sheppard's writings about the people, their art, and their lives helped put a human face on what was happening, and was instrumental in helping fuel the launch of a global movement against slavery in King Leopold's Congo.

The accounts of many Black novelists and poets of the time were published in African American **newspapers** such as the **Chicago Defender**, the **Baltimore Afro-American**, and the **Pittsburgh Courier**. These stories got wider distribution to smaller publications through syndication from the Associated Negro Press. Publications such as **Negro Digest**, **Ebony**, and *Jet* often had special features on travel by African Americans, particularly noting feats such as the exploits of the explorer Matthew Henson and other "firsts" in travel by African Americans, as well as stories by prominent Black Americans. **Martin Luther King, Jr.**, wrote about his pilgrimage to India, the home of his spiritual mentor Gandhi, in the pages of *Ebony*. The major outlets for African American literary and scholarly talent were **The Crisis**, the magazine published by the **NAACP**, and **Opportunity**, the magazine published by the Urban League.

During the 1930s, many left-leaning African American writers, such as Richard Wright, wrote for Communist and other left-leaning newspapers and reviews, such as *New Masses*, the *Daily Worker*, and *Partisan Review*.

The stories of these travelers, expressed in different styles, opened up the world to armchair and future travelers alike. The stories of runaway slaves inspired others to take their chance for freedom, as did the tales told by those who found greater opportunities in the migration north, the Black expatriates who found life more racially tolerant overseas, the Pan-African intellectuals, and those who traveled to Africa via programs such as Operation Crossroads Africa, the Peace Corps, or Africare, or as exchange students.

African Americans have continued to travel the world, inspired by the political, intellectual, and cultural currents and events of the time and traveling via different routes, to different places, for different reasons. And more of their writing specifically documents their travel experiences. "My journey to Africa was merely the logical extension of my journey to Europe. I had come seeking the answer to how I could face the lacerating racial whirlwind and yet make a life in America," wrote **Hoyt Fuller**, an educator, editor, critic, and author who is considered the godfather of the **Black Arts Movement**, in his book *Journey to Africa*, documenting his first trip to the continent in 1958.

Eddy L. Harris, who has been labeled a "memoirist-adventurer," is one of the best-known African Americans currently specifically doing travel writing. His work documents his journeys to places that are both geographically and emotionally foreign to him, from **Harlem, New York**, to Mississippi, to Africa. In recent years several African American journalists have penned memoirs about their time spent as foreign correspondents in Africa.

Travel writing and travel writing as literature have, in recent years, grown as fields of study. There is increasing work being done to recover the voices of Black American and other travelers from the African **diaspora** in books such as the anthology *A Stranger in the Village: Two Centuries of African American Travel Writing*, as well as in scholarly publications such as *Journal of African Travel Writing* and *Studies in Travel Writing*.

Commercially, the growth of the African American travel market has led to an increase in publications targeting this group. There are magazines such as *Ebony* and *Essence*, travel books, and, increasingly, the Internet, all of which have opened up new spaces for a new generation of African Americans and writers from the African diaspora to tell their stories as they travel the world. (*See* **Expatriate Writers; Paris, France**.)

Resources: James Baldwin, "A Stranger in the Village," in his *Collected Essays* (New York: Library of America, 1998); John Hope Franklin and Alfred A. Moss, Jr., *From Slavery to Freedom: A History of African Americans*, 8th ed. (Boston: McGraw-Hill, 2000); Hoyt W. Fuller, *Journey to Africa* (Chicago: Third World Press, 1971); Farah J. Griffin and Cheryl J. Fish, eds., *A Stranger in The Village: Two Centuries of African-American Travel Writing* (Boston: Beacon Press, 1998); Adam Hochschild, *King Leopold's Ghost: A Story of Greed, Terror, and Heroism in Colonial Africa* (Boston: Houghton Mifflin, 1998); Langston Hughes: *The Big Sea* (New York: Knopf, 1940); *I Wonder as I Wander* (New York: Rinehart, 1956); Margaret Walker, *Richard Wright: Daemonic Genius* (New York: Warner Books, 1988); Richard Wright, excerpt from

Black Power: A Record of Reactions in a Land of Pathos, in *A Stranger in the Village*, ed. Farah J. Griffin and Cheryl J. Fish (Boston: Beacon, 1998), 151–152.

Wilma Jean Emanuel Randle

Trethewey, Natasha (born 1966). Poet and professor. Trethewey's poetry reflects concern with absence and memory, with the work lives and the private lives of African Americans, and with the exploration of matrilineal heritage. **Rita Dove** chose Trethewey's first book, *Domestic Work*, to receive the Cave Canem Poetry Prize in 1999. In *Domestic Work* the microrelationships within a family reflect larger social and political relationships as Trethewey explores nuances of racism in her grandmother's life and in the various jobs her grandmother held.

In *Bellocq's Ophelia*, Trethewey's second book, she imagines a fictional life for an early twentieth-century prostitute whose photograph is in E. J. Bellocq's *Storyville Portraits*. His photos serve as inspiration for Trethewey as she creates a series of persona poems which tell the story of her main character's survival as Trethewey again infuses past history with present imagination to create poems which reflect a range of issues. Working in a variety of forms, Trethewey produces verse that is known for its strong rhythm and musicality as she gives voice to characters' secrets, which she says might otherwise be overlooked.

Trethewey grew up in the **Atlanta, Georgia**, area and earned an M.A. in English and creative writing from Hollins University and an M.F.A. in poetry from the University of Massachusetts. She has received a Grolier Poetry Prize and an NEA fellowship, and was a fellow at Radcliffe's Bunting Institute in 2000–2001. In 2003 she received a Guggenheim Fellowship for her work. She intends to use this fellowship to research a third book which explores **Civil War**–era memorials in **the South**, as she explores again the junctures between personal memory and public history.

Trethewey's poems have appeared in such **literary magazines** as *Agni, American Poetry Review,* **Callaloo**, *Kenyon Review, New England Review,* and *Southern Review.* She is also a member of the Dark Room Collective. At this writing, she teaches at Emory University in Atlanta.

Resources: Jill Petty, "An Interview with Natasha Trethewey," *Callaloo* 19, no. 2 (Spring 1996), 364–375; Natasha Trethewey: *Bellocq's Ophelia* (St. Paul, MN: Graywolf Press, 2002); *Domestic Work* (St. Paul, MN: Graywolf Press, 2000).

Elline Lipkin

Trice, Dawn Turner (born 1965). Novelist. With the success of her two published novels, Dawn Turner Trice, a native of **Chicago, Illinois**, has established her place within the African American literary tradition. She was influenced by such writers as **Ernest James Gaines, Langston Hughes, August Wilson**, and Richard Ford. It was their ability to tell a story, not crafty language and beautiful phrasing, that she admired most. The story is Trice's focus and, according to the critics, her stories are first-rate.

Only Twice I've Wished for Heaven (1996) was Trice's first novel. The story "contrasts two contiguous worlds separated by a fence" (Duboin, 117). The novel begins when Tempestt Saville and her parents move to Lakeland, a fictional community of affluent and educated African Americans. Thirty-fifth Street, on the other side of the fence, is a "microcosm of the decaying black ghetto" (115).

The fence is a significant symbol in the novel. Corinne Duboin, of the University of Réunion, suggests that the fence "symbolizes the great social and cultural divide within the African American community" (117). Trice explains how this divide was not always a challenge for African Americans. In **slavery** times and in the era of the **Civil Rights Movement**, "the thing was to get out to come back. So, it wasn't just that [African Americans] were saving [themselves], but [they] were getting out to come back and save other people" (117).

Important themes include community, the "elder" figure, and heaven. Miss Jonetta, the owner of a liquor store on Thirty-fifth Street, and the community of elderly men who frequent her store, befriend Tempestt. Tempestt is unhappy in Lakeland and regularly sneaks through a gap in the fence to visit these elders. Miss Jonetta and the men "represent a positive force" in the novel (119). Trice feels that it is the community and individuals like Miss Jonetta who can help restore ravaged communities.

When calamity befalls both communities, the main characters flee to places that represent Heaven in their minds. Miss Jonetta moves to **the South**, and the Savilles go west, to California, "looking for a new life" (122).

An Eighth of August (2000) is Trice's second novel. It centers around a tragedy that occurs in Halley's Landing, a fictional African American community, during an annual celebration of the signing of the Emancipation Proclamation. The novel is narrated by members of this community. Once again, Trice explores the themes of community and the role of the elderly figure, who helps guide others in the right direction.

Resources: "Dawn Turner Trice," *Contemporary Authors Online*, http://galenet.gale group.com/servlet/BioRC (Detroit: Gale, 2004); Corinne Duboin, "A New Voice in African American Literature: An Interview with Dawn Turner Trice," *Sources* 11 (2001), 115–127; Dawn Turner Trice: *An Eighth of August* (New York: Crown, 2000); *Only Twice I've Wished for Heaven* (New York: Crown, 1996).

Gladys L. Knight

Trickster. A character in African American tales of heroism that originated in African oral narratives in which animals took on the personalities of human beings and overcame difficult circumstances by defeating larger animals through the use of trickery. Often taking the form of a rabbit, spider, tortoise, or monkey, the figure of the trickster, reborn in various parts of the Americas, became a symbol of heroic action and potential power for enslaved Africans who felt powerless in the face of **slavery** and, specifically, the plantation system. This figure became central to the African American trickster tale, which was shared through word of mouth among the slaves in order to inspire perseverance, to communicate instructions on how to outwit and/or overcome the slave masters, and, most important, to provide examples of how to obtain materials for survival under circumstances marked by want.

Trickster tales, according to John W. Roberts, were also based on the everyday life of Africans, who had to deal with "subsistence-level existence as well as chronic shortages of basic material necessities occasioned by various factors peculiar to life on the African continent" (24). The slave experience, also marked by such conditions, allowed for the transformation of such tales into ones that reflected the need for survival strategies in a new world. Regarded by Whites as childish inventions, trickster tales were thus allowed to abound; and their heroes reflected the ingenuity one could employ in dealing with the harsh realities of deprivation. Viewing these heroes with awe and, in many cases, venerating them, African slaves and their offspring adopted the personalities and characteristics of the trickster and applied them to their own experiences during enslavement. In the words of Robert Hemenway, "Trickster tales, universal in all folklore, were especially popular [in the African American folkloric tradition] because they often emphasized the triumph of the weak over the strong; they seemed ready made for a slave situation in which foot speed—escape—was a persistent hope and tricks rather than physical force were the primary recourse for survival"(25). Roberts characterizes the reverence for the heroes of these tales as almost a deification when he writes that the "African conception of the trickster as a sacred being, usually a god, undoubtedly influenced African attitudes toward the adaptability of behaviors embodied in trickster tales in certain kinds of situations"(27).

The best-known animal trickster is Brer Rabbit, notorious for stealing from others in the animal and human kingdoms. In one of the most popular versions of his tale, Brer Rabbit steals water from a well. A farmer erects a "tar baby" near the well in order to trap the rabbit. When Brer Rabbit tries to steal water again, he becomes stuck in the sticky mass of the tar. Finally catching the rabbit, the farmer throws him into the briar patch, from which he escapes once again. In a few other versions, Brer Rabbit's outcome is less positive; he is punished severely for maliciously duping his own kind and for creating disorder within the animal community. As Roberts makes clear, a trickster was viewed as heroic only if his tricks purposefully reflected the "most advantageous behaviors for securing individual interests without disrupting the order and harmony of society" (29). Appropriate trickster behavior, then, did not willfully bring harm to the rest of the community. Given this, in adopting the appropriate behaviors of trickster figures such as Brer Rabbit, slaves sought to weaken the master's authority while seeking to avert retaliation and punishment. Speaking of the importance of Brer Rabbit to hero formation within the slave community, Hemenway characterizes it in this way: "Shaped by a long line of oral artists, Brer Rabbit is black from the tip of his ears to the fuzz of his tail, and he defeats his enemies with a superior intelligence growing from a total understanding of his hostile environment. He is the briar-patch representative of a people living by their wits to make a way out of no way" (9). Sharing trickster tales in secret and striving together for the rewards of the trickster, slaves often used these tales of heroism as a source of communal strength.

In addition to animal tricksters, Africans had a wealth of religious **folklore** from which to draw for the development of trickster tales in the Americas. The Yoruba in particular contributed to this tradition the characteristics of their most respected trickster deity, Eshu-Elegba (also known as Legba, Elegbara, Esu), who outmaneuvered his fellow deities to gain the respect of the creator god and to be granted the power to make things happen; he thus became the guardian of the crossroads, where choice, destiny, and morality are mediated through communication (Roberts, 18–19). Enslaved Africans applied these attributes to the invention of supernatural figures (also known as conjurers) who would circumvent the slavocracy and subvert the oppressive structure of the plantation system. Embodying elements of animal and cosmic tricksters, individuals such as **John the Conqueror** were born and functioned as "mediational" characters between and within the spirit and material worlds. As Deidre Badejo emphasizes, such a figure became "man, animal, demi-god and Nature" all at once (5). The result was "not only a literary figure who dupes for self-aggrandizement but also one who challenges an established social order and probes the question of fate" (10). This character would later influence the "badman" folk heroic tradition, in which the trickster "responded to victimization with violence" (Roberts, 206).

A White Southerner who romanticized the slave system with the creation of the character of Uncle Remus, Joel Chandler Harris, best known for his *Uncle Remus* tales, became one of the first and best-known collectors of trickster tales. Despite their emphasis on comic elements that appeared to denigrate slaves, the tales received wide attention in the nineteenth century; and their popularization resulted in the recognition of the African origins of the tales and of the trickster figure as a hero in African (and later African American) folk expression. **Charles Waddell Chesnutt**'s *The Conjure Woman* (1899) further added to the interest in tricksters and conjurers in Southern folklore. Modern retellings of particular tales featuring the trickster figure include **Zora Neale Hurston**'s *Mules and Men* (1935) and **Julius Lester**'s *Black Folktales* (1969).

The trickster figure continues to be used by contemporary writers and intellectuals. For example, poets such as Kamau Brathwaite and Louise Bennett have included references to Anansi the spider god in their verses. The novelist **Toni Morrison** rewrites the tale of Brer Rabbit and the tar baby in *Tar Baby* (1981); and Erna Brodber focuses on the supernatural communicative powers of tricksters within Black folk communities in *Myal* (1988) and *Louisiana* (1994). Finally, such literary theorists as Jay Edwards and **Henry Louis Gates, Jr.**, with his theory of "signifyin(g)," have highlighted the complex structures of trickster tales and the subversive elements in the language used by trickster figures in such narratives from the African oral tradition to the modern literary one. (*See* **Folktales**.)

Resources: Barbara Babcock-Abrahams, "'A Tolerated Margin of Mess': The Trickster and His Tales Reconsidered," *Journal of the Folklore Institute* 2 (1975), 147–186; Deidre L. Badejo, "The Yoruba and Afro-American Trickster: A Contextual Comparison," *Présence Africaine* 147, no. 3 (1988), 3–17; Jay Edwards, *The Afro-American Trickster Tale: A Structural Analysis* (Bloomington: Folklore Publications Group, Indiana University, 1978), 9–13; Arthur Huff Fauset, "American Negro Folk Literature," in *The New Negro*, ed. Alain Locke (New York: Albert and Charles Boni, 1925), 238–244; Henry Louis Gates, Jr., *The Signifying Monkey: A Theory of Afro-American Literary Criticism* (New York: Oxford University Press, 1988); Robert Hemenway, "Introduction: Author, Teller, and Hero," in *Uncle Remus: His Songs and Sayings*, by Joel Chandler Harris (1880; repr. New York: Penguin, 1982), 7–31; Annie Reed, "Brer Rabbit and the Briar Patch," in *Talk That Talk: An Anthology of African-American Storytelling*, ed. Linda Goss and Marian E. Barnes (New York: Simon and Schuster, 1989), 30–31; John W. Roberts, *From Trickster to Badman: The Black Folk Hero in Slavery and Freedom* (Philadelphia: University of Pennsylvania Press, 1989); Robert Farris Thompson, *Flash of the Spirit: African and Afro-American Art and Philosophy* (New York: Vintage Books, 1984); Roger M. Valade III, "Trickster Tale," in *The Essential Black Literature Guide* (Detroit: Visible Ink Press, 1996), 361.

Deonne N. Minto

Troupe, Quincy Thomas, Jr. (born 1943). Poet, editor, educator, and biographer. Quincy Troupe is best known for award-winning poetry, which blends **jazz** and be-bop rhythms, cadences, and language in order to explore social justice issues connected with being a person of color and, in particular, an African American man. Troupe has received the National Endowment for the Arts Award in Poetry (1978) and has twice won the American Book Award from the Association of American Publishers (in 1980 for *Snake-back Solos* and in 1990 for *Miles: The Autobiography*). He won the Peabody Award in 1991 for coproducing and writing *The Miles Davis Radio Project*, and he has twice been the winner of the World Heavyweight Championship Poetry Bout at the Taos Poetry Circus. In 1972 Troupe was awarded a $10,000 International Institute of Education travel grant, which he used to visit Senegal, Ivory Coast, Guinea, Ghana, and Nigeria. He also received a $6,000 grant from the New York State Council of the Arts in 1979. In 2002 he was named the first Poet Laureate of California; he subsequently resigned from the post and from his faculty position at the University of California at San Diego in response to controversy surrounding his falsification of his bachelor's degree on his curriculum vitae.

Quincy Troupe was born on July 23, 1943, to Dorothy Marshall and Quincy Troupe Sr., a Negro League baseball player. He grew up in **St. Louis, Missouri**, and later moved to Louisiana and then to **Los Angeles, California**. In 1964 he published his first poem, "What Is a Black Man?" in *Paris Match*. In Los Angeles he taught creative writing for the Watts Writers' movement from

1966 until 1968, and in 1968 published the anthology *Watts Poets: A Book of New Poetry and Essays*. He also served as associate editor of *Shrewd* magazine that year and taught creative writing at the University of California at Los Angeles and the University of Southern California. He has also taught creative writing and literature at Ohio University, where he was the founding editor of *Confrontation: A Journal of Third World Literature*, which published works by Chinua Achebe, **Toni Cade Bambara**, **Audre Lorde**, Herberto Padilla, Amos Tutuola, and **Alice Walker**, among others. Troupe also edited *American Rag*. He subsequently taught creative writing and literature classes at Richmond College, Columbia University, the University of California at Berkeley, California State University at Sacramento, the University of Ghana at Legon, and the University of California at San Diego.

In 1975 Troupe and Rainer Schulte edited the acclaimed *Giant Talk: An Anthology of Third World Writings*, a volume that includes poetry, **folktales**, short stories, and novel excerpts from African American, African, Native American, Caribbean, and Latin American authors. Troupe and Schulte define Third World writers as "those who identify with the historically exploited segment of mankind who confront the establishment on their behalf" (Slater).

Troupe's earliest poetic influences were Pablo Neruda, John Joseph Rabearivello, Aimé Césaire, Cesar Vallejo, **Jean Toomer**, and **Sterling A. Brown**. A *Publishers Weekly* review of Troupe's collection of poetry *Avalanche* noted that his poetry often manifests as a "cold, smacking, 'rush of objects.'" Troupe's first collection dedicated entirely to his own poetry, *Embryo, 1967–1971*, published in 1972, includes the poem "Impressions/of Chicago: For Howlin' Wolf," which demonstrates his flurry of music imagery and metaphor. In 1978 he published *Snake-back Solos: Selected Poems, 1969–1977*. Imagery of music saturates the collection and contributes to the varied tones in the poetry.

Troupe's other volumes of poetry are *Skulls Along the River* (1984); *Weather Reports: New and Selected Poems* (1991); *Avalanche: Poems* (1996); *Choruses: Poems* (1999); *Take It to the Hoop, Magic Johnson* (2000); *Transcircularities: New and Selected Poems* (2002); and *Little Stevie Wonder* (2005). In addition to the poetry collections, Troupe wrote *The Inside Story of TV's "Roots"* (with David L. Wolper), which explores the story behind the **Alex Haley** novel and subsequent miniseries (1978), and *Soundings* (1988), a collection of essays. He edited *James Baldwin: The Legacy* (1989), a collection of tributes from famous writers and others, compiled after **James Baldwin**'s death, and he recorded Baldwin's poetry for the Library of Congress on two separate occasions. Troupe has published numerous articles in magazines and journals. In 1989 Troupe and Miles Davis wrote the critically acclaimed *Miles: The Autobiography*. Troupe garnered the American Book Award for *Miles* and attracted a new throng of admirers. He went on to write *Miles and Me*, his reflections on interviewing Miles Davis for the autobiography. Douglas Henry Daniels of the *African American Review* called the book an "invaluable work."

Resources: Horace Coleman, "Quincy Thomas Troupe, Jr.," in *Dictionary of Literary Biography*, vol. 41, *Afro-American Poets Since 1955*, ed. Trudier Harris and

Thadious M. Davis (Detroit: Gale, 1985), 334–338; Douglas Henry Daniels, "Review of *Miles and Me*," *African American Review* 35, no. 1 (Spring 2001), 152–153; Tom Dent, "*Snake-back Solos*," *Freedomways* 20 (Second Quarter 1980), 104–107; Henry Louis Gates, Jr., and Nellie Y. McKay, eds., *The Norton Anthology of African American Literature* (New York: Norton, 1979), 2002–2007; Michael Harper, "Review of *Snakeback Solos*," *New York Times Book Review*, Oct. 21, 1979, pp. 18–21; "Quincy (Thomas) Troupe, (Jr.)," in *Contemporary Authors*, New Revision Series, vol. 126 (Detroit: Gale, 2004), 403–408; Review of *Avalanche*, *Publishers Weekly*, Mar. 18, 1996, p. 66; Jack Slater, "Review of *Giant Talk*," *New York Times Book Review*, Nov. 30, 1975, pp. 56–57; Quincy Troupe: *Avalanche: Poems* (Minneapolis, MN: Coffee House Press, 1996); *Choruses* (Minneapolis, MN: Coffee House Press, 1999); *Embryo Poems, 1967–1971* (New York: Barlenmir, 1972); *Little Stevie Wonder* (Boston: Houghton Mifflin, 2005); *Miles and Me* (Berkeley: University of California Press, 2000); *Skulls along the River* (New York: I. Reed Books, 1984); *Snake-back Solos: Selected Poems, 1969–1977* (New York: I. Reed Books, 1978); *Soundings* (New York: Writers & Readers, 1988); *Take It to the Hoop, Magic Johnson* (New York: Jump at the Sun, 2000); *Transcircularities: New and Selected Poems* (Minneapolis, MN: Coffee House Press, 2002); *Weather Reports: New and Selected Poems* (New York: Writers & Readers, 1991); Quincy Troupe, ed.: *James Baldwin: The Legacy* (New York: Simon & Schuster, 1989); *Watts Poets: A Book of New Poetry and Essays* (Los Angeles: House of Respect, 1968); Quincy Troupe and Miles Davis, *Miles: The Autobiography* (New York: Simon & Schuster, 1989); Quincy Troupe and Rainer Schulte, eds., *Giant Talk: An Anthology of Third World Writings* (New York: Random House, 1975); Quincy Troupe and David L. Wolper, *The Inside Story of TV's "Roots"* (New York: Warner Books, 1978); Mel Watins, "Hard Times for Black Writers," *New York Times Book Review*, Feb. 21, 1981, pp. 3, 26.

Alicia Kester

Truth, Sojourner (1797–1883). Itinerant preacher, abolitionist, feminist, social reformer, and singer. Sojourner Truth is best known for her speech "Ain't I a Woman?," delivered in May 1851 to the Women's Rights Convention in Akron, Ohio. Born into a slave-owning Dutch family in Ulster County, New York, probably in 1797, Truth was originally known as Isabella Baumfree. She was sold away from her parents at the age of nine. She was later married to a fellow slave named Thomas and birthed five children. In 1826, a year before **slavery** was outlawed in New York, she left the house of her master, Mr. Dumont, where she had experienced physical and sexual abuse and, with one of her children, found shelter with Isaac and Maria Van Wagenen. She worked as their domestic servant and successfully sued for the custody of another of her children who had been illegally sold into **the South** as a slave. The Van Wagenens paid her old master for the services of Truth and her child. She was known as Isabella Van Wagenen from this point until about 1843.

After her conversion to Christianity by way of a visitation from God, she dedicated her life to God's work, at first "under the influence of Millerite

Second Adventism" (Painter, "Sojourner Truth," 738). She moved to New York City in 1828 with her son. During her fourteen years there, Truth joined various churches but left that "Sodom" at God's command to go east as an evangelist (Gilbert). She set forth, with fairly traditional Christian beliefs, to "set the world right side up." She met Olive Gilbert, an abolitionist and feminist, and a friend of William Lloyd Garrison of the **Abolitionist Movement**. Gilbert recorded Truth's story in *The Narrative of Sojourner Truth: A Bondswoman of Olden Time*, published in Boston in 1850. Proceeds from the sale of the book helped maintain Truth's family financially. The sale of her photograph also earned income. She often said, "I sell the shadow to support the substance" (Samra).

Although the veracity of the account of her 1851 Akron speech, as transcribed by Frances D. Gage, the President of the Women's Rights Convention, has been questioned, this address established Truth's role as a cultural icon (Sánchez-Eppler; Samra). (Painter credits Gage with turning "ain't I a woman?" into a "refrain" in Truth's speeches in 1863 ["Sojourner Truth, 738]). Truth's lifelong illiteracy was, she said, the result of slavery, which robbed her of an education. In such statements as "I can tell you I can't read a book, but I can read de people" (Mabee and Newhouse), however, Truth occasionally revised the traditional notion of literacy. Because her speeches and her narrative were actually written by others, the authenticity of the accounts has sometimes been in question (Humez). Depending upon who transcribed Truth's autobiographical accounts and speeches, Truth's dialect may appear Northern or Southern, her views informed or uninformed.

In 1853, Truth and her grandson, Samuel Banks, made an uninvited visit to **Harriet Beecher Stowe** in Andover, Massachusetts, remaining for several days. Stowe later recorded her impressions in "Sojourner Truth, the Libyan Sibyl," an article published a decade later in *The Atlantic Monthly* (Stowe; Terry; Lebedun). Its subtitle refers to a statue inspired by Truth and sculpted by William Wetmore Story that was displayed at the World's Fair in London in 1862. Stowe records her conversations with and impressions of Truth's striking stature (she stood nearly six feet tall) and powerful personal presence. Truth informed Stowe that her name used to be Isabella but that when she left "the house of bondage," the Lord renamed her Sojourner Truth because of her mission as a traveling,

Sojourner Truth, 1864. Courtesy of the Library of Congress.

truth-declaring preacher. God made her, she says, "a sign unto this nation" of the sins against her people. In 1857, drawn to a Quaker-related group of reformers living in Battle Creek, Michigan, Truth moved there from Northampton, Massachusetts. From the 1850s to the 1870s, she continued to advocate at various meetings and rallies for the rights of African Americans and women. In 1864, a year after the Emancipation Proclamation, Truth visited **Washington, D.C.**, "to see the freedmen of [her] people." On October 29 of that year, she met with President Lincoln at the White House. The nature of their discussion and Lincoln's attitude toward Truth remain a matter of dispute. She thereafter worked with freed slaves in Washington, resettling some with her own money in Rochester, New York, and Battle Creek, Michigan. Scandalized that freed Blacks were still relying on the government in 1870, she promoted their education so that they might be better able to support themselves. She was also in favor of their settlement in the West, based on the model of the Indian reservation. She kicked off a resettlement campaign in February 1870 and toured New England and the mid-Atlantic states, collecting signatures in its support. The campaign was not successful.

Although Truth was reputed to have been involved with the **Underground Railroad**, no evidence for this claim exists. Tragically, Truth's grandson, Samuel Banks, died in 1875 at the age of twenty-four, depriving Truth of a beloved traveling companion. Truth also experienced severe health difficulties at this time, including the paralysis of her right side and permanent gangrenous ulcers on her legs. Frances Titus, a New England Quaker who also worked to bring freed slaves to Battle Creek, helped to support Truth financially and to revise her *Narrative*. The 1875 edition includes Truth's "Book of Life," a compendium of clippings and letters from her scrapbooks. Although Titus preserved these documents, which scholars have used, she also romanticized Truth, misrepresented various crucial dates, and poorly edited older documents. She did, however, endorse Truth's argument that the nation owed Blacks a debt for having profited for generations from their unpaid labor.

In her last years, Truth lived with her daughters in Battle Creek, Michigan, where she frequently had visitors. After several months of intense suffering, she died there before dawn on November 26, 1883. Nearly a thousand people attended her funeral, and some of Battle Creek's most prominent citizens acted as pallbearers. Titus's 1884 edition of Truth's *Narrative* includes a "Memorial Chapter." In one of the tributes to her in that chapter, **Frederick Douglass** describes Truth as "Venerable for age, distinguished for insight into human nature, remarkable for independence and courageous self-assertion, devoted to the welfare of her race, . . . [and] for the last forty years an object of respect and admiration to social reformers everywhere."

Resources: Olive Gilbert, ed., *The Narrative of Sojourner Truth: A Bondswoman of Olden Time* (New York: Penguin, 1998); Jean M. Humez, "Reading *The Narrative of Sojourner Truth* as a Collaborative Text," *Frontiers: A Journal of Women Studies* 16, no. 1 (1996), 29–52; Jean Lebedun, "Harriet Beecher Stowe's Interest in Sojourner Truth, Black Feminist," *American Literature: A Journal of Literary History, Criticism,* and Bibliography 46, no. 3 (Nov. 1974), 359–363; Carleton Mabee and Susan Mabee Newhouse, *Sojourner Truth: Slave, Prophet, Legend* (New York: New York University Press, 1993); Nell Irvin Painter: "Sojourner Truth," in *The Oxford Companion to African American Literature*, ed. William L. Andrews, Frances Smith Foster, and Trudier Harris (New York: Oxford University Press, 1997), 738; *Sojourner Truth: A Life, a Symbol* (New York: Norton, 1996); Matthew K. Samra, "Shadow and Substance: The Two Narratives of Sojourner Truth," *Midwest Quarterly: A Journal of Contemporary Thought* 38, no. 2 (Winter 1997), 158–171; Karen Sánchez-Eppler, "Ain't I a Symbol," review of Nell Irvin Painter, *Sojourner Truth, American Quarterly* 50, no. 1 (Mar. 1998), 149–157; Harriet Beecher Stowe, "Sojourner Truth, the Libyan Sibyl," *The Atlantic Monthly* 11 (Apr. 1863), 473–481; Esther Terry, "Sojourner Truth: The Person Behind the Libyan Sibyl," *Massachusetts Review: Quarterly of Literature, the Arts, and Public Affairs* 26, no. 2–3 (Summer/Autumn 1985), 425–444.

Carol Margaret Davison

Tubbee, Okah (1810–?). Musician, physician, and storyteller. Okah Tubbee's life as a Black slave is outlined in *A Sketch of the Life of Okah Tubbee (Called) William Chubbee, Son of the Head Chief, Mosholeh, of the Choctaw Nation of Indians* (1852). *A Sketch* was transcribed by his wife, Laah Ceil Manatoi Elaah Tubbee, and reflects aspects of several genres of the day: the religious-conversion narrative, the **slave narrative**, the captivity narrative, and stories of frontier exploration. Tubbee is a relatively obscure author now, despite the republication of his narrative by Daniel F. Littlefield, Jr., in 1988; the republication seems to have sparked no critical notice and has since gone out of print. Nonetheless, in his own era, Okah Tubbee gained renown as a musician and doctor in Natchez, Mississippi (his birthplace), as well as other cities and small towns.

Born around 1810, apparently a son of Franky (Frances), a Black slave who bore two other children to her master, James McCary, Okah Tubbee was originally named Warner. McCary died three years later and manumitted his two eldest children, Kitty and Robert, as well as Franky. He provided a large estate for the children and a stipend for Franky to continue caring for them. His will dictated that Warner remain in **slavery**, owned by his mother and siblings.

In the first sentence of his narrative, Tubbee recounts his recollections of childhood as "scenes of sorrow; though I have an imperfect recollection of a kind father, who was a very large man, with dark, red, skin and his head was adorned with feathers of a most beautiful plumage" (17). He claims that he was taken from his true father, whom he reveals to be a Choctaw chief, Moshulatubbee, which Littlefield refutes in his well-documented "Introduction." Throughout the narrative, Tubbee inserts pieces of evidence to prove his Choctaw parentage. He refers often to his temper and claims it as a matter of race in ways such as "all my Indian nature was aroused, and my very blood boiled in every vein" (27). Tubbee claims that his siblings were privately tutored and well dressed (Littlefield's research supports Tubbee's account), while he was made to serve as the family's slave.

Tubbee's is a discomforting tale that places racism in the hands of Blacks and that, surprising for its period, fails to condemn the enslavement of African Americans. Even after Tubbee flees slavery and has an opportunity to buy his manumission, he never speaks to the practice of slaveholding. Any readerly expectation that he would join forces with antislavery workers is in vain. Ultimately, Tubbee attempts to erase slavery by erasing his biological relationship to it.

Resources: Melissa Meeks and Natalia Smith, eds., *Documenting the American South* (Chapel Hill: Academic Affairs Library, University of North Carolina, 2002), http://docsouth.unc.edu/neh/tubbee/menu.html; Okah Tubbee, *The Life of Okah Tubbee*, ed. Daniel Littlefield (Lincoln: University of Nebraska Press, 1988); Laah Ceil Tubbee and Okah Tubbee, *A Sketch of the Life of Okah Tubbee (Called) William Chubbee, Son of the Head Chief, Mosholeh Tubbee, of the Choctaw Nation of Indians* (Toronto, 1852).

Pamela Ralston

Tubman, Harriet Ross (c. 1820–1913). Escaped slave, conductor on the **Underground Railroad**, Union Army spy and scout, nurse, and activist. Harriet Tubman was born Araminta Ross on the Brodas plantation in Dorchester County, Maryland, to parents who were descended from the Ashanti tribe of West Africa. She later changed her name to Harriet, her mother's name. At around the age of five, she became a house servant, and later a field slave. Her master often "sold her out" to other plantations, and she was beaten regularly (Shaw). An overseer struck her on the head with a two-pound weight when she tried to defend a fleeing slave at the age of twelve. From then on, she suffered from narcoleptic seizures or blackouts (Shaw). In 1844, when she was about twenty-five years old, she married John Tubman, a free African American man. She worked as a slave by day, but was allowed to stay with her husband at night.

Despite her injuries, Tubman was a strong and capable woman who could navigate by the stars and create wood-crafting because of her former field work. These skills came in handy when she escaped from **slavery** in 1849 and went to **Philadelphia, Pennsylvania**, because she heard that she was about to be sold following her master's death. Tubman did not tell her husband about her plans because she knew he would turn her in (Shaw). The only person she told was her sister. Eventually, she settled in Auburn, New York, among many supporters of the **Abolitionist Movement**. Because she wanted other slaves to be free as well, Tubman saved money and came back to **the South** approximately nineteen times as a conductor on the Underground Railroad. The Railroad consisted of a group of African Americans and White Americans who helped slaves escaped to the North through a series of tunnels, dirt roads, and hidden rooms in homes. Over the next ten years, Tubman personally helped free about 300 slaves, including all her family members, and she never lost an escapee. On her third trip back home to help slaves escape, she went to get her husband, only to discover he had remarried and did not want to leave with her. She nonchalantly moved on to free others.

Tubman's success rate had to do with her strategic planning, wit, and courage. All of her escapes occurred on Saturday nights because she knew the slave owners could not put up Wanted posters until Monday. Tubman went undetected because she seemed to be a harmless woman who walked and sang songs when in actuality she usually carried a gun. The songs' lyrics contained clues alerting slaves that she came to help them escape. Known as "The Moses of Her People," she was such a threat that slave owners offered a $40,000 reward for her capture. However, Tubman was never captured because of her ingenuity. Once she escaped capture by pretending to read her own Wanted poster. One legend claims that she had a narcoleptic blackout underneath one of her Wanted posters and never realized it.

To end **slavery**, Tubman worked with such abolitionists as **Frederick Douglass** and **William Still**. Fortunately, Tubman was too ill to participate in the doomed raid on Harper's Ferry with **John Brown** in 1859. Later that year, she was physically assaulted by the police when she helped a runaway slave named Charles Nalle escape to Canada. During the **Civil War**, Tubman's duties as a Union spy, scout, and nurse made her a major asset. On June 2, 1863, she organized and led the Combahee River raid in South Carolina that freed more than 750 slaves. It remains the only military raid in U.S. history that was planned and led by a woman. Even though Tubman fought valiantly for the Union cause, she was denied a pension for many years.

After the Civil War ended, Tubman settled with her family back in Auburn and married Nelson Davis in 1870. They lived together until his death eighteen years later. With Tubman's cooperation and assistance, Sarah Elizabeth Bradford wrote Tubman's biography, *Scenes in the Life of Harriet Tubman*, in 1869. Tubman tried to build a home for elderly ex-slaves in Auburn with the profits from this book and her military pension. Eventually, for lack of funds, she gave the land to the African Methodist Episcopal Zion Church, which completed the home in 1908. She later moved into the home, which today is known as the Harriet Tubman Home. Besides this endeavor, Tubman tried to establish schools in North Carolina for free Blacks and fought for many social issues such as women's rights. Tubman died of pneumonia, at around the age of ninety-three, on March 10, 1913. She

Harriet Tubman, c. 1870. Courtesy of the Library of Congress.

was buried with military honors in Auburn's Fort Hill Cemetery. Shortly after her death, a bronze plaque was placed at the Cayuga County Courthouse and a civic holiday was declared in her honor. In 1944, Eleanor Roosevelt christened a ship *Harriet Tubman*. The U.S. postal service issued stamps to honor her in 1978 and 1995. Numerous books about her and a 1978 movie, *A Woman Called Moses*, have celebrated Tubman's life.

Tubman's bravery and ingenuity, as she worked against seemingly staggering odds, make her an American hero. She freed herself and other African Americans. Many regard her feats as timeless and inspirational.

Resources: Susan Altman, "Harriet Tubman," in *Encyclopedia of African-American Heritage* (New York: Facts on File, 2001); "Harriet Tubman," *The New York History Net: The Harriet Tubman Home*, http://www.nyhistory.com/harriettubman/life.htm; K. B. Shaw, "Harriet Tubman," *SPECTRUM Home & School Magazine*, http://www.incwell.com/Spectrum.html; Paul Wendkos, dir., *A Woman Called Moses* (New York: Xenon 2 Studios, 1978; VHS format, 1999).

Devona Mallory

Turner, Darwin T. (1931–1991). Literary critic, poet, and educator. Darwin Theodore Turner, who gained prominence in the study of Black literature during the 1960s and who remains an influential figure in African American literature in the twenty-first century, was born in Cincinnati, Ohio. When he completed a B.A. in English (1947) at the age of sixteen, he became the University of Cincinnati's youngest graduate (to date, this record still stands). Turner remained at the University of Cincinnati, where he received an M.A. (1949), then earned a Ph.D. (1956) at the University of Chicago. Turner began his career as an educator at Clark College and subsequently taught at Morgan State College (now Morgan State University), Florida A&M University, North Carolina A&T College (now North Carolina A&T University), the University of Wisconsin at Madison, the University of Michigan, and the University of Hawaii. He joined the faculty at the University of Iowa in 1971, and twenty years later, at the time of his death, he was chair of the Afro-American Studies program there. Turner, who was president of the **College Language Association** (1963–1965), was active in many other professional organizations including the Modern Language Association of America, the National Council of Teachers of English, the Association for the Study of Afro-American Life and History, the National Council of Black Studies, and the Rockefeller Commission on the Humanities.

In addition to his distinguished teaching career and contributions to professional societies, Turner was a prolific scholar. He wrote *In a Minor Chord: Three Afro-American Writers and Their Search for Identity* (1971); *Theory and Practice in the Teaching of Literature by Afro-Americans* (1971), with Barbara Dodds Stanford; and *The Wayward and the Seeking: A Collection of Writings by Jean Toomer* (1980). Turner edited and compiled works including *Images of the Negro in America: Selected Source Materials for College Research Papers* (1965), edited with Jean M. Bright; *Black American Literature: Essay, Poetry, Fiction,*

Drama (1970); *Afro-American Writers* (1970); *Black Drama in America: An Anthology* (1971; 2nd ed. 1994); *Voices from the Black Experience: African and Afro-American Literature* (1972), compiled with Jean M. Bright and Richard Wright; *The Art of Slave Narrative: Original Essays in Criticism and Theory* (1982), edited with John Sekora; and the Norton Critical Edition of **Jean Toomer**'s *Cane: An Authoritative Text, Backgrounds, Criticism* (1988). Turner also wrote *Katharsis* (1964), a volume of poetry; contributed poems and many articles to journals and books, and wrote introductions to books by **Charles Waddell Chesnutt**, **Countee Cullen**, **Paul Laurence Dunbar**, **Zora Neale Hurston**, and Jean Toomer.

Turner represented the United States at the Second World Festival of Black and African Arts and Culture in Lagos, Nigeria, in 1977, and was awarded an honorary Doctor of Letters degree by the University of Cincinnati (1983); he received additional honors from the alumni associations of the University of Cincinnati and the University of Chicago, the College Language Association, the Middle-Atlantic Writers Association, and other organizations. A continuing tribute to Turner's legacy began on October 12, 1991, eight months after his death, when the University of Cincinnati renamed its Minority Scholars Program the Darwin T. Turner Scholars Program.

Resources: Primary Sources: John Sekora and Darwin T. Turner, eds., *The Art of the Slave Narrative: Original Essays in Criticism and Theory* (Macomb: Western Illinois University Press, 1982); Darwin T. Turner: *In a Minor Chord: Three Afro-American Writers and Their Search for Identity* (Carbondale: Southern Illinois University Press, 1971); "Langston Hughes" (Deland, FL: Everett/Edwards, 1972), tape recording; Darwin T. Turner, ed.: *Afro-American Writers* (New York: Appleton-Century-Crofts, 1970); *Black American Literature: Essays* (Columbus, OH: Merrill, 1969); *Black Drama in America: An Anthology*, 2nd ed. (Washington, DC: Howard University Press, 1994); *Cane* [by Jean Toomer]: *An Authoritative Text, Backgrounds, Criticism* (New York: Norton, 1988); *The Wayward and the Seeking: A Collection of Writings by Jean Toomer* (Washington, DC: Howard University Press, 1980); Darwin T. Turner and Jean M. Bright, eds., *Images of the Negro in America* (Boston: D. C. Heath, 1965); Darwin T. Turner and Barbara Dodds Stanford, *Theory and Practice in the Teaching of Literature by Afro Americans* (Urbana, IL: National Council of Teachers of English, 1971). **Secondary Sources:** Arthur P. Davis, J. Saunders Redding, and Joyce Ann Joyce, eds., *The New Cavalcade: African American Writing from 1760 to the Present*, vol. 2 (Washington, DC: Howard University Press, 1992), 254–255; Linda Metzger, ed., *Black Writers: A Selection of Sketches from Contemporary Authors* (Detroit: Gale, 1989), 553–554; Ann Allen Shockley and Sue P. Chandler, *Living Black American Authors: A Biographical Directory* (New York: Bowker, 1973), 160–161.

Linda M. Carter

Turner, Henry McNeal (1834–1915). Theologian and newspaper editor. Turner was a bishop in the African Methodist Episcopal (A.M.E.) Church from 1880 to 1915, a politician during the **Reconstruction**, the editor of several **newspapers**, a missionary, and an innovative theologian known for proclaiming, "God is a Negro!" (Bracey, 154–155). Born free in 1833 in South Carolina, Turner joined the A.M.E. Church in Louisiana in 1857. In 1862, he headed the church's missionary efforts in **the South**, convinced that African Americans should educate the slaves and freedmen. One year later, Turner became a chaplain in the Union Army. Angered by the mistreatment of African Americans, he supported the **Back-to-Africa Movement** as a means of restoring racial pride. In April 1868, Turner was elected to the Georgia House of Representatives, but he was removed from the position by the White legislators in September of the same year.

Drawing on his experiences and observations of American society, Turner wrote literature for **"racial uplift,"** to inspire pride in his African American readers. In 1872, he wrote "On the Present Duties and Future Destiny of the Negro Race," and in 1873, he published a scientific lecture titled *The Negro in All Ages*. In 1876, Turner served as the book manager of the A.M.E. publishing house, which also published the denominational newspaper, the A.M.E. *Christian Recorder*. He published a revised *Hymnbook of the African Methodist Episcopal Church* (1883).

A devoted civil rights advocate, Turner opposed the U.S. Supreme Court's decision in *Plessy v. Ferguson*, which established the "separate but equal" doctrine (Franklin and Moss). Turner published *The Genius and Theory of Methodist Polity* (1885) to bring uniformity to the A.M.E. Church discipline. In 1886, he started the *Southern Recorder*, a newspaper focused on the specific needs and concerns of Southern A.M.E. ministers. In 1892, Turner founded the official newspaper of the A.M.E. Church missionary department, the *Voice of Missions*, and in 1900, he started his own newspaper, the *Voice of the People*, which encouraged people of African descent to return to Africa. Throughout his career, Turner clashed with politicians, ministers, and congregants, and he engendered his share of controversy, but he never wavered from his goal of uplifting the African American race.

Resources: Stephen Ward Angell, *Bishop Henry McNeal Turner and African-American Religion in the South* (Knoxville: University of Tennessee Press, 1992); John Bracey et al., eds., *Black Nationalism in America* (Indianapolis: Bobbs-Merrill, 1970); John Hope Franklin and Alfred A. Moss, Jr., "Losing the Peace," in *From Slavery to Freedom: A History of African Americans*, 8th ed. (Boston: McGraw Hill, 2000), 272–290; Mungo M. Ponton, *The Life and Times of Henry M. Turner* (New York: Negro Universities Press, 1970); Edwin S. Redkey, ed., *Respect Black: The Writings and Speeches of Henry McNeal Turner* (New York: Arno, 1971); Henry McNeal Turner: *The Genius and Theory of Methodist Polity; or, The Machinery of Methodism, practically Illustrated Through a Series of Questions and Answers* (Philadelphia: Publication Department, A.M.E. Church, 1885); *The Hymnbook of the African Methodist Episcopal Church* (Philadelphia: Publication Department, A.M.E. Church, 1883).

Julius H. Bailey

Turner, Nat (1800–1831). Leader of a slave insurrection. Although life as a nineteenth-century slave in Southampton County, Virginia, might easily have rendered Nat Turner anonymous in history, his decision to mobilize a group of slaves in resisting involuntary servitude earned Turner a place among legendary figures of the African American past. His deeds secured his place not only in history but also in literature. As a child, Turner dazzled those around him with his intelligence and gifts of prophecy. He felt destined for something greater than the life of a slave, and so he devoted himself to his studies and his spiritual development in the hope of realizing that promise. Despite his talents, Turner found himself subject to circumstances that he, like other slaves, could do little to control. At age twelve, he faced the reality of all slave children, beginning a life of unremunerated toil. Work was hard and treatment was harsh, and owners traded their human chattel at will, separating family members and often severing such ties forever through distance, death, and adversity. Turner saw his mother, and later his wife, sold and sent away.

While Turner's personal restraint and religious outlook gave him the reputation of a trustworthy slave, he privately resented the constraints placed upon his liberty. Like his father before him, he became a fugitive slave at one point. Unlike his father, though, Turner voluntarily returned thirty days later on the basis of what he considered divine guidance urging him to help others escape captivity, not by flight but by resisting **slavery** as an institution.

Following the death of his owner, Turner found himself the property of a minor child of a slave master. Turner began to identify natural phenomena, such as lights in the sky and a solar eclipse, as messages from God that directed him to lead a slave rebellion. On the night and early morning of August 20–21, 1831, Turner and six other African American men attacked the home of his owner in Southampton County, Virigina. They killed the whole family. The ranks of the rebels swelled to about forty, and before a militia began to pursue them, they had killed at least fifty-five people. Some rebels were captured immediately, but Turner himself wasn't captured until about six weeks later. In jail, Turner gave a confession to Thomas R. Gray, who recorded it. Turner was sentenced to execution on November 5, 1831; he was hanged and then skinned on November 11, 1831 (Greenberg).

The insurrection in 1831 not only disproved the notion of slavery as a benevolent institution, but it also sparked fears of further unrest and violence throughout the slaveholding **South**. While Turner had demonstrated the potential force of slave revolt, his insurrection also resulted in the death of hundreds of African Americans who were tortured and murdered in the climate of suspicion and panic following the rebellion. In the wake of the trial and execution of participants in the uprising, slave legislation became even more restrictive regarding any behaviors Whites considered a threat to the order, such as group movement, assembly, and even literacy, since it helped slaves communicate freely among themselves.

With his reported final words, "I am ready," uttered just prior to his public hanging, Turner ended his life as he had lived it: brave and resolute. In the American tradition of the patriot Patrick Henry's "Give me liberty or give me death," Turner gave his life in his effort to expose the hypocrisy of slave

Composite of scenes of Nat Turner's rebellion, published in 1831. Courtesy of the Library of Congress.

trade within a democracy. In part due to his profile as a conscientious objector to slavery and its curtailment of human rights, Turner has been the subject of many stories, poems, plays, songs, and images.

By interpreting and supplementing the historical record, artistic representations of the Southampton insurrection keep Nat Turner's memory vibrant. Fictional treatments of Turner's life include such works as **Harriet Beecher Stowe**'s *Dred: A Tale of the Great Dismal Swamp* (1856), Daniel Panger's *Ol' Prophet Nat* (1967), and William Styron's *The Confessions of Nat Turner* (1967) (Davis). Poetry inspired by the incidents in Southampton County abounds, particularly among African American poets. Examples include **Sterling A. Brown**'s "Remembering Nat Turner," **Robert Hayden**'s "The Ballad of Nat Turner," **Alvin Aubert**'s "Nat Turner in the Clearing," and Ophelia Robinson's extended verse "Nat Turner." The same historical subject informs numerous plays written for the stage, from **Randolph S. Edmonds**'s *Nat Turner* to Robert O'Hara's *Insurrection: Holding History*. The story of Nat Turner also captures the imagination of musicians, as was the case with Corey Coke's spoken word performance on "mastablasta," a cut on his 1999 compact disc, *Coreyography*.

Of course, these portraits of Nat Turner and the raid that made him famous have often inspired controversy, since writers, dramatists, artists, and composers approach the topic in their own ways and frequently take liberties with the subject. Styron's novel, *The Confessions of Nat Turner*, was especially controversial. A great deal is at stake, however, when a cultural icon is depicted, because people may regard him differently, depending upon their perspectives. Nat Turner has been called a prophet, a fanatic, a criminal, an avenger, a leader, a visionary, a dissenter, and a rebel. However he may be viewed, he is not likely to be forgotten. Nat Turner continues to exert an influence on memories of the American and African American past. (*See* **Historical Fiction; Slave Narrative.**)

Resources: Mary Kemp Davis, *Nat Turner Before the Bar of Judgment: Fictional Treatments of the Southampton Slave Insurrection* (Baton Rouge: Louisiana State University Press, 1999); Eric Foner, ed., *Nat Turner* (Englewood Cliffs, NJ: Prentice-Hall, 1971); Scot French, *The Rebellious Slave: Nat Turner in American Memory* (New York: Houghton Mifflin, 2004); Kenneth S. Greenberg, ed., *Nat Turner: A Slave Rebellion in History and Memory* (New York: Oxford University Press, 2003); Stephen B. Oates, *The Fires of Jubilee: Nat Turner's Fierce Rebellion* (New York: Harper & Row, 1975); Albert E. Stone, *The Return of Nat Turner: History, Literature, and Cultural Politics in Sixties America* (Athens: University of Georgia Press, 1992).

Linda S. Watts

Turpin, Waters E. (1910–1968). Novelist, playwright, and college professor. Waters Edward Turpin, a pioneer of the African American family saga, was born in Oxford, Maryland. He was the only child of Simon and Rebecca (née Waters) Turpin, and he lived in Oxford until his family moved to New Jersey in 1922. The novelist Edna Ferber, who employed Turpin's mother as a domestic, encouraged his interest in writing. Turpin attended high school at Morgan Academy in **Baltimore, Maryland.** He then earned a B.A. from Morgan State College (now Morgan State University), an M.A. from Columbia University (1932), and an Ed.D. from Columbia (1960). Turpin was a welfare investigator for the Works Progress Administration in the early 1930s and then taught English and was a football coach at Storer College in Harpers Ferry, West Virginia, from 1935 to 1938. He left Storer to begin work on a doctorate. From 1940 to 1950, Turpin taught at Lincoln University in Pennsylvania; one of his students was Kwame Nkrumah, who later became president of Ghana. In 1950 Turpin accepted **Nick Aaron Ford**'s offer of a teaching post at Morgan State, where Turpin's wife, the former Jean Fisher, was a faculty member. Turpin taught there for eighteen years, until his death on November 19, 1968.

Turpin is best known for his three published novels. *These Low Grounds* (1937) is apparently the first African American novel to tell the story of four generations of an African American family. It was printed with Ferber's endorsement on the dust jacket, and **Ralph Ellison** made his debut as a writer when he reviewed the novel at the request of **Richard Wright**, who was the editor of *New Challenge*. *O Canaan!* (1939), a portrayal of African American migration from **the South** to **Chicago, Illinois**, during the **Great Depression**, was followed by *The Rootless* (1957), a representation of slave life on a

Maryland plantation. Three of Turpin's plays were produced during his life-time: *Let the Day Perish*; *Saint Michael's Dawn*; and the opera *Li'l Joe*, with lyrics by Turpin, were first produced in 1950, 1956, and 1957, respectively. Turpin and Ford edited two textbooks: *Basic Skills for Better Writing* (1959) and *Extending Horizons: Selected Readings for Cultural Enrichment* (1969). Turpin's short stories, poetry, essays, and book reviews were published in periodicals including the *Morgan State College Bulletin*, *Negro History Bulletin*, **Phylon**, and the *CLA Journal*. His manuscripts and documents are located in the Waters Edward Turpin Collection at Morgan State University.

Resources: Nick Aaron Ford: "Tribute to Waters Turpin," *CLA Journal* 7 (1969), 281–282; "Waters Turpin: I Knew Him Well," *CLA Journal* 21 (1977), 1–18; Burney J. Hollis, "Waters, Edward Turpin," in *Dictionary of Literary Biography*, vol. 51, *Afro-American Writers from the Harlem Renaissance to 1940*, ed. Trudier Harris and Thadious M. Davis (Detroit: Gale, 1987), 289–295; Margaret Ann Reid, "Waters Turpin," in *The Oxford Companion to African American Literature*, ed. William L. Andrews, Frances Smith Foster, and Trudier Harris (New York: Oxford University Press, 1997), 739–740; Elizabeth Thomas, "Waters Edward Turpin," in *Black Writers: A Selection of Sketches from Contemporary Authors*, ed. Linda Metzger (Detroit: Gale, 1989), 554–555; Waters Turpin: *O Canaan!* (New York: Doubleday, Doran, 1939); *The Rootless* (New York: Vantage, 1957); *These Low Grounds* (New York: Harper & Brothers, 1937); Waters Turpin and Nick Aaron Ford: *Basic Skills for Better Writing: A Guide and Practice Book for Those Who Intend to Master the Essentials of Good English* (New York: Putnam, 1959); *Extending Horizons: Selected Readings for Cultural Enrichment* (New York: Random House, 1969).

Linda M. Carter

Twain, Mark (1835–1910). Novelist, essayist, short story writer, and public persona. One of the most widely regarded authors of post–**Civil War** America, Twain produced novels that are considered American classics and, in recent years, have been read in ways that emphasize his deep engagements with **race** and imperialism.

Twain was born Samuel Langhorne Clemens in Missouri, along the bustling Mississippi River that would play a central role in many of his novels. His early years revealed his entrepreneurial and adventurous spirit; he worked at times as a local beat journalist, at times as a riverboat captain, and, concurrently with a broad American interest in oceanic travel, at times as an international travel writer. He spent most of his life on the verge of financial ruin, and used his talent as a writer of mostly satiric comedy to charm the reading public into supporting his career.

That Clemens openly used a pseudonym for his published works—most famously Mark Twain, but also Thomas Jefferson Snodgrass, Quentin Curtius Snodgrass, Sieur Louis de Conte, and Josh—points to the ironic pressure his writing put on the questions of authorship and identity. His novels are often saturated with dark comedy, presenting what on the surface seems a simple narrative, but one that masks complex and subtle social critique. His writing elicits laughter at the comedy of American life and tears for the tragedy of America's unfulfilled democratic promises. Through the lens of **satire**, Twain's texts level incisive appraisals of a range of issues; he tackles political corruption in a time of territorial expansion (in 1873's *The Gilded Age*), the violent reversal of the freedoms Blacks gained during **Reconstruction** (most notably in *The Adventures of Huckleberry Finn* [1884] but also in *Tom Sawyer Abroad* [1894]), the fraught logic of the "one drop" rule (in 1894's *Pudd'nhead Wilson*), and the barbarous contradictions of American imperialism in the Philippines (in 1901's "To A Person Sitting in Darkness"). In an introduction to *Pudd'nhead Wilson* (1959), **Langston Hughes** lauded Twain for not depicting Blacks stereotypically and praised the satiric narrative.

Huckleberry Finn is arguably Twain's most famous—and infamous—novel. Following in the footsteps of *The Adventures of Tom Sawyer* (1876), the narrative paints a picture of rural life along the Mississippi through the eyes of a boy coming into adulthood in a nation fraught with racial strife. The protagonist, Huck Finn, having fled a variety of family problems, finds himself on an island in the river where a fugitive slave named Jim has taken sanctuary. Huck and Jim enjoy living together for a few days, but when Huck returns to the mainland, he finds out the town has assumed he's been murdered by Jim. After a series of narrative twists which split up Huck and Jim and get them back together, and eventually lead to Jim being returned to the police, Huck is reunited with a more mature Tom Sawyer. Tom pledges to help Huck rescue Jim from the conditions of **slavery**, but when they take refuge in a backwoods cabin, Tom, now the embodiment of the patronizing cruelty of post-Reconstruction race relations, forces Jim to act in dehumanizing ways to gain his freedom. The novel closes with a series of seemingly discontinuous events, including Tom getting shot in the leg, Jim being recaptured, Jim's owner dying and bequeathing him his freedom, Huck's father dying, Tom's Aunt Sally offering to adopt Huck, and Huck deciding to "light out for the Territory" in order to avoid the barbarity of American civilization.

While some have seen the ending of the novel as rushed and unrealistic, Twain's notes to *Huck Finn* show the care he took in attempting to portray Jim's existence as not the piece of fugitive property his world would have seen him as, but rather as a compassionate and heroic human being. The novel's bawdy colloquial **vernacular** language, the characters' seemingly dangerous unchildlike behaviors, and the rampant use of the derogatory term "nigger" have kept the novel on many of America's "banned books" lists. But as the noted Twain scholar Shelley Fisher Fishkin has argued, *Huckleberry Finn* offers one of the most devastating critiques of America's institutionalized racism, and does so ironically, through the eyes of someone deeply embedded within its discourses. Fishkin, in *Was Huck Black?* (1993), has meticulously researched the vernacular language published while Twain was assembling the novel, and posits that Huck's character—subsequently lauded as a figure of American independence and autonomy—was based on a blend of two African American children Twain knew personally.

Whether or not one can viably claim Huck's "Blackness," it is undoubted that Twain's work continues to challenge America's racial norms, narrative conventions, and exclusivist constructions of national identity, and that his writing, like that of **Harriet Beecher Stowe**, is distinctively connected to central concerns of African American literature. His wry wit and incisive politics still speak to the most pressing contemporary concerns.

Resources: **Primary Source:** *The Oxford Mark Twain*, ed. Shelley Fisher Fishkin (New York: Oxford University Press, 1996), is a 29-volume edition that compiles 35 of Twain's individual works. Important works are listed here, along with their original date of publication: *The Innocents Abroad; or, The New Pilgrim's Progress* (1869); *The Gilded Age* (1873); *The Adventures of Tom Sawyer* (1876); *Life on the Mississippi* (1883); *Adventures of Huckleberry Finn* (1884); *A Connecticut Yankee in King Arthur's Court* (1889); *The Tragedy of Pudd'nhead Wilson and the Comedy of Those Extraordinary Twins* (1894); *Following the Equator and Anti-imperialist Essays* (1897, 1901, 1905). **Secondary Sources:** Ralph Ellison, *Shadow and Act* (New York: Random House, 1953); Shelley Fisher Fishkin, *Was Huck Black? Mark Twain and African-American Voices* (New York: Oxford University Press, 1993); Susan Gillman, *Dark Twins: Imposture and Identity in Mark Twain's America* (Chicago: University of Chicago Press, 1989); Langston Hughes, "Introduction" to *Pudd'nhead Wilson*, by Mark Twain (New York: Bantam, 1959), v–ix; Elaine Mensh and Harry Mensh, *Black, White, and Huckleberry Finn: Re-imagining the American Dream* (Tuscaloosa: University of Alabama Press, 2000); Hilton Obenzinger, *American Palestine: Melville, Twain, and the Holy Land Mania* (Princeton: Princeton University Press, 1999); R. Kent Rasmussen, *Mark Twain A to Z: The Essential Reference to His Life and Writings* (New York: Oxford University Press, 1996); Eric Sundquist, *To Wake the Nations: Race in the Making of American Literature* (Cambridge, MA: Belknap Press of Harvard University Press, 1993).

Keith Feldman

Tyree, Omar (born 1969). Novelist, publisher, lecturer, and performance poet. The author of eleven novels, Tyree is a spokesman for contemporary African American life. In recognition of this role, in 2001 he received the **NAACP** Image Award for an Outstanding Literary Work of Fiction for his seventh novel, *For the Love of Money* (2000). His novels explore the everyday experiences of Blacks in America. A graduate of Howard University, Tyree formed his own publishing company, MARS Productions, in 1991 and issued his first two novels, *Colored, on White Campus: The Education of a Racial World* (1992) and *Flyy-Girl* (1993) ("Reflections"). The characters in his novels are realistic portraits of men and women struggling with everyday problems: love, careers, families, and relationships. For example, in *A Do Right Man* (1997), the main character, Bobby Dallas, is a successful radio talk-show host who seems to have it all, except a woman to share his life. The novel explores what many Black men are experiencing in their lives, careers, and loves. The best-selling *For the Love of Money* (2000), a sequel to *Flyy Girl*, also deals with the themes of success and happiness. Beautiful, rich actress Tracy Ellison returns to her hometown of **Philadelphia, Pennsylvania**, and begins dealing with unresolved issues involving past loves and family ties.

Despite the overwhelming popularity of his novels, however, Tyree seems to feel that African American literature has become a victim of "feminization." To combat this, he has adopted the persona of the urban griot in order to entice the male audience to his message. According to a statement on his Web site, "In the annals of West African history, 'griot' (gree-oh) was the honored name bestowed on wise and knowledgeable storytellers." As the present-day urban griot, Tyree attempts to appeal to the "disenfranchised male readers... who read and write and think...with hardcore, fast-moving, plot-driven stories that males can take to naturally." The novels deal with such issues as "crime, sexuality, sports, drugs, and working within the system." Writing as the urban griot, Tyree produced the novel *One Crazy A** Night* (2003), which portrays a young Black couple who are kidnapped by a White supremacy group. MARS Productions has an "urban griot music division" to provide soundtracks for these urban-themed novels, the first of which is *Rising Up!* (2003) ("Urban Griot"). A new novel, *Cold Blooded*, by Tyree, writing as the urban griot, appeared in 2004. Along with pursuing his career as a novelist and the urban griot, Tyree lectures frequently.

Resources: Primary Sources: Omar Tyree: *Capital City: Chronicles of a D.C. Underworld* (Wilmington, DE: MARS Productions, 1994); *Colored, on White Campus: The Education of a Racial World* (Washington, DC: MARS Productions, 1992); *Diary of a Groupie* (New York: Simon and Schuster, 2003); *A Do Right Man* (New York: Simon and Schuster, 1997); *Flyy Girl* (Washington, DC: MARS Productions, 1993); *For the Love of Money* (New York: Simon and Schuster, 2000); *Just Say No!* (New York: Simon and Schuster, 2001); *Leslie* (New York: Simon and Schuster, 2002); *OmarTyree.com* (2003), http://www.omartyree.com; *One Crazy A** Night* (Charlotte, NC: MARS Productions, 2003); *Single Mom* (New York: Simon and Schuster, 1998); *Sweet St. Louis* (New York: Simon and Schuster, 1999); "The Urban Griot," *The Urban Griot: Read and Write and Think*, http://www.theurbangriot.com. **Secondary Sources:** Beth Farrell, "Review of *Leslie*, by Omar Tyree," *Library Journal*, Dec. 1, 2002, p. 196; Nikitta A. Foston, "Black Male Authors: Smart, Sexy and Successful," *Ebony*, Dec. 2002, 98+; Brett Johnson and Glenn Townes, "Raw and Uncut," *Black Issues Book Review*, July/Aug. 2002, 40+; "Omar Tyree" (interview), *Ebony*, Nov. 2002, p. 18; "Reflections on Success: Omar Tyree," *The Black Collegian Online* (July 23, 2003), http://www.blackcollegian.com/issues/30thAnn/reflectotyree2001-30.shtml; Curtis Stephen, "Review of *Diary of a Groupie*, by Omar Tyree," *Black Issues Book Review*, July/Aug. 2003, 55; Jeff Zaleski, "Review of *Just Say No!*," by Omar Tyree, *Publishers Weekly*, Aug. 6, 2001, p. 62.

Judith M. Schmitt

DUE DATE
